AWS Certified Cloud Practitioner (CLF-C02) Certification Guide

Second Edition

Build practical AWS cloud skills through real-world business scenarios and prepare with confidence

Rajesh Daswani

<packt>

AWS Certified Cloud Practitioner (CLF-C02) Certification Guide

Second Edition

Portfolio Director: Kartikey Pandey
Relationship Lead: Preet Ahuja
Project Manager: Sonam Pandey
Content Engineer: Apramit Bhattacharya
Technical Editor: Simran Ali and Sumant Jadhav
Indexer: Rekha Nair
Production Designer: Shantanu Zagade
Growth Lead: Amit Ramadas

First published: January 2022
Second edition: August 2026

Production reference: 1290726

Published by Packt Publishing Ltd.
Grosvenor House
11 St Paul's Square
Birmingham
B3 1RB, UK.

ISBN 978-1-83546-429-8
www.packtpub.com

To my wife, Divya, for her unwavering support, encouragement, and belief in me throughout this journey. To my daughter, Ryka, for inspiring me to keep learning, growing, and striving to be a better person every day. And to my parents, whose sacrifices, values, and determination laid the foundation for everything I have achieved.

– Rajesh Daswani

Foreword

Cloud computing changed how businesses build things. Teams can provision what they need in minutes and pay only for what they use. That shift has made cloud skills essential for almost anyone working in technology today, not just IT specialists.

I have known Rajesh Daswani for many years. He has always had a gift for making complex cloud topics simple. Whether he's teaching a class or speaking at an event, he focuses on helping people understand the "why", not just memorize the "what". He brings that same clarity to this book, and he has built something genuinely useful.

What sets this book apart is Belly Brew Co. Limited, the fictional company at the center of it. Instead of learning AWS services one by one in isolation, you follow Belly Brew Co. Limited through real business problems: a website that needs to scale, manufacturing data that needs fast analysis, and a CFO who needs convincing that cloud spend makes sense. You solve each problem the way a working cloud practitioner would.

This approach makes the material stick. You don't just learn what Amazon EC2 or S3 does. You learn when to reach for it and why, which is the skill employers actually care about once the exam is behind you.

The book still gets you ready for the AWS Certified Cloud Practitioner (CLF-C02) exam. It covers the material in full, with clear explanations and practice questions in every chapter. But it treats the exam as a milestone, not the destination.

Read it start to finish, or work through the chapters you need most. Either way, pay attention to the Belly Brew Co. Limited scenarios. They will teach you more about cloud thinking than any list of service definitions.

Rajesh has written a guide that respects the reader's time and intelligence. I'm glad to recommend it.

Ashish Prajapati

Customer Solutions Manager, AWS;

Founder, Become a Solutions Architect (BeSA)

Contributors

About the author

Rajesh Daswani is a cloud architect, trainer, and author with over 25 years of experience in information technology, specializing in cloud computing, infrastructure, networking, storage, and enterprise architecture. As a technical trainer, he has helped thousands of students and IT professionals develop practical cloud skills and achieve industry-recognized certifications across Amazon Web Services (AWS), Microsoft Azure, and Google Cloud.

Rajesh has held technical leadership, architecture, and training roles across a variety of industries and is passionate about simplifying complex technical concepts through real-world examples and hands-on learning. As the founder of IaaS Academy, he creates training content, certification resources, and project-based learning experiences designed to help aspiring cloud professionals build the skills needed for modern cloud careers.

When not teaching, writing, or designing cloud solutions, Rajesh can be caught watching reruns of his favorite Star Trek (TNG) shows. He also likes to be known as a food connoisseur, concocting his own mix of fusion dishes for family and friends.

About the reviewers

Ivan Barlog is an AWS Certified Solutions Architect and an AWS Community Builder on the Serverless track who helps small businesses design cloud-first architectures and modernize AWS systems. He provides consulting and technical due diligence for international clients, focusing on practical, cost-effective serverless solutions. Active in meetups and the AWS community, Ivan writes blog posts on AWS, TypeScript, and web technologies, and shares guidance through conference talks and mentoring.

Thu Kha Kyawe is a Cloud and Site Reliability Engineer specializing in AWS infrastructure, DevOps practices, and cloud automation. He has extensive hands-on experience architecting, deploying, and operating scalable, production-grade cloud environments, with a strong emphasis on infrastructure as code, CI/CD pipeline design, containerized workloads, observability, and system reliability.

His work focuses on building secure, resilient, and highly available distributed systems that support modern engineering teams. He holds AWS certifications and continually refines his expertise through real-world implementations, architectural design, and operational optimization initiatives. He has a strong interest in reliability engineering, automation strategy, and designing cloud platforms that are scalable, maintainable, and performance-driven.

Beyond his core engineering responsibilities, He actively contributes technical insights and practical knowledge to the broader cloud and DevOps community. He also served as a technical reviewer for the book *The Cloud DevOps Engineer's Guide* by providing professional review feedback and technical validation focused on AWS infrastructure, DevOps methodologies, cloud automation, and site reliability engineering best practices.

Tomica Kaniški is an accomplished IT professional and technology enthusiast with extensive experience in datacenter technologies, networking, containers, and virtualization across on-premises and multi-cloud environments. In his current role as a Cloud Security Architect at Atos, he partners with global enterprises in diverse industries to design and implement secure, resilient cloud solutions.

He holds numerous certifications from Microsoft, AWS, and Google Cloud, among others, and is passionate about continuous learning and knowledge sharing. His contributions to the global IT community through conferences, trainings, and publications have earned him multiple recognitions, including Microsoft MVP and Cisco Champion awards.

Tomica is currently expanding his focus into AI security, reflecting his commitment to staying ahead in emerging technologies. Outside of work, he enjoys hiking, reading, and photography — and occasionally moonlights as a rockstar in training.

Table of Contents

Chapter 4: AWS Accounts, Multi-Account Strategies, and AWS Organizations

Chapter 5: AWS Access Management 89

Chapter 7: AWS Networking Services, Part 1 – Virtual Private Cloud (VPCs) 161

Chapter 10: High Availability, Fault Tolerance, and Elasticity on AWS 275

Preface

Embarking on a career in cloud computing can be one of the most rewarding decisions you make. With the ever-changing landscape of **Information Technology** (**IT**), Cloud Computing, and the rapid rise of **Artificial Intelligence** (**AI**), there has never been a more exciting time to build a career in technology. Organizations of every size are transforming the way they design, deploy, and manage applications, and cloud technologies sit at the heart of that transformation.

Today, IT professionals across the world are racing to understand cloud computing services, AI, and **Machine Learning** (**ML**). The reason is simple: AI and ML solutions run on cloud infrastructure. Whether you are training machine learning models, deploying AI-powered applications, or managing the platforms that support them, a solid understanding of cloud technologies is no longer optional—it is essential.

While AI has made software development more accessible than ever, technology still requires strong engineering foundations. Almost anyone can vibe code an application that appears functional, secure, and scalable. However, look under the bonnet, and you will often find architectural weaknesses, security gaps, operational challenges, and cost inefficiencies that only a skilled cloud engineer, developer, or architect can identify and resolve. Understanding cloud infrastructure is what separates simply building applications from building them properly.

The *AWS Certified Cloud Practitioner (CLF-C02)* certification introduces you to the fundamentals of cloud computing and the core AWS services that power modern applications. It provides a solid foundation in cloud concepts, security, networking, storage, pricing, architecture, and operational best practices. More importantly, it equips you with the knowledge required to understand how the technologies shaping today's digital world are built and delivered.

At the same time, the technology industry has become increasingly competitive. As AI continues to automate routine tasks, employers are placing greater value on professionals who understand cloud platforms and can apply that knowledge to real business challenges. Upskilling in cloud and AI technologies is rapidly becoming a prerequisite for anyone seeking to build a successful and resilient career in IT.

This study guide is designed to do more than simply help you pass the AWS Certified Cloud Practitioner (CLF-C02) exam. It provides a structured learning experience that allows you to develop practical knowledge and apply what you learn through hands-on activities and real-world project exercises. By working through the projects in this book, you will gain valuable experience designing, building, supporting, and managing cloud-based solutions in a safe and controlled environment.

The project narratives encourage you to think like an engineer, make decisions based on business requirements, and develop solutions that deliver measurable value. In doing so, you will build the confidence to discuss cloud architecture, engineering principles, and development strategies with colleagues, hiring managers, and recruiters alike.

Whether your goal is to pass the certification exam, secure your first role in cloud computing, transition into a new technology career, or build a stronger foundation for working with AI-powered systems, this book has been written with one objective in mind: to help you develop the knowledge, skills, and confidence needed to succeed in the cloud-first world that lies ahead.

Who this book is for

This book is designed for anyone looking to build a rewarding career in computing and **Amazon Web Services** (**AWS**). It is particularly suited to aspiring cloud engineers, IT support professionals, system administrators, application developers, business analysts, project managers, technical sales professionals, and students and graduates who wish to begin a career in cloud technologies.

No prior experience with AWS is required. While a basic understanding of computers, some networking concepts, and general IT terminology may help, the materials in this study guide are presented in a way that allows complete beginners to follow along and develop their knowledge progressively

Whether you are preparing for the AWS Certified Cloud Practitioner (CLF-C02) exam, exploring a career transition into cloud computing, or seeking to understand cloud fundamentals and technologies that underpin AI and machine learning solutions, this study guide provides the knowledge, practical exercises, and real-world use cases to build confidence and succeed.

What this book covers

Chapter 1, Real-World Application – Customer Scenario, introduces you to a real-world use case for a fictitious company called Belly Brew Co. Limited. You play the role of a Cloud Practitioner and review the key business requirements, setting the scene for the upcoming chapters and giving you an opportunity to develop the practical skills required to design solutions that fulfil business goals and objectives. This chapter helps you appreciate how cloud engineers, architects, and developers review business requirements and define suitable technical solutions.

Chapter 2, What Is Cloud Computing?, introduces you to the fundamental concepts of cloud computing, including cloud service models and deployment models. You will also learn about the six advantages of cloud computing—an important topic that is tested in the AWS certification exam.

Chapter 3, Introduction to AWS and the Global Infrastructure, will help you understand the AWS Global Infrastructure and its various components, which is critical to knowing how and where to deploy your solutions in the cloud. Businesses must decide which AWS Regions to operate in and which infrastructure components are most suitable for their applications and workloads.

Chapter 4, AWS Accounts, Multi-Account Strategies, and AWS Organizations, shows that businesses often require multiple AWS accounts to separate application environments such as development, testing, and production. While some organizations operate a single AWS account, others may manage hundreds. As environments grow, administration can quickly become complex. AWS Organizations and AWS Control Tower provide the tools required to manage and govern a multi-account environment efficiently.

Chapter 5, AWS Access Management, explores authentication and authorization, which are critical security controls that ensure only authorized personnel can access your AWS accounts, resources, and applications. This chapter introduces several identity and access management services that enable you to define who can access what while following the principle of least privilege when assigning permissions to internal users and external customers.

Chapter 6, Amazon Simple Storage Service (Amazon S3), introduces you to one of the core services on AWS—Amazon S3. This object storage service offers far more than simply storing files, images, and videos. You will learn how to archive data for long-term retention, replicate data for disaster recovery, and even host static websites for serverless application architectures.

Chapter 7, AWS Networking Services, Part 1 – Virtual Private Cloud (VPCs), introduces you to networking in the cloud. Specifically, you will learn how to build isolated networks to host and protect resources such as Amazon EC2 instances and Amazon RDS databases. Designing your VPC with security in mind helps protect backend services while safely exposing frontend entry points to your application stack.

Chapter 8, AWS Compute Services – EC2, Lightsail, ECS, EKS, and Lambda, explores the wide range of compute services that AWS offers, and it introduces you to traditional virtual machines such as Amazon EC2, container platforms such as Amazon ECS and Amazon EKS, and serverless computing with AWS Lambda. Lambda can significantly reduce compute costs because you are only charged when your application code is executed.

Chapter 9, Databases on AWS, introduces you to databases in the cloud and explores both SQL and NoSQL database services, along with caching solutions that improve application performance. You will also learn about specialist database services designed for specific use cases.

Chapter 10, High Availability, Fault Tolerance, and Elasticity on AWS, introduces the AWS services used to design resilient, scalable, and highly available applications. It covers how load balancers, Auto Scaling, and related traffic management services help distribute demand, reduce single points of failure, and keep applications available as usage changes.

Chapter 11, AWS Networking, Part 2 – Route 53 and CloudFront, delves into more advanced networking concepts using services such as Amazon Route 53 for DNS name resolution and traffic routing, and Amazon CloudFront for content delivery. Together, these services help you distribute content globally with low latency and improved performance through caching.

Chapter 12, Application Integration, introduces the integration services and tools used to build modern architectures. Modern architectures focus on moving away from monolithic applications towards microservices and event-driven solutions. This approach enables different components of an application to scale independently, reduces administrative overhead, and ensures that failures in one component do not affect the entire application. For example, separating customer-facing frontend services from backend processing workflows helps prevent backend systems from becoming overloaded.

Chapter 13, Analytics on AWS, introduces several analytics services capable of supporting a wide range of workloads, from real-time data processing to running ad hoc queries using fully managed services with minimal operational overhead. Data is the modern currency, and the ability to analyze that data efficiently and derive meaningful insights is critical for every business.

Chapter 14, Machine Learning and Artificial Intelligence, introduces several AWS Machine Learning and Artificial Intelligence services that are available as fully managed offerings. From image and video recognition to text extraction, speech synthesis, and language comprehension, AWS provides a wide range of tools to help you build end-to-end AI and machine learning solutions.

Chapter 15, Automation, Deployment, and Additional AWS Services, introduces automation and deployment tools that help ensure the consistent and repeatable provisioning of AWS resources. Using **Infrastructure as Code** (**IaC**) and DevOps strategies such as **Continuous Integration and Continuous Deployment** (**CI/CD**), you can improve consistency across the entire application lifecycle. You will also learn how services such as AWS CloudFormation enable you to deploy infrastructure using code, providing a documented and repeatable configuration for your environment.

Chapter 16, Management and Governance on AWS, introduces several management and governance services, including tools for patch management, performance monitoring, auditing, and operational visibility. Designing and implementing cloud solutions is only one aspect of a cloud engineer's role. Once deployed, workloads must also be monitored, maintained, and governed. The services introduced in this chapter help ensure your infrastructure remains secure, resilient, and aligned with best practices.

Chapter 17, Security Fundamentals and Tools on AWS, focuses on implementing security across all layers of your application stack. You will learn about the AWS Shared Responsibility Model and how security responsibilities are divided between AWS and the customer. While AWS secures the underlying infrastructure, you remain responsible for securing your workloads, configurations, and data. This chapter also introduces services used for encryption, protecting **personally identifiable information** (**PII**), defending against network and application attacks, and much more.

Chapter 18, Cloud Economics and Pricing Strategies on AWS, introduces several cost optimization strategies and the tools available to help you monitor spending, forecast future costs, and manage your cloud investments effectively.

Chapter 19, AWS Cloud Adoption Framework (CAF) and Well-Architected Framework, introduces two important frameworks for building efficient cloud solutions. The AWS **Cloud Adoption Framework** (**CAF**) helps organizations plan and execute successful cloud transformations using proven methodologies and best practices. The AWS Well-Architected Framework focuses on designing secure, resilient, high-performing, and cost-optimized cloud workloads through a set of architectural best practices and design principles.

To get the most out of this book

To complete the exercises in this book, you will need access to an AWS Free Plan account. Instructions to create the free plan account are provided in *Chapter 4*.

Software/hardware covered in the book	Operating system requirements
AWS Command Line Interface (CLI) version 2	Windows, macOS, or Linux
Visual Studio Code	

Download and install Visual Studio Code, which is an **integrated development environment** (**IDE**), from – Follow the download instructions from the website for your operating system.

If you are using the digital version of this book, we advise you to type the code yourself or access the code from the book's GitHub repository. Doing so will help you avoid any potential errors related to the copying and pasting of code.

Download the example code files

The code bundle for the book is hosted on GitHub at `https://github.com/PacktPublishing/AWS-Certified-Cloud-Practitioner-CLF-C02-Exam-Guide`. We also have other code bundles from our rich catalog of books and videos available at `https://github.com/PacktPublishing`. Check them out!

Download the color images

We also provide a PDF file that has color images of the screenshots/diagrams used in this book. You can download it here:`https://packt.link/gbp/9781835464298`.

Conventions used

There are a number of text conventions used throughout this book.

`CodeInText`: Indicates code words in text, database table names, folder names, filenames, file extensions, pathnames, dummy URLs, user input, and Twitter handles. For example: "Mount the downloaded `WebStorm-10*.dmg` disk image file as another disk in your system."

A block of code is set as follows:

```
Resources:
  MyEC2Instance:
    Type: AWS::EC2::Instance
    Properties:
      # Use an Amazon Linux 2023 AMI us-east-1 Region (update AMI ID per region!)
      ImageId: [PROVIDE REGIONAL SPECIFIC AMI ID]
      InstanceType: t3.micro   # Define Instance Type
```

Any command-line input or output is written as follows:

```
$ mkdir bellybrew
$ cd bellybrew
```

Bold: Indicates a new term, an important word, or words that you see on the screen. For instance, words in menus or dialog boxes appear in the text like this. For example: "From the left-hand menu, select **IAM user groups under Access management**"

> **Note**
>
> Warnings or important notes appear like this.

> **Tip**
>
> Tips and tricks appear like this.

Get in touch

Feedback from our readers is always welcome.

General feedback: If you have questions about any aspect of this book or have any general feedback, please email us at `customercare@packt.com` and mention the book's title in the subject of your message.

Errata: Although we have taken every care to ensure the accuracy of our content, mistakes do happen. If you have found a mistake in this book, we would be grateful if you reported this to us. Please visit `http://www.packt.com/submit-errata`, click **Submit Errata**, and fill in the form.

Piracy: If you come across any illegal copies of our works in any form on the internet, we would be grateful if you would provide us with the location address or website name. Please contact us at `copyright@packt.com` with a link to the material.

If you are interested in becoming an author: If there is a topic that you have expertise in and you are interested in either writing or contributing to a book, please visit `http://authors.packt.com/`.

Share your thoughts

Once you've read *AWS Certified Cloud Practitioner (CLF-C02) Certification Guide, Second Edition*, we'd love to hear your thoughts! Scan the QR code below to go straight to the Amazon review page for this book and share your feedback.

`https://packt.link/r/1-835-46429-7`

Your review is important to us and the tech community and will help us make sure we're delivering excellent quality content.

Free benefits with your book

This book comes with free benefits to support your learning. Activate them now for instant access (see the "*How to Unlock*" section for instructions).

Here's a quick overview of what you can instantly unlock with your purchase:

Online Exam-Prep Tools

Ace your certification exam with exam-ready online resources

DRM-Free PDF Version

Download DRM-free PDF and ePub copies of this book.

7-Day Packt Library Access

Get 7-day unlimited access to 8,000+ books and videos. No credit card required.

Available for first-time Packt+ trial users only.

Next-Gen Reader Access

Read this book on Packt Reader with progress sync, dark mode and note-taking.

How to Unlock

Scan the QR code (or go to `packtpub.com/unlock`). Search for this book by name, confirm the edition, and then follow the steps on the page.

UNLOCK NOW

Note: Keep your invoice handy. Purchases made directly from Packt don't require one

Part 1

Building Real-World Skills for a Successful Career in Cloud Computing

Establishing yourself with credible skills in cloud computing is no longer simply a case of passing exams and getting a few certifications. Employers and hiring managers want to know what solutions you can build and, more importantly, why you chose the specific tools and services you did to build your solutions. They want to understand what business problems you were able to solve, and whether your solution is secure, scalable, and cost-effective.

The first part of this study guide introduces you to the world of Belly Brew Co. Limited, a fictitious company in the food and drinks industry. You will learn about the core requirements of a business that is looking to adopt cloud technologies to gain a competitive edge in the market. By understanding these requirements and building solutions to address the business objectives and goals, you gain hands-on practical experience that you can demonstrate at interviews and with end clients – proving that you have not just the theoretical knowledge but the practical experience to add value to the business.

This part of the book includes the following chapters:

- *Chapter 1, Real-World Application – Customer Scenario*
- *Chapter 2, What Is Cloud Computing?*
- *Chapter 3, Introduction to AWS and the Global Infrastructure*

1

Real-World Application – Customer Scenario

One of the most significant challenges in learning and understanding new technologies is gaining practical hands-on experience using the services and tools offered. While passing the exam and earning a certification is essential, knowing how to apply your newfound knowledge and build real-world solutions is what employers are interested in.

This second edition of the *AWS Certified Cloud Practitioner Study Guide* is designed to help you prepare for the **AWS Certified Cloud Practitioner (CLF-C02) exam** and develop practical skills in using AWS services and tools.

To help you gain much-needed hands-on experience, this study guide has been written around the business requirements of a fictitious company called **Belly Brew Co. Limited**.

This chapter will help you understand how to interpret client requirements, identify their business needs, and develop potential cloud solutions to address business problems. You will then implement some of those solutions through the step-by-step project guides documented in this book.

The following sections will cover the core details of this fictitious company for which you have been hired. We will set the scene for the business as you progress through the various chapters of this study guide; essential business requirements that Belly Brew Co. Limited is looking to fulfill with your help will be discussed. It is recommended that you keep this chapter handy while going through the various project exercises, enabling you to refer to Belly Brew Co. Limited's business requirements.

The following topics are covered in this chapter:

- About Belly Brew Co. Limited
- Current IT systems and issues that are of concern to the business
- Core business requirements for this engagement

Note

Free Benefits with Your Book

Your purchase includes a free PDF copy of this book along with access to an online cert prep platform designed to help you ace your AWS Certified Cloud Practitioner (CLF-C02) exam. Check the *Free Benefits with Your Book* section in the *Preface* to unlock them instantly and maximize your learning experience.

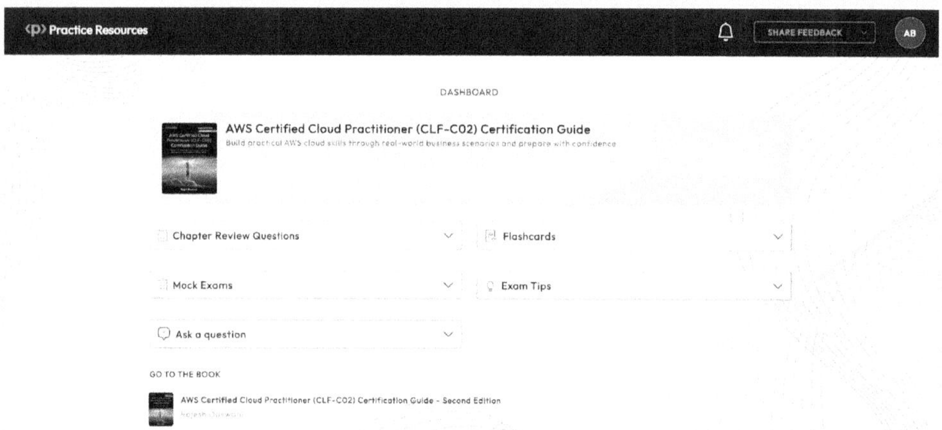

Figure 1.1: Dashboard interface of the online practice resources

Here's what you'll find on the online platform:

- 2 Mock Exams (65 questions)
- 50 Flashcards
- 30 Exam Tips
- 76 Chapter Review Questions

About Belly Brew Co. Limited

Belly Brew Co. Limited manufactures gut-friendly health beverages sold to customers via a network of participating supermarkets and grocery stores across the UK. The company has taken the UK soft drinks market by storm, embarking on an extensive marketing campaign to promote the benefits of gut-friendly beverages, as depicted in their new Kombucha line marketing campaign shown in *Figure 1.2*:

Figure 1.2: New product ranges from Belly Brew Co. Limited

The company plans to expand its product range to compete with the mainstream soft drinks industry and win a larger market share.

A selection of the beverages includes the following:

- **BB Kombucha**: Belly Brew Co. Limited's flagship product range. This is a fermented tea that contains probiotics with antioxidants. The selection includes a wide range of fruit flavors with low sugar content. This line is Belly Brew Co. Limited's primary offering that aims to compete with the much-recognized selection of soft drinks on the market.
- **Yoghurt Smoothies**: Blended yoghurt with fruits and other ingredients, offering a tasty drink packed with probiotics. Here again, a wide range of fruit flavors is offered.
- **Apple Cider Vinegar Tonic**: Diluted apple cider vinegar with water and honey beverage that may support gut health.
- **Coconut Water Kefir**: A dairy-free alternative to traditional kefir made by fermenting coconut water.

- **Bone Broth**: A rich broth made from simmering bones, connective tissues, and vegetables, which can be soothing to the digestive system.
- **BB Shots**: The range includes several gut-health-focused wellness shots, such as ginger, turmeric and cayenne, lemon and ginger, and chia seed with coconut water.

All primary departments, including sales, marketing, finance, HR, and R&D, are based at the company headquarters in London's West End. The company also has three manufacturing plants across the UK, located in Birmingham, Manchester, and Leeds, with additional cold storage facilities in Bradford.

The following map illustrates these locations in *Figure 1.3*:

Figure 1.3: Belly Brew Co. Limited head office and manufacturing plants

The company is undergoing a significant expansion plan thanks to new investment, which will be used to increase its product range and capacity. Furthermore, the marketing department has recently been granted a considerable budget to target the public with various campaigns and advertisements. Previously, their primary mode of winning sales was only through their distributors. Taking on the well-established conglomerates of the soft drinks industry will involve a lot of work and investment. The company must examine its current IT infrastructure and business applications to see if they can handle this vast expansion plan. The company is also looking to launch multiple websites and applications for the end customer to build brand awareness and loyalty.

The **Chief Technology Officer** (**CTO**) has raised concerns over the current internal IT ecosystem and feels it needs to be upgraded. This will be for both infrastructure and critical software applications. There is also a concern about managing costs, and the CTO would like to consider cloud-based solutions to avoid tying up precious capital in unnecessary hardware purchases.

To understand what needs to change, we first need to look at what Belly Brew Co. Limited already has in place. The next section explores its current core IT infrastructure and the key business applications that support its operations today.

Current IT systems and issues that are of concern to the business

Belly Brew Co. Limited hosts its entire IT infrastructure in the London-based offices. This comprises a series of physical servers running VMware hypervisors that host several virtual machines that run business applications and databases. However, their primary **customer relationship management** (**CRM**) software is a cloud-hosted **Software as a Service** (**SaaS**) based product. The company had also previously migrated its collaboration tools (including email, file storage, and meetings) to the Microsoft Office 365 platform. Apart from this, all other software applications run locally on virtual machines within their on-premises datacenter, many of which are on legacy hardware.

Each manufacturing plant across the country has a basic IT infrastructure primarily comprised of applications such as employee check-in and check-out tools, biometric applications for authentication, and various manufacturing automation and monitoring services that run from localized servers. Each manufacturing plant has network connectivity to the London HQ via IPsec **Virtual Private Network** (**VPN**) tunnels. Several different datasets are uploaded daily to central servers in London via these VPN tunnels.

Websites and marketing campaigns

Belly Brew Co. Limited's current primary website runs from a single physical on-premises server running the Apache web services platform. The server boasts an Intel Xeon Silver 4310 2.1GHz, 16GB RAM (memory), and 3x 1.6 TB SAS hard disks in a RAID 5 configuration and runs the Ubuntu server operating system. It was also purchased with additional Ubuntu premium support, and the total cost was just over £8,000. The company follows a three-year straight-line depreciation policy for all IT equipment. The finance department is keen to do away with procuring physical infrastructure and accounting for depreciation and loss of asset value over time. The concept of moving away to an **operational expenditure** (**OPEX**) investment mode in IT excites the department.

The website primarily promotes and advertises the company's current line of products and is aimed at the **business-to-business** (**B2B**) market. This is a static website with a simple enquiries form to enable potential new business customers to enquire about the product range and potentially conduct new business. Existing B2B customers rarely visit the website.

Manufacturing applications

The food and drinks manufacturing industry uses industry-grade equipment to mass-produce the company's product range, enabling it to achieve a lower cost per unit. Belly Brew Co. Limited must follow strict guidelines and procedures to ensure compliance with all health and safety regulations and to ensure that the products produced are fit and safe for human consumption.

Often, several applications are used to automate, control, and manage production lines, product packaging, labelling, and dispatch. In addition, businesses must regularly monitor their products and perform extensive testing and sampling to ensure that quality and safety levels are maintained. Belly Brew Co. Limited follows many tests and sampling procedures across the product range.

One such process involves monitoring each cask of freshly brewed kombucha throughout the fermentation cycle until it is bottled and distributed to supermarkets and grocery stores. The objective is to ensure that the pH remains within the acceptable safety range of 2.5 to 3.5. pH is a measure of how acidic or alkaline a solution is. Production staff collect pH readings at regular intervals using specialized monitoring equipment, and any cask that falls outside the acceptable range is immediately removed from the production batch for further investigation.

To support quality assurance and compliance requirements, measurement data for each cask is recorded daily in CSV (comma-separated value) files and exported to a central repository. A legacy application then analyzes the data and identifies any casks that fail to meet the required quality and safety standards.

Another test includes temperature monitoring of the brewing vessels, ensuring the beverage is within the acceptable range of 75-85 °F (24-29 °C), with 80 °F as the optimal temperature. Several other applications are running on legacy systems, which need to be considered for an upgrade and migration to the cloud.

Business applications

Belly Brew Co. Limited consumes several business applications, many of which are SaaS-based tools hosted on vendor cloud systems. These are split across internal systems and business-focused applications and include the following:

- CRM (SaaS-based application)
- Marketing and Advertising Toolkits (SaaS-based applications)
- Finance and Accounting software (On-premises servers)
- Probio Control Suite (monitoring applications located at manufacturing centers)
- Payroll and HR applications

Now that you have a high-level overview of the IT infrastructure and some core business applications, it's time to evaluate some of the business's more urgent requirements. Throughout this study guide, you will have an opportunity to address these requirements and formulate solutions that can be designed, built, and delivered via AWS.

Core business requirements for this engagement

This section examines two immediate business requirements for which the company would like to consider a cloud-based solution. As an AWS Cloud Practitioner, you will have the opportunity to analyze the requirements and formulate possible solutions using the knowledge gained from this study guide. In later chapters of this book, you will be asked to architect and implement two projects—one for each requirement. The requirements are detailed below, along with a **high-level design** (**HLD**) solution concept for your reference. As you progress through the study guide, you will use these requirements to build your architecture and implement the appropriate solutions.

Requirement 1 – Developing a customer-facing website that helps promote the company brand among the public

The company has strategically decided to decommission the existing website as it no longer sees its value. This well-established company has already secured a significant partnership with major supermarkets and grocery chains. Any new B2B clientele would comprise smaller startups in the UK anyway, and enquiries would come through well-established channels. Instead, the company has decided to design a new front-end website to promote its products to end customers.

High-level requirements

For the foreseeable future, the customer-facing website should only offer a *window-shopping* service for new products, blog articles on gut health, and a form to collect end-customer details for free sample trials and a free recipe book. Belly Brew Co. Limited would like to build a database of all regular and potential customers that will be used in marketing campaigns. The company also hopes to use this data to design surveys and generate feedback on its products, which can be used to innovate new lines for the business.

Purchase of actual products would still take place via supermarkets and grocery stores. The company will eventually look to sell its products on its e-commerce website, but this is not likely to happen for at least another 24 months.

High-level design solution

The website should be scalable and highly available. It should incorporate security best practices and design methodologies that align with corporate policies. The following high-level design diagram illustrates the architecture you will deploy in your AWS account.

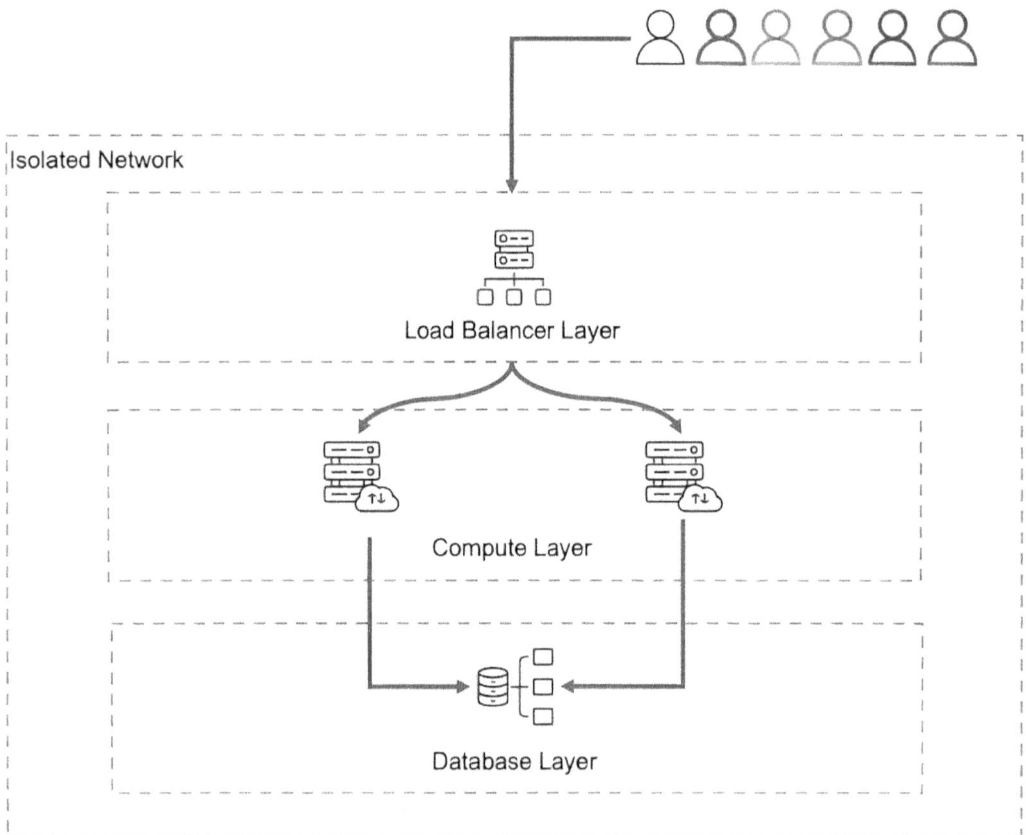

Figure 1.4: High-Level Design – Belly Brew Co. Limited's Corporate Website

This high-level design depicts a three-layer architecture enclosed in a private, isolated network. You will build a private network in your AWS account using the Amazon **Virtual Private Cloud** (**VPC**) service discussed in *Chapter 7*. AWS enables you to define isolated networks within the AWS cloud to separate your workloads from each other. This ensures application isolation, offers various security features, and allows you to fulfill compliance regulations. For example, you would not want your customer-facing website to be in the same network as your internal HR system to avoid security risks such as data breaches or unauthorized access to sensitive employee information.

The three-tier design would consist of:

- **Load Balancer Layer**: This layer will accept incoming traffic from end users on the Internet and direct them to internal servers hosting your web application. The load balancer ensures even distribution of traffic across multiple servers used to support your application. It can also perform health checks against your internal servers and ensure traffic is directed to only healthy servers. If a server fails, it can direct traffic from that server to another healthy server, ensuring high availability, which is a critical requirement for Belly Brew Co. Limited. You will learn how to set up load balancers for the website application in *Chapter 10*.
- **Compute Layer**: This layer will host virtual servers running a Linux operating system and be configured as web servers. The application will provide the business logic to enable visitors to the site to post their details, such as name and email address. The details will be used to send these visitors the free recipe eBook, and free trial coupons that can be exchanged for its beverages from supermarkets and grocery stores. Hosting multiple servers in the compute layer will ensure that if a server fails, the application can continue functioning from other remaining servers. You will also learn how to provision servers to automatically maintain a specific fleet size and scale your compute resources based on demand. You will learn how to provision and configure the required compute resources in *Chapter 8*.
- **Database Layer**: This layer will host databases that will be used to capture and store visitor details persistently. Databases represent an integral part of any application architecture, offering long-term persistent storage of data and enabling the ability to query vast amounts of data to extract business-critical information. When building your website application for Belly Brew Co. Limited, choosing the correct database is crucial. Equally important is the security and availability of that data. These concepts are discussed in *Chapter 9*. As part of the project, you will deploy a MySQL database to host visitor data for your website application.

This design gives Belly Brew Co. Limited a secure and scalable foundation for its customer-facing website. The next requirement shifts focus from public engagement to the company's internal R&D data analytics processes.

Requirement 2 – Improving R&D data analytics processes

The R&D department struggles with ad hoc and routine analysis of monitoring data generated at its manufacturing plants. Due to the use of old legacy systems, delays in obtaining various analytical data of their products during the manufacturing process result in delays on the production line. This means customers often don't get their deliveries on time, resulting in complaints.

High-level requirements

The daily analysis of Kombucha casks to identify any stock that fails the safety tests takes a long time. Currently, the monitoring tool, provided and managed by a third party, produces a printout of a report listing each Kombucha cask and whether it failed the safety check. Specifically, if the pH levels exceed 3.5 or drop below 2.5, the cask must be removed from production. A manual process needs to be carried out to review this report and identify any casks needing removal from production. It can sometimes take a while to determine which casks fail the safety checks. Belly Brew Co. Limited has a requirement to devise a viable solution that can speed up the analysis process of these reports and quickly identify casks that need to be removed from production.

Discussions with the third-party vendor that supplies the monitoring tool suggest that their application can be configured to post reports as a **comma-separated file** (**CSV**) to any storage platform in the cloud if required. This file structure allows you to capture data in a structured manner that can be easily manipulated using a tabular format. However, a solution is needed to consume and analyze the data in those files quickly.

All casks must be analyzed by 5 PM each day so that the night staff can send the casks for bottling. A history of daily reports needs to be maintained in case records need to be reviewed at a later stage.

High-level design solution

Belly Brew Co. Limited is looking for a simple yet robust solution that would allow it to analyze the data from the CSV files and produce a report that will quickly identify the casks that fail the safety checks within minutes. The following high-level design diagram illustrates the architecture you will deploy in your AWS account to fulfill the business requirements.

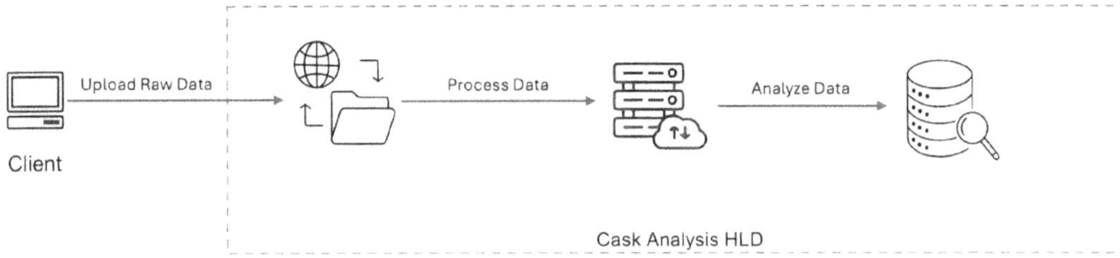

Figure 1.5: Belly Brew Co. Limited's Kombucha Casks Analytics

The components of this architecture are as follows:

- **Storage Layer**: Amazon S3 can store CSV-formatted reports. The third-party provider can post the CSV files to the S3 bucket. Amazon S3 is an object storage solution that can store virtually unlimited amounts of data as flat files, such as documents, images, and video. Amazon S3 is discussed in detail in *Chapter 6*.
- **Analytical Service**: To quickly query the data, the contents of the CSV file must be accessible by an analytical tool that can run SQL queries against the raw data and extract the information on which casks failed the safety checks. Amazon Athena is a tool designed to run queries against raw data held in Amazon S3 and forms part of AWS's analytical services on offer. Analytics is discussed in *Chapter 13*.
- **Compute Layer**: At a specific schedule, a computing service must update Amazon Athena with new data and then perform the query to extract information on the casks. The compute process must be triggered at defined schedules as required. AWS compute services are discussed in *Chapter 8*.

Together, these services provide a lightweight way to store the daily reports, query them quickly, and help the R&D team identify failed casks in time for the evening bottling process.

Summary

While learning new technologies will help you develop your career, employers are keen to see what real-world experience you can bring. Newly certified professionals must constantly battle the age-old catch-22 situation – you have the qualification but no experience, versus you have the experience but don't have the credentials. When learning something new, you often need the opportunity to apply your newfound knowledge to develop expertise and skill, understanding the intricate nuances of design, configuration, implementation, troubleshooting, and support.

This chapter introduced you to a scenario of a typical business that could benefit from moving its IT infrastructure and business applications to the cloud. The scenario discusses the business of a fictitious company called Belly Brew Co. Limited, which is looking to expand its business and develop its brand by developing and launching new product ranges, upgrading its technology consumption, and designing solutions that will enable it to become more agile and competitive in the market. The company's IT infrastructure and applications need a revamp. This includes the decision to design and launch a more customer-focused website and resolve some backend operation issues with its manufacturing processes around maintaining the health and safety of its products and addressing the cost concerns of the company.

This study guide will walk you through two project solutions Belly Brew Co. Limited can use to fulfill its business requirements. You will receive clear step-by-step instructions on architecting and deploying your solution in your AWS account. Using the knowledge gained from the theoretical concepts discussed in the following chapters and various AWS technologies and services, you will implement real-world solutions in response to Belly Brew Co. Limited's requirements.

The next chapter will introduce you to the key features and configurations of cloud computing and discuss its benefits.

2

What Is Cloud Computing?

In this chapter, you'll be introduced to cloud computing—what it is, along with a high-level overview of its service models and deployment methods. You'll explore how cloud computing has become the default choice for businesses seeking to use technology to solve problems, build innovative solutions, and serve customers more effectively. You'll also learn how cloud computing has leveled the playing field, empowering both large enterprises and small startups to build scalable, highly available, secure, and cost-effective applications.

Additionally, this chapter provides a high-level overview of virtualization and its critical role in making cloud computing what it is today: a way to access cutting-edge technology using a **pay-as-you-go model** rather than locking up capital in expensive on-premises hardware.

The following topics are covered in this chapter:

- Understanding cloud computing
- Exploring virtualization technologies
- Comparing cloud computing service models
- Choosing cloud deployment models
- Applying the six advantages of cloud computing

Understanding cloud computing

Traditionally, if you wanted to host business applications or e-commerce websites to promote your products on-premises, you would have to consider the cost of the physical hardware, its ongoing maintenance, and support. Hosting expensive infrastructure equipment also incurs costs associated with managing **heating, ventilation, and air conditioning** (**HVAC**), as well as expensive real estate space required to house the infrastructure. In addition, there are networking costs related to inbound internet connectivity, firewall, and security measures you must implement to avoid attacks and outages and ensure continuous connectivity and access for your customers.

Cloud computing is the **on-demand delivery** of IT services to customers and partners, usually through a network, such as the public internet. Businesses can access these services that enable them to provision IT resources such as compute, network, storage, databases, and software using a pay-as-you-go pricing model instead of procuring and maintaining physical infrastructure.

This enables businesses to consume IT services using an **Operating Expenditure** (**OPEX**) mode of investment instead of a **capital expenditure** (**CAPEX**) mode. Instead of procuring expensive hardware, businesses can *lease* the available capacity in the cloud provider's IT infrastructure to provide the required IT resources. This can help companies host those same applications without incurring unnecessary capital costs. Companies opting for cloud computing can thus invest their capital in more business-critical requirements, such as **research and development** (**R&D**) projects to build and design innovative products and services, fulfill compliance and regulatory requirements, marketing, and sales.

Cloud computing is much more than leasing infrastructure from a supplier. It offers flexibility and speed when provisioning required IT resources through a **self-service approach**. Rather than place service requests with the provider to have the necessary IT resources provisioned by remote engineers, businesses can access the provider's cloud environment and programmatically provision resources on their own. When those resources are no longer required, they can terminate them just as quickly, ensuring that they only pay for the resources they consume.

This is all possible thanks to virtualization technologies, which will be discussed in this chapter's *Exploring virtualization technologies* section, and the ability to interact with the cloud providers' IT ecosystem through a piece of technology called **Application Programming Interface** (**API**). An API enables two software components to communicate with each other over a set of defined rules and protocols. Another way to describe APIs is to think of them as messengers between the two software applications that facilitate necessary interaction between them. These APIs enable you to programmatically access services and request specific permitted actions, which also ensures security since you are only allowed to make authorized API calls.

By allowing you to directly interact with the cloud providers' systems programmatically and make authorized API calls, you can provision resources through this self-service model. There is no need to wait for the providers' remote engineer to provision those resources for you. You can securely access the provider's cloud environment through web and network interfaces and provision your required resources programmatically.

Consider a high-level overview of an online flight booking system to gain a deeper understanding of how APIs work. A high-level architecture design is depicted in *Figure 2.1*:

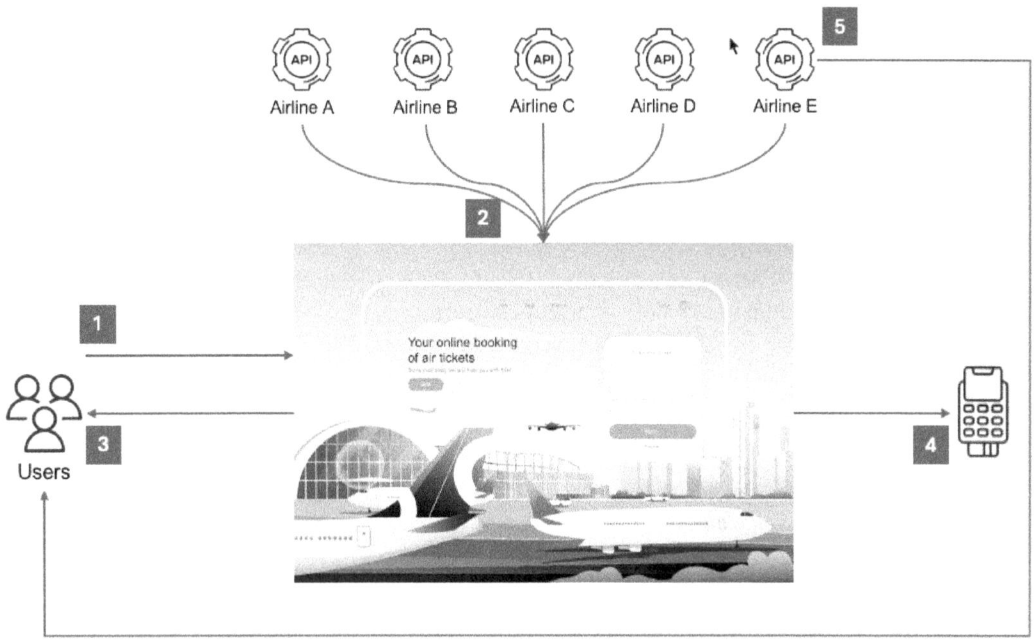

Figure 2.1: Flight Aggregator System making API calls to get flight ticket details

To book flights for your next vacation, you could use an aggregator website to search for flights to your destination offered by different airline companies. The key steps (as shown in *Figure 2.1*) would involve the following:

1. You provide your travel details, choice of cabin, and any meal preferences, and input these details into the aggregator website
2. The website you are interacting with records all your requirements and obtains available flight schedules and pricing data from the airline companies by making API calls to them
3. You are presented with a list of possible flights from the cheapest to the most expensive
4. You choose a particular airline and schedule and make the payment
5. The aggregator books the flight with the relevant airline company, and the airline issues your ticket and PNR number

This interaction between the aggregator and the airline company happens because the aggregator uses APIs to submit booking requests and retrieve flight information on your behalf. By agreeing on a common API interface, different companies can exchange information even though their underlying systems may be implemented differently. The following section provides an example of how API calls enable customers to interact with AWS.

Making API calls with AWS

Cloud providers like AWS expose approved and authorized APIs that enable programmatic calls to their various services, allowing you to interact with them and provision the required IT resources.

For example, as shown in the screenshot in *Figure 2.2*, your configuration choices in the web console result in the client application making API calls to backend services to provision the required resources. In this example, you are provisioning a virtual server running Amazon Linux, which you can then use to host your application.

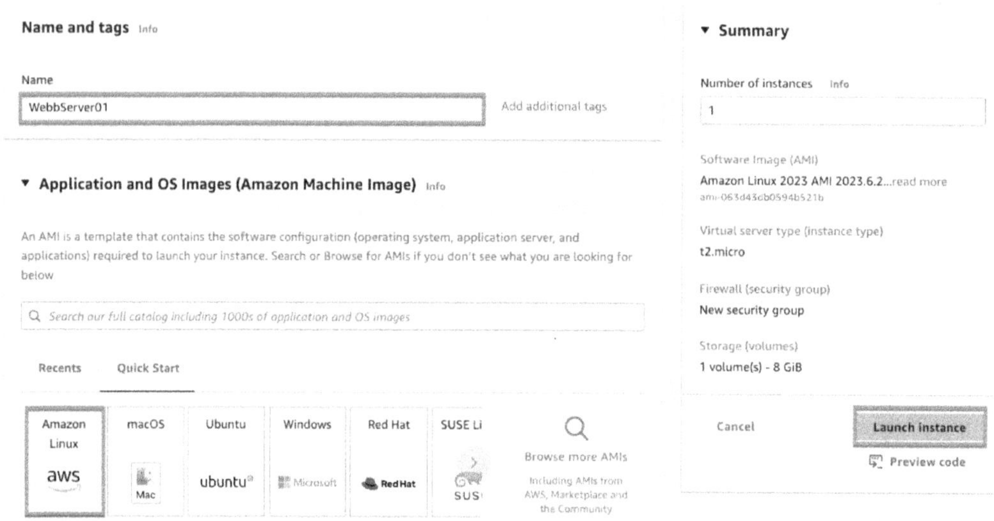

Figure 2.2: Web Console Screenshot – Launching an EC2 Instance

These APIs are made available securely and predictably so that only authenticated users can access them, and you can only make calls that are authorized, ensuring the overall security of the provider's environment simultaneously.

You can interact with the AWS ecosystem using the web management console and the **command line interface** (**CLI**). The CLI is a tool you install on your local computer that allows you to make API calls to services in your AWS account using approved commands.

You can also write code and build applications to programmatically interact with AWS using a supported language and the provider's **software development kits** (**SDKs**). This kit consists of tools, libraries, and documentation that enable you to choose a supported programming language to gain knowledge of the AWS ecosystem and make the right API calls.

In the next section, you will learn more about virtualization and how this piece of technology has been fundamental to the evolution of cloud computing.

Exploring virtualization technologies

Most modern applications function following a client-server model. Multiple users often access the same application simultaneously – for example, you and millions of others simultaneously access Netflix to binge-watch your favorite shows. This is made possible through the client-server model.

The following diagram in *Figure 2.3* depicts a high-level representation of this client-server model for illustration purposes.

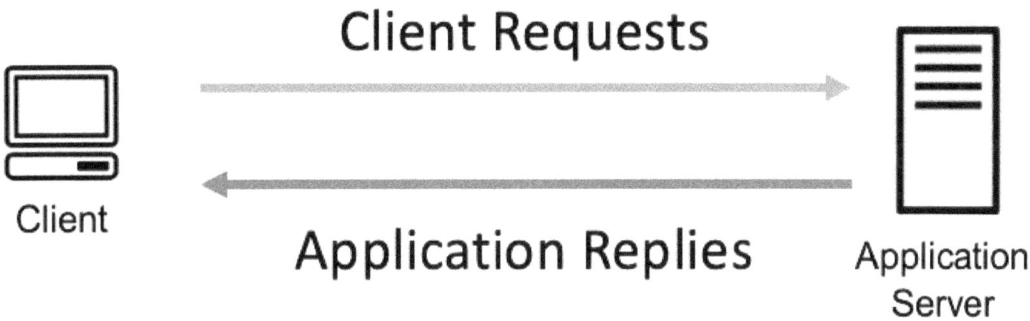

Figure 2.3: Client-Server relationship

As depicted in the diagram in *Figure 2.3*, you use client software on your local device to access the server application, such as a web browser interface or a fully blown desktop application. The client sends a request to the server, and the server responds to that request.

Applications that run on servers are specifically designed to handle many incoming requests. These servers run on physical hardware that is usually more powerful than your standard desktop, laptop, or mobile device. Additionally, the operating system installed on these servers is typically a variation of the standard desktop or laptop operating system. They are designed to serve multiple requests and host various applications. They are intended for server components in your client-server model. For example, you get two flavors of the Windows operating system—one for desktops/laptops, such as Microsoft Windows 11, and the other for servers, such as Microsoft Windows Server 2025.

Before the advent of virtualization technologies in the late 1990s and early 2000s, companies had to procure multiple physical servers and storage equipment to host a wide range of software services. Even though hardware technologies had drastically improved capabilities, businesses could not host numerous applications on the same physical server due to compatibility issues. Since each physical server would only host a single operating system with standard system files and libraries, any software installed on those servers must be compatible with the operating system and those system files. For example, if you want to host two applications—one running on Microsoft Windows and the other on Red Hat Linux—then you would need two physical servers.

When virtualization became a mainstream reality, thanks to the efforts of companies like IBM, VMware, and Microsoft, it redefined how businesses built, designed, and deployed their applications. Virtualization is a technology that uses software to create an abstraction layer of the physical hardware components, such as CPU, memory, network, and storage. This software allows you to divide your physical servers (and their components) into multiple virtual servers, or what is commonly known as **virtual machines** (**VMs**).

In *Figure 2.4*, the right-hand image depicts a typical virtualization architecture that makes use of a **Hypervisor** to enable the creation of virtual machines:

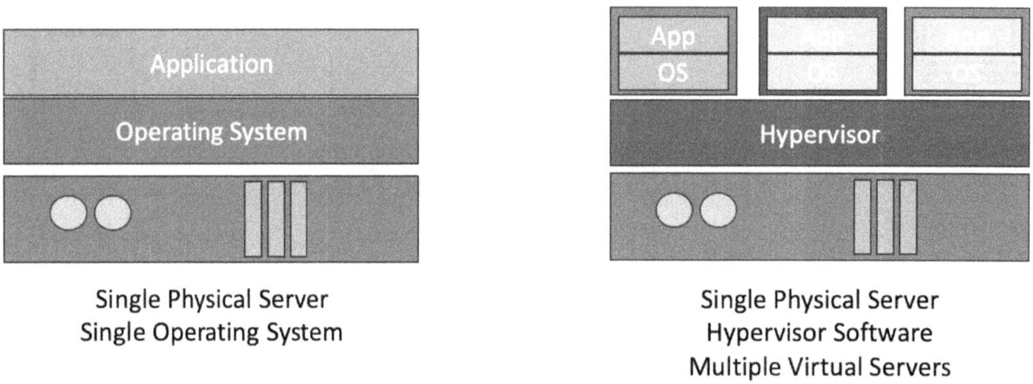

Figure 2.4: Physical Servers vs. Virtualization

Each virtual machine would have its own operating system, and all applications would be encased in a VM. This enables you to deploy multiple applications on the same physical server, even those that have compatibility issues with other applications.

In the diagram illustrated in *Figure 2.4*, the illustration on the right represents a single physical server using a Hypervisor. This is a virtualization technology that enables you to create virtual machines, each with its own operating system running on a single physical hardware. In this example, you are, in effect, running three virtual servers, each hosting an application on the same physical server.

Additional benefits of virtualization include:

- Hosting multiple applications on a single server better uses the hardware resources
- It reduces the energy consumption required to host fleets of servers and applications and is also more cost-effective

- Easier backup and recovery, thanks to the portability of virtual machine images
- Faster software installation and setup
- Reduced compatibility issues

Given the advancement of virtualization technologies, cloud vendors such as AWS can offer an almost endless supply of virtual machines to the rest of the world, enabling businesses to build highly available, scalable, and cost-effective solutions. This technology has undergone substantial innovation, enabling AWS to offer its customers managed platforms and services, as well as the concept of serverless architectures. We will discuss these more advanced solutions in subsequent chapters.

To understand how cloud services differ, it helps to look at the main service models that define how much responsibility you keep and how much the cloud provider manages for you. In the next section, you will learn about three different cloud computing service models, each offering various levels of control, flexibility, and management.

Comparing cloud computing service models

Businesses require a wide range of applications, and cloud computing offers the ability to offload the cost and complexity associated with hosting and managing those applications. Often, businesses will use a combination of **off-the-shelf** (**OTS**) products and specific line-of-business applications, some of which are designed and built in-house.

Cloud computing models offer a way to cater to all such variations. So, for example, many cloud providers offer productivity suites as a complete end-to-end software package. Examples include Microsoft Office 365, which offers a suite comprising word processing, spreadsheets, presentation software, and desktop-level databases, among many others. At the same time, businesses will often have special in-house developed or bespoke software solutions that must be deployed on a custom-built infrastructure. A cloud provider, such as AWS, can provide access to virtual infrastructure components comprising VMs, networks, storage, and databases.

Cloud computing services can be offered across three separate models. The model you choose for your project will depend on your application-specific needs and the level of control you require of the underlying infrastructure that supports your application stack. The following sections provide an overview of each of these model types.

Infrastructure as a service

Infrastructure as a Service (**IaaS**) is a cloud computing model that delivers virtualized components to enable you to build your cloud environments. These include compute, network, and storage services offering maximum flexibility, allowing you to define custom-built cloud networks with necessary security configurations. This model will enable you to deploy virtual machines hosting various operating systems, applications, and storage services to host and manage data. This model is closely related to traditional on-premises environments, except that you do not have direct access to the underlying hardware and can only define configuration items from the virtual machine's **operating system** (**OS**) layer upward.

Amazon Elastic Compute Cloud (**EC2**) is an example of IaaS. The service enables you to deploy virtual machines (servers) running a choice of Linux, Microsoft, or MacOS operating systems and comes in various configurations to support different use cases – capable of hosting standard websites through more intensive **high-performance computing** (**HPC**) applications.

Platform as a service

Platform as a Service (**PaaS**) is a cloud computing model that enables you to focus more on your application code and its development lifecycle rather than spend time and effort configuring underlying infrastructure resources. This is because when you supply your application code, you also provide details such as the language and framework used to build the application. You also provide details of any application requirements, such as high availability and scalability, and if you require a backend database.

The PaaS Service then provisions all the necessary infrastructure using the information provided by automated scripts. It provides an environment to host and support your application and manages its deployment and lifecycle.

With this service model, you can also easily manage your application's lifecycle and define different deployment strategies and processes for managing upgrades to the application code.

Most PaaS solutions, such as those offered by AWS, like AWS Elastic Beanstalk, also allow you to decide how the underlying resources should be configured. For example, if your application requires high availability, the service will provision the necessary load balancers and deploy virtual servers across multiple availability zones.

> Note
>
> Regions and availability zones are discussed in *Chapter 3*.

Ultimately, the provider is responsible for configuring and managing the underlying infrastructure components, including virtual machines, storage, network configurations, and databases, reducing your overall burden and allowing you to focus more on your application layer.

For example, you can use AWS Elastic Beanstalk to deploy a complete three-tier application architecture comprising a load balancer, front and backend compute layers, and a database solution. The PaaS service can be instructed to build the entire infrastructure stack, which includes application load balancers, virtual servers running the Linux operating system to host the application logic, and a backend database to host customer data.

> **Tip**
>
> Although outside the scope of the AWS Certified Cloud Practitioner Exam, if you are interested in building and deploying a sample three-tier application using AWS Elastic Beanstalk, you can review this detailed how-to guide on YouTube at `https://youtu.be/sAyCmAryjU4`

Software as a Service

Software as a Service (**SaaS**) is a cloud computing model that delivers a complete end-to-end software application, usually over the Internet. Hosting and managing any hardware or infrastructure component is unnecessary since you will not need to install the software locally in your environment. Most SaaS products are also accessible using a standard browser interface, although some offer fully functional client desktop applications.

For example, Microsoft Office 365 is a SaaS offering that enables you to access office productivity tools via the internet. One such tool is Microsoft Exchange, which provides email, calendar, and task services. You can access your email mailbox account directly on the Office 365 portal over the Internet using the online version of Microsoft Outlook, or install a desktop edition of the Outlook software to send and receive emails. Microsoft Outlook is the client software that connects to the server component of Microsoft Exchange.

The important distinction between hosting Exchange on premises and Office 365 is that you do not need to run your copy of Microsoft Exchange. You do not have to deploy your Exchange servers or worry about patching them or updating and upgrading the Exchange software when newer versions are released.

But while SaaS-based solutions remove much of the infrastructure provisioning and management from the customer to the vendor, certain applications may require end-user configuration for which you may need to hire **subject matter experts** (**SMEs**) who can configure the product. For example, with Microsoft Exchange, you will still need to set up your company Exchange account and domain names, necessary DNS records, set up users, groups, and mailboxes, and define specific security rules and permissions. These tasks would require you to either have in-house expertise or outsource the configuration and support of the service to a third party.

AWS also provides several SaaS-based products, such as Amazon WorkDocs and Amazon QuickSight. Amazon WorkDocs is a fully managed platform for creating, sharing, and enriching digital content. In contrast, Amazon QuickSight is a business intelligence tool designed to help build dashboards and visuals for data analysis. There are no servers to provision and no underlying infrastructure to manage.

In the case of our fictitious client, Belly Brew Co. Limited, a new customer-facing website that will promote its products and engage with the public must be built, designed, and deployed. This website can be hosted on an IaaS, PaaS, or even SaaS platform—AWS can offer both IaaS and PaaS solutions. For a SaaS-based solution, Belly Brew Co. Limited could consider using a fully managed web hosting platform offering website-building services like WordPress.

Choosing a suitable model depends on your business requirements and whether you are building an in-house solution or can subscribe to an **off-the-shelf** (**OTS**) product that fulfills your requirements. For in-house applications, you can opt for an IaaS model or a PaaS solution, though the latter would have some restrictions. For example, legacy systems may need to be refactored or re-architected since many PaaS solutions would support only modern languages and libraries.

> **Tip**
>
> You can learn more about the different approaches to migrations by reviewing this article at `https://iaas-academy1.teachable.com/p/understanding-the-7rs-of-aws-migration-a-quick-guide-for-aspiring-cloud-practitioners`

SaaS-based solutions take away much of the overhead in managing underlying infrastructure and the application lifecycle. You don't need to worry about designing, building, and deploying updates, releases, and bug fixes. This is the vendor's responsibility. However, at the same time, you do lose the flexibility in how that lifecycle is managed.

While IaaS gives you the flexibility to custom-design and build your underlying infrastructure that will host your application, it also means that you will need to employ the necessary expertise to correctly configure, support, and manage that infrastructure, as well as incur the required costs associated with it. The following table in *Figure 2.5* summarizes each cloud model and the breakdown of responsibility across each model.

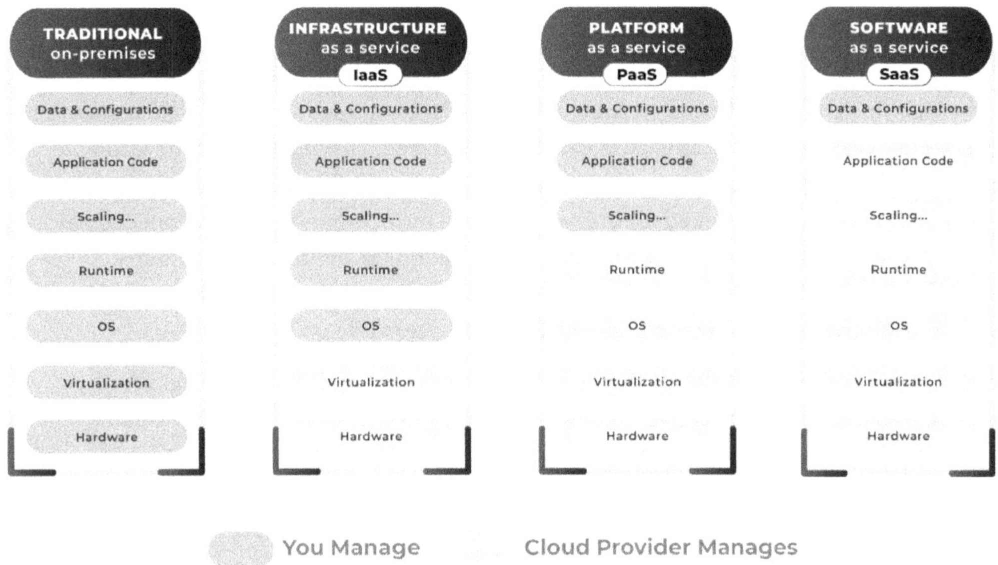

Figure 2.5: Cloud Computing Models and levels of customer responsibility and management

After understanding how responsibility is shared across IaaS, PaaS, and SaaS, it is equally important to consider where these cloud environments are hosted. This brings us to cloud deployment models and the advantages and trade-offs each model presents. In the next section, you will learn more about cloud deployment models, which examine where the environment's infrastructure is located and its key advantages and disadvantages.

Choosing cloud deployment models

Businesses have different requirements for hosting and managing their IT resources, applications, and workloads. Some applications are highly sensitive to latency issues caused by wide-area networks and must operate as closely as possible to other services or end users. At the same time, certain businesses must host all their IT services and resources in-house due to strict compliance and regulatory requirements. Yet another scenario could be that a business would need to host certain resources on-premises and others in the cloud due to technical requirements and/or cost control.

Businesses can choose between three primary cloud deployment models (**private**, **public**, and **hybrid**) for cloud computing deployment. These three deployment models are discussed next.

Private cloud

This configuration involves using virtualization solutions and software management tools to deliver self-service capabilities in resource provisioning, configuration, and management. Like normal cloud environments, end users can define and create resources from the available infrastructure to fulfill application requirements. The key difference here is that this cloud environment is usually designed for only internal use by an organization and not external customers. While this is much like a traditional on-premises environment, resource management software and self-service modeling are designed to increase the utilization of available resources and remove excessive administrative burdens.

Private cloud environments lack many features and the economies of scale that are often attributed to public cloud due to the investment made in the latter by dedicated cloud vendors such as AWS, Microsoft, and Google. Finally, building a private cloud solution would incur a sizable capital investment upfront, which is not ideal for many businesses. Nevertheless, some organizations would still need to host their applications within a private cloud environment for reasons such as regulatory laws or national security. Another technical reason would be the requirement for extremely low-latency connectivity.

Public cloud

A public cloud provider, such as AWS, offers access to an extensive range of IT technologies and services that end customers and partners can use to build solutions and host applications using a pay-as-you-go model. These providers enable you to design, build, and deploy your application natively in the cloud and facilitate migrating applications on-premises to the cloud through various tools and processes. The biggest advantage to using a public cloud service is that you do not need to procure expensive hardware and can move away from a CAPEX mode of investment in IT to an OPEX one.

Another key advantage is that cloud providers design and build innovative solutions that are accessible at affordable prices, leveraging economies of scale due to adoption by a large pool of customers. Cloud providers also offer access to globally located data center facilities, enabling you to build highly available solutions, access global markets, and fulfill disaster recovery strategies, enhancing global customer experience. These features would likely be cost-prohibitive for most companies if they only adopted traditional on-premises IT services. Small retail businesses, for example, can benefit from cloud computing by efficiently deploying their applications across the globe without having to procure real estate and expensive hardware in multiple regions, giving them access to a wider customer base.

Hybrid cloud

Hybrid cloud environments are a design pattern that bridges private and public clouds. Most companies will find themselves in this configuration simply because, traditionally, they may have built on an on-premises environment and are now looking to offload a portion of their IT services to the public cloud. Another reason for hybrid deployments is that certain business application components must reside on premises due to network bandwidth, latency issues, or compliance and regulatory laws. Hybrid cloud environments usually involve designing network and application connectivity between on-premises systems and the public cloud account.

Companies expanding their IT footprint generally try to identify public cloud options. This avoids CAPEX expenditure and grants access to cutting-edge technologies and services through a pay-as-you-go model.

With these deployment models in mind, we can now look more closely at why businesses adopt cloud computing in the first place and how those advantages can help Belly Brew Co. Limited become more agile and competitive.

Applying the six advantages of cloud computing

The cloud offers several benefits to businesses of all sizes, from new startups to well-established multinational companies. In this section, we review the six advantages of cloud computing:

- **Trade fixed expenses for variable expenses**: Traditional IT involves procuring expensive hardware and building in-house or co-located data center facilities to host and support your application portfolio. With the cloud, all hardware infrastructure components are procured and managed by the cloud vendor, leaving you to provision and consume virtualized IT resources such as virtual machines, storage volumes, and network services on a pay-as-you-consume model. Belly Brew Co. Limited can rapidly embark on its cloud journey, paying only for the resources it uses without worrying about purchasing any physical hardware.
- **Benefit from massive economies of scale**: Cloud providers like AWS serve thousands of customers across the globe, enabling them to architect, build, and deliver services at much lower costs, all thanks to the concept of economies of scale. If Belly Brew Co. Limited were to build its own in-house analytical tools, manage releases, bug fixes, and support, the costs associated would be much greater than if it used managed offerings from AWS.

- **Stop guessing capacity**: Traditional on-premises IT infrastructure design and build patterns often resulted in companies adopting a 'peak load provisioning' model. Because it is usually difficult to predict demand and capacity requirements, many businesses would spend extra to ensure they have additional capacity to handle peak load periods. This means that resources would often be underutilized and idle during low usage, wasting resources and money.
  Many providers, such as AWS, offer auto-scaling services that enable businesses to provision resources when required and just as quickly terminate them when demand drops, resulting in better cost management. Using auto-scaling services, Belly Brew Co. Limited could provision website application servers that would scale out when traffic to the website increases and scale back in when traffic drops, ensuring a cost-optimized architecture.
- **Increased speed and agility**: With traditional IT, you would have to wait for long lead times to deliver physical hardware, which must be installed and configured. This results in developers having to wait weeks or even months before they can get started on projects. With cloud computing, you can provision new resources such as servers, storage volumes, and network resources in seconds. The latter enables you to build a range of environments to cater to development, testing, and production quickly. Belly Brew Co. Limited can access cloud computing services to spin up the necessary infrastructure resources to host their new customer-facing website in minutes, all with high availability, scalability, and fault tolerance.
- **Stop spending money running and maintaining data centers**: Cloud computing enables businesses to focus on their core products and services and the applications that differentiate them from the competition. There is no need to focus on building, designing, and investing in the underlying infrastructure, enabling businesses to direct their precious capital to more important matters, such as designing better products and solutions or sales and marketing. With cloud computing, the company can consume cloud IT services and resources to build applications that enable it to better engage with its customers and ensure quality, on-time products, rather than focus time and money on data center activities.
- **Go global in minutes**: Cloud providers like AWS offer access to multiple global data centers across multiple regions. You can deploy your applications across these regions to ensure global reach over a low-latency network connection. Attempting to build a global presence in this manner is often cost-prohibitive for many organizations, had it not been for cloud computing.

These six advantages of cloud computing illustrate their critical benefits compared to traditional on-premises environments. Belly Brew Co. Limited can benefit from moving its workloads to the cloud, enabling it to design, build, and deploy solutions more quickly and at a more manageable pay-as-you-go price. Belly Brew Co. Limited's **Chief Finance Officer** (**CFO**) does not need to commit large amounts of capital to hardware procurement and can still benefit from cutting-edge technologies that can deploy applications that are accessible globally. Belly Brew Co. Limited can become more agile and deliver new innovative solutions for both its end customers and internal stakeholders.

Summary

This chapter examines the world of cloud computing at a high level. You learned about how traditional IT services have evolved into cloud computing thanks to the invention of virtualization technologies. Understanding the various cloud computing and delivery models with their features and specific use cases is critical for the exam since knowing which model is appropriate for particular use cases will be tested.

In practical terms, you will find that many companies have a hybrid cloud solution since the need to host infrastructure and data on-premises continues to be a requirement across various industries due to either compliance and regulatory requirements or simply because of latency-related issues. AWS offers many services to help build hybrid cloud environments across compute, storage, networking, and security foundations, such as authentication and authorization processes.

For most small to medium enterprises, looking after infrastructure, whether on-premises or in the cloud, is costly and incurs additional management overhead. This directs precious resources toward activities the business would rather not have to deal with. Building architectural solutions using PaaS and SaaS services removes much of the underlying heavy lifting associated with IaaS architectures. The goal of a cloud practitioner, then, should be to help businesses focus on their core products and services and, where possible, pass this heavy lifting on to AWS. Finally, you learned about the six advantages of cloud computing and how Belly Brew Co. Limited can benefit by moving its workloads to the cloud.

In the next chapter, we introduce you to the largest cloud provider, **Amazon Web Services** (**AWS**), and its global infrastructure.

Exam Readiness Drill – Chapter Review Questions

Apart from mastering key concepts, strong test-taking skills under time pressure are essential for acing your certification exam. That's why developing these abilities early in your learning journey is critical.

Exam readiness drills, using the free online practice resources provided with this book, help you progressively improve your time management and test-taking skills while reinforcing the key concepts you've learned.

HOW TO GET STARTED

- Open the link or scan the QR code at the bottom of this page
- If you have unlocked the practice resources already, log in to your registered account. If you haven't, follow the instructions in *Free Benefits with Your Book* section in this book's *Preface* and come back to this page.
- Once you log in, click the START button to start this chapter's quiz
- We recommend attempting a quiz multiple times till you're able to answer most of the questions correctly and well within the time limit.
- You can use the following practice template to help you plan your attempts:

Working On Accuracy		
Attempt	**Target**	**Time Limit**
Attempt 1	40% or more	Till the timer runs out
Attempt 2	60% or more	Till the timer runs out
Attempt 3	75% or more	Till the timer runs out
Working On Timing		
Attempt 4	75% or more	1 minute before time limit
Attempt 5	75% or more	2 minutes before time limit
Attempt 6	75% or more	3 minutes before time limit

The above drill is just an example. Design your drills based on your own goals and make the most out of the online quizzes accompanying this book.

Link to this Chapter's Quiz

You need to unlock the online practice resources to access the link below. Check the *Free Benefits with Your Book* section in the *Preface* for detailed instructions on how to do this. You only need to unlock the resources once.

Open Quiz `https://packt.link/clf_c02_ch2` or scan the QR code

3

Introduction to AWS and the Global Infrastructure

This chapter introduces the world of **Amazon Web Services** (**AWS**), which is the world's largest cloud provider today. In August 2006, it was one of the first providers to launch a virtual server infrastructure in the cloud, **Amazon Elastic Compute Cloud** (**EC2**). Amazon EC2 is a compute service that enables you to host applications on virtual servers running Microsoft Windows, Linux, and even macOS.

Today, AWS offers over 200 services to cater to every possible business need, enabling its customers to build end-to-end application solutions hosted on its platform. The best part is that these services can be consumed to host workloads on a pay-as-you-go model, eliminating the need to tie up vast amounts of upfront capital in highly depreciating hardware that incurs various hidden costs, too.

This chapter discusses the AWS Global Infrastructure, which is a vast collection of data center facilities spread across global locations that enable customers to access cloud services and resources in a manner that addresses latency concerns as well as regulatory and compliance requirements. You will learn about regions and availability zones and how these infrastructure offerings will enable you to build highly available, highly performant, and compliance-ready solutions in the cloud.

You will also learn how AWS's edge locations are designed to help customers reach a global customer base, thanks to its content delivery network service offering—Amazon CloudFront. This chapter concludes by examining how Belly Brew Co. Limited can benefit from AWS Global Infrastructure.

The following topics are covered in this chapter:

- Understanding AWS and its service ecosystem
- Exploring Regions, Availability Zones, and edge infrastructure
- Comparing AWS Support Plans
- Monitoring AWS Health events and service availability
- Using AWS documentation, Knowledge Center, and security resources

Understanding AWS and its service ecosystem

Amazon Web Services (**AWS**) is a public cloud provider that has been named a leader in 2023 by Gartner in its Magic Quadrant for Strategic Cloud Platform Services for thirteen consecutive years. With over 200 services across all three cloud computing models (IaaS, PaaS, and SaaS), AWS caters to almost every business requirement. These range from virtualized infrastructure solutions comprising compute, network, storage, and databases to cutting-edge technologies such as the **Internet of Things** (network of interconnected devices that collect, exchange, and act on data through the internet to enable automation and smarter services), machine learning, and artificial intelligence.

Furthermore, within each service offering comes a wide range of variations and features to fulfill almost any business requirement. For example, AWS provides relational and non-relational databases within its database offering. It offers databases designed for specific purpose-built application types, enabling customers to choose the right tool for the job.

In addition, the **AWS Partner Network** (**APN**) comprises a growing community of systems integrators specializing in AWS and its services and offering extensive capabilities to help businesses adopt cloud technologies.

AWS offers these services to customers of all shapes and sizes worldwide via its collection of data centers and infrastructure facilities. These data centers and the extensive range of core infrastructure services enable customers worldwide to access AWS cloud technologies. The following section will teach you more about the AWS Global Infrastructure.

Exploring the AWS Global Infrastructure

The AWS Global Infrastructure comprises several strategically placed data center facilities across the globe through which over 200 services are offered to its customers. AWS serves customers from almost every industry, ranging in size from small startups to giant conglomerates. Its global infrastructure architecture must provide customers with a scalable and secure infrastructure that offers high availability and durability.

The design of this global infrastructure must fulfill a wide range of use cases. These include customers who need to deploy applications closer to their end consumers, who may be in different parts of the world. These customers require single-millisecond latency connections to their applications or customers who must ensure that they fulfill data residency requirements by ensuring that data is stored within a particular geographical border.

These use cases vary drastically. For example, the infrastructure components and design architectures required by Netflix will differ from those of a small startup that delivers services to a local government organization.

To cater to this widely differentiated customer base while fulfilling regulatory, compliance, and legal guidelines, AWS has built a global infrastructure comprising different data center design patterns and required hardware components. This also includes making strategic decisions on where to buy and lease real estate space and how to use the vast collection of infrastructure hardware.

The following sections cover the various components of the AWS Global Infrastructure.

Regions

AWS Regions are geographical locations that host one or more data center facilities. You can think of a data center facility as a physical building that houses a range of infrastructure components such as computing, network, and storage services. A region is a strategically defined geographical area where AWS offers infrastructure, platform, and software services. These regions are strategically chosen to ensure low-latency access to customers based in and around that region. *Figure 3.1* is an image of the Regions currently deployed by AWS at the time of writing this book.

Figure 3.1: AWS Regions

The grey dots represent regions that are currently live, and the black ones are regions that will soon be available to AWS customers. A few more regions may be available by the time this book is published.

For example, AWS has a London region designed for UK-based customers with low-latency connectivity. However, as shown in *Figure 3.2*, customers in Northern Ireland may find that the Dublin region offers lower latency. This is simply because the physical distance from Northern Ireland to Dublin is less than it is to London. Thus, customers can choose the region that is closest to them.

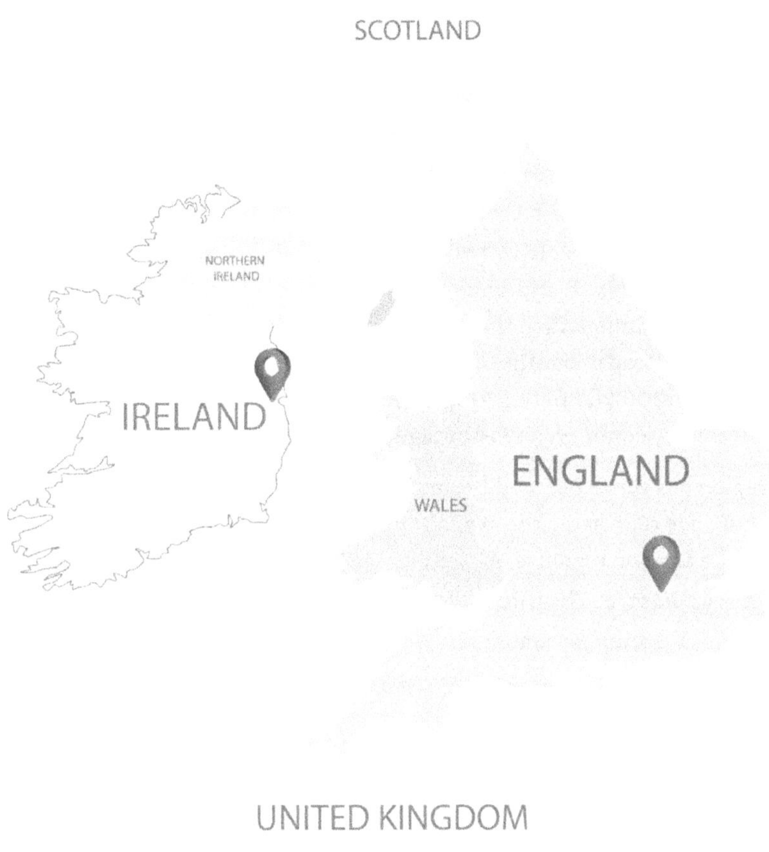

Figure 3.2: AWS regions in London and Dublin

Another reason for having multiple regions is to enable customers to fulfill data residency laws and regulatory requirements. This is because AWS will never replicate or move any data hosted in one region to another region. Since each region has its collection of infrastructure services, such as computing, network, and storage, which are isolated and separated from other regions, customers can rest assured that any data they host in one region will remain in that region unless, of course, the customer copies that data to another region.

So, some customers in the UK who are bound by these data sovereignty laws will be able to ensure that they fulfill those requirements by hosting their applications and data only in the London region. Taking this concept one step further, some customers in Northern Ireland may have no choice but to host their applications in the London region because they are bound by UK laws rather than the **European Union** (**EU**) or Irish laws. Those customers would not be able to use the services in the Dublin region, even though the Dublin region would offer lower latency.

Regions are further subdivided into availability zones. These are a collection of one or more data center facilities in large metropolitan areas within a geographical region, such as a country. These availability zones enable AWS to offer redundancy and high availability, which are discussed next.

Availability zones

Each region is subdivided into at least two distinct **availability zones** (**AZs**). Most regions have at least three availability zones, and some have even more. You can think of availability zones as metropolitan areas within which the regional data center facilities are physically located. Each AZ hosts its collection of **compute**, **storage**, and **network services**. These AZs are up to 60 miles or just under 100 kilometers from each other. This design reduces the possibility of all zones being affected by common power outages, fires, floods, or other disasters.

The London region has three availability zones. Each region has a designation code, and an extension of that code represents the availability zone names in that region. For example, the region code for the London region is `eu-west-2`. Similarly, the region code for the North Virginia region is `us-east-1`. The three availability zones within the London region are `eu-west-2a`, `eu-west-2b`, and `eu-west-2c`.

For some services, you can choose which availability zone to place your resources in. For example, when you deploy web applications and websites on AWS, they must run on some compute resource, such as a virtual server. A virtual server is a software-based representation of a physical computer that allows users to run operating systems and applications on a remote server, and it handles multiple requests for the service it offers. For example, a WordPress application on a server will answer visitor requests to view blog articles it hosts. One such compute service on AWS is the **Amazon Elastic Compute Cloud** (**EC2**) service, which enables customers to host virtual servers (EC2 instances) in the cloud.

When deploying this virtual server or EC2 instance, you must select the availability zone to deploy it in, as depicted in *Figure 3.3*.

Figure 3.3: Availability Zones in the London region

You also have the option to select '**No preference**', as displayed in the screenshot, if you want AWS to choose an availability zone for you. In this example, a subnet in availability zone `eu-west-2b` is being selected for the EC2 instance. A subnet represents a subset of the network range of the main network, known as a **Virtual Private Cloud** (**VPC**). These subnets are also known as sub-networks, meaning they are a smaller portion of the main network, specifically the VPC. VPCs and Subnets allow you to create private networks in the cloud, within which you host your resources, such as EC2 instances. A VPC spans the entire region, whereas a subnet, which is a subset range of that VPC, spans a single availability zone. VPCs and Subnets are discussed in more detail in *Chapter 7*.

In most cases, you would like to host your applications across multiple virtual servers. As a best practice, you must spread those servers across multiple availability zones in a region. This ensures that if one availability zone suffers an outage, your application running on the other virtual servers in the different availability zones continues to serve customers.

Interestingly, the availability zone names mentioned earlier are not the actual physical names/IDs of the zones. AWS will randomly map the availability zone names you reference to different physical zones, which changes from one AWS account to the next. Look at *Figure 3.4*, which lists the availability zones in the North Virginia region for two separate AWS accounts:

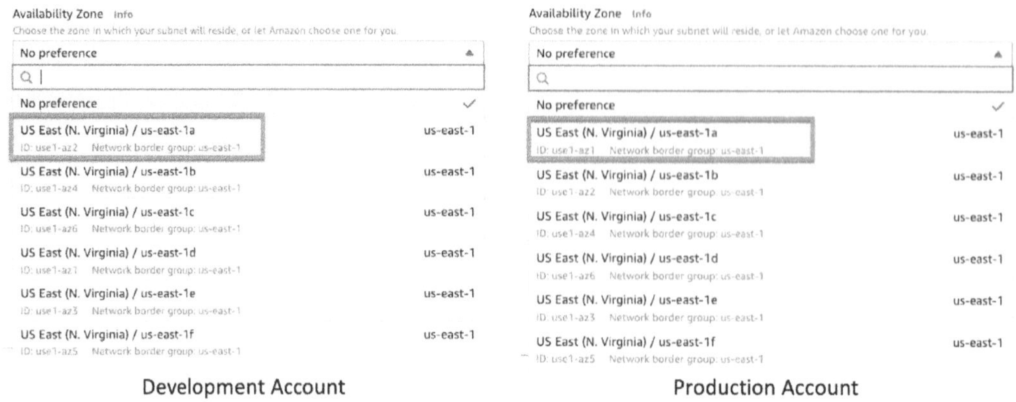

Figure 3.4: Availability zone names mapped to physical IDs of the zones

Notice that the Development Account availability zone `us-east-1a` (part of the `us-east-1` or North Virginia region) is mapped to the physical ID `use1-az2`, whereas the Production Account is mapped to `use1-az1`.

This is a crucial behind-the-scenes configuration feature because it ensures even distribution of resources across all availability zones, reducing the load on infrastructure services within a single zone. Consider an example where thousands of customers each have a single EC2 instance in the `us-east-1` region. The majority will choose the `us-east-1a` availability zone simply because it's at the top of the list. However, this would mean that the overall load of servers running in `us-east-1a` will be drastically higher when compared to the other zones. By randomly assigning the availability zone names to different physical zones in the region, you get a more even distribution of resources and better performance overall.

When you deploy an EC2 instance to host your website, you must choose a region and a specific availability zone in that region to host the instance. Furthermore, you must configure a private network in the AWS account that defines the IP Address boundary within which to host that instance. This requires you to specify a subnet (or a sub-network) that is tied to a given availability zone.

As per *Figure 3.5*, the Belly Brew Co. website is hosted on an EC2 instance running the Linux operating system in a public subnet in the `eu-west-2a` availability zone of the London region.

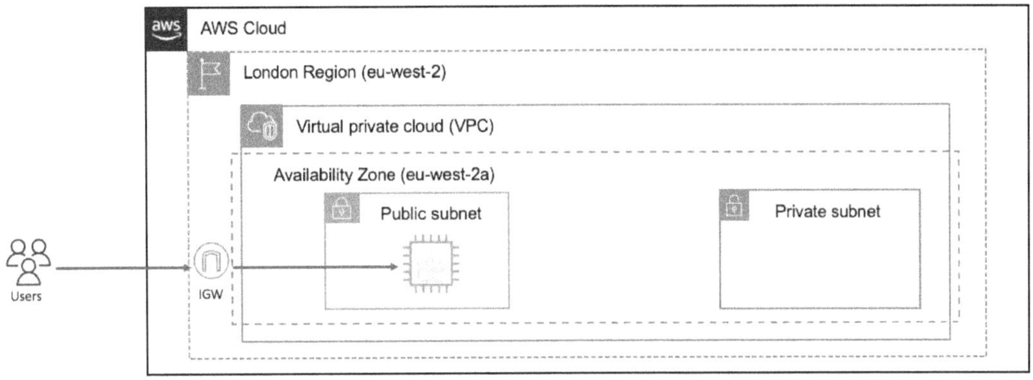

Figure 3.5: Hosting the Belly Brew Co. Limited website on EC2 in a subnet in the eu-west-2a AZ of the London region

This is a simple solution, but it has some security risks. Specifically, deploying a production web application in the public subnet is not recommended. *Figure 3.6*, later in this chapter, shows an alternative design where the EC2 instances are deployed in the private subnet.

A **subnet** is a network segment that defines an **Internet Protocol** (**IP**) address block of a larger network. This more extensive network is called a **Virtual Private Cloud** (**VPC**) on AWS, as illustrated in *Figure 3.5*. Customers can create isolated networks in their AWS account in the cloud, each hosting a different application stack to ensure isolation and separation. Within each VPC, you will have one or more subnets. So, for example, you can have one subnet host your application and another host your backend database. This further allows you to separate workloads that belong to an application stack.

Servers and other network devices require an IP address to communicate with each other. Devices that belong to the same subnet can usually communicate with each other by default because they are allocated private IP addresses from the same IP block range.

This is like your home network, comprising desktop computers, laptops, tablets, phones, and printers. Enabling inbound access to these devices would require you to create firewall rules on your home router/modem so that you can publish services such as your website on the Internet.

In the same way, you can create firewall rules for your VPC, enabling users on the Internet to access your website from the Internet, as depicted in *Figure 3.4*. Don't worry if this seems a bit complicated right now, as VPCs, subnets, and firewall rules are discussed in detail in *Chapter 7*.

The critical thing to remember is that, even though availability zones are isolated, they are close enough to enable synchronous replication with single-digit millisecond latency. Synchronous replication is where data is copied to another system, like a backup or secondary system, at the same time it is written to the main system. The opposite of synchronous is asynchronous, which is where data is first committed to the main system and then copied to the backup or secondary system.

When designing your application architecture, this allows you to distribute your workloads across multiple availability zones while ensuring low-latency connectivity between them. Using this concept, you can ensure your application is built for high availability. **High Availability** ensures that redundant systems or components are in place so that if one fails, others can take over to keep the application running without interruption. As well as building for high availability, you should design your applications to be fault-tolerant. This is where a system is designed to keep working even if some parts fail.

Figure 3.6 depicts a VPC with two private subnets – one in AZ `eu-west-2a` and the other in `eu-west-2b`. The decision to move the EC2 instances hosting the Belly Brew website into the private subnets, unlike the public subnets in *Figure 3.5*, is to increase the security posture of the architecture. This is discussed in detail in *Chapter 7*.

For now, what you will notice in this architecture is that users on the Internet can still access the Belly Brew website running on an EC2 instance in a subnet located in the `eu-west-2a` AZ, even if connectivity to the instance in `eu-west-2b` is severed due to some issue, such as a complete power outage. This is possible thanks to an **application load balancer** (**ALB**) that distributes incoming requests across healthy instances in multiple availability zones and subnets.

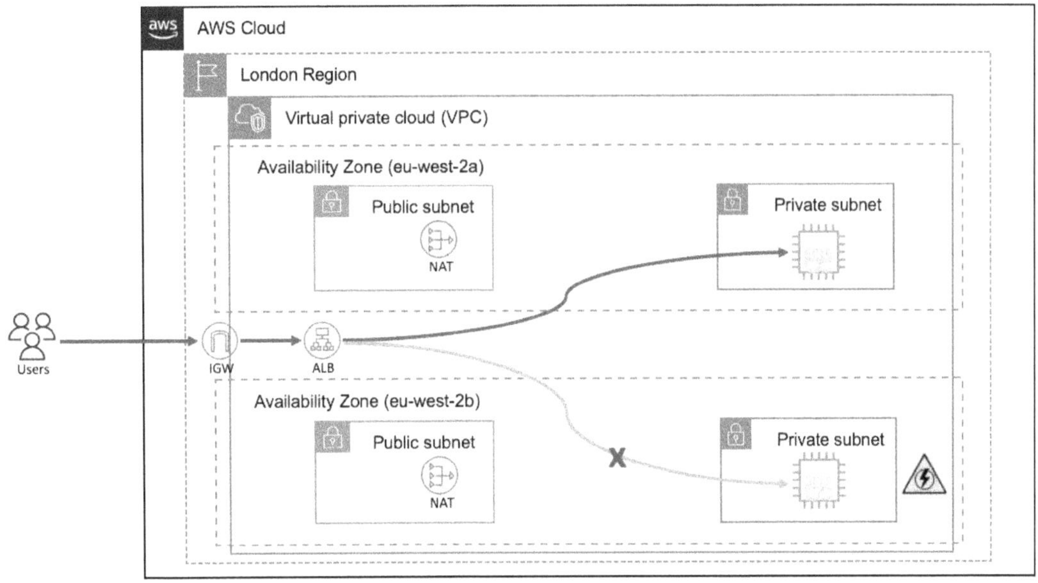

Figure 3.6: Application architecture built for high availability

By using AZs, you enable customers to build highly available and redundant application architectures. In the case of Belly Brew Co Limited, using two EC2 instances to host your website, where the EC2 instances are placed across two AZs, increases high availability and redundancy. The last thing Belly Brew wants is for customers to navigate to their website only to see an error message. You can take this one step further by distributing copies of your application across multiple regions. This can ensure low-latency access for your users worldwide, or if you need to adhere to different laws and regulations.

Access to multiple regions and the ability to distribute your application across these regions also facilitate global redundancy in the case of a regional outage.

An important consideration for the AWS Cloud Practitioner exam is the differences between services that are regional-based and those that are global. Most services allow you to create resources based on regional sources. This will enable you to fulfill any compliance and regulatory requirements, such as ensuring data resides in a specific region. Some services are, however, global, and the following sub-section provides a quick overview of these.

Global vs. regional vs. zonal services

Most AWS services require you to specify a region within which you can create resources for that service. For example, when you create an Amazon S3 bucket, which is used to store data in the cloud, you must first specify the region in which the bucket must be created. The data then resides in that region where the bucket has been made. In most cases, this also addresses data residency concerns and the fulfillment of any regulatory and compliance laws.

Some services require that you specify the Availability Zone within which you create a related resource. This is particularly true for EC2 instances (virtual servers you deploy in the cloud) and Amazon RDS instances (relational database instances).

Yet again, there are other global services. You do not need to specify the region in which you deploy a resource related to that service. This ensures that the resources you create within your AWS account are unique globally.

For example, with Identity and Access Management (AWS IAM), you can create IAM users that represent your colleagues who may need access to services and permissions to perform job functions in your AWS account. Each IAM user you create is unique in your AWS account globally and capable of accessing services and resources across all regions and availability zones as long as necessary permissions have been granted to that user.

While regions and availability zones form a substantial part of the AWS Global Infrastructure, Edge Locations are another component that enables customers to cater to a more global customer base efficiently. This infrastructure component is discussed next.

Edge locations and regional edge caches

In addition to regions and availability zones, the AWS Global Infrastructure comprises a globally distributed **point of presence** (**POP**) network. This network includes physical infrastructure components called **edge locations** and **regional edge caches**.

Multiple edge locations and regional edge caches are strategically placed across the globe in many countries and enable direct connection into AWS regions through its backbone high-speed network. One of the primary use cases of this network of edge locations and regional edge caches is that they offer content caching services that enable customers to reduce latency when uploading and downloading data from AWS.

You access this network via several services, including Amazon CloudFront (discussed in *Chapter 11*) and Amazon S3 Transfer Acceleration (discussed in *Chapter 6*).

Consider the use case of the Amazon CloudFront service. Assume you are hosting a website that distributes product training videos, each about 1GB in size, from a region such as North Virginia (`us-east-1`). Suppose you have a global customer base trying to access the training content. Customers in Australia may experience slower download speeds than those in North America.

To help elevate this poor performance, Amazon CloudFront enables access to required content via the AWS backbone network of edge locations comprising high-speed links. Furthermore, that content is cached locally at an edge location closer to the end consumer, as depicted in the following diagram in *Figure 3.7*.

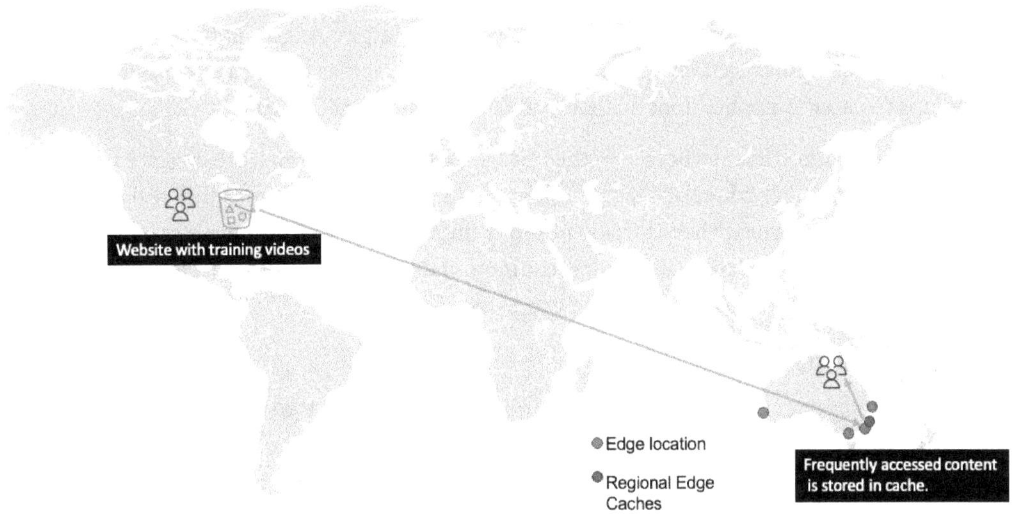

Figure 3.7: AWS CloudFront utilizing AWS POPs to distribute content

In this example, customers based in Australia can retrieve the content from the cache hosted in locations such as Sydney, Brisbane, Perth, and Melbourne. Once the content has been accessed at least once, a copy of the training video(s) can be cached locally, ensuring low-latency access to that data.

Regional edge caches

Caching content at edge locations needs to be efficiently managed. After all, there is always going to be some physical limit to how much data you can cache. To ensure efficient management of storage services, content that has not been requested for some time will be purged from these edge locations to make room for more popular content. If such content is then requested again, it must be retrieved from the origin and downloaded from the Amazon S3 bucket in North Virginia as per the preceding example.

However, AWS also offers regional edge caches strategically placed to allow less popular content to reside closer to the end consumer longer. If the content is requested within a set time frame, called a **time to live** (**TTL**), it will be retrieved from the regional edge cache. It will then be cached again at edge locations, and this approach avoids unnecessary traffic back to the origin.

AWS Local Zones

For many organizations, the existing collection of AWS Regions might still cause some latency issues depending on their application use case. Consider large cities or metropolitan areas where there is a requirement for specific ultra-low latency access to services running on AWS —perhaps to cater to applications such as gaming or video broadcasting.

AWS offers additional infrastructure in the form of **Local Zones**, which are distinct from regions and availability zones. AWS has created additional data centers within those areas that make up these local zones. These local zones may not host all services offered by AWS, but may carry most of the services that customers require in those specific locations. Only customers within close proximity to a local zone can access services within it.

AWS Wavelength

Yet another component of the AWS Global Infrastructure is **AWS Wavelength**. These infrastructure facilities are designed to offer low-latency and high-bandwidth connectivity for mobile devices and users. Wavelength zones involve deploying AWS compute and storage services within telecommunication houses offering 5G networks so that application traffic from 5G devices can reach application servers running at these facilities without leaving the provider's network. This drastically reduces latency and substantially improves application performance that requires edge-based computing and storage services.

AWS Outposts

Many businesses require proper hybrid solutions that enable them to run applications locally within their data centers or on-premises environments with access to cloud services. **AWS Outposts** is a fully-fledged infrastructure offering from AWS that enables you to host physical equipment and run several AWS services locally within your on-premises locations.

The core of this infrastructure offering comprises physical servers ranging from 1U and 2U form factors to 42U. The "**U**" stands for **rack unit**, a standard unit of measurement used to describe the height of servers and other equipment that fit into a rack. 1U is 1.75 inches (4.45 cm) in height. Contained within these racks are host machines, switches, and patch panels that can offer all the compute, storage, and network services locally. The service also connects back up to AWS for seamless management of those services and resources using the same AWS tools you already know. The benefits of the AWS Outposts offering include low-latency access to on-premises systems, local data processing, data residency, and application migration with local system interdependencies.

Regardless of which components of the AWS global infrastructure you must use to host your application solution, you must first create an AWS account to access AWS services and provision the required resources. An AWS account is essentially a resource container – a mechanism to access AWS services securely. AWS accounts are isolated by default from one another – this is why multiple customers can access the same set of services you need on AWS. Still, those other customers will not have any visibility into the resources you provision in your AWS account.

Your AWS account will give you direct access to all regions and availability zones, though you may need to request access for some regions depending on which country your business is hosted in. You will learn more about how to create your first AWS account in *Chapter 4*. As part of creating your AWS account, you must also select a support plan, which will be discussed in the next section.

Comparing AWS support plans

You must select a support plan when signing up for a Free Tier AWS account. By default, the **basic support plan** is provided with every AWS account you create and is free of cost. The other plans, Developer, Business, Enterprise-on-Ramp, and Enterprise, are chargeable. Understanding the features offered across the various plans is heavily tested in the AWS Certified Cloud Practitioner exam and is one you must learn.

The basic support plan

The basic support plan offers a base set of customer services but does not come with any technical support. Key features of this plan include:

- **Customer services and access to communities**: You can access customer services to resolve any issues related to your account, such as billing and payments, or if you are having problems signing into your account. The service can be accessed 24/7. In addition, you have free access to all documentation, whitepapers, and the AWS re:Post blog website.
- **AWS Trusted Advisor**: This service inspects the resources you deploy and the services you consume in your AWS account. It is an advisory service that analyzes your resources against six categories: Cost optimization, Performance, Security, Fault tolerance, Service limits, and Operational Excellence. The Trusted Advisor service is an excellent resource for identifying if your resources are configured in alignment with industry-recommended best practices. Note that the service is not entirely free and is tied to the support plan that you subscribe to. Customers on the Basic and Developer support plan get access to a few core checks, whereas customers on the Business, Enterprise on Ramp, and Enterprise plans get access to all checks across.
- **AWS Health:** This service offers a dashboard that reports on the availability and accessibility of all AWS services that may directly impact the resources provisioned in

your AWS account. It also provides details of any scheduled maintenance tasks or guidelines for upgrades and configuration changes that may affect your workloads.

While the Basic Support Plan is useful for account-level help and access to AWS guidance tools, teams that need technical support for development and test workloads may need to consider the Developer Support Plan.

The developer support plan

This support plan is designed for organizations running early development and test workloads on AWS, where some technical support may be required during standard business hours. In addition, you can get general guidance on how various services and resources should be configured.

This support plan is ideal for Belly Brew Co Limited during the development phase of their web application. This is because it is relatively cheap compared to the other plans, and you get technical support related to AWS technologies within standard business hours. While you can raise support tickets with AWS cloud support associates, note that they cannot discuss specific technical problems you might be facing at the application level for workloads you deploy on AWS. Furthermore, support is only available via web and chat. No telephone support is available under this plan. Consider upgrading your support plan if you run production-grade workloads requiring urgent resolutions.

The business support plan

This support plan gives you access to cloud experts 24/7 who can help you resolve technical issues you may be having with your AWS resources, which you use to host your applications in the cloud. If your production systems are currently down, you can get a guaranteed response from a cloud engineer via chat, email, or phone within one hour. You also get access to third-party software support, documentation, and forums. Given the business size and purpose of the website you will build on AWS for Belly Brew Co Limited, this plan is ideal for production-level workloads. This is because for a standard website that doesn't currently operate as an e-commerce web application, a one-hour response time in the event of production system outages might be acceptable. As a cloud practitioner, it would be necessary to discuss the various plans with Belly Brew and provide the pros and cons of each plan, including cost, to enable the business to make an informed decision.

The enterprise on-ramp support plan

This support plan is designed for customers with business-critical and production workloads where rapid response from experts is paramount. It offers many services on the Enterprise Plan, such as 24/7 technical support from cloud experts and access to a pool of technical account managers (TAMs) who can provide consultative guidance for your specific application use case.

This plan offers a response time of under 30 minutes for business-critical system outages.

The enterprise plan

This support plan is the créme de la créme that AWS offers its customers. For a higher fee, you get all the benefits of the previous plans plus access to a **dedicated technical account manager** (**TAM**), response to business/mission-critical issues within 15 minutes, proactive support in managing billing and cost optimization for your workloads, as well as access to AWS Incident Detection and Response for an additional fee.

As discussed earlier, this plan might not be necessary for Belly Brew Co Limited since you will be hosting a standard website that doesn't run e-commerce or business-critical applications. The cost of the Enterprise Plan is substantially high, and thus, the expense must warrant the benefit gained, which, in the case of Belly Brew, is not the case.

> Note
>
> The complete list of features across all plans is available at `https://aws.amazon.com/premiumsupport/plans/`.

In the next section, you will learn about the AWS Health service, which is designed to help you proactively monitor and manage your workload availability.

Monitoring AWS health events and service availability

The AWS ecosystem is vast, comprising infrastructure, platform, and software services catering to millions of customers across the globe. Occasionally, issues within this ecosystem may affect your workloads and applications. These can also include planned and scheduled tasks. AWS offers a health dashboard (see *Figure 3.8*) to help you monitor how these occasional issues or scheduled events may affect your workloads and applications.

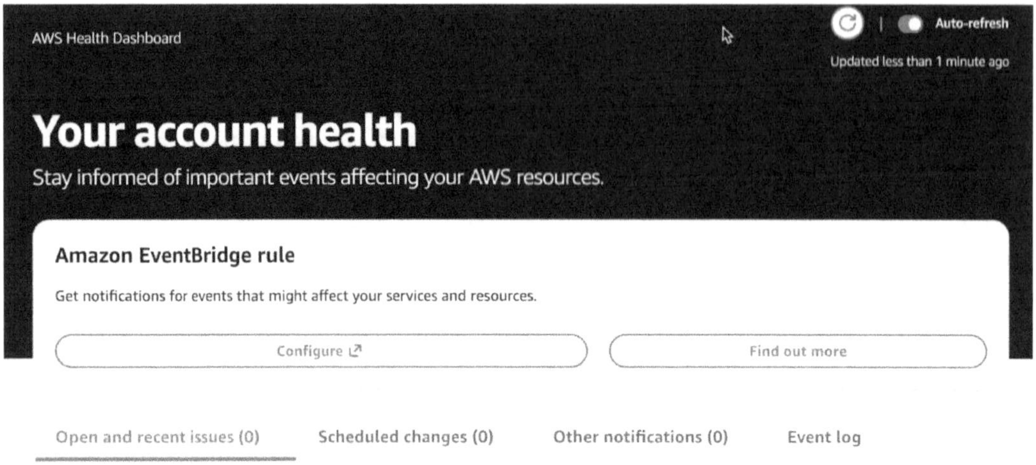

Figure 3.8: AWS health dashboard – Scheduled changes tab

In this example screenshot, you will note how AWS provides details of any open and recent issues, scheduled changes to infrastructure that might affect your workloads, and other notifications.

You can also use the AWS Health services to send Amazon EventBridge alerts to be notified of upcoming events. **Amazon EventBridge** is a service designed to capture events that occur with your applications and AWS resources and send events to targets that can take action based on the events. You can use Amazon EventBridge to build serverless event-driven applications on AWS. In addition, if you subscribe to the business, enterprise on-ramp, or enterprise support plans, you can use the AWS Health API to integrate with third-party event management systems.

Next, you will learn more about sources of documentation and knowledge centers available on AWS.

Using AWS documentation, Knowledge Center, and security resources

AWS offers a wide range of resources to help customers learn about its services with a deep level of technical detail, examples, use cases, and architectural references that align with industry-standard best practices. With example design patterns, sample codes, and complete references, you have access to all the information you need to build end-to-end solutions on the AWS platform. Some of these resources include the following:

- **AWS Documentation**: AWS offers extensive documentation across all its services. Most of the documentation around its various technology offerings will be broken down across category heads, such as User Guides, Developer Guides, API References, and others. The documentation offers include hands-on tutorials, AWS prescriptive guidance, the AWS Architecture Center, where you learn how to architect more in line with best practices and AWS recommendations, and the AWS Solutions Library, which contains vetted solutions and guidance for business and technical use cases.

  > **Note**
  >
  > The primary documentation can be found at `https://docs.aws.amazon.com/`

- **Knowledge Center**: The AWS Knowledge Center is a website that offers the most **frequently asked questions** (**FAQs**) and requests that AWS gets from its customers. It often comprises a series of queries submitted by other customers, for which AWS offers troubleshooting steps, and is an excellent webpage to bookmark.
  Queries are categorized by service. This is a valuable resource with questions like "Why aren't my Amazon S3 objects replicating when I set up replication between my buckets?" or "How do I troubleshoot a 403 Access Denied error I am getting from Amazon S3?"

  > **Note**
  >
  > The website is available at `https://repost.aws/knowledge-center/all`.

- **Security Resources**: AWS also offers a dedicated documentation page that contains a vast collection of articles, use cases, documentation, training materials, and whitepapers focused on ensuring you have all the information on how to build solutions in the cloud that are highly secure and fulfill security best practices

  > **Note**
  >
  > The site is available at `https://aws.amazon.com/security/security-learning/`

Summary

In this chapter, you discovered how the AWS Global Infrastructure is designed to help you build highly available, fault-tolerant, secure, and cost-effective solutions in the cloud. The AWS Global Infrastructure is designed to help you develop your solutions in a manner that ensures low-latency connectivity and can fulfill any compliance or regulatory requirements required by your business on concepts such as data privacy and data residency. Understanding the fundamental components of the AWS Global Infrastructure will help you build solutions for your clients by following industry-standard best practices with high performance, resilience, and security.

Belly Brew Co. Limited is a UK-based company that serves the UK market. In this scenario, you would want to host its website and other applications within the London region. The London region comprises three availability zones, enabling you to design your solutions with high availability in mind. Specifically, you can deploy websites and applications on compute resources such as EC2 instances provisioned across multiple availability zones within the London region. This will ensure high availability and redundancy despite an availability zone outage. Depending on Belly Brew's compliance and regulatory requirements, there is also the option to host a backup solution in Ireland. If there is a regional outage in London, customers can be redirected to the Dublin region, which will still provide relatively low latency.

Depending on the customer base and their locations, the use of Edge locations can also help cache content closer to end users—but this will depend on the type of content you plan to host for the Belly Brew website. For example, if you plan to host lots of videos, then using CloudFront would be ideal.

When setting up an AWS account, you must select a support plan—the minimum support package is the Basic Support Plan. If you require technical support or need instant access to expert AWS consultants, you should consider upgrading your plan according to your specific needs. Concerning the AWS Certified Cloud Practitioner exam, ensure you understand the fundamental offerings across all the support plans. For example, if you require a dedicated technical account manager (TAM), this is available only as part of the Enterprise Support plan. Also, the Basic Support Plan only offers a few core Trusted Advisor checks. We will discuss the Trusted Advisor service in detail later in this book.

In the next chapter, we will move from AWS infrastructure to AWS account structure, learning how accounts, multi-account strategies, AWS Organizations, and Control Tower help businesses separate workloads, manage access, control costs, and apply governance at scale.

Exam Readiness Drill – Chapter Review Questions

Apart from mastering key concepts, strong test-taking skills under time pressure are essential for acing your certification exam. That's why developing these abilities early in your learning journey is critical.

Exam readiness drills, using the free online practice resources provided with this book, help you progressively improve your time management and test-taking skills while reinforcing the key concepts you've learned.

HOW TO GET STARTED

- Open the link or scan the QR code at the bottom of this page
- If you have unlocked the practice resources already, log in to your registered account. If you haven't, follow the instructions in *Free Benefits with Your Book* section in this book's *Preface* and come back to this page.
- Once you log in, click the START button to start this chapter's quiz
- We recommend attempting a quiz multiple times till you're able to answer most of the questions correctly and well within the time limit.
- You can use the following practice template to help you plan your attempts:

Working On Accuracy		
Attempt	**Target**	**Time Limit**
Attempt 1	40% or more	Till the timer runs out
Attempt 2	60% or more	Till the timer runs out
Attempt 3	75% or more	Till the timer runs out
Working On Timing		
Attempt 4	75% or more	1 minute before time limit
Attempt 5	75% or more	2 minutes before time limit
Attempt 6	75% or more	3 minutes before time limit

The above drill is just an example. Design your drills based on your own goals and make the most out of the online quizzes accompanying this book.

Link to this Chapter's Quiz

You need to unlock the online practice resources to access the link below. Check the *Free Benefits with Your Book* section in the *Preface* for detailed instructions on how to do this. You only need to unlock the resources once.

Open Quiz `https://packt.link/clf_c02_ch3` or scan the QR code

Part 2

AWS Technologies and Services

This second part focuses on the core AWS services and technologies to help you build real-world cloud solutions. While each chapter covers core fundamental concepts and topics to help you prepare for the *AWS Certified Cloud Practitioner (CLF-C02)* exam, you will also develop hands-on skills in building solutions for Belly Brew Co. Limited incrementally. This enables you to appreciate how various cloud services can be chained together to build a complete end-to-end solution that is production-grade and deployable in the real world.

The experience you gain within these chapters while completing all project exercises is going to be extremely valuable in developing real-world experience you can boast about in your LinkedIn profiles, GitHub repos, and within the pages of your resume. In today's competitive world, it's no longer enough to simply have the skills – you must advertise your capabilities and be seen to be offered roles at top organizations.

You are encouraged throughout the chapters to think and build like an architect, configure and implement like an engineer, and troubleshoot and resolve like a support analyst, covering the majority of the roles you can consider embarking upon in your career.

This part of the book includes the following chapters:

- *Chapter 4, AWS Accounts, Multi-Account Strategies, and AWS Organizations*
- *Chapter 5, AWS Access Management*
- *Chapter 6, Amazon Simple Storage Service (Amazon S3)*
- *Chapter 7, AWS Networking Services, Part 1 – Virtual Private Cloud (VPCs)*
- *Chapter 8, AWS Compute Services – EC2, Lightsail, ECS, EKS, and Lambda*
- *Chapter 9, Databases on AWS*
- *Chapter 10, High Availability, Fault Tolerance, and Elasticity on AWS*
- *Chapter 11, AWS Networking, Part 2 – Route 53 and CloudFront*

4

AWS Accounts, Multi-Account Strategies, and AWS Organizations

AWS is a public cloud service provider that caters to a global customer base comprising start-ups and multi-national organizations, from the Big 4 accounting firms (Deloitte, EY, KPMG, and PwC) to Netflix. Individuals can also access these services for personal projects or merely to learn about the ecosystem and gain hands-on experience, proving skills to current and future employers.

Naturally, if customers across most countries can access AWS services and spin up resources, they would want to ensure very high levels of security so that one customer's resources are not accessible by another customer unless explicit permissions are granted. This chapter discusses the concept of an AWS account, which allows the separation and isolation of resources that belong to one customer from another.

With AWS, you can also create multiple accounts. There are several use cases for this, the most common being separating different workload environments such as development, testing, and production. However, with multiple accounts comes the overhead of additional management and administration, so the primary reason behind the AWS Organizations service is as a means to centrally manage these accounts from a security perspective and optimize costs. This chapter reviews the service's key fundamentals and showcases its core features.

The following topics are covered in this chapter:

- Understanding AWS accounts
- Architecting a multi-account strategy for your business

- Managing multiple AWS accounts with AWS Organizations
- Using AWS Control Tower for multi-account governance

In addition to security concepts related to protecting and managing your AWS account(s), this chapter also aligns with the exam *Task Statement 4.2: Understand resources for billing, budget, and cost management*, with a particular focus on AWS Organizations consolidated billing and allocation of costs in *Domain 4: Billing, Pricing, and Support*.

Understanding AWS accounts

An AWS account is a container for your AWS resources, where you can create, manage, and control access to the resources you provision. The account acts as an isolated boundary between other accounts you own and those of different customers. It also handles administrative functions such as access management and billing.

When you create an AWS account, you have access to the vast array of AWS services from which you can launch and manage resources – these include computing services, networks, storage, and databases that you need to host your applications. Each account is tied to a billing method, and any resources launched incur charges based on AWS pricing models. Each account also has a **Root User** who owns the account and has the maximum privileges to access any service and launch any resources. This root user can define who else in your organization can access services in your AWS account and what resources they can launch using an **Identity and Access Management** service.

You can start using AWS by creating a free plan account, as you will see in the next section.

The AWS free tier account

Getting started with AWS is easy. All you need to do is set up a free plan account. AWS recently changed its free tier offering, which means, unlike the previous 12-month free tier offer with specific free thresholds across different services, you are now allocated $100 worth of AWS credits at sign-up to use for your experimentation and learning efforts. A further $100 worth of credits is offered if you complete a set of five tasks using the AWS management console. Free plan accounts are designed for learning and experimentation and run for a maximum of six months. After six months, you must either convert the account to a paid plan account or AWS will close it down.

A credit or debit card is required to set up the account, but you are only charged if you exhaust your free credits. Another important point to note is that certain services are not available in the free plan account, and enabling or using those services will automatically exhaust your credits and convert your account into a paid plan account. For example, the AWS Organization service, designed to help you centrally manage multi-account environments, is not available under the free plan offering.

AWS offers many free services and trials to help customers test their products and embark on experimentation projects. Some services are provided free of cost for their lifetime usage. For example, you get unlimited access to **AWS License Manager**, where you can proactively define rules to manage, discover, and report third-party license usage. Another example is free access to AWS Control Tower, which allows you to set up and govern a new, secure multi-account AWS environment.

Regardless of which plan you are on, the following services are offered free up to the specified maximum usage per month:

- **Lambda**: 1 million requests/month plus 400,000 GB-seconds of compute. Genuinely generous
- **DynamoDB**: 25 GB storage, 25 write capacity units, 25 read capacity units
- **SNS**: 1 million publishes, 100,000 HTTP deliveries
- **SQS**: 1 million requests
- **CloudWatch**: 10 custom metrics, 10 alarms, 1 million API requests, 5 GB of Logs ingestion
- **KMS**: 20,000 symmetric request operations
- **Data transfer out**: 100 GB/month to the internet, aggregated across all services

> Note
>
> You can review the complete list of free tier options at `https://aws.amazon.com/free/`

In the next section, you will learn more about the use case of multi-account AWS environments and their benefits.

Architecting a multi-account strategy for your business

AWS advocates creating and using multiple AWS accounts for your workloads and their environments based on specific best practices. While it is possible to host numerous applications across its various environments, such as development, **user acceptance testing** (**UAT**), and production in a single account, this can quickly become very cluttered and complex, resulting in increased management overhead.

Depending on your industry, a single account with numerous applications and environments may also not fulfill specific compliance and regulatory requirements. Furthermore, AWS recommends that different teams and individuals in your organization are granted only the necessary permissions to complete their job function, thereby advocating the **principle of least privilege** (**POLP**) access.

For example, developers will need various access permissions in a development environment to spin up resources and access multiple services. However, they should have limited access to production environments since those environments are customer-facing. If all workloads and environments are in a single account, you must define highly complex identity and access management rules, which may be prone to errors and result in a less secure environment.

Another reason AWS recommends a multi-account strategy is to help limit the **blast radius** of any disasters occurring in an individual account. A **blast radius** refers to the extent of impact caused by a disaster, such as a failure, error, or security breach within a system, and is often used to describe the potential damage or containment of such events. Since an AWS account is naturally isolated from other AWS accounts, any misconfiguration of one account, such as the accidental exposure of the root user's credentials or a bug resulting in a repeat loop of resource creation, such as deploying multiple EC2 instances, will not affect other AWS accounts.

In *Figure 4.1*, you will note the number of accounts created for Belly Brew Co. Limited. In this example, you have a **development account**, a **UAT account,** and a **production account**. These accounts will be used to host the various environments of the new customer-facing website, which Belly Brew Co. Limited plans to launch soon. The development account is where the developers will have sufficient privileges to build the web application. The UAT account is where the application will be tested for technical processes and functional accuracy. The production account is used to host the finished product, which is accessible to customers.

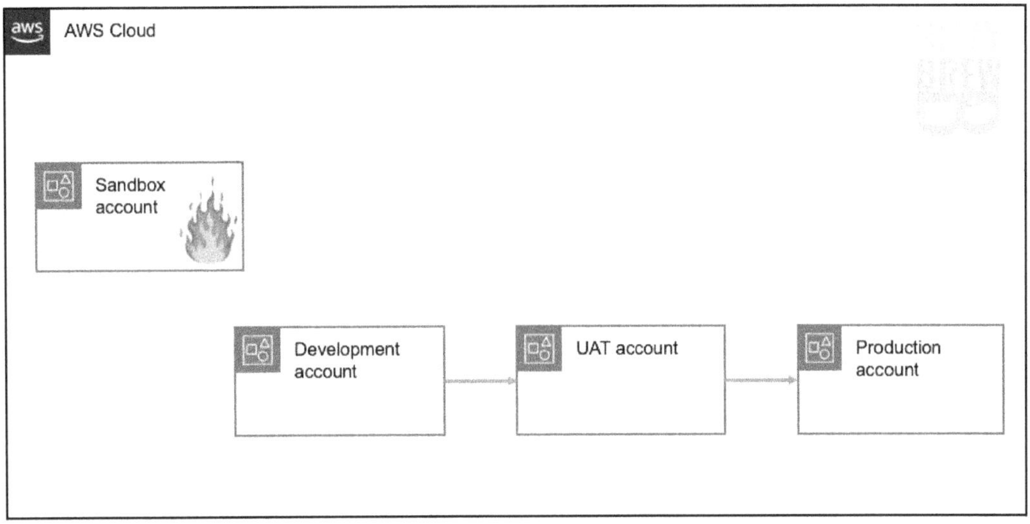

Figure 4.1: Belly Brew Co. Limited's multi-account strategy

There is also a **sandbox account** designed for developers to perform experimentation work to learn about the various AWS services. This is an isolated, secure environment used for testing, experimentation, or development without affecting production systems or data.

Belly Brew Co. Limited's developers will use the Sandbox account to experiment with the various AWS technologies, and any actions performed in this account will not impact workloads in the development, UAT, or production accounts. Using the **Identity and Access Management** (**IAM**) service will also ensure that developers are permitted to access only specific services relevant to their projects and job functions, preventing accidents and mistakes from resulting in unexpected costs. The AWS IAM service is discussed in *Chapter 5*.

The following are some key benefits of a multi-account architecture:

- **Isolation between applications and workloads**: You can isolate applications from different business units or clients using multiple accounts. This enables you to secure boundaries to fulfill any compliance and regulatory requirements.
- **Limited visibility and discoverability**: An AWS account acts as a natural boundary. This resource container is not accessible to any entity (users or applications) from other AWS accounts unless permissions are explicitly granted. This allows you to isolate certain accounts entirely, if required, and allow access from resources in different accounts.
- **Isolation of security and audit accounts**: By having multiple accounts, you can designate specific accounts to perform and host audit and security information of other

accounts. This ensures that critical data is stored away from accounts that might be compromised in a malicious attack.

- **Opportunity to host separate disaster recovery accounts**: Using a multi-account strategy, you can host separate accounts with duplicate workloads explicitly designed for **Disaster Recovery** (**DR**) and **Business Continuity Plan** (**BCP**) processes. In the event of a disaster in your primary accounts, you can switch to the DR accounts and continue business operations.

The switchover process will depend on your DR and BCP strategy, whether you opt for a Pilot light strategy or a multi-site active/active strategy. In a **Pilot light strategy**, you have a minimal version of an environment that is always running. In a disaster, additional resources can be rapidly spun up from this minimal setup to restore full operations. In a **multi-site strategy**, you have an exact duplicate environment, ideally running in a different region. In the case of a disaster, you switch over to the other site almost instantly.

> Note
>
> To learn more about AWS Disaster Recovery and Business Continuity Planning, refer to the AWS Disaster Recovery whitepaper available at `https://docs.aws.amazon.com/whitepapers/latest/disaster-recovery-workloads-on-aws/disaster-recovery-workloads-on-aws.html`

In the case of Belly Brew Co. Limited, the development version of the web application, which may have newer features, should not be accessible to end users and customers until they have passed the necessary testing and are officially released in the production account. Customers should only be able to access the live version of the web application in the production account. Additionally, the process of releasing the live version in the production account should always follow approved methods – developers shouldn't be able to release new updates without proper change control procedures that ensure minimum disruption and quick failback in case of issues.

While having multiple AWS accounts offers several benefits, you must have a means to efficiently create and manage these accounts, both from a security perspective and for cost optimization. AWS Organizations is a service designed for this specific purpose, and it is discussed in the next section.

Managing multiple AWS accounts with AWS Organizations

The **AWS Organizations** service is designed to help customers create and manage multiple AWS accounts to meet their various requirements, all from a central dashboard. The service offers security features to ensure the accounts align with corporate policies, regulatory requirements, and best practices. This is done by creating and applying various **Service Control Policies** (**SCPs**), which will be discussed shortly.

In addition, the service also provides a consolidated view of all billing and charges incurred by the various AWS accounts using a single billing console. You can also benefit from volume discounts for resource consumption across individual organization members' accounts.

The following are the critical steps required to create your AWS Organizations service:

1. Designate an existing AWS account or create a new AWS account to act as the management account for the AWS Organization Service. This management account is based at the root of your organization, as depicted in *Figure 4.2*.

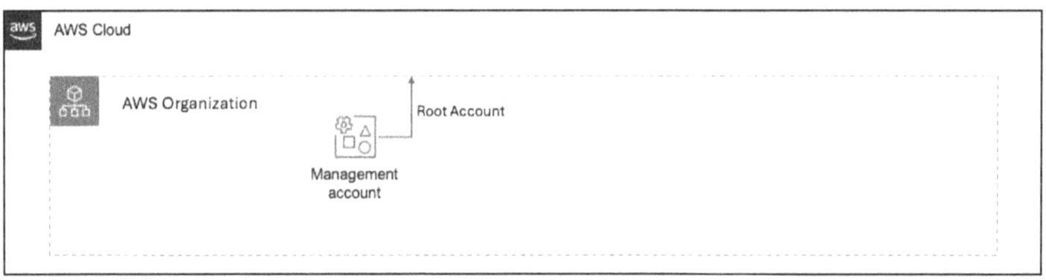

Figure 4.2: AWS Organizations with management account

   You must not use this account to host applications. Its sole purpose is to act as the management account for the Organization service as a recommended best practice.

2. Ensure you log into the account as the root user or an IAM user who will have administrative permissions and create the Organization from the AWS Organization dashboard
3. From the AWS Organizations dashboard, you can then invite other existing accounts that belong to your company or create new accounts for your organization from within the console
   For example, for Belly Brew Co. Limited, you could consider three separate accounts – one for development of the customer web application, one for testing the application from a functional and technical perspective, and one for production, where the application is deployed and live for end customers to access.

The management account is also used to install and set up any automation tooling that helps deploy guardrails and other standardization tools to help you centrally manage all your AWS accounts.

Next, you will learn more about how to structure your AWS Organization service using organizational units.

Organizational units

You can create **Organizational units** (**OUs**) to manage these accounts effectively within similar configurations. An OU is a logical group of one or more AWS accounts that share a common function—environmental, departmental, or any other grouping strategy you may wish to adopt. When deciding how to structure your AWS Organizations service, you must adopt a functional approach, ensuring that you fulfill specific security requirements rather than simply creating accounts based on your organization's hierarchy. Many businesses will have multiple AWS accounts that share similar workload types, such as requiring separate environments for development, UAT, and production. This would result in creating groups of accounts that share similar security requirements. For example, the security requirements for production accounts will differ from those for development accounts.

OUs can also be nested, which enables smaller units of management. For example, you can create OUs for your Workloads (applications) and then make two nested OUs to divide production workloads from pre-production.

Figure 4.3 depicts the Workloads OU, which contains Belly Brew Co. Limited's website application accounts nested in environment OUs for development, UAT, and production.

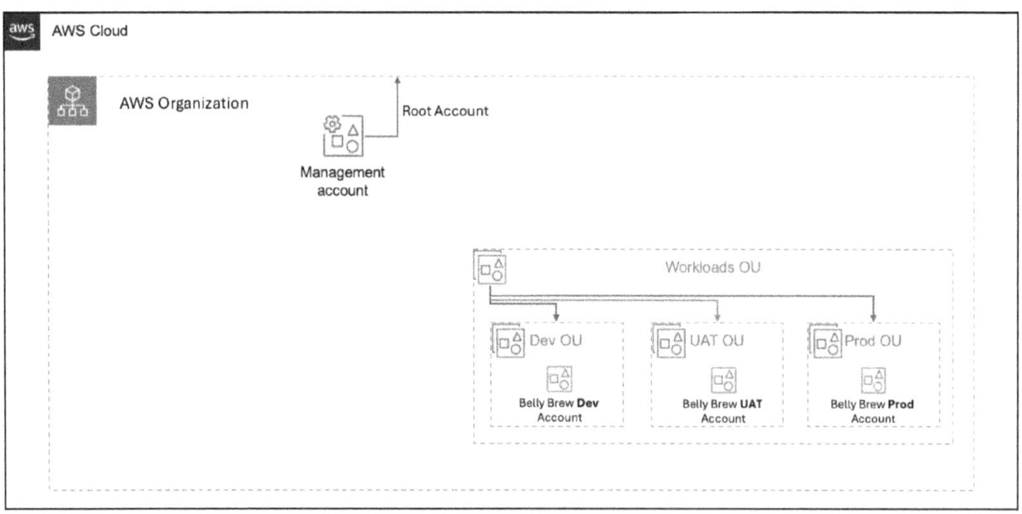

Figure 4.3: Belly Brew Co. Limited's OU structure

The steps involved in creating the OUs are as follows:

1. Within the AWS Organization service, you would create a Workloads OU. This is where your AWS accounts, which will be used to host the various applications and their environments (Dev, UAT, and Prod), will reside.
2. To ensure further categorization and easier management, you must create nested OUs for each group of accounts, such as Dev OU for development, UAT OU for user acceptance testing, and Prod OU for production
3. Next, you must move the appropriate AWS accounts into their relevant OU. This is done within the AWS management console.

In this example, Belly Brew Co. Limited has three separate AWS accounts representing the three environments of the Belly Brew Co. Limited customer web application. To ensure isolation and separation, these accounts are placed in their relevant OUs. Those OUs are further placed in the Workloads OU designed for application hosting and management.

AWS recommends having accounts and OUs for certain foundational services, such as security, audit logging, and shared infrastructure services, which host resources consumed across different departments and business units in your company.

Figure 4.4 depicts certain OUs and accounts you should consider incorporating into your multi-account architecture. However, this will depend on your business model and any compliance or regulatory requirements for the industry in which your business operates.

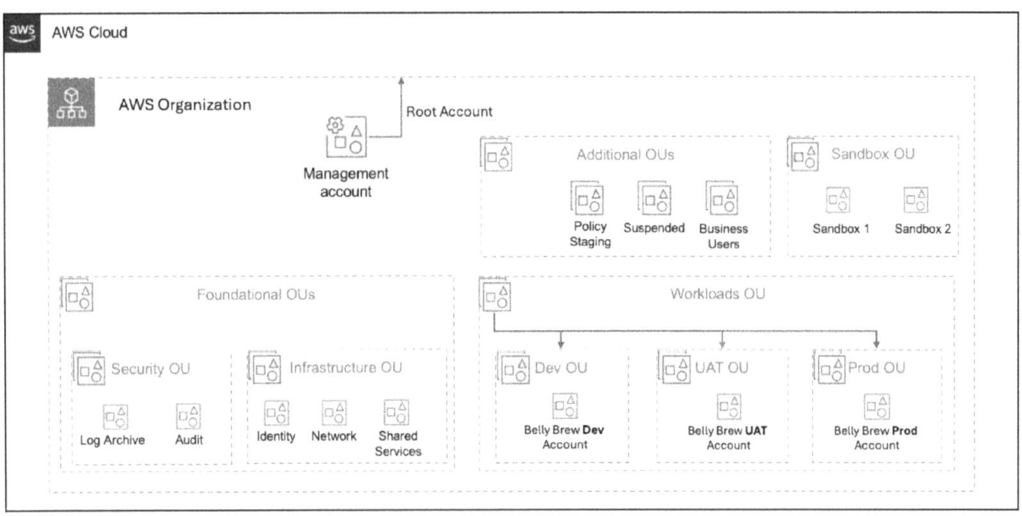

Figure 4.4: OU architecture with some AWS-recommended OUs and accounts

The following are some OUs and accounts you may wish to incorporate for Belly Brew Co. Limited as part of your AWS Organization architecture, as depicted in *Figure 4.4*:

- **Foundation OUs**: AWS recommends you have accounts for certain foundational services in any organization. These include security and infrastructure accounts that host applications for the company's internal business processes. These should ideally be separate from workloads designed for customer-facing applications. These can be divided into the following OUs and accounts:
- **Security OU**: This OU is designed to isolate your security and audit logging services with minimal access limited to your security team only to ensure data integrity. AWS recommends you have a Log Archive account and an Audit account. The Log Archive account can securely gather logging data from other accounts in the organization and is used by your security, audit, and compliance teams. The audit account can delegate admin access to AWS security tools and a dashboard accessible to specific teams for investigation and forensic analysis.
- **Infrastructure OU**: This OU is intended for AWS accounts that host shared infrastructure resources and are used by other accounts within the organization. Any organization, such as Belly Brew Co. Limited, will have a workforce – employees who work across different departments in the organization. One use case for an infrastructure account is to host an identities account that manages all workforce identities across the organization. Users would be assigned permissions to access other accounts based on their job function, which would be centrally managed in this infrastructure service account. This way, users do not need separate IAM accounts to access each individual AWS account. Instead, they would use cross-account access capabilities using their identity account credentials to access other AWS accounts.
- **Additional OUs**: These OUs would vary depending on the industry and organization. However, for most companies, including Belly Brew Co. Limited, you should consider the following OUs:
    - **Policy Staging OU**: AWS recommends a policy staging OU to safely test policies before applying them to the intended OUs or accounts. To avoid any unexpected behaviors, separating this OU and the accounts it contains is highly recommended. Policies applied to Belly Brew Co. Limited workloads OUs must ensure high levels of security while granting necessary access to your workforce to complete their job functions. For example, technical test teams should have sufficient access to the UAT account to perform application failover tests, but not necessarily have access to the production account.

- **Suspended OU**: Over time, you may stop using specific AWS accounts and no longer need them. However, for compliance and regulatory requirements, you may need to hold them in a separate OU until you permanently close the accounts down.
- **Business Users**: This OU is designed for individual business users or teams needing resources unrelated to the organization's customer-facing applications and workloads. For example, the HR department might host HR-related applications for time clocking of all the staff who work at the Belly Brew Co. Limited's manufacturing plants across the UK.

- **Sandbox OU Accounts**: These accounts are hosted in a Sandbox OU designed to allow developers to experiment with AWS technologies to build and break solutions. They can also be used for learning, developing, and researching new products and services. Being isolated from other OUs, any experimental disasters caused by the sandbox users will not impact the organization's production workloads.

Using OUs ensures you manage groups of AWS accounts that share common functions more efficiently. With nested OUs, you can create a hierarchical architecture that follows a natural flow of authority and control. However, note that you can nest OUs up to five levels deep, including the root and AWS accounts in the lowest-level OUs.

While separating accounts into various OUs can help isolate workload types, a mechanism is required to ensure that each account and the OU it's hosted in are adequately secured and managed. AWS offers **Service Control Policies** (**SCPs**) to help define security permissions and guardrails, determining what services can be consumed and what resources can be launched. The following section examines the fundamentals of SCPs in more detail.

Securing OUs and accounts with service control policies

AWS **Service Control Policies** (**SCPs**) are guardrails you can define for your AWS accounts, restricting what services can be consumed and what resources can be launched. With SCPs, you create policy documents using the **JavaScript Object Notation** (**JSON**) format, allowing you to define granular permissions on actions in your AWS member accounts.

However, SCPs do not directly define users' actions in your AWS accounts. They are guardrails defining the maximum permissions administrators can grant users and roles in a member account. Thus, in addition to creating SCPs, you must also define permissions assigned to your users and applications within an AWS account that align with the SCP. Only then can those users and applications access approved services and resources. These permissions are granted using the AWS IAM service or by creating resource-based policies. A diagram illustrating this concept is depicted in *Figure 4.5*:

Figure 4.5: SCPs and IAM policies

In this illustration, although Alice has been granted IAM permission to access the Amazon EC2 and S3 services in the Dev Account, she can only access Amazon S3 and create S3-related resources. This is because the Service Control Policy acts as a guardrail and doesn't explicitly permit the Dev Account to consume the Amazon EC2 service. Furthermore, although the SCP allows the Dev Account to consume the DynamoDB service, Alice has not been given the necessary IAM permissions to access DynamoDB and is thus denied access. Suppose another user in the Dev Account is assigned permission to access DynamoDB using an IAM policy. In that case, the user can access the service because the SCP permits the service in the Dev Account.

If an SCP denies specific actions, even if an IAM or resource-based policy allows them, the action will still be prevented. SCPs limit what permissions can be granted, and IAM or resource-based policies cannot exceed the boundaries defined by the SCPs. AWS IAM is discussed in detail in *Chapter 5*.

Tip

SCPs can be used to restrict specific actions that apply even to the root users of the individual member accounts. For example, you can prevent a root user of a member account from attempting to leave the organization once it has become a member.

SCPs are disabled by default. This means that to use the security features of the AWS Organization service, you must first enable the SCP policy service. In *Figure 4.6*, you will note that the service control policies are enabled.

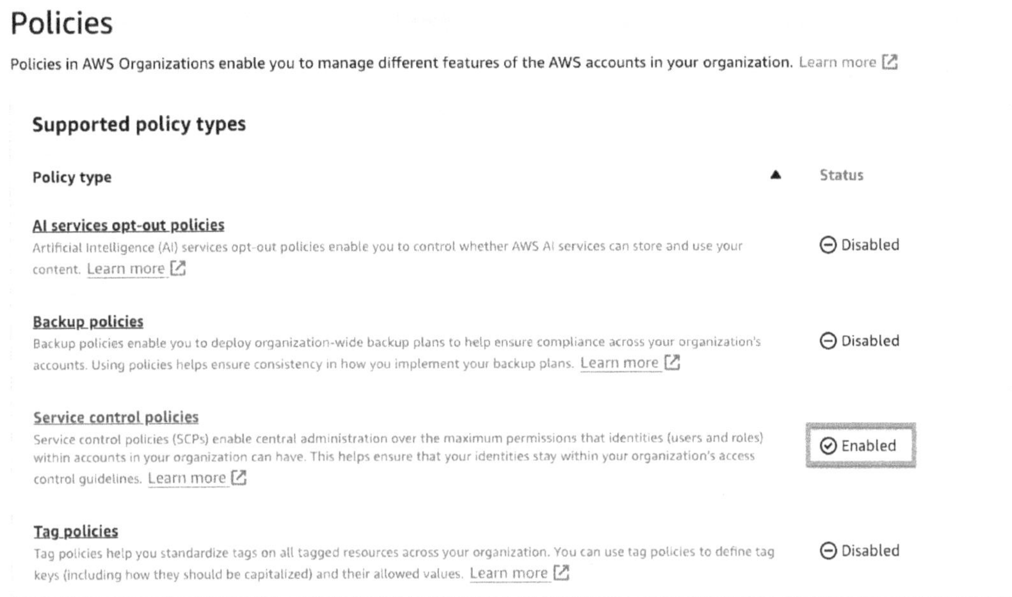

Figure 4.6: Service control policies status

Another factor to consider is that SCPs can be applied at all levels of the organization – at the root, the OUs and nested OUs, and finally, at the account level. This means that the policy must be applied at all layers of the hierarchy for it to be applicable. *Figure 4.7* illustrates this concept:

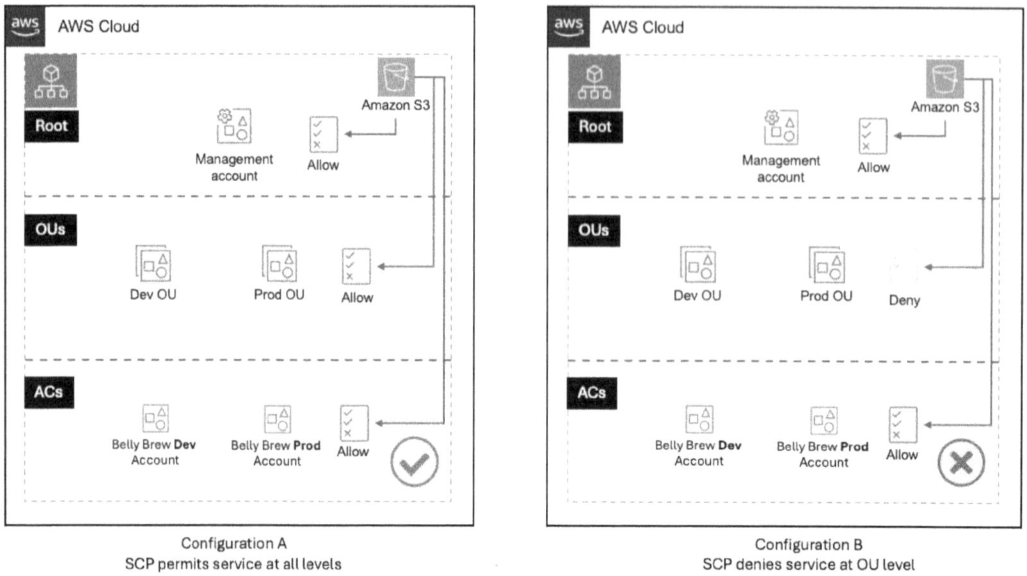

Figure 4.7: Applying SCPs at all levels

In *Figure 4.7*, you will note two different configurations. In **Configuration A**, the permissions to consume the Amazon S3 service are applied at all hierarchy levels. This ensures that Amazon S3 can be consumed in the Belly Brew Co. Limited Prod Account. However, in **Configuration B**, the permission to access the Amazon S3 service is being denied at the OU level, specifically the Prod OU. This results in the service being denied at the account level, even though there is explicit permission to allow this at the account level.

> **Note**
>
> AWS permissions follow a simple pattern. There is an implicit deny rule unless you explicitly configure an 'allow' rule. Furthermore, a 'deny' rule will always override an 'allow' rule.

It is important to note that when you enable SCPs, the default policy applied at the root level is `FullAWSAccess`. This overcomes the implicit deny security measure to allow you to start accessing services across all AWS accounts and organizations. The alternative would be a highly restrictive environment, which also risks denying access to any account. With the `FullAWSAccess` policy set by default, proper planning is required to ensure you deny services or regions you do not plan to use in your AWS Organization.

> **Note**
>
> Security features like SCPs do not restrict users or roles in the management account. This is to ensure you don't accidentally lock yourself out of your entire organization.

AWS Organizations offers much more than the security configurations of your multi-account architecture. Using AWS Organizations, you can optimize billing and cost management by benefiting from volume discounts and the ability to share certain resources across member accounts. This feature is discussed in the next section.

AWS Organizations, consolidated billing, and resource sharing

Each AWS account is usually linked to a payment method along with the contact information of the root user. You are charged against this billing method for any services you consume, and resources deployed (beyond any free-tier thresholds). The root user of every AWS account is responsible for the charges incurred in that account.

However, in a corporate setting, multiple teams may own and manage the resources in their respective AWS accounts. Still, the finance department usually handles the billing and payments. This allows the finance team to oversee all costs and enforce budgetary constraints. Any projects being worked on would need financial approval from the relevant heads and key stakeholders.

The AWS Organizations services offer the consolidated billing feature to help companies better manage costs across the various AWS accounts they own. The consolidated billing feature transfers all responsibility for expenses incurred and payments made to the management account. The feature offers a consolidated view of every service used in each account and itemized invoices per account.

Figure 4.8 shows an example of a management account's **Bills dashboard**.

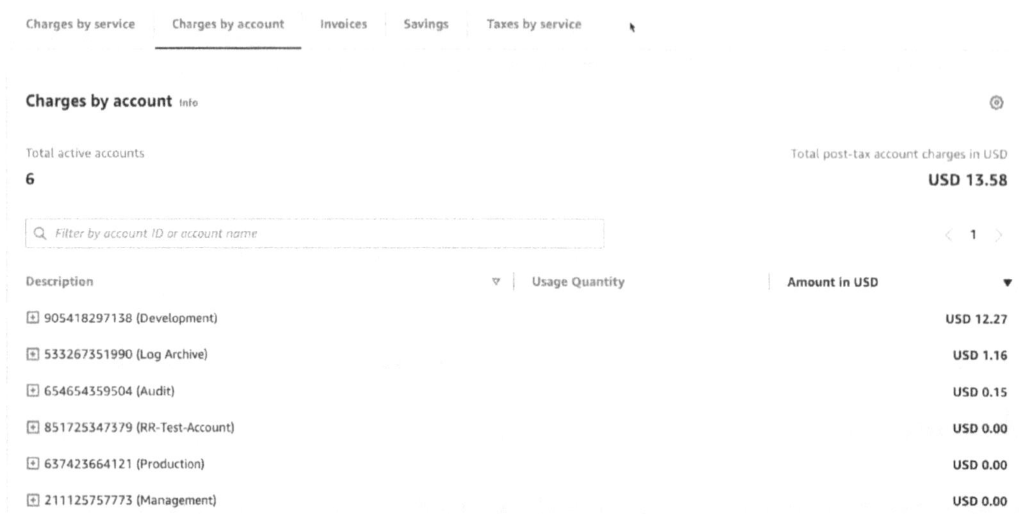

Figure 4.8: Bills dashboard of management account

As per the screenshot, the development account costs the organization the most. This is likely because of a project currently being under development. You will note that this organization has no charges yet for the production account.

Expanding the plus sign next to the account will also provide a breakdown of services consumed per region and the cost incurred, giving you a detailed itemized billing report.

Another key benefit of using AWS Organizations and the consolidated billing feature is the benefit of volume discounts. AWS offers volume discounts when you consume more of a service beyond specified thresholds. For example, as you consume more storage using the Amazon S3 service, the per-**gigabyte** (**GB**) rate decreases. This is explained in detail in the next section.

Volume discounts with AWS Organizations

Belly Brew Co. Limited will host a wide range of AWS accounts, including foundational accounts, workloads, and Sandbox accounts, to name just a few. By using AWS Organizations and the consolidated billing feature, the company will benefit from volume discounts.

A critical business process involves analyzing the daily production of Kombucha casks to ensure that the beverages manufactured fall within health safety limits. This is a manual process, as discussed in *Chapter 1*. Belly Brew Co. Limited wants to build an application to digitize the solution and avoid the manual process. This will likely create lots of data that will need to be stored. The plan is to host this data in an Amazon S3 bucket (an ideal object storage solution for raw data like documents, images, and videos).

At the same time, Belly Brew Co. Limited will have other accounts that consume storage for a wide range of use cases—log files stored in the log archive account, for example.

Assume that every month, the total data stored across these two accounts alone is as follows:

- **Log Archive Account**: 10TB (terabytes) of storage.
- **Belly Brew Co. Limited Manufacturing Operations Account**: 5TB of storage. Note that 1TB is 1000 GB.

Assume that the cost per 1GB is $0.20 for the first 10TB and only $0.05 for the next 20TB; the following tables depict the cost benefits of clubbing these accounts into an AWS Organization to benefit from volume discounts:

The following figure illustrates costs without configuring Belly Brew Co. Limited's AWS accounts as part of a single AWS Organization:

Without AWS Organization – Each Account Managed Separately		
AWS Account	**Total Storage Consumed**	**Cost**
Log Archive Account	10TB (10,000 GB)	$2,000 ($0.20 * 10,000)
Production Account	5TB (5,000GB)	$1,000 ($0.20 * 5,000)
Total Cost		$ 3,000

Figure 4.9: Without AWS Organizations

Figure 4.9 treats each account separately and not as part of the organization. The storage consumption of each account remains within the initial 10TB threshold and does not benefit from a volume discount, even though both accounts belong to Belly Brew Co. Limited.

The following figure illustrates costs after configuring Belly Brew Co. Limited's AWS accounts as part of a single AWS Organization:

With AWS Organizations (Log Archive and Production part of same Org)		
AWS Account	**Total Storage Consumed**	**Cost**
Log Archive Account	10TB (10,000 GB)	$2,000 ($0.20 * 10,000)
Production Account	5TB (5,000GB)	$250 ($0.05 * 5,000)
Total Cost		$2,250

Table 4.10: With AWS Organizations

Figure 4.10 treats each account as part of a single AWS organization. The storage consumption of the Log archive account consumed the initial 10TB threshold. Because the Production account consumes an additional 5TB of storage above the initial 10TB threshold for the entire organization, the per GB rate falls to $0.05 per GB. This results in an overall savings of $750, with the total cost being $2,250 instead of $3,000, as per *Figure 4.9*.

Another critical benefit of AWS Organizations is sharing resources across AWS member accounts. This feature is discussed in the next section.

Shared resources across accounts

Many organizations will have shared infrastructure services, which other teams or departments may need access to. Sharing resources like network subnets of a **Virtual Private Cloud** (**VPC**) across member accounts allows owners of those accounts to deploy their applications in the shared resource. To share such resources, you must first enable the **Resource Access Manager** (**RAM**) service in your AWS Organizations. You can then share resources with all the other accounts or specific accounts contained within one or more OUs.

Some resource types can also be shared with other AWS accounts not part of your organization. These include the **Backup Vault** in AWS Backup, which is used to securely store and organize backups created by AWS Backup. Sharing resources can also help optimize costs. For example, if you need to deploy virtual servers in the cloud, you can use the **Amazon Elastic Compute Service** (**EC2**). This service enables you to deploy virtual machines (virtual servers) running Windows, Linux, or the MacOS operating system. By default, these instances are purchased using a pay-as-you-go model known as **on-demand pricing**. On-demand pricing is where you pay for the resource hourly or by the second.

However, you can also purchase **reserved EC2 instances** (**RI**) contracts. This contract is a commitment to consume a particular virtual machine with specified attributes (CPU, memory, network capabilities) for one to three years. These reserved instance contracts are available at a substantial discount compared to the on-demand hourly price. With AWS Organizations, you can share reserved instances purchased in the management account with other member accounts of the organization. This means that if you happen to have spare RI capacity available, these contracts can be fully utilized in other member accounts that might need capacity. Amazon EC2 and **Reserved Instances** (**RIs**) are discussed in detail in *Chapter 8*.

While AWS Organizations and its core features enable you to streamline the management of a multi-account architecture, you must still make manual decisions and define configuration items such as OUs, SCPs, and more. Companies with hundreds of AWS accounts will still perform several tasks to ensure their organizational structure fulfills recommended best practices and security guidelines. This can all become very complex and time-consuming. AWS offers another solution to help create and manage your AWS multi-account architecture more efficiently, using industry-standard best practices and well-architected references. This service is called AWS Control Tower and is the topic of the next section.

Using AWS Control Tower for multi-account governance

AWS Control Tower is a fully managed service designed to help you build complex multi-account architectures using industry-standard best practices. The service uses the **AWS Landing Zone blueprints** to create a secure multi-account environment following well-architected references. These blueprints incorporate governance, data security, and audit logging capabilities.

AWS Control Tower offers predefined rules comprising preventive, detective, and proactive guardrails, allowing you to enforce compliance. Preventive guardrails help to avoid policy violations, while detective guardrails are designed to monitor your member accounts and notify you when a policy violation occurs. Proactive controls scan your resources before they are provisioned, ensuring that they are only provisioned if they are compliant with those controls.

The service also integrates with the AWS Account Factory, allowing you to create new AWS accounts from the AWS Organization service using a set of pre-configured settings that ensure consistency, as well as other services, such as the AWS IAM Identity Center (previously known as AWS Single Sign On, SSO), AWS CloudTrail, and AWS Config, offering auditing and governance features. Finally, a central dashboard allows you to monitor your multi-account environment and review all guardrail compliance statuses and governance metrics.

The AWS Control Tower builds on the AWS Organizations service by providing automated setup, governance, and best practices for multi-account environments. This makes architecting and deploying a multi-account environment much more effortless.

The next section of this chapter walks you through creating your first AWS account, which you will use throughout the remaining chapters to build solutions and gain the necessary technical skills.

Project task 4 – Setting up and securing your AWS development account

In the upcoming project tasks, you will create your first AWS account. This account will be called `bellybrewdevelopment`. You will use this account to carry out all upcoming project tasks and exercises to build hands-on experience on the AWS platform. In addition, you will also configure a billing alarm for your account.

As discussed in this book's *Preface*, you must complete all project tasks and exercises to maximize learning. You will be creating a free plan account for this purpose. The free plan account comes with a credit of US $100, which you can use to carry out all the exercises. Once you create a new free plan account, you can also complete a set of tasks to earn an additional US $100 in credits, giving you a total of US $200 worth of credits to use for your labs and experiential learning.

Note that for labs and exercises in this study guide, you will consume only a small percentage of the overall credits, and so will have lots left over for your own learning.

By the end of this book, you will also complete a clean-up process to terminate all the resources/services used in labs and project exercises. This will help ensure you do not incur any further charges. If your resources are left running, your charges will increase. To ensure this does not happen, you will also set up a billing alarm, which will notify you if you exceed the allocated budget amount.

Technical requirements

To complete the upcoming project tasks, you will need access to an email account (email address) not previously used to sign up for an AWS account. You will also need access to a mobile phone (for verification) and access to a credit or debit card.

Project task 4.1 – Creating a free-tier AWS account

In this project task, you will create your AWS free plan account.

1. Using your favorite web browser, navigate to the website `https://aws.amazon.com/free/`
2. Click the **Create a Free Account** button, which will present the AWS Sign-Up webpage
3. Provide an email address for your account. This email address must not have been previously used to set up an AWS account.
4. Next, you must choose a name for your account. Ensure you name this account as `bellybrewdevelopment` as per the following screenshot in *Figure 4.11*

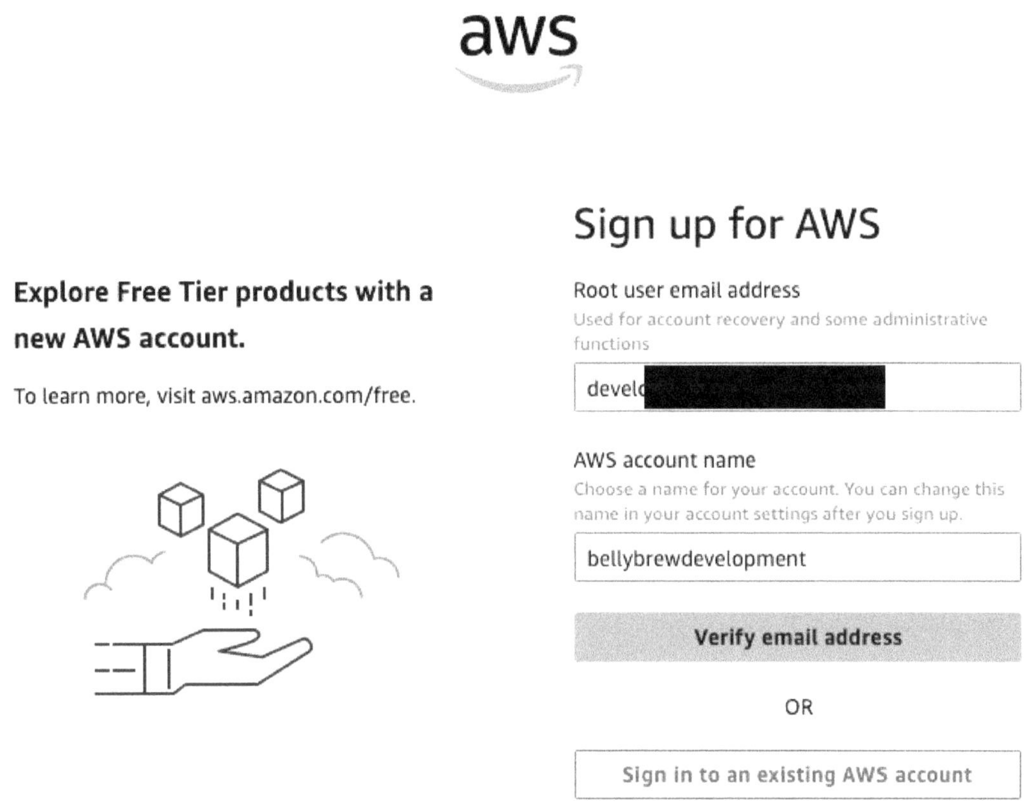

Figure 4.11: Sign up for AWS

5. Next, click the **Verify email address** button
6. You will receive a 6-digit PIN code to your email address. Copy this code and paste it in the verification code text box provided, and click **Verify** as per the screenshot in *Figure 4.12*

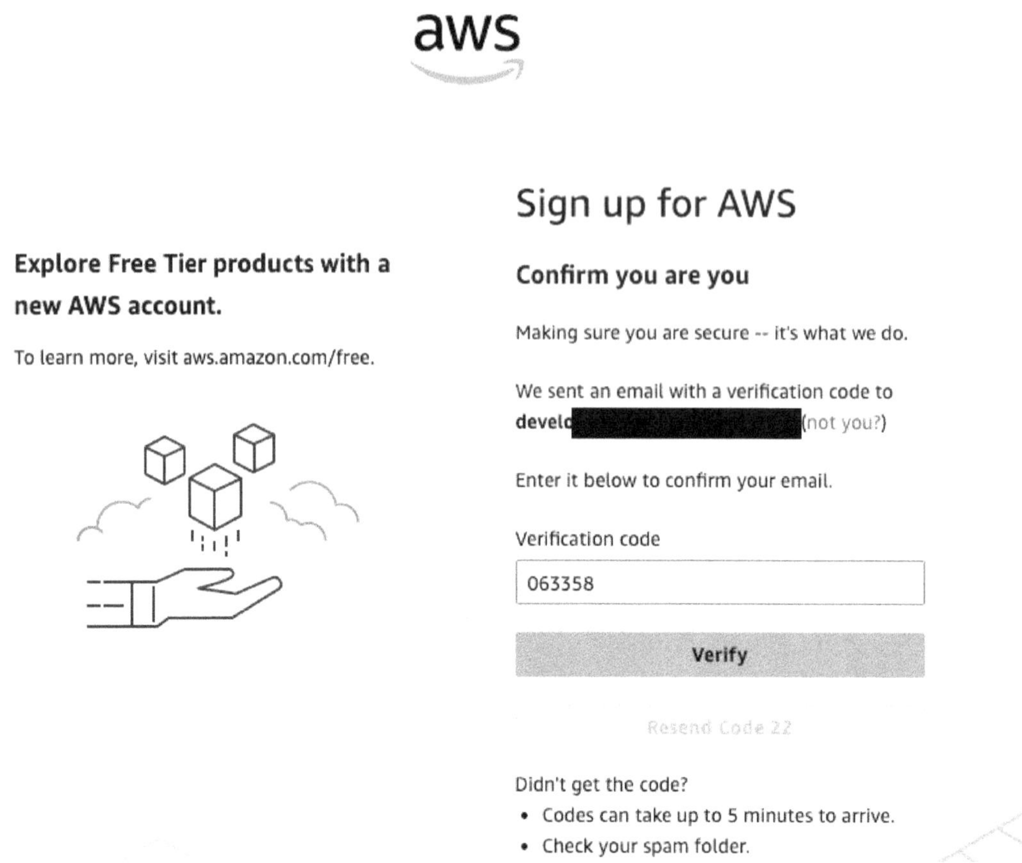

Figure 4.12: Email verification

7. On the next screen, you must provide a complex password for your AWS account. This is the root user's password. You must confirm the password and ensure you store it in a safe place. Click **Continue** after you're done
8. On the next screen, you will be prompted to select either the **Free Plan** or the **Paid Plan**. The Free Plan is only available if you are using a new email address, credit card, and billing information. Select the **Free Plan**, which gives you access to the AWS account for six months and the $200 credits ($100 when you sign up and a further $100 when you complete a set of tasks in your AWS account)
9. On the next screen, you must provide contact information. Under **How do you plan to use AWS?**, select the **Personal** option. You can choose the **Business** option if you wish to set up a business account.

10. Fill out the rest of the form by providing a valid mobile number and address. Finally, ensure you select the checkbox next to **I have read and agree to the terms of the AWS Customer Agreement** and click **Continue**
11. Next, you must provide your Billing Information. Ensure you provide your credit/debit card details and then click the **Verify and Continue** button.
12. On the next screen, you must verify your identity. Select **Text message (SMS)** under **How should we send you the verification code?**
13. Provide your mobile phone number, complete the security check, and click the **Send SMS** button
14. You should receive an SMS PIN to your mobile phone, which will need to be entered on the next screen in the **Verify code** text box
15. Once verified, you will be redirected to the AWS management console home page as per the following screenshot in *Figure 4.13*. You will also receive an email confirming that your AWS account is now active and ready to use.

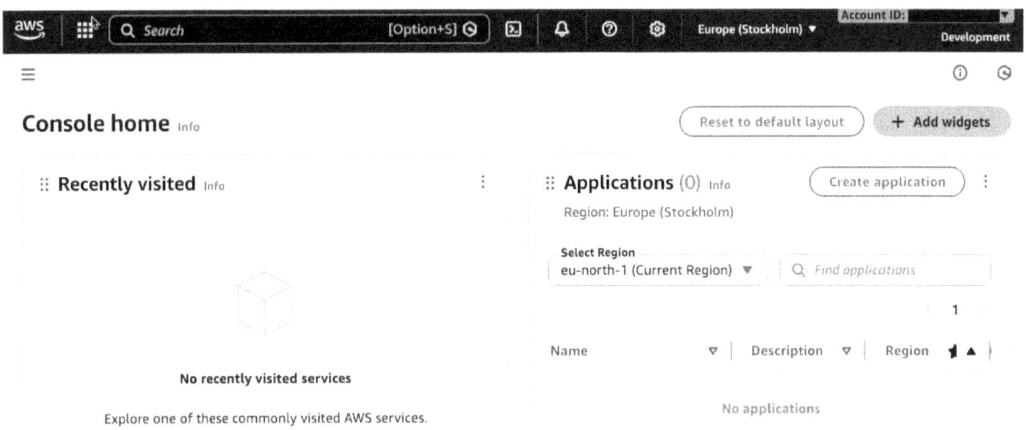

Figure 4.13: AWS management console

16. Log out of your account by clicking on the **Account Name** at the top left of the screen and clicking the **Sign out** button in the pop-up screen that appears

Now that you have set up your AWS Account, the next step is to further secure it using **Multi-Factor Authentication** (**MFA**). MFA is a security method that requires a user to verify their identity using two or more different factors instead of just a password.

Project task 4.2 – Securing your account with MFA

When you next log back into your AWS account, you will be prompted to set up your MFA security. You can use your mobile smartphone to set up your MFA. Download an authenticator app from the App/Play store such as Google Authenticator or Microsoft Authenticator and install it on your phone. The rest of this how-to guide uses the **Google Authenticator App**.

1. Log back into the AWS account again using your chosen email address and password. Ensure you are logging in using the **Root user** type as per the following screenshot in *Figure 4.14*

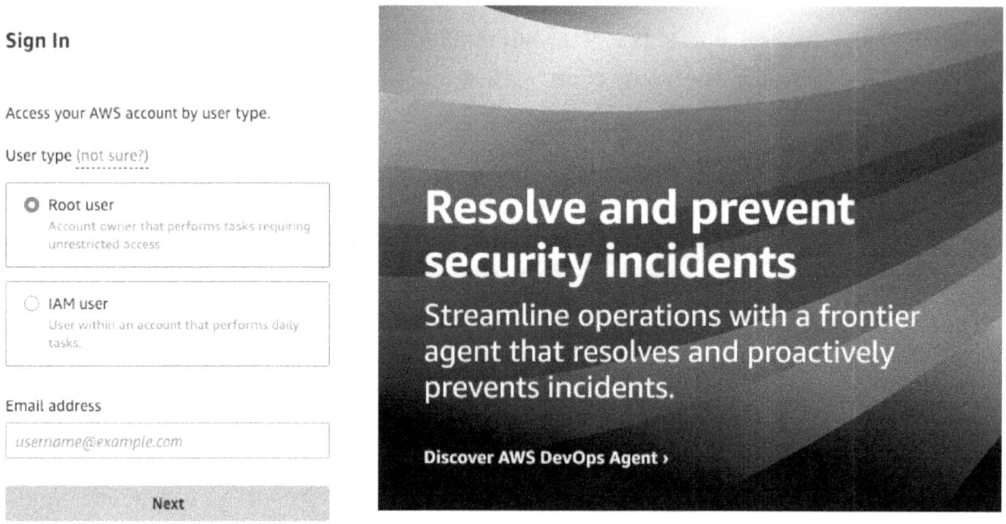

Figure 4.14: AWS sign-in page

2. While logging back in, you may be prompted to verify your identity, where AWS will send a verification code to your email address. Complete this verification process
3. Next, you will be prompted to secure your account with MFA as shown in the following screenshot:

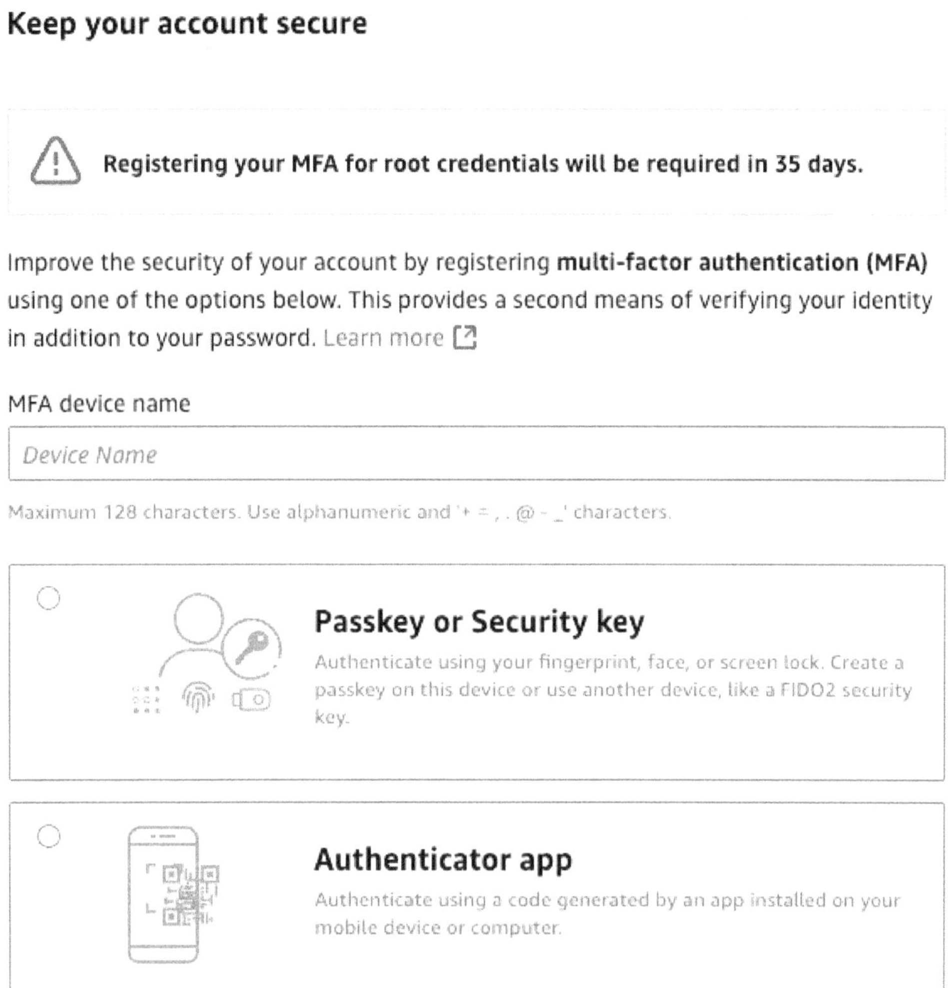

Figure 4.15: Secure your account with MFA

4. From the options provided, select the **Authenticator app** and click **Next**. The **Set up authenticator app** webpage will appear.
5. On your smartphone, launch the **Google Authenticator** app. Tap the **Plus (+)** icon on the app and select the option to **Scan a QR code**. This will launch the camera on your phone
6. On the AWS **Set up authenticator app** webpage, click the **Show QR code** link
7. Use the phone camera currently active in the Google Authenticator app to scan this QR code. The app will then create an entry for your AWS account

8. Next, you must enter two consecutive codes from your app into the webpage to complete the MFA registration as shown in *Figure 4.16*:

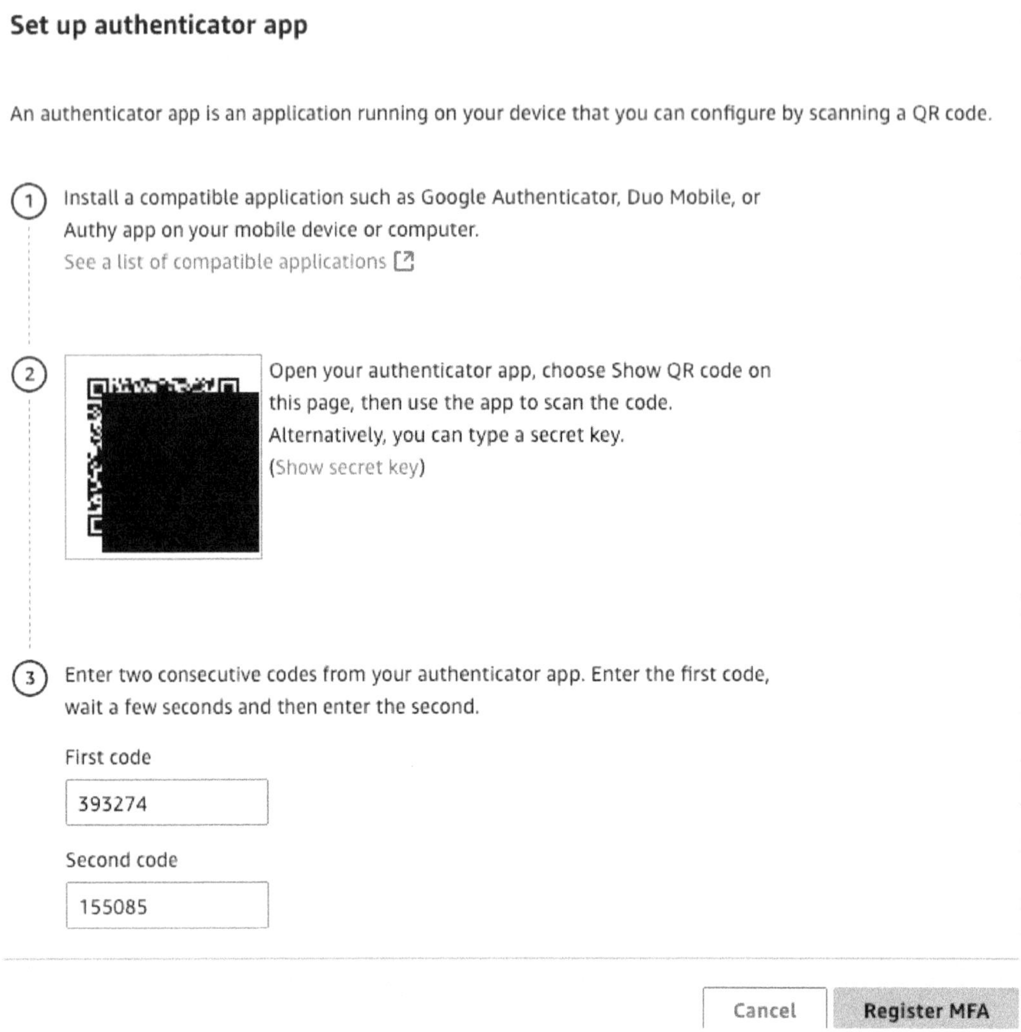

Figure 4.16: MFA registration

9. Click the **Register MFA** button. You should then receive a confirmation that you have now successfully registered your MFA device. Click the **Continue to console** button
10. Once you log into the web management console, scroll down to the Explore AWS widget to confirm that you now have the option to earn another $100 when you complete a set of five tasks, as shown in *Figure 4.17*:

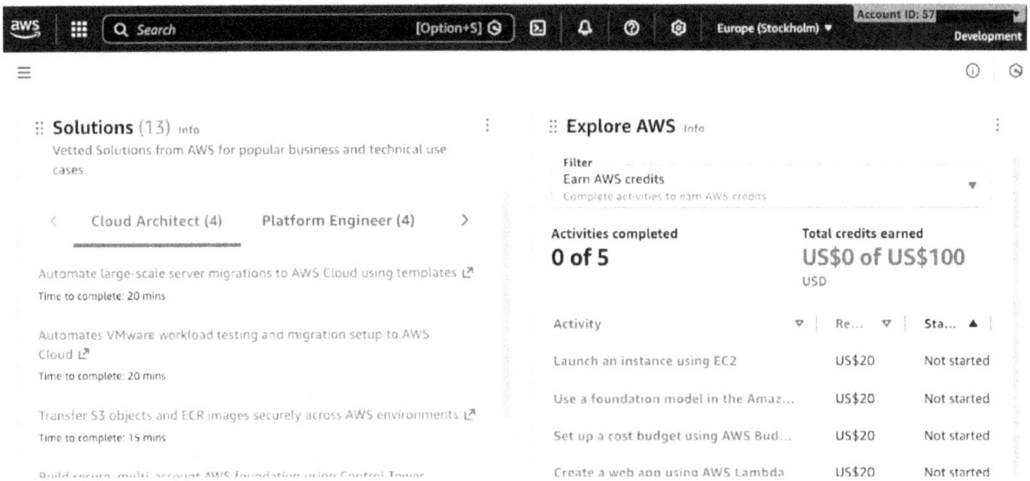

Figure 4.17: Confirmation of how to earn extra AWS credits

You must proceed to click each of the activities as shown in Figure 4.17. You will then be guided through the activity tasks with step-by-step instructions provided in the management console during the activity.

The next section walks through one of the activities – setting *up a cost budget using AWS Budgets*.

Project task 4.3 – Setting up AWS budgets

In this project task, you will create a monthly cost budget using AWS Budgets. This allows you to track your usage and costs in your AWS account, and you can choose to be alerted when you cross the budget threshold defined, or even when, based on current consumption levels, you are forecasted to cross the budget.

This task is also one of the five tasks you can complete following the step-by-step guidance provided in the AWS Management Console to earn extra credits. Each task completed earns you US $20 worth of credits, and if you complete all five tasks, you earn US $100 in addition to your sign-up credits of US $100, giving you a total of US $200.

1. While still logged into the AWS Management Console, scroll down to the **Explore AWS** widget and click the **Set up a cost budget using AWS Budgets** link
2. In the pop-up window that appears, click the **Start activity** button
3. You will be redirected to the **Billing and Cost Management** console, specifically the **Choose budget type** webpage, as shown in *Figure 4.18*

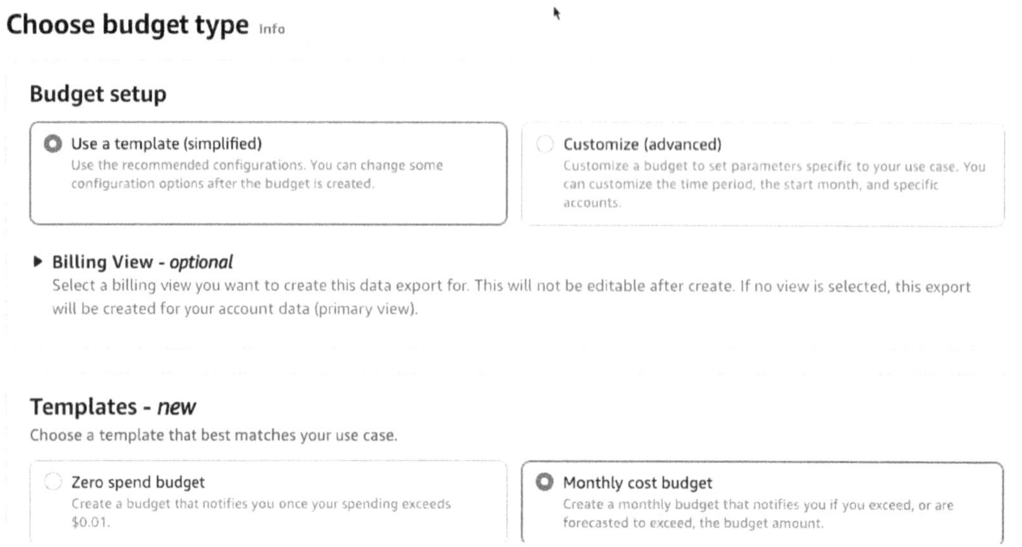

Figure 4.18: AWS cost budgets

4. You will also notice a tool tip providing you with step-by-step guides to complete this activity. Follow the steps of the tool tip and click **Next** as you progress through the steps, as shown in *Figure 4.19:*

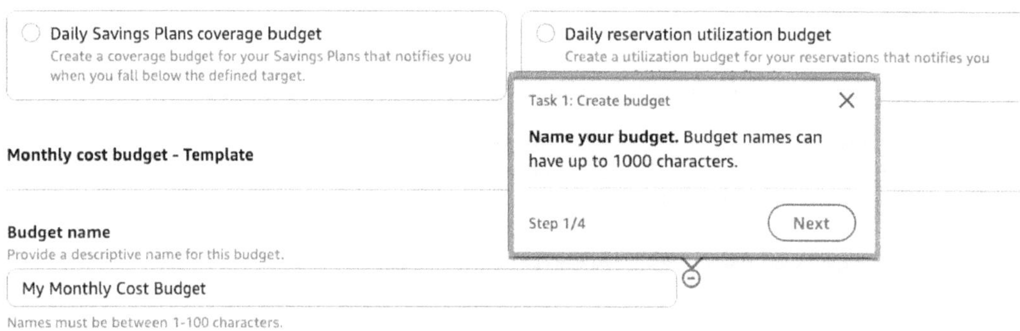

Figure 4.19: Creating AWS monthly budgets tutorial

5. Provide a name for your budget and then click **Next** in the tool tip for the next step
6. For the **Enter your budgeted amount ($)**, provide a value such as `$20`. It is strongly recommended that you allocate at least $20 for the exercises in this study guide. As you complete the various projects in this study guide, you will also be guided to terminate unwanted resources at the end of those exercises, ensuring that you do not incur any unnecessary charges against your credits. Click **Next** on the tool tip for the next step

7. Enter your email address in the **Email recipients** text box to have notifications sent to you. Click **Next** on the tool tip box
8. Click the **Create budget** button, and your budget will be created. You should see a notification congratulating you that you have now completed the tutorial.
9. You may need to log out and log back in, and then you will be able to see that you have had a credit of $20 added to your total credits. You can view your total credits allocated to your account by clicking on the **Account Name** (e.g., Development) at the top right-hand corner of the webpage, and you should see a pop-up window displaying your total credits earned so far, as shown in *Figure 4.20*:

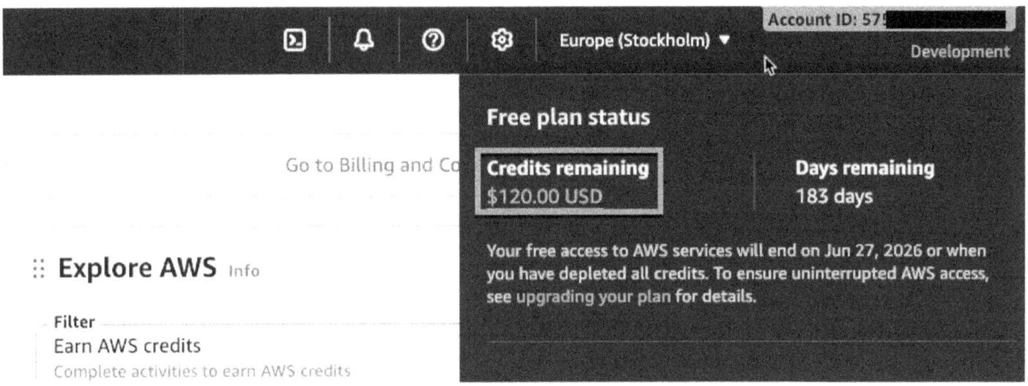

Figure 4.20: Total credits earned

It is strongly recommended that you follow the self-paced tutorials to complete the remaining four activities, allowing you to earn additional credits. Once you have completed the remaining activities, your account should have a total credit of US$200.

Furthermore, now that you have created a monthly budget, you will receive an alert to your email if you cross the threshold value. This should further alert you to terminate any unwanted resources, making sure you have credits left over for additional learning and experimental work.

Summary

An AWS account is a resource container that facilitates your ability to access AWS services and provision resources to host your applications and data. The architecture of an AWS account ensures that the resources you create within the account are visible to only those who have access to the account. This enforces stringent security, ensuring one customer cannot access the resources of another without appropriate permissions.

Customers can create numerous AWS accounts for different workloads and application stacks – they can also adopt strategies to separate environments of an individual application lifecycle by creating a separate account for each environment of the applications, such as one account for development, one for testing, and another for production. This ability to host different applications and environments of an application across different accounts ensures isolation and separation. Also, it reduces the blast radius of any disasters occurring in one account, preventing them from affecting resources in another. Businesses will also need to consider separating accounts from a compliance and governance perspective. For example, you would not want your customer-facing applications to necessarily reside in the same AWS accounts as your internal operations workloads.

As part of preparing for the AWS Certified Cloud Practitioner exam, understanding this basic concept is vital. Many businesses will have thousands of accounts, so naturally, you must also be able to manage multiple accounts efficiently. This chapter introduced you to the features of the AWS Organization service and core offerings, which are vital to ensuring reliable, cost-effective, and secure management of an organization's multi-account architecture. The importance of clubbing related accounts using OUs can help with efficient management. Using **service control policies** (**SCPs**), you learned how to restrict what services, resources, and actions can be taken in AWS member accounts. Furthermore, you also learned about the benefits of consolidated billing, which can help customers reduce overall costs resulting from volume discounts. In addition, the ability to share resources between member accounts can also further optimize your total spending in the cloud.

From a practical perspective, you learned how Belly Brew Co. Limited would use the AWS Organization service to separate the different environments of the customer-facing web application. In addition, the company would require accounts for foundational services and other internal business processes. SCPs will be crafted to ensure only approved services and resources can be created in those accounts. You would not want to give unrestricted access to spin up any resources in your corporate accounts, which could have cost implications as well as security issues.

In this chapter, you learned how AWS accounts, multi-account strategies, AWS Organizations, and AWS Control Tower help structure and govern cloud environments. In the next chapter, we will focus on securing access within those environments by using AWS Identity and Access Management, IAM users, groups, policies, roles, AWS Identity Center, Amazon Cognito, and AWS Directory Service.

Exam Readiness Drill – Chapter Review Questions

Apart from mastering key concepts, strong test-taking skills under time pressure are essential for acing your certification exam. That's why developing these abilities early in your learning journey is critical.

Exam readiness drills, using the free online practice resources provided with this book, help you progressively improve your time management and test-taking skills while reinforcing the key concepts you've learned.

HOW TO GET STARTED

- Open the link or scan the QR code at the bottom of this page
- If you have unlocked the practice resources already, log in to your registered account. If you haven't, follow the instructions in *Free Benefits with Your Book* section in this book's *Preface* and come back to this page.
- Once you log in, click the START button to start this chapter's quiz
- We recommend attempting a quiz multiple times till you're able to answer most of the questions correctly and well within the time limit.
- You can use the following practice template to help you plan your attempts:

Working On Accuracy		
Attempt	**Target**	**Time Limit**
Attempt 1	40% or more	Till the timer runs out
Attempt 2	60% or more	Till the timer runs out
Attempt 3	75% or more	Till the timer runs out
Working On Timing		
Attempt 4	75% or more	1 minute before time limit
Attempt 5	75% or more	2 minutes before time limit
Attempt 6	75% or more	3 minutes before time limit

The above drill is just an example. Design your drills based on your own goals and make the most out of the online quizzes accompanying this book.

Link to this Chapter's Quiz

You need to unlock the online practice resources to access the link below. Check the *Free Benefits with Your Book* section in the *Preface* for detailed instructions on how to do this. You only need to unlock the resources once.

Open Quiz `https://packt.link/clf_c02_ch4`or scan the QR code

5

AWS Access Management

Now that you have created your first AWS account, you must ensure that access to the account is secured and that only authorized individuals in your organization can consume services and provision required resources for your approved projects and workloads.

AWS offers several services to ensure you grant access to only authorized individuals and use the **principle of least privilege** (**POLP**) when assigning permissions and rights to those individuals. Furthermore, applications you deploy on AWS may require access to specific AWS services. For example, an application may need access to an Amazon S3 bucket to upload log files or a database to query customer records. Using AWS's suite of access management tools, you can ensure that those applications are granted only the necessary permissions for those services and resources to function correctly.

This chapter will teach you about the **AWS Identity and Access Management** service, a core component offering authentication and authorization services for your AWS account and the workloads you deploy. In addition, you will also learn about other authentication and authorization services and technologies that cater to a wide range of use cases — from implementing and managing federated access and single sign-on capabilities for your workforce to building a sign-up and sign-in solution for your applications.

This chapter discusses the importance of building access solutions according to the principle of least privilege, protecting the root user account, and using the appropriate tools based on the use case. This chapter will also showcase methods used to access the AWS account and how permissions are granted through policy documents.

The following topics are covered in this chapter:

- Managing access with AWS Identity and Access Management
- Centralizing workforce access with AWS Identity Center

- Managing application-user identities with Amazon Cognito
- Integrating Microsoft directory services with AWS Directory Service

Managing access with AWS Identity and Access Management

AWS Identity and Access Management (**AWS IAM**) is a core security service that enables you to securely control access to your AWS account. AWS IAM offers two key services: **authentication** and **authorization**. Authentication enables the identification and verification of a trusted identity, which can be an IAM user or an IAM role (discussed in the *IAM users* and *IAM roles* sections later in this chapter). This trusted identity authenticates against your AWS account by presenting a set of credentials that AWS IAM will verify and, if correct, grant access to the AWS account.

Now, although access to the AWS account has been granted through the authentication process, the identity still cannot perform any action in the account until you authorize it with specific permissions. Here, the identity is also known as a **principal**, which is any entity, such as human users, applications, or services, that can access a particular resource. Principals can be granted permissions via policies to access specific services and perform certain actions against those services.

With both authentication and authorization, you can decide who or what can access your AWS account, which services can be consumed, and what actions can be performed against the resources in your account.

For example, you can create a set of credentials for the principal (also an identity) 'Alice' to access your AWS account. Alice can then use these credentials to authenticate against your AWS account. Next, you can define policies (also known as permissions) so that Alice is authorized to access Amazon S3, which is an object storage solution, and download data from a specific S3 bucket. Similarly, you can authorize another principal, such as an application running on an EC2 instance (which is a virtual server), with the permission to update a database with customer orders.

Authorization requests can be made by principals in your AWS account or from other trusted AWS accounts.

Before examining the different types of principals you can define permissions for, it's important to appreciate the role of the root user, which represents the owner of your AWS account. The next section delves into this further.

The role of the root user account

The root user is the owner of the AWS account. It is represented by the email address and password you chose when setting up the AWS account. This root user is the absolute 'God' of your account, meaning that it has full unrestricted access to the services in the account and can launch any type of resources within the confines of the limits and quotas imposed by AWS. The only exception to this is that if the AWS account is a member of an AWS Organization, then you can use **Service Control Policies** (**SCPs**) to restrict specific access and permissions for the root user.

The root user can also perform certain actions that no other IAM user can. These include:

- Change your account settings.
- Close your AWS account. Only the root user can close the account.
- Amazon **Simple Storage Services** (**Amazon S3**). Certain actions on the Amazon S3 service, such as enabling multi-factor authentication for an Amazon S3 bucket
- Sign up for a US Gov Cloud account. This requires additional prerequisites.
- Viewing certain tax invoices.
- Restore IAM permissions—for any administrator user, if no other user has administrative access.
- Activate IAM access to Billing and Cost management – by default, only the root user can access this service. However, AWS strongly recommends that you do not use the root user account for day-to-day operations. Activating this feature enables you to grant permissions to other IAM users to access billing and cost information. An example use case for this is granting access to members of the Finance department.

AWS also recommends that you enhance the login security of the root user account by enabling multi-factor authentication. This ensures that a bad actor cannot easily gain access to your AWS account if they happen to know your email address and password. This feature is discussed in the next section.

The root user and multi-factor authentication

Multi-factor authentication (**MFA**) is the practice of using an additional authentication factor in addition to your standard username and password. MFA follows a principle of authenticating based on a minimum of two of the following factors:

- **What you know**: This is a standard authentication factor that requires the trusted identity to present a set of credentials (for example, username and password) to verify their identity. It's based on the idea that only the identity will have access to these credentials.

- **What you have**: This is an additional authentication factor that requires the trusted identity to possess some device (physical or virtual, like an app) that can be used to generate a one-time password (or PIN). This can also be a mobile number that would receive a text SMS with the PIN. It's based on the idea that only the identity would possess this device (or a specific mobile number).
- **What you are**: This is an additional authentication factor that requires the identity to verify their physical being, such as a fingerprint, retina scan, etc.

MFA thus refers to answering multiple challenges to verify your identity, such as *what you know* and *what you have* in the authentication process. AWS customers can also configure their accounts with a *what you are* type MFA by using a biometrics-enabled authenticator.

Using MFA drastically reduces the chances of a malicious attacker impersonating you. If the attacker has access to your credentials, hopefully, they will not have access to your physical or virtual device that generates those one-time PINs.

AWS enables its customers to configure MFA both for the root user as well as for IAM users, and most companies will implement MFA as a standard security protocol along with ensuring the use of password complexity to make brute force attacks difficult.

When you have hundreds or even thousands of users who need an IAM user ID to access your AWS account, ensuring that everyone chooses a complex password can be an administrative overhead. Luckily, AWS offers a feature to enforce this, and the next section covers this in more detail.

Enforcing password complexity

Password complexity refers to the ability to construct a password that is hard to guess. This involves combining letters, numbers, and symbols while containing a minimum set of characters. The password must not be made of dictionary words, and depending on the identity and management service, its security can be enhanced using passphrases.

AWS offers a feature that allows you to enforce rules on how passwords should be defined using the password policy feature located in the Account Settings section of the IAM dashboard, as depicted in *Figure 5.1*:

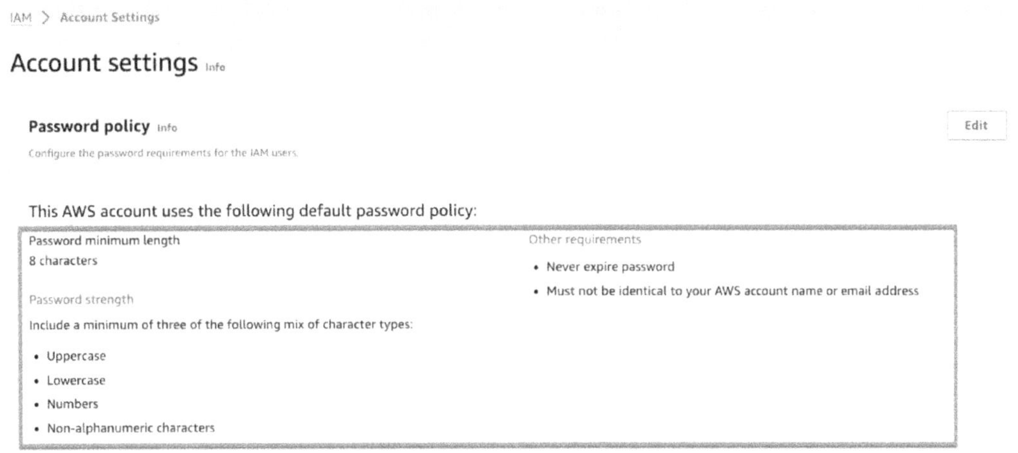

Figure 5.1: Password policy settings

As a company, you can define password complexity rules that apply to all IAM user accounts created in the AWS account. This makes it easier to fulfill compliance requirements.

In the next section, you will learn more about IAM users. These are identities that usually represent your human workforce and need access to your AWS account to design, build, and manage your products and services.

IAM users

An IAM user is an identity you create for a trusted human user to be able to authenticate against your AWS account. This IAM user can represent a development team member, server administrator, or the company's CEO. The trusted individual uses the IAM user's credentials to log into the AWS account and perform any tasks permitted based on permissions you assign using IAM policies (discussed later in this chapter).

IAM user credentials can also be used by non-human users, such as an application running on an EC2 instance that needs access to other services on AWS. However, this access method is not recommended, as managing credentials for non-human principals can be an administrative overhead. Furthermore, using IAM user credentials embedded in application code carries a much higher risk since the credentials are usually stored in plain text and could fall into the wrong hands. Instead, AWS recommends you use IAM roles for this use case, which will be discussed shortly.

When accessing your AWS account, IAM users must perform a login exercise and verify their identities using the credentials defined for their IAM user account. Depending on the method of access, AWS offers multiple credential types as follows:

- **Username and Password**: These credentials allow you to access your AWS Management Console. To sign in, you must provide the AWS `account ID` or the account alias in addition to the username and password. AWS lets you create a URL to customize your AWS Account ID (where you can substitute the ID for an alias). This URL is formatted as `https://My_AWS_Account_ID.signin.aws.amazon.com/console/`
- **Access Keys**: These comprise an access key ID (for example, `AKIAIOSFOFFD7EXAMPLE`) and a secret access key (for example, `wJalrXUvdFEMI/K4FDENG/bKxRflCYEXAMPLEKEY`). Access keys are used to access your AWS account programmatically using the **command-line interface** (**CLI**). This access method requires you to install the CLI tools on your local machine, which you can download from `https://aws.amazon.com/cli/`, and interact with AWS using commands and API calls. You can have a maximum of two access keys for each IAM user.
- **X.509 Certificates**: This method has been deprecated for most services. However, IAM users can still use X.509 certificates to authenticate for some AWS services like AWS IoT.

Often, different teams within a company share common job functions. While each team member will require an IAM user account, managing permissions becomes much easier when you group users into IAM groups and assign permissions at the group level. The next section discusses IAM groups in detail.

IAM groups

IAM groups allow you to manage user permissions more efficiently. Permissions are assigned to groups, and users who belong to those groups automatically inherit those permissions. For example, the development team might need access to a set of DevOps tools, while the infrastructure engineering team may require access to networking and compute services.

Rather than assigning permissions to each IAM user individually, you can place users into groups and assign the necessary permissions to the group. Users in the group will inherit the group's permissions, as shown in *Figure 5.2*:

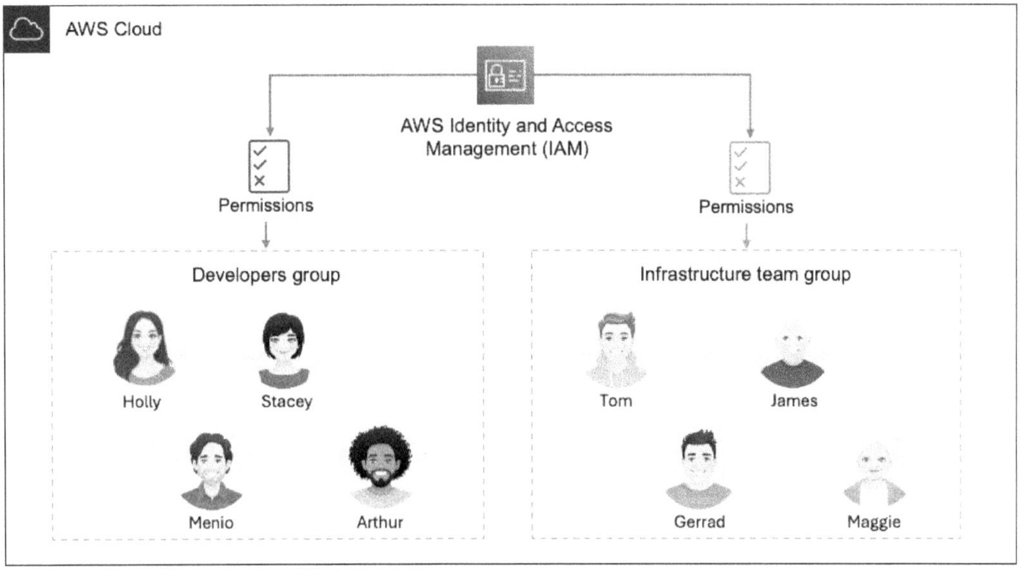

Figure 5.2: Using IAM groups to manage permission assignment

As per the diagram in *Figure 5.2*, assigning permissions to groups is easier than assigning these permissions directly to each user, as it involves fewer permissions and policy documents to manage. In this example, you only need to assign two sets of permissions to two groups. Users within the groups will inherit the permissions applied at the group level. This also reduces the management overhead when team members change roles or join and leave the company.

The next section will teach how permissions are assigned to IAM users and groups.

IAM policies

Permissions are assigned using IAM policy documents. There are two types of policies you can configure on AWS – IAM Policies and resource-based policies. IAM policies are known as identity-based policies, and they are directly assigned to identities such as IAM users, IAM roles (discussed in the *IAM roles* section), or groups of IAM users who need access to services and resources in your AWS account. IAM policy documents are written in **JavaScript Object Notation (JSON)** format.

With IAM policies, you can define permissions that cover specific granular actions that can be performed against resources. This allows you to apply the POLP, ensuring that the identity does not have more permissions than necessary for their job role.

For example, some users may be permitted to launch and configure EC2 instances, but only a few senior users should be allowed to terminate any EC2 instances.

IAM policies can be applied to IAM identities such as IAM users, IAM roles, and groups of users within the same account in which they were created.

There are three types of identity-based policies:

- **Managed AWS policies**: These are standard, pre-defined policy documents written in JSON and managed solely by AWS. These boilerplate policies can be used to standardize permissions for your identities. The policies are created independently of any identity and can be assigned to one or more identities in your AWS account. You cannot edit these policies.
- **Customer-managed policies**: These are policies you create and manage and assign to IAM Identities. Unlike many AWS managed policies, you can define more granular permissions against specific resources in your AWS account. You can have up to five versions of a customer-managed policy, allowing you to revert to previous versions if required.
- **Inline policies**: These policies are created for a specific identity, such as an IAM user. They are not independent of that identity and cannot be attached to other identities. This ensures a strict one-to-one relationship between an identity and a policy. AWS recommends using inline policies sparingly because they require more administrative effort than managed policies. They also make tracking what policies you have configured in your AWS account more difficult.

Figure 5.3 depicts the IAM policies dashboard. Note the policies with the Amazon icon, which signifies that they are managed by AWS.

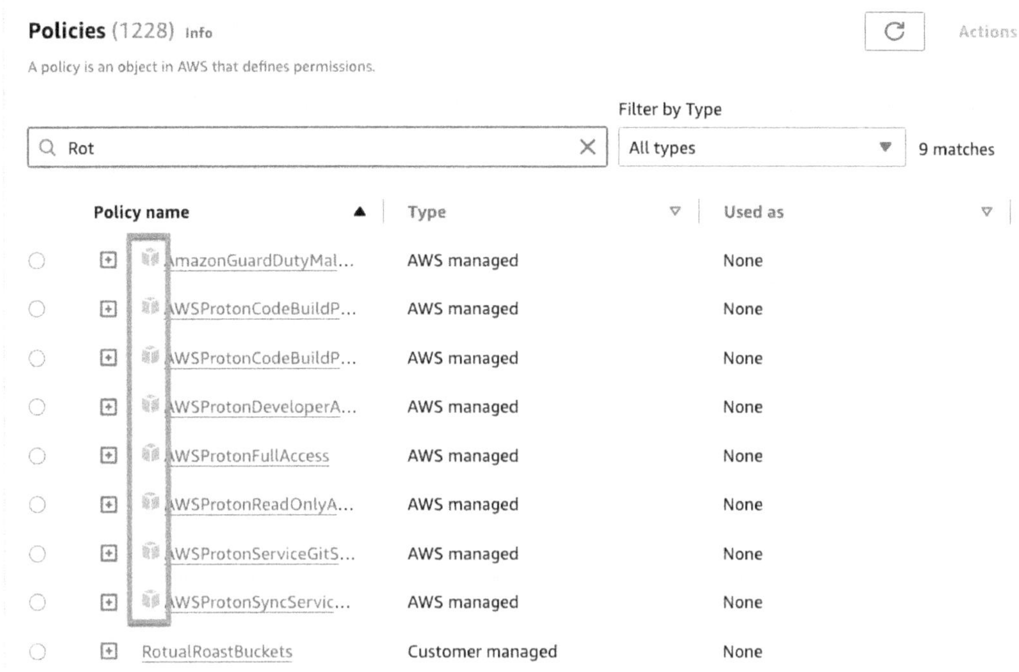

Figure 5.3: IAM policies

Belly Brew Co. Limited would require various managed policies to grant access to its various resources on AWS. For example, a developer may wish to host the Belly Brew Co. Limited website source code in an Amazon S3 bucket and ensure that only specific users and groups can access it. The following code snippet is an example of an IAM policy created for Belly Brew Co. Limited. The policy grants the `GetObject` access permission to the Belly Brew Co. Limited website source code bucket, enabling access to only its contents:

```
{
  "Version": "2012-10-17",
  "Statement": [
    {
      "Sid": "Stmt1727061999054",
      "Action": [
        "s3:GetObject"
      ],
      "Effect": "Allow",
      "Resource": "arn:aws:s3:::bellybrew-source-code/*"
    }
```

```
    ]
}
```

This policy grants the identity it is attached to the ability to read and download objects from the `bellybrew-source-code` S3 bucket.

Because this is an IAM policy, you do not need to specify the identity. Instead, you can attach the policy to the identity that needs the permissions specified in the policy. The following represents the anatomy of a typical IAM policy:

- `Version`: This is the currently supported version of the JSON document, which, at the time of writing this book, is 2012-10-17.
- `Statement`: This is the beginning of the policy statement. Under the statement block, you can have multiple permissions blocks, enabling you to apply various permissions across different AWS services and resources. The preceding code snippet shows only one statement block.
- `Sid`: The **Sid** (**Statement ID**) is an optional identifier that gives a unique name or label to individual statements within a policy. It can help distinguish between different statements, mainly when a policy contains multiple statements.
- `Effect`: This defines whether the statement block is going to allow some action or deny it. In this example, the `Effect` is set to `Allow`.
- `Action`: This is the specific permission you grant or deny to the identity to perform. The `Action` statement defines the AWS service and one or more actions that are permitted against resources of the Service. In this example, the service is Amazon S3, and the action permitted is `GetObject,` which would allow the identity to read/download the object from the bucket.
  The `Get` action, for example, includes several sub-operations, such as `GetObject`, that allow you to read/download objects. Another sub-operation is `GetBucketVersioning`, which enables you to retrieve a bucket's versioning state.
- `Resource`: This policy component defines the actual resource against which the identity is granted specific permission. In the previous code snippet, the ARN of the Belly Brew Co. Limited bucket is provided as `arn:aws:s3:::bellybrew-source-code/*. Note that the ARN is` followed by a slash (/) and an asterisk (*). This asterisk, also known as a wildcard, states that the identity can access all contents of the `bellybrew-source-code` bucket.
  Likewise, if you set the ARN to a wildcard (asterisk) and do not define a specific bucket, then the identity can perform the said action against all buckets in the AWS account. In

that case, the resource policy component would look like the following snippet, where the `Resource` element is set to an asterisk (*):

```
{
  "Sid": "Stmt1727076398268",
  "Action": "s3:*",
  "Effect": "Allow",
  "Resource": "*"
}
```

- `Condition`: You can also define conditional statements in your policy so that the policy is only applicable if the condition is met. An example might be to restrict identities from creating new S3 buckets once the request comes from a source IP address that represents your corporate network. This way, you add a layer of security to ensure that requests come from authorized sources.

Sometimes, when you apply specifically complex policies to Identities, there may be issues because those policies have not been defined correctly. You can use the IAM policy simulator to help you troubleshoot your policies and identify potential access or permissions issues. This is discussed in the next section.

IAM Policy Simulator

The IAM Policy Simulator is a tool for analyzing whether your IAM users, groups, or roles can perform specific actions with their assigned permissions. This is particularly useful when troubleshooting complex permission sets and trying to identify the root cause of any missing permissions.

> **Note**
>
> You can access the simulator at `https://policysim.aws.amazon.com/`. You must log in to your AWS account to use the service.

In *Figure 5.4*, you will note the permissions defined for an IAM user called Bob. The user only has a single policy attached, granting full access to the Amazon DynamoDB service. When running tests to see if Bob can perform the `GetObject` action against the Amazon S3 service, the results show **Denied**.

Figure 5.4: IAM Policy Simulator

This is because Bob has not been granted permission to access Amazon S3. While this example is simple, imagine troubleshooting more complex policies. The IAM Policy Simulator also lets you test your new policies to ensure they perform as expected. You can then test out the policy before deploying it on AWS.

In the next section, you will learn more about another IAM identity feature: IAM Roles.

IAM roles

An IAM Role is like an IAM user, except it is created independently of any specific human user. Whereas an IAM user account is usually made for a particular person, IAM roles are intended to be assumed by one or more principals who need access to specific services and resources in your AWS account.

Authorized principals can access a particular resource by assuming the role if the role has been configured to trust that principal and it has permissions for the resource. This means that an IAM role is configured with a trust policy that identifies the principal who can assume the role. Additionally, an IAM policy is attached to the role, defining the permissions the role grants to the principal.

IAM roles only grant temporary credentials to principals who assume them. The **AWS Security Token Service** (**AWS STS**) entirely manages these credentials. You do not create usernames and passwords or access keys (long-term credentials) for IAM roles. Instead, the AWS STS service assigns temporary credentials to the principal who assumes the role. These temporary credentials will include an access key ID, a secrets access key, and a security token. The security token expires after a short period, and the AWS STS service renews the credentials before expiry if the principal is still permitted access. This all happens transparently to the end user.

IAM roles are used in various scenarios, some of which will be covered in the following subsections.

Cross-account access

In *Chapter 4*, you learned about the importance of a multi-account architecture. While having multiple accounts offers more significant levels of security and isolation between your workloads, how you configure access to those accounts is very important. The last thing you want is for your workforce to have multiple IAM user accounts, one in each AWS account, to grant them access to the various environments and applications you host.

Instead, you can configure cross-account access for your workforce using IAM roles. Using this approach, you create all your IAM users within a single AWS account and grant them permissions to assume IAM roles of other AWS accounts with the required level of access. So, in the case of Belly Brew Co. Limited, you might create the IAM user accounts in a separate AWS account – you can call it the Identities AWS Account – and configure roles with relevant permissions in the Development and Production accounts, allowing those IAM users the ability to assume the roles. The permissions granted via those IAM roles would be based on their job function and group membership within the Identities account.

Figure 5.5 illustrates the workflow:

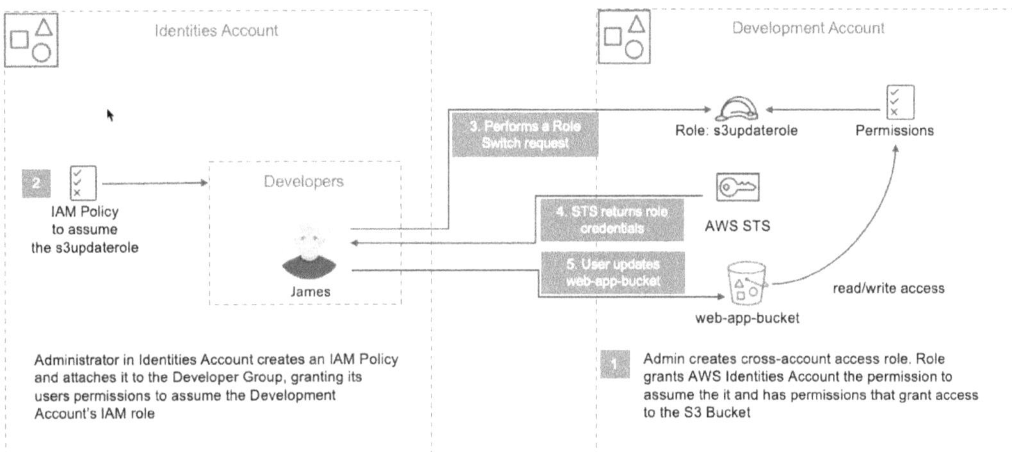

Figure 5.5: IAM roles for cross-account access

The diagram illustrates how James in the Identities account can access the `web-app-bucket` in the Development account without having to create a duplicate IAM user account for James in the latter account. The following is a breakdown of the workflow as per the diagram in *Figure 5. 5*:

1. An administrator in the Development account creates an IAM role called `s3updaterole` that grants access to the web-app-bucket. This role must have a trust policy to trust IAM users from the Identities account
2. An administrator in the Identities account creates an IAM policy allowing IAM users who are members of the Developers group to assume the `s3updaterole` role
3. The developer performs a **Switch role** operation by assuming the IAM role from the Development Account
4. The **Security Token Service** (**STS**) of the Development Account grants temporary credentials to the developer
5. The user can then switch roles to the `s3udpaterole`. If the user uses a web console to access the S3 bucket in the Development account, the user can choose the Switch Role option from the navigation bar, as per *Figure 5.6*.

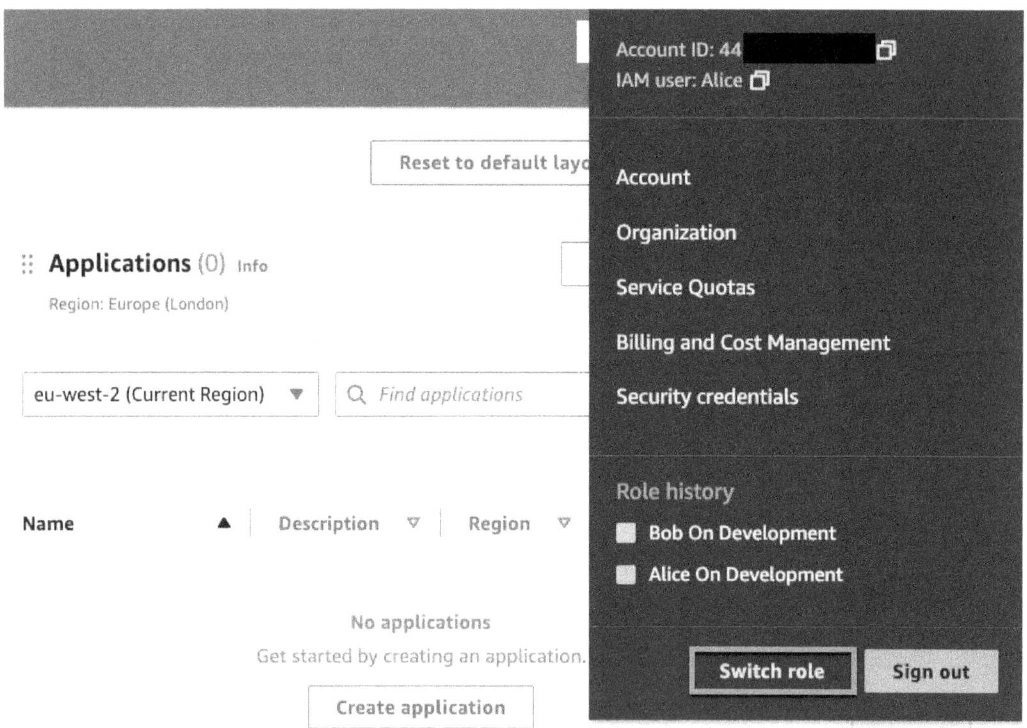

Figure 5.6: Role switch operation

If using the CLI or AWS API, the user must call the `AssumeRole` function to obtain credentials for the `s3updaterole` role by specifying the role's ARN.

> **Note**
>
> Note that when switching roles, you must know the destination **AccountID** and the **role name** you need to assume.

Another use case for IAM roles is granting users from external identity providers (outside the AWS ecosystem) temporary credentials to access services and resources in your AWS accounts. This is made possible by using identity federation, which will be discussed in the next section.

IAM roles for identity federation

Identity federation is the process of granting access to identities authenticated by external, trusted **identity providers** (**IDPs**) to services and resources within your AWS account.

For example, Belly Brew Co. Limited has an on-premises IT environment that spans its head offices and manufacturing plants across the UK. Employees at Belly Brew Co. Limited use the on-premises identity provider, in this case Microsoft Active Directory, to authenticate against on-premises workloads. Some of those users, such as developers and systems administrators, now require access to resources in the AWS accounts. Rather than creating additional credentials in the AWS accounts for those users (IAM user accounts), which would require the users to remember multiple usernames and passwords, you can use identity federation to authenticate those users against your AWS environment.You can then define IAM roles that specify the permissions those users will have in your AWS accounts.

AWS Identity Federation supports SAML 2.0 (Security Assertion Markup Language 2.0), allowing you to establish trust between your organization, acting as the **identity provider** (**IdP**), and AWS as the service provider. Using SAML, your users can access the AWS Management Console through federated **single sign-on** (**SSO**) or gain federated access to execute AWS API operations.

AWS Identity Federation also supports web identity federation with **OpenID Connect** (**OIDC**) providers such as Google and Facebook. This is usually used to provide authentication and authorization for mobile and web-based applications. However, AWS recommends you use Amazon Cognito for this scenario. This service has several additional features and security tools, which will be discussed later in this chapter.

Another use case for IAM roles is the ability to grant temporary access to non-AWS workloads, which will be discussed next.

IAM roles anywhere

Previously, when you created IAM roles, they could only be assumed by identities in your AWS account or other AWS accounts, as in the case with cross-account access discussed previously.

However, IAM roles could only be assumed by applications running on an AWS service, such as an EC2 instance. An example scenario would be an application hosted on an EC2 instance that requires access to an Amazon S3 bucket to upload log files.

But what about applications running on-premises or third-party cloud providers, which may also require access to AWS services and resources? In this scenario, you would be embedding long-term credentials, such as access keys, in your application code or using some environmental variables to host these keys, but the security risk of this approach means that it does not follow industry-standard best practice. This is because you are potentially storing access keys in plain text within the application source code.

AWS now offers IAM Roles Anywhere, which addresses this issue – a service that allows you to create a trust anchor to establish a trust relationship between the IAM Roles Anywhere service and a **Certificate Authority** (**CA**) that issues X.509 certificates for your organization. The on-premises server would present the certificate that the AWS IAM roles anywhere service validates and maps the server to a specific IAM role. The on-premises server is then granted permissions to access AWS services and resources as defined in the IAM policy attached to the role.

To generate these X.509 certificates, you can either use a CA using **AWS Private Certificate Authority** or a **CA** from your **public key infrastructure** (**PKI**) provider.

Using IAM Roles Anywhere, you can authenticate non-AWS workloads using the trust anchor and obtain temporary credentials from the IAM Role to access permitted AWS services and resources.

So far, you have learned that IAM roles allow users and applications that run on resources such as EC2 instances to access other AWS services and resources. But what about granting the resources of one AWS service the ability to access the resources of another AWS service? In the next section, you will learn more about service roles that allow one AWS service to access another service with specific permissions required for your application workflow.

AWS service roles

A service role allows an AWS service to perform actions against another service and its resources on your behalf. Using a service role, you can define a set of permissions the AWS service needs to interact with other AWS services and resources in your account. You get to decide the actions the service can take against another resource.

For example, a spreadsheet is stored in an Amazon S3 bucket (a storage platform). You need to process the data in the spreadsheet and update a backend database table running on Amazon DynamoDB (a NoSQL database solution). To help automate the process, you could use a Lambda function (which offers serverless compute capabilities) and write code to extract the data from the spreadsheet, process it, and then update the database.

The Lambda function will need permission to read the raw data from the S3 bucket and write the processed data to the DynamoDB table. To facilitate this, you would create an appropriate IAM role (with the necessary permissions) and associate it with the Lambda function. When the function executes, it assumes this service role, allowing it to read data from the S3 bucket and write to the DynamoDB table.

While creating identities and assigning appropriate levels of permissions following the principle of least privilege is critical, monitoring the list of live and active identities in your AWS account is equally important. Many organizations tend to have identities, such as IAM user accounts, continue to exist long after they are required. This poses a security risk if someone manages to guess the username and password of an unused IAM user account or if the access keys fall into the wrong hands. In the next section, you will learn about a tool you can use to actively manage your IAM identities.

The AWS credentials report

You can download the AWS credentials report to monitor a list of all IAM users you have created in your AWS account. This **comma-separated values** (**CSV**) file, depicted in *Figure 5.7*, is updated every four hours and enables you to audit your IAM user security posture.

user	arn	user_creation_time	password_enabled	password_last_used	password_last_changed	mfa_active	access_key_1_active
<root_accour	arn:aws:iam::	2023-07-29T10:00:29Z	TRUE	2024-09-26T13:46:45Z	2023-07-29T11:04:41Z	FALSE	FALSE
Alice	arn:aws:iam::	2023-09-10T11:29:15Z	TRUE	2024-09-25T12:52:28Z	2024-04-09T07:45:44Z	FALSE	TRUE
Dorian	arn:aws:iam::	2023-09-07T17:43:55Z	TRUE	no_information	2023-09-07T17:43:55Z	FALSE	FALSE
john	arn:aws:iam::	2024-09-04T05:26:27Z	TRUE	no_information	2024-09-04T05:26:28Z	FALSE	FALSE

Figure 5.7: AWS credentials report

Using this report, you can identify critical information about your IAM user accounts, such as whether they have been configured with web console access, CLI access, set up with multi-factor authentication, etc. You can also identify the last time the IAM user logged into the AWS account, which can help identify stale and unused accounts.

In *Figure 5.7*, you will note that MFA has not been enabled for any IAM accounts. Furthermore, even the root user account has yet to be configured with MFA, which poses an extremely high risk to the account. A malicious attacker would need to guess the email address and the password to gain full administrative rights to the account. AWS highly recommends you configure MFA for the root user.

The AWS Credentials Report can give auditors a detailed breakdown of your IAM user and root user configuration. It can also form part of your compliance reporting and documentation.

In the next section, you will learn about another identity and access management service specifically designed for managing your workforce identities across multiple AWS accounts in your AWS Organization.

Centralizing workforce access with AWS Identity Center

In the previous section, you learned how to design cross-account access for IAM user accounts using IAM roles. This allows users in one AWS account to access services and resources in other AWS accounts and prevents the creation of duplicate IAM user accounts in multiple AWS accounts. Using IAM roles in this scenario to enable cross-account access offers several benefits, including enforcing the principle of least privileged access and reducing the management overhead associated with managing multiple (duplicate) IAM user accounts for the same individual.

However, the cross-account design approach is cumbersome to set up. For every AWS account the IAM user needs access to, you must create a specific IAM role with the necessary permissions and trust policies. While creating IAM roles to allow users from other third-party external accounts (such as business partners or service providers) is a viable option for this use case, AWS offers an alternative solution for managing your workforce users' access to your AWS Organization's member accounts. This alternative is the AWS Identity Center.

Previously dubbed the **AWS Single Sign On** (**SSO**) service, **AWS Identity Center** is explicitly designed to manage your organization's workforce identities. The service offers a single space from which you can create and assign groups of users and their permissions to AWS accounts in your AWS Organizations. These permissions can be assigned based on job function or any other security protocol your company follows. In addition, with its single sign-on capabilities, the Identity Center makes it much easier to federate with external identity providers. It seamlessly allows you to define access permissions through the various AWS accounts in your organization.

Once configured, your workforce can access a single portal to authenticate against all your AWS accounts (if the necessary group memberships and permission sets have been granted in the Identity Center). A screenshot of a typical portal is depicted in *Figure 5.8:*

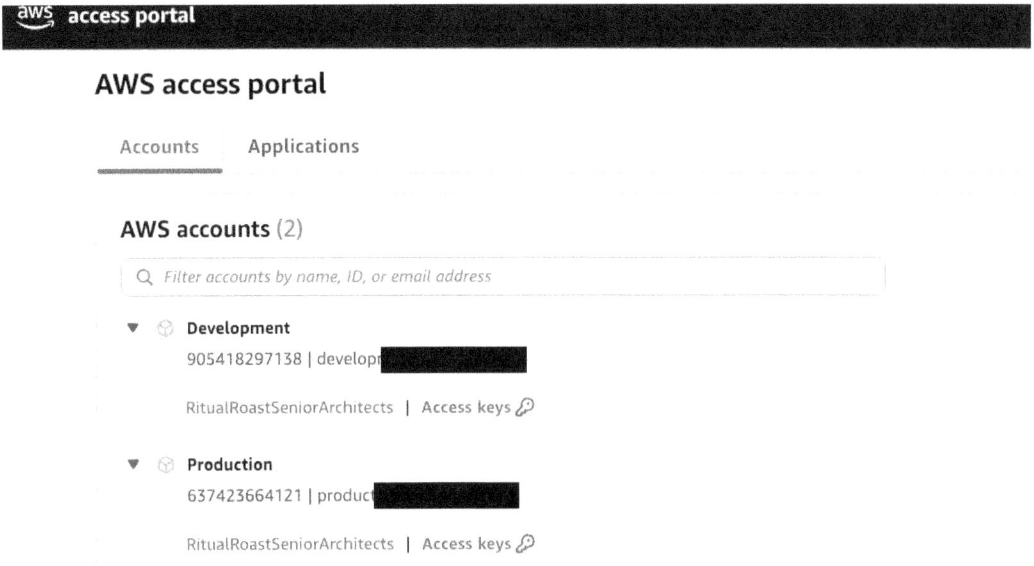

Figure 5.8: AWS Access Portal – IAM Identity Center

You must still use the **AWS Identity and Access Management Service** (**AWS IAM**) to manage all your IAM roles. The Identity Center is designed to manage your company's workforce identities alone. The best part is you do not need to create and manage individual IAM roles or worry about Account IDs and Role names when you try to access other AWS accounts in the Organization.

In addition to granting your workforce access to your organization's various AWS member accounts, the AWS Identity Center can also be configured to provide seamless access to applications that those workforce users require, using the same **single sign-on** (**SSO**) capabilities. Applications such as Amazon Q Developer and Amazon Redshift offer integration with the AWS Identity Center. Your workforce users can also be granted access to third-party applications using SSO, such as Office 365, Salesforce, and many more.

In addition to managing identities for your workforce users, you must also decide how to manage application end users. These users are not part of your technical workforce but are end consumers of the applications you host on AWS. These users can be internal or external to the organization, such as customers.

While IAM and AWS Identity Center are designed to help you configure authentication and authorization for your organization's employees, you also need to consider how end users and customers will authenticate with the applications you host on AWS.

Customers only need to authenticate with the application itself, not with the underlying AWS services or resources. This reflects a clear separation of roles: customers authenticate with the application they use, while employees—such as developers and cloud engineers—authenticate with the AWS platform to configure and manage the resources that host the application.

The next section provides an overview of Amazon Cognito, a service designed to help you build an identity platform for your application users.

Managing application-user identities with Amazon Cognito

So far, you have learned how to create and manage identities that form part of your workforce. These identities represent users who need access to your AWS accounts to design and build solutions for your company. They also include users in your business who need access to the AWS accounts to manage security, auditing, and cost management.

In addition to these users, you need a mechanism to authenticate and authorize end users of the web and mobile applications you host on AWS. These users can be considered customers of your application, whether they are internal to the organization or external customers who purchase access to your products and services.

AWS offers Amazon Cognito, a service that provides a **customer identity and access management** (**CIAM**) service for your web and mobile applications. The service takes the burden of building an identity and access management solution for your applications by offering a wide array of features that you can integrate with your application authentication and authorization processes. These include a customizable **user interface** (**UI**) for sign-up and sign-in web pages for your applications, enabling self-registration capabilities and multi-factor authentication support.

With Amazon Cognito, you can create a user pool of identities (scalable to millions of users) or integrate with social identity providers like OpenID (OIDC), such as Facebook, Google, and Amazon. You can also integrate with SAML 2.0-compatible providers, such as Microsoft Active Directory.

There are two types of pools you can create with Amazon Cognito:

- **Amazon Cognito user pools**: Offer authentication services to your application, allowing it to host millions of users or federate with third-party identity providers, such as Apple, Facebook, and Google. For federated access, the user pool manages tokens issued by the identity provider. Amazon Cognito user pools also allow tracking user devices, locations, and IP addresses.

- **Amazon Cognito identity pools**: Allow authorization to access AWS services and resources such as Amazon DynamoDB, Amazon S3, and Lambda serverless components. Using IAM roles, you can enforce the principle of least privileged access to AWS services. Amazon Cognito identity pools also enable you to define access for unauthenticated (guest) users who may be permitted to access specific resources. This can be useful when you build a web application that offers free vs. premium paid-for services.

In addition to user identity management for internal workforce and application authentication requirements, AWS also offers services to facilitate integration with Microsoft identity and access management services, specifically Microsoft Active Directory. The next section provides an overview of this offering.

Integrating Microsoft directory services with AWS Directory Service

The Microsoft industry-recognized Active Directory Service is a critical identity and access management solution that underpins the very essence of identity management within the Microsoft ecosystem.

Almost every Microsoft infrastructure application and service requires an Active Directory environment for user authentication and authorization, application management, and security integration. Customers who wish to host Microsoft infrastructure applications on AWS often require an Active Directory environment to be present. In the past, this would mean deploying Active Directory on virtual machines accessible to those applications over appropriate network connectivity.

AWS offers **AWS Directory Service for Microsoft Active Directory** (**AWS Managed Microsoft AD**). This fully managed service reduces the administrative burden of hosting your own AD servers in the cloud.

AWS Managed Microsoft AD offers the full spectrum of Active Directory services running as a highly available pair of domain controllers across two availability zones connected to your virtual private cloud (Amazon VPC). AWS will manage the administration of the servers, including software updates, backup, and data replication. With this deployment in place, you can host Microsoft directory-aware applications, including Microsoft SharePoint, Exchange, SQL Server-based applications, and more. The service also allows integration with Amazon RDS for Microsoft SQL Server and the ability to configure trust relationships with on-premises Active Directory environments for an authentic hybrid cloud experience.

In addition, you can join **Amazon Workspace Windows desktops** to the Active Directory domain to enjoy benefits such as enhanced management and security of your virtual desktops in the cloud. Amazon Workspaces is a fully managed end-user computing service that enables you to deploy virtual Linux and Windows desktops in the cloud, accessible using thin client machines or even web browser interfaces.

This section provided an overview of the AWS Directory Services for Microsoft Active Directory and how to integrate Microsoft AD-aware applications within your AWS environments. In the next section, you will have the opportunity to work in your AWS Development account, where you will set up IAM users and groups. You will also learn how to access the AWS account and its services using the **command line interface** (**AWS CLI**).

Project task 5 – Setting up access to the Belly Brew Co. Limited AWS environment

In this set of project tasks, you will create an IAM group and an IAM user account for a senior developer. You will assign the senior developer **Administrative Access** permissions via the group membership to complete all project tasks in this study guide.

Later, you will configure your local machine with the AWS CLI tools so that you can access the AWS Development account programmatically.

Technical requirements

To successfully perform the following tasks, you must first have completed all the project tasks in *Chapter 4*.

Project task 5.1 – Creating an IAM group and an IAM user account

In this project task, you will create an IAM group called `SeniorDevelopers`. You can then create an IAM user account called 'Alice' for a fictitious senior developer working for Belly Brew Co. Limited. You will then add Alice to the Developers group assigned with the `AdministratorAccess` IAM policy. Going forward, you will log in as the IAM user Alice for most project tasks in this study guide.

Ensure you are still logged into your **AWS Development** account as the root user before performing the following steps:

1. From the search bar at the top of the AWS management console, search for IAM and navigate to the IAM web console, as depicted in *Figure 5.9*:

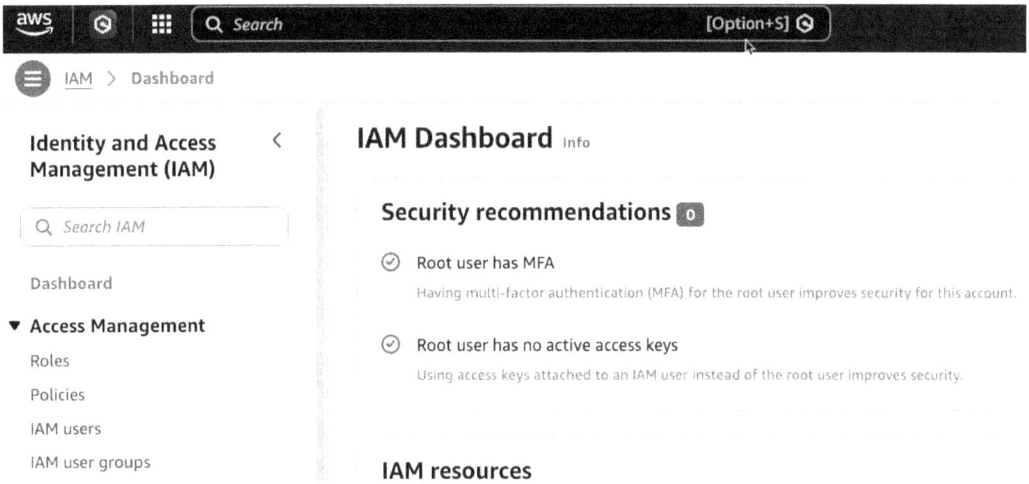

Figure 5.9: AWS IAM web console

2. From the left-hand menu, select **IAM user groups** under **Access management**
3. Next, from the right-hand pane, click the **Create group** button
4. In the text box under **User group name**, type in the name `SeniorDevelopers`
5. Next, scroll down and select the check box next to `AdministratorAccess` under Policy name as per *Figure 5.10*:

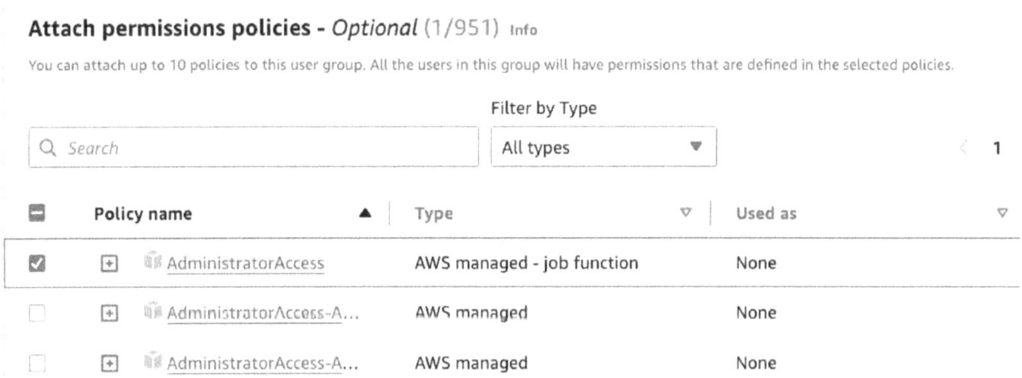

Figure 5.10: IAM policies

6. Scroll further down the webpage and click the **Create user group** button
   You have now created a user group called `SeniorDevelopers` and attached the IAM policy `AdministratorAccess` to this group. Next, you will create an IAM user account for 'Alice' and make her a group member.

7. From the left-hand menu, select **IAM users** under **Access management**
8. In the right-hand pane, click the **Create user** button
9. Next, for the **User name**, type in `Alice`
10. Click to select the checkbox next to **Provide user access to the AWS Management Console – optional**
11. You may be prompted to confirm whether you are creating a user in the Identity Center or an IAM user. In most cases, you would use the Identity Center to create your workforce identities. However, for this exercise, please select the **I want to create an IAM user** option for this project task.
12. Next, select **Custom password** and provide a password of your choice, ensuring complexity such as a combination of upper-case letters, lower-case letters, numbers, and symbols
13. Untick the check box next to **Users must create a new password at next sign-in – Recommended**. Click **Next**.
14. In the **Set permissions** section, select the option to **Add user to group**
15. From the list of **User groups**, select **SeniorDevelopers** and click **Next**
16. In the **Review and create** webpage, click the **Create user** button
17. The user **Alice** has now been created and added to the **SeniorDevelopers** group. You will then be presented with the Retrieve password webpage. Make sure to note down the Console sign-in URL and Alice's password as per *Figure 5.11*:

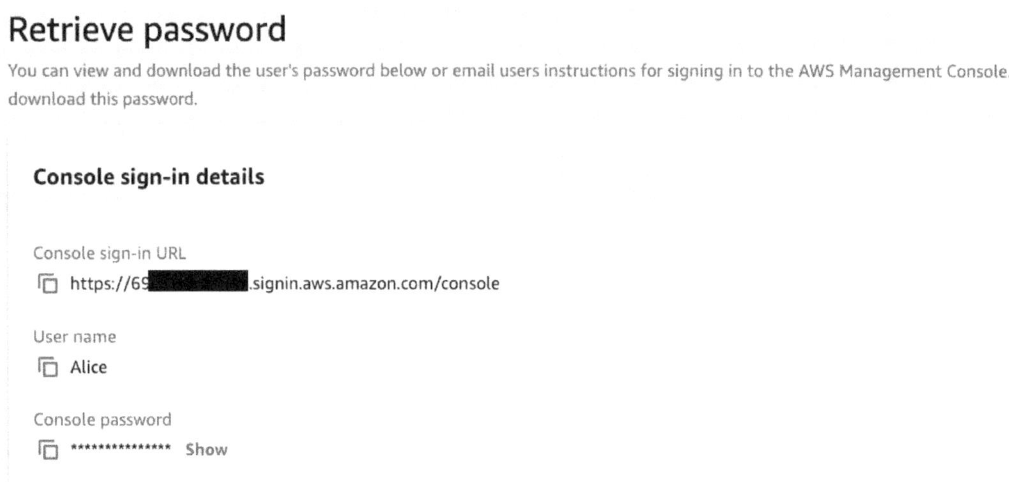

Figure 5.11: Retrieve password webpage when creating an IAM user

18. The sign-in URL is simply a URL constructed using your AWS account ID. If you do not know the URL, and you need to log in as an IAM user, you can navigate to the standard sign-in page and choose the option to log in as an IAM user as per *Figure 5.12*. You must, however, provide the account ID for the AWS account in which the IAM user was created.

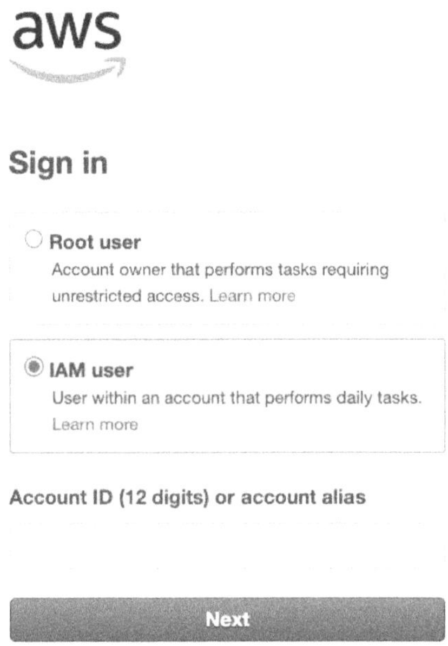

Figure 5.12: AWS Sign-in page

19. You can find your AWS account ID by clicking the drop-down arrow next to your account name in the top right-hand corner of the screen when you are logged in as the root user, as per the following screenshot in *Figure 5.13*

Figure 5.13: Account ID

20. Ensure you note down your AWS account ID, as you will need this when logging in as an IAM user. Alternatively, make a note of the sign-in URL, as discussed earlier, or save it as a bookmark.

Now that you have created an IAM user account for Alice, you can log in as Alice for all future project tasks in this study guide. AWS highly recommends that you do not use the root user account for day-to-day use and instead configure an IAM user (or an Identity Center user) with the necessary permissions for day-to-day tasks.

In the next project task, you will learn how to access the AWS Development account using the **command line interface** (**CLI**).

Project task 5.2 – Installing and configuring the AWS CLI on your local computer

To complete this project task, you must download and install the AWS CLI on your local computer. Depending on your operating system, you must download the correct installer and/or run through a series of commands to install the CLI.

Perform the following steps:

1. Navigate to the following webpage: `https://docs.aws.amazon.com/cli/latest/userguide/getting-started-install.html`.

2. In the left-hand menu, click **Install/Update**, under the **Get started** section. In the right-hand pane of the webpage, you should find links to the installation instructions for your specific operating system. Select your computer's operating system and follow the instructions provided on the webpage. See screenshot in *Figure 5.14:*

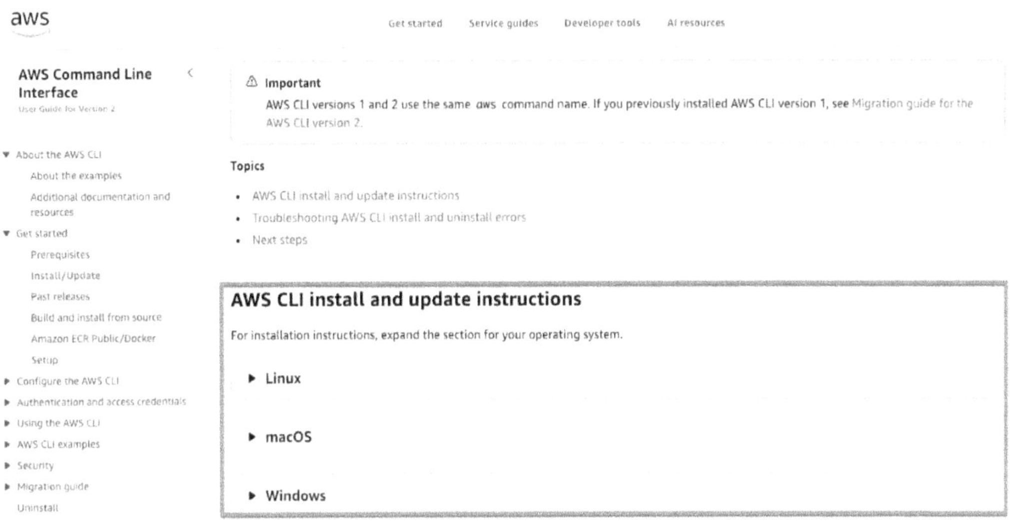

Figure 5.14: AWS CLI installers

3. For both Windows and MacOS, you must download the installer, double-click on it, and run through the guided installation process, accepting all default values
4. For Linux, you must follow a series of instructions and commands to complete the installation, as per the guide provided on the webpage
5. To test that your installation has been completed successfully, you can launch the terminal window on your Mac OS or Linux computer and run the command `aws --version`, and press enter. For Windows, launch the command prompt and run the command `aws --version` and press *Enter*
6. You should get a response with the current version of the AWS CLI installed on your computer, as per *Figure 5.15*:

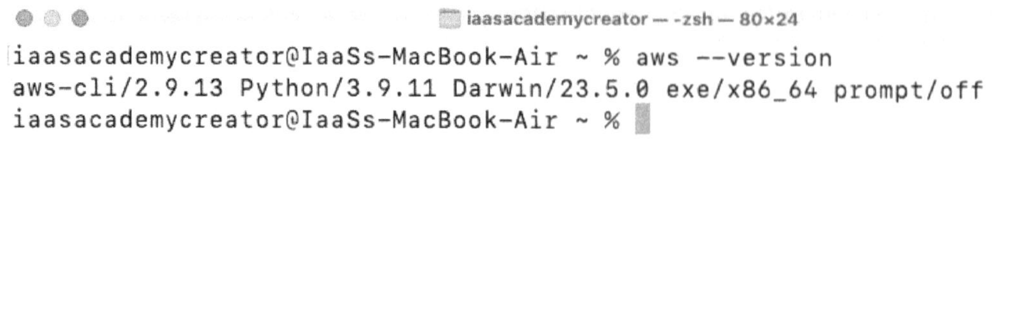

Figure 5.15: MacOS Terminal Window with the command aws --version

Once you have confirmed the installation of the CLI on your computer, you will need to configure it with access credentials for your AWS account. This is discussed in the next project task.

Project task 5.3 – Configuring the AWS CLI on your computer

To configure the CLI tool you have installed on your computer, you will need to generate a set of Access Keys. You cannot use your IAM username and password with the CLI tool. Instead, you must configure the tool with an Access Key ID and a Secret Access Key.

Perform the following steps:

1. Ensure that you are logged out of the AWS management console if you are still logged in as the root user
2. Using the IAM sign-in link, you made a note of at the end of *Project Task 5.1*, navigate to the IAM sign-in page for your AWS account
3. Log in as the IAM user Alice and ensure you provide the password you chose for this IAM user account
4. Once logged in, click the drop-down arrow next to the Account Name on the top right-hand corner of the screen and select **Security credentials** as per the following screenshot in *Figure 5.16*:

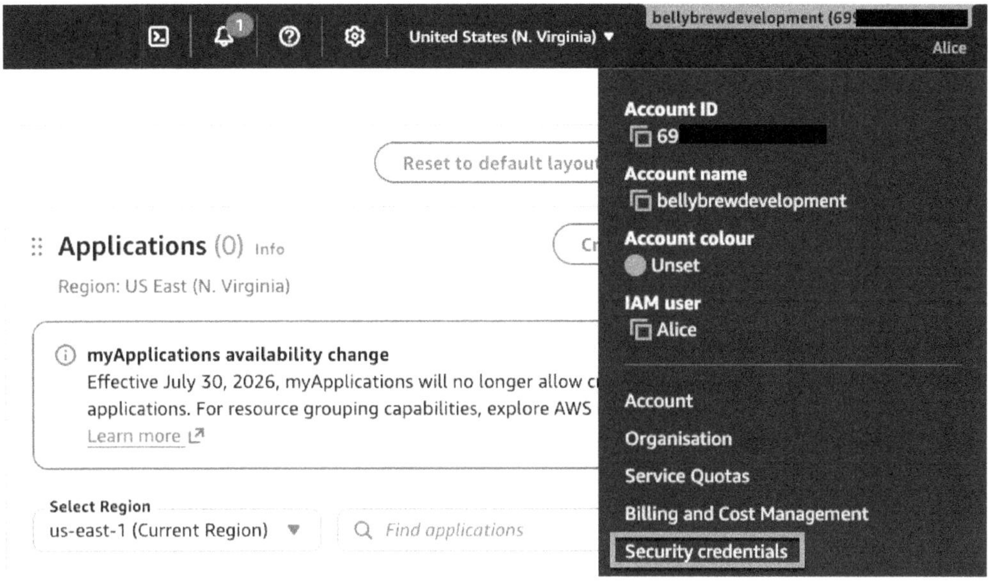

Figure 5.16: Access Security credentials for IAM user 'Alice'

5. Here, you will create an access key ID and a secret access key for programmatic access using the CLI. On the My security credentials webpage, scroll further down and click on the **Create access key** button in the Access keys section.
6. Next, select the **Command Line Interface (CLI)** under **Use case**
7. Scroll down to the bottom of the webpage and click the box to confirm that you wish to proceed with creating an access key. Click **Next**.
8. Provide a description for this access key. For example, you can describe its use case as `"Programmatic access for Alice."`
9. Click the **Create access key** button
10. AWS will generate a set of access keys comprising an access key ID and a secret access key. You will have the option to download these keys in a `.csv` file format. Ensure you download this file, which will contain your access keys.
11. Now that you have downloaded the credentials, you must configure the CLI tool installed on your computer with the access keys

12. On your computer, launch the command prompt if you are using a Windows operating system or the terminal if you are using MacOS or Linux
13. In the command prompt/terminal window, type in the command `aws configure`
14. You will be prompted to enter the AWS Access Key ID. From the CSV file you downloaded, copy and paste the Access key ID and press *Enter*
15. Next, you will be prompted to enter the AWS Secret Access Key. Copy the key from the CSV file and paste it into the terminal/command prompt, and then press enter.
16. Next, you will be prompted to enter the Default region name. For the region name, enter `us-east-1` and then press *Enter*. This is the North Virginia region, where most project tasks will be performed.
17. Next, for the Default output format, press *Enter* to accept the default configuration and press enter

    Your AWS CLI tool has now been configured with Alice's credentials per the screenshot in *Figure 5.17*. You can access your AWS Development account using the command-line interface.

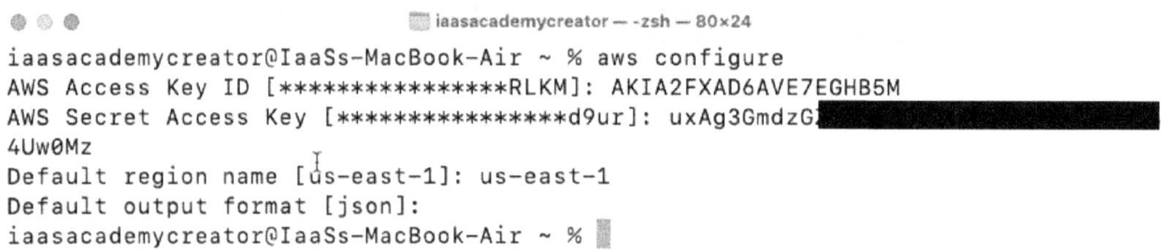

Figure 5.17: AWS CLI tool configured with Alice's credentials

18. To test the CLI, type in the following command in your terminal/command prompt:

```
aws iam list-users
```

19. You will get a response with the list of IAM users. For now, only Alice will be listed because that is the only IAM user in the AWS Development account. See *Figure 5.18*:

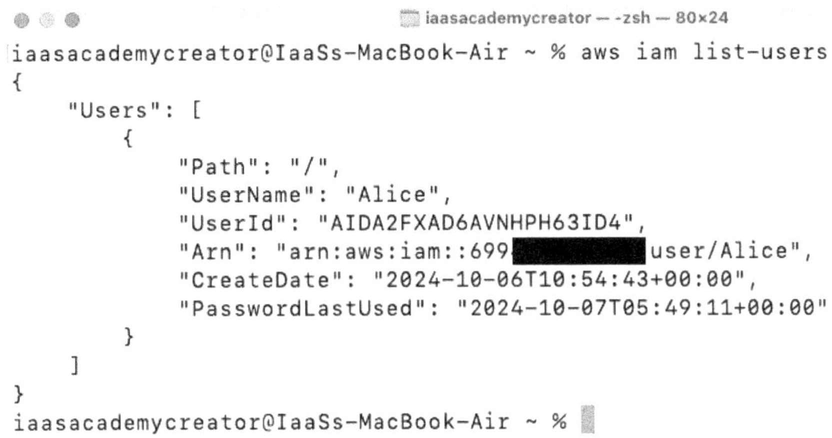

Figure 5.18: Results of CLI command AWS IAM list-users

As the IAM user Alice, you now have access to AWS Development using both the command line interface and the web console. You will use this account for upcoming project tasks.

Finally, it is strongly recommended that you delete the downloaded CSV file so there are no credentials lying in the Downloads folder that other applications may have access to.

Summary

AWS Identity and Access Management is a critical security service designed to ensure that only authorized principals can access services and resources in your AWS account. The service also enables you to configure strict password policies to enforce complexity and enhance login security using multi-factor authentication. AWS recommends that both IAM and root user accounts be configured with MFA.

It is paramount to understand the importance of applying the principle of least privileged access, which reduces the risk of accidental configuration or recourse by unauthorized personnel. In addition, limiting access to only authorized services and resources ensures that the blast radius of any disasters caused by leaked credentials, which have come into the possession of bad actors, is reduced.

In addition to enabling access to your workforce, you must design authorization for other principals, such as services and applications that must interact with AWS resources. For example, an application running on a web server may need access to a backend database. AWS recommends that for such use cases, you must use IAM roles to grant temporary credentials with only the necessary permissions required for the interaction. This prevents the need to manage long-term credentials, such as access keys, which can pose a security risk and increase administrative burden. IAM roles are also designed to enable entities external to the AWS account to access services and resources through a trust policy, allowing you to design cross-account access for third parties.

To manage your workforce identities, especially if you have an AWS Organization service to manage multiple AWS accounts, use the Identity Center. You can create and manage workforce identities with single sign-on capability. Rather than create duplicate identities in each AWS account for the same individual, you can have a single Identity Center account that grants the individual access to multiple AWS accounts in your organization.

Finally, you can build a **customer identity management system** (**CISM**) for your application end users using AWS Cognito. The service enables you to integrate a sign-up and sign-in feature into your applications, enabling your end users and customers to self-register for access to your application. Amazon Cognito offers you the ability to create and manage a user pool within the service or integrate with third-party open identity providers such as Google and Facebook for identity federation. Additionally, you can configure identity pools to grant users direct access to resources running on services such as Amazon S3 and Amazon DynamoDB. Amazon Cognito Identity Pools can also be used to grant unauthenticated or guest access to certain resources. This can be particularly useful when you want to offer certain services on trial or for free.

Ultimately, any reputable identity and access management service must ensure it offers stringent authentication and authorization features that protect your cloud environment and the applications you host within it. AWS offers a diverse set of services to fulfill a wide range of customer requirements across its identity solutions.

Exam Readiness Drill – Chapter Review Questions

Apart from mastering key concepts, strong test-taking skills under time pressure are essential for acing your certification exam. That's why developing these abilities early in your learning journey is critical.

Exam readiness drills, using the free online practice resources provided with this book, help you progressively improve your time management and test-taking skills while reinforcing the key concepts you've learned.

HOW TO GET STARTED

- Open the link or scan the QR code at the bottom of this page
- If you have unlocked the practice resources already, log in to your registered account. If you haven't, follow the instructions in *Free Benefits with Your Book* section in this book's *Preface* and come back to this page.
- Once you log in, click the START button to start this chapter's quiz
- We recommend attempting a quiz multiple times till you're able to answer most of the questions correctly and well within the time limit.
- You can use the following practice template to help you plan your attempts:

Working On Accuracy		
Attempt	**Target**	**Time Limit**
Attempt 1	40% or more	Till the timer runs out
Attempt 2	60% or more	Till the timer runs out
Attempt 3	75% or more	Till the timer runs out
Working On Timing		
Attempt 4	75% or more	1 minute before time limit
Attempt 5	75% or more	2 minutes before time limit
Attempt 6	75% or more	3 minutes before time limit

The above drill is just an example. Design your drills based on your own goals and make the most out of the online quizzes accompanying this book.

Link to this Chapter's Quiz

You need to unlock the online practice resources to access the link below. Check the *Free Benefits with Your Book* section in the *Preface* for detailed instructions on how to do this. You only need to unlock the resources once.

Open Quiz `https://packt.link/clf_c02_ch5`or scan the QR code

6

Amazon Simple Storage Service (Amazon S3)

Storage services are a significant component of cloud computing because almost every application needs somewhere to host its data. Although cloud service providers like AWS have offered cheap storage services due to economies of scale, you must evaluate your storage requirements and design an appropriate storage lifecycle as an organization. Regulatory and compliance requirements might require you to store data for as long as 7 to 10 years. However, you must purge unwanted data from your storage systems to ensure effective cost management and data security.

Storage services can host various data formats, from unstructured data such as documents, emails, images, and video to structured formats such as lists and tables in a database. AWS offers various storage options, each designed for specific data formats. This chapter introduces storage concepts and then discusses a particular storage architecture: object storage with Amazon **Simple Storage Service** (**Amazon S3**).

Amazon S3 is one of AWS's flagship products, offering almost unlimited storage capacity and a wide range of features to meet your application requirements. It is an object storage solution offering very high levels of availability due to its distributed architecture, durability, and scalability. It is even possible to host a static website on Amazon S3, which functions well as part of a serverless design architecture.

Belly Brew Co. Limited can use Amazon S3 to host a wide range of data, including archival data such as accounting and trading information, data on its manufacturing processes, reports such as accounting data or information on its safety checks for auditing purposes, and digital assets for its websites, such as images and videos.

The following topics are discussed in this chapter:

- Exploring storage options on AWS
- Working with Amazon S3
- Connecting on-premises storage to AWS with Amazon Storage Gateway
- Moving data and extending storage to the edge with the AWS Snow Family

Exploring storage options on AWS

Storage services are delivered using infrastructure and storage management software that enable you to write to and read from a storage medium such as a hard drive, solid-state drive, USB device, magnetic tape, and others. However, how the data is stored on the device and accessed by your application is determined by the type of storage you use. The type of storage also determines its use case since you have varied levels of durability, reliability, efficiency, and latency when accessing your data.

Three primary storage types are available, and AWS offers services to support each type. These are discussed next.

Block storage

Block storage is an architectural design that divides and stores your data into fixed-sized blocks on physical storage devices like **hard drives** (**HDDs**) and **solid-state drives** (**SSDs**). It operates at a lower level, dealing directly with raw storage blocks on physical disks. Each block has a unique address and is used to identify the location of your data. The architecture makes it possible to store blocks that belong to the same data across multiple locations or disks and are managed by underlying software, often known as the storage subsystem.

The storage subsystem allocates, organizes, and accesses blocks on the physical storage drives. It uses tools like **Logical Volume Managers** (**LVM**), RAID controllers, and others to manage data at the block level. When you attempt to access your data, this storage subsystem retrieves all the individual blocks and presents the data to you as a complete file after reassembling the blocks in the correct order.

Data can be stored on **direct-attached storage devices** (**DAS**) such as a hard drive connected to your computer or across a fast network interface such as a **storage area network** (**SAN**) supported by iSCSI or Fibre Channel.

The primary benefits of block storage include data redundancy and replication, which provide fault tolerance, high performance through caching and load balancing, and maintaining data integrity through error-checking. The low latency and high-performance data access capability make it ideal for hosting database solutions, operating systems, and applications that are sensitive to latency. It is also suitable for hosting **virtual machines (VMs)**, which require isolated, independent block storage volumes.

On AWS, block storage options include **Elastic Block Store** (**EBS**) and **Instance Store**. EBS volumes can be attached to your **Elastic Compute Cloud** (**EC2**) instances – virtual servers you deploy in the cloud running Linux, Windows, or MacOS operating systems. EBS volumes are network-attached, like the SAN storage option. Instance Store volumes are carved out of physical storage attached to the host machine on which you launch your EC2 instances. Given that EBS volumes are network attached, they can be a bit slower than Instance Store volumes. However, EBS volumes are persistent, whereas Instance Store volumes only exist as long as the EC2 instance (virtual server) is in the running state. Once the instance is stopped, the Instance Store volume is destroyed. For these reasons, Instance Store volumes are considered temporary storage.

File storage

File Storage is another storage architecture in which your data is organized and managed as files within a hierarchical directory (folder) structure. You can think of file storage as organizing your filing cabinet with folders and sub-folders within which your documents reside.

The data structure uses file systems like **NFS** (**Network File System**) or **SMB/CIFS** (**Server Message Block/Common Internet File System**) to store, organize, and retrieve your data. Using protocols like NFS and SMB, you can create file shares, making it easy to share your data. Applications running on your virtual servers in the cloud can use file storage to share data too.

Retrieval of your data requires you to know the unique path and name within the directory structure and identify the folders (and sub-folders, if necessary) to access the file.

Due to the nature of file storage, metadata (information used to describe the data) may be limited. In addition, due to operating system limitations, you might experience performance issues if your directory hierarchy runs through deeply nested subdirectories. Other performance issues result from introduced latency when accessing files over a network, which is usually slower than block storage.

It is also essential to appreciate that file storage represents a higher layer of abstraction above block storage. Ultimately, all data is stored on block devices, such as direct-attached storage or network-attached devices.

File storage is handy for file sharing, media storage and streaming, collaboration, and document management.

AWS offers a few file storage services. These are:

- **Amazon Elastic File System** (**EFS**): This fully managed file system is designed to let you share data across Linux-based virtual machines. You can access the file system from your on-premises network over a **VPN** (**Virtual Private Network**) or AWS Direct Connect. Due to its fully managed offering, you do not need to pre-provision storage volumes. Instead, the file system will grow as you add data and shrink as you delete data, ensuring cost optimization.
- **Amazon FSx for Lustre**: This is a fully managed high-performance file system for compute-intensive workloads. It is designed to handle large datasets up to petabytes in size. Using a familiar file-folder hierarchy, the Luster file system offers a high throughput and low latency. Amazon FSx for Luster integrates with Amazon S3 (Amazon Simple Storage Service), allowing easy import and export of data between Amazon S3 and the Luster File System. Amazon S3 can be used to store data, and when you need to process it, you can import it into FSx for Luster. It is ideal for workloads such as machine learning, big data analytics, and high-performance computing (HPC) applications.
- **Amazon FSx for Windows File Server**: This service offers Microsoft Windows-based EC2 instances file-sharing capabilities. The service runs on fully managed Windows-based servers in the background. It requires the presence of Microsoft Active Directory to provide authentication and access control, and enables customers to host their Windows-based file-sharing solution in the AWS cloud.

Object storage

Object storage is designed especially for cloud storage applications. The architecture presents **a flat-file structure** and stores your data as **objects** in their entirety, with extensive metadata information and globally unique identifiers, making them ideal for storing structured, semi-structured, or unstructured data types. Due to its flat file structure, there are no folders or directories to manage. This also means you avoid the limitations of extensively nested directories, which affect performance and scalability.

The architecture lends itself to horizontal scaling, which involves adding more nodes to your storage pool. This means you can store virtually unlimited amounts of data, making it ideal for data lakes, big data, large files, and more.

Access to your data can be done using API calls (e.g., RESTful APIs), and this makes object storage ideal for web-based applications by allowing access from anywhere over the Internet. Many companies use object storage to host digital assets such as media files (images, video, and documents) since object storage is much cheaper than file storage solutions.

While object storage solutions offer high scalability and almost unlimited data storage, they have certain limitations. These include higher latency than file storage systems, especially when accessing small files and applications requiring frequent read/write operations.

Like file storage, object storage presents an abstraction layer for the underlying block devices, and this presents performance overhead due to the need to process metadata and API calls. Other disadvantages of object storage include limitations on individual object sizes (Amazon S3 has a maximum object size of 50TB). Also, while the flat file namespace makes storing almost unlimited amounts of data easy, it is less intuitive than the file-folder hierarchical structure of file storage solutions. You also cannot host applications or databases on Amazon S3 due to its higher latency issues and lack of computing capability.

AWS offers Amazon Simple Storage Service (Amazon S3), an object storage solution that allows you to store almost unlimited amounts of data cost-effectively. With Amazon S3, you create buckets (containers) and place your objects in a flat file structure. You can then access your data via the web console, through the CLI, or programmatically by making API calls.

In the next section, you will learn more about Amazon S3 and its core features.

Working with Amazon S3

Amazon S3 is one of AWS's most popular products, offering a robust, highly durable, scalable, and cost-effective object storage solution. With Amazon S3, customers can store almost unlimited amounts of data at a fraction of the cost compared to hosting a similar solution on premises.

Amazon S3 is designed to offer 99.999999999% (that's eleven 9s) of durability. This means that if you store 10,000,000 objects in Amazon S3, then on average, you might expect to experience the loss of a single object every 10,000 years. This is possible because your data is replicated across multiple storage devices and availability zones within a given region. Another critical factor is that while AWS will replicate your data across multiple availability zones in the region you host it, it will never replicate data to other regions unless you configure it to do so. This ensures you can maintain data privacy and sovereignty if such regulatory requirements bind your business.

In the next section, you will learn more about Amazon S3 buckets and objects—the nuts and bolts of the product.

Buckets and objects

Buckets are containers you create in Amazon S3 that can host unlimited objects in the cloud. You can have up to 100 buckets per AWS account. However, this is just a soft limit and can always be increased to 1,000 buckets by getting approval from the AWS support team.

When creating buckets, you must specify the region in which you host that bucket. Your choice of region will depend on factors such as:

- Location of end users who will need to access your bucket to optimize for latency
- Any data residency laws your company may need to follow
- Minimizing costs

Buckets traditionally have a **globally unique namespace** – a feature that enables them to be accessed over the Internet. This means that bucket names must be unique across all AWS accounts. For example, if you create a bucket called `belly-brew-kefir-recipes`, no other AWS user can use that exact name.

This global uniqueness also means that every object stored in a bucket has a unique address. For example, the image file *strawberries-and-cream-smoothie.jpg* stored in the *belly-brew-yoghurt-recipes* bucket in the North Virginia region can be accessed using the following URL:

`https://belly-brew-yoghurt-recipes.s3.us-east-1.amazonaws.com/strawberries-and-cream-smoothie.jpg`.

This format is known as a **virtual-hosted style endpoint**, which follows the structure:

`https://bucket-name.s3.region-code.amazonaws.com/key-name`

Recently, AWS introduced an enhancement to simplify bucket naming by allowing you to create general-purpose buckets within an account's regional namespace.

With this approach, you can choose a bucket name prefix and AWS automatically ensures uniqueness by appending a suffix that includes your account ID and Region. For example: `mybucket-123456789012-us-east-1-an`

In this case:

- `mybucket` is your chosen prefix
- `123456789012-us-east-1-an` is the AWS-generated account regional suffix

This means you no longer need to worry about global naming conflicts. The same prefix can be reused across different accounts, but only your account can use your specific suffix.

Buckets can also be accessed using **website endpoint URLs**. This access method is made possible when the bucket is being used to host a static website, which you will learn more about later in this chapter. Depending on the region where the bucket is hosted, your website endpoint will be in one of the following two formats:

- `s3-website dash (-) Region`: http://**bucket-name**.s3-website-**region-code**.amazonaws.com
- `s3-website dot (.) Region`: http://**bucket-name**.s3-website.**region-code**.amazonaws.com

The default index document configured for your website will be presented upon navigating to the URL.

When creating buckets, you must adhere to the following naming rules:

- Bucket names must be between 3 and 63 characters in length.
- Bucket names must be in lowercase letters. They can only contain numbers, dots (.), and hyphens (-).
- Bucket names must begin and end with a letter or number and must not have any spaces between the characters.
- Bucket names must not be formatted as an **Internet Protocol Address** (**IP Address**) such as 192.168.1.1.
- Bucket names used with the Amazon **S3 Transfer Acceleration** (**S3TA**) service cannot have dots (.) in their names. You will learn more about S3TA later in this chapter.
- You cannot have nested buckets (buckets within buckets).

Any data stored in an Amazon S3 bucket is treated as an object. Each object can range between zero (0) bytes and five terabytes (TB).

Objects comprise a **key** (name of the file/object) and its **value** (representing the data held in binary). Keys can be up to 1,024 bytes long and consist of letters, numbers, and certain special characters like dots (.) and hyphens (-). You access objects through URLs or by making API calls for programmatic access. For example, you can issue the `s3:GetObject` API call when using the AWS CLI.

In the next section, you will learn more about how to manage objects in your Amazon S3 buckets.

Managing objects in your buckets

As previously discussed, Amazon S3 is an object storage solution with a flat file structure. This means that objects are ultimately stored in the root of the bucket without a real directory-style hierarchical structure. This can make navigating and traversing objects in the bucket cumbersome, especially if you have hundreds or thousands of them.

Amazon S3 offers a solution using **prefixes** and **delimiters**, which can help you manage and browse your objects in a simulated hierarchical fashion. This allows you to create a path-like structure that can be used to organize objects within a bucket. Because Amazon S3 doesn't have a traditional file system, you use prefixes to group related objects by adding path segments.

For example, you might want to store recipes categorized under 'current' and 'archive' as follows:

- Current recipes:
    - /bbgutrecipes/current-recipes/raspberry-kombucha-v3.doc
    - /bbgutrecipes/current-recipes/strawberry-kombucha-v3-v3.doc
    - /bbgutrecipes/current-recipes/pineapple-smoothy-v3.doc
- Archive recipes:
    - /bbgutrecipes/archive-recipes/ raspberry-kombucha-v2.doc
    - /bbgutrecipes/ archive-recipes/ strawberry-kombucha-v2.doc
    - /bbgutrecipes/ archive-recipes/ pineapple-smoothy-v2.doc

You will note that version 2 of the recipes is categorized under the archive-recipes prefix, whereas version 3 of the recipes is currently used by the Belly Brew Co. Limited team and categorized under the current-recipes prefix.

When using the Amazon S3 console to navigate your objects, the use of these prefixes simulates a folder structure, which makes navigation easier, as per the following screenshot in *Figure 6.1*:

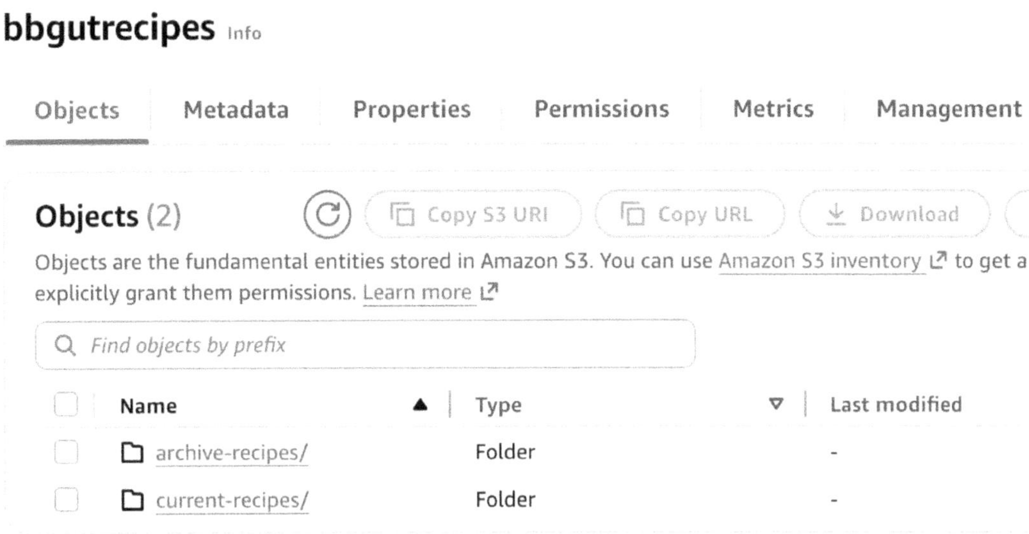

Figure 6.1: Bucket with prefixes

While this architecture allows you to better manage your objects, the fact is that the keys of the object itself now comprise prefixes and delimiters. For example, the version 3 recipe of the raspberry kombucha now has a key (name) of *current-recipes/*`raspberry-kombucha-v3.doc`. Ultimately, all objects are stored in a flat file structure. One exception to this is when using a particular bucket type called an S3 directory bucket, discussed later in this chapter.

One benefit of using prefixes and delimiters is that they help you limit search results to only those keys that begin with a specific prefix. This allows you to perform list operations such that keys with a common prefix are returned as a single result, reducing the number of requests made and saving on cost.

Prefixes can also enhance performance when you access objects. Amazon S3 offers 2,500 PUT/COPY/DELETE or 5,500 GET/HEAD operations per second per prefix. By using prefixes to categorize your objects, you can increase overall performance. For example, if you have five prefixes to categorize five different collections of objects, you can achieve a total read performance of 27,500 (5,500 * 5) read requests per second for your GET operations.

As an organization, you may have different data sets with varying access patterns. For example, you may have a subset of data that you need to access frequently and another set of data that you just want to store as archives, accessing them only on rare occasions. Furthermore, you may also have some data sets where the access pattern is difficult to predict. AWS offers storage classes for such varying use cases, which are discussed in the next section.

Choosing the right Amazon S3 storage class

With Amazon S3, you can store unlimited data in an S3 bucket. However, not all data is treated the same. Usually, only a subset of data tends to be accessed very frequently. Some data sets must be accessed instantly, especially with applications that are sensitive to latency. Other data sets are stored for archival purposes, where instant access is not required. As an example, the graphics design team at Belly Brew Co. Limited creates certain digital assets for its monthly online newsletters, comprising documents, images, and videos. This month's newsletter webpage will need instant access to those digital assets so that when end users access the webpage, those digital assets are rendered with the website. Since the webpage only showcases the current month's newsletter, previously used digital assets for previous months' newsletters do not need to be instantly accessible. However, the company may still choose to store them for reference.

Amazon S3 offers a feature called **storage classes** to separate frequently accessed data from infrequent ones. The service also provides classes used for archival data – data that is rarely accessed and where delays in access may also be acceptable. Choosing the most suitable storage class impacts your total cost. This is because, at a minimum, you are charged for the total amount of storage consumed as gigabytes per month (GB/month), any data transferred out of the region in which the bucket is hosted, and the total number of requests made.

AWS provides the following storage classes, and understanding their core features and limitations is critical to prepare for the AWS Certified Cloud Practitioner exam.

The following table in *Figure 6.2* gives you a complete list of storage classes on AWS.

Storage Class	**Use Case**	**Durability**	**Availability**	**AZs**	**Min. storage duration**	**Min. object size**
Standard	Frequently accessed data (more than once a month) with millisecond access	99.999999999%	99.99%	>=3	None	None

Storage Class	Use Case	Durability	Availability	AZs	Min. storage duration	Min. object size
Standard (IA)	Long-lived, infrequently accessed data (once a month) with millisecond access	99.999999 999%	99.9%	>=3	30 Days	128KB
S3 Intelligent -Tiering	Data with unknown and unpredictabl e access patterns*	99.999999 999%	99.9%	>=3	None	None
S3 One Zone-IA	Re-creatable, infrequently accessed data ideal as secondary backup	99.999999 999%	99.95%	1	30 Days	128KB
S3 Express One Zone	Single-digit millisecond data access for latency-sensitive applications within a single Availability Zone	99.999999 999%	99.95%	1	None	None

Storage Class	Use Case	Durability	Availability	AZs	Min. storage duration	Min. object size
S3 Glacier Instant Retrieval	Long-lived, archive data accessed once a quarter with millisecond access	99.999999 999%	99.9%	>=3	90 Days	128KB
S3 Glacier Flexible Retrieval	Long-lived archive data accessed once a year, with retrieval times of minutes to hours	99.999999 999%	99.99% (After restoring objects)	>=3	90 Days	NA**
S3 Glacier Deep Archive	Long-lived archive data accessed less than once a year, with retrieval times of hours	99.999999 999%	99.99% (After restoring objects)	>=3	180 Days	NA***

Table 6.1: AWS S3 Storage Classes

Note the asterisk signs in the table:

- * Objects less than 128KB are not monitored and are always stored in the Frequent Access tier

- ** Retrieval requires 40 KB of additional metadata for each archived object; 32 KB charged at the S3 Glacier Deep Archive rate and 8 KB charged at the S3 Standard rate
- *** Retrieval requires 40 KB of additional metadata for each archived object; 32 KB charged at the S3 Glacier Flexible Retrieval rate and 8 KB charged at the S3 Standard rate

The following provides a summary of the various storage classes on AWS:

Storage classes designed for frequently accessed data

If you need instant access to your data with millisecond latency and you will be making frequent requests for your data, then the following storage class is recommended:

- **Amazon S3 Standard**: This is the default storage class offering millisecond latency for applications that require instant access. Examples include web applications. Data is always replicated across at least three availability zones, and you get 99.99% availability. Unlike other infrequent access storage classes, you are not charged a retrieval fee, which makes this class ideal for frequently accessed data.
- **Amazon S3 Express One-Zone**: As of 2026, this is one of the latest storage classes added to the Amazon S3 service. Data is stored in a single availability zone of your choice, designed to deliver single-digit millisecond access. This is further made possible because you can place your compute resources in the same availability zones as the bucket, reducing the physical distance between the two types of resources. It is specially designed for latency-sensitive applications and uses a particular bucket type known as the **S3 directory bucket**. Unlike standard S3 buckets, which store objects as flat files, this newer bucket type organizes data into a directory hierarchy that can scale horizontally. It also isn't affected by the current prefix limitations.
- **Reduced Redundancy** (**RRS**): This storage class is designed for reproducible noncritical data, such as thumbnail images or larger original images you might use for your YouTube video chapters. Amazon no longer recommends using this storage class because while it offers the same availability as the Standard storage class, it only provides 99.99% (that's four 9s) of durability.

Storage classes designed for infrequently accessed data

These two storage classes are cheaper than the Amazon S3 Standard class because they are designed for infrequently accessed data while offering millisecond latency access. AWS understands that customers may have a vast collection of data they seldom access, but one that requires instant access when needed. AWS offers them a lower price point for not frequently accessing this data. To deter customers from misusing this storage class and ensure they are used for infrequent access only, AWS enforces an object retrieval cost. In addition, these storage classes are for objects of at least 128 KB in size, and while you can store smaller objects, each object is billed as if it were at least 128 KB.

- **Amazon S3 Standard-IA (Infrequent Access)**: This infrequent access storage class is designed for critical objects that cannot be recreated. You can have 99.9% availability, and your data is stored redundantly across at least three availability zones.
- **Amazon S3 One Zone-IA (Infrequent Access)**: This storage class is cheaper than the S3 Standard-IA because objects are hosted in one availability zone only, reducing availability to 99.5%. If, on rare occasions, an availability zone experiences an outage, you must wait for it to come back online before you can access your data. AWS recommends you use this storage class only for objects you can recreate, such as for secondary backup copies of your data.

Storage classes designed for archival or rarely accessed data

AWS offers three classes designed for long-term (archival) storage requirements. In return, you pay less to host your data in Amazon S3. These storage classes are cost-effective if you use them as intended – rarely accessing your data and storing it for a longer term. However, you still get the same levels of durability.

- **S3 Glacier Instant Retrieval (IR)**: Although you may rarely access data hosted in this storage class, you might still need instant access to it. This storage class offers millisecond retrieval for your critical data when you needed most. However, the minimum storage duration is 90 days. If you store data for less than this, you are charged for the entire 90-day period.
- **S3 Glacier Flexible Retrieval**: This storage class is cheaper than Glacier IR since data is not instantly available. It is designed for data you may need to retrieve once or twice a year. There is a 90-day minimum storage period and a retrieval fee. You must follow a retrieval process, which can take some time, ranging from minutes to hours, depending on the retrieval tier you choose, as follows:
    - **Expedited retrieval**: This is designed to retrieve a subset of your data within 1 to 5 minutes. You can use this tier when you urgently must get access to archival data, which is the most expensive of the tiers.
    - **Standard retrieval**: This is designed for objects that need to be restored within a 3-to-5-hour window. This tier is cheaper than Expedited retrieval.
    - **Bulk retrieval**: This tier is designed for customers who have massive data sets and can take 5 to 12 hours. There is no retrieval fee for this tier.

- **S3 Glacier Deep Archive**: This storage class is the cheapest option available on AWS and is designed for long-term archive storage. Ideally, where you must keep data for many years to fulfill compliance or regulatory requirements or for disaster recovery and backup purposes, the minimum storage duration is 180 days. This storage class has two retrieval tiers as follows:
    - **Standard retrieval**: This is designed for objects that must be restored within a 12-hour period
    - **Bulk retrieval**: This tier enables customers to retrieve data within 48 hours

Storage class designed for unknown access patterns

Sometimes, it isn't easy to know what the access pattern for your data might be. You may need to access your data frequently for a few weeks when it is first created, and then suddenly find that you have not accessed it for some time. After a short period, your access patterns may change again, and you need to access the same dataset daily. AWS offers a storage class that places your objects in the most cost-effective storage class, which changes as your access patterns change, for a small monitoring and automated tiering fee at the object level. This class is not ideal for small objects, as you are charged for a minimum object size of 128 KB. This storage class is known as Amazon S3 Intelligent Tiering.

- **Amazon S3 Intelligent Tiering**: When you store your data in this class, it is automatically moved between three access tiers based on access patterns as follows:
    - **Frequent Access**: This access tier is for objects you access frequently and newly uploaded objects
    - **Infrequent Access**: Objects not accessed for 30 consecutive days are automatically transitioned into this storage class, which is cheaper than the Frequent Access tier
    - **Archive Instance Access**: This access tier further reduces your cost, and objects are transitioned into this tier when they haven't been accessed for 90 consecutive days

The tiers above offer instance access to your data with millisecond latency. In addition to these, the S3 Intelligent-Tiering storage class also offers two optional archive tiers as follows:

- **Archive Access**: Amazon S3 provides the archive access tier for data that can be accessed asynchronously and where instant access is not required. When activated, objects not accessed for 90 consecutive days will be transitioned into this access tier, bypassing the Archive Instance Access tier.
- **Deep Archive Access**: This archive tier is designed for objects that have not been accessed for 180 consecutive days and offers the cheapest option of the Intelligent access tiers. Access to your data is asynchronous and not instant.

Choosing the suitable storage class is critical for your business and can affect overall storage costs. Your choice will also depend on your access patterns and whether you need the ability to access your data with millisecond latency. Where access patterns are unknown, Amazon S3 offers the Intelligent-Tiering storage class, which automatically uses machine learning to transition your data into the most cost-effective storage class.

In the next section, you will learn more about bucket policies and enforcing authentication and access rights at the bucket level.

Access permissions

By default, access to your AWS bucket is private. Only the resource owner or the root user of the AWS account can access the bucket in Amazon S3.

To allow other users or applications to interact with the bucket you create in S3, you must define a set of permissions. In *Chapter 5*, you learned how to create IAM policies that can grant access to users, groups, and roles in your AWS account to resources such as S3 buckets. In addition to IAM policies, you can also define resource-based policies. These policies are directly attached to the resource, such as an S3 bucket. With Amazon S3, resource-based policies are called **bucket policies**. Bucket policies are also written in JSON, like IAM policies.

A fundamental difference between IAM and resource-based policies is that you must define a `principal` element in the latter. This allows you to identify the principal who has permission to carry out the actions described by the `action` statements in the policy. The following bucket policy, as per the screenshot in *Figure 6.2*, illustrates this concept with an example:

```
{
  "Id": "Policy1730533776208",
  "Version": "2012-10-17",
  "Statement": [
    {
      "Sid": "Stmt1730533774777",
      "Action": [
        "s3:GetObject",
        "s3:ListAllMyBuckets",
        "s3:ListBucket"
      ],
      "Effect": "Allow",
      "Resource": [
        "arn:aws:s3:::bellybrew-source-code",
        "arn:aws:s3:::bellybrew-source-code/*"
      ],
      "Principal": {
        "AWS": [
          "arn:aws:iam::6994████████:user/Bob"
        ]
      }
    }
  ]
}
```

Figure 6.2: Resource-based (Bucket Policy) example

As per the screenshot in *Figure 6.2*, you will note that the principal element is defined as an IAM user named 'Bob'. This user will have access to list buckets in the AWS account, list the contents of the `bellybrew-source-code` bucket, and be able to retrieve (download) objects from the bucket.

IAM policies are limited in scope because they can only grant permissions to users and roles within the account in which they were created. Of course, you can enable users and resources in other AWS accounts to assume the role, but the policy itself can only be attached to identities in the account in which it was created.

This makes perfect sense since IAM policies, by their very nature, must be attached to an IAM identity. However, if you need to grant direct access to principals outside your AWS account, such as an IAM user from another AWS account or an application hosted in an external AWS account, you can use bucket policies. This is because you can provide the full **Amazon Resource Name** (**ARN**) of the user or role from the external account in the principal element of the JSON document.

One thing to note, though, is that the principal in the external account must have permission to access the same service in the account it belongs to before you can grant it access to a related resource in your account.

Another critical benefit of bucket policies is the ability to define the principal element with a wildcard or an asterisk (*). This denotes anyone or anything as the principal. The following JSON snippet illustrates the principal's use of a wildcard:

```
{
  "Version": "2012-10-17",
  "Statement": [
    {
      "Effect": "Allow",
      "Principal": "*",
      "Action": "s3:GetObject",
      "Resource": "arn:aws:s3:::bellybrew-source-code/*"
    }
  ]
}
```

In the preceding JSON snippet, you will note that the principal element is set to a wildcard (*). This grants anonymous access to retrieve objects from the bucket. This is often used when you want to host public-facing static websites on your Amazon S3 bucket, which is discussed next in this chapter.

Static website hosting

In addition to hosting data for your organization, Amazon S3 offers several other features and capabilities. One such feature is the ability to host complete websites for your organization. The only limitation is that the service offers only a **static website hosting** capability. That means that since Amazon S3 doesn't have any runtime or compute component, you cannot run server-side scripts. However, if designed with other AWS services and resources, static websites hosted on Amazon S3 can provide all the functionality you need for your web applications.

For example, Belly Brew Co. Limited could host their primary customer-facing website on Amazon S3. The frontend components could easily be hosted using standard **Hypertext Transfer Protocol** (**HTML**) files, **Cascading Style Sheets** (**CSS**), **Portable Document Format** (**PDFs**), images, and videos. You can also host JavaScript or client-side scripts that can run in the client browsers to offer additional features and interactivity. Suppose you require forms of data input and processing. In that case, you can use HTML forms to collect data, which can be passed on to backend compute resources such as EC2 instances or Lambda functions to be processed and manipulated for specific use cases. Through websites hosted on Amazon S3, you can access backend **Application Programming Interfaces** (**APIs**) to interact with backend compute resources or other AWS services such as databases and analytical tools.

The best thing about Amazon S3 static website hosting is that it is highly scalable and available. You do not need to worry about capacity provisioning, as AWS takes care of this seamlessly. Amazon S3 can handle large volumes of end-user traffic and is often a better solution than traditional web server architectures running on a fleet of **Elastic Compute Cloud** (**EC2**) resources, depending on your use case.

The following examples are ideal for Amazon S3 static website hosting:

- **Product pre-launch websites**: If you need to advertise or promote a new product that you plan to launch soon, then Amazon S3 website hosting is ideal. In most cases, such websites are designed to provide product information and may collect some data for newsletters or notification purposes. Because it can often be challenging to know how well your new product will be received, hosting such a website across a fleet of EC2 instances may be more costly since you may need to scale out fast and utilize many servers to advertise the launch of your product successfully.
- **Offloading**: If you plan to launch a dynamic web application and require compute capability with server-side scripting, you must choose a compute service such as EC2 to deploy your web application on. However, even in such scenarios, you could offload the hosting of your digital assets, such as images, videos, and documents, to download to an Amazon S3 bucket, which will be cheaper from a storage cost perspective. An excellent example would be hosting all your training videos on using the new product in an S3 bucket rather than block or file storage attached to the webservers.
- **'Lite' version of website or "Under Maintenance" banners**: You can also use Amazon S3 static website hosting as a failover solution if your main website running on compute resources such as EC2 experiences an outage.

Amazon S3 Static Website hosting powers millions of websites and web applications online. In this study guide, you will learn how to host Belly Brew Co. Limited's *Coming Soon website* using static website hosting later in the project section of this chapter.

Protecting your data while storing it in the cloud is paramount to every customer. While Amazon S3 offers eleven 9s of durability, you must still take the necessary steps to prevent data loss from accidental deletion or overwrites. In the next section, you will learn about another feature known as **versioning**, which can help mitigate this type of disaster.

Amazon S3 versioning

You may often have multiple copies of your data, such as documents you update regularly. If you make changes to an object (such as a document) and upload it to an Amazon S3 bucket using the same Key (name), it overwrites the previous copy of that object. This is because the versioning feature is not enabled by default. If you need to protect earlier copies of your data as you regularly perform updates, you can enable versioning. This adds a **version ID** to every upload action you perform for that object, effectively creating a new version of it.

You can then access previous versions of the same object and restore them if there is an issue with the current version or refer to earlier versions as required. With versioning enabled, you also mitigate the risk of accidental deletions. This is because if you perform a standard delete operation without specifying the version ID of a particular object version, Amazon S3 doesn't delete the object; it simply hides the object from view in the management console by adding a delete marker to the object. You can then restore the object to view by deleting the delete marker.

Versioning must be used carefully as it incurs additional costs due to increased storage consumption.

While versioning can help you prevent accidental deletions and allow you to maintain multiple versions of an object, it cannot prevent issues that might cause the bucket to get deleted, or if there is a regional disaster in which the bucket is hosted. To address such concerns, AWS also offers another feature called Cross-Region Replication, which is discussed next.

Cross-region and same-region replication

As discussed previously, AWS will never replicate objects hosted in one region to another region to ensure that you abide by any regulatory or data sovereignty laws. However, nothing can stop you from replicating objects across regions if your business use case requires it and if you are not affected by such laws.

Customers can configure **Cross-Region Replication** (**CRR**) to copy objects from buckets in one region to another asynchronously. If required, you can also set up bidirectional replication, ensuring your buckets are always in sync. CRR can be used for the following use cases:

- **Reduce latency**: You can reduce latency by copying objects to buckets located in regions closer to end users. This is particularly noticeable with huge files, and if you do not make use of a content delivery network such as Amazon CloudFront (discussed later in *Chapter 11*).
- **Increase operational efficiency**: If you have applications that need to interact with the data in your Amazon S3 bucket, placing those buckets closer to where you host your application will increase operational efficiency. This also means that if you host your applications across multiple regions, a copy of the data in each area would be beneficial. Cross-regional replication can make it extremely easy to ensure that your application has fast and reliable access to data when needed.
- **Fulfil regulatory or compliance requirements**: Your organization may need to comply with regulatory requirements that stipulate a copy of your data is hosted in another region to ensure security against any major disasters. Cross-region replication can help fulfill this requirement very easily.

Interestingly, you can also configure bucket replication across buckets hosted in the same region. This is known as **Same-Region Replication** (**SRR**). Often, companies may wish to implement SRR for use cases such as log aggregation, replicating data between development and testing environments, or across AWS accounts. You may also be required to set up SRR for your buckets for compliance requirements and protection from accidental bucket deletions.

A prerequisite to configuring bucket replication is that you must also enable versioning. Finally, you can replicate objects between two buckets, where the replicas are stored in a different storage class in the destination bucket than the original data in the source bucket. This can help you reduce your overall costs, where you might have the original data in Amazon S3 Standard but the replicas in Amazon S3 Standard-IA.

Managing your objects' lifecycle is another essential factor when working with lots of data. Companies often have vast amounts of data, consuming storage using more expensive storage classes and incurring unnecessary costs when, in fact, some of the data can be moved to cheaper storage classes or deleted altogether as they are no longer required. The following section discusses a solution offered by AWS.

Amazon S3 lifecycle management

Like every resource or application, data, too, has a lifecycle. A dataset might initially be highly popular and in constant demand, with the need to access it frequently and instantly. Over time, demand may reduce depending on the type of data and its use case, and eventually, the dataset may become obsolete or even meaningless. For example, Belly Brew Co. Limited rarely accessed accounting records older than 48 months. They also no longer need the log files from an old server that used to host their previous customer relationship management software. With Amazon S3, you can store an unlimited amount of data. This makes it very easy to hoard data in your Amazon S3 buckets. However, you are charged for the total amount of monthly storage consumed.

To help you better manage your data lifecycle, AWS offers the Lifecycle Management feature. This tool allows you to define rules (called transition actions) to automatically move data not frequently accessed into cheaper storage classes after a set period, including Glacier storage classes, for long-term retention. You can also use the Lifecycle Management tool to expire data (called expiration actions), which results in deleting it from Amazon S3 altogether. This is particularly useful when you no longer need that data, as it has passed any regulatory compliance period.

For example, you may transition data into the Standard-IA storage class after 60 days, then into Glacier Deep Archive after 180 days, and finally expire the data after 7 years.

Amazon S3 Lifecycle Management actions can be applied to the entire bucket or a subset of data by defining a prefix. You can also use one set of rules for current data and another for previous versions.

When it comes to securing your data, you have also learned about how authorization plays a vital role in using IAM policies and bucket policies. To protect against accidental deletions, you learned about versioning, and to ensure you keep secondary copies of your data, you can use replication. However, you must also consider how data can be secured at rest in the Amazon S3 buckets. In the next section, you will learn more about securing your data using encryption at rest.

Amazon S3 encryption

Encryption converts data into a coded format to prevent unauthorized access, ensuring that only those with the correct decryption key can read the original information. It is widely used in cybersecurity to protect sensitive data during storage or transmission.

Data encryption must be performed both in transit (in-flight between two systems) using protocols like **Secure Socket Layer/Transport Layer Security** (**SSL/TLS**), and at rest (while it resides on a storage medium such as a hard drive).

Amazon S3 offers a few options for protecting data at rest:

- **Server-side encryption**: When you upload (create) an object in Amazon S3, it is encrypted before being committed to disk. When you download/retrieve an object, it is automatically decrypted if you are authorized to access the object. There are four mutually exclusive server-side encryption options available to use on AWS:

   - **Server-side encryption with Amazon S3-managed keys (SSE-S3)**: This is the default encryption option, and all new objects uploaded to Amazon S3 are encrypted at rest. Each object is encrypted with a unique key, then with a master key that is regularly rotated. It uses the 256-bit Advanced Encryption Standard (AES-256) encryption algorithm.
   - **Server-side encryption with AWS Key Management Service (AWS KMS) keys (SSE-KMS)**: This server-side encryption option provides integration with the Amazon Key Management Service (AWS KMS). You can use the AWS-managed keys or create and manage your own CMKs (customer-managed keys). It offers additional features, such as integration with AWS CloudTrail, enabling you to maintain an audit trail of how and when the keys were used.
   - **Dual-layer server-side encryption with AWS Key Management Service (AWS KMS) keys (DSSE-KMS)**: This server-side encryption option is like SS3-KMS but applies two individual layers of encryption instead of one. The feature enables you to analyze data in Amazon S3 using an encryption method that fulfils various compliance and regulatory requirements.
   - **Server-side encryption with customer-provided keys (SSE-C)**: This server-side encryption option is used when you must follow specific requirements that stipulate you create and manage the encryption keys entirely, and AWS manages the encryption. When you retrieve data from Amazon S3, you must then provide the same encryption key as part of your request.
- **Client-side encryption**: This option involves encrypting your data on the client-side and then uploading the encrypted data to Amazon S3. You handle the full encryption and decryption process.

So far, you have discovered several features that help you to protect your data and manage costs. When you upload massive amounts of data into Amazon S3, you may also want to improve the speed at which your upload operations are completed. In the next section, you will learn about the Amazon S3 Transfer Acceleration service, which can help you with this.

Amazon S3 Transfer Acceleration (S3TA)

Amazon S3 buckets are regionally based. However, the data may need to be accessible across the globe. Due to the infrastructure architecture of the Internet, some users may experience longer and variable upload and download speeds, especially if they are located a considerable distance from your S3 bucket.

To improve performance and speed of access, you can enable your buckets with a feature known as **Amazon S3 Transfer Acceleration** (**S3TA**). This service routes your uploads via AWS's globally distributed edge locations and backbone network. Doing so logically shortens the distance between your end users and the physical location of the S3 bucket.

Using Amazon S3TA comes at an additional cost. You can use a comparison tool, as depicted in the screenshot in *Figure 6.3*, to simulate the transfer speeds from your browser to see if using the service would be beneficial for your requirements.

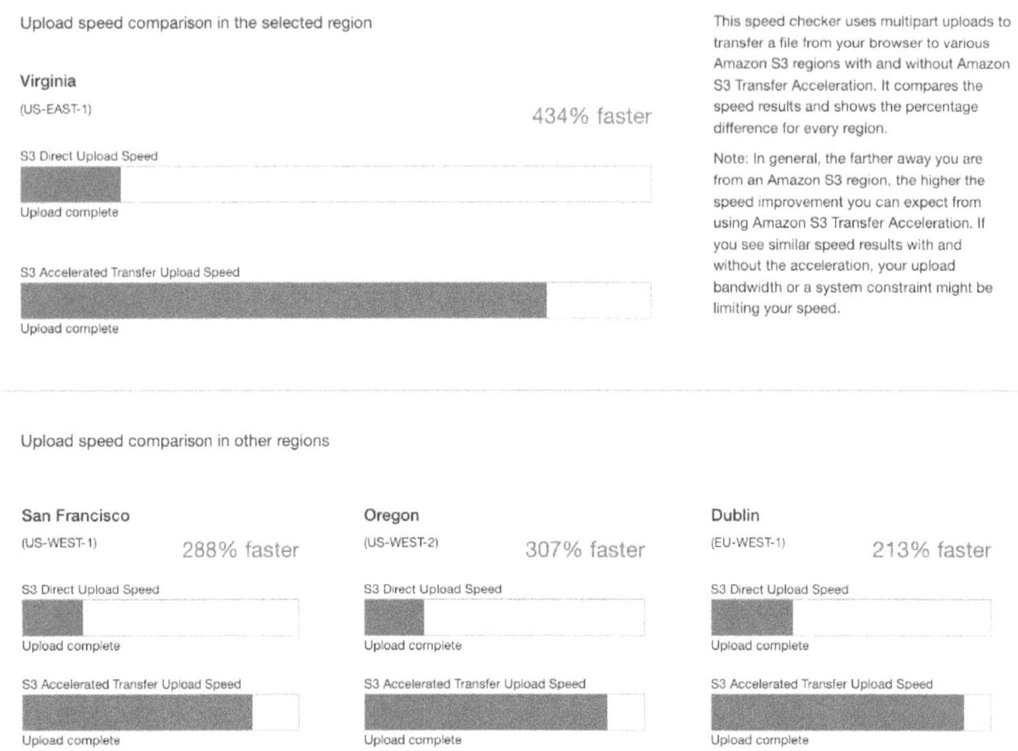

Figure 6.3: S3TA speed test

The Amazon S3TA tool is available at `https://s3-accelerate-speedtest.s3-accelerate.amazonaws.com/en/accelerate-speed-comparsion.html`

In this section, you learned about the Amazon S3 service and its core features that enable you to secure your data, optimize costs, and enhance performance. In the next section, you will learn more about building a hybrid cloud storage solution that enables you to connect your on-premises workloads with Amazon S3 in the cloud. This is often an essential requirement for most companies since hosting on-premises storage solutions to cater to very low-latency access is still a huge requirement. At the same time, companies want to offload a substantial portion of their data into the cloud to benefit from the wide range of features and benefits discussed earlier. The next section provides an overview of the Amazon Storage Gateway service that enables you to build hybrid cloud storage solutions.

Connecting on-premises storage to AWS with Amazon Storage Gateway

Amazon Storage Gateway is an on-premises hybrid cloud solution that enables you to connect your on-premises infrastructure to cloud storage services on the AWS platform. It uses industry-standard storage protocols such as **Network File System** (**NFS**), SMB, and **Internet Small Computer Systems Interface** (**iSCSI**) to seamlessly connect your virtual machine resources on-premises to the cloud. Your on-premises workloads can then work directly with cloud storage, uploading and downloading data as required.

To ensure security and privacy, you can configure the storage gateway to use secure IPsec **virtual private network** (**VPN**) tunnels or AWS Direct Connect.

To deploy the storage gateway service, you can install the virtual machine on VMware ESXi or Microsoft Hyper-V hypervisors. You can also procure hardware appliances for a seamless plug-and-play experience.

AWS Storage Gateway offers the following three options, which you can use depending on your use case:

- **File Gateway**: Also known as the Amazon S3 File Gateway, this option uses industry-standard NFS and SMB protocols to store and retire objects directly in Amazon S3. You configure file shares and associate them with your Amazon S3 buckets. Files written to the file share are available in the bucket as objects with full prefix paths. Existing objects in the bucket are accessible as files in the file system.
- **Volume Gateway**: This option enables you to connect your on-premises servers and applications to cloud storage on AWS using the iSCSI protocol. Using this service, you can mount storage volumes on your on-premises servers. Volume Gateway is available in two options:
    - **Cached volumes**: Most of your data is stored in Amazon S3, and a subset of data is hosted locally on premises for frequent access requirements. This offers higher cost savings since you do not need to host vast amounts of storage hardware on premises.

  - **Stored volumes**: This option is ideal if you need low-latency access to your entire dataset. The stored volume option is then used to asynchronously back up your data to the cloud as point-in-time Elastic Block Store (EBS) volumes.
- **Tape Gateways**: If your business manages backups using traditional tape storage infrastructure with software solutions such as Veritas BackupExec, NetBackup, or Commvault, this storage gateway solution is an excellent replacement. Using the concept of virtual tapes and virtual tape drives, you can use the Tape Gateway option to durably store your backups in Amazon S3 Glacier Flexible Retrieval or Glacier Deep Archive. Because your backup application is presented with a virtual tape infrastructure using the iSCSI protocol, it works seamlessly, allowing you to continue operating your backup solution.

In this section, you were given an overview of using the AWS Storage Gateway to build a hybrid cloud storage solution. However, you may also be required to quickly transfer a large amount of data from your on-premises locations to Amazon S3. Another use case is where you may need to extend your hybrid cloud solutions to run storage and compute services in locations with unconditioned environments or mobile environments such as construction sites, ships, factory floors, military camps, etc. The following section introduces an edge computing solution and data transfer technology known as the Amazon Snow Family, which fulfills this requirement.

Moving data and extending storage to the edge with the AWS Snow Family

The Snow Family offers technologies to protect data at the edge or enable customers to move petabytes of data to and from the AWS cloud. Two key services are the AWS Snowcone and the AWS Snowball services.

AWS Snowcone

The AWS Snowcone device is a rugged, small-form-factor edge computing and storage device designed for use in the field. It's lightweight and can fit in a small backpack as well as be delivered by a drone to remote locations. The device comes with either an 8TB HDD or a 14TB SSD and has 2 vCPUs with 4GB of usable memory. You can use it to move data to AWS offline by shipping the device or online using the AWS DataSync service. It is mainly designed to be installed and run in harsh conditions, such as oil rigs, factory floors, fields, and forests with little or no connectivity.

AWS Snowball Edge

AWS Snowball Edge devices are designed to migrate large amounts of data to the AWS cloud and offer computing capabilities that enable the processing of data on-premises. These devices encrypt your data at rest as well as feature a **Trusted Platform Module** (**TPM**) that can detect unauthorized modification to the hardware, software, or firmware.

Amazon Snowball Edge comes with two options:

- **Snowball Edge Storage Optimized**: These devices offer larger storage capacity and are ideal for data migration tasks. Specifically, the storage-optimized options are available in two flavors: **AWS Snowball Edge Storage Optimized 80TB** and **210TB**. The 80TB version offers an 80TB HDD drive and a 1TB SSD usable drive, with 40 vCPUs and 80GB of usable memory. The 210TB version comes with 210TB NVMe SSD storage, 104 vCPUs and 416GB of memory.
- **Snowball Edge Compute Optimized**: This device offers higher computing capabilities and is ideal for use cases such as machine learning, analytics, and other computing tasks. With 28TB of SSD storage, the device has 104 vCPUs and 416GB of memory.

> **Note**
>
> AWS often changes and updates its line of products and services. At the time of writing this book, AWS Snowball Edge is no longer available to new customers. Existing customers, however, can continue to use the service. This service is slowly being replaced by the new **AWS DataSync** for online transfers and **AWS Data Transfer Terminal** for secure physical transfers. The content on Snowball Edge is included in this chapter purely for exam preparation purposes.

In the next section, you will have an opportunity to work with the Amazon S3 service in your own AWS account and complete a project task.

Project task 6 – Deploying a static website using Amazon S3 for Belly Brew Co. Limited

The directors at Belly Brew Co. Limited have requested a minimal website to be hosted on AWS with a "coming soon" message. The website should showcase some of the newer product ranges, but, for now, must function as a simple static site to promote the company. You have been asked to design a **proof of concept** (**POC**) of how the new website will be hosted on Amazon S3 and how it will be accessed. Since this is just a demonstration to seek approval from the stakeholders, you do not need to configure the company's domain name to point to the website or implement SSL/TLS connectivity for now.

In the following project task, you will create an Amazon S3 bucket and configure it with a static website hosting service. You will deploy the website and configure it with settings to demonstrate that it can be accessed from the Internet.

Technical requirements

You must download the source files from our GitHub repository at `https://github.com/PacktPublishing/AWS-Certified-Cloud-Practitioner-CLF-C02-Exam-Guide` to complete the project task. The required files are in the `chapter6` folder. The website source code files are available to you as a zipped folder, which you will need to extract on your computer using an unzip utility. Both Mac and Windows computers have an inbuilt unzip utility. There is also a sample JSON policy document, which you will need to configure your bucket policy. Download both files and have them handy on your desktop.

While you can open source code files and JSON documents using basic text editors such as Notepad on Windows or TextEdit on macOS, it is recommended that you use an Integrated Development Environment (IDE) such as Visual Studio Code. An IDE provides useful features such as syntax highlighting, code formatting, and easier navigation, making it simpler to work with code throughout the exercises in this book. To get started, download Visual Studio Code from `https://code.visualstudio.com`, choose the version for your operating system, and follow the standard installation process. Once installed, you can use it to open, edit, and save the files used in this book. You must carry out the exercise in the AWS account that you named `bellybrewdevelopment` in *Chapter 4*. You must also log in to your AWS account as the IAM user 'Alice' you created in *Chapter 5*.

Remember, to log in as an IAM user, you must provide your AWS account ID. You can obtain this by logging in as the root user first and noting the Account ID by clicking on your Account Name in the top right-hand corner of the AWS Management Console. You can then log out and log back in, selecting the option to log in as an IAM user from the main AWS sign-in page.

Project task 6.1 – Creating an Amazon S3 bucket

In this project task, you will create the Amazon S3 bucket that will act as the storage container for Belly Brew Co. Limited's static website files:

1. From the main AWS management console, search for "S3" in the search bar at the top of the webpage and navigate to the Amazon S3 service
2. Ensure that you are in the North Virginia region by selecting it from the top right-hand corner of the webpage, as shown in *Figure 6.4*

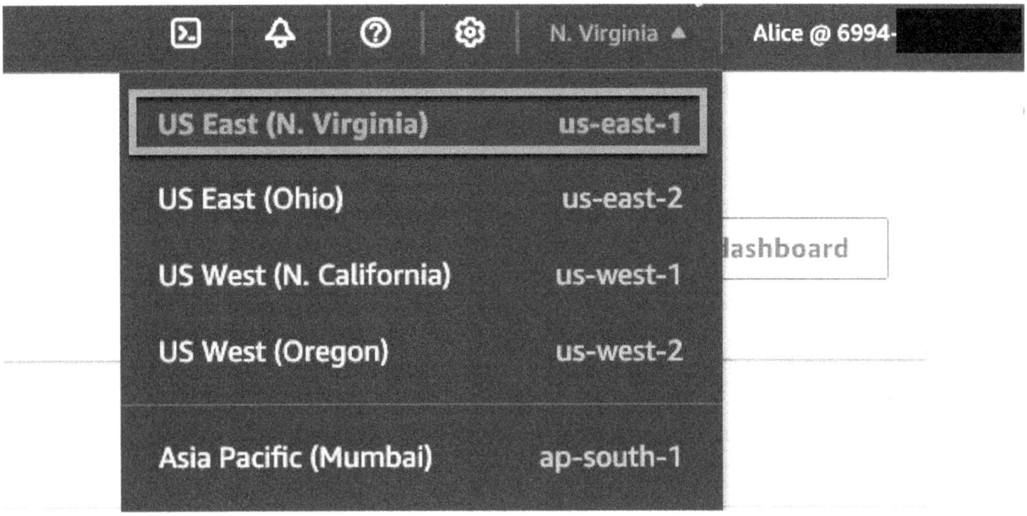

Figure 6.4: Selecting the North Virginia region

3. From the left-hand menu, click **General purpose buckets** under **Buckets**
4. In the right-hand pane, click the **Create bucket** button
5. Next, provide a name for the bucket, such as `belly-brew-coming-soon`. Select the **Global namespace** option and type in a name for the bucket in the text box under **Bucket name**. Note that you will not be able to select the same name as it has been used for this tutorial. Amazon S3 bucket names are unique globally, and you must select another name of your choice. You can always use the same name and simply prepend or append your name to the name "belly-brew-coming-soon" to get a unique name.
6. Scroll a bit further down till you reach the **Block Public Access settings for this bucket** section. Ensure that the **Block all public access** setting is unticked. This ensures that the bucket and its contents can be made publicly available. If this setting is enabled, then users on the Internet will not be able to access the website even if you have a bucket policy that allows anonymous access.
7. You must also tick the option **I acknowledge that the current settings might result in this bucket and the objects within becoming public**

8. Scroll a bit further down the webpage and note that Bucket versioning is set to the **Disabled** state. Leave this setting as it is, as you do not need to enable versioning.
9. For now, leave the remaining sections, such as Encryption and Advanced settings, at their default configuration settings. At the bottom of the webpage, click the **Create bucket** button

You will see a message confirming that the bucket has been successfully created. In the next project task, you will configure the bucket with static website hosting.

Project task 6.2 – Configuring static website hosting

In this project task, you will configure the bucket you created with the static website hosting feature.

1. While still in the Amazon S3 management console, select **General purpose buckets** from the left-hand menu
2. In the right-hand pane, click the bucket you created in *Project Task 6.1*
3. Select the **Properties** tab
4. Scroll toward the bottom of the webpage and click the **Edit** button in the **Static website hosting** section
5. Select the **Enable** option
6. Under **Hosting type**, click the option to select **Host a static website**
7. Next, you must provide the file names for the index and error documents. The error document is the webpage that your users will be redirected to if there is any issue with the static website or if the index page cannot be found. For the **Index document**, type in the name `index.html`. For the **Error document**, type in the name `error.html`
8. Click the **Save changes** button on the webpage

Your bucket has now been configured with static website hosting. In the next project task, you must define a set of permissions to ensure that users on the Internet can access the website. This is done using a bucket policy, which grants anonymous access for the `GET:Object` action.

Project task 6.3 – Creating a bucket policy

In this project task, you will configure a bucket policy for your Amazon S3 bucket to enable public access to the website.

1. While still in the Amazon S3 Console, click **General purpose buckets** from the left-hand menu and then click the bucket you created earlier from the right-hand pane
2. Click the **Permissions** tab
3. Scroll further down the webpage and click the **Edit** button in the **Bucket policy** section

4. Copy and paste the contents of the `bucket-policy.json` file you downloaded from the GitHub repository into the Policy text area. You can use Visual Studio Code (or any other text editor) to open the file.
5. You must change the **[Bucket Name]** placeholder to the name of your bucket as depicted in the screenshot in *Figure 6.5*

```
{
  "Id": "Policy1730702426202",
  "Version": "2012-10-17",
  "Statement": [
    {
      "Sid": "Stmt1730702424764",
      "Action": [
        "s3:GetObject"
      ],
      "Effect": "Allow",
      "Resource": "arn:aws:s3:::[Bucket Name]/*",
      "Principal": "*"
    }
  ]
}

```

Figure 6.5: Bucket Policy Sample

6. Scroll down to the bottom of the webpage and click the **Save changes** button

In the next project task, you will upload the source code files for the website.

Project task 6.4 – Uploading website files to S3 bucket

In this project task, you will upload the website source code files from your desktop to the S3 bucket. Ensure that you have extracted the files from the zipped folder. You must upload the files and folders as they appear in the unzipped folder to the root of the S3 bucket.

1. While still in the Amazon S3 web console, click **General purpose buckets** from the left-hand menu
2. In the right-hand pane, click the bucket you created earlier

3. Click the **Upload** button in the right-hand pane
4. In the **Upload** webpage that appears, drag and drop all the contents of the unzipped folder into the **Files and folders (0)** section of the webpage as depicted in the screenshot in *Figure 6.6*

Figure 6.6: Upload website source code to S3 bucket

5. Click the **Upload** button at the bottom of the webpage. Depending on your Internet connection, the upload should take about a minute, and you should see a message stating it has been completed successfully.

In the next project task, you will access the website from the static website URL.

Project task 6.5 – Accessing the website

In this project task, you will access the website using the Amazon S3 static website URL.

1. While still in the Amazon S3 web console, click on **General purpose buckets** in the left-hand menu
2. In the right-hand pane, click the Amazon S3 bucket you have configured with static website hosting

3. Click the **Properties** tab
4. Scroll to the bottom of the webpage till you get to the **Static website hosting** section
5. You should be able to click the **Bucket website endpoint** link as per the following screenshot in *Figure 6.7*

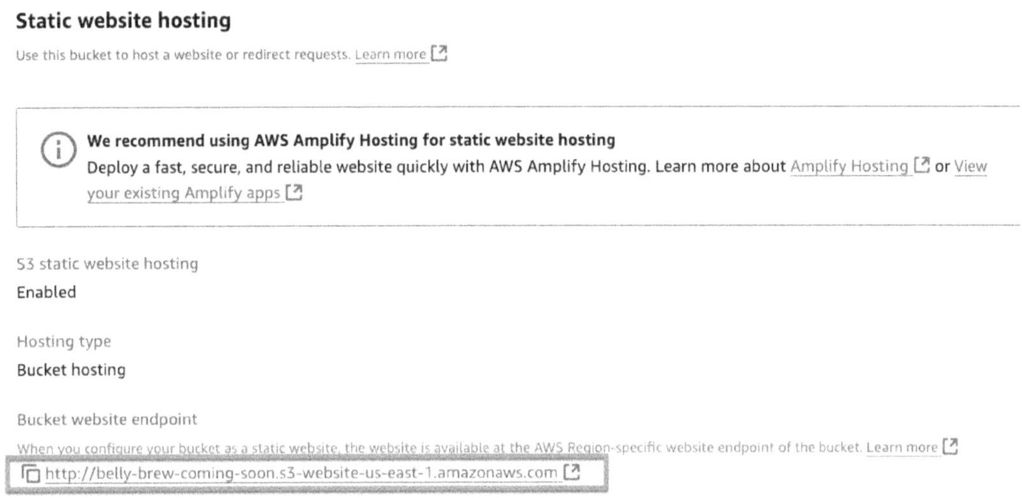

Figure 6.7: Static website hosting endpoint link

6. Click the endpoint URL to launch your website. Depending on the web browser you are using, you may get a warning that the site is not secure. This is perfectly fine, as you have not configured the website for HTTPS traffic. Go ahead and continue to the website, ignoring the warning, and you should find the Belly Brew Co. Limited coming soon webpage load as per the following screenshot in *Figure 6.8*.

Figure 6.8: Belly Brew Co. Limited static website

7. You can scroll through the website and review it

In this project task, you successfully configured and set up an Amazon S3 static website hosting service for Belly Brew Co. Limited's coming soon webpage. You discovered that it was necessary to disable the Block Public Access setting and configure a bucket policy to allow anonymous access to the website. This was necessary to make the website publicly accessible.

Generally, the frontend of your web applications will be publicly accessible. You can then incorporate authentication and authorization services for users to sign up to and sign in to the website to access more premium content or place orders if this were an e-commerce web application. Note that in this current state, the architecture excludes some critical real-world design patterns. For example, you would want to use a custom domain name to access the website and ideally use HTTPS (instead of HTTP), which enforces encryption in transit. Furthermore, you would want to host a caching service to make the website accessible over a low-latency connection using a content delivery network such as Amazon CloudFront, which is discussed in *Chapter 11*.

Summary

Amazon S3 is an object storage offering from AWS that comes with a vast array of features to help businesses manage their entire data. The architecture means that it can offer 99.999999999% (eleven 9s) of durability and extremely high levels of availability, depending on the storage class you store your data in.

In this chapter, you learned about the features of Amazon S3, including how to secure your data with bucket policies and encryption options—a critical requirement for every business that wishes to consider cloud storage to host their data. This chapter also includes crucial topics you are likely to be tested on in the exam, such as how versioning can help prevent accidental deletions and how cross-region replication can facilitate ensuring your data is closer to end consumers. You also learned how lifecycle management can help you manage the lifecycle of your data effectively and also optimize cost savings for the organization.

Amazon S3 offers static website hosting, a service that powers millions of websites and is suitable for many use cases. Using Amazon S3 to host your front-end website can also help you architect serverless solutions, which you will learn more about as you progress through this study guide.

The chapter also discusses the AWS Storage Gateway Service, enabling you to build hybrid cloud storage solutions for your business requirements. With options for managing files directly in Amazon S3 from local on-premises file gateways through to continuing your backup solutions with the tape gateway, this service ensures you can have access to cloud data with low-latency access.

Finally, you learn about the AWS Snow Family, a service that extends edge storage and compute services and enables you to transfer petabyte-scale data to AWS quickly.

Exam Readiness Drill – Chapter Review Questions

Apart from mastering key concepts, strong test-taking skills under time pressure are essential for acing your certification exam. That's why developing these abilities early in your learning journey is critical.

Exam readiness drills, using the free online practice resources provided with this book, help you progressively improve your time management and test-taking skills while reinforcing the key concepts you've learned.

HOW TO GET STARTED

- Open the link or scan the QR code at the bottom of this page
- If you have unlocked the practice resources already, log in to your registered account. If you haven't, follow the instructions in *Free Benefits with Your Book* section in this book's *Preface* and come back to this page.
- Once you log in, click the START button to start this chapter's quiz
- We recommend attempting a quiz multiple times till you're able to answer most of the questions correctly and well within the time limit.
- You can use the following practice template to help you plan your attempts:

Working On Accuracy		
Attempt	**Target**	**Time Limit**
Attempt 1	40% or more	Till the timer runs out
Attempt 2	60% or more	Till the timer runs out
Attempt 3	75% or more	Till the timer runs out
Working On Timing		
Attempt 4	75% or more	1 minute before time limit
Attempt 5	75% or more	2 minutes before time limit
Attempt 6	75% or more	3 minutes before time limit

The above drill is just an example. Design your drills based on your own goals and make the most out of the online quizzes accompanying this book.

Link to this Chapter's Quiz

You need to unlock the online practice resources to access the link below. Check the *Free Benefits with Your Book* section in the *Preface* for detailed instructions on how to do this. You only need to unlock the resources once.

Open Quiz `https://packt.link/clf_c02_ch6`or scan the QR code

7

AWS Networking Services, Part 1 – Virtual Private Cloud (VPCs)

In the **information technology** (**IT**) world, networking technologies have been pivotal in connecting our world. With this technology and its fundamental principles and processes, the Internet as we know it came into existence.

Businesses, from home office start-ups to large multinationals, depend on this vital IT service to communicate within their organizations and with external entities such as partners, suppliers, and customers. Without networking, your colleague sitting a few desks away from you would have to save a file to a disk and then pass that disk to you so you can insert it into your computer to access a file you are collaborating on. This would be highly inefficient. Instead, with networking, you and your colleague can save and access the file in a shared location on a local network or even on the Internet.

Networking does more than enable devices to communicate with each other. IT networks represent boundaries of communications, such that devices within a network are free to communicate with each other, but access to and from external networks can be restricted. Networks can be configured to communicate with other networks – that's how the Internet works. It's a collection of many small networks, all interconnected. The term "Internet" itself comes from "inter-networking." These smaller networks, which may belong to different organizations, individuals, or service providers, connect using standardized communication protocols such as **TCP/IP (Transmission Control Protocol/Internet Protocol)**.

In this chapter, you will learn how IT networks play a fundamental role in enabling different resources (devices) that host various parts of your application to communicate with each other. Specifically, you will learn how to create cloud networks in your AWS account called **Virtual Private Cloud (VPC)** to host and manage your application resources. Amazon VPCs are designed to help you build secure networks in the cloud within which you can host your application resources and define exactly how they are accessed from the Internet or via private connections from your on-premises locations. Depending on your use case, your resources, such as web servers, application servers, and databases, may require access to and from the Internet. You will learn how to build secure VPCs that ensure only specific authorized traffic is permitted into and out of your VPC. This chapter will also provide a deep-dive analysis of how networking works and discuss concepts for designing and building secure networks in the cloud.

The following topics are discussed in this chapter:

- Understanding on-premises corporate networks
- Explaining IP addressing and subnet masks
- Comparing network sizes and IP address classes
- Building virtual networks with Amazon VPC
- Securing VPC traffic
- Connecting VPCs with VPC peering
- Centralizing VPC connectivity with AWS Transit Gateway
- Securing hybrid connectivity with VPNs
- Connecting on-premises networks with AWS Direct Connect

Understanding on-premises corporate networks

Every business will have some on-premises network. Even a small start-up is likely to have a home office network comprising various devices that need to communicate with each other. Your home office may look like the diagram in *Figure 7.1*.

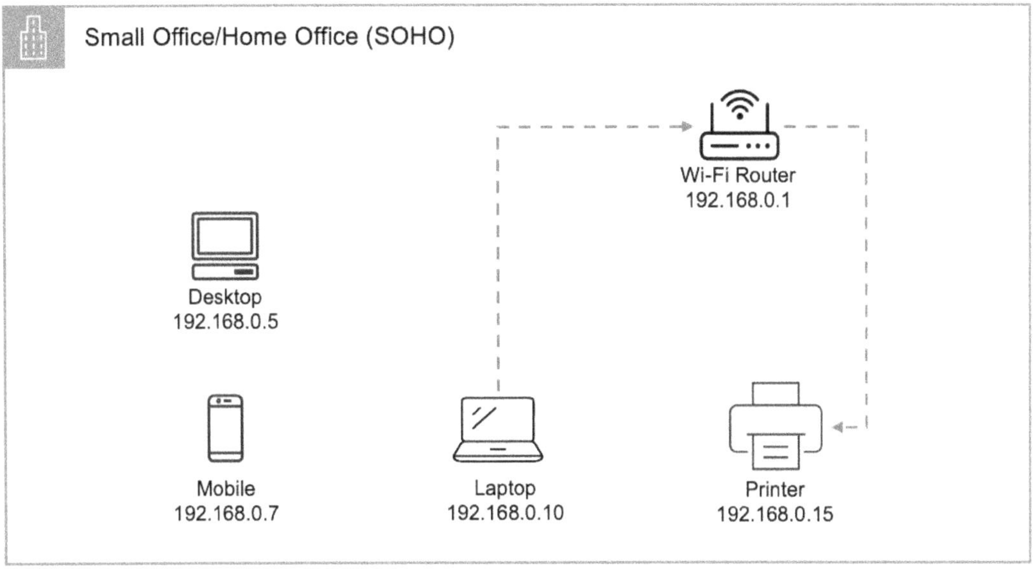

Figure 7.1: Small Office/Home Office (SOHO) setup

As depicted in the diagram, even a home office would require a network setup to ensure the devices can communicate. In this illustration, the devices are connected using the WIFI router, enabling communications between them. With this networking technology, a user can send data from the laptop to the printer to print a document. You will note in the diagram that each device also has an IP address, such as the laptop with 192.168.0.10 and the printer with 192.168.0.15. If the IP addressing has been defined and configured correctly, the devices in this SOHO (Small Office Home Office) network can communicate with each other, in this case using the WIFI router, which offers wireless connectivity. Network connectivity can also be provided using wired connections, with cables connected from each device to a central switch to which all other devices connect.

While the SOHO network depicted in *Figure 7.1* is simple, networks can get very complex depending on the number of devices they need to support and the use case. The following section provides a high-level overview of a typical business network architecture.

Basic corporate networks

Most businesses must host more complex networks with extra security in mind. This is because a company will host several applications, some of which might be more sensitive than others and require isolation and separation. Furthermore, the business must serve different departments, external users, and customers. You would not want your customers getting access to your staff payroll application now, would you? To ensure higher levels of security and isolation of workloads, business networks are often divided into small, separate networks designed for specific use cases.

A high-level example of such a network is illustrated in the following diagram in *Figure 7.2*:

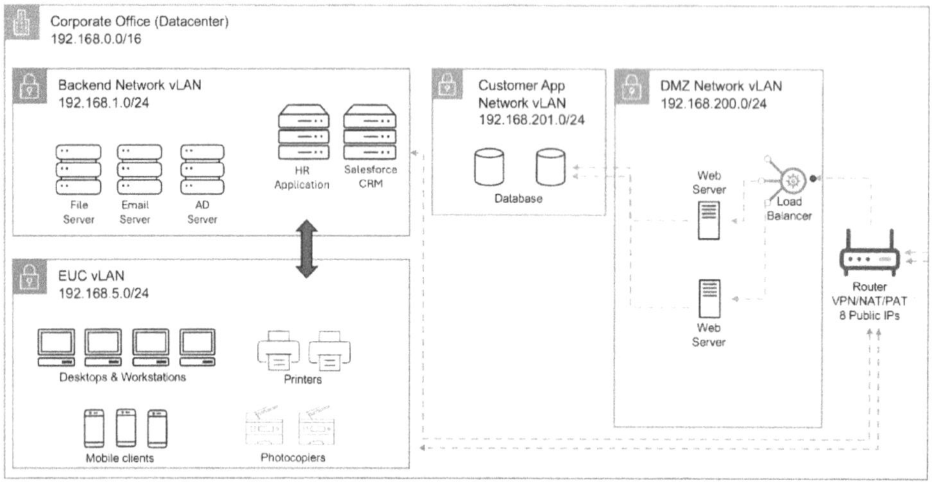

Figure 7.2: Example of corporate network

As depicted in *Figure 7.2*, the corporate network has several small sub-networks. These small sub-networks are also known as **virtual local area networks** or **vLANs**. These virtual LANs are designed to isolate workloads but allow inbound and outbound communication from other vLANs over specific types of traffic if required. Networks tend to experience a lot of traffic, usually in the form of broadcast traffic. Broadcast traffic is a type of network communication where a message is sent to all devices in a specific network. Think of it like someone shouting a message in a room full of people; everyone hears it, even if it's not meant for them.

For example, when a device connects to a network and asks, "Who is the main server?" it uses broadcast traffic to send that question to all devices. Only the correct device (the server) will respond, but everyone else still hears the question.

Broadcasts are beneficial in small networks but can cause congestion in larger ones if overused, like shouting in a crowded space all the time. By placing workloads in isolated virtual networks, you can define what traffic is permitted inbound from other networks, reducing this *noise*. This also helps you separate workloads unrelated to each other to enhance security and enforce compliance.

As per the diagram, two networks are designed to host customer-facing applications: the web servers served behind a Load Balancer located in the **demilitarized zone** (**DMZ**) and the databases hosting customer data in the Customer App Network vLAN. A DMZ network is one where your resources may have direct exposure to the Internet to allow users and applications direct access to them. For example, in our diagram, users from the Internet can access the customer's website via the Load Balancer. This Load Balancer is placed in the DMZ, as depicted in the diagram. The load balancer distributes incoming traffic from customers on the Internet across the two web servers through which customers can access their data and services. A DMZ must only host those resources which need direct Internet access to ensure higher levels of security. Hence, the databases are hosted in a separate vLAN, which is internal in the Customer APP Network vLAN. This ensures that customers can access those databases only via the web servers in the DMZ. The web server would only allow those users who successfully authenticate against the application to access the database.

Furthermore, within the corporate network, internal vLANs provide resources and applications for internal business requirements. In this illustration, you will note the Backend Network vLAN, which hosts servers and applications for internal business use cases. You will also note that the EUC (End User Computing) vLAN is designed to host client devices such as staff members' laptops, desktops, printers, and photocopiers.

In the next section, you will learn more about how these virtual LANs are created from the more extensive corporate network using IP addressing and subnetting.

Explaining IP addressing and subnet masks

By now, you know that network devices such as laptops, desktops, phones, tablets, and printers can communicate if placed in a network that allows connectivity over a wired or wireless connection. In addition to this physical connectivity, each device requires a unique IP address to communicate. In the same way, as you cannot have the same mobile number used on two separate smartphones simultaneously, you cannot have two network devices with the same IP address communicate in the same network.

However, IP addresses do more than act as telephone numbers for your devices. IP addresses allow you to create the network logically. This means that even if you have devices connected physically, say over a wired/wireless connection, it's how the IP address is configured on those devices that allows the communication to occur. As per the following diagram, even though the laptop and desktop computers are in the same physical network, they cannot communicate because their IP addresses are not in the same logical network. This ability to build logical networks within a physically connected space allows you to create separate virtual LANs, as discussed earlier.

This is all thanks to Subnet Masks, which enable you to define smaller logical networks within the larger physical network. Before examining how subnet masks are used to build logical *sub-networks*, it's essential to understand the fundamentals of IP addresses. There are two versions of IP addresses: IPv4 and IPv6. These are discussed in the next section.

IP address version 4 (IPv4)

The standard IP address you might be familiar with is IPv4. This was the first general release IP addressing system and took the form of **four decimal numbers separated by dots**. An example of an IPv4 address is `192.168.1.7`. Each decimal notation is called an octet, ranging between 0 and 255 in decimal. Computers, however, use binary numbers to communicate. This is a base 2 number comprising only zeros and ones. Thus, the IP address you are familiar with must be converted into binary for your computer.

Each octet in your IP Address represents 8 bits in binary, which can range from eight zeros to eight ones (00000000 to 11111111). Since there are four octets, an IPv4 address comprises 32 bits in binary (8 bits x 4 octets).

Take the example of the IP address `192.16.1.7`. In binary, each octet would be converted into 8 bits of zeros and ones, depending on the value of the octet. The following diagram in Figure illustrates what this IP address looks like as a binary representation.

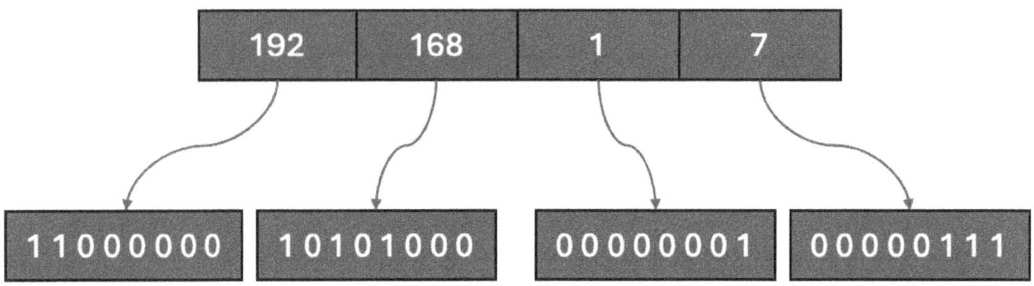

Figure 7.3: IP address represented as binary bits

Understanding the fundamentals of IP addressing and how this conversion to binary takes place will help you appreciate how logical networks are built. Take the example of the IP address `192.168.1.7`. Conversion of this IP address to its binary equivalent requires knowing the place value of each binary bit in decimal. The position of each bit in the octet represents a power of 2, starting with '0' at the far right and ending with '7' at the far left of each octet.

To illustrate this conversion, let's take the last octet of the IP address `192.168.1.7`, which is '7' in this case. To convert this number into binary, start by reviewing the following table to identify the placeholder values of each bit in binary:

X represents a '0' or '1' in binary

Bit Position	7th	6th	5th	4th	3rd	2nd	1st	0th
Binary Bit	X	X	X	X	X	X	X	X
Power of 2	2^7	2^6	2^5	2^4	2^3	2^2	2^1	2^0
Place Value	$X*2^7$ or X*128	$X*2^6$ or X*64	$X*2^5$ or X*32	$X*2^4$ or X*16	$X*2^3$ or X*8	$X*2^2$ or X*4	$X*2^1$ or X*2	$X*2^0$ or X*1

Figure 7.4: Binary bit place values in decimal

Since there are only 8 bits in binary per octet, the maximum place value for the far left bit you can define is 2 to the power of 7 (2^7). This is because you start at 2 to the power of 0 (2^0) in the far right.

Starting from the right and moving to the left, the value of each bit can be either a '0' or the resulting power of 2 in decimal, based on the bit position. So, for example:

- The first value of the first bit is either equal to '0' or '1'. If X is 1, it is 2 to the power of 0 (2^0), which is 1.
- The second bit is double the first bit and is either equal to '0' or '2'. If X is 1, it is 2 to the power of 1 (2 ^ 1), which is 2.
- The third bit is double the second bit and is either equal to '0' or '4'. If X is 1, then it is 2 to the power 2 (2 ^ 2), which is 4.
- The fourth bit is double the third bit and is either equal to '0' or '8'. If X is 1, then it is 2 to the power of 3 (2^3), which is 8, and so on.

To calculate the decimal values of the binary representation, you must first identify which of the Xs should be converted to a '1' and which to '0' in binary. The decimal value is then derived by adding up all the place values of each bit as follows:

$$Decimal = (X*128) + (X*64) + (X*32) + (X*16) + (X*8) + (X*4) + (X*2) + (X*1)$$

So, to calculate the binary representation of **'7'** from the IP address 192.168.1.7, you must identify which of the 'Xs' should be converted to zeros and which ones to ones. You can only convert those bits to ones whose value will be equal to or less than your decimal number. Furthermore, you must convert the minimum number of bits to get to your decimal representation, since you will add up the decimal equivalent of the bits converted to ones. So, for example, as shown in *Figure 7.5*, you would perform your conversions as follows:

- From the left, ignore all bits that would yield a decimal value greater than '7'. In this case, you will start converting the binary bit in **position 2** to one. This is because 2 to the power of 2 (2^2) is 4. The value of 4 is less than 7.
- Next, you can convert the binary bit in **position 1** to a one. This is because 2 to the power of 1 (2 ^ 1) is 2. Adding up the place values for the bits in these two positions will yield a '6' (4 + 2).
- Since the decimal value of '6' is still less than our IP octet of '7', you can now convert the binary bit from **position 0** to a one. Here, 2 to the power of 0 (2 ^ 0) is 1. Adding this to your earlier value of '6' results in 7, the fourth octet of our IP address `192.168.1.7`

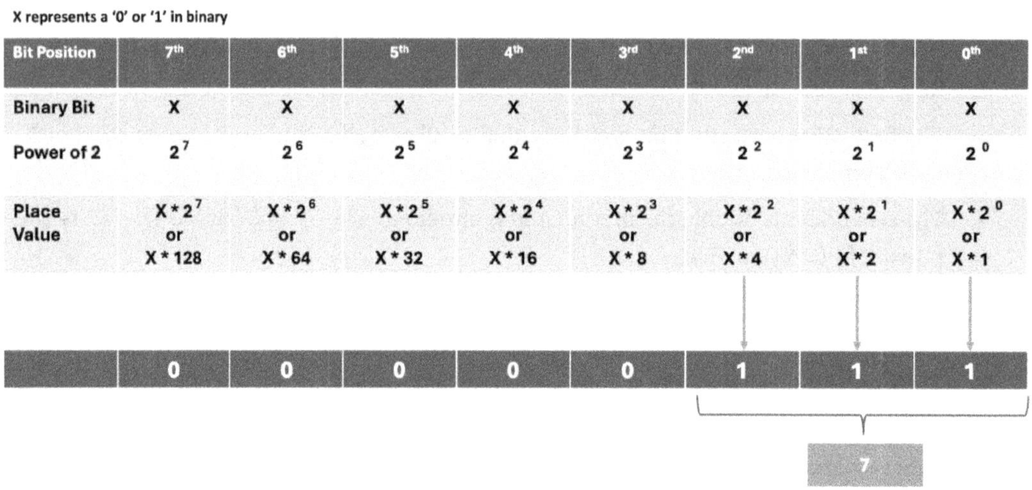

Figure 7.5: Converting an IP address to binary

Hence, the binary representation of 7 is 00000111. Converting the remaining octets in the IP address `192.68.1.7` gives 11000000 10101000 00000001 00000111.

While IPv4 addresses are used mainstream across company networks and even the Internet, they do, however, come with certain limitations. These are discussed in the next section.

IPv4 address limitations

As previously mentioned, the IPv4 address space comprises 32 bits. This means that the maximum number of IP addresses in this version is 2^32, giving you 4,294,967,296 IP addresses. On the surface, you might assume that this is a large number of IP addresses. However, almost every device is now connected to a network, including the Internet. These include your home computers, laptops, printers, scanners, and smart devices like your doorbell. You would agree that these 4 billion odd IP addresses are insufficient.

The largest network is the Internet, and every device that must connect to the Internet must have a unique IP address. However, an important fact is that while billions of devices must connect to the Internet, users and applications on the Internet do not need to connect to those devices directly. As depicted earlier in *Figure 7.2*, the desktops and laptops in the EUC vLAN may require internet access, but you wouldn't want strangers on the Internet connecting to the devices from the Internet inbound.

Realizing this simple fact, the Internet Assigned Numbers Authority (IANA) devised a brilliant plan to allocate a range of IP addresses for private use only. These IP ranges are not routable over the Internet, which means you cannot connect to them directly from the Internet. Businesses and homes can use these private IP address ranges to configure their internal private networks. Since these networks are private, you can use the same set of ranges across all businesses and homes without worrying about conflicting IP addresses.

The IANA has defined the following IP address ranges for private use:

- `10.0.0.0/8`: IP address range: 10.0.0.0 – 10.255.255.255
- `172.16.0.0/12`: IP address range: 172.16.0.0 – 172.31.255.255
- `192.168.0.0/16`: IP address range: 192.168.0.0 – 192.168.255.255

An additional IP Address range designed for internal networks that host devices running the Microsoft Windows Operating System is the Automatic Private IP Addressing (APIPA) range. This is particularly useful if you do not configure your internal devices with any of the private IP address ranges mentioned earlier. This range is from 169.254.0.0 to 169.254.255.255

The remaining address ranges are considered public addresses and are considered routable over the Internet with certain exceptions.

The key benefit of these private IP address ranges can be illustrated in the following illustration in *Figure 7.6*:

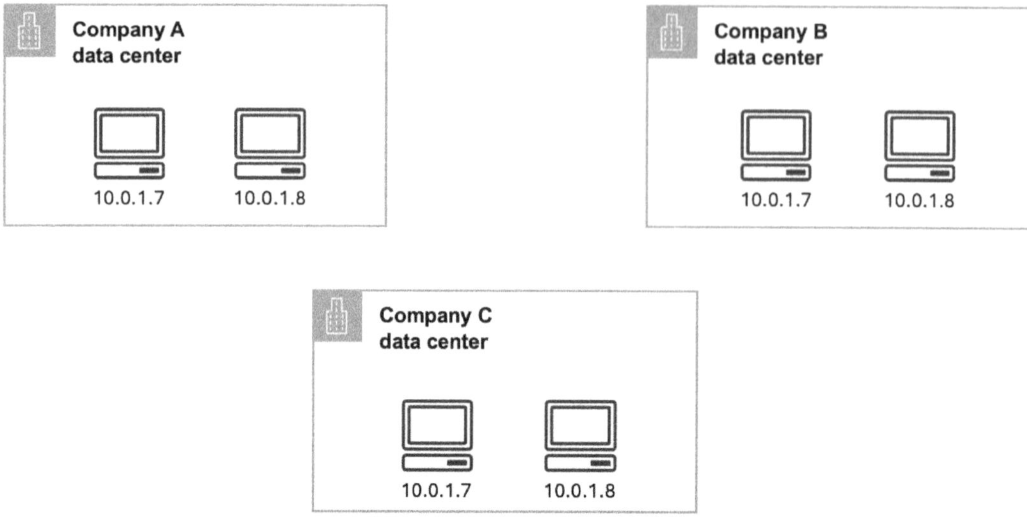

Figure 7.6: Private IP address ranges used by businesses for internal networks

As depicted in *Figure 7.6*, you will note that all three companies have allocated the same range of IP addresses from the `10.0.0.0/8` network. However, conflicting IP addresses do not arise since these businesses are not connected. This also means that companies can use this private IP address range for their internal networks, saving the scarce public ranges for only those devices that need to route traffic over the Internet. Furthermore, given that these private ranges are not routable over the Internet, it enhances your internal network security. A user on the Internet cannot connect to the IP address `10.0.1.7`, for example, since the traffic to this address will not traverse the public Internet.

The next question is obvious: if these IP address ranges are not routable on the Internet, then how can these devices access the Internet? Most devices in your corporate network will need Internet access, if only to download updates and patches like updated anti-virus definitions or software. The following section explains how these devices can access the internet.

Secure internet access

In *Figure 7.6*, it was discussed that businesses can use private IP address ranges that are not routable over the Internet, which offers enhanced security and enables the conservation of public IP addresses. However, businesses still need Internet access. Almost every network device will need some Internet access for a wide range of use cases. For example, a staff member may want to browse the Internet or send and receive emails. To enable this Internet access, public IP addresses would be required. However, assigning devices in the internal network with public IP addresses would defeat the purpose of the private IP address ranges defined by the IANA.

Instead of exposing internal devices such as laptops, desktops, printers, etc., by giving them public IP addresses, you could configure a relay device that would allow internal devices to access the Internet through it in a manner that ensures only that relay device would require a public IP address. This device (or software application) is known as **Network Address Translation**, or **NAT** for short.

In the following illustration in *Figure 7.7*, internal devices across the three companies can now access the Internet using NAT service, which can be configured on a router that offers this capability. The NAT device maintains an internal table of requests from internal devices to services on the Internet and forwards that traffic, advertising only its public IP address. Responses are received by the NAT device, which are then relayed back to the original requester, as depicted for Company A in the diagram, where the client machine with private IP `192.168.1.8` needs to access the AWS platform. The response from the platform would be sent to the NAT device, which would then relay it back to the client machine.

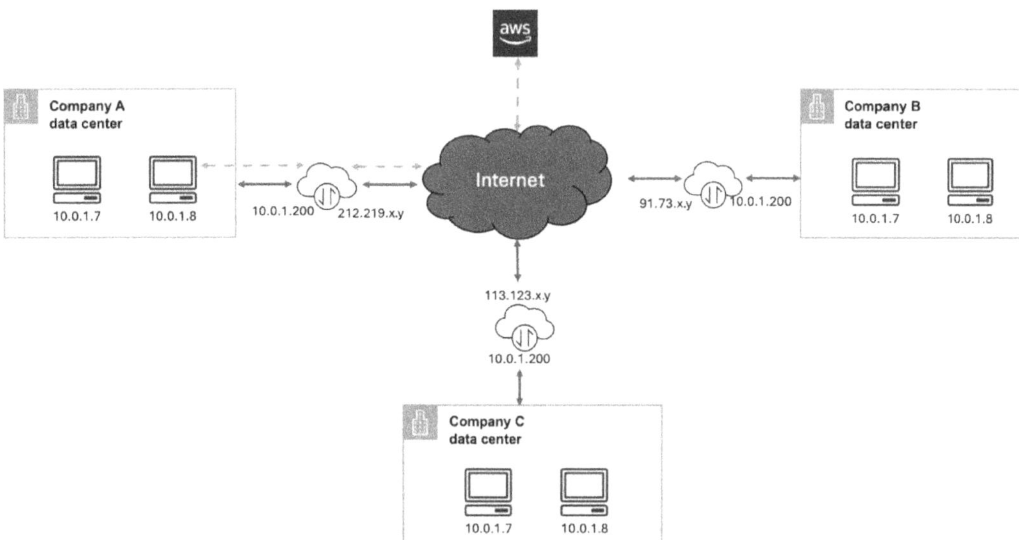

Figure 7.7: Private IP address ranges businesses use with Internet access via NAT services

As per *Figure 7.7*, network devices such as computers can access the internet without a public IP address. The NAT device maintains a table to ensure that responses to any Internet-hosted resource can be relayed to the correct device.

While private IP address ranges have enabled billions of devices to access the Internet, it is not a permanent solution. More and more devices now need direct Internet access, and a revision of the IPv4 address scheme was essential. This led to the development of **IPv6** (**Internet Protocol version 6**) by the **Internet Engineering Task Force** (**IETF**) in the 1990s. The following section provides a high-level overview of this newer version.

Overview of IPv6

The IETF designed a new version of the IP Address system known as IPv6. This version uses a 128-bit addressing system, giving you 2^128 addresses. This is enormous, far exceeding the **4.3 billion** addresses in IPv4 (2^32). IPv6 addresses are denoted in hexadecimal format rather than standard decimal since the numbering system would be very long. This newer version can ensure that every device on Earth (and beyond) can have a unique address, allowing for better scalability, security, and efficiency in networking.

While IPv6 is the answer to the drawbacks in IPv4, most networks still need to be able to use the older version of IP addressing, partly due to compatibility and interoperability with legacy devices that may not be IPv6-aware.

An important concept is that networks often need to be isolated. Network boundaries ensure the isolation and separation of networks, usually required for security, compliance, and operational efficiency. Furthermore, networks can be of varying sizes, determining how many devices can be hosted in that network. These concepts are discussed in detail in the following section.

Comparing network sizes and IP address classes

The IETF designed different classes of IPv4 addresses to help cater to various network sizes and use cases. Initially, there were five classes defined. This was known as the classful addressing scheme. Classes A to C represent generic unicast IP addresses (with certain exceptions). A unicast IP address uniquely identifies a single device on a network, allowing direct one-to-one communication.

Class D comprises multicast addresses. A multicast IP address sends data to multiple devices simultaneously within a specific group rather than to a single destination. Class D (`224.0.0.0` to `239.255.255.255`) is reserved for multicast traffic in IPv4, enabling efficient group communication. This is ideal for applications like **live video streaming** (e.g., IPTV or video conferencing), where data needs to be efficiently delivered to multiple recipients simultaneously using multicast. Class E (`240.0.0.0` to `255.255.255.255`) is reserved for experimental and future use in IPv4 and is not typically assigned for standard networking.

Classes A to C define standard network sizes. This is achieved by masking a portion of the IP address to represent the network. This also ensures your ability to create isolated networks that cannot directly communicate with each other unless you add a routing mechanism between the two networks.

The following standard classes have the following configurations:

- **Class A**: The first octet (first 8 bits) of a class A address represents the network portion, where the remaining three octets (24 bits) define the host portion. Furthermore, the first bit of a Class A network is always set to '0' in binary since the IP range for a Class A starts at '0'. The remaining 7 bits in the first octet define the number of networks in this class. Thus, taking 2 to the power of 7 (2^7) will give you 128, the total number of possible networks you can have in a Class A. It is important to remember that two networks within this range cannot be used to host devices. The first network is `0.0.0.0`, and the second is `127.0.0.0` (up to `127.255.255.255`). This is because:
    - **0.0.0.0** represents a reference point rather than a network. It means a default route and is used to signify any network, like a wildcard for routing purposes.
    - **127.0.0.0** is known as the loopback address and is used for local communication within a device. Any data packet sent to 127.x.x.x never leaves the device – it is often used for troubleshooting or testing applications locally.

  The total number of possible host machines in a Class A network is calculated as follows: (2^24) - 2 = 16,777,214. You must subtract 2 IP addresses because the first IP address represents the network ID, and the last IP address represents the broadcast IP.

- **Class B**: The first two octets (first 16 bits) of a class B address define the network portion, and the remaining 16 bits can be used for the host portion. The first two bits are also set to 10 in a class B network, meaning that this class's starting IP address is 128. This means the remaining 14 bits (16 minus the two bits set to '10') define the number of networks in a Class B range. Therefore, the total possible networks you can have in a Class B is 16,384 (2^14).
  The remaining 16 bits are used for possible host IP addresses and are calculated as follows: (2^16) - 2 = 65,534. You must subtract 2 IP addresses because the first IP address represents the network ID, and the last IP address represents the broadcast IP address per network in this class.

- **Class C**: The first three octets (first 24 bits) of a Class C address define the network portion, and the remaining 8 bits represent the host portion. In a Class C network, the first three far-left bits are set to 110, meaning that this class's starting range of IP addresses is 192. Furthermore, the remaining 21 bits define the number of networks in a Class C. This gives you 2,097,152 (2 ^ 21) possible networks.
  The remaining 8 bits are used for possible host IP addresses and are calculated as follows: (2^8) - 2 = 254. Again, remember that the first IP address in the network is the network ID, and the last IP address is used for broadcast traffic.

Figure 7.8 provides a visual representation of these classes:

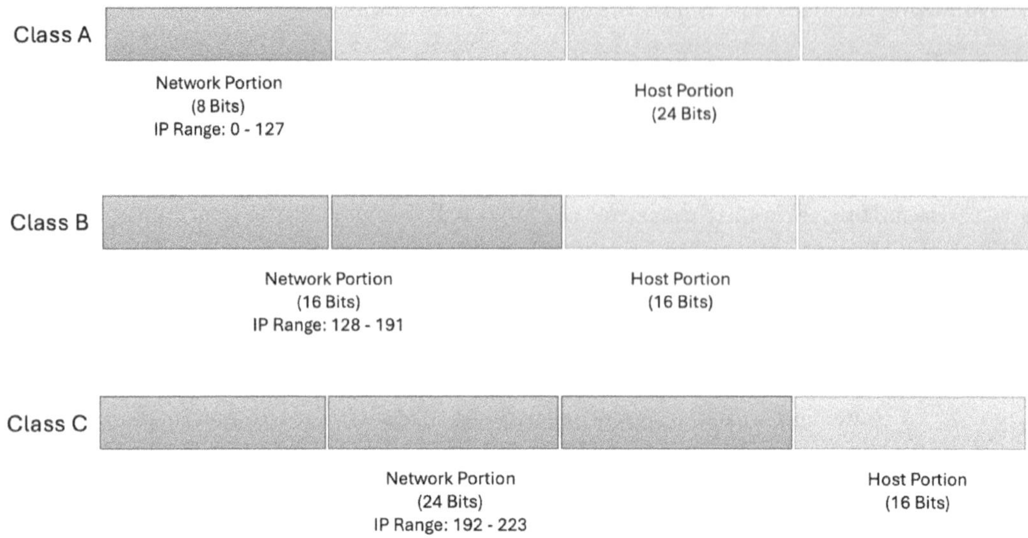

Figure 7.8: Classful Addressing System

As per the diagram in *Figure 7.8*, the number of class A networks is much smaller than that of class C. However, each class A network can hold massive amounts of host devices per network compared to class C.

These IP addresses were originally assigned strictly according to **classful** network design architecture. However, this approach came with severe limitations, such as the inability to create custom network sizes. With the scarcity of public IP addresses, classful network design proved inefficient. For instance, a small company might only need one public IP address to enable its internal network of users to access the Internet via a NAT device. With classful networks, they would be compelled to be assigned a Class C address at a minimum, providing the business with 254 public IP addresses, which represents a complete waste of this scarce resource.

An alternative solution that was devised is the **classless interdomain routing system** (**CIDR**), which allows you to build custom network sizes and subnetworks. Before looking at how custom network sizes can be built, it is essential to understand how these networks are created using the IP addressing system. For example, how can an IP address `192.168.6.8` be on a different network than `172.31.5.4`? This is all thanks to masking an IP address into a network portion and a host portion using Subnet Masks, which is the topic of the next section.

What are subnet masks?

A subnet mask is a 32-bit number like an IP address. However, subnet masks *mask* an IP address to determine which portion of an IP address belongs to the **network** and which portion belongs to the **hosts**. Ultimately, subnet masks are thus used to define network boundaries and the number of IP addresses per network. This allows you to use subnet masks to create standard classful networks, as previously discussed, as well as custom network sizes and sub-networks.

A subnet mask consists of **two parts**:

- **Network Portion** (set to **1s**) → Identifies the network
- **Host Portion** (set to **0s**) → Identifies the specific hosts within the network

The decimal notation of a subnet mask range is `255.0.0.0` to `255.255.255.255`. A logical `AND` operation is performed between an IP address and a chosen subnet mask to determine the network it belongs to. Devices on the same network using the same subnet mask can communicate with each other freely, whereas communication with other networks would require some form of traffic routing. This allows you to isolate traffic between different networks and enhance security.

The Class A, B, and C networks are created using a set of standard subnet masks. Based on earlier discussion, you would guess that the IP address `10.0.0.5` belongs to a Class A network, since the first octet '10' falls within the 0–127 IP address range. However, using subnet masks, you can define an IP address such as `10.0.0.5` as part of a Class B network instead. This is achieved by using an appropriate subnet mask to mask off the first two octets for the network portion and the remaining two octets to represent the host portion, which, as you now know, is a standard Class B configuration.

For example, take the IP address `10.0.0.5`. If you associate it with a subnet mask of `255.255.0.0`, it technically falls within a Class B network, as depicted in the following diagram in *Figure 7.9*:

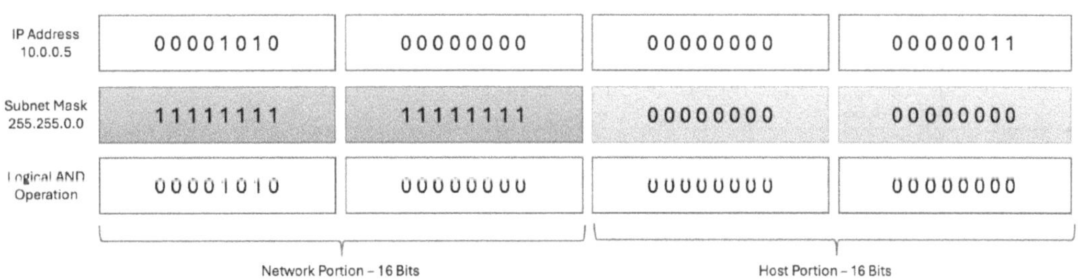

Figure 7.9: IP address and subnet mask conversion for 10.0.0.5

A logical `AND` operation is calculated using the following process:

- A '0' and '0' equals '0'
- A '0' and '1' equals '0'

- A '1' and '0' equals '0'
- A '1' and '1' equals '1'

Based on the results of the logical AND operation in *Figure 7.9*, you will note that if any of the first two octets of the IP address were to change, this would yield a different result for the logical AND operation block. So, for example, if the IP address were to change from `10.0.0.5` to `15.0.0.5`, the logical AND operation would result in a different sequence of binary numbers as depicted in *Figure 7.10*:

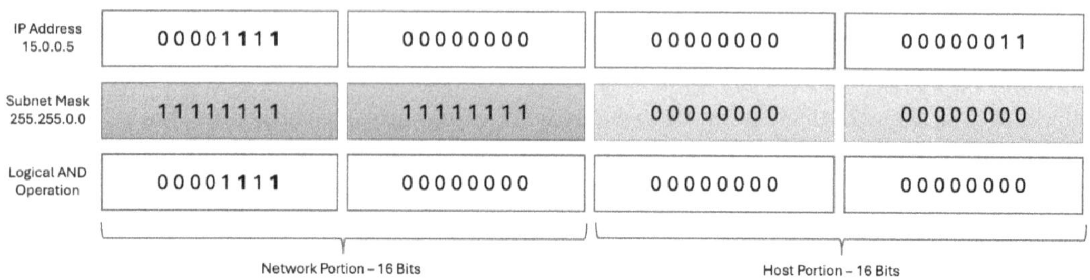

Figure 7.10: IP address and subnet conversion for IP 15.0.0.5

Since the first two octets represent the network portion because of the subnet mask, the resulting change in the first block of the logical AND operation would effectively denote a different network compared to the previous `10.0.0.5` IP address in *Figure 7.10*.

Furthermore, because the host portion in the subnet mask is set to all zeros and is only represented by the last two octets (last 16 bits), any variation in these octets of the IP address will keep it within the same network.

For example, if you perform the same exercise for the IP address `15.0.0.32`, you will see that it is in the same network as the IP address `15.0.0.5`, as per *Figure 7.11*:

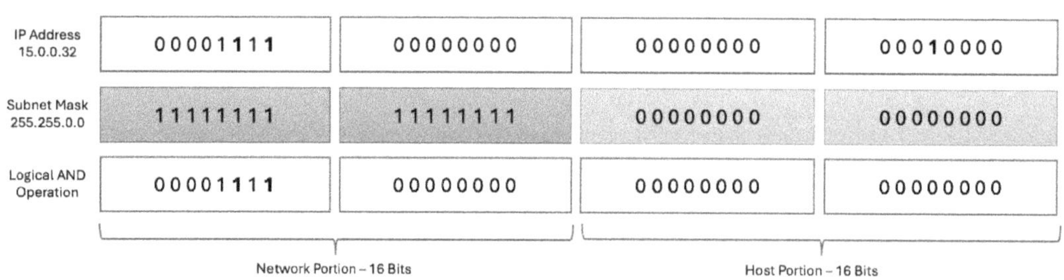

Figure 7.11: IP address and subnet conversion for IP 15.0.0.32

Comparing the logical AND operations, you will note that the sequence of binary numbers is the same for both *Figure 7.11* and *7.10*, proving that the IP addresses `15.0.0.5` and `15.0.0.32` belong to the same network defined by the subnet mask of `255.255.0.0`.

Now, while subnet masks can help define different network sizes and identify which IPs belong to which network, often you may wish to divide a larger network into small *sub-networks*, as previously discussed in the section 'Basic Corporate Networks' and depicted in *Figure 7.2*. To achieve this, you would use subnet masks to divide existing networks further into small networks through a process known as **subnetting**, which will be discussed in the next section.

What is subnetting?

Previously, you used fixed-length subnet masks to mask off portions of your IP address to define network and host portions. You would mask off the first octet of the IP address for a Class A network, the first two octets for a Class B network, and the first three octets for a Class C network. So, for a class A network, you could use the subnet mask `255.0.0.0` to mask off the first octet of your IP address for the network portion. Any changes in the first octet of an IP address would yield a different network. For example, when using a subnet mask of `255.0.0.0`, the IP address `10.0.0.0` is on a different network than `31.0.0.0`.

Subnetting is a process by which you can use a subnet mask to divide a more extensive network into smaller *subnetworks (subnets)*. This is particularly useful when you have different workload types that need to be isolated from each other, or you want to reduce broadcast traffic, allowing only permitted network connections between these workloads. For example, you have a more extensive corporate network and want subnetworks for your backend databases, frontend web servers, and a network for your employee workforce.

Subnetting involves *borrowing* bits from the host portion of an IP address range to create these smaller subnetworks. These borrowed bits effectively enable you to create subsets of your larger primary network. The subnetworks are therefore part of the larger primary network, but traffic between the subnetworks can be restricted to ensure isolation of workloads, enhance security, and ensure operational efficiency.

Take the example of a business that needs eight subnetworks, each capable of hosting 30 IP addresses for a maximum of 30 devices per network. The company could use a standard Class C IP address range of `192.168.0.0`, with a subnet mask of `255.255.255.0`. The resulting eight networks could be:

- **Network 1**: 192.168.1.0 (subnet mask: 255.255.255.0)
- **Network 2**: 192.168.2.0 (subnet mask: 255.255.255.0)
- **Network 3**: 192.168.3.0 (subnet mask: 255.255.255.0)
- **Network 4**: 192.168.4.0 (subnet mask: 255.255.255.0)
- **Network 5**: 192.168.5.0 (subnet mask: 255.255.255.0)
- **Network 6**: 192.168.6.0 (subnet mask: 255.255.255.0)

- **Network 7**: 192.168.7.0 (subnet mask: 255.255.255.0)
- **Network 8**: 192.168.8.0 (subnet mask: 255.255.255.0)

The eight networks defined would fulfill this requirement for the business, giving eight individual networks for its various workloads. However, each network can host up to 254 devices using a standard Class C configuration. The total number of IP addresses in each network is 256 (2^8, given that eight bits in the last octet are reserved for host IPs in a Class C configuration).

> **Note**
>
> Recall that you can only host 254 devices, even though there are 256 IP addresses in total in a Class C network, because the first and last IP addresses cannot be used. The first IP address of any network is the network ID, and the last IP address is reserved for broadcast traffic.

This may not be an issue when using private IP address ranges, but applying the same approach to the limited number of public IP addresses creates a lot of wastage. Furthermore, most internet service providers (ISPs) and cloud providers charge a fee for public IP addresses.

To illustrate how subnetting works, consider a network built with the IP address range of `192.168.1.0` and a subnet mask of `255.255.255.0`. The following diagram in *Figure 7.13* illustrates this class C network and its binary representation.

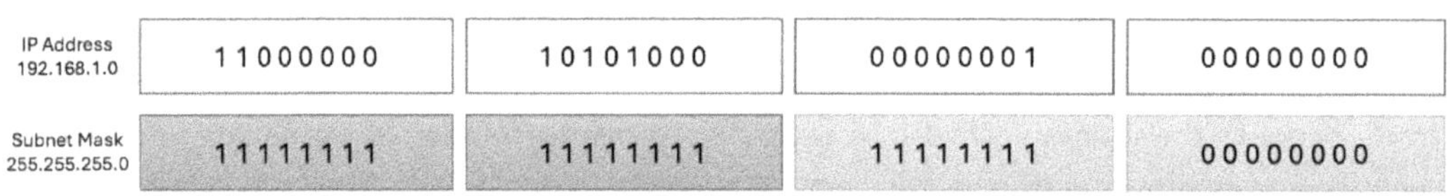

Figure 7.12: IP Address Class C Network

This network has 256 IP addresses and can host 254 devices. However, the business requires eight subnetworks, each with a capacity to host up to 30 devices. The IP address range `192.168.1.0` can be further divided into subnetworks by borrowing bits from the fourth octet (the host portion) to represent the subnetworks that fall within the original Class C network.

If you were to borrow just three bits from the far left of the fourth octet (the host portion), you could create eight subnetworks within the `192.168.1.0` larger network. The following formula derives this:

Number of subnets = 2 ^ (number of host bits borrowed)

In this example, 2^3 = 8, giving you eight subnetworks as the business requires. By borrowing 3 bits, you now have 5 bits left to represent the host portion. This will define the total number of IP addresses available in each subnetwork. This number can be calculated using the formula:

Number of IP addresses per subnetwork = 2 ^ (Number of host bits remaining)

In this example, 2^5 = 32, each of the eight subnetworks can have a maximum of 32 IP addresses. Remember that for every network, you have one IP address reserved for the network ID and one IP address for the broadcast IP. Thus, the total number of usable IP addresses for host devices is 30 (32 - 2).

Note that when borrowing bits from the host portion of the IP range, you have a different subnet mask than the original network. This is illustrated in *Figure 7.13*:

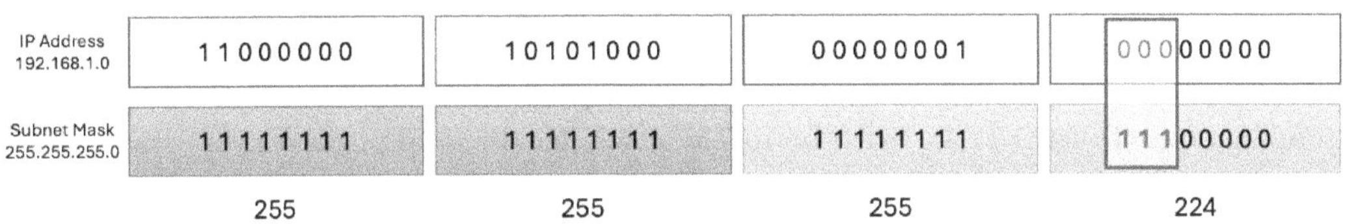

Figure 7.13: Subnet mask of new subnetworks created

Using a subnet mask of `255.255.255.224`, derived from the fact that you have borrowed three bits to represent the network, you create eight subnetworks within the more extensive Class C network, which has a subnet mask of `255.255.255.0`.

Figure 7.14 illustrates the binary representation of the eight networks created using a subnet mask of `255.255.255.224` and showcases the starting IP addresses of each:

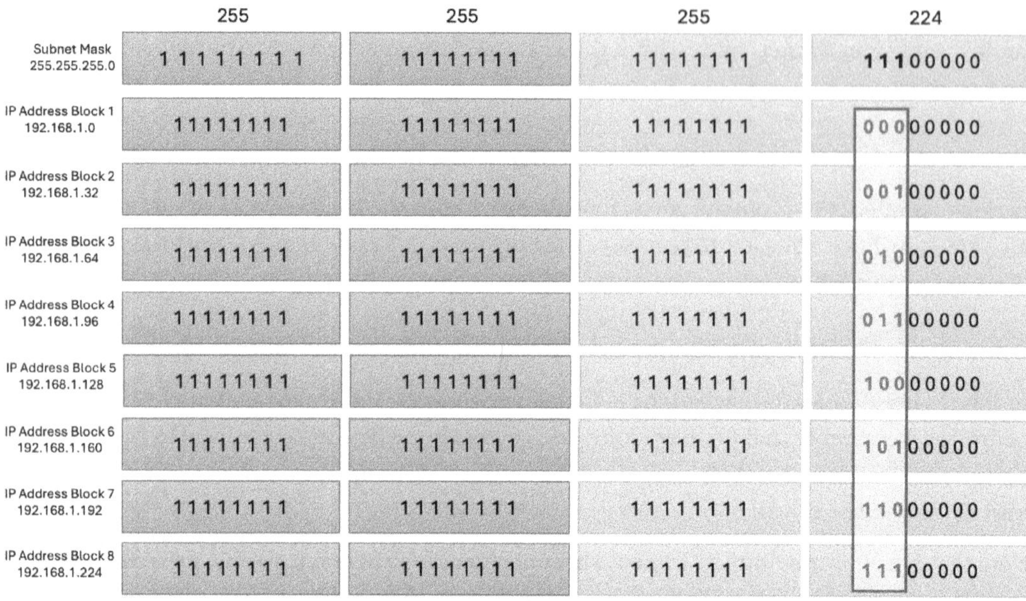

Figure 7.14: Creation of eight subnetworks

Note the pattern difference in each of the IP blocks depicted in binary. The different combinations of *ones* and *zeros* in the borrowed bits define the eight possible networks when using only three bits from the fourth octet to create subnetworks. Furthermore, each of the IP blocks representing a subnetwork consists of 30 usable IP addresses as per the following:

- **Network 1**: 192.168.1.0 (IP Addresses: 192.168.1.0 to 192.168.1.31)
- **Network 2**: 192.168.1.32 (IP Addresses: 192.168.1.32 to 192.168.1.63)
- **Network 3**: 192.168.1.64 (IP Addresses: 192.168.1.64 to 192.168.1.95)
- **Network 4**: 192.168.1.96 (IP Addresses: 192.168.1.96 to 192.168.1.127)
- **Network 5**: 192.168.1.128 (IP Addresses: 192.168.1.128 to 192.168.1.159)
- **Network 6**: 192.168.1.160 (IP Addresses: 192.168.1.160 to 192.168.1.191)
- **Network 7**: 192.168.1.192 (IP Addresses: 192.168.1.192 to 192.168.1.223)
- **Network 8**: 192.168.1.224 (IP Addresses: 192.168.1.224 to 192.168.1.255)

Using the subnet mask, you can also identify which network a particular IP address in the range belongs to. For example, the IP Address `192.168.1.130` would be part of the `192.168.1.28` network with a subnet mask of `255.255.255.224`. This is made clearer when you examine the binary representation of the IP address `192.168.1.130` and perform a logical AND operation with the subnet mask as depicted in *Figure 7.15*:

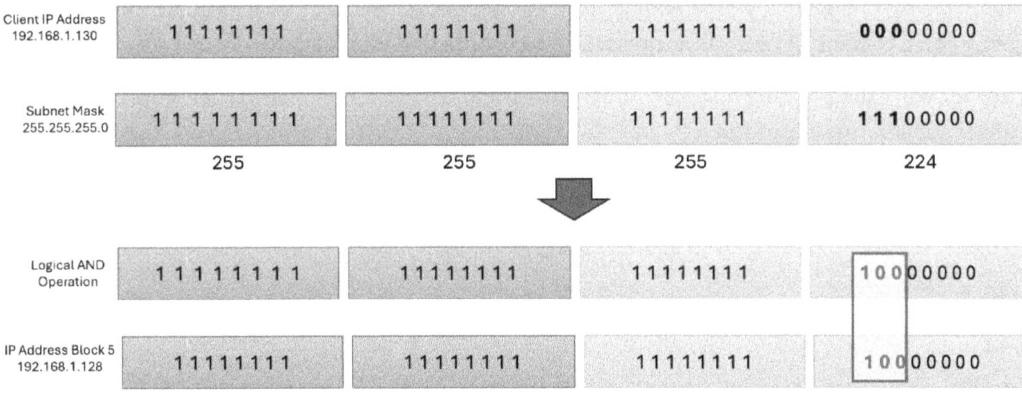

Figure 7.15: Illustrating how IP address 192.168.1.130 falls within the IP address block 5 network

The binary representation of the IP address `192.168.1.130` falls within the IP Address Block 5 network as illustrated through the binary pattern in the diagram.

Using a subnet mask, you can define multiple networks and subnet networks. However, the process is cumbersome as per the discussion so far. Another method of determining network sizes and the number of IPs hosted per network is to use a **CIDR** (**Classless Interdomain Routing**) notation. This is discussed in the next section.

Classless Inter-Domain routing

Using CIDR notations, you can easily define networks of different sizes just as you use subnet masks. Network devices convert the CIDR notation into the subnet mask for your subnet. **CIDR notations** use a suffix (`/n`) to indicate the number of bits used for the network portion of an IP address. So, for example, `192.168.1.0/24` means that you are using 24 bits out of the 32-bit range to represent the network. This is the same as using the first three octets or a subnet mask of `255.255.255.0`, which is a Class C network.

Furthermore, given that /24 indicates the number of network bits, the remaining 8 bits (32 - 24) define the total number of IP addresses you can have in that network. This is calculated as 2 ^ 8, which equals 256. Remember that a network's first and last IP addresses are reserved for network ID and broadcast; you have 254 usable IP addresses.

Most modern devices allow you to define networks and IP ranges using this CIDR notation, which is much easier to handle. Furthermore, you can easily define variable-length subnet masks with CIDR. So, in the earlier example of the IP address `192.168.1.0` with a subnet mask of `255.255.255.224`, you are borrowing 3 bits from the fourth octet. The CIDR notation for the same network would be `192.168.1.0/27` (24 bits from the first three octets plus three bits borrowed from the fourth) for the subnetworks. Working out the number of subnetworks is calculated by taking 2^3, which equals eight subnetworks. Finally, you have 5 bits remaining, giving you a total of 32 (2^5) IP addresses or 30 usable IP addresses.

The following diagram in *Figure 7.17* illustrates standard CIDR blocks and their equivalent subnet mask representations:

CIDR NOTATION	SUBNET MASK	NUMBER OF HOSTS (USABLE)
/30	255.255.255.252	2
/29	255.255.255.248	6
/28	255.255.255.240	14
/27	255.255.255.224	30
/24	255.255.255.0	254
/16	255.255.0.0	65,534

Figure 7.16: Standard CIDR notation and equivalent subnet masks

CIDR notations and subnet masks both define network boundaries, but CIDR is more than just an alternative notation for subnet masks. CIDR is a broader concept that includes both **subnetting** and **route aggregation**, which is also known as **supernetting**. CIDR allows ISPs to summarize multiple networks into one route, reducing the size of global routing tables. For example, instead of advertising `192.168.0.0/24`, `192.168.1.0/24`, and `192.168.2.0/24`, an ISP can summarize them as `192.168.0.0/22`.

Now that you have learned about the fundamentals of networks, IP addressing, subnet masks, and CIDRs, it's time to look at how to design and build virtual networks in the cloud. Many AWS services require you to provide them within isolated networks you define, enabling you to apply firewall rules to dictate what type of traffic is allowed into those networks. This is where the AWS **Virtual Private Cloud** (**VPCs**) come in, and is the topic of the next section.

Building virtual networks with Amazon VPC

A **Virtual Private Cloud** (**VPC**) is a virtual network within your AWS account that enables you to isolate and manage workloads efficiently. You can create multiple VPCs, each dedicated to a specific application stack. For instance, one VPC could host a customer loyalty application, including all necessary resources such as compute, storage, networking, and databases, while another VPC supports an internal business intelligence tool. This segmentation enhances security and ensures compliance by isolating workloads.

When you create a VPC, it spans the entire AWS region where it is deployed. This allows resources within the VPC to be distributed across multiple availability zones using the subnets you define. Since subnets operate at the availability zone level, you can deploy redundant application components across zones to ensure high availability. As shown in *Figure 7.17*, resources within a VPC can communicate seamlessly over AWS's high-speed network, even if they physically reside in different subnets that belong to that VPC. This is possible because all subnets within a VPC share the same IP address CIDR block.

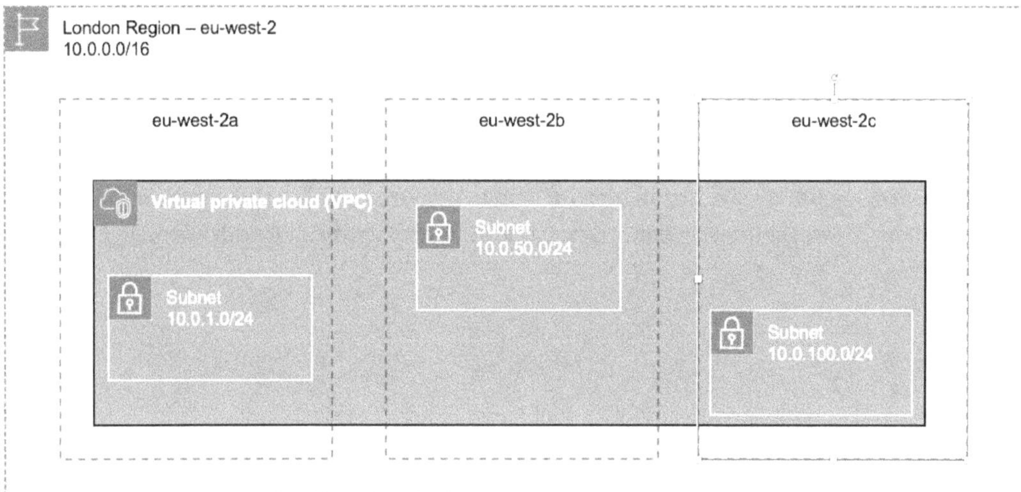

Figure 7.17: VPCs span entire regions, and subnets span specific availability zones

These subnets are logically part of the same VPC but are physically hosted on hardware located in different data centers across multiple availability zones. The ability to create such logical networks over distances, enabled by high-speed links and network connectivity, ensures redundancy in the event of an availability zone failure.

For example, suppose you host a replica of your application across these subnets, and the availability zone `eu-west-2a` experiences an outage. In that case, customers can still access the application servers running in the other two subnets, which are physically located in the remaining availability zones.

Subnets can be either private or public. Public subnets allow you to host resources that can be assigned public IP addresses and made directly accessible from the Internet. These typically include resources you want to expose publicly, such as a management server for remote access or a load balancer. In contrast, private subnets restrict direct inbound Internet access. However, resources in a private subnet can still access the Internet through a **Network Address Translation** (**NAT**) service, which is discussed in detail in a later section.

The following section provides a detailed explanation of how to configure your VPC for Internet access.

Internet access

VPCs can be configured with Internet access, allowing you to publish applications and make them accessible to end users or customers on the Internet. To enable Internet access for your VPC, you must deploy an **Internet Gateway** (**IGW**)—a highly available, AWS-managed service. Additionally, you need to configure the **route tables** to ensure that traffic from the VPC destined for the Internet is directed to the Internet Gateway.

As depicted in *Figure 7.18* and discussed earlier, a VPC can be configured with **public subnets** with a direct route to the Internet Gateway via an associated route table. You will note that the route table has a route to the Internet referenced as the IP CIDR 0.0.0.0/0; its target is the **Internet Gateway** (**IGW**). This configuration allows resources within these subnets to connect to the Internet. However, these resources must be assigned a **public IP address** or an **Elastic IP** (**EIP**).

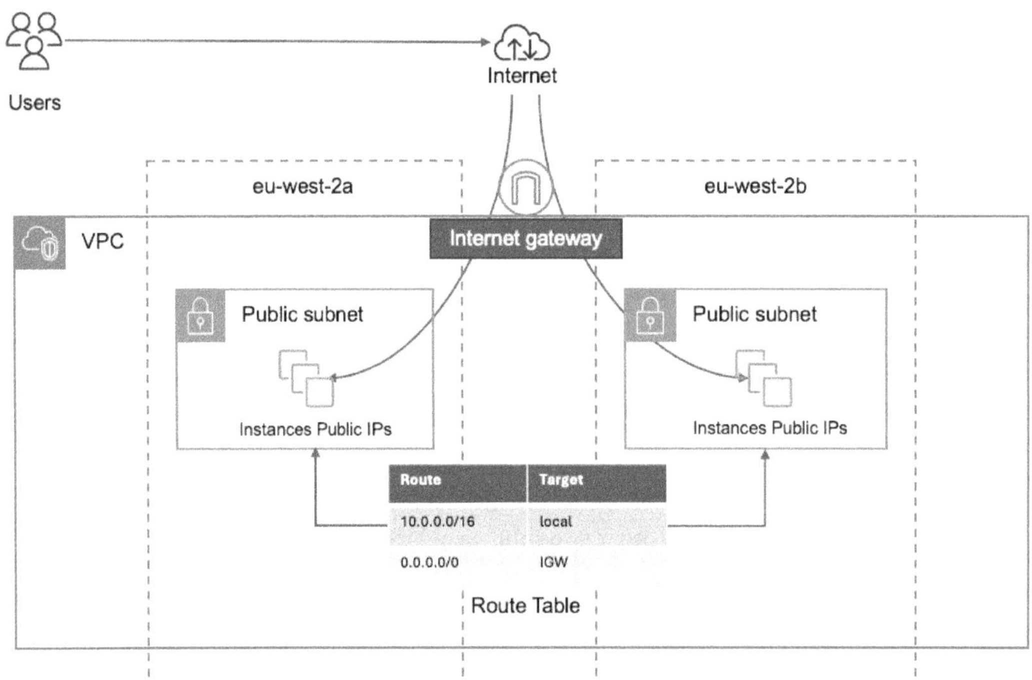

Figure 7.18: Enable internet access for VPCs

An **Elastic IP** (**EIP**) is a static, public IPv4 address you can allocate and associate with an instance in your VPC. Unlike a standard public IP, which changes if the instance is stopped and restarted, an EIP remains constant until you manually release it. This makes EIPs useful for applications that require a fixed public IP address, such as hosting services or failover scenarios. However, AWS charges for EIPs, so it's best to release any that are not actively used.

The **Internet Gateway** acts as a bridge, allowing resources with public IPs to send and receive traffic directly from the Internet. The gateway enables responses to reach the intended resource by maintaining the mapping between its public and private IP addresses.

In addition to resources in public subnets, you may have resources in **private subnets** that also need Internet access—for example, to download software updates or critical patches. These resources do not have a public IP since they must remain private while still being able to reach the Internet. This setup is similar to how a typical home network works: devices like laptops and desktops do not have public IP addresses but can still access the Internet via a home router or modem. This capability is made possible through a service known as **Network Address Translation** (**NAT**), which is the focus of the next section.

Network address translation (NAT)

At the beginning of this chapter, you discovered how corporate networks are divided into smaller subnetworks. In AWS, when you build VPCs, you deploy certain specific resources in public subnets, also known as the **DMZ**, while others are placed in **private subnets** for security. By deploying resources in a private subnet, you ensure they are not directly accessible from the Internet. These resources include database servers and application servers, which should only be accessible through frontend web servers or load balancers. This setup ensures that any traffic to backend services is proxied through frontend web servers, preventing direct exposure to the Internet.

However, some application servers in private subnets still require Internet access, for example, to download software updates, security patches, or product updates. Since these servers do not have public IP addresses, you need a mechanism to allow outbound Internet access. This is where **Network Address Translation** (**NAT**) comes in.

As illustrated in *Figure 7.19*, the NAT service acts as an intermediary, allowing resources in private subnets to access the Internet without being directly exposed. AWS provides the NAT Gateway, which must be deployed in a public subnet and assigned an Elastic IP address. Outbound traffic from private subnet resources is forwarded to the NAT Gateway, which then routes the traffic to the Internet.

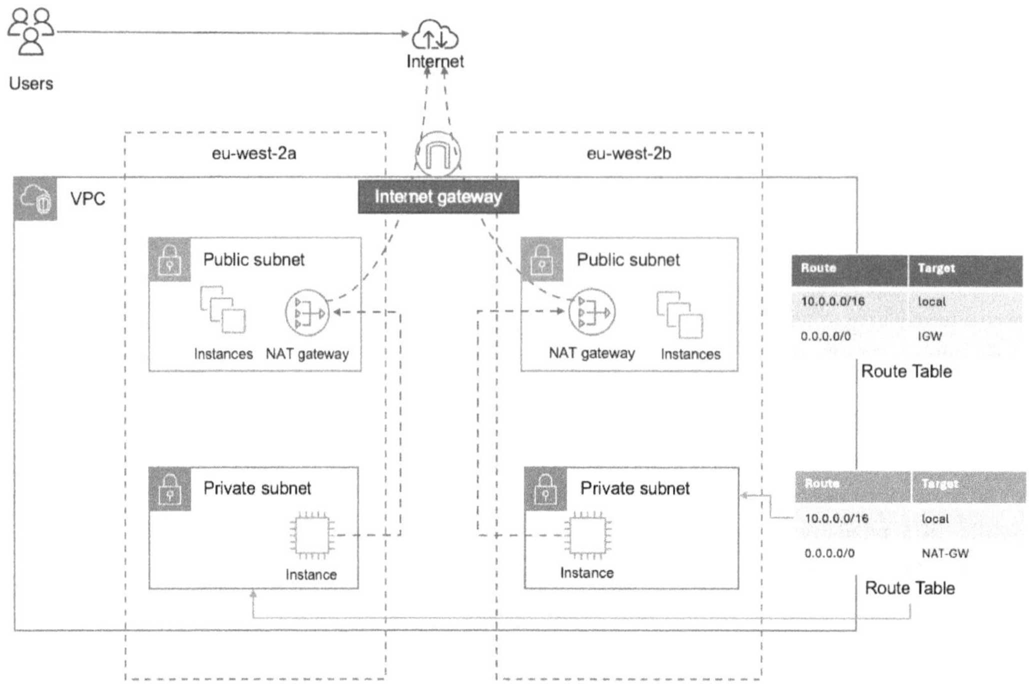

Figure 7.19: Internet access for resources in private subnets via NAT gateway

To enable this process, you must configure the route table for the private subnets to direct Internet-bound traffic to the NAT Gateway instead of the Internet Gateway. The NAT Gateway performs a one-to-many mapping, translating requests from multiple instances' private IP addresses to its public IP address before forwarding them to the Internet. When responses are received, the NAT Gateway relays them back to the original requesting instance in the private subnet.

While Internet Gateways and NAT Gateways enable you to provide Internet access to resources in your VPC, you must also consider what type of traffic you allow inbound and outbound from your VPC. Restricting traffic to only what is required for your application's specific use case is critical in preventing malicious attacks. VPC security is discussed in the next section.

Securing VPC traffic

When configuring your VPC, AWS provides multiple security features to control the flow of traffic into, out of, and within your cloud network. These features help ensure that only authorized traffic reaches your applications and resources.

For instance, you may allow inbound traffic to your web servers from the internet on port 80 (HTTP) and/or port 443 (HTTPS). HTTPS ensures encrypted connections to your web servers.

Once a request reaches the web server, it may need to communicate with a backend MySQL database to store and retrieve data. You can allow traffic from the web servers to the database on port 3306 (MySQL's default port) to enable this. By restricting access to only approved sources—such as the web servers—you prevent unauthorized resources inside and outside the VPC from connecting directly to the database.

AWS provides two key firewall services to help secure your VPC: **Security Groups** and **Network Access Control Lists** (**NACLs**), discussed in the following subsections.

Security groups

Security Groups act as virtual firewalls that control inbound and outbound traffic at the resource level. They are primarily used with resources such as EC2 instances, Lambda functions, ECS containers, and RDS database instances, all requiring a network interface to communicate within a VPC, other networks, or the internet.

As shown in *Figure 7.20*, a Security Group is associated with a resource's network interface, allowing you to specify which traffic (ports and protocols) is permitted for both inbound and outbound communication. Since every resource has at least one primary network interface, you must attach one Security Group to define the allowed traffic flows.

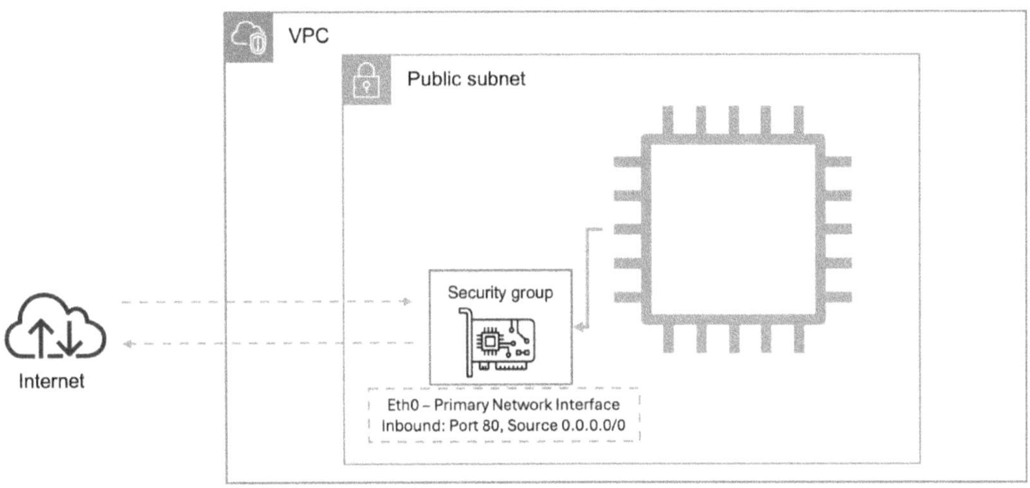

Figure 7.20: Security group associated with EC2 instance

The diagram showcases an inbound rule that allows traffic on port 80 (HTTP) from the Internet. This would allow users on the Internet to access your website hosted on this server. You can have up to five security groups associated with an instance.

Each VPC has a default Security Group that allows inbound connectivity from itself on all protocols and ports. This is a default setting that ensures multiple resources, such as EC2 instances attached to the default group, can communicate with each other on any port.

Security Groups act as stateful firewalls, meaning that if you define an outbound rule to allow access to the internet on ports 80 and 443, the responses to those requests will automatically be allowed inbound. Conversely, suppose you define an inbound rule to allow users from the internet to access a web server on port 80, as shown in *Figure 7.20*. In that case, the corresponding outbound responses are automatically permitted.

Security Groups operate on a **deny-by-default** principle, meaning you must define inbound rules before any traffic can reach the resources attached to the Security Group. Additionally, **explicit deny rules cannot be configured**.

For example, if you allow inbound traffic from the entire internet (`0.0.0.0/0`) on a specific port, you **cannot** then deny inbound traffic on port 80 from a specific IP address range. If you need to block traffic from a particular source explicitly, you must use NACLs, which are discussed in the next section.

Network access control lists (NACLs)

Network Access Control Lists (NACLs) act as firewalls at the subnet level, allowing you to define exactly what traffic is permitted into and out of a subnet. Within the subnet, resources have Security Groups attached to them for additional traffic restrictions at the resource level.

NACLs are often considered a secondary firewall solution, providing an additional layer of security alongside Security Groups. By default, AWS creates a default NACL that allows all inbound and outbound traffic. However, organizations typically create custom NACLs that deny all traffic by default and then explicitly define which ports and protocols are allowed inbound and outbound.

NACLs are particularly useful when different types of resources exist within a subnet, ensuring only permitted traffic flows in and out.

Unlike Security Groups, NACLs support explicit deny rules. This is possible due to the way NACLs process traffic:

- Inbound and outbound rules are evaluated in order, based on rule numbers (lower numbers have higher priority)
- As shown in *Figure 7.21*, an inbound rule numbered **50** denies traffic from a specific IP CIDR block (192.168.5.0/24) on port 443

Inbound rules (3)

Filter inbound rules

Rule number	Type	Protocol	Port ra...	Source	Allow/Deny
50	HTTPS (443)	TCP (6)	443	192.168.5.0/24	Deny
100	HTTPS (443)	TCP (6)	443	0.0.0.0/0	Allow
*	All traffic	All	All	0.0.0.0/0	Deny

Figure 7.21: Example NACL inbound rules

- However, a higher-numbered rule (**100**) allows inbound traffic on port 443 from the entire internet
- This configuration enables general internet users to access the website on port 443 while blocking devices from the specified IP CIDR range from reaching the web server

You will also notice a catch-all entry with the rule numbered as a wildcard (*****). This rule denies all other types of traffic, ensuring that only traffic on port 443 (HTTPS) will be permitted inbound.

A key feature of Network Access Control Lists (NACLs) is that they are **stateless**. Unlike **Security Groups**, which automatically allow return traffic, **NACLs require explicit inbound and outbound rules** for bidirectional traffic flow. If you allow inbound traffic, you must also define a corresponding outbound rule to permit the response traffic.

You can create multiple VPCs in your AWS account across all regions. Sometimes, you may wish to have resources in these VPCs communicate with each other. While this can be done via the Internet Gateway, you should also ensure that communications between VPCs do not traverse the public Internet. This can be achieved by using a feature known as VPC Peering, which is the topic of the next section.

Connecting VPCs with VPC peering

A VPC peering connection is a private network link between two VPCs, allowing resources in one VPC to access those in another. Peering connections can be within the same region or across regions, enabling organizations to build global-scale network architectures. This is especially useful for data sharing across regions, whether for **disaster recovery** (**DR**) purposes or to bring resources closer to end customers in a distributed setup.

While AWS manages the underlying infrastructure to ensure high availability and fault tolerance, users must manually configure peering connections, update route tables, and adjust NACLs and Security Groups to allow traffic between the connected VPCs.

However, standard VPC peering has limitations. Each peering connection must be explicitly defined, meaning that if multiple VPCs need to communicate, each connection must be set up individually. As per the diagram in *Figure 7.22*, transitive routing is not supported, preventing traffic from automatically flowing between peered VPCs.

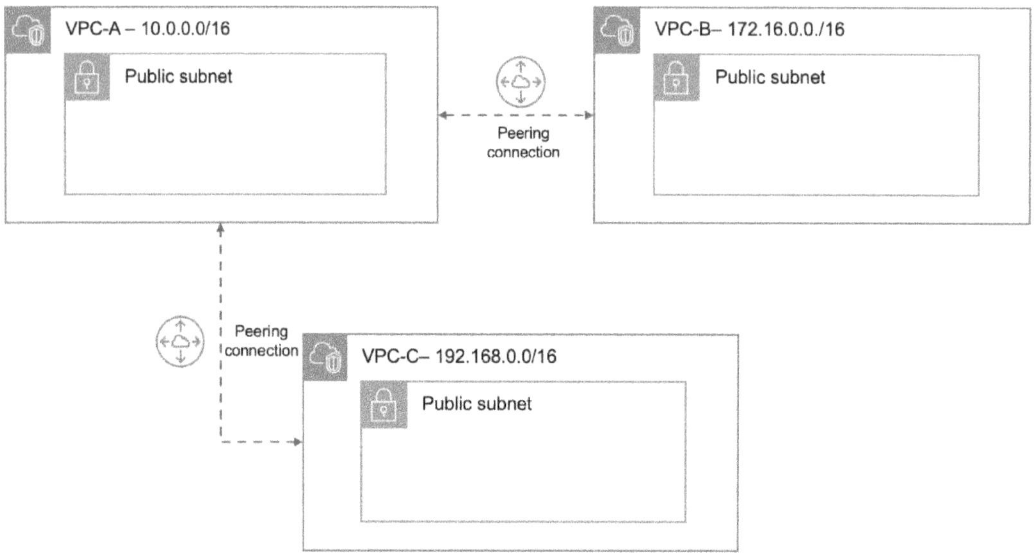

Figure 7.22: VPC peering configuration

In *Figure 7.22*, you can see that there is an explicit peering connection between VPC A and VPC B, as well as between VPC A and VPC C. However, it is important to note that even though VPC A is connected to both VPC B and VPC C, resources in VPC B cannot communicate with resources in VPC C unless there is a direct peering connection between them.

This requirement to define explicit peering connections can soon become very complex and add administrative overhead. As discussed in the next section, AWS offers another service to help address this.

Centralizing VPC connectivity with AWS Transit Gateway

AWS VPC Transit Gateway is designed to help connect multiple VPCs both within and across regions through a standard hub-and-spoke model. As depicted in *Figure 7.23*, this simplifies the network architecture as new VPCs peered to the gateway need just a single connection to route traffic to other VPCs in the configuration. Unlike VPC Peering, which requires direct connections between VPCs, Transit Gateway provides a high-performance, scalable interconnect with optimized routing.

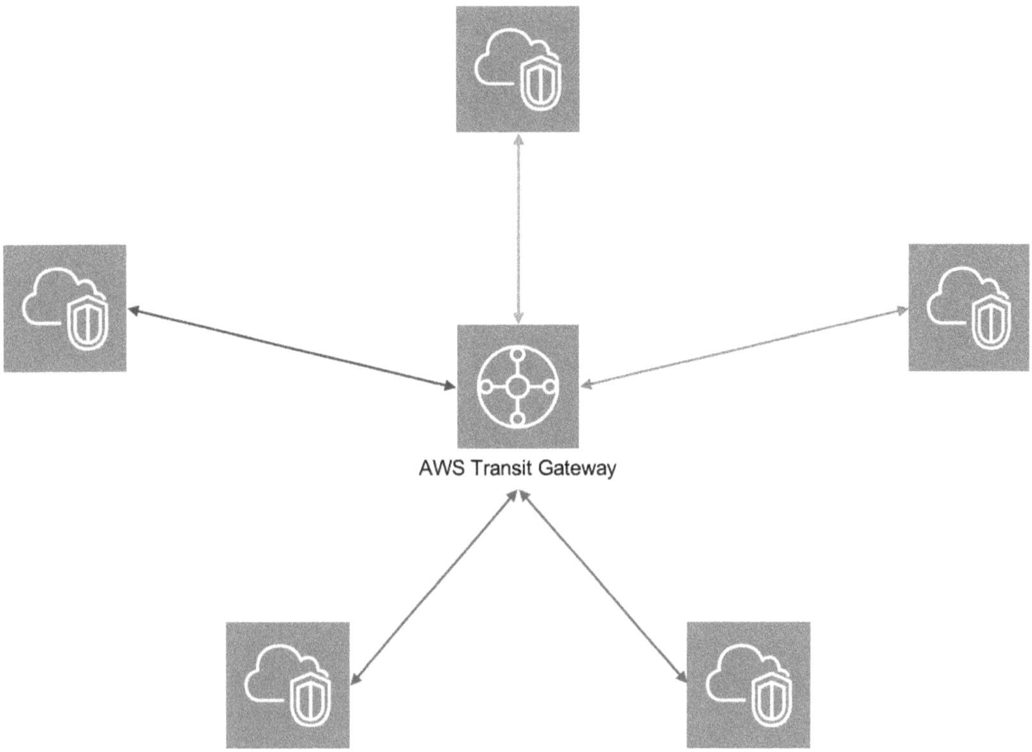

Figure 7.23: VPC transit gateway

Your VPC Transit Gateway can also be used to connect to an on-premises network, enabling you to easily access all other VPCs through it.

As well as enabling connectivity between VPCs, you may wish to connect to your VPC from on-premises locations and data centers. You must secure this connection, and this is where you can configure **Virtual Private Networks** (**VPNs**), which is discussed in the next section.

Securing hybrid connectivity with VPNs

Many companies need to securely connect to their AWS-hosted VPCs to carry out various tasks. While connecting over the Internet is an option, organizations often prefer a more secure connection, especially for backend operations. You can configure a **Virtual Private Network** (**VPN**) connection to facilitate this. This connection traverses the public Internet but secures data using AES-128 or AES-256-bit **Internet Protocol Security** (**IPSec**) encryption, ensuring that data transfers remain unreadable by unauthorized parties. Often referred to as establishing a secure VPN tunnel, this approach enhances overall security.

As depicted in *Figure 7.24*, you can set up a site-to-site VPN connection by configuring a VPN Gateway and attaching it to your VPC. Additionally, you must deploy a customer gateway, a hardware or software service located on the on-premises network that connects to the VPG over the Internet. Once the VPN connection is established, you must configure the necessary route table to ensure traffic is properly routed across the VPN connection.

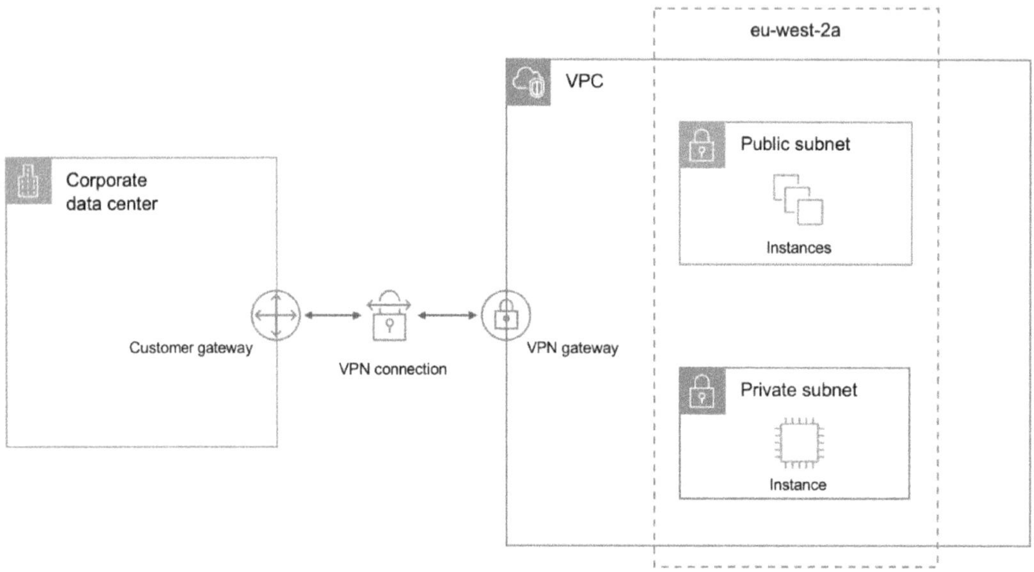

Figure 7.24: IPSec site-to-site VPN tunnel

IPSec VPN tunnels are designed to encrypt the traffic between the VPC and your on-premises data center. However, the bandwidth would be limited by your Internet connection from your on-premises location. Further, there is a hard limit set by AWS, which caps at 1.25 Gbps per tunnel. You can use the AWS Direct Connect service discussed in the next section if you require more bandwidth and a dedicated connection that bypasses the public Internet.

Connecting on-premises networks with AWS Direct Connect

Direct Connect is a service that enables you to connect your corporate data center to your VPC and other public services offered by AWS over a dedicated fiber optic network connection. This network connection is completely private and does not traverse the public Internet.

This solution is more expensive but helps address higher bandwidth requirements. With Direct Connect, you can configure dedicated connections offering speeds of 1, 10, or 100 Gbps.

While understanding the fundamentals of VPCs is essential, getting hands-on experience will help you build much-needed practical skills. The following section covers creating a VPC in your AWS account.

Project task 7 – Building a multi-tier network with Amazon VPC

In *Chapter 1*, it was discussed that Belly Brew Co. Limited needed a customer-facing web application, which would be used to advertise its wide range of products. The website must be capable of capturing current and potential customers' contact details, which can be used for marketing campaigns. To encourage viewers to part with their contact details, the website will offer a free recipe e-book for new sign-ups, and the contact details will be used to deliver free product trial vouchers regularly, which they can redeem at their favorite store.

In the following project exercise, you will build a VPC following best practices, which will be used in later chapters to host this web application. The VPC must meet strict security guidelines, ensuring only permitted traffic is allowed inbound. Furthermore, necessary security groups and NACLs must be configured to ensure that only authorized resources are allowed to update the database and provide a secure means to deliver the eBook.

The following diagram in *Figure 7.25* illustrates the core VPC architecture you will build for Belly Brew Co. Limited:

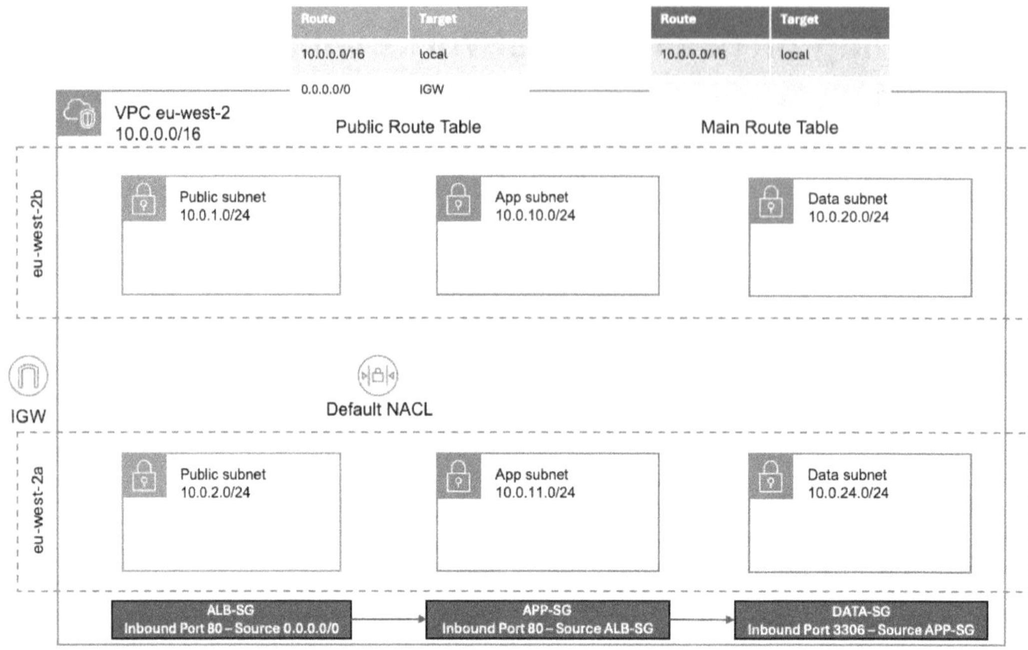

Figure 7.25: Belly Brew Co. Limited – VPC architecture

As part of this architecture, you will build a VPC with subnets spread across two availability zones to ensure redundancy and high availability in the London region. The following key components represent your VPC design:

- Each AZ will host three subnets:
    - One public subnet will be used to host public-facing resources such as load balancers. Load balancers are discussed in *Chapter 10*, and they enable you to accept incoming traffic from the Internet and then distribute it securely across internal web/app servers.
    - One pair of private subnets to host compute resources that will host your web application. These will be your *app* subnets.
    - A second pair of private subnets will host a backend database that will be used to capture visitors' contact details. These will be your data subnets.

  This architecture ensures that your web/app servers and your database servers are not directly exposed on the internet. Instead, incoming traffic needs to first reach your load balancers, which will be responsible for distributing that traffic evenly across multiple resources in the app subnet, across multiple AZs, as illustrated in *Figure 7.26*.

- Your VPC will be configured with an Internet Gateway to allow inbound and outbound access to the Internet.
- Your VPC will be configured with appropriate route tables and routes to direct traffic within the VPC and externally. Note that the Main Route Table in this chapter will not be configured with an Internet route. Instead, you will configure a NAT gateway in *Chapter 10*. This ensures you incur minimum charges, as the NAT gateway does not fall within the free tier offering. Don't worry; once you complete the project exercises in *Chapter 10*, you will delete the resources as part of a clean-up exercise.

Finally, you will configure your security groups to ensure that only authorized traffic from permitted sources can access your web application and backend database.

Technical requirements

To complete the project tasks in this chapter, ensure that you have completed all previous exercises in earlier chapters. Log in to your AWS Development account as the IAM user Alice to complete the project tasks.

Project task 7.1 – Creating a VPC

In this project task, you will create the base VPC architecture in the London region.

1. Log in to your AWS Development account as the IAM user Alice
2. From the search bar at the top of the management console, search for and navigate to the VPC service. You will be redirected to the **VPC dashboard**.
3. In the right-hand corner of the webpage, select **London** from the region drop-down list if you are not already in the London region
4. From the left-hand menu, select **Your VPCs**
5. In the right-hand pane, click the **Create VPC** button
6. Ensure that **VPC only** is selected under **Resources to create**, and then provide a name for your VPC in the text box labeled **Name tag – optional**. For example, you can name your VPC as `belly-brew-vpc`
7. Next, set the **IPv4 CIDR** to `10.0.0.0/16`
8. Leave all other settings at their default values and click the `Create VPC` button at the bottom of the webpage

Your VPC will now be created, and you will see a message on the webpage confirming the creation of the VPC with a unique ID. In the next project task, you will configure public and private subnets as discussed earlier.

Project task 7.2 – Creating subnets for your VPC

In this project task, you will create six subnets: two public subnets and four private subnets.

1. Ensure you are still logged into your AWS development account and in the VPC dashboard
2. From the left-hand menu, select **Subnets**
3. In the right-hand pane, click the **Create subnet** button
4. Select the VPC you created in *Project Task 7.1* from the **VPC** drop-down list
5. In the **Subnet settings** section, you will need to provide details for each subnet:
    a. For the **Subnet name**, provide a name for your public subnet, such as `belly-brew-vpc-public-sub-01`
    b. For the **Availability Zone**, select `eu-west-2a` from the drop-down list
    c. For the **IPv4 subnet CIDR block**, provide the CIDR (as depicted in Figure 7.26) for the first public subnet, which should be `10.0.1.0/24`. See the screenshot in *Figure 7.26*:

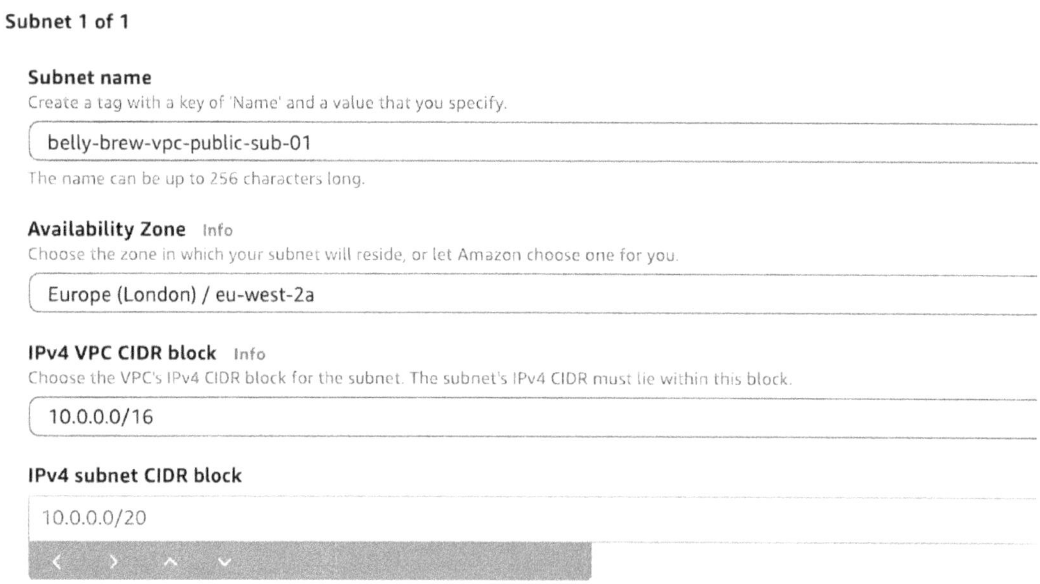

Figure 7.26: Creating subnets

6. Next, as you need to provide details for another five subnets, do not click the **Create subnet** button just yet. Instead, click the **Add new subnet** button at the bottom of the

webpage to define subnets for the second public subnet and the remaining four private subnets. Repeat *Step 5* for each of the rows in the following table:

Subnet name	Availability Zone	IPv4 subnet CIDR block
belly-brew-vpc-public-sub-02	eu-west-2b	10.0.2.0/24
belly-brew-vpc-app-sub-01	eu-west-2a	10.0.10.0/24
belly-brew-vpc-app-sub-02	eu-west-2b	10.0.11.0/24
belly-brew-vpc-data-sub-01	eu-west-2a	10.0.20.0/24
belly-brew-vpc-data-sub-02	eu-west-2b	10.0.21.0/24

Table 7.1: Subnet details for the Belly Brew VPC

7. Once you have all the subnets defined, click the **Create subnet** button at the bottom of the webpage

Your subnets will now be created, and you will see confirmation once they are complete. In the next project task, you will deploy an Internet gateway and attach it to the VPC.

Project task 7.3 – Creating an internet gateway

1. From the left-hand menu, select **Internet gateways**
2. In the right-hand pane, click the **Create internet gateway** button
3. Provide a name for the Internet gateway in the text box provided in the **Internet gateway settings** section. You can give a name like `belly-brew-vpc-igw`
4. Click the **Create internet gateway** button
5. You will be redirected to a page where you will see confirmation that the Internet gateway has been created. You must now attach it to the VPC. In the right-hand pane, click the **Actions** button and select **Attach to VPC**
6. Select the VPC you created in *Project Task 7.1* from the search box under **Available VPCs**
7. Click the **Attach internet gateway** button. Your Internet gateway will now be attached to the VPC, and you will receive a confirmation.

In the next project task, you will define route tables for public and private subnets.

Project task 7.4 – Configuring route tables

When you create a VPC, a default route table (main route table) is automatically created and associated with every subnet you create in the VPC. These route tables define routes that allow traffic to flow within the VPC across subnets and external networks, including the Internet. Because public and private subnets must be separated, you need to create separate route tables for your public subnets.

For this project task, you will create a route table for your public subnets, enabling resources to access the Internet directly via the Internet Gateway you created in *Project task 7.3*. You will then associate the private subnets with the main route table, which currently contains only a local route for internal communication. Later, in *Chapter 10*, when you deploy a NAT Gateway, you will add an indirect route to the Internet for internal resources in the main route table, using the NAT Gateway as the target for Internet access.

1. Ensure you are still logged into your AWS Development account and the VPC dashboard
2. From the left-hand menu, select **Route tables**
3. In the right-hand pane, you will notice two route tables, with the term 'Yes' in the **Main** column, as depicted in *Figure 7.27*. These are the *main route tables*: one for the default VPC, which is created in every region and one for the VPC you created in *Project Task 7.1*

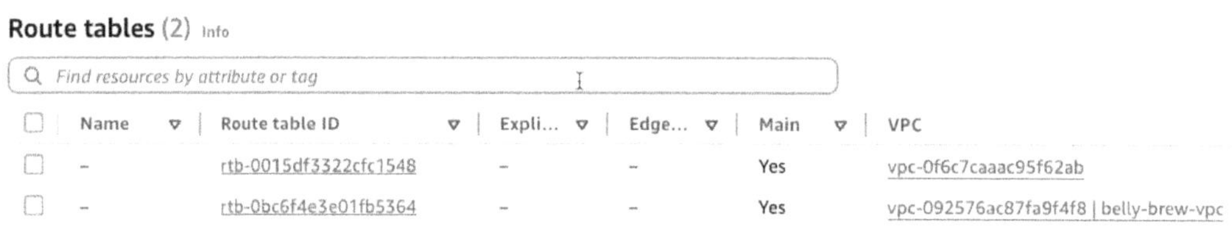

Figure 7.27: Main route tables

4. Notice which main route table belongs to your VPC by cross-referencing the VPC column. Use your mouse to hover over the **-** in the name column to get the option to edit the name of the routing table. Click on the pencil icon that appears to provide a name for your main route table. You can name the route table as `belly-brew-vpc-main-rt`. Doing so will allow you to identify the route table later easily.
5. Next, click the **Create route table** button
6. Provide a name for your public route table. You can name it.
7. Select the Belly Brew VPC you created in *Project Task 7.1* from the drop-down list, labeled VPC
8. Next, click the **Create route table** button at the bottom of the webpage. Your new route table will now be created and once done, you will be redirected to its details page.
9. While in the **belly-brew-vpc-public-rt** route table details page, click the **Routes** tab

10. Notice that there is only a single route: the local route. Click the **Edit routes** button.
11. In the webpage that appears, click the **Add route** button
12. For the **Destination**, type in `0.0.0.0/0` (this represents all external routes, including the Internet)
13. For the **Target**, select **Internet Gateway** and then click in the search box that appears to select the Internet gateway you created in *Project Task 7.3*, as per the screenshot in *Figure 7.28*:

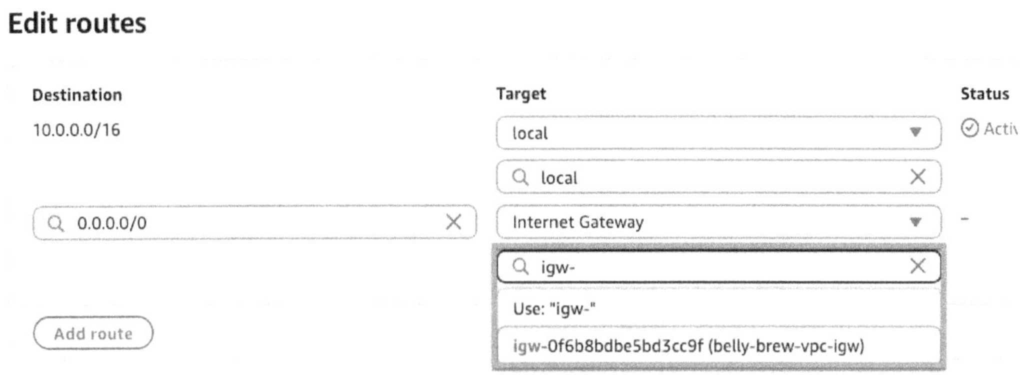

Figure 7.28: Editing routes in the public route table

14. Click the **Save changes** button. Your public route table will now be updated as depicted in the screenshot in *Figure 7.29*:

Figure 7.29: Updated public route table

15. Next, click the **Subnet associations** tab
16. Click the **Edit subnet associations** button in the **Explicit subnet associations** (0) section
17. From the available subnets, select both public subnets you created in *Project Task 7.2*
18. Click **Save associations**. You will see a confirmation that both public subnets have now been associated with the public route table.

Your public subnets have now been associated with the public route table. This table ensures that resources deployed in the public subnet can access the Internet directly via the Internet gateway. Those resources must have a public IP address, as previously discussed.

In the next project task, you will configure security groups for your application's three-tier architecture.

Project task 7.5 – Configuring security groups

In this project task, you will create three security groups to define how inbound traffic is allowed into your resources, which you will deploy in subsequent chapters. As per the illustration in *Figure 7.30*, you must ensure that only authorized resources can communicate with your backend resources.

Figure 7.30: Security groups

As depicted in *Figure 7.30*, traffic will be allowed inbound from the internet on port 80 (HTTP) to the load balancer, which you will deploy in Chapter 10. This is defined as part of the inbound rules created for the **ALB-SG** security group. This load balancer will then distribute the inbound request for your Belly Brew Co. Limited web application to the application servers you deploy in the App Subnets. The **APP-SG** security group attached to the application servers will ensure that only the load balancer can forward HTTP requests to it as specified in the Source configuration of that security group. Finally, the **DATA-SG** security group attached to your database instances will ensure that only the application servers can send traffic to it on port 3306, which is the default port for the MySQL database engine.

1. Ensure you are still logged into your AWS development account as the IAM user Alice, and in the VPC dashboard in the London region
2. From the left-hand menu, select **Security groups**
3. In the right-hand pane, click the **Create security group** button

4. You will be presented with the configuration page for a new security group. Provide a name for your Load Balancer's security group in the **Security group name** text box. You can provide a name like `belly-brew-vpc-alb-sg`.
5. Allow inbound traffic on port 80 from the Internet to Load Balancers
6. Ensure you select the Belly Brew VPC from the VPC drop-down list
7. Next, click the **Add rule** button in the **Inbound rules** section
8. For the rule Type, select **HTTP**
9. In the drop-down list under the **Source** column, select **Anywhere-IPv4**
10. Scroll a bit further down and click the **Add new tag** button in the **Tags – optional** section
11. Provide a key-value pair to label your security group. Set the **Key** to "Name" and the **Value** to "belly-brew-vpc-alb-sg". This will label the name of your security to easily identify it.
12. Scroll to the bottom of the webpage and click **Create Security Group**. You will get a confirmation stating that the security group was successfully created.

> **Note**
>
> You do not need to create any Outbound rules, as by default, all Outbound traffic is allowed.

Next, you will create a security group for the application servers:

1. From the left-hand menu, select **Security groups** again
2. In the right-hand pane, click the **Create security group** button
3. For the Security group name, provide a name like `belly-brew-vpc-app-sg`
4. Provide an appropriate description, such as "Allow inbound traffic on port 80 from Load Balancers"
5. Select the **Belly Brew VPC** from the VPC drop-down list
6. Click the **Add rule** button in the Inbound rules section
7. Select **HTTP** from the drop-down list in the **Type** column
8. Select **Custom** from the drop-down list in the **Source** column
9. From the search box next to Custom, make sure you select the load balancer security group you created following *Steps 2 to 12* earlier, as depicted in *Figure 7.31*:

Figure 7.31: Creating the application servers' security group

10. Scroll further down and click the **Add new tag** button in the **Tags – optional** section
11. Provide a key-value pair to label your security group. Set the **Key** to "Name" and the **Value** to "belly-brew-vpc-app-sg". This will label the name of your security to identify it easily.
12. Scroll to the bottom of the webpage and click **Create Security Group**. You will get a confirmation stating that the security group was successfully created. Next, you will create a security group for the database servers:
13. From the left-hand menu, select **Security groups** again
14. In the right-hand pane, click the **Create security group** button
15. For the **Security group name**, provide a name like `belly-brew-vpc-data-sg`
16. Provide an appropriate description, such as "Allow inbound traffic on port 3306 from App Servers"
17. Select the **Belly Brew VPC** from the **VPC** drop-down list
18. Click the **Add rule** button in the **Inbound rules** section
19. Select **MySQL/Aurora** from the drop-down list in the **Type** column. You will be deploying a MySQL database for the Belly Brew Co. Limited web application
20. Select **Custom** from the drop-down list in the **Source** column
21. From the search box next to **Custom**, select the application server security group you created following steps 14 to 24 earlier
22. Scroll further down and click the **Add new tag** button in the **Tags – optional** section
23. Provide a key-value pair to label your security group. Set the **Key** to `Name` and the **Value** to `belly-brew-vpc-data-sg`. This will label the name of your security to identify it easily.
24. Scroll to the bottom of the webpage and click **Create Security Group**. You will get a confirmation stating that the security group was successfully created.

Your security groups have now been created to ensure traffic is allowed only from authorized sources. In upcoming chapters, you will build on this architecture and use other AWS services to deploy a fully functional web application for Belly Brew Co. Limited.

The following section provides a summary of this chapter.

Summary

AWS Virtual Private Cloud is a service that enables you to build secure, isolated networks in your AWS account to host your application workloads. This allows you to separate workloads for various reasons, including compliance and security. A VPC spans an entire AWS region, enabling access to all **Availability Zones** (**AZs**) within that region to host your applications. You create subnets within specific AZs, allowing you to define subnetworks in the VPC when deploying your applications. This setup lets you host replica workloads across multiple subnets and AZs, enhancing high availability in case of an AZ outage.

Multiple VPCs within a region or across different regions can be connected using **VPC Peering**, which enables routing traffic between VPCs over AWS's private network. This reduces costs associated with internet traffic and enhances security. You can also host different components of your applications across multiple VPCs—for example, compute services in one VPC with a peering connection to another VPC hosting backend databases. This approach adds security layers by restricting access to specific VPCs based on administrative and engineering needs. For example, you might ensure that database administrators only have access to VPCs hosting databases while restricting access to web servers.

For more complex network connectivity, AWS offers the **VPC Transit Gateway**, which provides a hub-and-spoke model to connect multiple VPCs. This eliminates the need for individual peering connections, reducing operational complexity.

You can also connect your VPCs to on-premises locations using VPNs or AWS Direct Connect. The latter provides higher bandwidth and routes traffic over private networks, bypassing the public internet entirely.

Ultimately, VPCs are designed to help you build secure, private networks in the cloud, isolating workloads and ensuring that only authorized inbound and outbound traffic reaches your applications.

Exam Readiness Drill – Chapter Review Questions

Apart from mastering key concepts, strong test-taking skills under time pressure are essential for acing your certification exam. That's why developing these abilities early in your learning journey is critical.

Exam readiness drills, using the free online practice resources provided with this book, help you progressively improve your time management and test-taking skills while reinforcing the key concepts you've learned.

HOW TO GET STARTED

- Open the link or scan the QR code at the bottom of this page
- If you have unlocked the practice resources already, log in to your registered account. If you haven't, follow the instructions in *Free Benefits with Your Book* section in this book's *Preface* and come back to this page.
- Once you log in, click the START button to start this chapter's quiz
- We recommend attempting a quiz multiple times till you're able to answer most of the questions correctly and well within the time limit.
- You can use the following practice template to help you plan your attempts:

Working On Accuracy		
Attempt	**Target**	**Time Limit**
Attempt 1	40% or more	Till the timer runs out
Attempt 2	60% or more	Till the timer runs out
Attempt 3	75% or more	Till the timer runs out
Working On Timing		
Attempt 4	75% or more	1 minute before time limit
Attempt 5	75% or more	2 minutes before time limit
Attempt 6	75% or more	3 minutes before time limit

The above drill is just an example. Design your drills based on your own goals and make the most out of the online quizzes accompanying this book.

Link to this Chapter's Quiz

You need to unlock the online practice resources to access the link below. Check the *Free Benefits with Your Book* section in the *Preface* for detailed instructions on how to do this. You only need to unlock the resources once.

Open Quiz `https://packt.link/clf_c02_ch7`or scan the QR code

8

AWS Compute Services – EC2, Lightsail, ECS, EKS, and Lambda

At the core of every application lies a compute resource — the technology that powers computational processing and data operations. Computing capacity has evolved significantly over time. In the early days, this was provided by physical servers. A server is a computer or software system that delivers resources, services, or data to other computers, known as clients, over a network. However, physical servers had limited processing power, memory, and storage capacity. Due to these constraints—and challenges related to application compatibility, such as shared libraries and runtime environments—businesses typically dedicate a single physical server to each application. As a result, organizations maintained large banks of servers to support their various business applications, often requiring significant real estate, either on-premises or in co-located data centers, to accommodate their extensive infrastructure.

With the advent of virtualization and an increase in compute resources such as CPU (Central Processing Unit) capacity, memory, and storage, it was now possible to host multiple virtual machines (virtual servers) on a single physical host machine. This means that you can now run multiple applications on a single physical server, all isolated from each other within their own virtual machines. This avoided compatibility issues while reducing the overall footprint of physical hardware.

In this chapter, you will explore Amazon **Elastic Compute Cloud** (**EC2**). This service enables you to deploy virtual machines, providing the compute capacity needed to run applications ranging from simple websites to advanced artificial intelligence and data analytics workloads. Additionally, you will learn about other AWS compute services, including containerization, which offers a more efficient alternative to traditional virtual machines, and serverless architectures powered by event-driven compute services, which significantly reduce administrative overhead and provide a highly cost-effective solution.

The following topics are covered in this chapter:

- Understanding Amazon Elastic Compute Cloud
- Configuring EC2 instances with Amazon Machine Images
- Comparing EBS, instance store, EFS, and FSx storage options
- Choosing EC2 pricing options
- Deploying simple workloads with Amazon Lightsail
- Running containers with Amazon ECS and Amazon EKS
- Building event-driven applications with AWS Lambda
- Extending AWS compute to on-premises environments with AWS Outposts

Understanding Amazon Elastic Compute Cloud

Amazon Elastic Compute Cloud (**Amazon EC2**) is one of AWS's core service offerings, allowing you to launch virtual servers in the cloud. You can deploy servers running various operating systems, including a wide range of Linux distributions (such as Ubuntu, Red Hat, and Amazon Linux), Windows Server, and even macOS. Access to these virtual machines is provided at the operating system level, enabling you to configure the guest OS to suit your application's needs—install tools, manage patches, and perform upgrades.

Virtual machines run on virtualization software known as a **hypervisor**. You may be familiar with hypervisors in on-premises environments, such as VMware or Microsoft Hyper-V. Amazon EC2 instances run on a customized version of the Nitro Hypervisor. This customization minimizes overhead and offloads most virtualization tasks to dedicated hardware, allowing EC2 instances to achieve near-bare-metal performance.

Hypervisor software allows you to partition physical hardware into virtualized representations of physical components such as CPU, memory, and storage, presenting them as virtual machines—each isolated from the others and functioning as a complete server. In an on-premises environment, you can access the hypervisor layer to create virtual machines, select virtual components, and configure them to meet your specific requirements. For example, you might configure a virtual machine with two virtual CPU cores, 6GB of memory, and 1TB of root volume capacity. Each virtual machine hosts its own guest operating system, applications, and utilities as required, preventing conflicts due to compatibility issues.

With Amazon EC2, the underlying hypervisor is abstracted away from you. Instead, you access a self-service portal (or use the CLI) and choose from various configuration options, including CPU capacities, memory allocations, networking bandwidth, storage types, and operating systems. These EC2 instances are categorized into instance families, types, and sizes for easy selection and comparison.

For example, within the *general-purpose* family, several instance types provide different combinations of compute, memory, storage, and networking capacity. The M5 type, for instance, is powered by Intel Xeon® Platinum 8175M or 8259CL processors and is well-suited for modern applications. It offers up to 384 GiB of memory and supports a maximum network bandwidth of 25 Gbps with Enhanced Networking. On the other hand, the T2 type delivers a baseline level of CPU performance with burst capabilities when needed. It is designed for low-latency interactive applications, small to medium-sized databases, and product prototypes.

You also have instance sizes for each instance type—these define the amount of virtual CPU (vCPU), memory, supported storage type, maximum network bandwidth, and block storage EBS bandwidth. For example, the m5.large comes with 2 vCPUs, 8 GiB of memory, and up to 10 Gbps of network bandwidth. The m5.xlarge, on the other hand, offers 4 vCPUs and 16 GiB of memory. Your choice will be based on your application requirements.

The following screenshot in *Figure 8.1* depicts a small subset of the available instance sizes for the M5 instance type:

Instance Size	vCPU	Memory (GiB)	Instance Storage (GB)	Network Bandwidth (Gbps)	EBS Bandwidth (Mbps)
m5.large	2	8	EBS-Only	Up to 10	Up to 4,750
m5.xlarge	4	16	EBS-Only	Up to 10	Up to 4,750
m5.2xlarge	8	32	EBS-Only	Up to 10	Up to 4,750
m5.4xlarge	16	64	EBS-Only	Up to 10	4,750

Figure 8.1: Example instance sizes for the M5 instance type

AWS offers other EC2 instance families in addition to the general-purpose one, and these are listed as follows:

- **General purpose**: Designed for a balance of compute, memory, storage, and networking capacity and ideal for a wide range of application types.
- **Compute-optimized**: Designed for high-performance computing (HPC) and workloads like batch processing, media transcoding, and high-performing web servers.
- **Memory-optimized**: Designed for workloads that require large amounts of memory and workloads that process large data sets.

- **Accelerated computing**: These instances used hardware accelerators or co-processors to perform complex functions. They are ideal for floating-point number calculations, graphics processing, and data pattern matching.
- **Storage optimized**: These instances are designed for workloads that require high sequential read and write access to vast datasets and where low-latency, random I/O operations per second (IOPS) to applications are critical.

You will find the complete list of available instance families, types and their size offerings at `https://aws.amazon.com/ec2/instance-types/`. Depending on your application requirements, you must select the most appropriate instance to ensure performance levels and capabilities.

In addition to hardware resources, virtual machines—such as EC2 instances—require an **operating system** (**OS**) to serve as the interface between the hardware and software applications. The OS enables users to interact with the system and run applications. Common operating systems include Linux, macOS, and Microsoft Windows. You typically select an OS image to install when setting up a virtual machine in an on-premises environment. This image is often in the form of an ISO file, which contains all the necessary files for the OS installation on the VM. On AWS, this image file takes the form of an AMI (Amazon Machine Image), which is discussed in the next section.

Configuring EC2 instances with Amazon Machine Images

Amazon Machine Images (**AMIs**) are preconfigured templates or images that include the operating system and any additional software, configurations, or utilities required for your applications. AMIs are stored as snapshots in Amazon **Elastic Block Store** (**EBS**), like a **virtual hard disk** (**VHD**) image used in on-premises virtualization. They contain all the necessary system files, application data, and settings to launch an instance. Additionally, AMIs define block device mappings, specifying the storage volumes to be attached to an instance, and include access permissions that determine who can use the AMI.

AWS offers several pre-configured AMIs as part of its Quick Start AMIs, and these include many commonly used operating systems, including Ubuntu, Red Hat Linux, SUSE, and variations of the Microsoft Server operating systems, starting with Windows Server 2008 to Windows Server 2022 at the time of writing this chapter.

The following screenshot in *Figure 8.2* is a list of some common AMIs offered by AWS as part of the Quick Start toolkit:

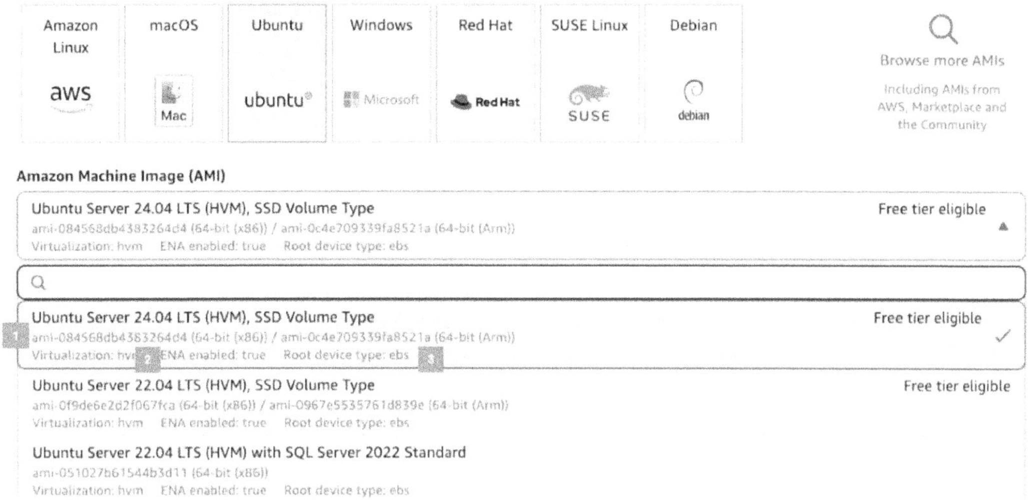

Figure 8.2: Quick start AMI templates offered by AWS

As shown in *Figure 8.2*, AWS offers a variety of AMI templates that support multiple operating systems. The AMI highlighted in the image includes several key features, along with the latest version of the Ubuntu Server operating system, which, at the time of writing, was Ubuntu 24.04 LTS. These features include:

1. **AMI ID and Architecture**: Every AMI has a unique AMI ID and is built for a specific CPU architecture. The highlighted Ubuntu AMI is designed for Intel-based x86-64-bit architecture.
2. **Elastic Network Interface** (**ENI**) and Elastic Network Adapter (ENA): When launched, all EC2 instances are assigned an Elastic Network Interface (ENI)—a virtual network card that provides connectivity (similar to a Wi-Fi card in a laptop). Elastic Network Adapters (ENAs) offer high-performance networking, supporting up to 100 Gbps speeds. The AMI used for your instance must be ENA-compatible to leverage this performance boost.
3. **Root Device and Storage**: The root device for this AMI snapshot is an Elastic Block Store (EBS) volume, which functions like a computer's local hard drive and hosts the operating system. EBS storage is discussed further later in this chapter.

In addition to the Quick Start AMIs available through the web console, there are other sources of AMIs:

- AWS Marketplace: AWS offers a marketplace where many third-party vendors sell software applications bundled as ready-to-use AMIs. Companies such as McAfee, Citrix, and F5 provide a wide range of software applications and tools packaged as

AMIs, making it easier for customers to deploy solutions within their VPCs and AWS accounts. Pricing is based on the hourly charge for the application plus the cost of the specific EC2 instance type on which the AMI is running. More details about the AWS Marketplace and the variety of third-party software solutions available can be found at the AWS Marketplace - `https://aws.amazon.com/marketplace`

- Community AMIs: Many communities supporting open-source software solutions and operating systems publish their AMIs on AWS. These are generally free, but you will still incur costs for the instances they run on. For example, you can find specific Linux distributions, such as CentOS, a popular AMI businesses use to host applications. However, it is essential to note that AWS does not provide support or warranties for community AMIs, so caution is advised when selecting one.
- Creating Your Own AMI: You can create your own AMIs tailored to your business requirements. For example, if you need to deploy multiple instances with a specific operating system configuration, settings, and required applications, you can build an EC2 instance with these exact specifications and then create an AMI of the instance. The AMI creation process also generates snapshots of the EBS volumes attached to the instance. This AMI can then deploy additional instances in your AWS account. Building custom AMIs to streamline deployment is known as using prebaked or golden AMIs. Instead of starting with a base AMI and manually installing software at instance launch, a prebaked AMI enables you to launch EC2 instances that are ready to use immediately, reducing boot time and configuration overhead.

AMIs are stored as block storage snapshots, specifically within the Amazon **Elastic Block Store** (**EBS**) service. Block storage, such as EBS volumes, functions as virtual hard disk drives for your EC2 instances, hosting and running the operating system as well as any applications. Additionally, EBS volumes are commonly used to store data that is local to the instance.

In the next section, you will learn more about AWS Elastic Block Store and how it forms a critical component of your EC2 instances.

Comparing EBS, instance store, EFS, and FSx storage options

Block storage is used for both physical and virtual servers (virtual machines) because it offers low latency, high performance, and direct access to the underlying hardware—features that are essential for operating systems, databases, and applications requiring fast data access.

More importantly, an operating system needs a file system (e.g., NTFS, ext4, XFS) to manage files and folders. This also defines how the OS will manage access and security of data stored on the volume. It must also be able to partition and format a storage volume to make it bootable—something that file storage like Amazon EFS or object storage services like Amazon S3 cannot provide.

AWS offers the **Elastic Block Storage** (**EBS**) solution, which functions similarly to attaching a storage volume as a virtual hard disk from a **Storage Area Network** (**SAN**) in an on-premises environment. You can create a volume with the desired capacity and attach it to a virtual machine as either a root volume (which is made bootable and typically hosts the operating system) or a data volume. Once connected, you format it with a file system that the operating system recognizes.

AWS EBS volumes are categorized into Solid State Drives (SSDs) and Hard Disk Drives (HDDs).

SSDs are optimized for transactional workloads that require frequent, low-latency read/write operations (measured in IOPS). They are ideal for boot volumes, databases, and latency-sensitive applications. However, HDDs are optimized for sequential throughput and are better suited for large streaming workloads such as log processing and data warehousing.

The following SSD volume types are offered as part of EBS:

- **gp3**: At the time of writing this chapter, gp3 volumes are the latest generation of low-cost SSD volumes offered by AWS. These volumes are ideal for most transactional workloads, provide low latency, and are well-suited as boot volumes. Compared to the previous generation (gp2), gp3 volumes are 20% more cost-effective and allow independent scaling of volume performance regardless of volume size. They offer a baseline performance of 3,000 IOPS, which can scale up to a maximum of 16,000 IOPS. Regarding capacity, gp3 volumes can be provisioned between 1 GiB and 16 TiB. AWS recommends migrating from gp2 to gp3 for better cost efficiency and performance.
- **io1**: Provisioned IOPS SSDs (io1) offer higher performance and are designed for critical I/O intensive workloads such as databases, which are often sensitive to consistent levels of performance and consistency. These volumes range from 4GiB to 64TiB, and you can provision between 100 IOPS and 64,000 IOPS. Note that you can achieve up to 64,000 IOPS only on Nitro Systems, whereas on other systems, the maximum performance is up to 32,000 IOPS.
- **io2 Block Express**: Built on the next generation of EC2 storage architecture, the io2 Block Express is designed for the most demanding I/O-intensive applications. It is ideal for critical workloads such as Oracle databases, SAP HANA, Microsoft SQL Server, and similar high-end applications. You get sub-millisecond average latency, and storage capacity of up to 64TiB, performance of up to 256,000 IOPS, and volume throughput of up to 4,000 MiB/s.

HDDs are optimized for streaming workloads, where the focus is on throughput. HDD storage options include:

- **st1**: This low-cost magnetic storage is ideal for frequently accessed, throughput-intensive sequential workloads and large datasets. Ideal applications include Amazon EMR, ETL, data warehouses, and Kafka. Volume size ranges from 126GiB to 16TiB.
- **sc1**: Also known as cold HDD, this storage option offers the lowest cost per GiB and is ideal for less frequently accessed workloads. Sc1 offers a maximum of 250 MB/s per volume and ranges between 125GB to 16TB in size.

> Note
>
> HDD volumes do not support boot volumes. For bootable drives, you must select SSD volumes.

The following are some additional features of AWS **Elastic Block Store** (**EBS**) volumes:

- EBS volumes are connected over a storage network and can be attached to or detached from an EC2 instance. If an instance experiences a failure, you can detach the EBS volumes and attach them to another instance to continue accessing the data stored on them.
- You can take snapshots of your EBS volumes as part of your disaster recovery and backup strategy. The first snapshot of a volume is always a full backup, while subsequent snapshots are incremental, capturing only the changes made since the last snapshot. These snapshots are stored in Amazon S3 and fully managed by AWS. Additionally, snapshots can be copied across regions, allowing you to create new volumes in different regions. They can also be shared with other AWS accounts.
- EBS volumes are network-attached storage that provide persistent block-level storage for EC2 instances. They exist independently of any instance's lifecycle.

In the next section, you will learn about another type of block storage—instance store volumes—and understand their use case. These volumes are directly attached to the physical host on which your EC2 instance is deployed.

AWS EC2 instance store volumes

AWS instance store volumes are local storage drives physically attached to the host where your EC2 instance is deployed.

The primary benefit of instance store volumes is their ultra-high throughput and low latency, making them ideal for workloads requiring fast, temporary storage. Another advantage is that they are included in the cost of supported EC2 instances, whereas EBS volumes incur separate charges.

However, instance store volumes are not persistent. Data stored on them remains available only while the instance is running on the same physical host as the volume. If you stop and restart an EC2 instance, AWS may launch it on a different host, and all instance store volumes will be lost. AWS recommends that instance store volumes be used only for temporary data.

While block storage is typically used to host the operating system and install applications on EC2 instances, it is not ideal for sharing data and files between instances.

Often, you may have a central repository of data that needs to be accessible by multiple EC2 instances. While it is possible to configure file shares on an EBS-backed EC2 instance using NFS (Network File System) or SMB (Server Message Block) protocols, this approach is cumbersome and can experience performance issues, primarily if instances are distributed across different Availability Zones in a region. This is because EBS volumes are availability zone-specific and need to be attached to instances in the AZ it is deployed in.

Instead, AWS offers dedicated file storage solutions designed specifically for shared access. The following section introduces two such offerings:

- **Amazon Elastic File System** (**EFS**) – A scalable, fully managed NFS file system for Linux instances
- **Amazon FSx for Windows File Server** – A fully managed file system that provides SMB-based shared storage for Windows workloads

Let's look at them in more detail in the following subsections.

Amazon Elastic File System

Amazon **Elastic File System** (**EFS**) allows you to create a shared file system within a region and configure mount points accessible across multiple Availability Zones. EC2 instances within these Availability Zones can mount the EFS file system, providing a common directory structure for shared file access.

Amazon EFS is designed for Linux-based EC2 instances and supports the NFS protocol for file sharing. Once configured, you create a file system and set up mount targets in each Availability Zone where instances need access.

An architectural illustration in *Figure 8.3* depicts this use case.

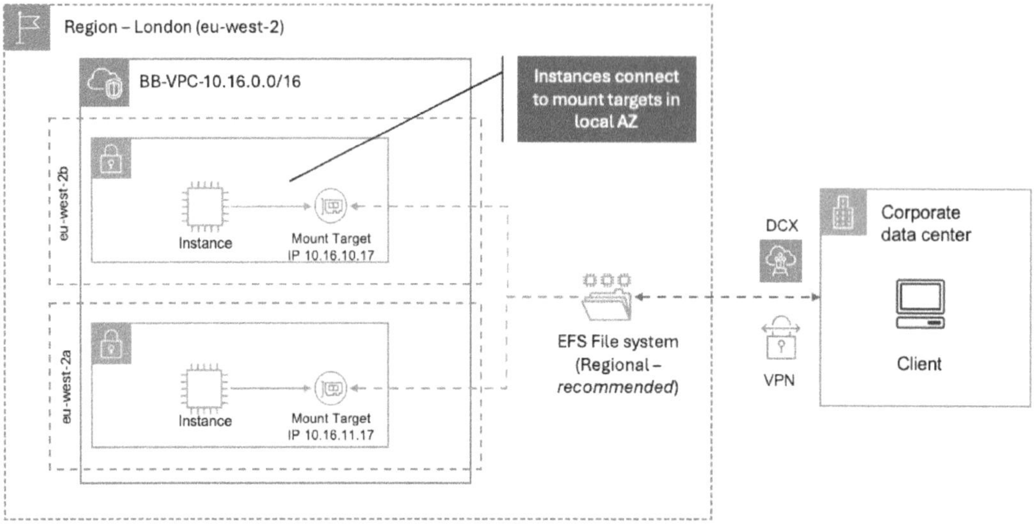

Figure 8.3: Configuring EFS with mount targets

As shown in *Figure 8.3*, Amazon EFS is a regional service that allows you to configure mount targets in Availability Zones. EC2 instances within those zones can mount the file system to share common files and data.

Additionally, you can connect to Amazon EFS from your on-premises network using AWS Direct Connect or IPSec VPN.

Unlike Amazon EBS volumes, Amazon EFS does not require you to provision storage upfront. Instead, EFS dynamically scales up and down based on usage, ensuring you only pay for the storage you consume. However, EFS file systems cannot be used as boot volumes or formatted like traditional drives. For such requirements, you must use EBS volumes.

While it is technically possible to access EFS from Windows instances, AWS only provides official support for Linux-based instances.

Amazon FSx for Windows File Server

Amazon FSx for Windows File Server provides a fully managed, native Windows file system hosted on AWS-managed Windows file servers. It integrates seamlessly with Microsoft Active Directory, allowing you to apply the same security policies for granting access to file shares and data across your Windows environment. FSx for Windows File Server natively supports the **Server Message Block** (**SMB**) protocol, which is widely used in Windows environments for network file sharing. Advanced features such as **volume shadow copy** (**VSS**), which offers data consistency versioning capability and the ability to scale your file system with DNS integration using **Distributed File Systems** (**DFS**), are all integrated as part of the service. Additionally,

Amazon FSx is ideal for typical workloads such as home directories, content management, and software build sharing.

In this section, you explored the various storage options available for Amazon EC2 instances, *including* block storage and file storage solutions.

You learned that **Amazon Elastic Block Store** (**EBS**) volumes function as direct-attached block storage, providing low latency and the ability to be formatted according to your operating system's requirements. Remember that only SSD-based EBS volumes can be used as boot volumes, while HDD-based EBS volumes are optimized for sequential data access.

Additionally, you reviewed file storage options and discovered that **Amazon Elastic File System** (**EFS**) is designed for Linux instances, enabling shared access to common files. In contrast, FSx for Windows File Server is the recommended solution for Windows-based instances.

In the next section, you will learn about the different EC2 pricing options available and discover their use cases.

Choosing EC2 pricing options

AWS offers a variety of pay-as-you-go pricing options for its EC2 service. You don't need to make a significant upfront investment in physical servers. Instead, based on your business requirements, you only pay for the hours your compute resources are in use. If you stop an instance but keep it in your account, you won't incur compute charges while it remains in a stopped state. This pricing model is the On-Demand pricing option and is the default method for procuring compute capacity on AWS. The following pricing options are available:

On-demand pricing options

The on-demand pricing option is the default pricing model for launching EC2 instances. You are charged an hourly rate, billed per second (with a minimum charge of 60 seconds), for the duration your instance remains in the running state. This charge includes all bundled operating system licensing costs unless you choose to bring your own enterprise licensing agreement. It also covers any bundled applications that come with the instance.

The on-demand pricing model is ideal for customers who require the flexibility to consume compute resources on a pay-as-you-go basis. Customers can deploy instances in their AWS account and are only billed for compute costs while the instances run—this pricing option best suits short-term, spiky, or unpredictable workloads. For example, suppose you need to deploy a set of test servers to run application test cases for a few weeks before rolling out a production application. In that case, On-Demand pricing offers a cost-effective solution. Since these instances are only needed for a few weeks or months and are likely to be used during business hours, this model minimizes unnecessary expenses.

> **Note**
>
> The on-demand pricing option only applies to the cost of computing capacity. It does not include the cost of any attached block storage volumes. For block storage, you are charged based on the total amount of provisioned storage, even if the instances are in a stopped state.

However, the on-demand pricing option may not be the most cost-effective choice if you require instances for long-running workloads, such as production e-commerce applications that need to operate 24/7 throughout the year. AWS provides discounted pricing options for long-running instances if you are willing to commit to a long-term contract. In such cases, **Reserved Instance pricing** becomes a more suitable option, which will be discussed next.

Reserved instance pricing option

This pricing model offers significant cost savings—up to 72% off the On-Demand price—for customers who commit to a 1-year or 3-year agreement for a specific compute capacity. Designed to encourage long-term commitments, Reserved Instance pricing is ideal for workloads that require continuous operation 24/7 throughout the year, such as corporate websites, e-commerce platforms, and global customer-facing applications.

It is important to note that Reserved Instances are not actual EC2 instances that you provision. Instead, they represent a pricing agreement that grants the customer the right to run a specific EC2 instance configuration in a designated AWS region for a fixed term (1 year or 3 years) at a discounted rate. Once you launch an instance matching the reserved configuration within the specified region (or an Availability Zone, depending on the Reserved Instance type), the Reserved Instance pricing is applied automatically instead of the standard On-Demand rate.

There are two Reserved Instance pricing options:

- **Standard Reserved Instance**: This option provides the highest discount—up to 72%—depending on the length of the commitment and whether you make an all-upfront payment (discussed later). While Standard Reserved Instances offer significant cost savings, they come with limited flexibility. You can modify certain attributes, such as:
    - The Availability Zone within the same region
    - The instance size (within the same instance family)
    - The network type

However, you cannot change the instance family, operating system, or tenancy model. If your requirements change, you can sell Standard Reserved Instances on the **AWS Reserved Instance Marketplace**, provided you meet the eligibility criteria. This marketplace allows you to sell unused Standard Reserved Instances to other AWS customers. You can sell your Reserved Instances when you no longer require those instances, at the end of a project, or if your business requirements change.

- **Convertible Reserved Instance**: This option offers greater flexibility at a lower discount than Standard Reserved Instances. With Convertible Reserved Instances, you can exchange your instance for another Convertible Reserved Instance with a different:
  - Instance family
  - Operating system
  - Tenancy model

  However, unlike Standard Reserved Instances, Convertible Reserved Instances cannot be sold on the AWS Marketplace.

The amount you pay upfront is a key factor in obtaining the maximum discount for Reserved Instances. AWS offers three payment options to suit different budgeting needs. An example of a standard 3-year reserved instance pricing option for a t2.micro Amazon Linux-based instance is displayed in the following screenshot in *Figure 8.4*:

Seller	Term	Effective rate	Upfront price	Hourly rate	Payment option	Offering class	Quantity available	Desired quantity	Normalized units per hour
AWS	36 month	$0.004	$115.00	$0.00	All upfront	Standard	Unlimited	1	0.5
AWS	36 month	$0.005	$0.00	$0.005	No upfront	Standard	Unlimited	1	0.5
AWS	36 month	$0.005	$66.00	$0.002	Partial upfront	Standard	Unlimited	1	0.5
3rd party	27 month	$0.005	$88.45	$0.00	All upfront	Standard	1	1	0.5

Figure 8.4: Reserved instance pricing options for a 3-year Amazon Linux t2.micro instance

With the **All upfront** option, you pay the total cost of the 1-year or 3-year term in advance at the contract's start. This eliminates monthly or hourly billing, providing the most significant possible discount, depending on the tenure of the contract. In *Figure 8.4*, you will note that the effective rate for selecting this option is $0.004 per hour, which is the cheapest of all other options.

The **Partial upfront** option allows you to pay a portion of the total cost at the beginning of the contract, with the remainder billed monthly at a discounted rate. This approach helps reduce monthly expenses while still offering substantial savings.

If you prefer not to make any upfront payments, the **No upfront** option lets you pay monthly at a discounted hourly rate throughout the contract term. While this still offers savings compared to On-Demand pricing, the discount is lower than what you would receive with **All upfront** or **Partial upfront** payments.

You will also note an offer from a third-party provider, possibly another AWS customer reselling a Standard Reserved Instance with a 27-month remaining contract.

Another pricing option offered by AWS is the Spot Instance Pricing Option, which is discussed next.

Spot instance pricing options

AWS frequently has excess compute capacity, aiming to sell it to maximize economies of scale. Customers occasionally require additional capacity, often for stateless workloads such as ad-hoc batch jobs, **extract, transform, and load** (**ETL**) operations, or media processing. AWS offers Spot Instances specifically designed for temporary and flexible workloads to encourage the use of this surplus capacity.

AWS Spot Instances provide the most significant cost savings, offering discounts of up to 90% off the On-Demand price. AWS determines the Spot Instance price based on current supply and demand, which fluctuate over time. As a customer, you can specify a maximum price at or above the prevailing Spot price when requesting a Spot Instance. Typically, you would set your maximum price slightly above the current Spot price to account for minor fluctuations, ensuring continued access to the instance. However, you are always charged at the prevailing Spot price. If the Spot price rises above your specified maximum price, AWS will terminate your instance with a minimum two-minute warning, as other customers may be willing to pay the higher price for the available capacity.

Amazon EC2 generates an instance rebalance recommendation signal to alert you when a Spot Instance is more likely to be interrupted. This notification allows you to proactively redistribute your workloads across other existing or newly launched Spot Instances rather than waiting for the standard two-minute interruption notice.

When you launch EC2 instances, you are deploying virtual servers on shared physical hardware by default. This means the host machine on which your EC2 instance is deployed shares hardware resources with other EC2 instances that might belong to other customers. While firewall configurations prevent you from accessing compute resources that belong to other customers and vice versa, you may have a regulatory requirement to ensure that all your virtual servers are deployed on a physical host consisting of instances that belong only to you. The next section explains Dedicated Hosts, which is a pricing option that fulfills this requirement.

Amazon EC2 Dedicated Hosts and Dedicated Instances

Amazon EC2 Dedicated Hosts provide a fully dedicated physical server exclusively for your use. This ensures that the underlying hardware is isolated from other AWS customers while still allowing you to share instance capacity across multiple AWS accounts. Dedicated Hosts offer complete control and visibility over instance placement on the host, along with host affinity, which ensures that workloads remain on the same physical machine. It also means that you can **bring your own licenses** (**BYOL**) to the platform. This is particularly beneficial for software that requires licensing on a per-socket, per-core, or per-VM basis. Many enterprise-grade applications have strict licensing conditions tied to the physical infrastructure, making Dedicated Hosts an ideal solution. Billing is based on the host, irrespective of the number of instances running on it.

Amazon EC2 Dedicated Instances is a similar offering to Dedicated Hosts except that the physical host is dedicated to a single AWS account, and you cannot share instance capacity with other accounts. You also do not have visibility into sockets and cores, and cannot have host affinity for your instances. There is only partial support for BYOL, specifically Microsoft SQL Server with License Mobility through Software Assurance, and Windows **Virtual Desktop Access** (**VDA**) licenses. However, dedicated instances fulfill the requirement of workloads needing isolated hardware, which is particularly useful for highly regulated environments.

Amazon EC2 is a fundamental compute service in AWS that enables you to deploy virtual machines in the cloud. It offers extensive flexibility, allowing you to configure instances with various operating systems, networking features, storage options, and data transfer settings. However, if you require a straightforward virtual server to run standard **off-the-shelf** (**OTS**) software with predictable monthly pricing, Amazon Lightsail provides a simpler alternative. The next section will cover Amazon Lightsail in more detail.

Deploying simple workloads with Amazon Lightsail

Amazon Lightsail provides preconfigured Linux and Windows virtual servers in the cloud, enabling customers to launch and manage common web applications quickly. Designed for simplicity and ease of use, Lightsail automatically configures networking, access, and security settings according to AWS best practices.

While configuration options are limited, Lightsail offers the advantage of a predictable, fixed monthly pricing model based on instance type, operating system, and bundled applications. It is well-suited for small business applications such as file storage, accounting software, simple web applications running on WordPress or Magento, and LAMP stack deployments. Additionally, Lightsail is an excellent option for managed service providers and resellers who need a hassle-free hosting solution without the complexity of hardware management.

Although virtual machines have significantly shaped modern cloud computing, they have limitations. Each virtual machine requires its own guest operating system, consuming additional resources. To address this challenge, AWS offers container-based compute solutions, which provide a more efficient and scalable alternative. The concept of containerization is explored in the next section.

Running containers with Amazon ECS and Amazon EKS

Traditional **virtual machines** (**VMs**) are deployed on bare-metal hardware configured with a hypervisor. The hypervisor abstracts and manages physical resources such as CPU, memory, and storage, enabling multiple VMs to run on the same hardware. Each VM functions independently, requiring its own operating system, libraries, and runtime environments to support its applications.

Due to compatibility requirements, multiple VMs are often deployed to host different application environments. For example, as illustrated in *Figure 8.5*, a development VM may have the latest software versions for building new features, applications, or experimentation. In contrast, a production VM may need to run an older, stable version. Multiple VMs must be provisioned for each environment to avoid compatibility issues and ensure isolation.

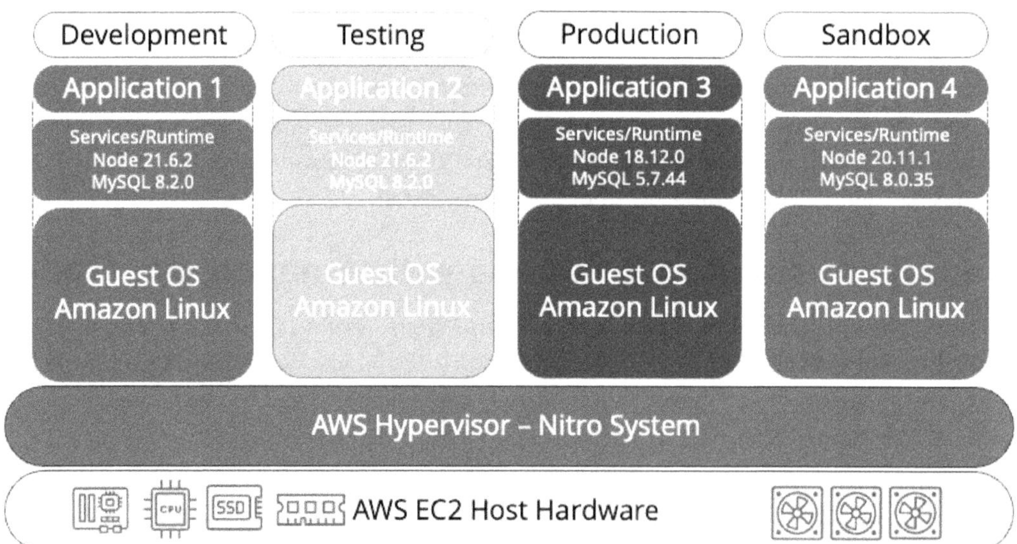

Figure 8.5: VMs hosting different versions of software for various environments

Each VM also includes its own guest operating system (Windows or Linux), which must be patched, managed, and monitored. This increases administrative overhead and leads to higher resource consumption.

Containerization is a more efficient and agile approach to provisioning compute capacity. This technology enables applications to run in isolated user spaces, known as containers, which share the same underlying operating system. Containers package all necessary dependencies, including binaries, libraries, configuration files, and runtime environments, ensuring consistency across different environments.

Since containers are abstracted from the host operating system while maintaining secure, isolated access, they allow for significantly higher density than traditional VMs. As illustrated in *Figure 8.6*, this results in more efficient resource utilization and improved scalability.

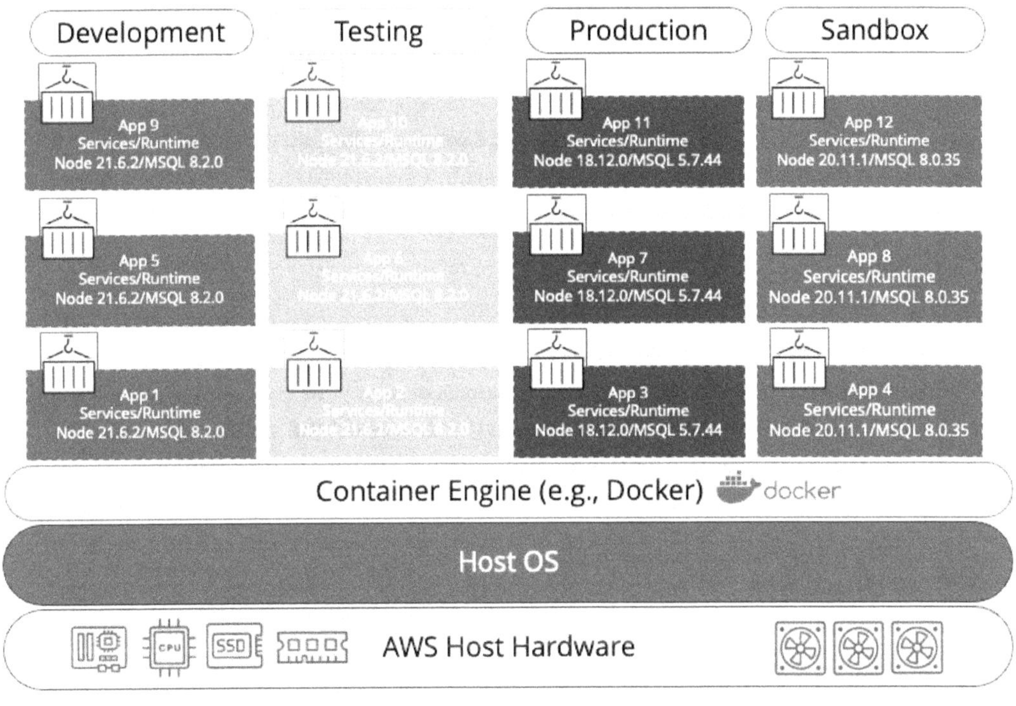

Figure 8.6: Containers running on the Docker engine

You would use a container engine to manage containers, and Docker is one of the world's most popular technologies for building, deploying, and managing containers.

Containerization significantly reduces overhead by allowing multiple containers to share the same underlying host operating system, rather than requiring each instance to have its own kernel, as with virtual machines.

As illustrated in *Figure 8.6*, containers leverage a container runtime, such as the Docker engine, to access the host OS while maintaining isolation. This eliminates the need for full guest operating systems, making the application footprint much smaller than VMs. As a result, containerized applications benefit from improved performance, faster startup times, and more efficient resource utilization than traditional VM-based architectures.

AWS offers two fully managed container orchestration services that allow you to deploy Docker-style applications – **Amazon Elastic Container Service** (**ECS**) and **Amazon Elastic Kubernetes Service** (**EKS**). These two services are discussed next.

Overview of Amazon Elastic Container Service

Amazon ECS is a fully managed container orchestration service that enables you to deploy, manage, and scale containerized applications. With Amazon ECS, you do not need to install and operate your own container orchestration software or manage and scale clusters of virtual machines. The service offers all these capabilities as a fully managed service, enabling you to focus on building and deploying your container images.

As part of the service, AWS also offers the **Elastic Container Registry** (**Amazon ECR**), a fully managed container image registry service. With seamless integration to Amazon ECS, you can build and manage all your container images, define their access permissions and deploy those images as containers on Amazon ECS.

Amazon ECS offers two deployment options:

- **Amazon Fargate (Fargate launch type)**: This option is **serverless** because you do not need to manage any underlying EC2 instances to host your containers. You package your application, specify the CPU, memory, and networking parameters, and AWS provisions the necessary container infrastructure within a secure, isolated environment accessible only via your VPC. AWS automatically places ECS tasks on the cluster, scales them as needed, and fully manages the underlying environment.
- **EC2 launch type**: This option allows you to manage a cluster of EC2 instances and manually schedule the placement of containers. You have complete control over the underlying instances, including the ability to patch, update, and optimize their configurations.
- **Amazon ECS Managed Instances**: This option allows you to run containers on EC2 instances while letting AWS handle much of the infrastructure management for you. AWS manages tasks such as instance provisioning, patching, and capacity management, while you still retain control over the type of instances used for your workloads. This is useful when you want more control than Fargate provides, such as

choosing GPU-optimized or network-optimized instances, but do not want to manage every aspect of the underlying EC2 fleet yourself.

Choosing between ECS launch options:

- The EC2 launch type is best suited for long-running applications that require manual auto-scaling management or cost optimizations through Reserved Instances
- The Fargate launch type is ideal for periodic or unpredictable workloads, offering on-demand scaling and minimal administrative overhead since AWS handles infrastructure management
- Amazon ECS Managed Instances is probably the best of both worlds in that AWS manages the instances, such as patching, capacity provision, workload placements, but you still get to choose the configuration like instance types, GPU and network optimized instances as well as access reserved capacity

In the next section, you will learn about the Amazon Elastic Kubernetes Service.

Amazon Elastic Kubernetes Service (Amazon EKS)

Kubernetes is an open-source and vendor-agnostic container orchestration service. Like ECS, it offers container orchestration, scaling, and management of applications across clusters of machines. Amazon EKS is AWS's offering of the Kubernetes service, which comes with existing tooling and plugins from partners and the Kubernetes community. This means you can also easily migrate existing Kubernetes clusters to AWS. Note that with EKS, you need to pay for the control plane, but there is no additional charge for ECS.

While containerization improves resource efficiency and performance, AWS also offers another compute service called AWS Lambda. This serverless compute solution executes code in response to events or triggers, enabling the development of event-driven architectures. Serverless computing with AWS Lambda is explored in the next section.

Building event-driven applications with AWS Lambda

AWS Lambda is a serverless compute offering that allows you to run code in response to an event or a trigger. Also known as **Function as a Service** (**FaaS**), AWS Lambda functions can be invoked to run code and be architected as part of your serverless architecture, including other technologies such as storage, databases, and network connectivity.

Depending on your application type and architecture, you can handle all compute and processing tasks using Lambda functions rather than spin up EC2 instances to perform any computational work or process data. There are limitations, however, to consider, but it is possible to build a complete end-to-end application using Lambda to handle the compute layer.

The following architecture, shown in *Figure 8.7*, illustrates how AWS Lambda could be used to build a complete web application solution.

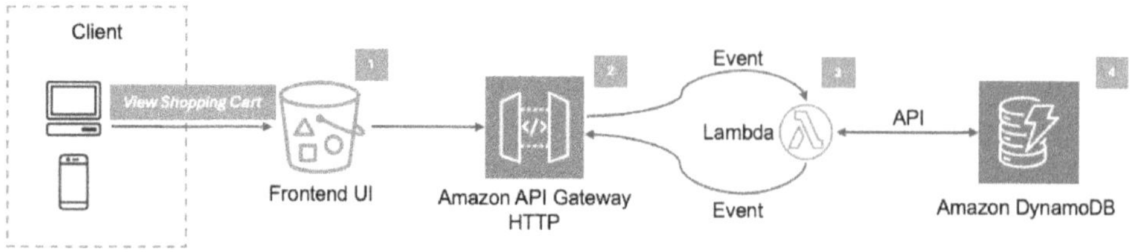

Figure 8.7: AWS serverless architecture with AWS Lambda

As shown in *Figure 8.7*, AWS Lambda provides compute services in response to events representing state changes. The architecture is structured as follows:

1. The client visits a website hosted on an Amazon S3 bucket configured with static website hosting. The example shown in the diagram is that of an e-commerce front-end **user interface** (**UI**).
2. Amazon API Gateway enables developers to easily create, publish, and manage APIs. The application would call specific APIs, such as `GET` or `PUT`, when retrieving product lists or adding products to the cart, respectively.
3. API Gateway would then trigger the relevant AWS Lambda function. In this example, when users request to view their shopping cart, as illustrated in *Figure 8.7*, the Lambda function executes code to retrieve the relevant data from the backend database.
4. Amazon DynamoDB hosts the web application's backend data, including customer information, product details, and order records. DynamoDB is ideal for storing large volumes of unstructured data and does not require extensive prior schema configurations. *Chapter 9* explores DynamoDB in greater detail.

AWS Lambda functions are executed when triggered or invoked by another AWS service and do not run independently. This means their use cases are based on event-driven architectures, which may also include scheduled events.

AWS Lambda is designed for short-running tasks rather than prolonged backend processing. As such, there are certain limitations on where Lambda functions can be used. For example, a Lambda function can run for 15 minutes per invocation, and a single function can use up to 10,240 MB of memory. In most cases, simple web requests such as retrieving a list of products from an e-commerce website take no more than 1 second, and so the 15-minute timeout limit is plenty for such use cases. The best part about Lambda is that you only pay when your code executes. This is much more cost-effective than EC2 instances, which often run idle as you wait for events to occur.

So far, this chapter has focused extensively on hosting applications in the cloud – using a wide range of compute services, including virtual machines with Amazon EC2, containerization with Amazon ECS and EKS, and serverless event-driven compute offerings such as AWS Lambda. However, many organizations may wish to bring cloud resources to their on-premises environment – this may be because of compliance and governance reasons or technical requirements such as having ultra-low latency access to these resources. The next section introduces AWS Outpost, which offers a solution to this requirement.

Extending AWS compute to on-premises environments with AWS Outposts

AWS Outposts allow customers to deploy cloud resources such as EC2 instances, S3 storage, and RDS databases on-premises. These resources run on AWS-supplied physical infrastructure, which includes racks, servers, storage, and networking equipment. All resources are managed using the same AWS management tools and services as in the cloud.

The physical infrastructure consists of a 42U rack, 48 inches deep, capable of housing 1U or 2U servers where your resources are provisioned. From a connectivity perspective, AWS Outposts extend your Amazon VPC from the AWS Region to your on-premises environment by defining "Outpost subnets." These subnets provide access to VPC components such as internet gateways, endpoints, and transit gateways. An Outpost acts as an extension of an Availability Zone in the associated Region, allowing you to benefit from its high availability and resilience.

In the next section, you will launch some EC2 instances, configure connectivity, and access those instances to remotely administer them.

Project task 8 – Deploying EC2 instances in public and private subnets of your VPC

In the upcoming project tasks, you will learn how to deploy and administer Linux-based EC2 instances within the VPC you created in *Chapter 7*. You will launch one instance in the public subnet and one in the private, as depicted in *Figure 8.8*:

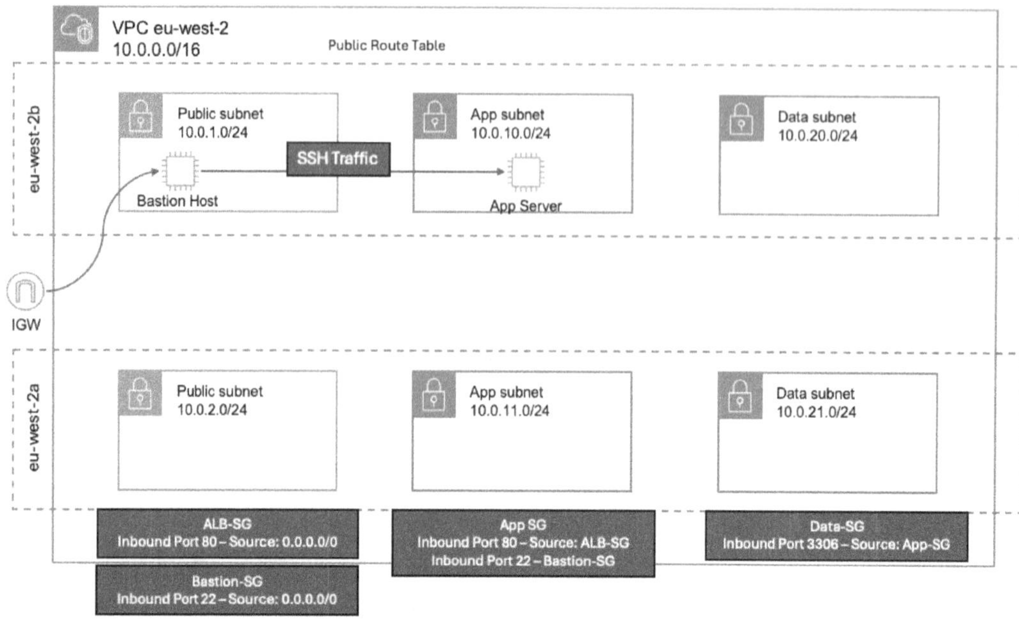

Figure 8.8: Deployment of two EC2 instances in Belly Brew Co. Limited's VPC – A bastion host and an app server

As depicted in *Figure 8.8*, you will deploy two EC2 instances—one in the public subnet and one in the private subnet. Additional configurations will be required to ensure you can connect to both instances.

- The EC2 instance in the public subnet will require a public IP address and act as a Bastion Host - A bastion host is a server used to securely access and manage resources in a private subnet by acting as a gateway for administrative tasks, typically via SSH or RDP. To ensure connectivity to the server, you will also create a new security group that will allow inbound traffic on port 22 for SSH from the Internet. Think of the bastion host as a *jumpbox* machine to access other computers in the private subnet since there is no direct access to them.
- Once you connect to this bastion host, you will then be able to access the EC2 instance in the private subnet remotely. To ensure connectivity is permitted, you will update the App-SG security group to allow inbound connections on port 22 for SSH.

Technical requirements

To complete the project tasks in this chapter, ensure that you have completed all previous exercises in earlier chapters and have access to the VPC you created in *Chapter 7*. Log in to your AWS Development account as the IAM user Alice to complete the project tasks.

Project task 8.1 – Creating a security group for the bastion host EC2 instance

In this project task, you will create a new security group for the Bastion host. Security groups are used to control the type of traffic you allow inbound and outbound. These restrictions reduce the attack surface, enabling you to monitor and audit traffic on the ports and protocols you define in the security group rules. You will allow inbound traffic on port 22 for SSH. This security group will be attached to the Bastion host EC2 instance later in this project exercise. Then you will update the App-SG security to allow inbound traffic on port 22, SSH from the Bastion host security group, ensuring that only the Bastion host can remotely connect to the EC2 instance deployed in the App subnet.

1. Log in to your AWS account to ensure you are in the London (`eu-west-2`) region, where you have previously deployed Belly Brew Co. Limited's VPC
2. Navigate to the VPC management console by searching for the service in the top search bar and clicking on the appropriate link
3. From the left-hand menu, select **Security groups** from the **Security** section
4. In the right-hand pane, click **Create security group**
5. Next, provide a name for the security group such as "`belly-brew-vpc-bastion-host-sg`"
6. Provide an appropriate description, such as "`Allow inbound SSH connections from the internet to Bastion host`"
7. Ensure you select Belly Brew Co. Limited's VPC from the **VPC** drop-down list that you created in *Chapter 7*
8. Next, click the **Add rule** button in the **Inbound rules** section
9. Set the **Type** to **SSH**, and then for the **Source**, select **Anywhere-Ipv4**, as per the screenshot in *Figure 8.9*:

Figure 8.9: Configuring a new security group for Bastion host EC2 instance

10. Next, click **Add new tag** in the **Tags – optional** section
11. For the Key, type in Name, and for the Value type in `belly-brew-vpc-bastion-host-sg`
12. Scroll down to the bottom of the webpage and click the **Create security group** button

In the next project task, you will update the App-SG security group to allow inbound SSH traffic on port 22 from the Bastion Host security group.

Project task 8.2 – Updating the App-SG security group

In this project task, you will update the App-SG security group to allow inbound traffic on port 22 for SSH. The source of that traffic would be any instances associated with the Bastion Host security group you created in *Project Task 8.1*. This ensures that access to the EC2 instances in the private subnet can only be initiated from the bastion host, reducing the attack surface and therefore improving your security posture.

1. Ensure that you are still logged into your AWS Development account and in the VPC management console in the London region
2. From the left-hand menu, click **Security groups** in the **Security** section
3. In the right-hand pane, select the **belly-brew-vpc-app-sg** security group you created in *Chapter 7*
4. In the bottom half of the pane, select the **Inbound rules** tab as per the following screenshot in *Figure 8.10*:

Figure 8.10: Updating the belly-brew-vpc-app-sg security group

5. Click **Edit inbound rules**
6. In the Edit inbound rules webpage that appears, click **Add rule**
7. For the Type, select **SSH**, and for the Source, click the search box and scroll down and select the **belly-brew-vpc-bastion-host-sg** security group as per the following screenshot in *Figure 8.11*:

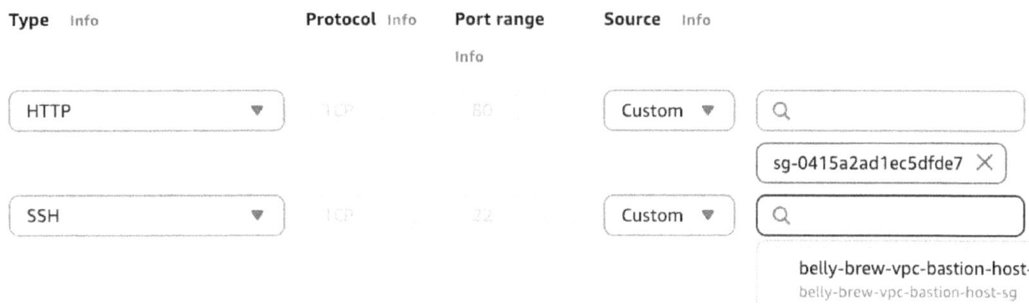

Figure 8.11: Creating a rule for SSH traffic

8. Click **Save rules**

In the next project task, you will launch your EC2 instance in the public subnet, which will act as the Bastion Host.

Project task 8.3 – Launching your bastion host instance

In this project task, you will launch a Linux EC2 instance in the public subnet, which will act as your bastion host to allow you to access instances in the private subnet. The bastion host will be associated with the security group you created in Project Task 8.1 to ensure inbound SSH connections from the Internet are allowed.

1. Ensure that you are still logged into your AWS Development account and in the London region
2. From the search bar at the top of the web console, search for **EC2** and then click on it (using the right mouse button) to open the EC2 dashboard in another browser tab. Ensure you are still in the London region.
3. From the left-hand menu, click **Instances**
4. In the right-hand pane, click the **Launch instances** button
5. Provide a name for your instance, such as `bb-bastion-host-01`
6. Select **Amazon Linux 2023 AMI** from the **Amazon Machine Image (AMI)** drop-down list in the **Application and OS Images (Amazon Machine Image)** section
7. Next, select **t3.micro** for the **Instance type**
8. In the **Key pair (login)** section, click the **Create new key pair** link
9. In the dialog box that appears, provide a key pair name such as `bb-keys`
10. Ensure **RSA** is selected as the **Key pair type** and the **Private key file format** is set to `.pem`

11. Click **Create key pair**. This will create your private keys and they will be downloaded to your downloads directory. You will need these keys later.
12. Click the **Edit** button in the **Network settings** section
13. Select Belly Brew Co. Limited's VPC from the drop-down list under **VPC – required**
14. Next, for the subnet, select **belly-brew-vpc-public-sub-01** from the **Subnet** drop-down list
15. Ensure that **Auto-assign public IP** is set to **Enable**
16. For the **Firewall (security groups)**, click the option **Select existing security group**
17. Next, select the **belly-brew-vpc-bastion-host-sg** security group from the drop-down list under **Common security groups**, as depicted in the following screenshot in *Figure 8.12*:

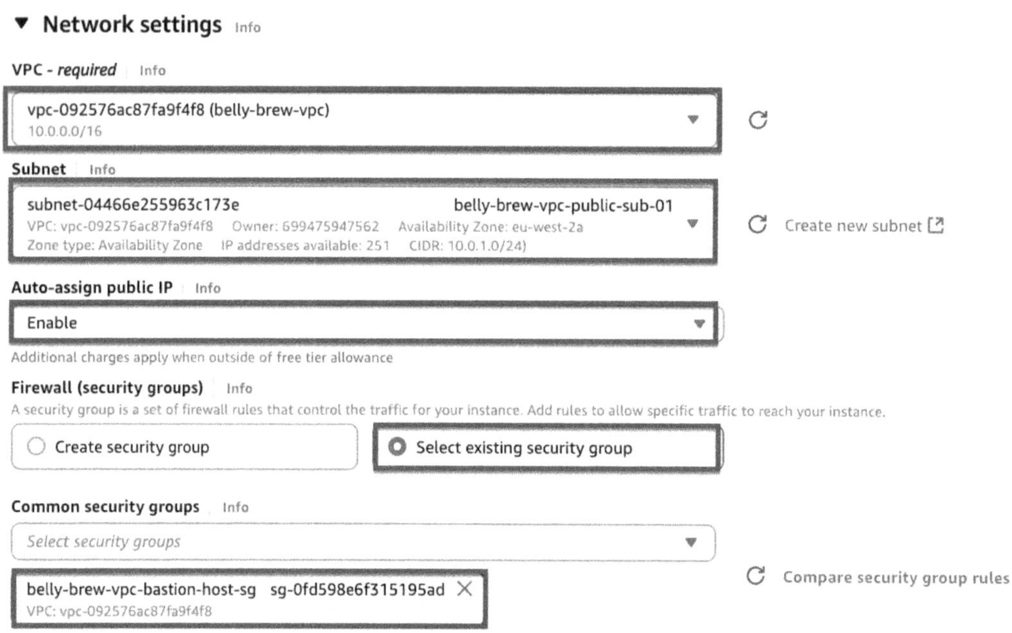

Figure 8.12: Network settings for bastion host EC2 instance

18. Next, in the right-hand pane, click **Launch instance**. You may need to scroll to the bottom of the page to see the button.

19. Your instance will now launch. Navigate back to the list of instances by clicking the **Instances** link in the breadcrumb at the top of the webpage
20. Click the refresh button to see your instances in the list if necessary. You should wait until your instance is running and the **Status check** updates the status to **3/3 checks passed**, as depicted in the following screenshot in *Figure 8.13*:

Figure 8.13: Instance details update

Your instance is now up and running, and you can proceed to launch another instance in the private subnet as part of the next project task.

Project task 8.4 – Launching your app instance in a private subnet

In this project task, you will launch another instance in the private subnet and remotely connect to it via the bastion host instance you deployed in *Project Task 8.3*.

1. Ensure that you are still logged into your AWS Development account and in the EC2 management console in the London region
2. From the instances window, click **Launch instances**
3. Provide a name for your instance, such as `belly-brew-app-srv-01`
4. Ensure that **Amazon Linux 2023 AMI** is selected as your **Amazon Machine Image (AMI)**
5. Next, select **t3.micro** from the **Instance type** drop-down list
6. From the **Key pair name – required** drop-down list, choose the **bb-keys** you created in Project Task 8.3
7. Next, click the **Edit** button in the **Network settings** section
8. Select the **belly-brew-vpc** from the **VPC – required** drop-down list
9. Next, for the subnet, select **belly-brew-vpc-app-sub-01** from the **Subnet** drop-down list
10. Ensure that **Auto-assign public IP** is set to **Disable** (as backend instances do not need a public IP)

11. For the **Firewall (security groups)**, click the option **Select existing security group**
12. Next, select the **belly-brew-vpc-app-sg** security group from the drop-down list under **Common security groups** as depicted in *Figure 8.14*:

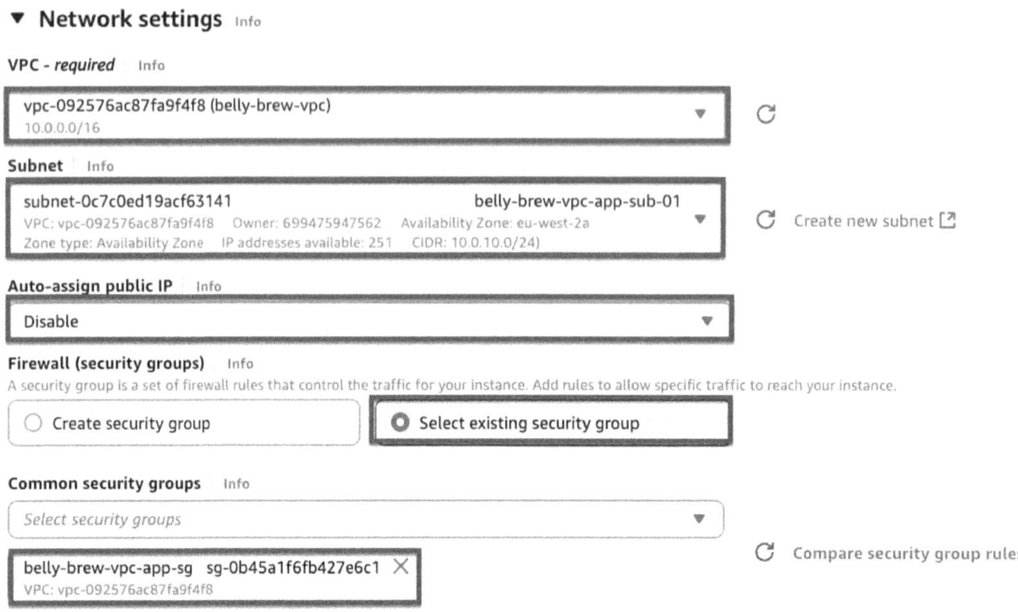

Figure 8.14: Network settings for bastion host EC2 instance

13. Next, in the right-hand pane, click **Launch instance**. You may need to scroll to the bottom of the page to see the button.
14. Your instance will now launch. Navigate back to the list of instances by clicking the **Instances** link in the breadcrumb at the top of the webpage
15. Click the refresh button to see your instances in the list if necessary. You should wait until your instance is running and the **Status check** updates the status to **3/3 checks passed**.

In the next project task, you will connect to your EC2 instances.

Project task 8.5 – Connecting to the bastion host instance

In this project task, you will use a feature known as EC2 Instance Connect to remotely access the bastion host server.

1. Ensure that you are still logged into your AWS Development account and in the EC2 management console in the London region
2. From the left-hand menu, click the **Instances** link under the **Instances** section

3. In the right-hand pane, select the bastion host instance you launched earlier by clicking on the check box next to the instance
4. Click the **Connect** button at the top of the webpage
5. In the Connect to instance webpage that appears, ensure that the EC2 instance **Connect** option is selected and then click the Connect button at the bottom of the webpage
6. A new webpage will open up in another browser tab, and you have access to the bastion host shell as per the screenshot in *Figure 8.15*:

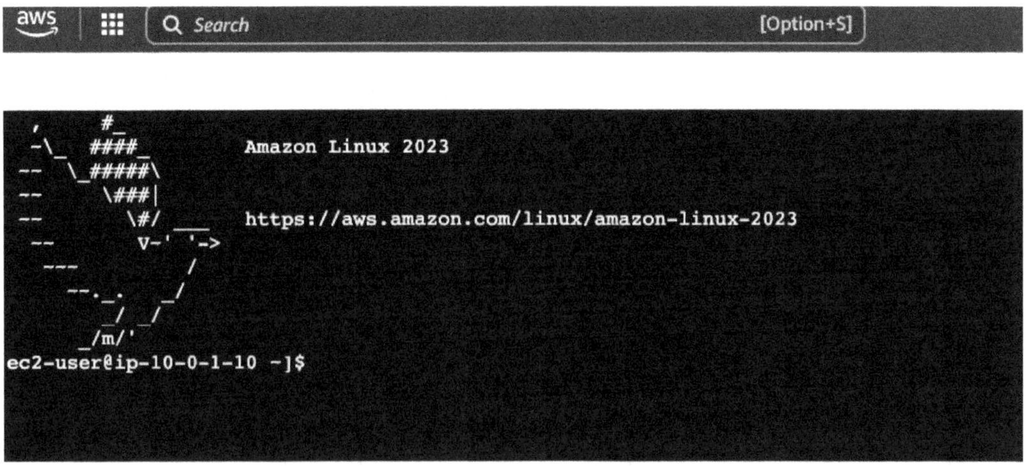

Figure 8.15: Remote shell interface of the bastion host instance

7. Type in the command `sudo su` and press enter to elevate your privileges to root

You have now logged into the bastion host instance. In the next project task, you will configure your bastion host so that from that server, you will be able to remotely access the instance in the private subnet using SSH.

Project task 8.6 – Connecting to belly-brew-app-srv-01 instance from the bastion host

In this project task, you will create a `.pem` file on the bastion host server and use that private key to remotely access the instance in the private subnet.

1. Earlier, you downloaded the `.pem` file when you launched the bastion host instance in *Project task 8.3*. This should be available in your downloads folder. Navigate to this folder and open the file in a text editor of your choice, such as TextEdit, Notepad or even Visual Studio Code. You can also use Visual Studio Code per the screenshot in

Figure 8.16. Highlight and copy the entire contents. (Make sure you include the `-----BEGIN RSA PRIVATE KEY-----` and the `-----END RSA PRIVATE KEY-----`)

Figure 8.16: Bb-keys .pem file content

2. Navigate back to the webpage where you are remotely connected to the bastion host instance
3. Type in the command `pwd` and press **Enter**. You should find that you are in the `/home/ec2-user` directory.

4. Next, create a file called `bb-keys.pem` using the `nano` command. Nano is a text editor - simply type `nano bb-keys.pem` and press **Enter**.
5. The application GNU nano 8.3 will launch with your file open to edit. Paste in the contents of the `.pem` file you copied earlier from the clipboard.
6. Save the file by typing in and pressing the `CTRL` and `X` combination keys on your keyboard. Then press `Y` (for yes) to save and press **Enter**.
7. To verify that the file has been saved, type in the command `ls` and press **Enter** as per the following screenshot in *Figure 8.17*:

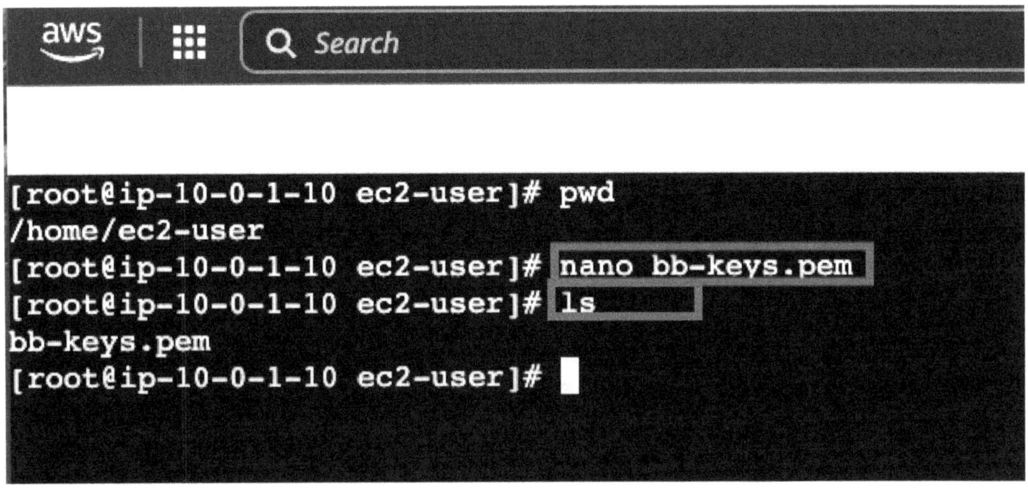

Figure 8.17: Creating a local copy of your pem file on the bastion host server

8. Next, type in the command `chmod 600 bb-keys.pem` and press **Enter**
9. Next, from the EC2 Instances web console in the other browser tab, select the **belly-brew-app-srv-01** instance by clicking the checkbox next to it
10. In the bottom half of the pane, make a note of the **Private IPv4 address** as per the following screenshot in *Figure 8.18*:

Figure 8.18: Note the Private IPv4 address of the app server

11. In the other browser tab where you are remotely logged into the bastion host server, type in the command `ssh -i "bb-keys.pem" ec2-user@private ipv4 address` (replace with the private IPv4 address that you noted for your server)
12. You may get a warning message asking you whether you want to continue. Type in yes and press **Enter**
13. You will now be connected to the **belly-brew-app-srv-01** instance over an SSH connection as per the following screenshot in *Figure 8.19*:

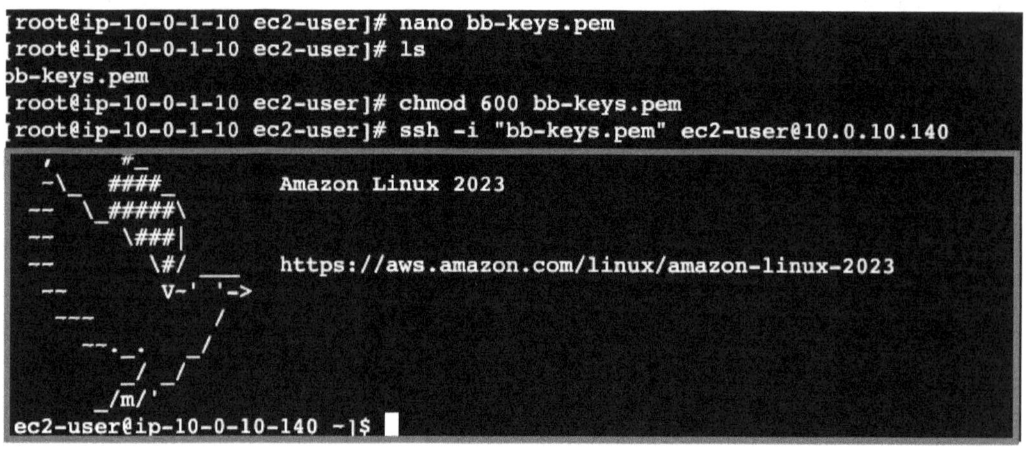

Figure 8.19: Successful connection to your private EC2 instance via the bastion host

You have now successfully connected to an EC2 instance in the private subnet using a bastion host in the public subnet. In the next project task, you will perform a clean-up exercise.

Project task 8.7 – Cleaning up

In this project task, you will terminate the EC2 instances to avoid any unnecessary costs.

1. Ensure that you are still logged into your AWS Development account and in the EC2 management console in the London region
2. From the left-hand menu, click the **Instances** link under the **Instances** section
3. In the right-hand pane, select both instances by clicking on their relevant checkboxes
4. From the **Instance state** drop-down list, click **Terminate (delete) instance**
5. Click the **Terminate (delete)** button

Your instances will now be terminated.

Summary

In this chapter, you explored a variety of AWS compute services, beginning with Amazon EC2, AWS's core virtual server offering. You learned about Amazon Machine Images (AMIs), which serve as templates that include the operating system, necessary software, and current patch levels—allowing you to launch EC2 instances as fully functional servers. You discovered that AMIs are available through Quick Start, the AWS Community, and the Marketplace, and that you can also build custom AMIs to meet your organization's specific needs.

You also examined the different EC2 instance types and families, understanding how each type corresponds to hardware characteristics like CPU, memory, and networking performance. Your learning continued with an overview of EC2 storage options such as Amazon EBS, Amazon EFS, and Amazon FSx, helping you understand how to attach persistent storage to your instances.

Additionally, you looked at the range of EC2 pricing models and learned how to select the most cost-effective option for your applications. Depending on your workload's requirements, you explored how to take advantage of discounted pricing options like Reserved Instances, Spot Instances, and Dedicated Hosts.

To wrap up, you were introduced to other AWS compute services beyond EC2. You considered the advantages of using containers for application deployment and learned that using serverless solutions like AWS Lambda to build event-driven architectures is best.

In the following chapter, we will move from the compute layer to the data layer, learning how AWS database services store, protect, scale, and migrate the data that those applications depend on.

Exam Readiness Drill – Chapter Review Questions

Apart from mastering key concepts, strong test-taking skills under time pressure are essential for acing your certification exam. That's why developing these abilities early in your learning journey is critical.

Exam readiness drills, using the free online practice resources provided with this book, help you progressively improve your time management and test-taking skills while reinforcing the key concepts you've learned.

HOW TO GET STARTED

- Open the link or scan the QR code at the bottom of this page
- If you have unlocked the practice resources already, log in to your registered account. If you haven't, follow the instructions in *Free Benefits with Your Book* section in this book's *Preface* and come back to this page.
- Once you log in, click the START button to start this chapter's quiz
- We recommend attempting a quiz multiple times till you're able to answer most of the questions correctly and well within the time limit.
- You can use the following practice template to help you plan your attempts:

Working On Accuracy		
Attempt	**Target**	**Time Limit**
Attempt 1	40% or more	Till the timer runs out
Attempt 2	60% or more	Till the timer runs out
Attempt 3	75% or more	Till the timer runs out
Working On Timing		
Attempt 4	75% or more	1 minute before time limit
Attempt 5	75% or more	2 minutes before time limit
Attempt 6	75% or more	3 minutes before time limit

The above drill is just an example. Design your drills based on your own goals and make the most out of the online quizzes accompanying this book.

Link to this Chapter's Quiz

You need to unlock the online practice resources to access the link below. Check the *Free Benefits with Your Book* section in the *Preface* for detailed instructions on how to do this. You only need to unlock the resources once.

Open Quiz `https://packt.link/clf_c02_ch8`or scan the QR code

9

Databases on AWS

At the heart of most applications, you will need to store, organize, analyze, and manipulate data in some form or another. Most applications will have a data store component where application-related data is hosted, and often you would use a *database* for this. This database is designed to help you organize data in a manner that makes it possible to derive information that consumers of your application require. For example, an e-commerce store will have a database component that stores a customer's previous orders, allowing you to use cutting-edge artificial intelligence and machine learning tools to build a personalized application that can make intelligent recommendations for future purchases. Critical to offering any of these functionalities is the raw data that needs to be stored in a manner that can be easily consumed.

In this chapter, you will learn the basics of databases, compare relational databases and non-relational databases, and their appropriate use cases. In addition, you will learn about certain industry-specific database solutions and get a thorough grounding in the architectural design patterns, best practices, and security strategies when hosting sensitive and critical corporate information. The topics covered in this chapter include:

- Understanding database concepts and models
- Working with relational databases on AWS
- Securing database credentials with AWS Secrets Manager
- Using Amazon DynamoDB for NoSQL workloads
- Improving database performance with Amazon ElastiCache
- Building data warehousing solutions with Amazon Redshift
- Migrating databases with AWS Database Migration Service

Understanding database concepts and models

There are several database types and models, catering to the wide range of different application requirements, such as the need for extensive complex queries or ultra-low latency, through to databases that must support complex entity relationships and the more modern vector-style databases to support artificial intelligence (AI) applications.

Perhaps one of the most common database models is the relational database, often referred to as SQL-based databases. Relational databases are often compared to a spreadsheet – the storage of structured data in a table, where rows define individual database records and columns represent the attributes that provide specific details or properties of each record, such as name, age, or email address, in a typical customer database. The following diagram in *Figure 9.1* depicts a typical table that stores customer details for an e-commerce company.

CustomerID	First_Name	Last_Name	Address	Town	Post_Code
CS7001	Alice	Brown	21 Hamilton Ave	London	WC1B 4RP
CS7001	Bob	Smith	12 Shelly Road	Oxford	OX1 1AA
CS7002	Holly	McDonald	33 Hazelwood Avenue	Wimbledon	SW19 1YT
CS7003	John	Major	108 Cavendish Avenue	High Gate	HA1 2IU

Figure 9.1: Customer contact table

As depicted in *Figure 9.1*, the *Customer Contact Details* table contains multiple records, each providing a specific customer's address information. The columns represent individual pieces of data that collectively offer meaningful insight into a customer's physical address.

A primary key is a crucial column in any relational database. A primary key is an attribute that holds a unique value for every record, enabling you to identify each one uniquely—no two records can share the same primary key. In this table, the primary key is labeled as **CustomerID**—a unique string that is not repeated elsewhere in the table. For example, you can easily identify **Holly McDonald** by using the **CustomerID** `'CS7002'` in a query to retrieve her address details.

Another key feature of relational databases is the ability to have multiple tables, each storing a specific set of data that can be linked to other tables through **joins**. This design enables the creation of a highly efficient and scalable database architecture.

For example, in *Figure 9.1*, the *Customer Contact Details* table contains information about customers and their contact details, including their home addresses. Now, imagine if each customer's order information were included in the same table. This approach would lead to inefficiencies due to data duplication, such as repeating the address details for every order a customer places.

An example of what this might look like is shown in *Figure 9.2*:

CustomerID	First_Name	Last_Name	Address	Town	Post_Code	Order Details	Qty	Amount
CS7001	Alice	Brown	21 Hamilton Ave	London	WC1B 4RP	Product 1701	2	$300
CS7002	Bob	Smith	12 Shelly Road	Oxford	OX1 1AA	Product 1789	1	$150
CS7002	Bob	Smith	12 Shelly Road	Oxford	OX1 1AA	Product 1777	1	$250
CS7002	Bob	Smith	12 Shelly Road	Oxford	OX1 1AA	Product 7878	5	$750
CS7003	Holly	McDonald	33 Hazelwood Avenue	Wimbledon	SW19 1YT	Product 7765	1	$350
CS7004	John	Major	108 Cavendish Avenue	High Gate	HA1 2IU	Product 5049	1	$333

Figure 9.2: Duplicate data example

As illustrated, the contact details for **Bob Smith** are repeated for each order he placed. This repetition is highly inefficient and results in unnecessary use of storage and system resources.

Instead, by leveraging the ability to host multiple tables, each focused on a specific area of the overall data set, you can achieve greater efficiency and improved data management. These tables can then be joined using **primary keys** and **foreign keys**, allowing queries to be executed more efficiently.

For example, in *Figure 9.3*, you'll notice there are two tables: one for *Customer Contact Details* and another for *Orders* placed by customers. The *Orders* table has its unique primary key, called **OrderID**. It also includes a column that links each order back to the customer who placed it—this is known as the **foreign key**.

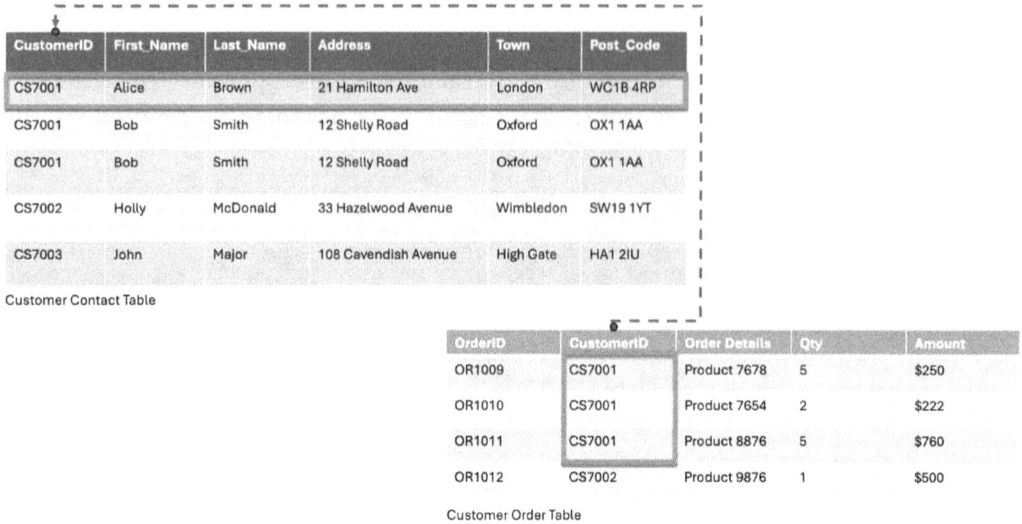

CustomerID	First_Name	Last_Name	Address	Town	Post_Code
CS7001	Alice	Brown	21 Hamilton Ave	London	WC1B 4RP
CS7001	Bob	Smith	12 Shelly Road	Oxford	OX1 1AA
CS7001	Bob	Smith	12 Shelly Road	Oxford	OX1 1AA
CS7002	Holly	McDonald	33 Hazelwood Avenue	Wimbledon	SW19 1YT
CS7003	John	Major	108 Cavendish Avenue	High Gate	HA1 2IU

Customer Contact Table

OrderID	CustomerID	Order Details	Qty	Amount
OR1009	CS7001	Product 7678	5	$250
OR1010	CS7001	Product 7654	2	$222
OR1011	CS7001	Product 8876	5	$760
OR1012	CS7002	Product 9876	1	$500

Customer Order Table

Figure 9.3: Join between the customer order table and the customer contact table

The example illustrated in *Figure 9.3* shows that **Alice Brown** has placed three orders. Rather than using a single table with extensive data duplication, you can structure the database using multiple related tables connected through joins. This approach allows you to reference data in one table from another without repeating the same information.

In this example, there's no need to duplicate Alice's contact details for each order she places. Instead, by mapping the **OrderID** in the Orders table to the **CustomerID** in the Customer Contact table, you can easily identify who placed each order. This structure enables more efficient queries and ensures data consistency.

In the *Orders* table, the column **CustomerID** acts as a foreign key, linking back to the primary key in the *Customer Contact Details* table.

You can then run queries across your tables to retrieve all the necessary related information. For example, if you want to generate a statement of account, you can query the order details for a specific customer and list them in the statement. At the same time, you can retrieve the customer's contact details to complete the statement, making it ready to be sent to the customer.

The term *relational* in *relational database* refers to the concept of **relations**, which in database theory are essentially **tables**.

- Each **table (relation)** stores data about a specific entity, such as Customers or Orders

- These tables are related to each other using **keys**:
    - **Primary keys** uniquely identify records in a table
    - **Foreign keys** establish relationships between different tables
- You can query across multiple tables using joins, thanks to these relationships

To query relational databases, you use a special language called a **structured query language**, or **SQL** for short. SQL is used to interact with databases, enabling you to create tables and relationships, insert, update, and delete data in tables, and run queries across multiple tables. Typical databases that utilize the SQL language include MySQL, Microsoft SQL Server, and Oracle.

Relational databases are also referred to as **Online Transaction Processing** (**OLTP**) databases. This type of database is designed for transactional workloads, which involve frequently adding, updating, and deleting small amounts of data. A common term used in this context is **CRUD**, which stands for **Create, Read, Update, and Delete**.

Relational databases, or **Relational Database Management Systems** (**RDBMS**), perform these CRUD operations in response to requests from your applications. Examples of transactional applications include an e-commerce website that processes customer orders or an employee database used by an HR application.

In the next section, you will learn more about Relational Databases on AWS.

Working with relational databases on AWS

Relational databases, such as MySQL or Microsoft SQL Server, must run on a compute resource, such as an Amazon EC2 instance. You need to install the database engine, after which you can interact with it using either a **command-line interface** (**CLI**) or a **graphical user interface** (**GUI**).

It's important to understand that a relational database requires core infrastructure components—compute, storage, and network connectivity—to be accessible and usable by your applications.

While installing and configuring a database engine like MySQL or Oracle on an EC2 instance is a valid approach, AWS offers a fully managed solution called **Amazon Relational Database Service** (**Amazon RDS**). Amazon RDS is an OLTP database designed for transaction-based workloads, such as student enrolment applications for universities or databases used in e-commerce applications. As another example related to the client requirements of Belly Brew Co. Limited, Amazon RDS can be used to host stock inventory data for its gut-friendly beverages, which will be updated regularly as orders are fulfilled and stock is replenished.

The key difference is that with Amazon RDS, you do not need to manage the underlying virtual machines or infrastructure that host the database engine—AWS handles it for you.

With EC2 self-hosting, AWS only manages the underlying physical host layer and the hypervisor software. You are responsible for managing, configuring, and securing the EC2 instances on which you install your chosen database engine. The following diagram in *Figure 9.4* illustrates the key differences between hosting your own database engine on EC2 instances vs. using the Amazon RDS service.

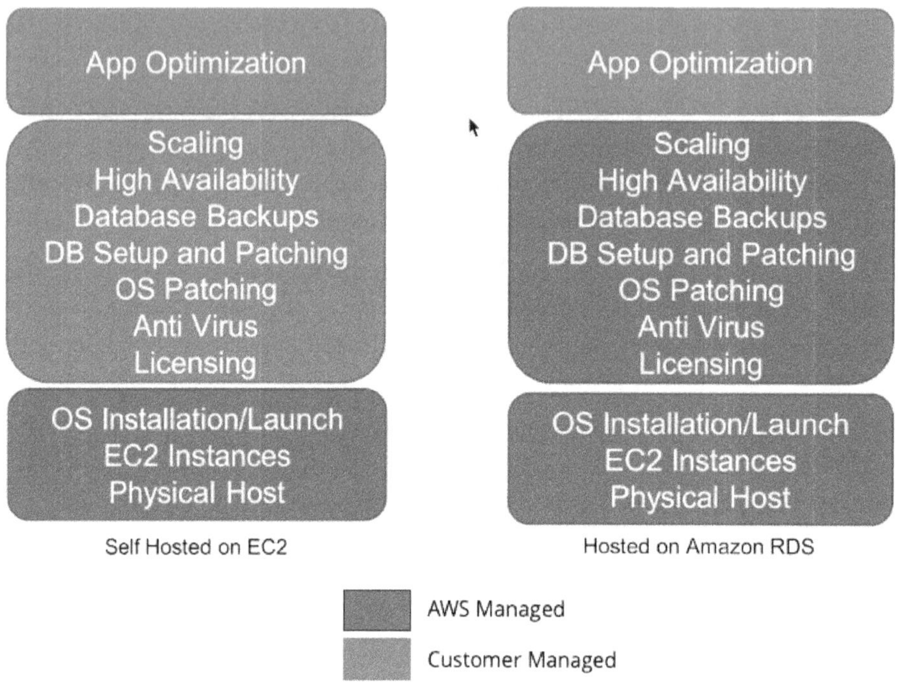

Figure 9.4: Self-hosted on EC2 vs. Amazon RDS

With Amazon RDS, AWS handles the administrative burden of installing, configuring, patching, and upgrading the database. This is achieved by abstracting away the underlying database administration tasks.

You still retain control over how the database is configured—such as the amount of CPU and memory allocated or how much storage is provisioned—by making API calls via the AWS Management Console or CLI.

You simply select the desired instance type and storage options, and AWS provisions the required resources for you.

Additionally, you can access the database using client tools or your application via AWS SDKs (Software Development Kits). However, you do not have access to the underlying operating system or the software components of the database engine that AWS provisions.

Amazon RDS offers several database engines that suit a wide range of businesses and enable companies to easily migrate their workloads to the cloud. These are:

- MySQL
- PostgreSQL
- Microsoft SQL
- Oracle
- IBM DB2

Amazon also offers its proprietary database, which is Amazon Aurora. This database offering comes with unparalleled high performance and availability, and has three variants (compatibility): Aurora for MySQL, PostgreSQL, and DSQL.

In the next section, you will learn about the core features of Amazon RDS.

Amazon RDS compute and storage options

To deploy a database using the Amazon RDS service, you must launch an RDS instance with your chosen engine. This instance runs on compute resources solely managed by AWS, and you do not have access to the underlying operating system or the database application software. Once your database instance has been provisioned, you can use client tools and utilities, or application code, to connect to the database instance and create one or more databases. Within each database, you can create one or more tables according to your application requirements.

To provision your Amazon RDS database, you must select an instance configuration from the available options. AWS offers three different classes to choose from – each with a range of various instance types that define the amount of CPU, memory, and other features, such as optimized writes and network bandwidth.

These include the following:

- **Standard classes (including the m classes)**: designed for a balance of compute, memory, and network resources, and ideal for most modern applications
- **Memory-optimized classes (including the r and x classes)**: designed for the most demanding applications, which require increased memory and are optimized for memory-intensive applications
- **Burstable classes (includes t classes)**: designed for non-production workloads and offer baseline performance levels with the ability to burst to full CPU usage during occasional spikes in demand

The following screenshot in *Figure 9.5* illustrates the available instance classes to choose from when provisioning your database instance.

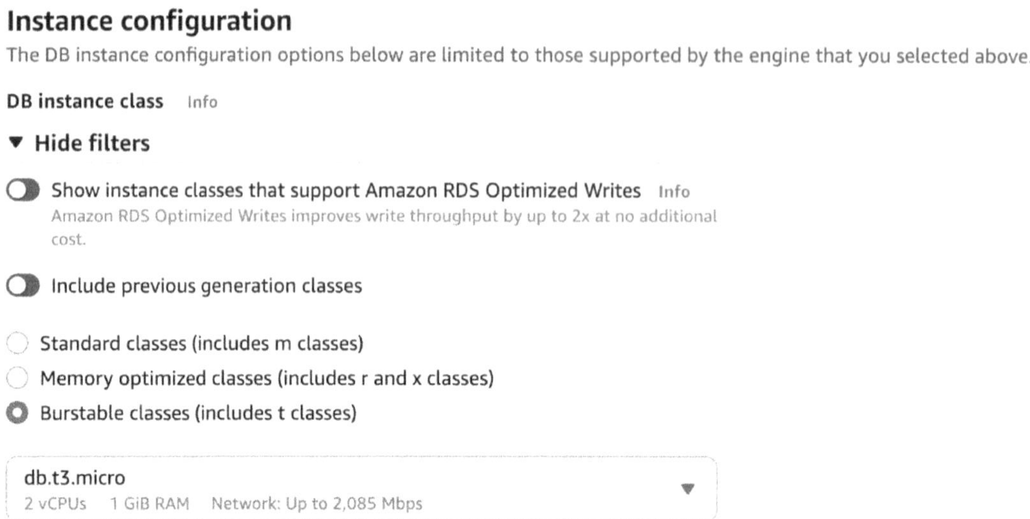

Figure 9.5: Instance configuration options

Once you select the class, you can then choose the appropriate instance size from the drop-down menu – this provides a selection of types offering varying levels of CPU, memory, and additional features, such as high-bandwidth networking, where applicable.

In addition to compute capacity, you must allocate storage for your database. AWS stores RDS database data on **Amazon Elastic Block Store (EBS)** volumes. You can modify the allocated storage capacity independently of the database instance class, allowing you to increase storage without changing the compute resources assigned to the database. This allows you to increase storage capacity without changing the instance type. The volume's throughput and IOPS (input/output operations per second) depend on the type of EBS volume you provision. These include:

- **General Purpose SSD (gp2/gp3):** Ideal for most database workloads that do not require extremely high IOPS. General-purpose SSD volumes support between 20 GiB and 64 TiB of storage for MariaDB, MySQL, and PostgreSQL. For Microsoft SQL Server and Oracle, the range is 20 GiB to 16 TiB.
    - **gp2** volumes provide performance based on the size of the volume, delivering a baseline of 3 IOPS per GiB and allowing smaller volumes to burst performance when additional throughput is required.

    - **gp3** volumes provide a baseline of 3,000 IOPS and 125 MiB/s throughput, with the ability to provision additional IOPS and throughput independently of storage capacity. This allows you to optimize performance without increasing storage size.
- **Provisioned IOPS SSD (io1/io2)**: Ideal for production-grade applications that require fast and consistent I/O performance. With Provisioned IOPS SSDS, you specify both the IOPS rate and the volume size, up to 64 Tib, depending on the database engine.

Amazon Aurora, however, offers significantly higher limits and capabilities, which will be discussed later in this chapter.

The best part is that you can scale your storage as needed, and Amazon RDS also offers **storage autoscaling**, which allows you to provision additional storage automatically when required.

> Note
>
> Amazon RDS Storage Autoscaling automatically increases database storage when required, up to a maximum limit that you define. Storage can only scale up; once additional storage has been allocated, it cannot be reduced without migrating to a new database instance.

Like EC2 instances, you must deploy your Amazon RDS databases in a VPC. This ensures that you can configure your database with the necessary network security settings to allow access only to authorized resources.

The following section explains some best practices to consider when deploying your Amazon RDS database.

Deploying an Amazon RDS database instance in a VPC

In most cases, you should deploy your database in private subnets within your VPC, as they are likely to contain sensitive data that must only be accessed by authorized applications. Placing databases in public subnets is rarely necessary and poses a significant security risk.

Using a VPC allows you to configure various network security components, ensuring that only specific applications running on other AWS resources can directly connect to the database.

Refer to the architectural diagram in *Figure 9.6*. Belly Brew Co. Limited's application is deployed on EC2 instances within the App Subnets. This application needs to connect to the backend database, which is deployed in the Data Subnet, also a private subnet.

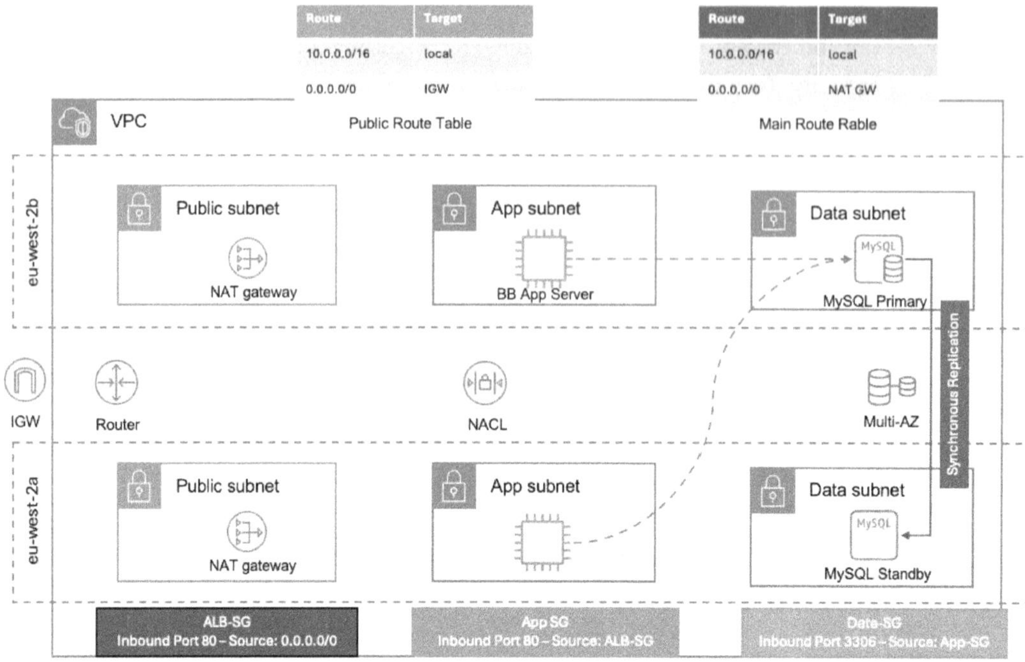

Figure 9.6: Deploying Amazon RDS MySQL DB instance in VPC

As depicted in *Figure 9.6*, EC2 instances hosted in the App Subnets (private subnets) need to connect to the MySQL database instances deployed in Amazon RDS. To enable this connectivity, the security group attached to the database instances, **Data-SG**, permits inbound traffic on port 3306, which is the default port for MySQL. The source of this traffic is restricted to any instance associated with the **App-SG** security group. This ensures that only resources related to the **App-SG** are allowed to send traffic to the MySQL database instances.

You will notice that only a single database instance has been configured in this VPC. This is because, with relational databases, there can only be one primary (or master) instance that is both writable and readable. However, this setup can act as a single point of failure. If the database instance fails, you may lose all your data. That's where AWS backup and recovery options come into play, which is the topic of the next section.

Backup and recovery

Your database is one of the most critical elements of your application — it hosts valuable data that your business depends on. AWS enables you to recover from the loss of any resource that hosts this data, such as your database instance, by allowing you to back up critical data and store that backup securely. In the event of a disaster, you can recover from the backup and launch new RDS database instances, minimizing the loss incurred.

However, backups are typically performed at regular intervals, such as every four hours or daily. Determining how often you should back up your data requires an understanding of your **Recovery Time Objective** (**RTO**) and **Recovery Point Objective** (**RPO**).

These two parameters will help you design a recovery strategy that meets your business requirements:

- **RTO**: This represents the amount of time (in hours) it takes to recover from a disaster and return to a working state. The recovery time includes provisioning a new database instance and performing a restore operation, which depends on the volume of data being restored.
- **RPO**: This defines the amount of data (measured as a factor of time) you are willing to lose in the event of a disaster. For example, if you cannot afford to lose more than four hours of data, then you must back up your data at least every four hours. The shorter the RPO, the less data is at risk of being lost during a failure.

Based on your RTO and RPO requirements, you can define your backup strategy. Amazon RDS offers two types of backup options: automatic backups and manual snapshots.

- **Automatic backups** are generated and managed by AWS. When enabled, these backups occur daily, and AWS provides a maximum retention period of 35 days. You can configure the retention period between 1 and 35 days. Older backups are automatically deleted after the set retention period. You can restore your database from these automatic backups at any time within the retention window. When you delete your database, AWS automatically deletes the associated automatic backups.
- **Manual snapshots** require you to initiate the backup manually. You should do this before making a significant change to your application or database, so you have a recent backup to revert to in case of failure. Unlike automatic backups, manual snapshots are *not* automatically deleted — you must manually delete them when they are no longer needed. Additionally, backups can be copied across AWS regions, allowing you to restore a copy of your database in another region if necessary.

AWS stores backups of your database in Amazon S3. You do not have direct access to these buckets. Instead, you must perform a restore operation from Amazon RDS to restore from backups.

While backups and restores enable you to recover from disasters such as a database instance failure, they do not provide high availability. Restoring a backup can take time, depending on the size of the database, which may result in your customers being unable to access the application until the restore process is fully complete. To address this limitation, AWS offers a feature known as **multi-AZ deployments**, which is discussed in the next section.

Amazon RDS multi-AZ options

When you deploy an Amazon RDS database, you can deploy a single instance in a specific subnet, which means that the instance resides in a single availability zone. Now, while backups and restore operations can help you recover from disasters, they don't offer instant failover capabilities in the event of a database instance failure or an availability zone outage.

Amazon RDS offers a feature known as **multi-AZ**, which involves having a primary instance of your database in one availability zone and one or two standby copies of the database in another availability zone. Data from the primary instance is replicated to the standby copy. AWS offers two options for configuring your RDS database with multi-AZ as follows:

Multi-AZ DB instance deployment

In a multi-AZ DB instance deployment, you have one *primary database instance* that handles all read and write requests. Resources such as EC2 instances must access this primary instance to perform read or write operations. This instance is deployed in a specific subnet within an Availability Zone. A *standby copy* of the database is automatically deployed in a different Availability Zone, and data is *synchronously* replicated from the primary to the standby instance as depicted in *Figure 9.7*:

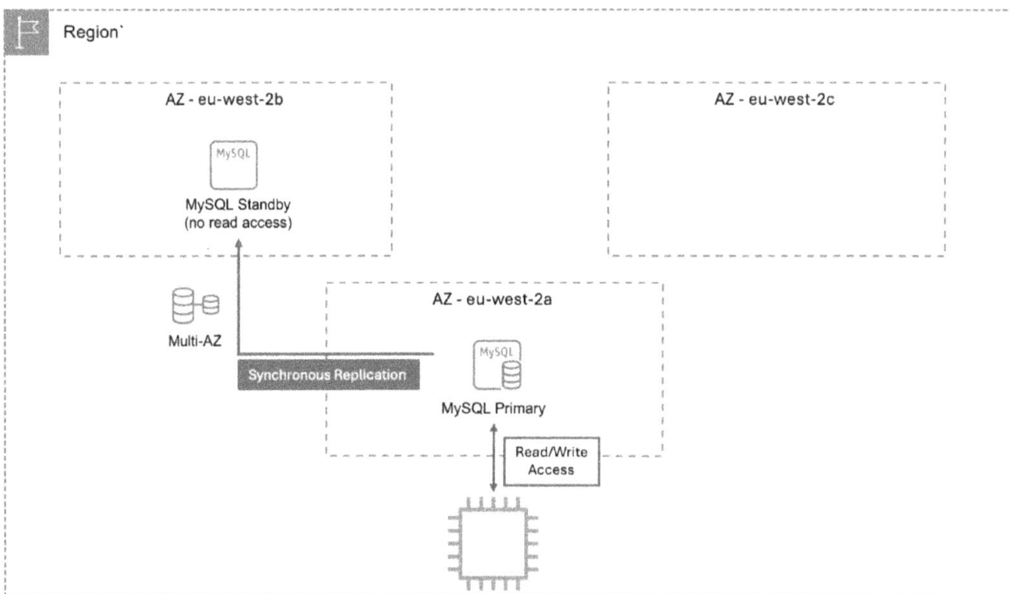

Figure 9.7: Amazon RDS multi-AZ instance deployment

The standby instance is not accessible when a multi-AZ instance configuration is in use. In the event of a failure of the primary instance, *AWS automatically initiates a failover* to the standby instance. Your applications running on your EC2 instance can then connect to the standby, which is promoted to become the new primary instance. A new standby instance replaces the old primary instance.

Since connectivity to the database is managed using a *DNS endpoint*, AWS handles the backend redirection to the new IP address during failover. This means you *do not need to reconfigure* your applications after a failover.

Multi-AZ DB cluster deployment

Amazon RDS also offers the Multi-AZ DB Cluster deployment feature, which provides additional capabilities compared to the Multi-AZ instance deployment option. In this configuration, replication is **semi-synchronous**—meaning the primary DB instance waits for at least one replica (not necessarily all) to acknowledge receipt of the data, though not necessarily confirmation of durability (i.e., writing the data to disk). This approach improves durability over asynchronous replication while reducing the performance impact typically associated with fully synchronous replication.

According to the diagram in *Figure 9.8*, the Multi-AZ DB Cluster deployment consists of two read-replica DB instances, in addition to the primary writeable DB instance.

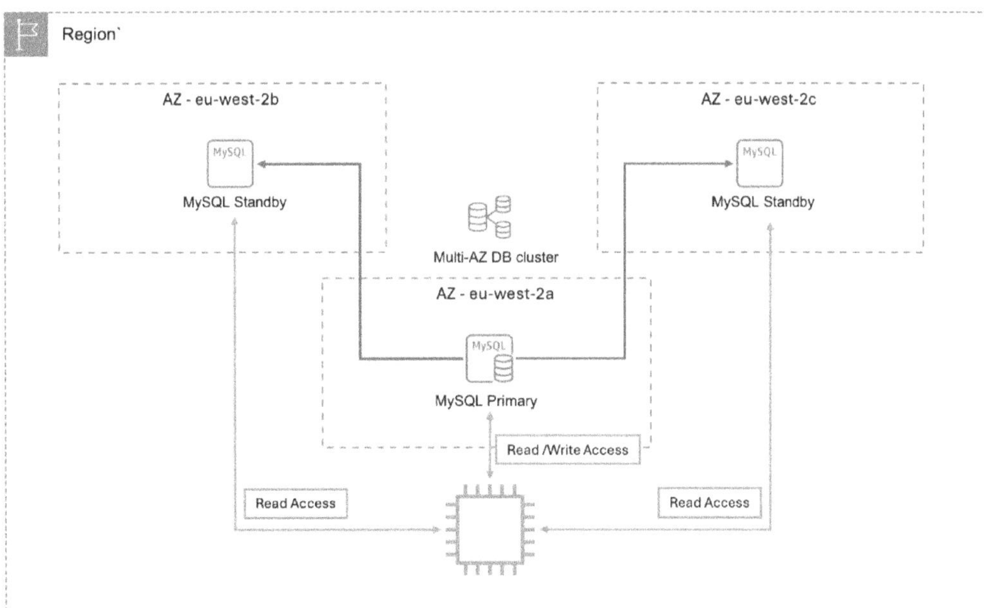

Figure 9.8: Amazon RDS multi-AZ DB cluster

These three instances are distributed across three separate Availability Zones, providing high availability, increased read capacity, and lower write latency compared to the multi-AZ DB instance deployment.

Note

While Multi-AZ deployments provide high availability and low RTO, they do *not* protect against data corruption—any corruption on the primary is likely replicated to the standby. Regular backups, whether automated or manual, are essential, especially before making changes. **Using both multi-AZ and backups ensures greater data protection and recovery options**.

Amazon RDS offers a single writable instance of your database by default. This means that the primary master copy of the database must be online and accessible to commit any write operations. As a Cloud Practitioner, you must consider how well your database can scale to handle increasing load. For relational databases, such as Amazon RDS, running engines like MySQL or PostgreSQL, you can only scale out your read requests using a feature known as **read replicas**. This is discussed in the next section.

Amazon RDS read replicas

An Amazon RDS Read Replica is a read-only copy of a database that applications can use to perform read queries. The replica is created by taking a snapshot of the primary instance and launching a new read-only instance from that snapshot. Asynchronous replication from the primary database to the read replica ensures that data changes committed to the primary instance are eventually reflected on the replica.

This setup reduces the load on the primary database by offloading read traffic to the replicas. It also enables continued support for read queries during planned maintenance on the primary instance.

As shown in *Figure 9.9*, you can create multiple read replicas from a single primary DB instance, allowing you to scale out your read workloads to meet increasing demand.

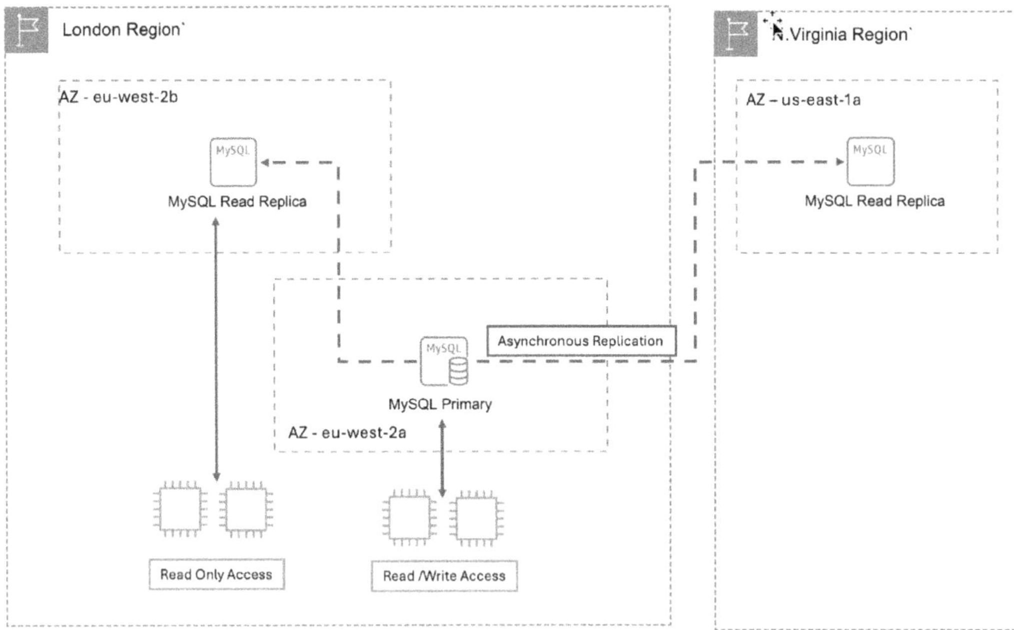

Figure 9.9: Amazon RDS read replicas

As shown in *Figure 9.9*, you can also create read replicas of your database instance in other AWS regions. In this example, a read replica is deployed in the N. Virginia region, replicating from a primary instance located in the London region. This configuration is useful for disaster recovery purposes and for supporting workloads in other regions that require low-latency access to your data.

In the event of a major disaster, a read replica can be promoted to function as a standalone primary database instance. This promotion severs the replication link to the original primary instance, effectively creating a new independent master database.

In addition to the standard open source and third-party engines offered by Amazon RDS, you also have Amazon Aurora, which is AWS's proprietary database engine that is compatible with MySQL and PostgreSQL engines. A brief overview of Amazon Aurora is provided in the next section.

Introduction to Amazon Aurora

Amazon Aurora is AWS's proprietary MySQL-compatible and PostgreSQL-compatible relational database service, designed for enterprise-grade workloads and production environments. It offers a comprehensive set of features, including high availability, automatic healing, and seamless scalability, to meet diverse business requirements. It is designed to be up to five times faster than standard MySQL and up to three times faster than PostgreSQL.

Aurora achieves these capabilities through its unique architecture, which automatically replicates data across a minimum of three Availability Zones. The architecture is depicted in the following diagram in *Figure 9.10*. You will note that the Aurora service provisions instances and a shared cluster volume across three availability zones.

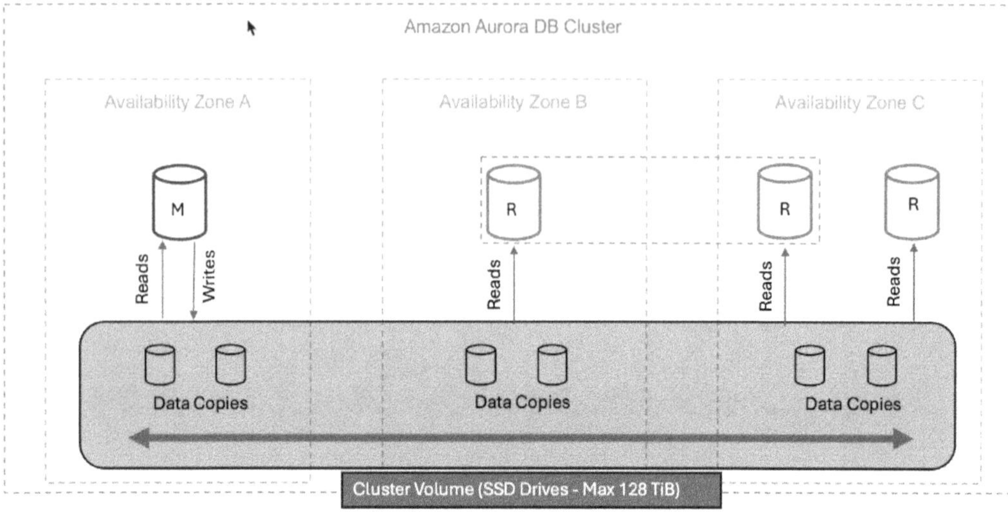

Figure 9.10: AWS Aurora DB cluster

Aurora offers built-in fault tolerance and supports up to 15 low-latency read replicas to efficiently scale read-intensive workloads. These read replicas not only help scale read operations but also provide multi-AZ capabilities. In the event of a failure of the primary instance, Aurora can instantly fail over to one of the read replicas. Unlike standard Amazon RDS, which uses EBS volumes attached to specific database instances, Aurora uses a shared storage architecture. It supports up to 128 TiB of storage per database and includes an auto-healing feature. Amazon Aurora is provisioned as a database cluster, which is discussed in the next section.

Amazon Aurora DB clusters

When launching an Amazon Aurora database, you provision a **DB cluster** that consists of one or more **DB instances** and a **cluster volume**. This cluster volume spans multiple **Availability Zones** and hosts copies of the cluster data.

The DB cluster is composed of two types of DB instances:

- **Primary DB instance**: Supports both read and write operations and performs all data modifications to the cluster volume. The primary instance is accessible via the **cluster endpoint**.
- **Aurora Replicas**: You can create up to 15 Aurora Replicas in addition to the primary instance. Although these replicas connect to the same cluster volume, they are used only for read operations. Applications can connect to them via the **reader endpoint**.

Aurora Replicas are designed to handle read queries and can also be used for failover if the primary instance fails.

When provisioning Amazon Aurora, you must select a **DB instance class**, which can be either **burstable** or **memory-optimized**, with various instance types offering different levels of CPU, memory, and network capacity. Additionally, Amazon Aurora is also available as a **serverless option**, which is discussed in the next section.

Amazon Aurora Serverless

Amazon Aurora Serverless v2 is a fully managed service that includes built-in autoscaling capabilities, allowing it to automatically adjust database capacity based on workload patterns and application demand. You are charged only for the resources consumed by your DB cluster, helping you avoid overprovisioning unless explicitly required by your application.

You do not need to specify the instance class, type, or size for your Aurora Serverless database. Instead, you define Aurora Capacity Units (ACUs), which Amazon Aurora uses to provision the required capacity. Each ACU provides approximately 2 GiB of memory along with a corresponding amount of CPU and network bandwidth. You specify a minimum and maximum number of ACUs for your cluster, and Amazon Aurora will scale within this range—adding or removing capacity based on application load.

Interestingly, the ACU count can scale down to zero, allowing the cluster to pause after a period of inactivity. This can be highly cost-efficient, as when your cluster is paused, you are only charged for the storage consumed.

Aurora Serverless is ideal for development and testing environments, as well as production workloads with unpredictable usage patterns. For example, an e-commerce website might experience increased traffic during the winter or rainy seasons. Another use case is deploying a new web application when its popularity is still uncertain. Once usage trends are clearer, you can decide whether to transition to a standard Aurora deployment or continue using the serverless architecture.

Databases store persistent or temporary data that is accessed by applications, which typically require authentication using credentials such as usernames and passwords. Hardcoding these credentials in the application is a poor practice. Instead, Amazon recommends using AWS Secrets Manager to securely retrieve database credentials dynamically. This will be covered in the next section.

Securing database credentials with AWS Secrets Manager

AWS Secrets Manager enables you to securely store and retrieve secrets such as database credentials, API keys, OAuth tokens, and other sensitive information. Your application can be configured to dynamically retrieve the necessary secret data to perform various operational tasks, such as authenticating to a backend database using credentials stored in Secrets Manager.

According to the diagram in *Figure 9.11*, your application requires permissions to access the secret stored in Secrets Manager and use that data to authenticate against the backend database. This approach eliminates the need to hardcode sensitive database credentials in the application code, which are often stored in plain text. It also prevents accidental exposure of credentials when application code is uploaded to public repositories like GitHub.

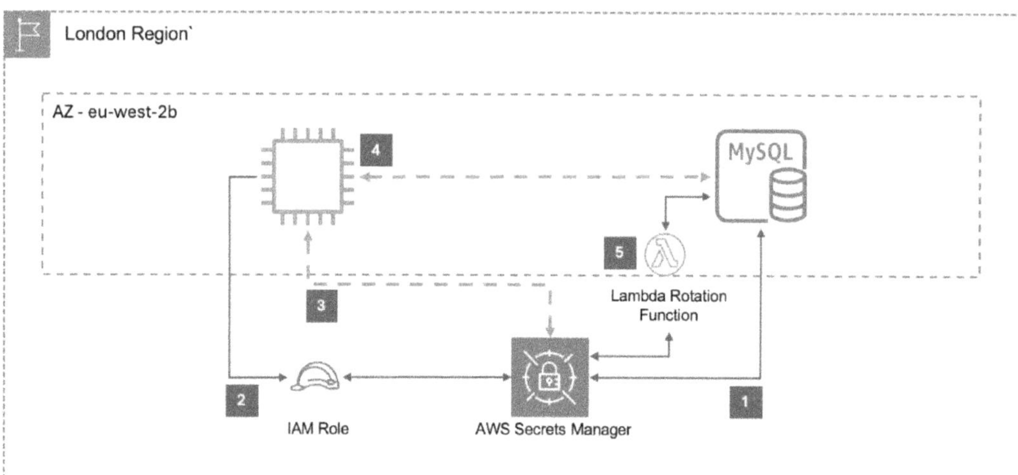

Figure 9.11: AWS Secrets Manager and application architecture

As shown in *Figure 9.11*, the high-level workflow for using AWS Secrets Manager is as follows:

1. AWS Secrets Manager is configured to store and manage the credentials of the MySQL database
2. The application, hosted on an EC2 instance, is configured with an **IAM role** that allows it to access the specific secret stored in AWS Secrets Manager

3. The application makes calls to AWS Secrets Manager using **AWS SDKs** (**Software Development Kits**) to retrieve the database credentials dynamically
4. The application uses the retrieved credentials to authenticate with the MySQL database
5. A Lambda function is provisioned if you configure the secret to rotate at regular intervals. This function updates both the secret stored in AWS Secrets Manager and the corresponding credentials in Amazon RDS.

AWS Secrets Manager also offers a powerful feature that allows you to set an **automatic rotation schedule** for your secrets. This ensures you do not rely on long-term credentials that are more likely to be compromised. Additionally, because the credentials are not stored within the application, rotating the secret does not require you to update or redeploy your application code.

Relational databases, also known as SQL databases, are designed to help you build an array of related tables with complex joins, enabling efficient and powerful queries. However, they require that data be stored in a structured format with a strictly defined schema.

The **schema** refers to the table structure consisting of rows and columns, where rows represent individual items and columns represent attributes whose values provide context to those items. In most cases, this schema must be defined at the outset, and making changes to it later can be challenging. Additionally, all data must conform to this structured format.

Relational databases, such as Amazon RDS, also have specific performance limitations, particularly when handling highly scalable or high-throughput workloads.

To address such use cases, AWS offers other database options, including **NoSQL** (**Non-Relational**) databases like **Amazon DynamoDB**. DynamoDB stores data as key-value pairs in JSON document format, and it does not require a strict, predefined schema.

The following section provides a high-level overview of **Amazon DynamoDB**.

Using Amazon DynamoDB for NoSQL workloads

Amazon DynamoDB is AWS's NoSQL, non-relational database solution, capable of delivering single-digit millisecond latency. The service operates from within the AWS public space, so you do not need to place instances in your VPC. Your compute resources can connect to DynamoDB tables by making API calls to the database.

Thanks to its serverless architecture, there is no need to specify instance classes, types or sizes. You also do not need to specify storage volume capacity. Instead, you define **provisioned capacity** in terms of **read capacity units** (**RCUs**) and **write capacity units** (**WCUs**), which AWS uses to provision the necessary infrastructure. Alternatively, you can opt for **on-demand**

capacity, where AWS dynamically provisions capacity based on your application's demand. All data is stored on **solid-state drives** (**SSDs**), and the underlying storage is replicated across multiple Availability Zones, ensuring durability and availability.

NoSQL databases, such as DynamoDB, support both semi-structured and structured data, including key-value pairs and document data models defined in **JSON** (**JavaScript Object Notation**) format. A fundamental difference between DynamoDB and Amazon RDS is that with DynamoDB, you do not need to specify a strict schema. The schema can be modified on the fly and updated as needed. Each item in a DynamoDB table does not require a value for every attribute. To get started, you only need a **primary key** and, optionally, a **sort key** to define the uniqueness of each item stored in the table.

AWS DynamoDB offers excellent performance and resilience features, making it ideal for modern web-based and mobile applications. It is the database of choice for gaming, streaming, and financial services applications. DynamoDB is well-suited for use cases with strict availability requirements, eliminating the need for manual scaling of instances or storage capacity.

Some key features of DynamoDB include:

- **DynamoDB Accelerator** (**DAX**): DAX is a fully managed caching feature that enhances the performance of your DynamoDB tables. It significantly reduces response times from milliseconds to microseconds for frequently accessed data. Unlike traditional caching solutions, DAX is easy to configure and does not require your application to manage both the cache and the database separately. This feature is particularly effective for read-heavy or bursty workloads, designed for eventually consistent reads and it minimizes the need to overprovision read capacity units.
- **DynamoDB Global Tables**: This feature provides a fully managed, multi-region, and multi-active database architecture that enables you to localize read and write operations. Global Tables allow you to deploy replicas of your table in multiple AWS regions. Each application can write to its local copy, and data is automatically replicated across regions to keep all tables in sync. This makes Global Tables ideal for applications that require high availability and low-latency access across geographically dispersed regions.
- **DynamoDB Streams**: This feature captures a time-ordered sequence of item-level changes that occur in your DynamoDB tables. With Streams, you can view and react to data modifications before the change, after the change, or both. DynamoDB Streams stores recent changes to your items over a rolling 24-hour period. This enables you to add real-time processing and additional intelligence to your application's business logic.

While DynamoDB DAX provides in-memory caching capabilities for DynamoDB tables, you may also require a similar caching solution for Amazon RDS databases. In such cases, Amazon ElastiCache is an ideal service, and the next section introduces its key features and benefits.

Improving database performance with Amazon ElastiCache

While DynamoDB DAX provides an in-memory caching solution for DynamoDB tables, you may wonder about caching options for Amazon RDS.

Amazon ElastiCache is an in-memory caching service that can be used with Amazon RDS to improve read performance by storing frequently accessed data in memory, reducing the need to query the backend database directly.

Caching services such as ElastiCache improve read performance because your application does not need to call the backend database to retrieve frequently accessed data. This also reduces the load on your Amazon RDS instances.

AWS offers three in-memory caching engines: **Valkey**, **Memcached**, and **Redis**.

- **Redis** is designed for complex data structures and supports features such as Multi-AZ deployment, data encryption, replication, and automatic failover
- **Memcached** is optimized for simpler data types but supports large nodes with multiple cores and threads, and it scales out effectively
- **Valkey** is an open-source alternative to Redis. It can handle a variety of workloads, such as caching, session stores, and message queues, and can act as a primary database

In the next section, you will learn about **Amazon Redshift**, which is designed for analytical workloads.

Building data warehousing solutions with Amazon Redshift

Data warehousing solutions like Amazon Redshift are designed to help businesses pull data from other relational databases or storage platforms and perform complex data analytics.

For example, you can combine data across customer orders, inventory systems, supplier contacts and agreements, and financial data to analyze trends, demand, and return on investment (ROI). Data warehousing solutions also help you build **Business Intelligence** (**BI**) platforms, enabling business executives to make informed decisions.

Unlike Amazon RDS, which is an **Online Transaction Processing** (**OLTP**) solution, data warehousing platforms like Amazon Redshift are designed for **Online Analytical Processing** (**OLAP**).

Instead of organizing data as rows—where each item is created and managed as a transaction—Redshift uses a **columnar storage format** to analyze large datasets efficiently. It can scale up to **petabytes** of data and supports **massively parallel processing** (**MPP**) for high-performance querying.

You have two options for launching your Amazon Redshift data warehouse:

- **Provisioned Cluster**: This is a cluster of nodes comprising one **leader node** and one or more **compute nodes**
    - The leader node manages all communication between the application and the compute nodes
    - The compute nodes *execute* compiled code provided by the leader node and return intermediate results for final aggregation
    - You can have up to *128 compute nodes* in your cluster, and you can choose both the node type and the number of nodes
    - The cluster is always on, whether you're querying it or not, and you are billed accordingly
- **Redshift Serverless**: This is ideal for those just starting out or with unpredictable workloads
    - Redshift automatically handles cluster provisioning and scaling based on query load
    - You only pay for the compute used, measured in **Redshift Processing Units** (**RPUs**)
    - There is no need to manage infrastructure, making it easier and more cost-effective for ad hoc analysis or variable usage patterns

Another solution offered by AWS is **Amazon Redshift Spectrum**. This service allows you to run SQL queries directly against data stored in Amazon S3 buckets. Redshift Spectrum is an extension of your Redshift cluster, enabling you to query S3 data alongside your Redshift tables in a single SQL query. This is particularly useful when you want to combine historical (cold) data stored in S3 with frequently accessed (hot) data in Redshift for seamless, integrated analytics.

Although AWS provides a wide range of database services, many companies still need to migrate their on-premises databases to the AWS Cloud. AWS offers several tools and services to move critical business data, and in the next section, you will learn about **AWS Database Migration Service** (**AWS DMS**).

Migrating databases with AWS Database Migration Service

Amazon offers the **Database Migration Service** (**DMS**), which is commonly used to help businesses migrate their on-premises databases to the AWS Cloud. You can migrate existing databases to Amazon RDS, DynamoDB, or Redshift easily using a managed service that handles all the heavy lifting for you.

You no longer need to perform a manual backup of your on-premises database and then restore it in the cloud. This process usually results in a more extended outage period. Instead, with AWS DMS, AWS helps you to configure a source endpoint for the source database and a target endpoint for your target database. Using replication, the data and any changes are migrated across to the target database. When you are ready to switch over, you simply point your application to the new target database endpoint.

You can perform a **one-time migration** or even configure **continuous replication** to migrate ongoing changes from your on-premises database over a defined period.

With AWS DMS, you can perform:

- **Homogeneous migrations**, such as MySQL to MySQL or Oracle to Oracle
- **Heterogeneous migrations**, such as Oracle to Microsoft SQL Server

For heterogeneous migrations, you must first use the **AWS Schema Conversion Tool** (**AWS SCT**) to convert the schema of the destination cloud database before performing the migration.

AWS DMS simplifies database migrations by reducing the complexity, risk, and downtime traditionally associated with moving databases to the cloud. Whether you are migrating between similar database engines or converting to a different database platform, AWS DMS provides a managed solution that helps you transfer data securely and efficiently. By combining AWS DMS with the AWS Schema Conversion Tool for heterogeneous migrations, organizations can modernize their database environments and accelerate their cloud adoption journey with minimal disruption to business operations.

In the next section, you will have an opportunity to build out an Amazon RDS database for Belly Brew Co. Limited. The database will be used to host customer contact information for its upcoming marketing campaigns. As part of the website you will build using this study guide, you will need to provision an Amazon RDS for MySQL database. This database will be used to capture customer contact data, which the marketing team will find invaluable.

In the next project section of this chapter, you will launch an Amazon RDS for MySQL database within the VPC you previously created for Belly Brew Co. Limited.

Project task 9 – Launching an Amazon RDS MySQL database

In this project task, you will deploy an Amazon RDS MySQL database that will be used to fulfill the requirements discussed in *Chapter 1*, specifically as highlighted in the *Requirement 1* section.

The MySQL database will be used to store existing and potential customer contact details, which will be used for future marketing campaigns. To encourage members of the public to share their contact details, a website will be deployed as a frontend to the database offering a free gut-friendly recipe ebook. In the future, the same contact details will be used to offer free product trials, newsletters, and vouchers.

Technical requirements

To complete the project exercises in this chapter, ensure that you have completed all the labs in all previous chapters. Log in to your AWS Development account as the IAM user Alice to complete the project tasks.

Project task 9.1 – Configuring an RDS database subnet group

In this project task, you will configure a database subnet group. This is a collection of subnets where Amazon RDS will be able to deploy your MySQL database instance. You must have a minimum of two subnets across two availability zones to form a subnet group. As per *Chapter 7*, you have already created two subnets for your database across availability zones `eu-west-2a` and `eu-west-2b` of the `belly-brew-vpc`.

1. Ensure that you are logged into Belly Brew Co. Limited's Development account and are in the London region
2. From the search bar at the top of the webpage, search for RDS and then select the **Aurora and RDS** link from the search results to access its console
3. From the left-hand menu, click **Subnet groups**
4. In the right-hand pane, click the **Create DB subnet group** button
5. Provide a name for your subnet group, such as `belly-brew-db-subnet-group`
6. Next, provide a description of your choice
7. Select Belly Brew Co. Limited's VPC you created in *Chapter 7* from the **VPC** drop-down list

8. Next, in the **Add subnets** section, select **eu-west-2a** and **eu-west-2b** from the **Availability Zones** drop-down list
9. Next, select the two data subnets you have previously created from the **Subnets** drop-down list as per the following screenshot in *Figure 9.12*:

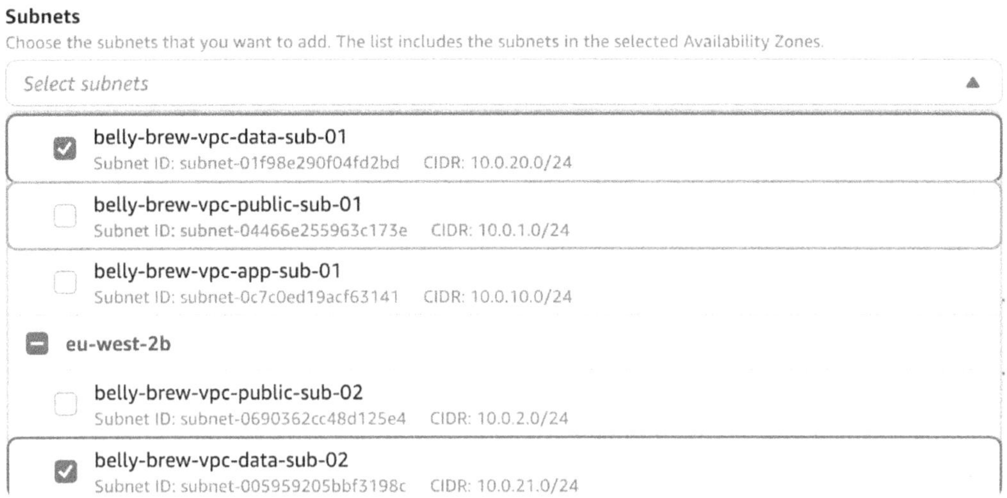

Figure 9.12: Belly Brew Co. Limited's data subnets

10. Scroll to the bottom of the webpage and click the **Create** button

Your database subnet group will now be created, and you should receive a notification confirming this.

In the next project task, you will deploy an Amazon RDS MySQL database in your VPC.

Project task 9.2 – Deploying Amazon RDS MySQL database

In this project task, you will deploy your Amazon RDS MySQL database. For this lab exercise, you will deploy a single instance of the database rather than a multi-AZ one to ensure you remain within the free tier usage of your AWS account. In a real-world production environment, consider using multi-AZ and read replicas based on your specific use case.

1. Ensure you are still logged into your AWS account and in the **Aurora and RDS** console
2. From the left-hand menu, click **Databases**
3. In the right-hand pane, click the drop-down arrow on the **Create database** button
4. Select **Full configuration**
5. Next, for the **Engine options**, ensure you select **MySQL** as the **Engine type**
6. Scroll down the webpage a bit further and select **Dev/Test** in the **Templates** section

7. In the **Deployment options** under **Availability and durability,** select **Single-AZ DB instance deployment (1 instance)**
8. In the **Settings** section, set the name of the **DB instance identifier** as `bellybrewdb`
9. Next, in the **Credentials Settings** section, set the **Master username** to `admin`. Select the **Self managed** option under **Credentials management**.
10. Next, type in a password of your choice in the text box below **Master password** and repeat the same password in the text box below **Confirm master password** – ensure you make a note of it, otherwise your application will not be able to connect to the database
11. In the **Instance configuration** section, ensure that **Burstable classes** (includes t classes) is selected and from the drop-down menu, select the **db.t4g.micro** instance type
12. Leave the storage settings at their default values
13. Next, select Belly Brew Co. Limited's VPC you created in *Chapter 7* from the **Virtual private cloud (VPC)** drop-down list in the **Connectivity** section. Doing so will automatically select the **belly-brew-db-subnet-group** you created in *Project Task 9.1* as per the screenshot in *Figure 9.13*:

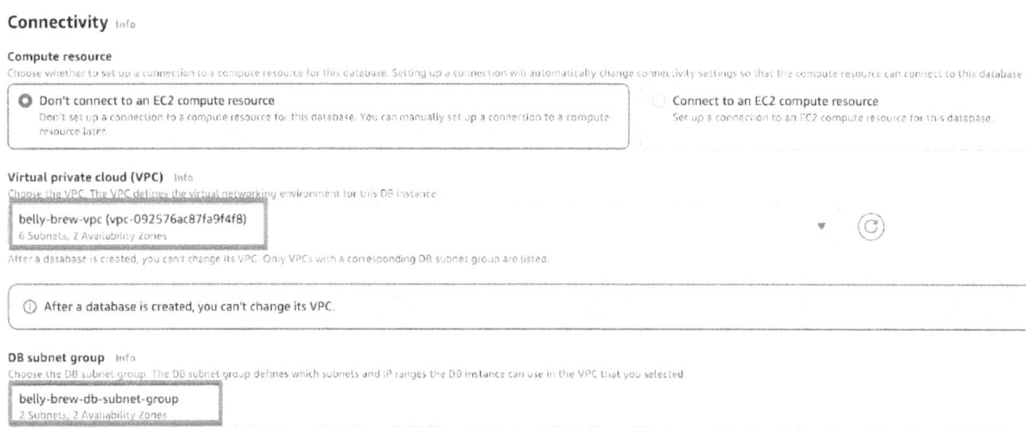

Figure 9.13: Amazon RDS MySQL VPC selection

14. Ensure that **No** is selected under **Public access**
15. Next, for the **VPC security group (firewall)**, delete the **default** security group by clicking the **x** icon next to it. Select the `belly-brew-vpc-data-sg` security group from the **Existing VPC Security Groups** drop-down list. Recall that you have configured this security group earlier in *Chapter 7*.

16. Ensure that **No preference** is selected under **Availability Zone**. AWS will deploy your database instance in one of the designated availability zones and subnets of the subnet group.
17. Next, as you scroll down, you will notice the first **Additional configuration** section. If you expand this, you should see that the default port (`3306`) for MySQL is already populated. Leave this setting at the default value.
18. Next, scroll further down the webpage until you get to the second **Additional configuration** section. In this section, you must provide a name for your database in the text box labeled **Initial database name**. For example, you can use the same name as the database identifier you provided earlier, such as `bellybrewdb`, as per the following screenshot in *Figure 9.14*

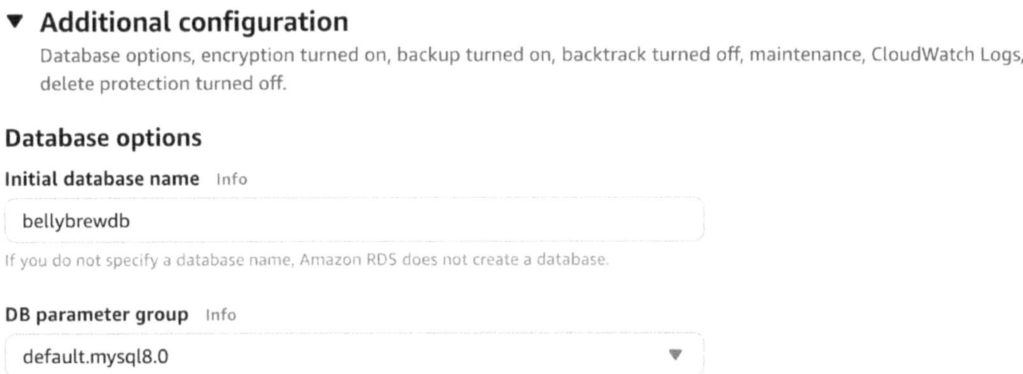

Figure 9.14: Initial database name

19. Next, ensure that **Enable automated backups** is selected, and then set the Backup retention period to 1 day
20. Accept all the remaining configuration settings at their default values and then scroll to the bottom of the webpage. Click the **Create database** button.

Your database will now be created. This can take up to 10 minutes. Once created, you will be able to view the database details in the console as shown in the following screenshot in *Figure 9.15*:

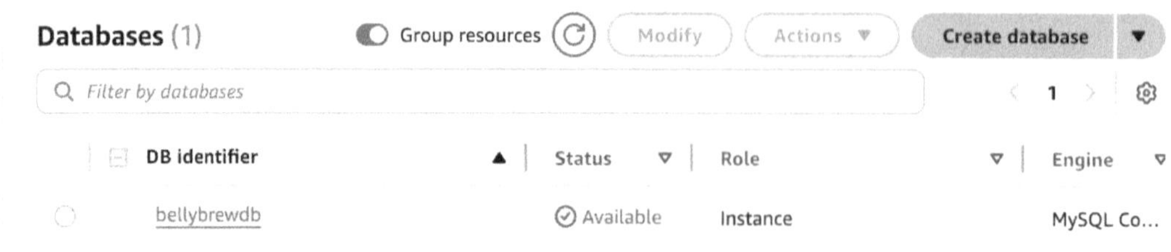

Figure 9.15: RDS MySQL database for Belly Brew Co. Limited

Clicking the database link in the **DB Identifier** column will allow you to review the database configuration details. For example, as shown in the following screenshot in *Figure 9.16*, you can review the **Connectivity & Security** settings.

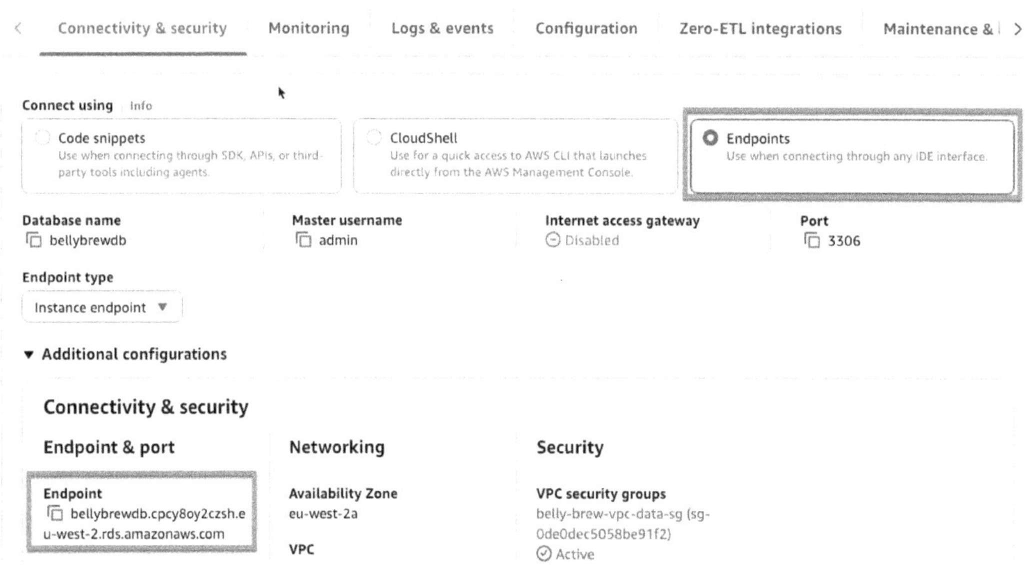

Figure 9.16: Connectivity and security settings

You must make a note of the database **Endpoint**, which you will need to configure your application with to access the database. You will also need the database name you chose earlier, as well as the username and password you defined for the database. These details will be required in *Chapter 10*.

Summary

In this chapter, you learned about various AWS database services available to support a wide range of use cases. You discovered some fundamental differences between SQL and NoSQL (Relational vs. Non-Relational) databases and their specific use cases.

Amazon RDS is a relational database service that supports various engines such as MySQL, PostgreSQL, Microsoft SQL Server, and Oracle. AWS also offers its own proprietary database called Amazon Aurora, designed for enterprise-grade applications and offering a suite of features to meet modern application requirements. Amazon Aurora provides six copies of the database using a clustered storage solution spread across three Availability Zones and includes advanced features such as self-healing capabilities.

You learned about the importance of designing your database solution for high availability using multi-AZ deployments and for scaling read operations using read replicas. You also learned about the importance of configuring both automatic and manual backups to mitigate the impact of major disasters or data corruption issues.

You then learned how DynamoDB is particularly useful for cutting-edge mobile and web applications, where applications require single-digit millisecond latency and data structures need to be flexible without a strict schema. This NoSQL offering from AWS also includes advanced features such as a built-in in-memory caching service called **DynamoDB Accelerator** (**DAX**) and the ability to deploy a multi-master (multi-active) database solution across multiple regions.

In addition, you learned about Amazon ElastiCache, which provides in-memory caching engines such as Redis and Memcached. For data warehousing solutions, AWS offers the Amazon Redshift service, available both as a provisioned cluster and as a serverless solution. Amazon Redshift Spectrum also allows you to query data stored in Amazon S3 directly, without having to import it into a Redshift cluster.

Finally, you learned about the AWS **Database Migration Service** (**DMS**), which enables migration of on-premises databases using both homogeneous and heterogeneous migration options. The latter requires the use of the AWS **Schema Conversion Tool** (**SCT**). DMS supports both one-time migrations and ongoing replication from a source database to a destination database.

In the next chapter, we will learn how to make the application highly available, fault-tolerant, and elastic using Elastic Load Balancing, Auto Scaling, AWS Secrets Manager, and Amazon SES.

Exam Readiness Drill – Chapter Review Questions

Apart from mastering key concepts, strong test-taking skills under time pressure are essential for acing your certification exam. That's why developing these abilities early in your learning journey is critical.

Exam readiness drills, using the free online practice resources provided with this book, help you progressively improve your time management and test-taking skills while reinforcing the key concepts you've learned.

HOW TO GET STARTED

- Open the link or scan the QR code at the bottom of this page
- If you have unlocked the practice resources already, log in to your registered account. If you haven't, follow the instructions in *Free Benefits with Your Book* section in this book's *Preface* and come back to this page.
- Once you log in, click the START button to start this chapter's quiz
- We recommend attempting a quiz multiple times till you're able to answer most of the questions correctly and well within the time limit.
- You can use the following practice template to help you plan your attempts:

Working On Accuracy		
Attempt	**Target**	**Time Limit**
Attempt 1	40% or more	Till the timer runs out
Attempt 2	60% or more	Till the timer runs out
Attempt 3	75% or more	Till the timer runs out
Working On Timing		
Attempt 4	75% or more	1 minute before time limit
Attempt 5	75% or more	2 minutes before time limit
Attempt 6	75% or more	3 minutes before time limit

The above drill is just an example. Design your drills based on your own goals and make the most out of the online quizzes accompanying this book.

Link to this Chapter's Quiz

You need to unlock the online practice resources to access the link below. Check the *Free Benefits with Your Book* section in the *Preface* for detailed instructions on how to do this. You only need to unlock the resources once.

Open Quiz `https://packt.link/clf_c02_ch9`or scan the QR code

10

High Availability, Fault Tolerance, and Elasticity on AWS

Businesses strive to ensure that their software applications are always available and experience minimal downtime. This is particularly critical when end customers need access to those applications, such as customers of an e-commerce business. Any downtime can impact not only sales but also the company's reputation. Therefore, designing solutions that are highly available or even fault-tolerant is essential for most businesses.

If you deploy your application on a single EC2 instance supported by a single database instance, you create a **single point of failure**. If there are any hardware or software issues with the EC2 instance, or if the Availability Zone in which it is deployed goes offline, your customers will be unable to access the application. Modern architectural patterns, therefore, incorporate **high availability** into their design. This often involves having multiple EC2 instances serving the same application, ideally deployed across multiple **Availability Zones** (**AZs**) within a region.

Using the multi-AZ option for your Amazon RDS database is another example of avoiding single points of failure. If your primary instance fails, AWS performs a failover to the standby instance, which maintains an up-to-date copy of your data. Your RDS database remains highly available, although there may be a few seconds of downtime during the failover process.

Fault tolerance takes this concept one step further, ensuring that your application continues to operate even if a component fails. In this case, Amazon RDS Multi-AZ alone is insufficient, as the failover process still introduces a brief period of downtime. Instead, you might re-architect your solution to use DynamoDB Global Tables, which offer the level of fault tolerance required. If a region goes offline, traffic can be redirected to another region with a copy of the DynamoDB table, maintaining seamless access.

You also want your application to be scalable, ensuring you have sufficient resources to handle changes in demand. You must be able to scale out as demand increases and scale in as it decreases. Scaling out may involve adding more EC2 instances to your fleet and distributing the load across the increased compute capacity. Conversely, when demand drops, you want to scale back and terminate unused EC2 instances to reduce costs and avoid waste. This ability to dynamically adjust resources in response to fluctuating demand is known as **elasticity**.

You'll also implement your first capstone project for Belly Brew Co. Limited, giving you real-world experience. As discussed in *Chapter 1*, Belly Brew Co. Limited wants to deploy a customer-facing website to engage with existing and potential customers. The website will offer a free gut-friendly recipe eBook in exchange for visitors sharing their contact details. The marketing team can then use these details for future campaigns.

You will have the opportunity to build a complete end-to-end three-tier architecture and deploy this website in your own AWS account. You have already configured several resources that will be used in this chapter's project section, such as the VPC and the MySQL database deployed in earlier chapters.

This chapter introduces you to the tools and services that help you design for both high availability and elasticity. It covers the following topics:

- Designing for high availability with Elastic Load Balancers
- Connecting Elastic Load Balancers to VPC resources
- Scaling EC2 workloads with AWS Auto Scaling
- Supporting application delivery with AWS Secrets Manager and Amazon SES

Designing for high availability with Elastic Load Balancers

One way to ensure high availability is by hosting multiple resources that serve the same application, such as several EC2 instances running the same web application. However, you need a mechanism to distribute incoming customer traffic across these resources in a way that ensures even load distribution across the fleet. This enables you to distribute incoming traffic effectively and deliver a consistent experience for all users. Amazon **Elastic Load Balancers** (**ELBs**) are designed for precisely this purpose.

ELBs can distribute traffic across multiple EC2 instances, containers, IP addresses, and even Lambda functions. If a particular EC2 instance fails, for example, the load balancer will redirect traffic to other healthy instances in the fleet.

Amazon load balancers detect failed instances by performing health checks—ongoing checks on instances and the applications running on them to verify they are healthy and responsive. The load balancer only routes traffic to instances that pass these health checks, indicating they are live and operational.

Amazon Elastic Load Balancers are regional services that can route traffic to resources across multiple AZs within a region. You deploy your load balancer in a VPC and specify which AZs will host your load balancer nodes. The following section explains how to deploy your load balancer in a VPC.

But before exploring the different types of AWS Load Balancers, it's helpful to understand the **Open Systems Interconnection** (**OSI**) model, which is a framework used to describe how data travels across a network.

Overview of the OSI model

Published in 1984, the **OSI model** outlines the process by which data flows through a network system. The OSI model is divided into **seven layers**, with each layer responsible for a specific part of the network communication process and utilizing various protocols at that layer.

Different hardware and software components that enable data transfer operate at varying layers of the OSI model. For example, packet-filtering firewalls, which inspect IP addresses, ports, and transport layer protocols such as **TCP** and **UDP**, operate at **Layer 3 (Network Layer)** and **Layer 4 (Transport Layer)**. In contrast, application firewalls that perform content filtering operate at **Layer 7 (Application Layer)**.

Figure 10.1 illustrates the seven layers of the OSI model:

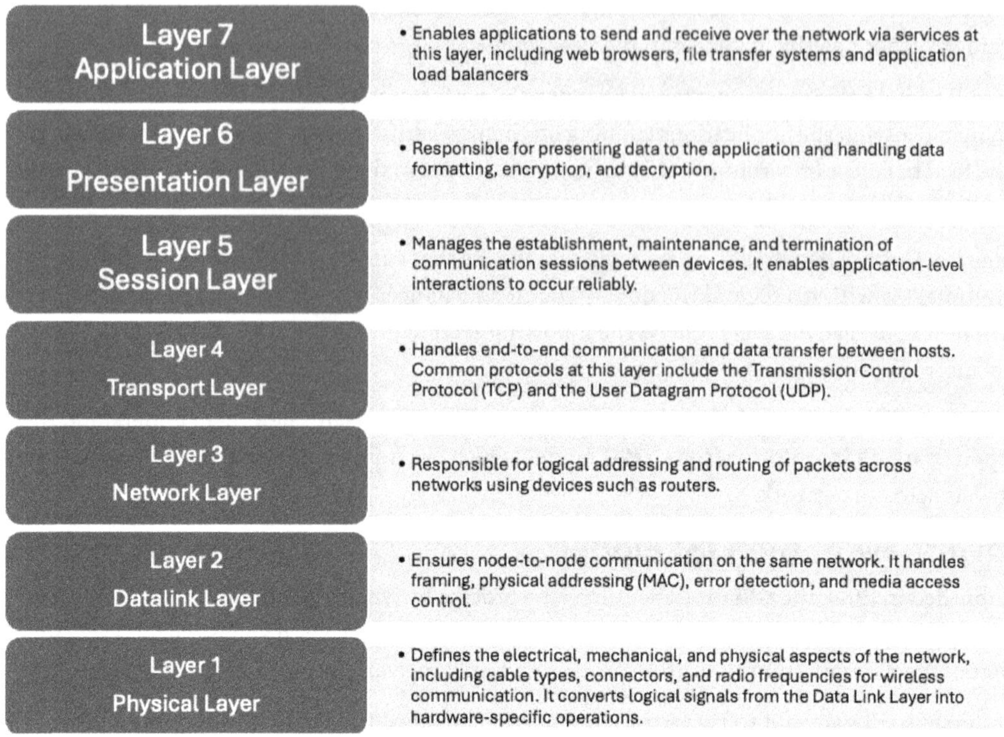

Figure 10.1: OSI Model

The OSI model helps developers, system engineers, and architects understand how communication flows between an end user and an application. It also helps when deciding where different security protocols and controls should be implemented across the networking stack.

The following table illustrates which service you will consume and what layer of the OSI model it operates at:

Architecture Component	**OSI Layer**
Route53/DNS	Layer 7
Load Balancers	Layer 7
Security Groups	Layer 3/4
VPC networking	Layer 3

Architecture Component	OSI Layer
EC2 application	Layer 7
RDS connectivity	Layer 4/7

Table 10.1: AWS Services and related OSI layers

Understanding the OSI model will help you appreciate the architectural decisions made when building the Belly Brew Co. Limited customer-facing website. As you work through this project, you will see how each AWS service and resource plays a role in enabling users on the Internet to submit their email address and receive a copy of the recipe eBook. This includes the networking components, security firewalls, application processing, and backend database connectivity.

Now that you have seen where load balancing fits within the wider networking stack, let's look at how Elastic Load Balancers are deployed inside a VPC and connected to the resources that serve your application.

Connecting Elastic Load Balancers to VPC resources

Amazon Load Balancers are deployed within your VPC and distribute traffic across multiple resources, such as EC2 instances. You can configure the load balancer to support various AZs within the region and define whether it is *internet-facing* or *internal-facing*. The key differences between the two options are as follows:

- **Internet-facing ELBs**: Accept inbound traffic from the internet and distribute it to resources deployed in either public or private subnets
- **Internal-facing ELBs**: Handle traffic originating from within your VPC, such as from resources in public subnets, and distribute it to resources located in private subnets

Figure 10.2 illustrates an example of an Internet-facing load balancer with load balancer nodes deployed across public subnets in Availability Zones `eu-west-2a` and `eu-west-2b`.

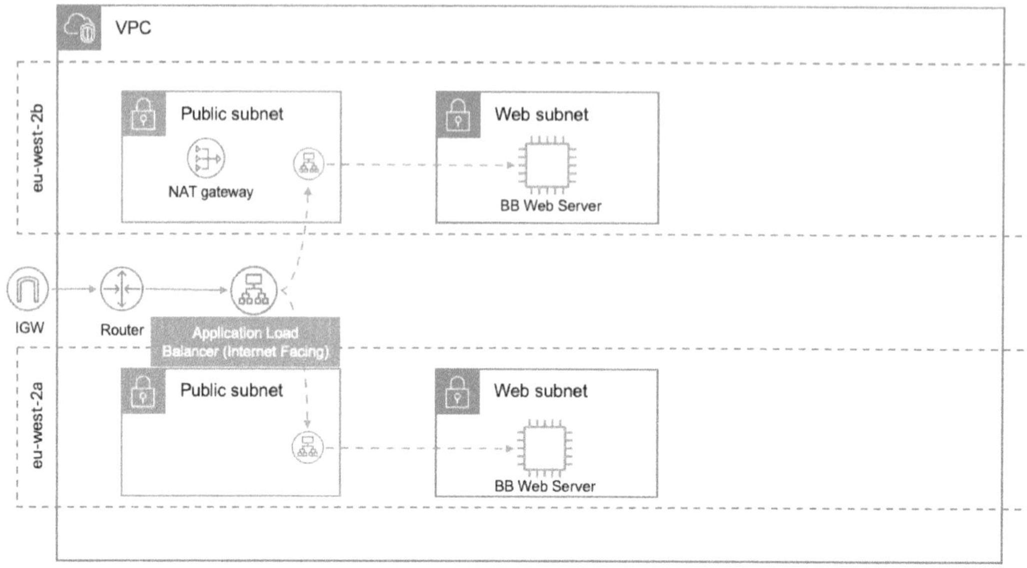

Figure 10.2: Application Load Balancer distributing traffic to EC2 instances in app subnets

As depicted in the diagram, an **application load balancer** (**ALB**) is deployed as an internet-facing load balancer. Here, you must select the public subnets within which AWS will deploy managed application load balancer nodes that will distribute inbound internet traffic within the designated AZs to EC2 instances in the private subnets. These EC2 instances might host the front-end web servers, for example.

Internal load balancers further distribute the traffic that reaches your web servers to backend resources such as middleware or app servers. As depicted in *Figure 10.3*, traffic from your web servers needs to be distributed to backend application servers, and here an internal load balancer can help manage the even distribution to backend servers.

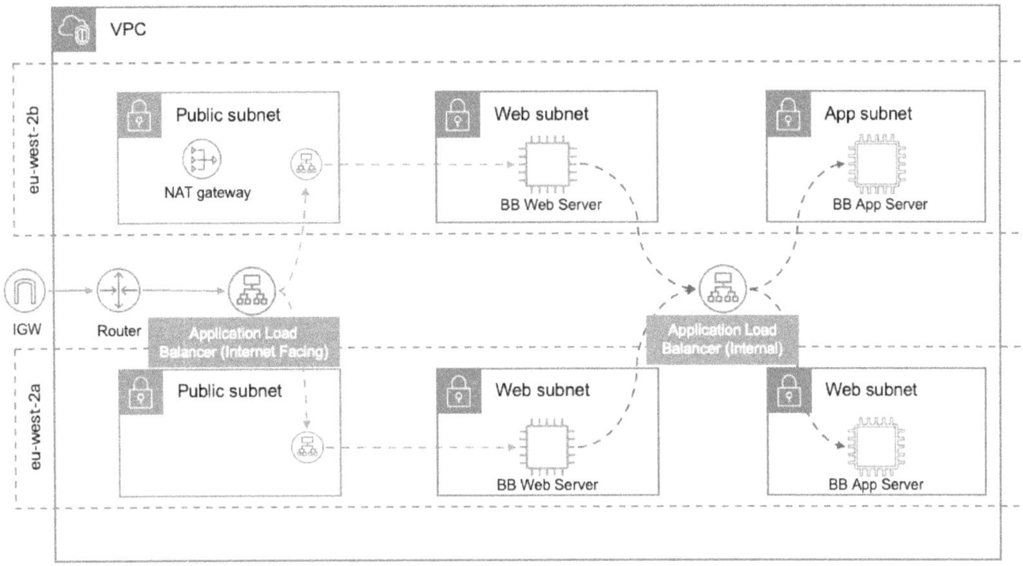

Figure 10.3: Three-tier architecture with internet-facing and internal load balancers

To ensure that a load balancer can receive traffic, it's essential to set up its security group with appropriate inbound rules. These rules must define the port, protocol, and source from which the traffic is permitted. Additionally, the security groups attached to the target instances must allow incoming traffic from the load balancer. This is typically achieved by specifying the load balancer's security group ID as the source in the targets' security group rules.

AWS offers four types of elastic load balancers, which are discussed in the following subsections.

Application Load Balancer

AWS Application Load Balancers (**ALBs**) operate at the application layer (Layer 7) and are specifically designed to route incoming client traffic based on content using the HTTP and HTTPS protocols. ALBs support distributing traffic to a variety of targets, including EC2 instances, containers, and AWS Lambda functions. As illustrated in *Figure 10.2* and *Figure 10.3*, you can deploy these targets across multiple AZs, helping to ensure high availability and fault tolerance in the event of an AZ failure.

Some key benefits of ALBs include the following:

- Support for path-based routing, allowing you to forward requests based on the **Uniform Resource Locator** (**URL**) in the request
- Support for host-based routing, enabling you to forward requests to specific targets based on the host portion of the URL

- Support for routing requests to multiple applications running on the same EC2 instance using different port numbers
- Support for registering Lambda functions as targets, as well as containerized applications

An ALB includes a configuration component called a **listener**, which defines how incoming requests are routed to registered targets. Listener rules consist of a priority, conditions, and actions. When the conditions of a rule are met, the corresponding action is executed. You also specify the protocol and port used to connect to your targets within the listener configuration.

The targets that receive routed requests are defined within **target groups**. An ALB can have one or more target groups, which can consist of EC2 instances, IP addresses (for containers), or Lambda functions. You can also route traffic to targets located outside your VPC.

This flexibility in routing to multiple target groups allows you to create complex routing architectures for different components of your application. For example, for an e-commerce website, one target group can route traffic to servers hosting your corporate pages (e.g., `www.mycompany.com`), while another target group handles the e-commerce section (e.g., `shop.mycompany.com`). You can even register the same target with multiple target groups, as illustrated in *Figure 10.4*.

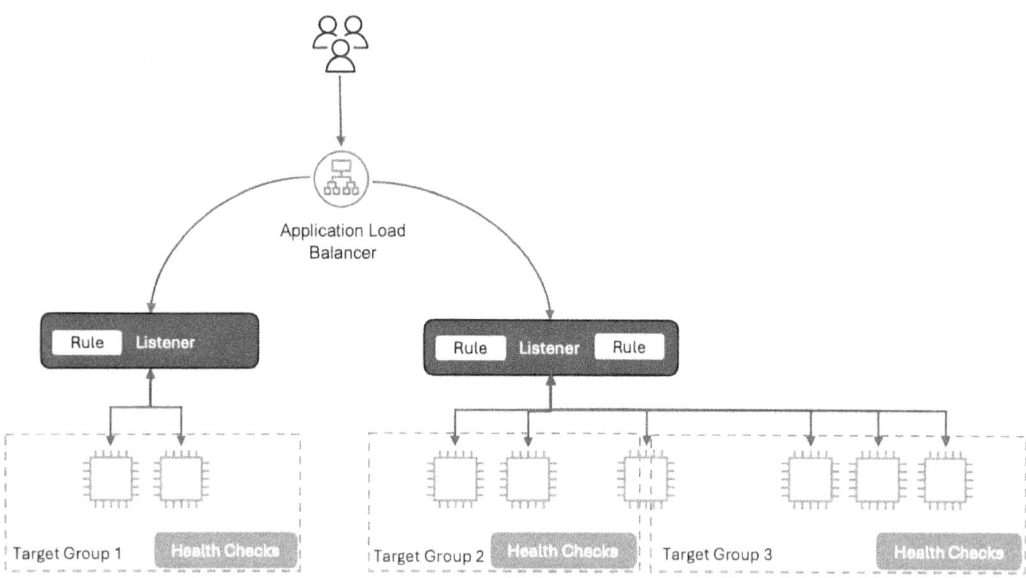

Figure 10.4: Application Load Balancer with multiple listeners and target groups

In addition to defining listener rules to route traffic to appropriate targets within a target group, ALBs also perform health checks on those targets to determine whether they are in a healthy state. Only targets that respond successfully to these health checks receive traffic. Any target that fails to respond is marked as *unhealthy* and is excluded from the target group. This ensures that the ALB routes client requests only to healthy targets, helping prevent users from encountering errors such as "Page cannot be found" or similar messages.

Next, you will learn about the AWS **Network Load Balancer** (**NLB**).

Network Load Balancer

Network Load Balancers (**NLBs**) operate at **Layer 4** of the OSI model and can handle millions of requests per second. NLBs are designed to load balance TCP and UDP traffic while maintaining ultra-low latencies. A key feature of NLBs is their ability to preserve the source IP address, allowing backend servers to see the original client IP—an essential requirement for specific applications.

NLBs also support both static IP addresses and Elastic IP addresses, the latter allowing you to assign a fixed IP per AZ. Unlike ALBs, NLBs do not inspect application-layer content, meaning they are unaware of cookies, content types, or custom headers.

Just like ALBs, NLBs perform health checks on registered targets and only route traffic to targets that are in a healthy state.

Some key benefits of NLBs include the following:

- Ability to handle highly volatile workloads and millions of requests per second
- Support for static IP addresses and one Elastic IP address per subnet
- Ability to register targets by IP address, including targets outside your VPC (e.g., on-premises resources)
- Support for routing traffic to multiple applications running on the same instance using different ports
- Support for containerized applications, such as those running on Amazon ECS

NLBs are particularly well-suited for high-performance, low-latency workloads, making them ideal for use cases like gaming, live streaming, and high-frequency trading.

In the next section, you will learn more about Gateway Load Balancers.

Gateway load balancer

Gateway Load Balancers (**GWLBs**) help you deploy, scale, and manage third-party virtual appliances, which are typically purchased from the AWS Marketplace. These appliances are commonly used for tasks such as security inspection and traffic analysis for data entering and leaving your VPC. Examples include third-party firewalls, **Intrusion Detection Systems** (**IDS**), and **Intrusion Prevention Systems** (**IPS**).

As shown in *Figure 10.5*, traffic entering your VPC is first routed to these virtual appliances by the GWLB. The traffic is inspected, and if it passes the checks, it is then forwarded to backend resources such as EC2 instances hosting your application. If the traffic does not meet the inspection criteria, it is dropped, and the backend resources are unaware of the presence of the appliance in the traffic path.

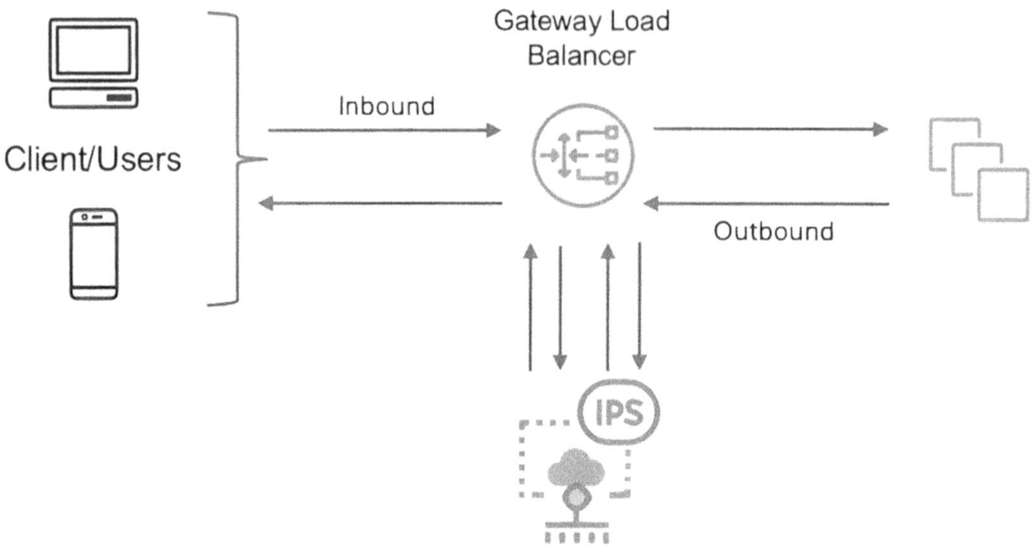

Figure 10.5: GWLB redirects traffic to the IPS device for inspection before forwarding to backend resources

GWLBs operate at **Layer 3** of the OSI model and provide a single entry and exit point for all traffic directed to these services. The load balancer uses a protocol called **GENEVE** (**Generic Network Virtualization Encapsulation**, over `port 6081`) to send traffic to and from the virtual appliances.

You will learn about the Classic Load Balancer next.

Classic Load Balancer

The **Classic Load Balancer** (**CLB**) is a previous-generation load balancer that can handle traffic at both **Layer 4** and **Layer 7** of the OSI model. However, it offers significantly fewer features compared to ALBs and NLBs.

AWS recommends migrating any existing CLBs to either ALBs or NLBs, depending on your use case, unless you have applications running in the EC2-Classic network that cannot be migrated due to specific constraints.

CLBs can handle HTTP, HTTPS, TCP, and SSL traffic and distribute incoming application traffic across multiple EC2 instances in multiple AZs.

While load balancing helps improve high availability and distribute traffic across multiple resources, such as EC2 instances, you still need a mechanism to scale those resources based on demand automatically. That brings us to the **Auto Scaling service**, which provides this capability and is going to be covered in the following section.

Scaling EC2 workloads with AWS Auto Scaling

One of the biggest challenges in deploying software solutions is effectively managing demand. Before the advent of virtualization and cloud technologies, companies would cater to unexpected demand by following the concept of **peak load provisioning**. This involves allocating extra compute and infrastructure resources based on the maximum expected demand (or peak load) rather than typical usage. This is like investing in a bus with 50 seats just because once a year, all 50 might be needed, even if most days only 10 people ride it.

With peak load provisioning, you ensure customer satisfaction and system stability during traffic spikes such as Black Friday sales or product launches. However, for most of the time, the extra capacity remains underutilized, leading to higher fixed and operational costs.

AWS offers **auto scaling** capabilities for its core services, enabling you to benefit from **dynamic load provisioning**. In this model, resources *scale out* or *scale in* based on actual demand, making it a far more cost-efficient approach:

- Scaling out involves provisioning additional resources, such as extra EC2 instances, to accommodate an increase in demand
- Scaling in means terminating unwanted resources because demand is low

Auto scaling is a regional service that allows you to scale across multiple AZs within a given region. This not only helps manage unexpected demand but also ensures high availability in the event of an entire AZ outage. Auto scaling automatically provisions additional resources when demand crosses the specified thresholds you define. If demand drops below a defined threshold, auto scaling can terminate unnecessary resources, ensuring efficient resource utilization and cost optimization.

In *Figure 10.6*, two additional EC2 instances were added to the fleet across AZs `eu-west-2a` and `eu-west-2b` due to an increase in average CPU utilization exceeding 80% for more than 15 minutes.

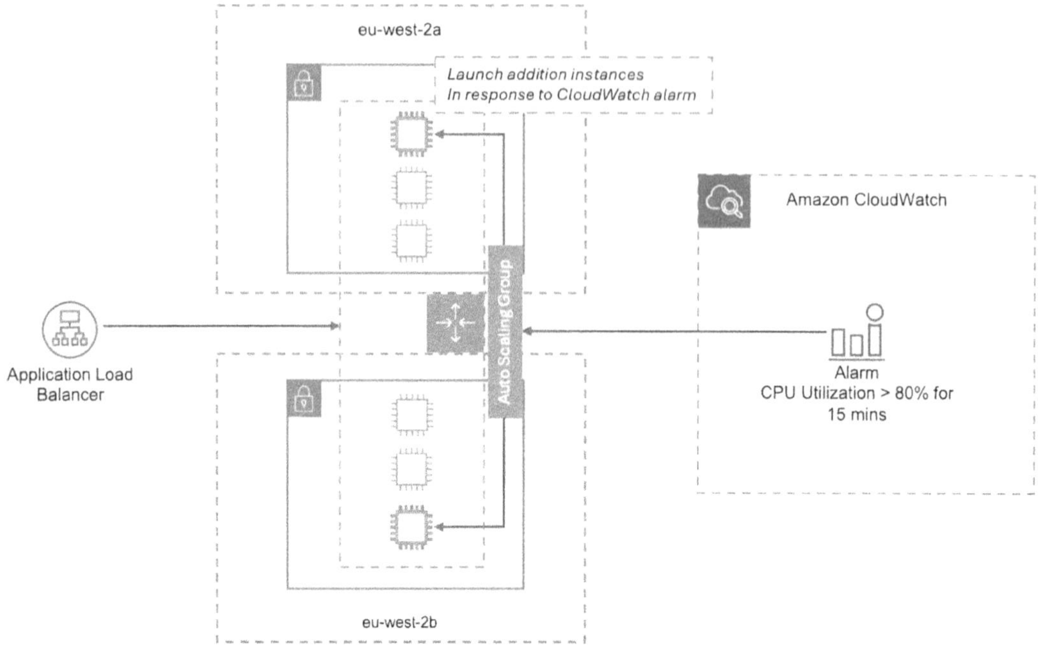

Figure 10.6: Auto Scaling Group responds to a CloudWatch alarm and launches additional instances

Auto Scaling performs scale-out or scale-in operations based on the threshold values and scaling policies you define. In this diagram, the auto scaling service has been configured to scale out if the average CPU utilization of the fleet exceeds 80% for 15 minutes or more.

Amazon CloudWatch is an AWS service that monitors and reports on a wide range of metrics, enabling you to assess the health of your resources. These metrics include CPU utilization, disk read/write operations, and network bytes in/out. Amazon CloudWatch is discussed in more detail in *Chapter 16*.

In the coming sections, you will learn more about some of the core components of the Amazon auto scaling service.

Auto scaling groups

When configuring auto scaling for your fleet of EC2 instances, you define an Auto Scaling group. This group manages all instance launches, terminations, monitoring, and scaling operations based on your specified configuration. You'll need to provide the following settings:

- **Minimum number of EC2 instances**: This is the lowest number of EC2 instances that must always be running in your fleet. AWS ensures that the instance count does not fall below this value.

- **Desired number of EC2 instances**: This represents the optimal number of instances you want running at any given time. AWS strives to maintain this desired capacity. If that's not possible (e.g., due to resource limitations), AWS will ensure that at least the minimum capacity is maintained. Note that the desired capacity can be equal to the minimum capacity.
- **Maximum number of EC2 instances**: This is the upper limit on the number of EC2 instances in your fleet. The auto scaling service can scale up to this number in response to increased demand, but will never exceed it. This cap helps prevent runaway scaling due to application bugs or malicious activity, reducing the risk of service disruption or unexpected costs.

The auto scaling service launches and terminates EC2 instances based on the scaling policies you define, the monitored metrics, and any alarms that are triggered. Auto scaling can also respond when an instance fails a health check, automatically replacing the unhealthy instance. You can use either the EC2 health checks on their own or combine them with the ELB health checks (as discussed earlier) to determine the health status of an instance.

The following section outlines the different scaling policies you can define.

Auto scaling policies

AWS provides several scaling policies that you can configure for your auto scaling groups. These policies determine when and how your EC2 instances scale in or out. The available options include:

- **Maintain current instance levels**: You can configure your auto scaling group to always maintain a consistent number of EC2 instances across multiple AZs. If an EC2 instance fails, auto scaling automatically replaces it to preserve the desired fleet size.
- **Manual Scaling**: You can manually adjust the minimum, desired, or maximum number of EC2 instances in the group. Auto Scaling will automatically make the necessary changes to match your updated settings.
- **Scheduled Scaling**: You can schedule scaling actions to launch or terminate EC2 instances at specific times. This is useful for predictable workload changes, such as scaling up on Black Friday for e-commerce demand or increasing capacity on the last Tuesday of the month to support payroll processing.
- **Dynamic Scaling**: When demand is unpredictable, dynamic scaling automatically adjusts capacity in response to real-time metrics. It initiates scale-out or scale-in actions in response to threshold breaches. For example, if average CPU utilization exceeds a defined level for a set duration, auto scaling adds more instances. If utilization drops below a specified threshold, it removes instances to optimize costs.

Dynamic scaling includes three types of policies:

- **Target Tracking Scaling Policy**: This policy adjusts capacity to maintain a specific target metric. For example, if your team determines that 45% average CPU utilization delivers optimal performance, auto scaling will automatically add or remove instances to keep utilization at that level—ensuring a balance between performance and cost.
- **Step Scaling**: This method utilizes a predefined set of steps to adjust capacity according to the extent to which the metric exceeds the threshold. Larger breaches trigger more significant scaling actions.
- **Simple Scaling**: This type of policy increases or decreases capacity based on a single scaling metric and a cooldown period after each action.

- **Predictive Scaling**: This policy uses machine learning to forecast future traffic trends based on historical usage and scheduled actions. It proactively adjusts capacity ahead of time, ensuring your application is ready for upcoming demand spikes.

When setting up your auto scaling groups and scaling policies, you must specify how the service should provision your EC2 instances, such as the operating system to use, any software applications to install, and specific configurations to apply at launch. To do this, you need to define a **Launch Template**, which is discussed in the next section.

EC2 launch templates

To set up your auto scaling group, you must configure a launch template. This template defines how your EC2 instances will be provisioned. For example, you must specify:

- An **Amazon Machine Image** (**AMI**)
- Instance type
- Key pair
- Security groups
- Block device mappings (if needed)

You can also assign IAM roles to the instance profile to grant permissions for AWS services, such as enabling your application running on EC2 instances to upload and download objects from an S3 bucket or update a DynamoDB database table. Additionally, you may include startup scripts that run when the instance launches. This process, known as **bootstrapping**, allows you to execute custom scripts written in Bash (for Linux) or PowerShell (for Windows). Within the **user data** section of the template, you can script the installation of tools, libraries, software, utilities, and more.

Launch Templates offer several advanced features, including:

- Defining multiple versions of a template to support different deployment environments
- Hosting variations of templates for different use cases
- Launching both **Spot** and **On-Demand** instances
- Specifying multiple instance types or even multiple launch templates

Now that you have a solid understanding of high availability, scalability, and the tools used to build a resilient and elastic architecture, the following section introduces a few additional services that are important for the AWS Certified Cloud Practitioner exam. These services are also included in this chapter because they will be used in the **capstone project** later.

Supporting application delivery with AWS Secrets Manager and Amazon SES

AWS offers more than two hundred services, all designed to help you build resilient, reliable, scalable, and cost-effective solutions. This chapter introduces you to two additional services that you must learn about to prepare for the AWS Certified Cloud Practitioner exam. The services introduced in this section are also part of the architecture design for your first capstone project for Belly Brew Co. Limited.

AWS Secrets Manager

AWS Secrets Manager is a fully managed service designed to help you securely store and access **secrets**, such as database credentials, access keys, API keys, and other sensitive information that must be protected.

The service allows you to store sensitive data in an encrypted format, which can only be accessed by entities with appropriate permissions. Access to these secrets is provided via API calls, enabling your application to retrieve them at runtime as needed programmatically. This is a far more secure approach than hardcoding secrets in plain text within your application code.

For example, if your application needs to update a backend database, it must first authenticate using a set of credentials. Instead of hardcoding these credentials in plain text within the application code and increasing security risk, the application can dynamically retrieve them from Secrets Manager at runtime. This ensures that sensitive information is not stored in plain text within the source code.

AWS provides additional tools for storing and managing sensitive data, such as environment variables and API keys, like **AWS Systems Manager Parameter Store**. However, AWS Secrets

Manager offers a key advantage: it allows you to automatically rotate sensitive credentials, such as Amazon RDS usernames and passwords, at defined intervals.

This feature utilizes an AWS Lambda function to automatically rotate credentials and update the associated database with the new values, much like you would regularly update your username and password. This automated rotation significantly enhances security by reducing the risk of credential compromise.

Customers can still use AWS Systems Manager Parameter Store. This service is ideal when you simply need a secure, centralized repository to store configuration values like environment variables and API keys without the need for automatic credential rotation.

Amazon Simple Email Service

Amazon Simple Email Service (**Amazon SES**) is a cloud-based tool that enables you to send high volumes of email directly from your applications. Whether you're delivering transactional messages, promotional campaigns, or newsletters, SES helps you reach a large audience efficiently. It offers flexible deployment options, allowing you to choose from dedicated, shared, or custom IP addresses. Plus, with built-in reporting and analytics, you get valuable insights into email performance and deliverability.

While understanding the theory behind these AWS services is essential for the Cloud Practitioner exam, hands-on experience is what truly sets you apart in the real world. In the next section, you'll get the chance to build a complete, end-to-end solution for Belly Brew Co. Limited. This project brings back the business scenario from *Chapter 1* and gives you a practical opportunity to apply what you've learned in your first capstone project.

Project 10 – Architecting and deploying Belly Brew Co. Limited's marketing campaign website

In *Chapter 1*, Belly Brew Co. Limited defined its initial requirement for a customer-facing website to promote the company brand to the public. A key functionality of this requirement was to gather the contact details of existing and potential customers for use in marketing campaigns.

To encourage customers to share their contact details, the marketing team has decided to offer a free e-book on gut-friendly recipes, along with the promise of regular product trials and discount coupon giveaways. Belly Brew Co. Limited's internal development team would build the website, but your role as a Cloud Practitioner is to design and architect a solution on AWS to host that website. Critical to this solution is ensuring that the website is highly available, scalable, and secure.

Figure 10.7 represents the architecture of the solution you will build as part of this project exercise:

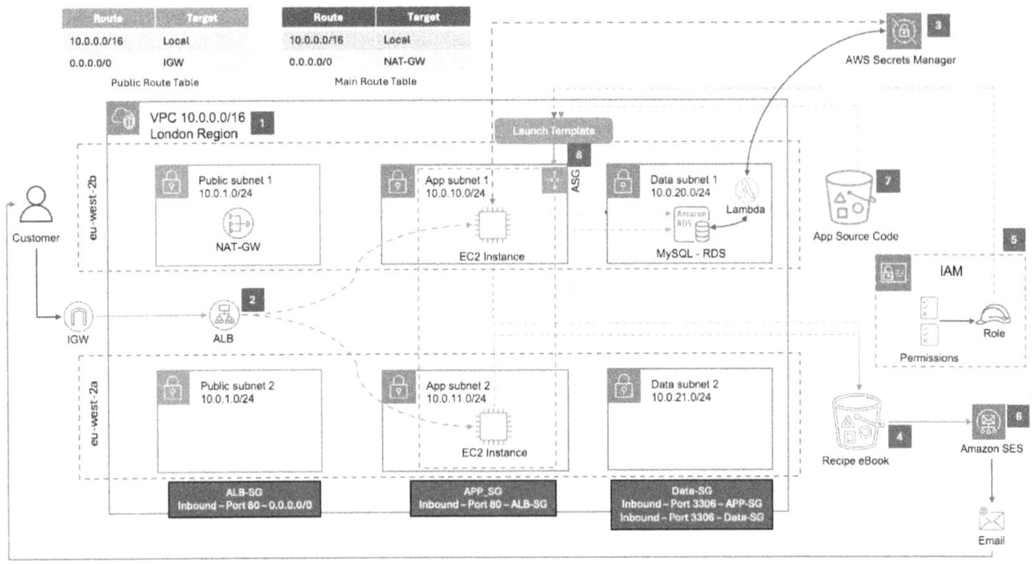

Figure 10.7: Belly Brew Co. Limited's customer-facing website

As depicted in the diagram in *Figure 10.7*, the following are the core components you will build out for this project:

1. **Amazon VPC**: In *Chapter 7*, you built a base VPC for Belly Brew Co. Limited as part of *Project task 7*. In this chapter, you will configure additional VPC components as follows:
   a. Deploy a NAT Gateway in **Public Subnet 1** to enable EC2 instances in the private subnet to access the internet and download updates, tools, and utilities. These EC2 instances will also use the NAT Gateway to access AWS public services such as Amazon S3 and Secrets Manager.
   b. Update the **Main Route Table** to configure a route to the internet via the NAT Gateway. The private subnets will use this route to allow EC2 instances to access the internet.
   c. Note that the database security group, **Data-SG**, will need to be updated with an additional inbound rule allowing traffic on port 3306 from itself. This is necessary because when you configure Secrets Manager with rotation enabled, AWS automatically creates a Lambda function that gets associated with this security group by default. By allowing inbound traffic on port 3306 from the RDS

security group itself, the Lambda function can connect to the Amazon RDS database and update the MySQL credentials.

2. **Application Load Balancer**: To ensure high availability, you will deploy multiple EC2 instances across two Availability Zones within the App subnets. As part of this solution, you will also deploy an ALB to distribute incoming customer traffic evenly across the instances in *App Subnet 1* and *App Subnet 2*. Additionally, you will need to create a **target group** that auto scaling will use to register the EC2 instances as targets.
3. **AWS Secrets Manager**: You previously provisioned the Amazon RDS MySQL database in *Chapter 9*, as part of *Project task 9*. The database was configured with a standard username and password for authentication, which you recorded. In this project task, you will configure a secret in AWS Secrets Manager to securely store and manage the database credentials. You will also configure a 7-day rotation policy to automatically rotate credentials at regular intervals, thereby enhancing the security of your database.
4. **Amazon S3 – Recipe eBook**: You will create another Amazon S3 bucket to host the free recipe eBook, which Belly Brew Co. Limited will email to all users who sign up on the website. The eBook will be automatically sent using Amazon SES and the **pre-signed URL** feature.
5. **IAM Roles**: To ensure that your website running on EC2 instances can connect to AWS Secrets Manager, Amazon S3, and Amazon SES, you must configure an IAM role with the appropriate permissions
6. **Amazon SES**: Amazon SES allows you to send email marketing campaigns to your registered users. In a production environment, you must configure Amazon SES to send emails to any email address registered with your business. However, this requires additional configurations and approval from AWS. For this project exercise, you will configure Amazon SES to send emails to a single, specified email address, demonstrating the application's functionality.
7. **Amazon S3 – Source Code**: You will create an Amazon S3 bucket to host the source code for the website. This code is available from the Packt GitHub repository at `https://github.com/PacktPublishing/AWS-Certified-Cloud-Practitioner-CLF-C02-Exam-Guide`. The source code will be used to deploy the application to EC2 instances via the Auto Scaling Launch Template.
8. **AWS Auto Scaling**: You will configure the AWS EC2 Auto Scaling service to automatically deploy a minimum of two EC2 instances (one in each app subnet across two AZs). You will not configure any scaling policies for this project; instead, you will set the minimum, desired, and maximum number of EC2 instances to 2.

To ensure that the EC2 instances are automatically configured to host the application, you will configure a Launch Template with all the necessary parameters to deploy the Belly Brew Co. Limited website application. The application source code will need to be updated with specific parameters tailored to your configuration. These include:

a. Amazon S3 bucket name for hosting your recipe eBook

b. The name of the secret you have configured in AWS Secrets Manager

In the next section, you will learn about the technical requirements needed to complete this project task.

Technical requirements

To complete the project exercises in this chapter, ensure that you have completed all the labs in all previous chapters. Log in to your AWS Development account as the IAM user Alice to complete the project tasks.

Ensure you download the source code `bellybrewcode.zip` and `user_data.sh` files from the GitHub repository and save them to your desktop for easy access. You must also download the `recipes.zip` folder, which contains the free recipe eBook that you will host in an Amazon S3 bucket.

You will need to make some minor edits to the application source to account for your environment settings. You must use an **integrated development environment** (**IDE**) such as Visual Studio Code to do this.

Project task 10.1 – Updating Belly Brew Co. Limited's VPC configuration

In this project task, you will update the existing Belly Brew Co. Limited's VPC configuration. These will include updating the database security group, deploying a NAT Gateway, and configuring the main route table.

Follow these steps:

1. Log in to your AWS Development Account as the IAM user Alice and navigate to the **VPC management console**
2. Ensure you are in the London region
3. From the left-hand menu, click on **Your VPCs**
4. Ensure you still have access to the `Belly Brew VPC` you configured in *Chapter 7*
5. From the left-hand menu, click on **NAT gateways**
6. In the right-hand pane, click the **Create NAT gateway** button

7. On the **Create NAT gateway** webpage, provide a name for your NAT gateway, such as `bb-nat-gw`
8. `Under Availability mode, select the Zonal option`
9. Select the `belly-brew-vpc-public-sub-01` subnet from the **Subnet** drop-down list
10. Under **Elastic IP allocation ID**, click on the **Allocate Elastic IP** button to assign an Elastic IP to your NAT gateway
11. Scroll further down the webpage and click the **Create NAT gateway** button. Your NAT gateway will take a couple of minutes to get created and become **Available** as depicted in the following screenshot in *Figure 10.8*:

Figure 10.8: NAT gateway configuration details

Now that the NAT gateway is in the **Available** state, you must update the main route table with a route to the Internet via the NAT gateway using the following steps:

1. From the left-hand menu, click on **Route tables**
2. In the right-hand pane, select the main route table. This is the route table with the word **Yes** in the **Main** column, associated with the `belly-brew-vpc`.
3. In the bottom half pane of the main route table, click on **Routes**
4. Click the **Edit routes** button
5. On the **Edit routes** webpage, click the **Add route** button
6. Next, select the IP range `0.0.0.0/0` from the search bar on the left
7. Next, select **NAT gateway** from the **Target** drop-down list, and in the search box that appears underneath, select the **NAT gateway** you created earlier
8. Click the **Save Changes** button

Your main route table has now been updated with a route to the Internet via the NAT gateway. Next, you must update the database security group.

This is how you do that:

1. In the left-hand menu, click on **Security groups** under the **Security** section
2. In the right-hand pane, select the database security group. If you followed the instructions in *Project task 7.5* from *Chapter 7*, this should be labeled as `belly-brew-vpc-data-sg`
3. In the bottom half of the right-hand pane, click on **Inbound rules**
4. Click the **Edit inbound rules** button
5. On the **Edit inbound rules** webpage that appears, click the **Add rule** button
6. Select the MySQL/Aurora option from the **Type** drop-down list and ensure **Custom** is selected as the **Source**
7. Next, in the search box next to **Custom**, ensure that you select the `belly-brew-vpc-data-sg` security group as per the following screenshot in *Figure 10.9*

Figure 10.9: Updating the database security group

8. Next, click on the **Save rules** button

Your VPC is now configured with the additional settings to complete this project. The provisioning of the NAT gateway and associated route table configuration will ensure that the EC2 instances that will be provisioned via the Auto Scaling groups in *Project task 10.8* will be able to access external networks to download source code files and install any necessary applications. The NAT gateway will also be used by AWS Lambda to connect to AWS Secrets Manager for credential rotation. In the next project task, you will configure the load balancer that will be used to distribute inbound traffic to your EC2 instances.

Project task 10.2 – Configuring an Application Load Balancer

In this project task, you will configure the ALB, which will distribute incoming web requests across your EC2 instances deployed in the App Subnets. These are the steps you must follow:

1. Search for and navigate to the EC2 console using the search bar at the top of the AWS management console
2. Ensure that you are still in the London region on the EC2 console webpage
3. From the left-hand menu, scroll down and click on **Target Groups** under **Load Balancing**
4. In the right-hand pane, click the **Create target group** button
5. On the **Create target group** webpage that appears, ensure that **Instances** is selected under **Target type** in the **Settings – immutable** section
6. Next, provide a **Target group name**, such as `bb-target-group`
7. For the **Protocol**, ensure that **HTTP** is selected from the drop-down list and set the **Port** to `80`
8. Next, from the **VPC** drop-down list, select Belly Brew Co. Limited's VPC (`belly-brew-vpc`)
9. Ensure that the **Protocol version** is set to `HTTP1`
10. In the **Health checks** section, ensure that `HTTP` is selected from the **Health check protocol** drop-down list
11. Set the **Health check path** to / (slash)
12. Expand the **Advanced health check settings** section and ensure that the following settings are configured:
    a. **Healthy threshold**: `3`
    b. **Unhealth threshold**: `2`
    c. **Timeout**: `5` seconds
    d. **Interval**: `10` seconds
    e. **Success codes**: `200`
13. Click **Next** at the bottom of the webpage

14. On the **Register targets - recommended** webpage that appears, scroll down and click the **Next** button. You will not be registering any targets now, as the auto scaling service will be configured to register the targets automatically.
15. On the **Review and create** webpage, scroll to the bottom of the page and click **Create target group**

Next, you will configure the application load balancer:

1. From the left-hand menu, click **Load Balancers**, in the **Load Balancing** section
2. In the right-hand pane, click the **Create load balancer** button
3. On the **Compare and select load balancer type** webpage, click the **Create** button under **Application Load Balancer**
4. Next, on the **Create Application Load Balancer** webpage that appears, provide a name for the load balancer, such as `bb-alb`
5. Next, for the **Scheme**, ensure the `Internet-facing` option is selected. Also ensure that `IPv4` is selected as the **Load balancer IP address type**
6. In the **Network mapping** section, select Belly Brew Co. Limited's VPC (`belly-brew-vpc`) from the **VPC** drop-down list
7. Select both `eu-west-2a` and `eu-west-2b` under **Availability Zones and subnets**
8. Ensure that you also select the public subnets under each zone as depicted in *Figure 10.10*:

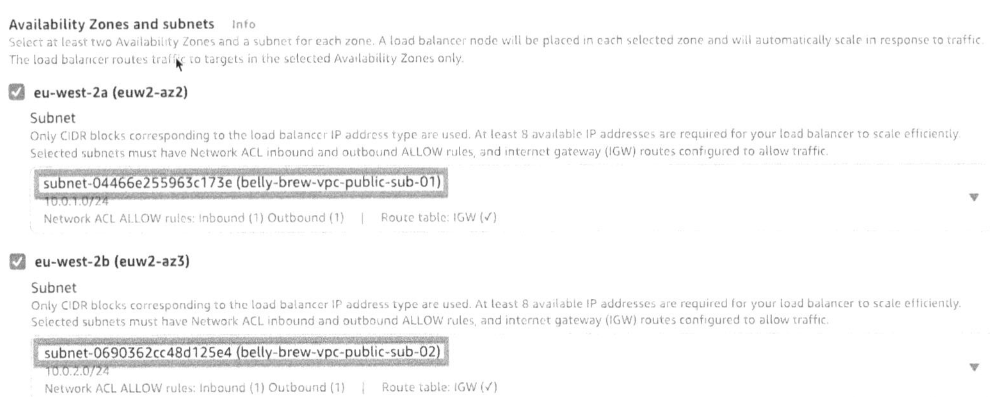

Figure 10.10: Select Belly Brew Co. Limited's public subnets for your load balancer

9. Next, under **Security groups**, select the load balancer security you created in *Project task 7.5* in *Chapter 7*. This should be `belly-brew-vpc-alb-sg`. Also, remove the default security group by clicking on the **X** icon next to it, as it's not required.

10. Under **Listeners and routing**, ensure that the **Protocol** is set to `HTTP`, with **Port** set to `80`. Select the target group you created earlier (`bb-target-group`) from the drop-down in the **Default action** section
11. Scroll to the bottom of the webpage and click the **Create load balancer** button

Your application load balancer will now be created. This will take a couple of minutes, and you should see the **Status** as `Active` as per the following screenshot in *Figure 10.11*:

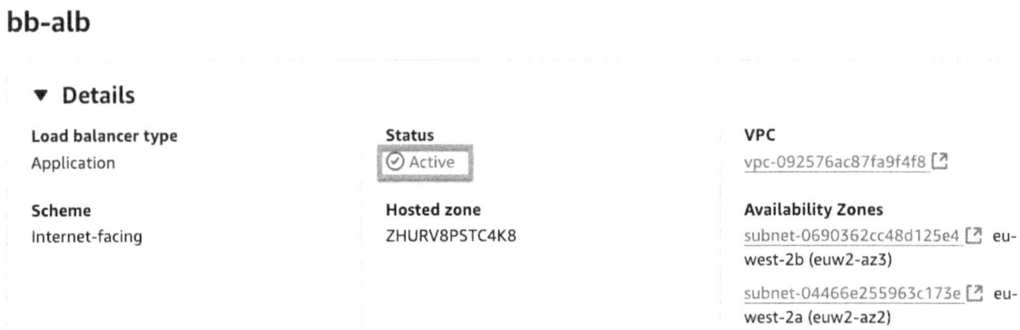

Figure 10.11: Application Load Balancer active status

Your application load balancer is now ready. Later, when you configure the auto scaling group, the service will register your EC2 instances to the target group, and the load balancer will distribute incoming traffic to those instances.

In the next project task, you will create a secret in AWS Secrets Manager to store and manage the Amazon RDS database credentials. This will be used by your application to dynamically retrieve those credentials when accessing the backend database.

Project task 10.3 – Creating a secret in AWS Secrets Manager

In this project task, you will create a secret to update and manage your Amazon RDS MySQL credentials. You will also configure a rotation policy to update the credentials every seven days.

1. From the top search bar on the AWS management console, search for and navigate to **AWS Secrets Manager**
2. Ensure that you are still in the London region
3. On the **AWS Secrets Manager** webpage, click the **Store a new secret** button
4. On the **Choose secret type** webpage, select the option `Credentials for Amazon RDS database`

5. Next, in the **Credentials** section, provide the database username and password you configured when you created Belly Brew Co. Limited's database in *Chapter 9*
6. Scroll down and in the **Database** section, select Belly Brew Co. Limited's Database (`bellybrewdb`) as per the following screenshot in *Figure 10.12*:

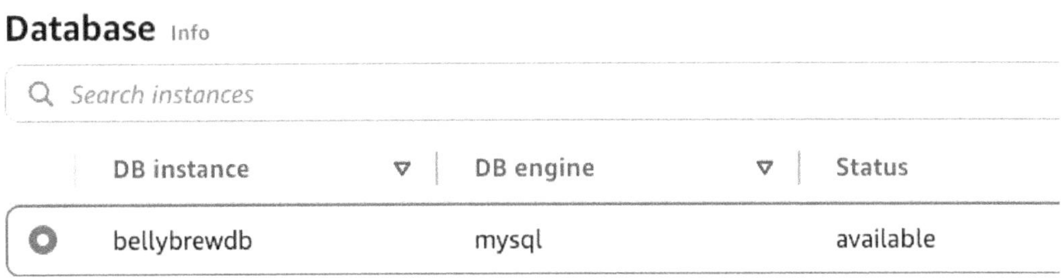

Figure 10.12: Belly Brew Co. Limited's database

7. Click **Next**
8. Provide a name for your secret in the **Secret name and description** section. For example, you can name your secret `bb-db-secret`
9. Scroll a bit further down the webpage and click **Next**
10. Click the toggle switch to turn **Automatic rotation** on in the **Configure automatic rotation** section
11. Next, in the **Rotation schedule**, ensure that the **Schedule expression builder** is selected
12. Set the **Time unit** to `Days` and the **Days** to `7`
13. Scroll down to the **Rotation function** section. Here, provide a name for your **Lambda rotation function**, for example, `bb-rotation`. AWS Secrets Manager will add a prefix to the name with the word `SecretsManager`. Note that the function name, including the prefix, must be a maximum of 64 characters. This Lambda rotation function, created by AWS, is responsible for updating the database credentials. It will also update the secret stored in AWS Secrets Manager.
14. Ensure that **Single user** is selected as the **Rotation strategy**
15. Next, click **Next**
16. Scroll to the bottom of the **Review** webpage and click the **Store** button

AWS will store the secret `bb-db-secret`. It will take a few minutes to configure the rotation settings. After a few minutes, you can refresh the page and then click on the secret name, `bb-db-secret`. You will note the **Secret details** as per the following screenshot in *Figure 10.13*:

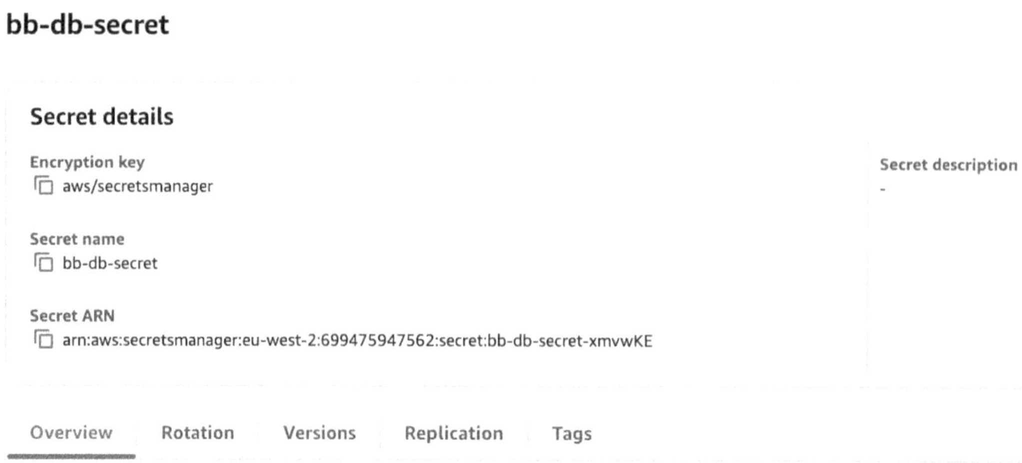

Figure 10.13: Belly Brew Co. Limited's RDS secret details

> **Note**
>
> Make a note of the **Secret ARN**. You will need this ARN when configuring IAM roles with the necessary permissions in *Project task 10.5*.

After a few minutes, the **Rotation** status will be enabled, as shown in the following screenshot in *Figure 10.14*:

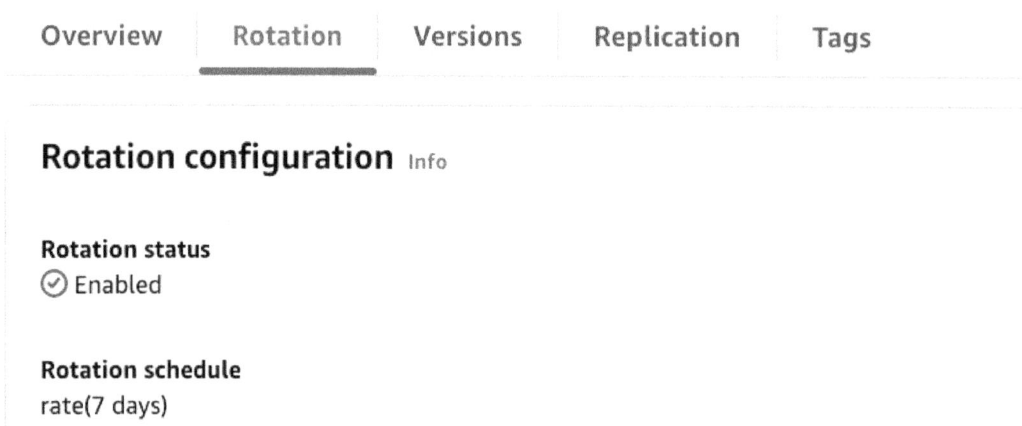

Figure 10.14: Secret rotation status enabled

Your secret is now configured for rotation and securely stored in AWS Secrets Manager. Later, you will update the application code with the secret name so that it can dynamically retrieve the database credentials to connect to the backend database.

In the next project task, you will create an Amazon S3 bucket that will be used to host the Belly Brew Co. Limited recipe eBook. Later, the application running on the EC2 instance will access the bucket and generate a pre-signed URL to send the eBook to users who register on the website.

Project task 10.4 – Creating an Amazon S3 bucket for recipe eBook

In this project task, you will create an Amazon S3 bucket to host the recipe eBook, which will be sent to all end users who subscribe to the website.

1. In the top search bar of the AWS Management Console, search for and navigate to Amazon S3
2. Ensure that you are still in the London region
3. From the left-hand menu, click on **General-purpose buckets**
4. In the right-hand pane, click the **Create bucket** button
5. Ensure the **Global namespace** is selected as the **Bucket namespace** option. Provide a suitable name for your bucket. Remember, bucket names are unique across the AWS ecosystem, so no two buckets can have the same name. For example, to complete this project guide, a bucket with the name `belly-brew-recipes` is being created
6. Leave all the remaining settings at default values and click the **Create bucket** button at the bottom of the webpage
7. You will then be redirected to the webpage listing all your general-purpose buckets in your AWS account. Click on the bucket you just created to navigate to the bucket webpage as per the screenshot in *Figure 10.15:*

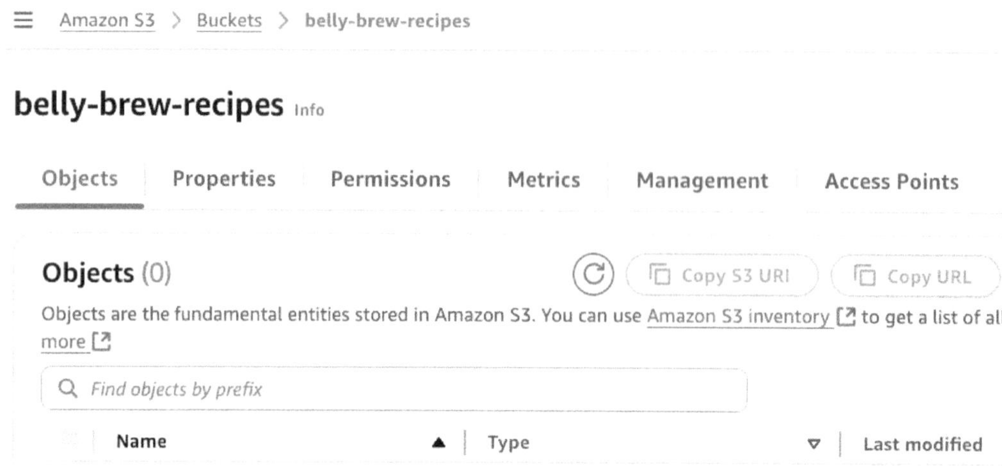

Figure 10.15: Belly Brew Co. Limited's recipes bucket

On your desktop, you should have downloaded the Belly Brew Co. Limited's recipe eBook from the GitHub repository. Ensure that you unzip the folder to extract the top-level folder and the recipe eBook contained within it. The folder structure is `recipe-book/ebook.pdf`.

8. While in the **belly-brew-recipes S3 bucket** webpage, click on the **Create folder** button on the far right
9. Provide a name for your folder, such as **recipe-book**
10. Scroll to the bottom of the webpage and click the **Create folder** button
11. Next, click the folder you just created to navigate into it
12. Click the **Upload** button on the far right of the webpage
13. On the **Upload** webpage that appears, click on the **Add files** button
14. In the File Explorer (Windows) or Finder (MacOS) tool that appears, navigate to the folder on your desktop containing the extracted recipe book and double-click on it
15. The `ebook.pdf` file will be listed in the **Files and Folders** section on the webpage
16. Scroll to the bottom of the webpage and click the **Upload** button
17. Once the upload completes, you should see an **Uploaded succeeded** message as shown in *Figure 10.16:*

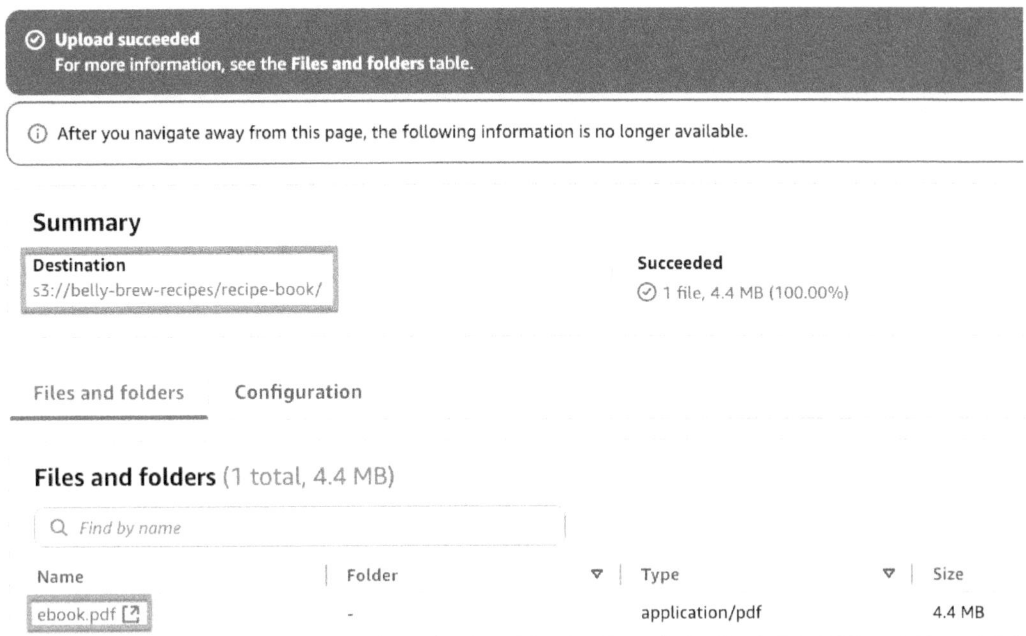

Figure 10.16: Upload of eBook to Amazon S3

Your recipe eBook has now been uploaded to the Amazon S3 bucket. Make a note of the bucket name and the path to your file. In this example, the eBook is in the `recipe-book` folder. Note that your bucket name will be different.

The Belly Brew Co. Limited website application that is running on your EC2 instances needs to access various other AWS services, such as AWS Secrets Manager, Amazon S3, and the Amazon SES service. To ensure the instances have the necessary permissions, you must create an IAM role that will be added to the instance profile for those EC2 instances. The next project task walks you through this process.

Project task 10.5 – Configuring IAM roles

In this project task, you will configure the necessary IAM roles to allow the EC2 instances to communicate with several services, such as AWS Secrets Manager, Amazon S3, and Amazon SES.

Here's what you have to do:

1. In the search bar at the top of the AWS Management Console, search for and navigate to the **IAM** service
2. From the left-hand menu, click on **Roles**
3. In the right-hand pane, click the **Create role** button
4. For the **Trusted entity type**, select `AWS service`
5. In the **Use case** section, select `EC2` from the drop-down list under **Service or use case**
6. Click **Next**
7. On the **Add permissions** webpage, search for and select the following permissions:
    - `AmazonS3FullAccess`
    - `AmazonSESFullAccess`
8. Click **Next**
9. Provide a name for the role, such as `bb-iam-role`
10. Scroll down the webpage and click the `Create role` button

Next, you must add additional permissions for the role to enable your web application to access the secret in AWS Secrets Manager. This will enable the application to authenticate against the backend MySQL database on Amazon RDS. This is how that is done:

1. Navigate back to the list of IAM roles. You can click on the **Roles** link again on the left-hand menu. In the right-hand pane, search for the **bb-iam-role** role. Click on the role to access its settings as shown in *Figure 10.17*:

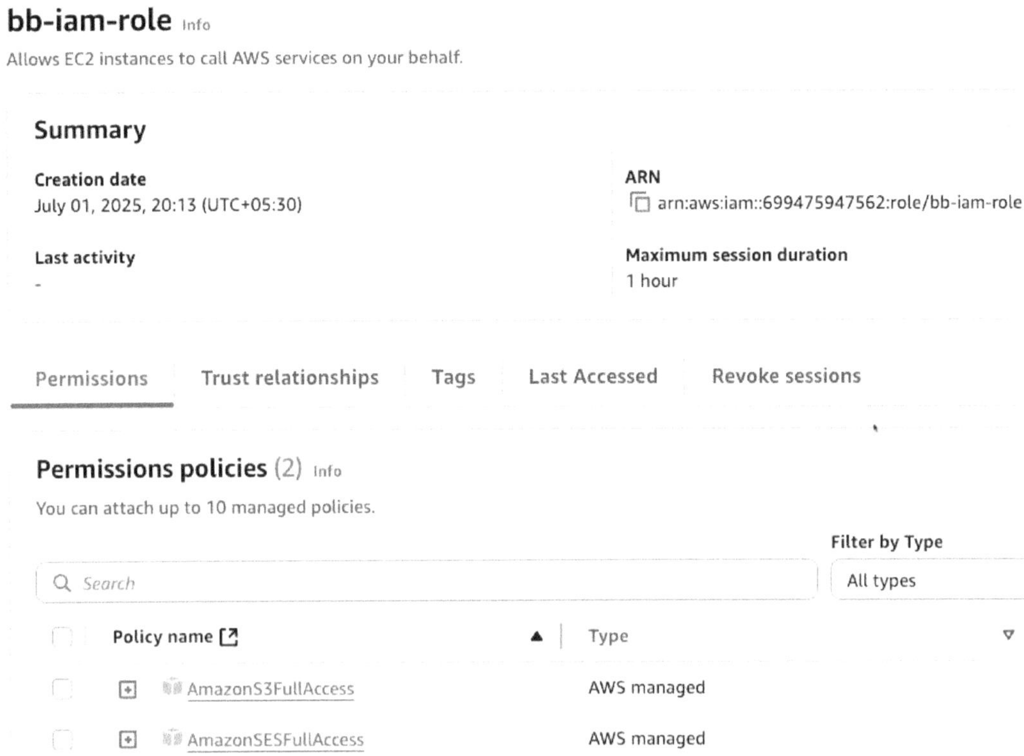

Figure 10.17: IAM role with permissions for Belly Brew Co. Limited's web app

2. In the **Permissions policies** section, select `Create inline policy` from the drop-down list under **Add permissions** in the far right of the section
3. On the **Specify permissions** webpage that appears, select the `Secrets Manager` service from the drop-down list in the **Select a service** section
4. Under **Actions allowed**, expand the **Read** option under **Access level**

5. Select the action `GetSecretValue` as shown in the following screenshot in *Figure 10.18*:

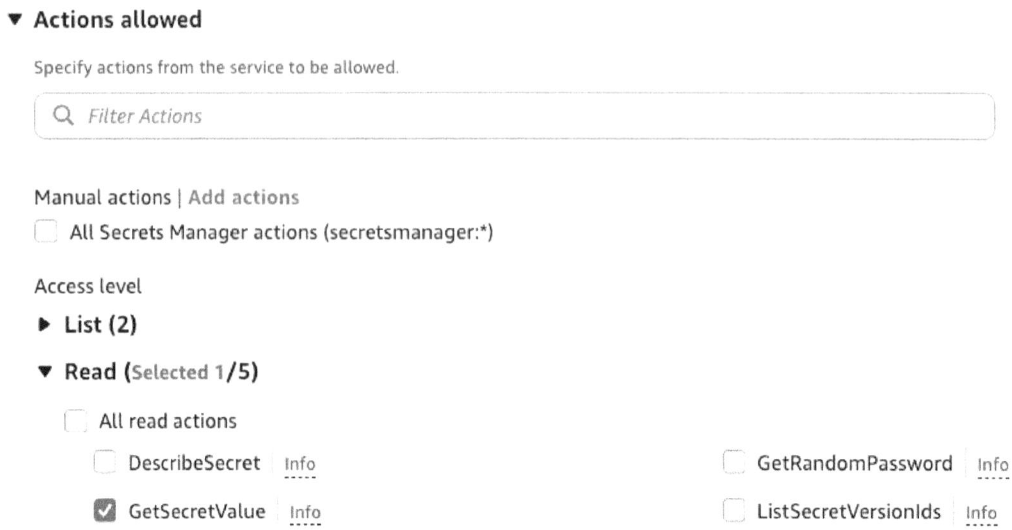

Figure 10.18: Configure permissions for IAM role to grant access to Secrets Manager secret

6. Scroll further down to the **Resources** section
7. Click **Add ARNs**
8. In the **Specify ARNs** dialog box that appears, paste the secret ARN you made a note of in *Project task 10.3* in the text box labeled **Resource ARN**, replacing the default text that was there. This will automatically populate the **Resource region** and **Resource secret** values as per the following screenshot in *Figure 10.19*:

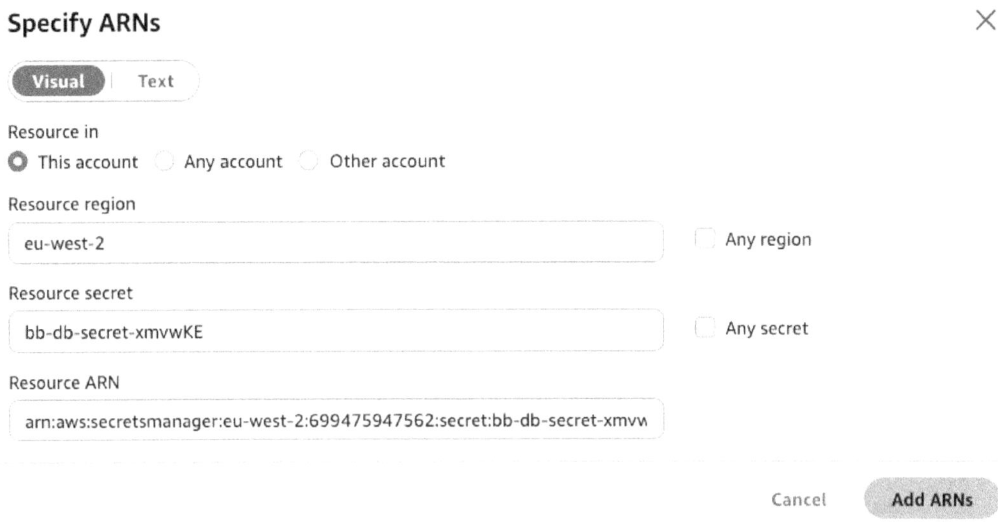

Figure 10.19: Specify the ARN of the Belly Brew secret

9. Click the **Add ARNs** button
10. Click **Next**
11. In the **Review and create** webpage that appears, provide a name for the policy, such as `bb-secret-iam-policy`
12. Click the **Create policy** button

Your IAM role has now been configured with an inline policy to grant read access to the secret you created in *Project task 10.3*.

With the IAM role now in place, which will be used by your EC2 instances, the next project task is to configure Amazon SES to send your customers the email containing a link to the recipe eBook. The next project task provides step-by-step instructions to configure Amazon SES in a sandbox environment.

Project task 10.6 – Configuring Amazon SES

In this project task, you will configure Amazon SES to send emails containing the eBook link to anyone who registers on Belly Brew Co. Limited's website.

> **Note**
>
> Note that Amazon places your Amazon SES service in sandbox mode when you create your AWS account. This is to help prevent fraud and abuse. In sandbox mode, you can only send messages to email addresses or domains that have been verified.

> Furthermore, there is a restriction of a maximum of 200 messages per 24-hour period, and you can only send a maximum of 1 message per second.
>
> For production environments, request production access from the Account Dashboard.

The following steps will guide you through the process of configuring Amazon SES:

1. From the search bar at the top of the AWS Management Console, search for and navigate to the Amazon SES service
2. From the left-hand menu (click the hamburger icon if it's not visible), click on **Identities** under the **Configuration** section
3. In the right-hand pane, click the **Create identity** button
4. Next, on the **Create identity** webpage, select the **Email address** option in the **Identity details** section
5. Provide an email address you have access to in the text box under **Email address**
6. Click the **Create identity** button at the bottom of the webpage
7. In a separate browser tab, navigate to your email account. You should receive an email from AWS asking you to verify your email address, as shown in the following screenshot in *Figure 10.20*. Ensure you click on the link provided to verify your email.

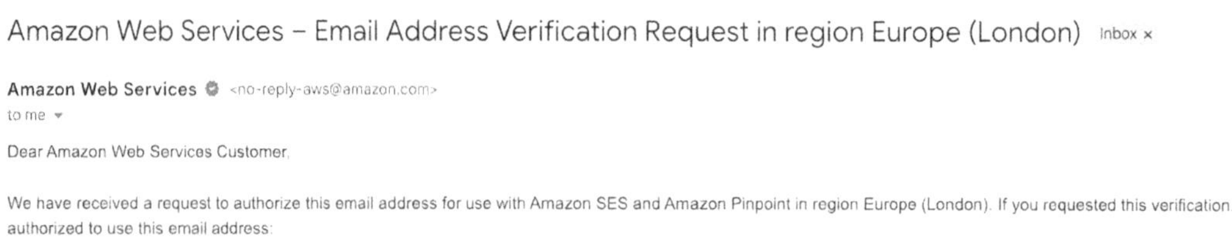

Figure 10.20: Verify your email address

8. Next, navigate back to the **Amazon SES Identities** webpage and refresh the page
9. You should find that the email address now has a verified status as per the following screenshot in *Figure 10.21*:

Figure 10.21: Verified identity status

You can now send emails to this address. You will use the same email address as the `From:` address, as well.

In the next project task, you will create another Amazon S3 bucket, which will be used to host the application source code. The Auto Scaling service, which you will deploy in *Project task 10.8*, dynamically provisions the required EC2 instances. As part of that process, the application source code must be downloaded and configured on the instances. This requires you to host the source code in a supported repository. In this case, you will be using an Amazon S3 bucket as that repository.

Project task 10.7 – Creating additional Amazon S3 buckets

In this project task, you will create an additional Amazon S3 bucket that will serve as the application source code repository. You should have downloaded the source code from the GitHub repository and extracted the files as per the following screenshot in *Figure 10.22*:

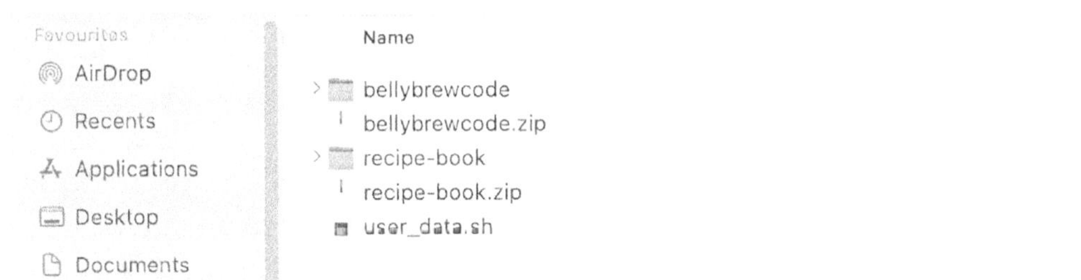

Figure 10.22: Application Source Code and Recipe eBook

Note the following:

- The `bellybrewcode.zip` should be decompressed (extracted) to reveal the `bellybrewcode` folder. Within this folder is another folder called `bellybrew`, which contains all the application source code.

- The `recipe-book.zip` folder, when decompressed (extracted), will reveal the `recipe-book` folder containing the ebook that you uploaded in *Project task 10.4*.
- The `user_data.sh` is the bash script you will use to configure your EC2 instances to host the web application.

The following is the list of instructions to follow:

1. In your Windows file explorer or MacOS Finder window, navigate to the contents of the `bellybrew` folder
2. Using your favorite IDE, such as Visual Studio Code, open the `index.php` file. This contains the main source code of the application. A screenshot is depicted in *Figure 10.23* for your reference.

```
Volumes > Extreme SSD > IaaS Academy > Packt > AWS Cloud Practitioner CLFC02 > Chapter 10
<?php
$responseMessage = null;

if ($_SERVER['REQUEST_METHOD'] === 'POST') {
    try {
        // Validate email
        $email = trim($_POST['email'] ?? '');
        if (!filter_var($email, FILTER_VALIDATE_EMAIL)) {
            throw new Exception("Invalid email address.");
        }

        // Load AWS SDK
        require 'aws.phar';
```

Figure 10.23: Screenshot of the index.php file

3. You must edit this code as follows:

    a. At line number 75, you must provide the secret name of the secret you created in *Project task 10.3*. See the screenshot in *Figure 10.24*. You can get the secret name from AWS Secrets Manager by simply navigating to the service and clicking on Secrets.

```
    // Load the Secrets Manager client
    $secretsClient = new Aws\SecretsManager\SecretsManagerClient($awsConfig);

    try {
        // Fetch secret by name
        $result = $secretsClient->getSecretValue([
            'SecretId' => '[PROVIDE SECRET NAME HERE]'
        ]);

```

Figure 10.24: Provide your secret name, replacing the placeholder shown

b. At line number `157`, provide the bucket name that contains the recipe book, replacing the placeholder

c. At line number `158`, provide the file name and path of the recipe eBook, replacing the placeholder. For example, the full path would be `recipe-book/ebook.pdf` – see screenshot in *Figure 10.25*:

```
149 /**
150  * Sends the recipe book email via AWS SES with a presigned S3 download link.
151  */
152 function sendRecipeBookEmail($email, $awsConfig) {
153     try {
154         $s3 = new Aws\S3\S3Client($awsConfig);
155 
156         $cmd = $s3->getCommand('GetObject', [
157             'Bucket' => '[PROVIDE YOUR RECIPE EBOOK BUCKET NAME]',
158             'Key'    => '[PROVIDE YOUR eBOOK PATH, e,g, recipe-book/ebook.pdf]'
159         ]);
160 
```

Figure 10.25: Provide the bucket name and file path of your recipe book

d. At line number `166`, replace the example email address with the email address you verified in *Project task 10.6*

4. Save the file with the changes made
5. Next, back in your AWS Management console, search for and navigate to the **Amazon S3 service**
6. Ensure that you are still in the London region
7. From the left-hand menu, click **General purpose buckets**
8. In the right-hand pane, click the **Create bucket** button

9. Provide a name for your bucket, for example, `bb-app-source-code` – remember bucket names must be unique, so you will need to choose another name
10. Scroll to the bottom of the webpage and click the **Create bucket** button. You should receive a notification on the webpage stating that the bucket has been successfully created.
11. Click the bucket you just created to open its details page; it should look similar to what is shown in *Figure 10.26*:

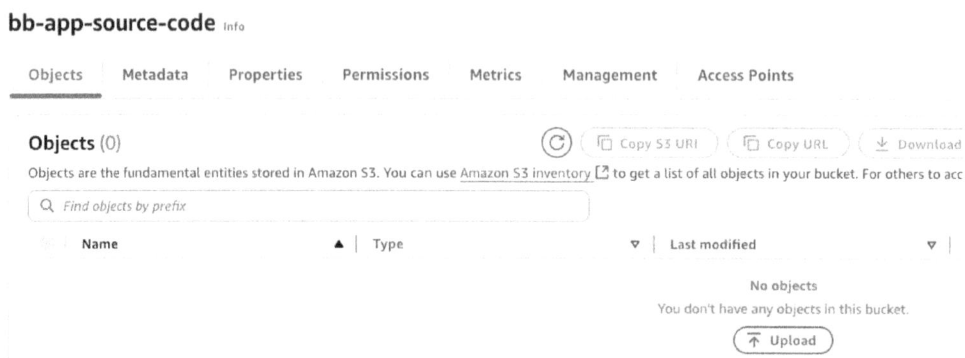

Figure 10.26: Amazon S3 bucket for application source code

12. Click the **Upload** button. This will open the **Upload** webpage of the bucket.
13. In the File Browser (Windows) or Finder (MacOS), navigate to the contents of the extracted source application source code. Recall that the source code is in the `bellybrew` subfolder of the extracted zip folder called `bellybrewcode.zip`
14. From your file browser or Finder tool, drag and drop the `bellybrew folder` into the `Files and folders (0)` area of the webpage as per the following screenshot in *Figure 10.27*:

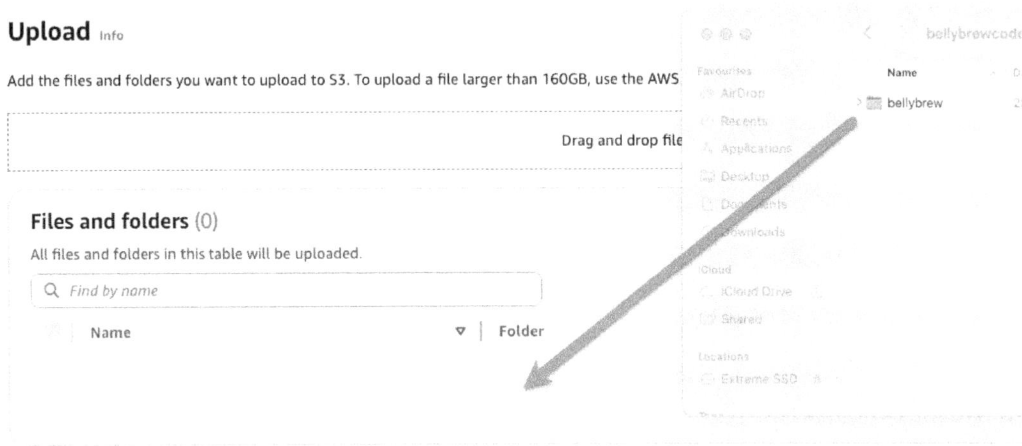

Figure 10.27: Upload the application source code folder to the Amazon S3 bucket

15. Scroll to the bottom of the webpage and click the **Upload** button. The files and folder structure will be uploaded to the bucket.
16. Click the **Close** button once the upload is complete

Your application source code has now been uploaded to the Amazon S3 repository. Next you will configure the Auto Scaling service to provision your EC2 instances, and create a user-data script that will be used to download and deploy this application source code to the EC2 instances provisioned by the Auto Scaling Group.

Project task 10.8 – Launching an AWS auto scaling group

In this project task, you will create a launch template and an auto scaling group to automatically deploy the application to a couple of EC2 instances, which will be deployed into the app subnets of Belly Brew Co. Limited's VPC. The EC2 instances will be configured with the necessary IAM roles to connect with the relevant backend services. The application code in the `index.php` file has also been updated with the required settings of your environment to ensure functionality.

From the GitHub repository, you should have also downloaded the `user_data.sh` bash script file. This file will need to be updated as per your environment and then used to deploy the application on the EC2 instances, which are deployed by the auto scaling group.

The following instructions detail the steps to follow to create an Auto Scaling Group for your application:

1. Using your IDE, such as Visual Studio Code, open the `user_data.sh bash` script file as per the following screenshot in *Figure 10.28:*

```
index.php    $ user_data.sh ×
Volumes > Extreme SSD > IaaS Academy > Packt > AWS Cloud Practitioner CLFC02 > Chapter 1
1   #!/bin/bash
2   # Update the system
3   sudo dnf update -y
4
5   # Install Apache
6   sudo dnf install -y httpd
7
8   # Install PHP and required extensions
9   sudo dnf install -y php php-cli php-common php-mysqlnd php-pdo php-gd php-
10
11  # Start and enable Apache
12  sudo systemctl start httpd
13  sudo systemctl enable httpd
14
```

Figure 10.28: Extract of user_data.sh script

2. You must update this script file by replacing the placeholder at line number 22 with your bucket name. Ensure that the bucket name is followed by a slash (/) and the folder name, which should be `bellybrew` as shown in the following screenshot in *Figure 10.29*. This command, `aws s3 cp`, will copy the application source code files from the Amazon S3 bucket to the html directory on the EC2 instances that are being deployed.

```
15  # Install AWS CLI (if not already installed)
16  sudo dnf install -y awscli
17
18  # Clear existing content in /var/www/html (optional)
19  sudo rm -rf /var/www/html/*
20
21  # Pull application code from S3 (replace <YOUR_BUCKET_NAME> and <YOUR_APP_FOLDER_OR_FILE> accordingly)
22  aws s3 cp s3://[YOUR BUCKET NAME]/bellybrew /var/www/html/ --recursive
23
```

Figure 10.29: Update user_data.sh script with your app source code bucket name

3. Next, save the file

4. Back in the web browser, from the search bar at the top of the AWS Management Console, search for and navigate to the **EC2** service
5. From the left-hand menu, click on **Launch Templates** in the **Instances** section
6. Next, in the right-hand pane, click the **Create launch template** button
7. Provide a name and description for your launch template. For example, you can name the template `bb-app-launch-template`
8. Click the **Quick Start** tab under **Application and OS Images (Amazon Machine Image)**
9. Next, select the **Amazon Linux** icon and ensure that the AMI is **Amazon Linux 2023 kernel-6.1 AMI**
10. Select `t3.micro` from the **Instance type** drop-down list
11. Ensure that the **Key pair name** is set to `Don't include in launch template`
12. Scroll further down and, in the **Network settings** section, ensure you select the `Select existing security group` option. From the **Security groups**, select the App Security Group you created in your VPC from the drop-down list as per the following screenshot in *Figure 10.30*:

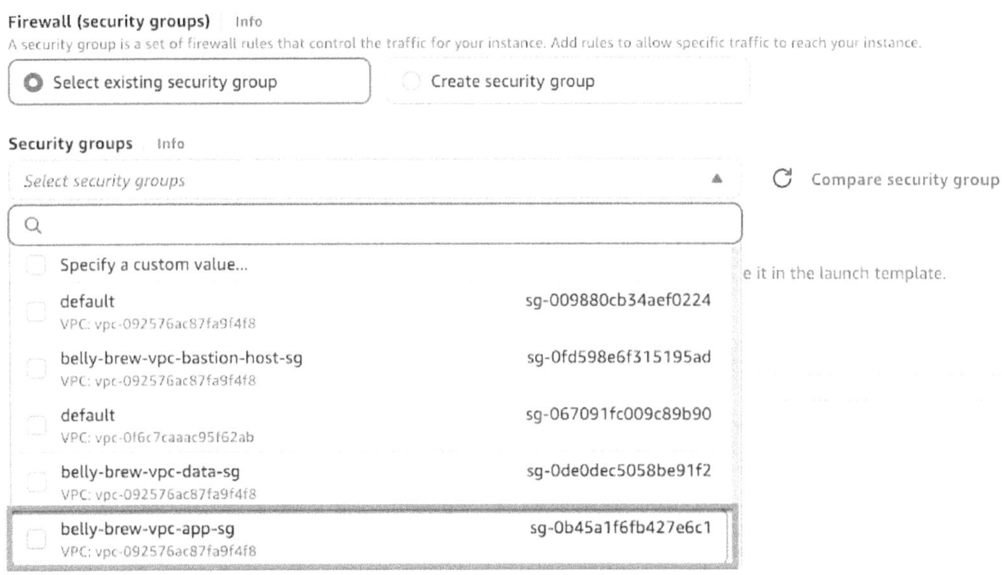

Figure 10.30: Select the App Security Group for your EC2 instances

13. Scroll down and expand the **Advanced details** section
14. Select the `bb-iam-role` you created in *Project task 10.5* from the **IAM instance profile** drop-down list. This is the IAM role you created with the necessary permissions for the application running on the EC2 instances to access various services.
15. Scroll further down to the **User data – optional** section. Copy and paste the `user_data.sh` code you edited earlier into the provided text area.
16. Click the **Create launch template** button
17. Click the **View launch template** button at the bottom of the webpage to see a list of launch templates you have, as shown in *Figure 10.31*:

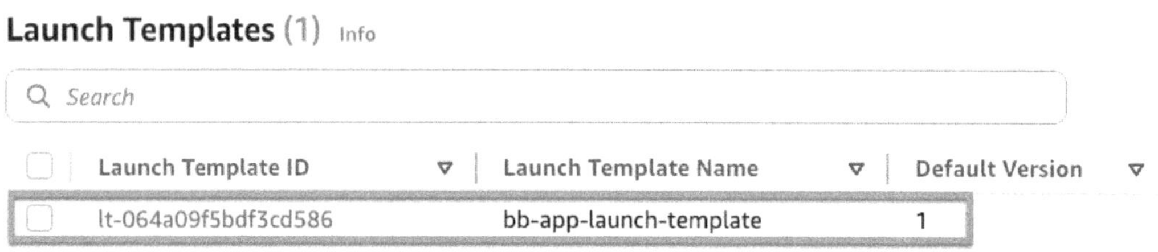

Figure 10.31: Launch template for Belly Brew Co. Limited's web application

Your launch template has now been created and forms the basis of your auto scaling group configuration. Next, you will configure the Auto Scaling Group service.

This is how you must do it:

1. From the left-hand menu, click on **Auto Scaling Groups** in the **Auto Scaling** section
2. In the right-hand pane, click on the **Create Auto Scaling group** button
3. Provide a name for your Auto Scaling Group, such as `bb-app-asg`
4. Select the launch template you created earlier from the **Launch template** drop-down list
5. Click **Next**
6. In the **Network** section, select Belly Brew Co. Limited's VPC you created in *Chapter 7*
7. Select the two App subnets you created in that VPC. You should have `belly-brew-vpc-app-sub-01` and `belly-brew-vpc-app-sub-02` as in *Figure 10.32*

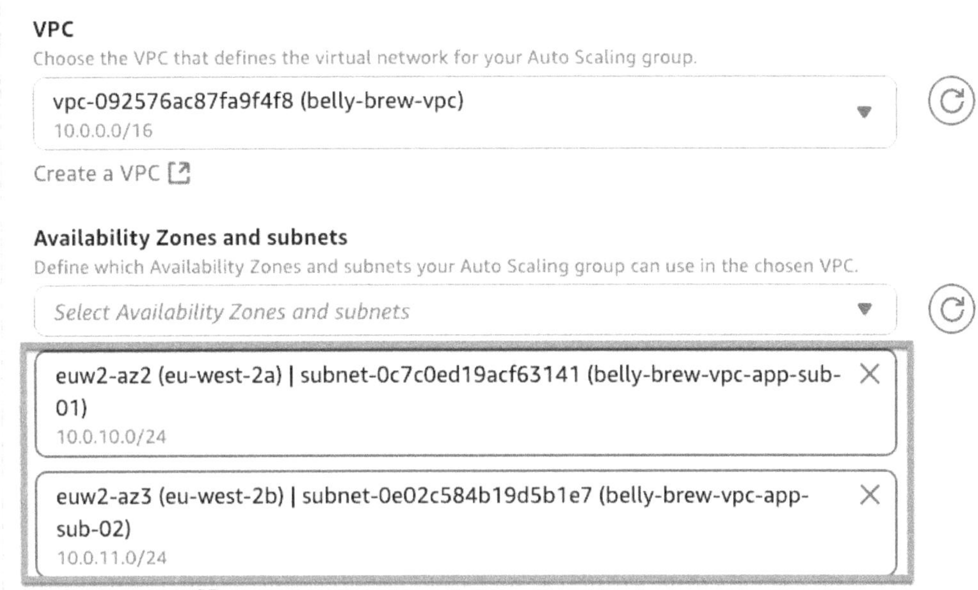

Figure 10.32: App subnets in Belly Brew Co. Limited's VPC

8. Accept the default settings under **Availability Zone distribution – new** and click **Next**
9. In the **Load balancing** section, ensure you select the option **Attach to an existing load balancer**
10. Select the `bb-target-group | HTTP` from the **Existing load balancer target groups** drop-down list you created in *Project task 10.2*. This will be the target group that the load balancer will register the EC2 instances it deploys to. This will ensure that inbound traffic to the Application Load Balancer is distributed to the instances deployed by the Auto Scaling service
11. Next, under **Health checks**, ensure that you select the option **Turn on Elastic Load Balancer health checks**
12. Click **Next**
13. Under **Group size**, set the **Desired capacity** to 2
14. For **Scaling**, set the **Min desired capacity** to 2 and the **Max desired capacity** to 2. This will ensure you always have two instances deployed – one in each App subnet and one in each Availability Zone. Should an EC2 instance in one subnet fail, the Auto Scaling service will replace it to maintain the desired capacity of 2. Additionally, for this configuration, you will not need to set any scaling policies.
15. Scroll down to the bottom of the webpage and click **Next**

16. In the **Add notification - optional** webpage, click **Next**
17. In the **Add tags – optional** webpage, click the **Add tag** button and set the **Key** to `Name` and the **Value – optional** to `bb-appservers`
18. Click **Next**
19. Review your configuration, and at the bottom of the webpage, click the **Create Auto Scaling group** button

Your Auto Scaling group will now provision two EC2 instances in each of the App subnets as depicted in the following screenshot in *Figure 10.33*:

Figure 10.33: Auto scaling group configured to deploy two EC2 instances

The EC2 instances will be configured with the Apache web services, and the application code will be deployed to those instances. The instances will also be registered as targets for the target group you configured earlier, which means that the load balancer will also be able to perform health checks against those instances. If the EC2 instances respond with a healthy check status, the load balancer will distribute incoming web requests across the instances in a round robin fashion, evenly distributing the load. You must wait for around 5 minutes for the deployment to complete.

Your infrastructure has been provisioned, and your application is fully deployed. In the next project task, you will access the application using the Application Load Balancer URL. You can then test the application to see if it functions as expected, enabling you to submit your email address and get an email with a link to the Belly Brew Co. Limited gut-friendly recipe eBook.

Project task 10.9 – Testing the application

In this project task, you will test the application and identify if the website performs as expected. This is how you can do it:

1. While still in the EC2 management console, click on **Auto Scaling Groups** from the **Auto Scaling** section in the left-hand menu
2. In the right-hand pane, click on the **bb-app-asg** auto scaling group you just created
3. Click the **Activity** tab. You will note that two EC2 instances were successfully deployed as per the following screenshot in *Figure 10.34*:

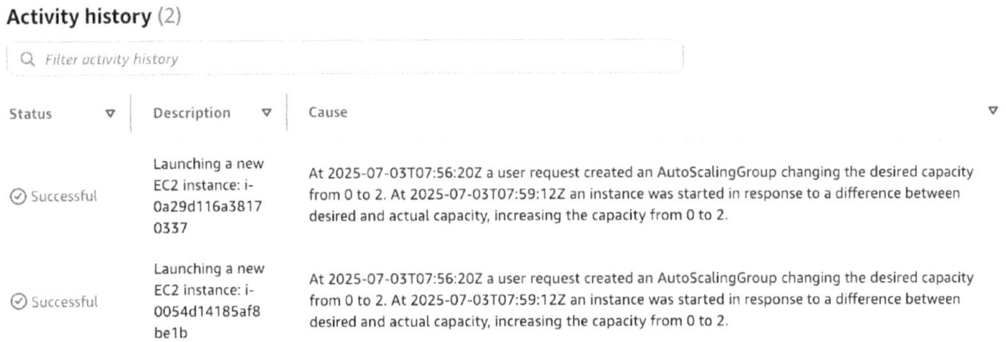

Figure 10.34: Auto scaling group activity history

4. From the left-hand menu, click on **Target Groups** in the **Load Balancing** section
5. In the right-hand pane, click to open the **bb-target-group** you configured earlier
6. The two EC2 instances you deployed using the Auto Scaling group should be in a healthy state as shown in *Figure 10.35*:

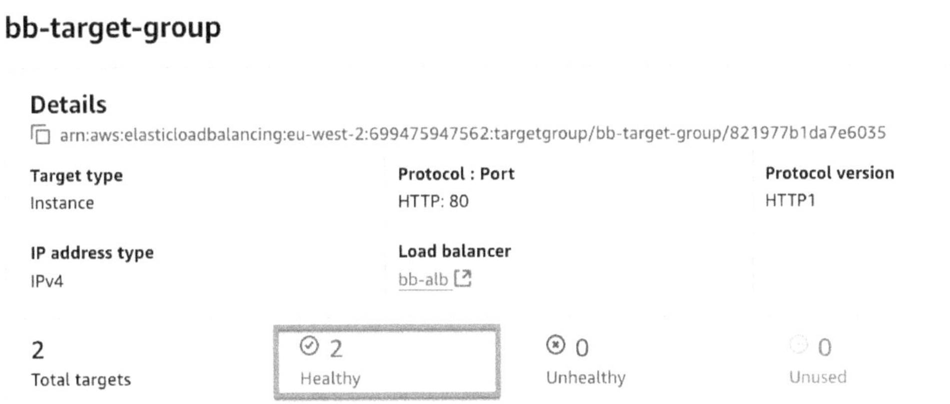

Figure 10.35: EC2 instance reports healthy status

7. From the left-hand menu, click **Load Balancers** in the **Load Balancing** section
8. In the right-hand pane, click the **bb-alb** application load balancer
9. Note the details of the load balancer as per the following screenshot in *Figure 10.36*:

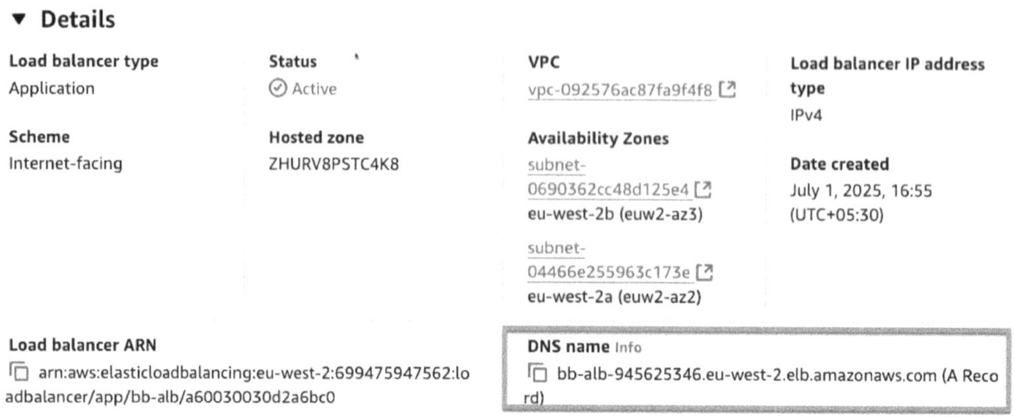

Figure 10.36: Belly Brew Co. Limited's Application Load Balancer DNS name

10. Copy the **DNS name** and paste it into a new browser tab in your Internet browser. You may need to check the address in your browser tab to ensure that the protocol used is http and not https. If the webpage does not load, click into the address bar of the browser tab and if the URL starts with https, delete the 's' and press enter.
11. The application should open, revealing Belly Brew Co. Limited's website as per the following screenshot in *Figure 10.37*:

Figure 10.37: Belly Brew Co. Limited's website application

12. Scroll down Belly Brew Co. Limited's webpage until you get to the customer signup section. You will note the form on the webpage where customers would provide their contact details and, in return, get a free recipe eBook as per the following screenshot in *Figure 10.38*:

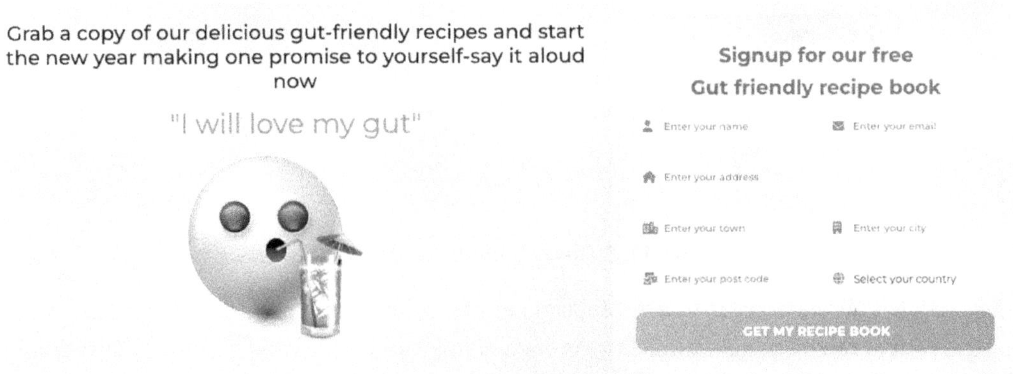

Figure 10.38: Website form encouraging customers to provide their contact details for a free recipe eBook

13. Go ahead and fill out the form using the same email address you verified for *Project task 10.6*
14. When you click the **GET MY RECIPE BOOK** button, you should see a message confirming that data has been saved and the email has been sent successfully
15. Log in to your email account to check for a message giving you a download link to access the eBook. Note that because the sender and recipient of the email are the same, the email message may end up in your spam folder. You should find an email like the following screenshot in *Figure 10.39*:

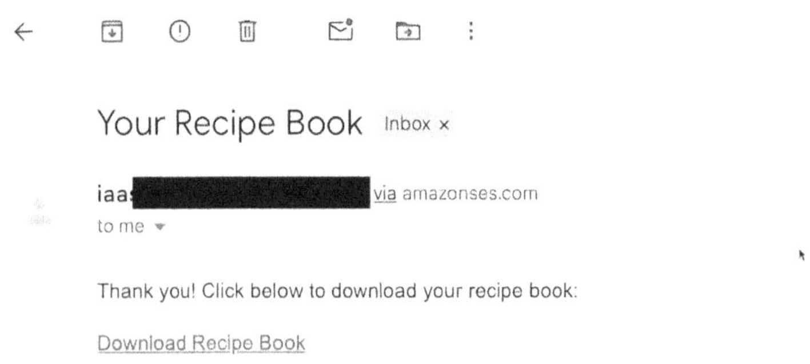

Figure 10.39: Email containing link to free recipe eBook

16. Note that the email is sent via amazonses.com. Click on the download link to access your recipe eBook. This link is a pre-signed link and is only valid for a short duration.

Congratulations! You have now completed the first capstone project of this study guide and fulfilled Belly Brew Co. Limited's first requirements.

Feel free to review your deployment and configurations of the various services further to better understand how each of these different services was used to build your final solution.

As part of this project, you have deployed several AWS resources. In the next project task, you will terminate those resources to avoid consuming any more AWS credits or incurring any unnecessary costs.

Project task 10.10 – Cleaning up

In this final task, you will terminate several services deployed, ensuring you do not incur any unnecessary charges.

This is what you have to do:

1. **Delete the Auto Scaling Group:**
    1. In the EC2 Management Console, click on **Auto Scaling Groups** in the **Auto Scaling** section from the left-hand menu
    2. In the right-hand pane, select the **bb-app-asg** auto scaling group
    3. Select the **Delete** option from the **Action** drop-down list
    4. Confirm the deletion of the auto scaling group by typing `delete` in the text box and clicking the **Delete** button. This will also terminate your EC2 instances.

2. **Delete the Load Balancers and Target Group:**
    1. From the left-hand menu, click **Load Balancers** in the **Load Balancing** section. In the right-hand pane, select the **bb-alb** load balancer, and then select the **Delete load balancer** option from the **Actions** drop-down list.
    2. In the dialog box that appears, type in `confirm` to confirm the deletion and click the **Delete** button
    3. Next, from the left-hand menu, click **Target Groups** in the **Load Balancing section**. In the right-hand pane, select **bb-target-group**. Next, select **Delete** from the **Actions** drop-down list. Click the **Delete** button to confirm deletion.
3. **Delete the Secret from AWS Secrets Manager and disable the rotation policy**
    1. From the search bar at the top of the AWS Management Console, search for and navigate to **CloudFormation**. AWS uses CloudFormation to create and deploy a Lambda function that is responsible for rotating the secret in Secrets Manager.
    2. In AWS CloudFormation, you will note that there are two Secret Manager stacks. Select the second stack (NOT the Nested one) in the right-hand pane. Click the **Delete stack** button and confirm the deletion by following the instructions in the dialog box that appears. This process will take a few minutes to complete. You can click on the refresh button to confirm that the stacks have been deleted. The nested stack will also get automatically deleted.
    3. From the search bar at the top of the AWS Management Console, search for and navigate to AWS Secrets Manager
    4. From the left-hand menu, click on **Secrets**
    5. In the right-hand pane, click on the **bb-db-secret** details page. Select **Delete secret** from the **Actions** drop-down list.
    6. In the dialog box that appears, set the **Waiting period** to 7 days and click the **Schedule deletion** button
4. **Delete the Amazon RDS database**
    1. From the search bar at the top of the AWS Management Console, search for and navigate to Amazon RDS
    2. From the left-hand menu, click **Databases**
    3. In the right-hand pane, select Belly Brew Co. Limited's database (`bellybrewdb`)
    4. Select **Delete** from the **Actions** drop-down list
    5. De-select the option to **Create final snapshot**
    6. De-select the option to **Retain automatic backups**

7. Select the option **I acknowledge that upon instance deletion, automated backups, including system snapshots and point-in-time recovery, will no longer be available**
8. Type `delete me` in the confirmation text box and click the **Delete** button. The database will take a few minutes to delete
9. Once the database has been deleted, you must also delete the database subnet group. From the left-hand menu, click on **Subnet groups**. In the right-hand pane, select Belly Brew Co. Limited's subnet group (*belly-brew-db-subnet-group*). Click the **Delete** button and then click the **Delete** button again in the dialog box that appears.

5. **Delete the NAT Gateway from your VPC**
   1. In the search bar at the top of the AWS Management Console, search for and navigate to the VPC console
   2. From the left-hand menu, click on **NAT gateways**
   3. In the right-hand pane, select the **bb-nat-gw** and click the **Delete NAT gateway** button from the **Actions** drop-down list
   4. Type `delete` in the dialog box that appears and then click the **Delete** button. This will take a few minutes to delete
   5. Next, you must update the Main Route Table as the NAT gateway no longer exists. From the left-hand menu, click on **Route tables**
   6. In the right-hand pane, select the main route table (`belly-brew-vpc-main-rt`)
   7. Click on the **Routes** tab and click **Edit routes**
   8. Click on the **Remove** button next to the entry for the route with the destination `0.0.0.0/0`
   9. Click the **Save changes** button

At this stage, you have terminated all resources to ensure you do not incur any charges. If you like, you can also empty the S3 buckets and delete them too. However, Amazon does give you 5GB of free storage.

This project has provided you with an opportunity to build a real-world end-to-end solution, understanding the choices made in architecture, design, and the build process, as well as how you go about implementing the final solution. You have gained practical experience in designing for high availability and scalability as well as incorporating security best practices and cost optimization strategies.

As a Cloud Practitioner, understanding the importance of trade-offs, which services to consume, and how to build and support your workloads is crucial to building a successful career in cloud computing.

Summary

When building solutions to host in cloud environments such as AWS, you must design your application to be highly available, resilient to failures, and scalable. Furthermore, to ensure cost optimization, you should provision your resources on an as-needed basis, fulfilling demand as it arises.

On AWS, you can configure Elastic Load Balancers to distribute incoming traffic across multiple EC2 instances, ECS containers, and Lambda functions to ensure high availability. If a particular EC2 instance fails, the load balancer will stop sending requests to that instance and instead route traffic only to healthy instances. This ensures that end users do not experience outages.

AWS offers various types of load balancers:

- **Application Load Balancers** (**ALB**): Designed to handle HTTP/HTTPS traffic
- **Network Load Balancers** (**NLB**): Designed to handle TCP/UDP traffic and are capable of processing millions of requests per second
- **Gateway Load Balancers** (**GLB**): Designed to manage traffic for virtual appliances, typically sourced from the AWS Marketplace

In addition to achieving high availability, it is equally important to ensure that your application is scalable. The AWS EC2 Auto Scaling service allows you to scale out or scale in based on demand. You can configure scheduled scaling, dynamic scaling, and predictive scaling as needed.

AWS offers several scaling policies to suit your application's needs, including target tracking and step scaling. These policies can be defined using metrics such as CPU utilization, request count per target from the load balancer, and many others. Building your solutions using these tools and services to ensure high availability and scalability is critical for any business or organization.

In the next chapter, you will discover some advanced networking concepts designed to help you build solutions for global presence and make your application accessible across multiple regions.

Exam Readiness Drill – Chapter Review Questions

Apart from mastering key concepts, strong test-taking skills under time pressure are essential for acing your certification exam. That's why developing these abilities early in your learning journey is critical.

Exam readiness drills, using the free online practice resources provided with this book, help you progressively improve your time management and test-taking skills while reinforcing the key concepts you've learned.

HOW TO GET STARTED

- Open the link or scan the QR code at the bottom of this page
- If you have unlocked the practice resources already, log in to your registered account. If you haven't, follow the instructions in *Free Benefits with Your Book* section in this book's *Preface* and come back to this page.
- Once you log in, click the START button to start this chapter's quiz
- We recommend attempting a quiz multiple times till you're able to answer most of the questions correctly and well within the time limit.
- You can use the following practice template to help you plan your attempts:

Working On Accuracy		
Attempt	**Target**	**Time Limit**
Attempt 1	40% or more	Till the timer runs out
Attempt 2	60% or more	Till the timer runs out
Attempt 3	75% or more	Till the timer runs out
Working On Timing		
Attempt 4	75% or more	1 minute before time limit
Attempt 5	75% or more	2 minutes before time limit
Attempt 6	75% or more	3 minutes before time limit

The above drill is just an example. Design your drills based on your own goals and make the most out of the online quizzes accompanying this book.

Link to this Chapter's Quiz

You need to unlock the online practice resources to access the link below. Check the *Free Benefits with Your Book* section in the *Preface* for detailed instructions on how to do this. You only need to unlock the resources once.

Open Quiz `https://packt.link/clf_c02_ch10`or scan the QR code

11

AWS Networking, Part 2 – Route 53 and CloudFront

When you type a URL into a web browser and are instantly presented with a website, what happens behind the scenes is quite remarkable. The servers hosting these websites on the Internet are accessible via a **public IP address**, which was discussed in *Chapter 7*. However, what you enter into the browser's address bar is a **domain name** in **Uniform Resource Locator** (**URL**) format—such as `https://iaasacademy.com`, a website I own and use to deliver Cloud Computing courses.

The "magic" happens thanks to a service called the **Domain Name System** (**DNS**), which translates URL-style domain names into their associated IP addresses. This translation allows your browser to locate and connect to the correct server hosting the website you wish to access. You can think of DNS as the Internet's phone book—designed to resolve human-readable domain names into machine-readable IP addresses, enabling devices like your desktop, laptop, or even smartphone to connect to the services provided by web servers hosting a wide variety of websites and applications.

But DNS does more than map domain names to IP addresses. In this chapter, you will learn how to scale your network architecture by integrating resources across multiple AWS regions—a crucial strategy for organizations aiming to enhance global availability, performance, and resilience. You will learn how **Amazon Route 53**, AWS's DNS service, can be used to implement intelligent routing strategies across your globally distributed infrastructure. These routing policies enable you to direct user traffic based on latency, geographic location, and health checks, making them ideal for supporting multi-region deployments. Such configurations are key to delivering low-latency access and establishing robust disaster recovery solutions.

In addition, this chapter introduces **Amazon CloudFront**, a globally distributed **Content Delivery Network** (**CDN**) service. CloudFront accelerates the delivery of your content, such as static assets, video streams, and APIs, by caching it at **edge locations** within the AWS Global Infrastructure. This reduces the physical distance between your application and your users, leading to lower latency and faster load times. By the end of the chapter, you will understand how to architect applications that offer high availability and optimized performance to a global user base.

The following topics are discussed in this chapter:

- Understanding how Amazon CloudFront works
- Introducing Amazon Route 53, DNS, and routing policies
- Introducing the AWS Global Accelerator

Understanding how Amazon CloudFront works

Amazon CloudFront is AWS's content delivery network service designed to distribute content with low latency by leveraging the caching functionality of edge locations. The service uses AWS edge locations and regional edge caches to route traffic over the AWS global backbone network and store cached content closer to users.

CloudFront is optimized for delivering both static and dynamic content, such as documents, images, and videos, to users. When a user requests content distributed via CloudFront, they are routed to the nearest edge location with the lowest latency to retrieve the content as quickly as possible. If the content is already cached at the edge location, it is delivered directly from there. Otherwise, the request is forwarded over the AWS backbone network to the origin server (such as an Application Load Balancer, Amazon EC2, or Amazon S3). The retrieved content is then cached at the edge location for a specified **Time to Live** (**TTL**) duration.

Without CloudFront, requests travel over the standard public internet, encountering multiple hops and routes, as illustrated in *Figure 11.1*:

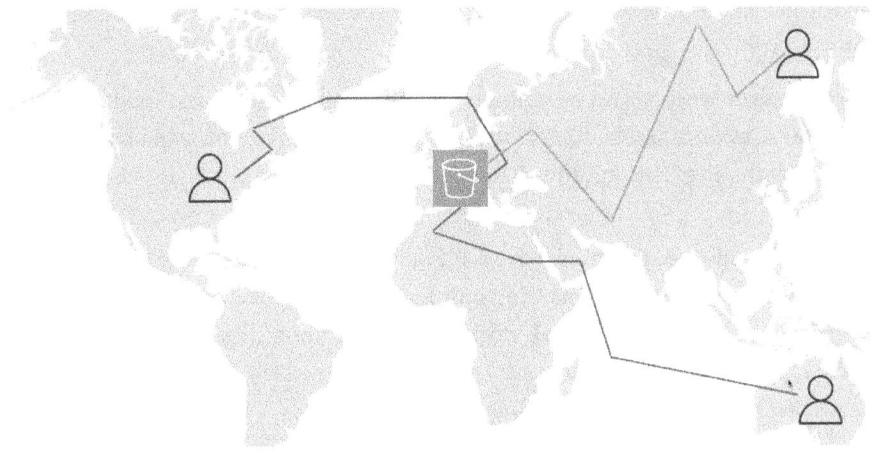

Figure 11.1: Without Amazon CloudFront

In this example, users requesting to access content in an Amazon S3 bucket in the London region might encounter multiple hops and routes. This slows down the overall transfer rates and occasionally also prevents connectivity due to faulty routers on the Internet.

With CloudFront, however, users' requests are routed to the nearest edge location and then through the optimized AWS backbone network, as depicted in the following diagram in *Figure 11.2*:

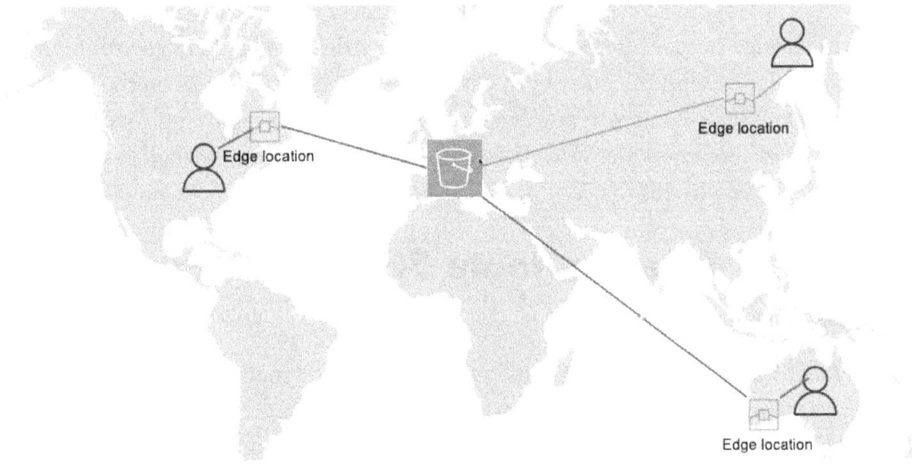

Figure 11.2: With CloudFront distribution

This reduces the number of intermediary networks the request traverses, reducing latency and improving performance. The AWS network also provides higher data transfer speeds, allowing users to access content more quickly.

The following are some examples of use cases where you would benefit from using the Amazon CloudFront service:

- **E-commerce website**: An e-commerce website can use Amazon CloudFront to distribute product assets, such as images and descriptions, more quickly to end users browsing the site. This improves the customer experience and helps keep users engaged.
- **Online fitness app**: An online fitness platform uses Amazon CloudFront to deliver workout videos smoothly, ensuring uninterrupted playback even when thousands of users are streaming during peak workout hours. Additionally, because videos are cached at local edge locations, users don't need to retrieve the content from the origin server each time, further improving performance.
- **Customize at the Edge**: You can integrate CloudFront with Lambda (also known as **Lambda@Edge**) to customize content delivery based on a variety of parameters. You can also authenticate users at the edge, enabling faster logins and signups.

To use Amazon CloudFront, you create a distribution point, which defines your origin endpoint. That origin can be an EC2 instance, a load balancer, an S3 bucket, etc. The distribution point created using CloudFront is a special URL that you then give to your users and takes the form of `d123456abcdef8.cloudfront.net`. Using this distribution point, users are directed to an edge location closest to them and then routed to the origin over the AWS backbone network, as illustrated in *Figure 11.2*.

Another critical edge service offered by AWS is Route 53, designed to help you configure DNS settings essential for communication both within the VPC and externally on the public Internet. Amazon Route 53 offers features such as routing policies and traffic shaping, which you use to build resilient and highly available solutions across multiple regions. The next section introduces you to this service.

Introducing Amazon Route 53, DNS, and routing policies

Amazon Route 53 is AWS's Domain Name System service, designed to translate human-readable names into IP addresses that computers use to communicate over a network. When you type `https://iaasacademy.com` in your browser window, you are directed to the IaaS Academy training website. What happens behind the scenes is quite amazing. *Figure 11.3* showcases a flowchart of the process:

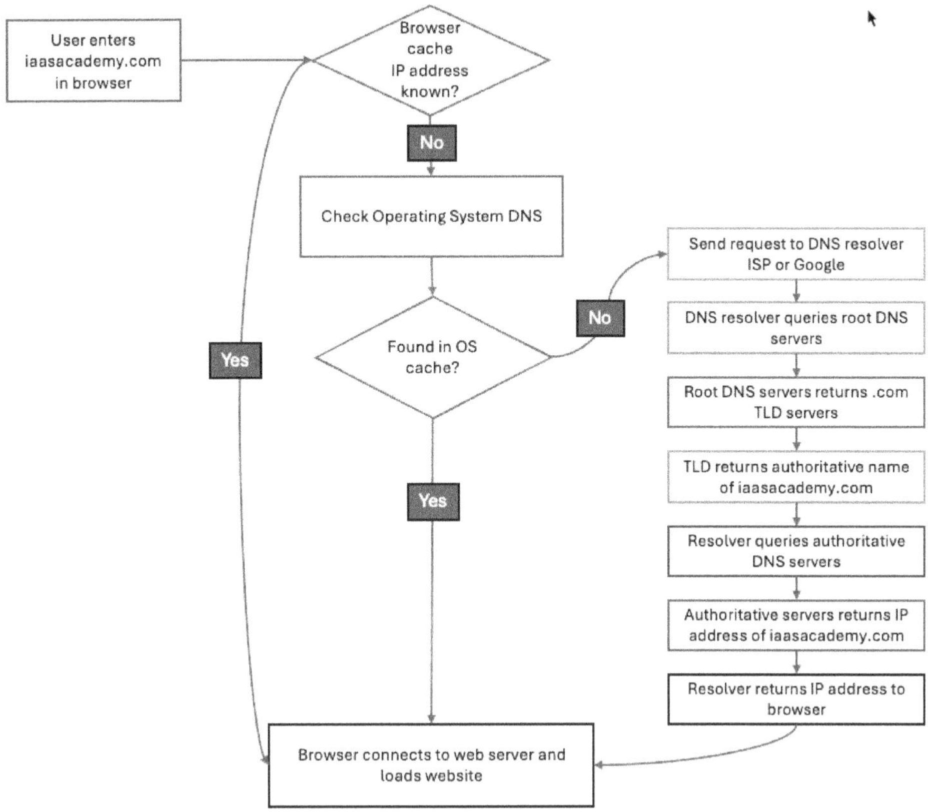

Figure 11.3: Flowchart of DNS name resolution process

Here is a high-level overview of the steps involved in DNS name resolution:

1. Your browser first checks its local cache to see if it already knows the IP address of the IaaS Academy website. If it doesn't, it passes the request to the local operating system cache.
2. If the name-to-IP address mapping is not cached (likely because you haven't visited the website before), your browser sends the request to a DNS Resolver. This is a DNS server that performs recursive queries on your behalf and is usually hosted by your local ISP, although you may also use Google's DNS servers.
3. The DNS Resolver then queries the **root DNS servers** to determine which **top-level domain** (**TLD**) servers (.com) are responsible for `iaasacademy.com`
4. The root DNS servers do not store the IP address for iaasacademy.com. Instead, they return the details (Name Server records and IP addresses) of the TLD servers for .com.

5. The DNS Resolver then queries the .com TLD servers to find out which authoritative name servers are responsible for `iaasacademy.com`
6. The TLD servers respond with the IP addresses of the authoritative DNS servers (Name Servers) that host and manage the DNS records for `iaasacademy.com`. If you host your domain name with Amazon Route 53, these would be the Route 53 name servers.
7. The DNS Resolver then sends the request to those authoritative servers and finally obtains the IP address of `iaasacademy.com`
8. Your browser receives the IP address and establishes a connection to the website, allowing you to continue your training on AWS technologies

This entire process happens in just a few seconds over the public Internet. Furthermore, the results are cached at the DNS Resolver, within your browser, and in your operating system, ensuring that future requests are completed much faster.

Amazon Route 53 offers the following core services:

- Domain registration
- Creation and management of Hosting Zones
- DNS Routing
- Health Checks

Let's look at these in a bit more detail.

Domain Registration

Amazon Route 53 offers full domain name registration services that you can use to purchase your own domain names. When you purchase a domain name, you register it under a TLD such as **.com**, **.co.uk**, **.org**, **.in**, etc.

Domain names are available on a first-come, first-served basis. This means that many common names may already be taken by someone else, as each domain name must be unique on the Internet.

As part of the registration process, you also select a lease duration for your domain name, which can range from 1 to 10 years. You must renew this lease before it expires, or you risk losing the domain to someone else. In fact, some businesses bulk-purchase popular names and then resell or auction them at a much higher price.

Next, you will learn how to manage DNS records for your domain names using **Hosted Zones**.

Amazon Route 53 hosted zones

When you purchase a domain name with Route 53, you must create a hosted zone to manage its records. A hosted zone is essentially a database, often called a **zone file**, that contains all the resource records you define for your domain name.

Here are some common record types you can create:

Record Type	Description
A/AAAA Records	Map a name to an IP address. For example, www.example.com → w.x.y.z. An A record maps a name to an IPv4 address, whereas an AAAA record maps it to an IPv6 address.
CNAME Records	Canonical name records map one name (alias) to another name. For example, you could map blog.example.com to www.example.com so that both resolve to the same resource.
MX records	Mail exchange records point to mail servers that handle email traffic.

Table 11.1: Example of DNS records

With Route 53, you can create two types of hosted zones:

- **Public Hosted Zones**: Define how you want to route traffic for your domain across the public Internet. For example, instead of giving users the Amazon S3 static website endpoint (`http://belly-brew-coming-soon.s3-website-us-east-1.amazonaws.com/`), you can create a DNS record in Route 53 that points a friendly domain name like `bellybrew.co.uk` to the S3 bucket. This makes it much easier for users to remember and access your site.
- **Private Hosted Zones**: Define how you want to route traffic within private networks, such as one or more VPCs. For example, you could use `devserver.example.com` to point to the private IP address of an EC2 instance in a VPC.

Hosted zones enable you to define DNS records for specific domain names as well as create routing policies for how traffic is directed to the resources that will host your application. Depending on the type of traffic and protocol used to connect to your application, you will need to create the appropriate record type. In addition to standard DNS records, as depicted in *Table 11.1*, AWS also offers the option to create **alias records**, which are used to route traffic to AWS-specific resources. This is discussed next.

Alias records

In addition to standard DNS records, Route 53 supports **alias records**, which are designed to map your domain directly to specific AWS resource endpoints, such as:

- An Application Load Balancer
- An Amazon S3 bucket configured for static website hosting
- An Amazon CloudFront distribution

Alias records are especially useful for mapping the **zone apex** (the root domain, without a hostname). For example, the zone apex of `www.iaasacademy.com` is simply *iaasacademy.com*.

This allows you to use branded, corporate DNS names directly with AWS resources.

In the next section, you will learn more about Amazon Route 53 routing policies, which can be used to build global network routing with options for resilience and reduced latency.

Amazon Route 53 routing policies

Amazon Route 53 provides several routing policies that let you define how traffic is directed to your resources. These policies allow you to split traffic between multiple resources, improve performance by routing users to the lowest-latency endpoints, or configure active-passive failover solutions for high availability.

The main routing policies are:

- **Simple Routing Policy**: The most basic policy. You define one record per DNS name, but that record can point to multiple resources. For example, you could map `www.iaasacademy.com` to several EC2 instances with different public IP addresses. Route 53 returns all available IP addresses to the client, which will then randomly select one to connect to.
- **Failover Routing Policy**: This policy enables an active-passive setup. You designate one resource as primary and another as secondary. Health checks monitor the primary resource, and if it fails, Route 53 automatically routes traffic to the secondary resource. This is particularly useful for ensuring resilience against Availability Zone or Regional outages.
- **Geolocation Routing Policy**: Routes traffic based on the geographical location of your users. For example, visitors from France can be directed to resources in the Paris Region, while visitors from the UK are directed to resources in the London Region.
- **Latency Routing Policy**: Routes traffic to the resource that offers the lowest latency from the user's location. This is commonly used when you have copies of your website deployed in multiple AWS Regions and want each user to connect to the fastest one.

- **Weighted Routing Policy**: Splits traffic between multiple resources based on weight values you assign. For example, if you deploy a new version of your application, you might send 10% of traffic to the new resource and 90% to the existing one. Over time, as you gain confidence, you can gradually shift all traffic to the new version.
- **Geoproximity routing policy**: This policy lets you send users to resources that are closest to them geographically. You can also manually adjust the traffic distribution using what is known as bias. For example:
  - If you want to send more traffic to your U.S. servers, you can increase the bias for that region.
  - If you want to send less traffic to Europe (such as during maintenance), you can decrease the bias for Europe.

  This policy type is used to steer traffic between regions depending on location and your chosen settings. You shift more or less traffic to a resource by adjusting the **bias** value.

Amazon Route 53 also allows you to perform health checks against your resources. Certain routing policies, like the failover routing policy, will send traffic based on the results of those health checks. Health checks are discussed next.

Amazon Route 53 health checks

Amazon Route 53 includes a health check feature that ensures traffic is only routed to resources and endpoints that respond as healthy. By default, Route 53 checks the health of your resources every 30 seconds, but you can reduce this to every 10 seconds at an additional cost.

The health checking service helps you detect unhealthy resources and can redirect traffic to other healthy resources, both within and across regions. This supports high availability and service continuity. For example, if you configure a failover routing policy between a primary site and a secondary site, you must set up health checks to monitor the primary site. If the primary site goes down, Route 53 automatically directs customer requests to the secondary site.

There are three types of health checks you can configure:

- **Health checks to monitor an endpoint**: These checks the health of resources such as an Application Load Balancer or the IP address of an EC2 instance.
- **Health checks to monitor other health checks**: This groups multiple health checks and evaluates the overall health based on a minimum number of healthy responses. If

the number of healthy resources falls below your defined threshold, Route 53 can act (e.g., rerouting traffic).

- **Health checks to monitor CloudWatch alarms**: You can create health checks that follow CloudWatch alarms. For example, you might set up an alarm to trigger if the number of EC2 instances behind a load balancer falls below a set value. If the alarm is triggered, Route 53 can mark the load balancer as unhealthy and route traffic elsewhere.

Amazon CloudFront integrates well with Amazon Route 53 for routing users' traffic over the Internet to the CloudFront distribution point, as depicted in the following diagram in *Figure 11. 4*:

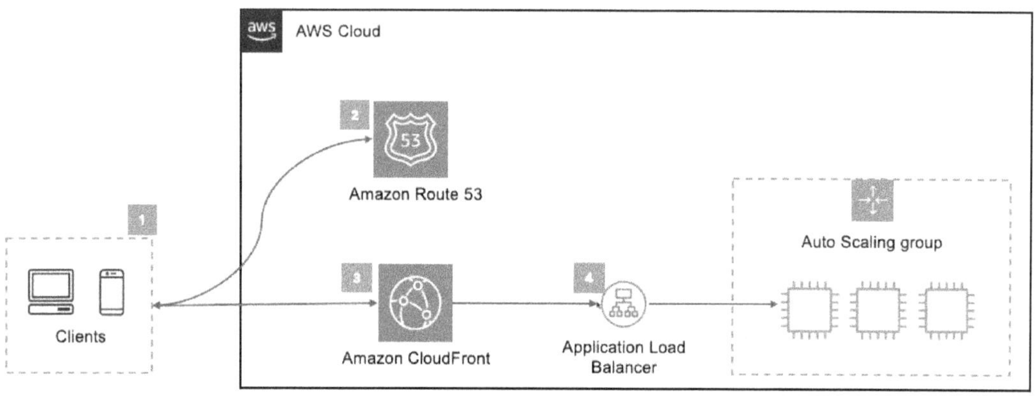

Figure 11.4: Integrating CloudFront with Route 53 to route users' traffic to the application load balancer

For example, in the case of our client, Belly Brew Co. Limited, *Figure 11.4* depicts how end users' requests to access the web application hosted on the EC2 instances are routed via the CloudFront distribution point. The following is a breakdown of the individual components of the request:

1. Users connect using a client, such as a web browser, to search for the Belly Brew Co. Limited website
2. Suppose the website DNS name is hosted on Amazon Route 53 with an entry for the CloudFront distribution point that has an endpoint for the application load balancer shown in the diagram. In that case, it will return the CloudFront distribution URL to the end user.

3. The user's browser will then connect to the CloudFront distribution point URL, which will forward that traffic to the Application Load Balancer URL
4. The application load balancer will then route the request to one of the three EC2 instances using a round robin fashion by default. Users will then be able to access the website using the company's DNS name.

Amazon CloudFront, in this example, is being used to cache content such as images and videos locally at Edge Location, vastly improving the user experience. It also increases your web application's reliability due to its globally distributed collection of edge locations. This not only improves transfer speeds and lowers latency but also improves availability due to its caching capability.

Another service that AWS offers, which improves the performance and availability of applications by using the AWS global network to route user traffic, is the **AWS Global Accelerator**. This service is discussed in the next section.

Introducing AWS Global Accelerator

The AWS Global Accelerator is a network service designed to provide better network performance to your application for your global users. The service improves the availability of your application by directing your users' traffic through the AWS backbone network via an edge location closest to them, thereby reducing latency.

The Global Accelerator allows you to assign two anycast IPv4 addresses that act as fixed entry points for your application endpoints, which could be Network Load Balancers, Application Load Balancers, Amazon EC2 instances, or Elastic IP addresses. You associate these IP addresses with multiple endpoints in one or more regions. Users who connect to those addresses are then routed via the endpoint that is most optimal in terms of location, latency, and health.

An anycast IP address is one that is shared between multiple servers and locations, but traffic is routed via the closest edge location in terms of network hops/latency. For example, if an anycast IP address is associated with a service that needs to be made available in London as well as Tokyo, a user in Tokyo will connect to the Tokyo network service, not London, avoiding unnecessary latency over the public Internet.

Do not confuse the Global Accelerator with Amazon CloudFront. The Global Accelerator is designed to improve network performance and route traffic to application endpoints. In contrast, Amazon CloudFront is a content distribution solution designed to cache content closer to the end user.

In the next section, you will have the opportunity to complete a lab exercise where you will implement a CloudFront distribution for the Belly Brew Co. Limited 'Coming soon' website.

Project task 11 – Configuring a CloudFront distribution for Belly Brew Co. Limited

In *Chapter 6*, you deployed a static website on Amazon S3 to promote the Belly Brew Co. Limited. That was a simple 'Coming soon' website that was designed to promote the upcoming release of their customer-facing web application. The site was deployed on an S3 bucket in the N. Virginia region. However, you anticipate that users across the globe may access the website too, and have decided to serve the website via a CloudFront distribution.

In this project task, you will configure and deploy a CloudFront distribution that will be used for the same website, as per the following diagram in *Figure 11.5*:

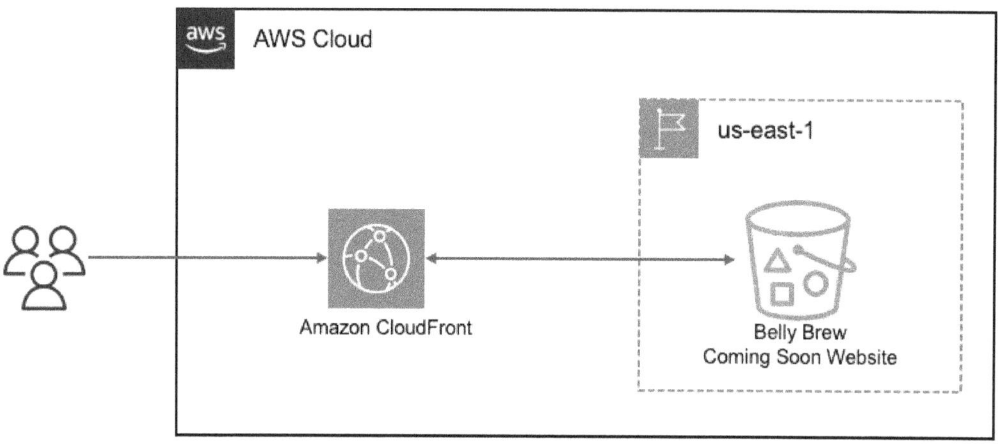

Figure 11.5: Create and configure a CloudFront distribution

This will ensure that the site is available over low-latency connectivity across the globe due to the use of edge locations and regional edge caches. Content will be cached locally at the edge location, making the end user experience a lot faster and more engaging.

Technical requirements

To complete the project exercises in this chapter, ensure that you have completed the project exercises in *Chapter 6*. Log in to your AWS Development account as the IAM user Alice to complete the project tasks.

Project task 11.1 – Creating a CloudFront distribution

In this project task, you will navigate to the AWS CloudFront console and configure a distribution for the Belly Brew Co. Limited's coming soon website, which should be accessible from the Amazon S3 service.

Follow these steps to configure the CloudFront distribution:

1. Ensure that you are logged into the AWS management console and are in the N. Virginia region
2. In the top search bar of your management console, search for and navigate to the Amazon S3 service
3. Confirm that the S3 bucket you created for the static website in an earlier chapter is still available, as per the following screenshot in *Figure 11.6*:

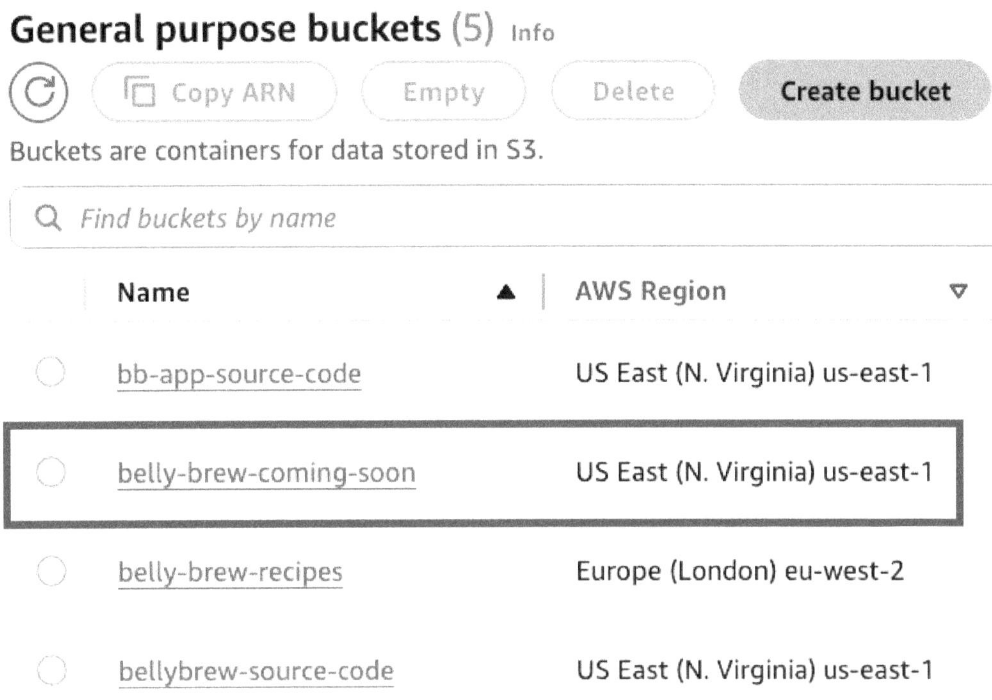

Figure 11.6: Amazon S3 bucket hosting Belly Brew Co. Limited static website

4. Next, from the search bar at the top of the webpage, search for and navigate to the CloudFront console
5. From the left-hand menu, click **Distributions** and then in the right-hand pane, click the **Create distribution** button
6. Next, you must select a plan (Free, Pro, Business, Premium, Pay as you go), select **Pay as you go,** and click **Next**
7. Provide a name for your distribution, such as `bellybrewcloudfront`

8. Next, provide an appropriate description of your choice
9. Under **Distribution type**, select the **Single website or app** option
10. Click **Next**
11. Select **Amazon S3** as the **Origin type**
12. Next, click the **Browse S3** button in the **Origin** section of the webpage to find your S3 bucket hosting the static website
13. In the **Select S3 location** pop-up window that appears, select the bucket that hosts your static website as per the following screenshot in *Figure 11.7*:

Figure 11.7: Select the belly-brew-coming-soon bucket

14. Click **Choose**. Remember, your bucket name will be different from the one you see in the screenshot because bucket names must be unique on the Internet.
15. You see a prompt indicating that, because this bucket has been configured with static website hosting, you should use the s3 website endpoint rather than the bucket endpoint. Go ahead and click the **Use website endpoint** button. This will update the format of the S3 origin automatically to the website endpoint address of your bucket.
16. Leave the remaining settings at their default values and click **Next**

17. On the **Enable security** webpage, accept the defaults and click **Next**
18. Next, review your configuration and click the **Create distribution** button at the bottom of the webpage
19. Your distribution will now be created. Click the **Distribution** link in the breadcrumb just below the search bar at the top of the management console

Your CloudFront distribution will take a few minutes to deploy. Check the status page regularly by clicking the refresh button. Once deployed, you will see the last modified date of the distribution, and the **Status** will be set to **Enabled**.

Project task 11.2 – Testing the CloudFront distribution

In this project task, you will test the distribution and confirm that you can access the application.

Follow these steps to test the CloudFront distribution:

1. While still in the CloudFront distribution webpage, click on your distribution ID as per the following screenshot in *Figure 11.8*:

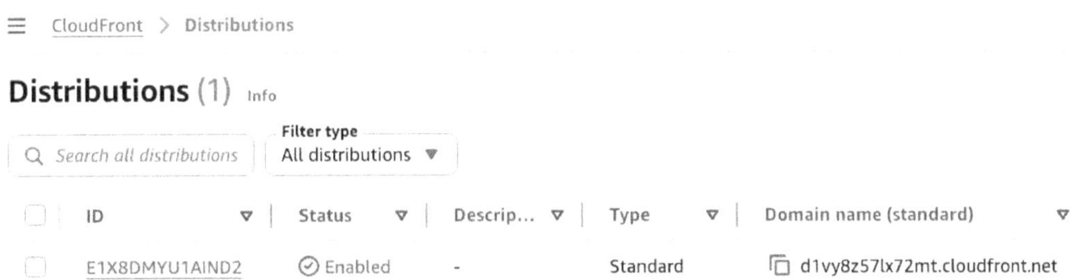

Figure 11.8: CloudFront distribution list

   You will note the domain name for the distribution as depicted in the screenshot. Your domain name might be different. Copy this name to the clipboard and then paste it into a new browser tab.

2. The Belly Brew Co. Limited 'Coming soon' webpage should load correctly as per the following screenshot in *Figure 11.9*:

Figure 11.8: Belly Brew Co. Limited 'Coming soon' website

You can now provide your CloudFront distribution domain name to anyone so that they can access the website.

Now that you have configured your CloudFront distribution for the Belly Brew Co. Limited's Coming soon page and tested its functionality, the next project task will walk you through the steps of deleting the distribution point. This is to avoid incurring any unnecessary charges against your AWS credits.

Project task 11.3 – Cleaning up

In this project task, you will delete the CloudFront distribution to avoid any unnecessary charges.

Follow these steps to delete the CloudFront distribution:

1. From the CloudFront console, select the check box next to the distribution you created in *Project Task 11.1*
2. In the top right-hand corner of the webpage, click the **Disable** button. You must disable the distribution first before you can delete it.

3. In the pop-up dialog box that appears, confirm you want to disable the distribution. This will take a few minutes to complete
4. Once disabled, you can select the checkbox next to the distribution again and click the **Delete** button to remove it from your AWS account. In the pop-up page that appears, click the **Delete** button again.

Now that you have successfully completed this project task, the next section provides a summary of what you have learned.

Summary

This chapter explained how Amazon Route 53 and Amazon CloudFront work together to improve website performance, resilience, and global distribution. Route 53 provides you with the ability to register your company's domain names, perform DNS resolution, map human-friendly domain names to IP addresses, and support advanced routing policies such as failover, latency-based, and weighted routing policies.

Organizations use these services and features to build highly available and fault-tolerant systems that automatically reroute users to healthy or geographically closer resources. Another key edge service offered by AWS is Amazon CloudFront. This acts as a global **Content Delivery Network** (**CDN**), caching content at AWS edge locations to minimize latency and accelerate content delivery. Combined with health checks and integration options such as Lambda@Edge, these services form the foundation for building scalable, secure, and high-performance applications for worldwide users.

For Belly Brew Co. Limited, you discovered how these AWS services can help deliver their website and digital content with faster load times and greater resilience, improving your customer experience and engagement. By serving their "Coming Soon" site through CloudFront, Belly Brew Co. Limited ensures that global visitors encounter minimal delays regardless of their location, while Route 53 allows them to use a friendly domain name (e.g., `bellybrew.co.uk`) instead of a raw S3 bucket address.

As their business grows, they can also adopt routing policies for disaster recovery or expand into multi-region deployments to serve customers across the U.K. and beyond. Ultimately, these services give Belly Brew Co. Limited the technical backbone to build an engaging, reliable online platform to support their brand growth and customer base.

The next chapter introduces you to Application Integration services on AWS. These services are designed to help you design and build different architectural patterns for your applications depending on their use case. You will learn about monolithic, microservices, and event-driven architectures, which are important topics for the AWS Certified Cloud Practitioner exam.

Exam Readiness Drill – Chapter Review Questions

Apart from mastering key concepts, strong test-taking skills under time pressure are essential for acing your certification exam. That's why developing these abilities early in your learning journey is critical.

Exam readiness drills, using the free online practice resources provided with this book, help you progressively improve your time management and test-taking skills while reinforcing the key concepts you've learned.

HOW TO GET STARTED

- Open the link or scan the QR code at the bottom of this page
- If you have unlocked the practice resources already, log in to your registered account. If you haven't, follow the instructions in *Free Benefits with Your Book* section in this book's *Preface* and come back to this page.
- Once you log in, click the START button to start this chapter's quiz
- We recommend attempting a quiz multiple times till you're able to answer most of the questions correctly and well within the time limit.
- You can use the following practice template to help you plan your attempts:

Working On Accuracy		
Attempt	**Target**	**Time Limit**
Attempt 1	40% or more	Till the timer runs out
Attempt 2	60% or more	Till the timer runs out
Attempt 3	75% or more	Till the timer runs out
Working On Timing		
Attempt 4	75% or more	1 minute before time limit
Attempt 5	75% or more	2 minutes before time limit
Attempt 6	75% or more	3 minutes before time limit

The above drill is just an example. Design your drills based on your own goals and make the most out of the online quizzes accompanying this book.

Link to this Chapter's Quiz

You need to unlock the online practice resources to access the link below. Check the *Free Benefits with Your Book* section in the *Preface* for detailed instructions on how to do this. You only need to unlock the resources once.

Open Quiz `https://packt.link/clf_c02_ch11`or scan the QR code

Part 3

Application Decoupling, Analytics, and AI/ML Services

The third part focuses on building real-world solutions that align with architectural best practices, such as decoupling application components and implementing integration patterns that enable functions to be separated and scaled independently. These include queuing services like Amazon SQS, notification services such as Amazon SNS, and event-driven architectures. This approach helps avoid monolithic design patterns, where tightly coupled dependencies can lead to widespread outages and a poor customer experience, particularly in complex application workflows.

This section also introduces data analytics, machine learning, and artificial intelligence services, enabling you to work with business data without worrying about the underlying infrastructure. These fully managed SaaS offerings allow you to focus on building innovative applications faster and more efficiently while reducing operational overhead.

This part of the book includes the following chapters:

- *Chapter 12, Application Integration*
- *Chapter 13, Analytics on AWS*
- *Chapter 14, Machine Learning and Artificial Intelligence*

12

Application Integration

There are three main architectural patterns when designing your applications: **monolithic**, **microservices**, and **event-driven**. Recall the project you designed and built for Belly Brew Co. Limited in *Chapter 9*. What you designed and deployed was a monolithic architecture. The application consisted of a front-end user interface that allowed members of the public to submit their email addresses on a sign-up form. The backend would process that data and update the Amazon RDS database with the user's contact details. The same application would then generate a presigned URL to email across to the user, so that they could download the free recipe eBook.

Although the architecture comprised several isolated components like the Amazon RDS database and Amazon SES to handle mass email messaging, the application itself runs as a single unit on the EC2 instances you deployed in your VPC. While this monolithic architecture has the advantage of being simple to develop and deploy, suitable for small applications, it is difficult to scale specific parts of the application independently and is harder to update and maintain. Sure, you have deployed the same application across multiple EC2 instances, across multiple AZs, offering high availability. Nevertheless, with this type of architecture, any component failure is likely to bring down the entire application stack.

In this chapter, you will learn why decoupling your application from traditional monolithic structures reduces the impact when making component changes, ensuring that updates and upgrades to new features can be released faster and with minimal impact.

You will learn how designing your applications as microservices, which involves breaking an application into smaller, independent services that each perform a specific business function, results in a more agile architecture. You will also learn about event-driven architectures, which is where applications are designed to react to events asynchronously, such as when someone places an order or there is a system update. Event-driven architectures improve scalability, reduce dependencies between services, and support real-time processing.

The following topics are discussed in this chapter:

- Understanding the application of notification services with Amazon SNS
- Decoupling your application architecture with Amazon SQS and Amazon MQ
- Designing event-driven workflows using the Amazon EventBridge services
- Visualizing and architecting application components using Amazon Step Functions

Understanding the application of notification services with Amazon SNS

Amazon Simple Notification Services (**Amazon SNS**) is a push-based notification service that follows a **publisher–subscriber (pub/sub) model**. In this model, a publisher sends messages to subscribers via a central channel called a **Topic**. With Amazon SNS, one component of an application can notify other components when an event or action occurs. The subscribing components can then process the message and take appropriate action. Messages are pushed directly to subscribers via a Topic and are not temporarily stored; however, retries can be configured to ensure messages are successfully delivered to subscribing components.

Amazon SNS allows you to design a message notification feature for your application that can handle high throughput, many-to-many messaging between distributed systems, microservices, and event-driven architectures.

For example, suppose you want to be notified if your IAM users delete sensitive data stored in a specific Amazon S3 bucket. To achieve this, you can create an event notification on the bucket to send an alert when the event type `s3:ObjectRemoved:Delete` occurs. In this example, the subscriber could be the email address of an administrator or the bucket owner. This type of messaging is known as **Application-to-Person** (**A2P**).

In another example, you can configure an Amazon S3 bucket to host images that end users upload. Each time a new image is uploaded, an `s3:ObjectCreated:*` event occurs. You can configure Amazon SNS to send a notification of this event to a Topic. A Lambda function can then subscribe to this Topic, triggering it to process the image, such as adding a watermark. This type of messaging is known as **Application-to-Application** (**A2A**).

When using Amazon SNS, your subscribers must be a supported endpoint type, which is depicted in *Figure 12.1*:

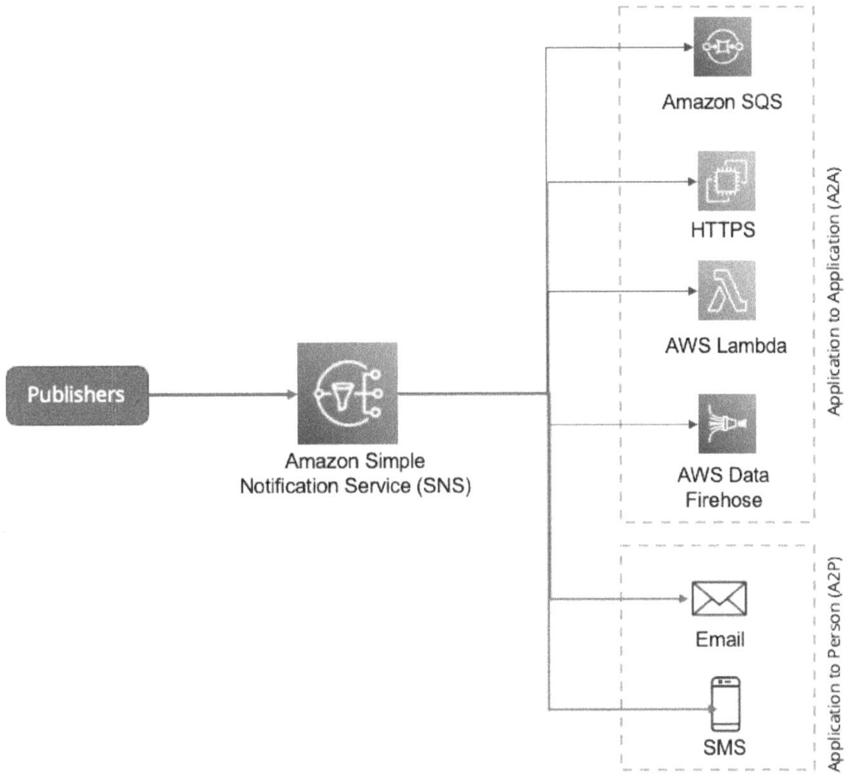

Figure 12.1: SNS endpoints and supported protocols

Amazon SNS A2A endpoints include Amazon SQS, HTTP/S endpoints, AWS Lambda, and Amazon Kinesis Data Firehose. Data from Kinesis Firehose can then be offloaded and stored in Amazon S3, Redshift, or other third-party services. You will learn more about Amazon Kinesis in *Chapter 13*.

Amazon SNS A2P endpoints include email, mobile text messaging, and mobile push endpoints.

Amazon SNS can send messages to multiple endpoints in parallel. This process is known as **fanout processing**, which is discussed in the next section.

Amazon SNS fan-out scenario

Amazon SNS is designed to send out notifications to multiple subscribing endpoints in parallel via topics. This means multiple components of your application process the same notification for their specific functions as part of the overall architectural design. For example, in *Figure*

12.2, a notification or an order placed on an e-commerce website is being sent in parallel to multiple endpoints.

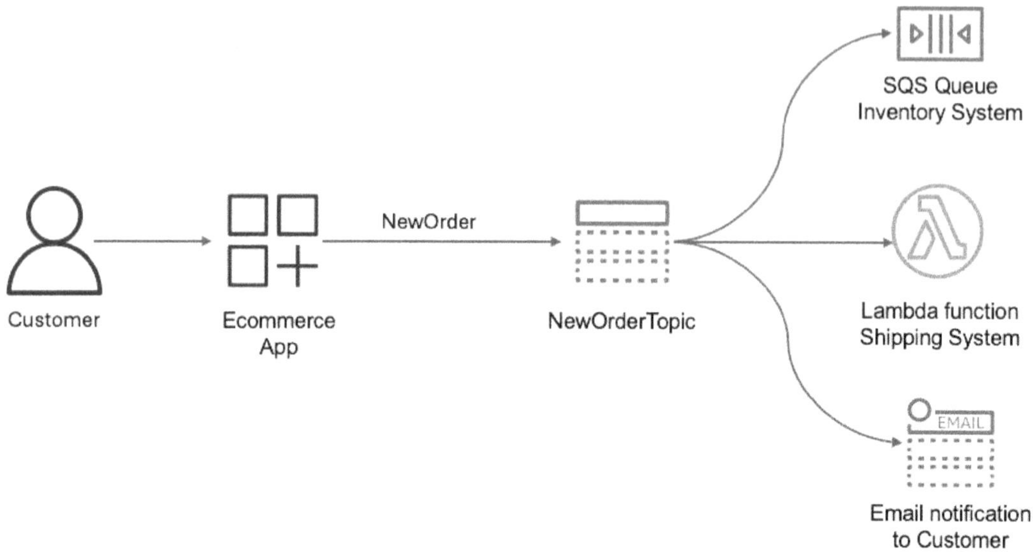

Figure 12.2: Amazon SNS fan-out scenario

Upon placing a successful order via the application, a new order notification is sent to the Amazon SNS **NewOrderTopic**. That notification is then pushed out to the following endpoints:

- The SQS Queue is used to host details of a new order so that a backend component can then retrieve the information and update the inventory system
- A Lambda function may subscribe to the topic so that each time a new order is placed, it triggers a shipping workflow in the shipping component of the application
- An email endpoint is used to inform the customer that the order has now been dispatched to them

Each system can operate independently, and all systems receive the message at the same time in a fan-out architecture.

While Amazon SNS is a push-based notification system, sometimes you need a queuing solution to hold messages so that backend components can process them as and when they are ready. This further decouples your architecture stack and lends itself well to a microservices design architecture. The next section introduces you to the Amazon **Simple Queue Service** (**Amazon SQS**), which offers such a queuing solution.

Decoupling your application architecture with Amazon SQS and Amazon MQ

Amazon SQS is a fully managed message queuing service designed to help you build decoupled architectures on AWS. With Amazon SQS, you can build distributed systems that lend themselves well to a microservices architecture, where each component works independently of the others. Using a queuing mechanism, one component of your application (such as the frontend) can submit requests or tasks to a queue that other components (such as the backend) can fetch and process whenever there is available capacity. This means that each component can scale independently, and updates or upgrades can be released for each component without affecting the others in the application.

Figure 12.3 shows an example of a media transcoding application that uses both Amazon SNS and Amazon SQS to process videos uploaded by end users.

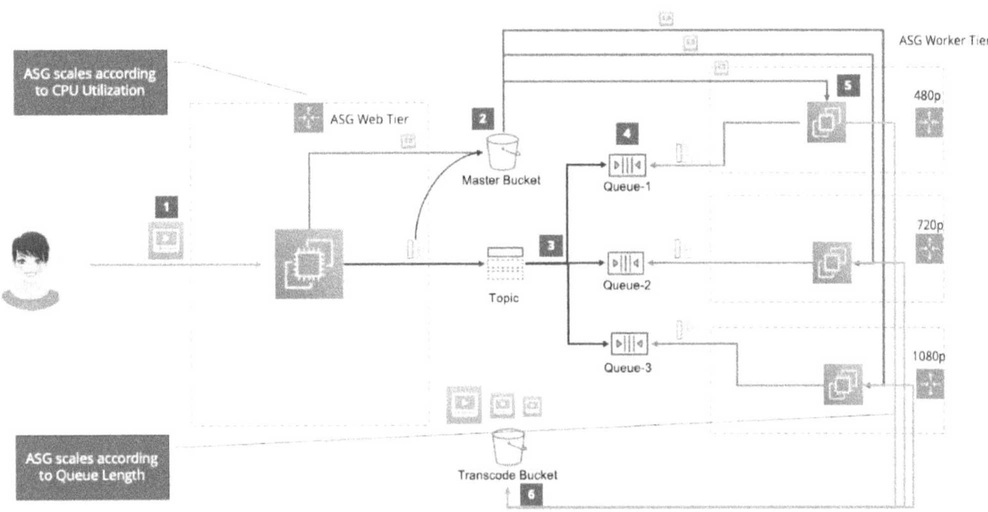

Figure 12.3: Amazon SNS fan-out scenario

It uses a frontend user interface to enable uploads and backend instances to process those video files. The application converts the raw video files into various formats and resolution sizes. Each layer of the application stack (frontend and backend) can scale independently. For example, the frontend scales based on metrics such as CPU utilization, while the backend scales based on the number of messages held in the Amazon SQS queue.

If the frontend experiences many requests, resulting in CPU utilization rising above a specified threshold, the Auto Scaling service deploys additional instances. Similarly, if the number of messages in the Amazon SQS queue rises above a given threshold, the backend EC2 instances scale out to accommodate demand and avoid extensive delays in processing requests.

Here is a breakdown of the application workflow:

1. Users upload their video files using a frontend user interface hosted as a website on a fleet of EC2 instances running in an Auto Scaling group
2. The videos are uploaded to a *master* Amazon S3 bucket, which generates a `CreateObject` event that triggers a notification message to an Amazon SNS topic
3. Simultaneously, the SNS topic has multiple Amazon SQS subscribers – one for each video format and resolution size. The messages are pushed forward by the SNS topic to these SQS Queues
4. The SQS queues will host these messages for a default period of up to 4 days, which can be increased to a maximum of 14 days
5. The relevant backend fleets of EC2 instances will regularly poll the queue they have been configured to access and pull those messages. The application will then be able to retrieve the relevant videos from the *master* Amazon S3 bucket.

The app servers will convert those videos into the required format and resolution and upload them to the *transcoded* S3 bucket as depicted in the diagram. The use of Amazon SQS queues ensures that messages can be held in the queue for a period until the backend resources have capacity to process those videos and reformat them. The frontend website does not need to depend on the availability of the backend application servers in this design configuration, offering a decoupled architecture for your application.

Next, you learn more about the types of Amazon SQS queues you can configure and their key features.

Types of Amazon SQS queues

Amazon SQS offers two types of queues: **Standard** queues and **First In First Out** (**FIFO**) queues.

Amazon SQS standard queues

Amazon SQS Standard queues are designed to handle a nearly unlimited number of API calls per second, and messages are delivered at least once. Because of the distributed nature of the queuing system, your application must be able to handle duplicate copies of a message being delivered. In addition, messages may not be delivered in the same order in which they were added to the queue. So, your application should also be able to handle messages that are out of order. The benefit of this design is that the service can scale to support very high transaction volumes.

Standard queues are useful when you need to process a very high number of transactions per second. However, there is a quota on the number of in-flight messages for a standard queue. A common example of using a standard queue is processing a large volume of credit card validation requests for an e-commerce application.

Amazon SQS FIFO queues

Amazon SQS FIFO queues preserve the exact order of messages. With FIFO queues, messages are processed exactly once, and duplicates are not introduced. The trade-off is that throughput is limited to 300 transactions per second, or up to 3,000 transactions per second if you use batching (10 messages per batch). FIFO queues are ideal when the order of events must be preserved and duplicates cannot be tolerated.

Here is a simple use case for an Amazon SQS FIFO queue:

Let's consider the case of online movie ticket booking. When you're buying movie tickets online, requests need to be handled in the order they come in. For example:

- At 10:01 AM, Person A tries to book Seat 12 and completes the payment
- At 10:02 AM, Person B also tries to book the same seat and attempts payment

Without FIFO handling, person B might get the seat even though person A was successful in completing the transaction 1 second earlier.

With an SQS FIFO queue, the system processes Person A's request first, completes the booking, and only then moves on to Person B. This ensures the seat goes to the person who booked it first, keeping things fair and preventing double bookings.

While Amazon SQS is a queuing system native to the AWS platform, many organizations use other message brokering services, such as Apache ActiveMQ, for their on-premises application. Companies that wish to migrate their applications to the cloud can use the Amazon MQ service for easier migrations. Amazon MQ is discussed in the next section.

Introduction to Amazon MQ

Amazon MQ is a managed message broker service designed to help application components communicate and exchange information. It enables different services to talk to each other directly, even if they are written in different programming languages or run on different platforms.

Many organizations already use message brokers within their on-premises environments to support existing applications. A common example is **Apache ActiveMQ**, a popular Java-based message broker.

When clients migrate their on-premises applications to the cloud, they may prefer to continue using services that are compatible with existing third-party brokers instead of re-architecting their applications for Amazon SQS. That's where Amazon MQ fits in — it offers compatibility with industry-standard APIs such as **JMS** (**Java Message Service**) and protocols including **AMQP 1.0** (**Advanced Message Queuing Protocol**), **MQTT** (**Message Queuing Telemetry Transport**), OpenWire, and **STOMP** (**Simple Text Oriented Message Protocol**).

Amazon MQ is ideal when you simply want to perform a lift-and-shift migration of existing legacy or on-premises applications that rely on existing broker protocols and APIs.

In the next section, you will learn about event-driven architectures that enable services to react asynchronously to events, reducing tight coupling and improving scalability, flexibility, and real-time responsiveness.

Designing event-driven workflows using Amazon EventBridge services

Amazon EventBridge is a fully managed event bus service that can be used to route real-time events from one application component to another. The targets of these events can include AWS Lambda, Amazon Kinesis, HTTP/S endpoints, Amazon SQS queues, Amazon SNS topics, and more.

With Amazon EventBridge, you can create an application architecture that reacts to events from upstream components, ensuring that resources are only consumed when those events occur. This has the added benefit of reducing overall costs. For example, you can invoke a Lambda function only when an event occurs, rather than running an EC2 instance hosting a backend application that sits idle and incurs unnecessary costs.

Events can be **system events**, such as an EC2 instance changing state from *running* to *stopped*, or **application events**, such as when a user uploads a video to an Amazon S3 bucket.

With EventBridge, you define **rules** that specify matching patterns for incoming events. When a matching event occurs, the rule sends the event to a target for further processing. For example, *Figure 12.4* depicts monitoring an EC2 instance state change.

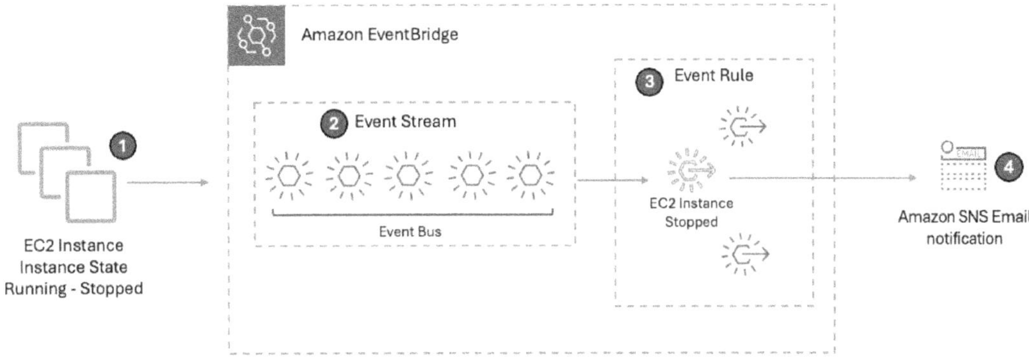

Figure 12.4: Amazon EventBridge

As depicted in *Figure 12.4*, the following steps represent the workflow:

1. An EC2 instance changes state from *running* to *stopped* (and vice versa)
2. These events are recorded in an event stream using the default event bus, which is available in your AWS account. You can also create custom event buses for custom applications.
3. A rule allows you to match an event to a target for processing. In this example, the rule is configured to filter events where the EC2 instance state changes from *running* to *stopped*.
4. The rule then sends the event notification to an Amazon SNS topic, which has an email subscriber (such as an administrator) who needs to be notified whenever an EC2 instance is stopped

In addition to monitoring real-time events, you can also schedule EventBridge rules to trigger events at designated times during the day, week, or month, or by using a rate expression. For example, you could configure a Lambda function to run every 10 minutes.

A common use case for this is configuring EventBridge to trigger a Lambda function that stops all development EC2 instances at 6 PM on weekdays after copying all log files, and then restarts them at 8 AM the following weekday.

This helps reduce costs, especially if the development servers are running on **On-Demand EC2 instances**, where you are charged by the second when the instance is in the *running* state.

Building a distributed application often involves designing a workflow that invokes and triggers various components. Often, you need to define this workflow in a specific order and to run automatically in sequence. AWS offers Step Functions, which is a service that lets you coordinate multiple AWS services into workflows, and this is discussed in the next section.

Visualizing and architecting application components with AWS Step Functions

AWS Step Functions is an orchestration service that you can use to design and build task-based application workflows. The service uses the concept of *states*, which represent the condition of your application at a given point in time while the user interacts with it. While in a particular state, you can perform specific tasks that define how your application functions. For example, a state may require calling a Lambda function to process some data.

States can make decisions based on input, perform specified actions, and produce outputs that are either consumed by other states or bring the application workflow to an end.

States can be any of the following types:

- **Success** or **Fail state**: Execution stops with either a success or a failure
- **Wait state**: A timeout is initiated to allow a process to complete before proceeding to the next state
- **Parallel state**: The state performs parallel executions – for example, completing an order fulfillment process while simultaneously sending an email to the customer
- **Map state**: Allows you to iterate over a list of items and process each one
- **Choice state**: Chooses between branches of execution
- **Task state**: Focuses on carrying out a specified task and may call other AWS services, such as AWS Lambda, to perform the task

Figure 12.5 illustrates an example of how AWS Step Functions can help you design a workflow of state machines as a series of event-driven steps.

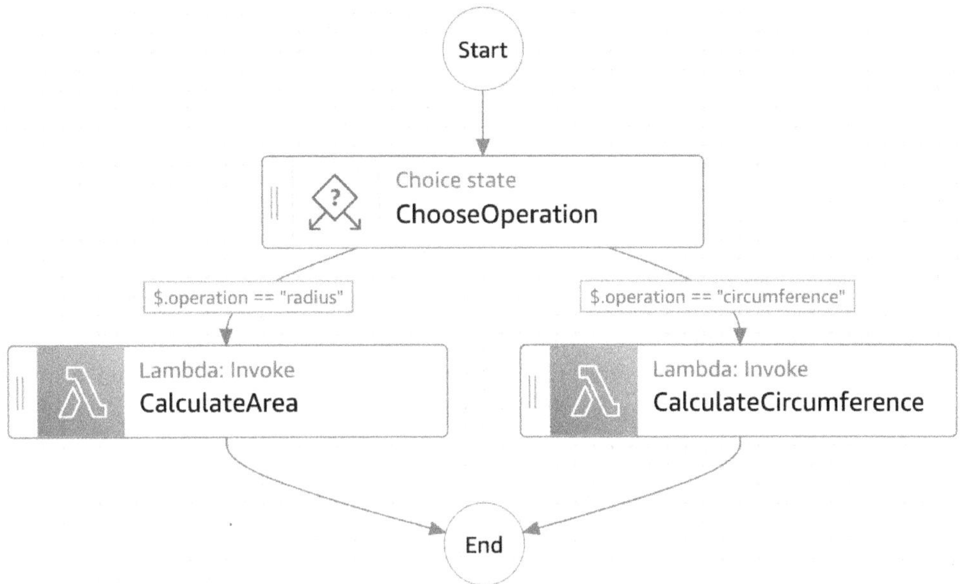

Figure 12.5: Example Step Functions workflow

In the example illustrated in *Figure 12.5*, an AWS Step Functions **state machine** has been created with the following workflow:

1. The user starts the app and provides two inputs:
    - The "operation," which can be either to calculate the area or the circumference
    - The "value" that the user inputs is the circle's radius (positive integer)
2. The state machine begins execution at `ChooseOperation`
    - `ChooseOperation` (**Choice state**)
        1. If operation is "radius", go to `CalculateArea`
        2. If operation is "circumference", go to `CalculateCircumference`
3. CalculateArea (Task state):
    1. Calls the `CalculateCircleArea` Lambda function
    2. Uses the input value as the radius

    3. Lambda returns the **area** of the circle (πr^2)
    4. Execution ends
4. CalculateCircumference (Task state):
    1. Calls the `CalculateCircumference` Lambda function
    2. Uses the input value as radius
    3. Lambda returns the **circumference** of the circle ($2\pi r$)
    4. Execution ends

AWS Step Functions enables you to build complex distributed application architectures easily with the help of state machines. You can use the visual interface of the Step Functions management console, where you drag and drop states, tasks, and define inputs and outputs, or configure your state machine using the **Amazon States Language** (**ASL**). This is a simple JSON-based language used to define workflows in AWS Step Functions.

Finally, there are two types of Step Functions workflows you can create. These are:

- **Standard workflow**: These have exactly one workflow execution and run for up to 1 year. So, if you have long-running jobs that may also require any human interactions as a manual approval process, then this workflow type is recommended. You are charged on a per-state transition basis, and each time a step in your execution is completed. With standard workflows, you also get execution history and visual debugging.
- **Express workflow**: These are for shorter durations up to a maximum of five minutes and offer *at least one* workflow execution. Express workflows are ideal for automated tasks and event rate workflows, such as stream data processing and IoT data ingestion and processing. Execution history can be sent to CloudWatch logs.

In the next section, you will have the opportunity to gain hands-on experience with the Amazon EventBridge service to build out a small event-driven solution.

Project task 12 – Notifying an admin when someone launches an EC2 instance

In this project task, you will take the role of a senior administrator monitoring your AWS account. The Belly Brew Co. Limited developers have been granted permissions to launch EC2 instances for development work. However, you want to be notified each time a developer launches a new EC2 instance.

In this project task, you can use the AWS EventBridge service to monitor events that occur in your EC2 platform. You will configure an SNS topic that will be used to send out alerts to an administrator's email address every time an EC2 instance is launched in your account or enters a *running* state.

Figure 12.6 provides an architectural overview of the project:

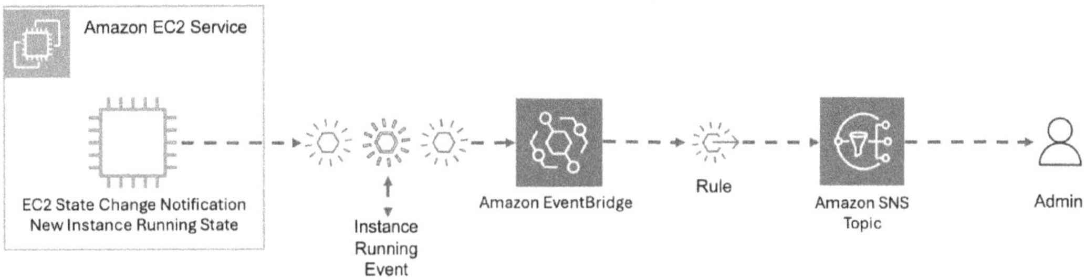

Figure 12.6: EventBridge project

An EventBridge rule is configured to send out the notification to an Amazon SNS topic. The administrator who has subscribed to the topic will then get the notification.

Technical requirements

To complete the project exercises in this chapter, ensure that you are logged in to your AWS Development account as the IAM user Alice to complete the project tasks.

Project task 12.1 – Creating an Amazon SNS topic

In this project task, you will create an Amazon SNS topic that will be used as the access point to capture any notifications of instances launched (or entered the running state). This will then be sent to subscribers, which can be an email endpoint of the administrator.

1. Ensure you are logged into the AWS Development account and in the London Region
2. From the search bar at the top of the AWS Management Console, search for and navigate to the Amazon SNS service
3. You will be presented with the Amazon SNS splash screen as shown in the following screenshot in *Figure 12.7*

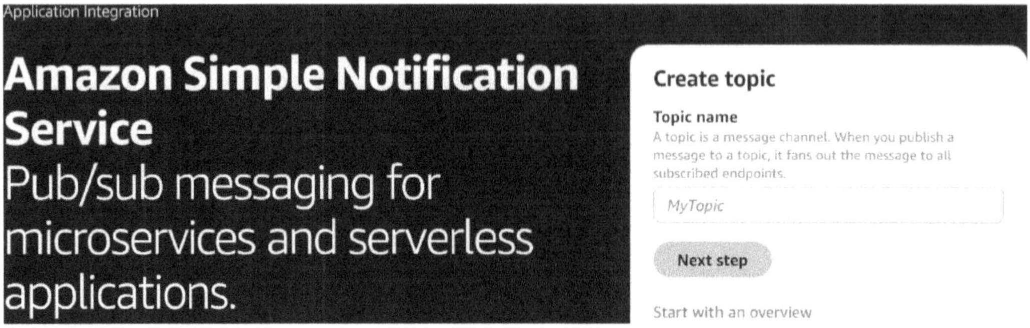

Figure 12.7: Amazon SNS Create topic splash screen

4. Provide a name for your topic in the right-hand text box as per the screenshot in *Figure 12.7*, and then click **Next step**
5. In the following screen that appears, select **Standard** under **Type**
6. You can optionally provide a display name
7. Scroll to the bottom of the webpage and click **Create topic**
8. From the left-hand menu, click **Topics**
9. In the right-hand pane, click the topic you just created to open its details page
10. Under **Subscriptions**, click the **Create subscription** button
11. You will be redirected to the **Create subscription** webpage. You must choose the **Email** from the drop-down list under **Protocol**.
12. Next, provide a valid email address that you have access to in the **Endpoint** text box
13. Scroll to the bottom of the webpage and click **Create subscription**
14. Next, you must confirm the subscription by logging into your email account and confirming the subscription in the email sent to you by AWS. Note that sometimes the notification email from AWS might end up in your spam folder, so check there if necessary.

Your subscription and the Topic have now been created. In the next project task, you will create the EventBridge rule. The EventBridge service monitors all incoming events for every action that takes place in your account.

Project task 12.2 – Creating an EventBridge rule

In this project task, you will create an EventBridge rule to monitor the EC2 instance events and identify any EC2 instances that are launched and/or enter a running state. Here's what you will need to do:

1. Ensure you are still logged into your development account and in the London region
2. From the search bar at the top of the management console webpage, search for and navigate to EventBridge
3. From the left-hand menu, click **Rules** under the **Buses** section
4. In the right-hand pane, click on the **Create rule** button
5. Click on the Advanced builder option under Builder mode
6. Provide a name for your rule, such as `EC2LaunchNotifier`, and click **Next**
7. Next, ensure that **AWS events or EventBridge partner events** is selected as the **Event source**
8. Scroll further down the webpage and ensure that **AWS services** is selected under **Event source**
9. For the **AWS service**, select `EC2` from the drop-down list
10. Next, for the **Event type**, select `EC2 Instance State-change Notification` from the drop-down list
11. Under **Event Type Specification 1**, select **Specific state(s)** and then from the drop-down list select `running`. See the following screenshot in Figure *12.8* for reference

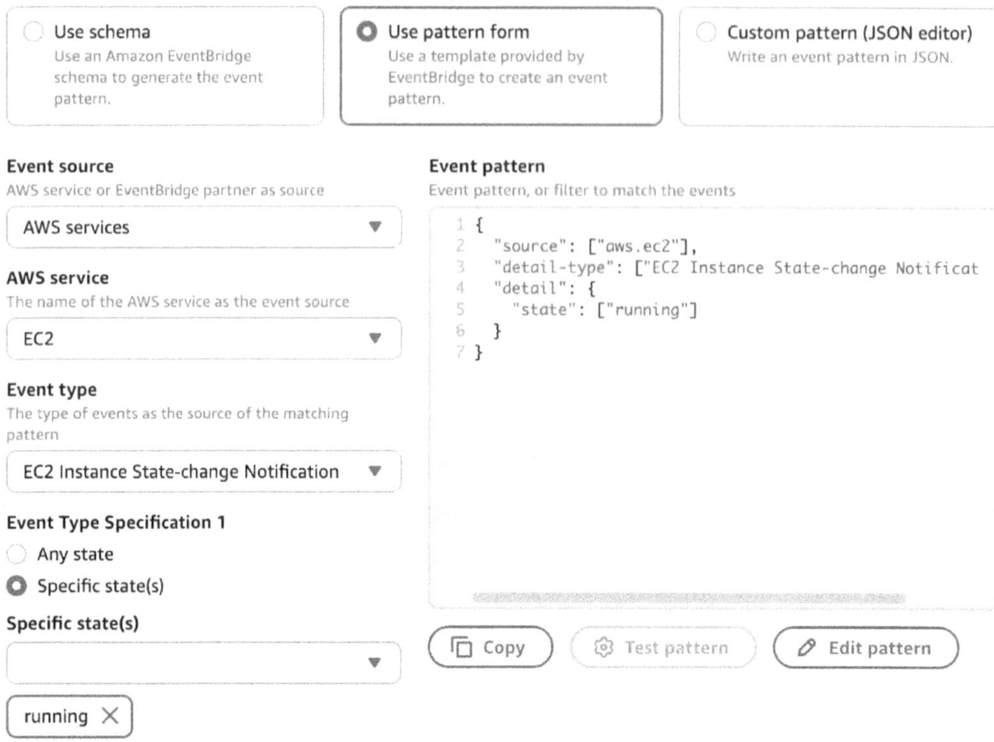

Figure 12.8: EventBridge event pattern configuration

12. Click **Next**
13. Select `AWS service` under **Target types** in the **Select target(s)** section
14. Select `SNS topic` from the drop-down list under **Select a target**
15. Next, select the topic you created earlier in *Project Task 12-1* from the drop-down list under **Topic**
16. Click **Next**. (You can optionally add tags and then click **Next**.)
17. Review your configuration in the **Review and create** webpage
18. Click the **Create rule** button at the bottom of the webpage

Now that your EventBridge rule has been configured, you can test out the configuration. In the next project task, you will launch an EC2 instance and test the EventBridge rule. Because the rule you created is monitoring any EC2 instances that enter the 'running' state, it should trigger the SNS notification services, resulting in an email being sent to the email address you provided in *Project Task 12.1*.

Project task 12.3 – Launching an EC2 instance

In this project task, you will launch an EC2 instance and test out the EventBridge rule to see if you get an alert notification in your email.

Here is how you do it:

1. Ensure you are still logged in to the AWS Management Console
2. From the search bar at the top of the webpage, search and navigate to **EC2**
3. From the left-hand menu, click on **Instances**
4. In the right-hand pane, click the **Launch instance** button
5. Provide a name for your EC2 instance, such as `TestEC2Instance`
6. Next, select `Amazon Linux` under **Quick Start** in the **Application and OS Images (Amazon Machine Image)**
7. Select `t3.micro` from the drop-down list under **Instance type**
8. Select `Proceed without a key pair (Not recommended)` from the drop-down list in the **Key pair (login)** section of the webpage
9. Scroll to the bottom of the webpage and click the **Launch instance** button. Your EC2 instance will now launch.
10. From the left-hand menu, click on Instances again to view your instances. Wait for a few minutes for the instance to launch completely and enter the running state.
11. Log in to your email account, and you should receive an email confirming that an EC2 instance was launched, as shown in *Figure 12.9*:

Figure 12.9: Email confirming the launch of an EC2 instance and its entry into the running state

In the next project task, you will terminate the resources you created as part of the cleanup exercise. Since you have now successfully completed the task, there is no requirement to have the EC2 instances you launched earlier, thereby ensuring you do not incur any unnecessary usage of your AWS credits (or costs).

Project task 12.4 – Cleaning up

Now that you have successfully tested out that EventBridge and Amazon SNS can be configured to send you alerts on any EC2 instance entering a running state, you must terminate unwanted resources.

Here is how that is done:

1. While still logged into the AWS Management console and in the EC2 dashboard, click on **Instances** from the left-hand menu
2. In the right-hand pane, select the EC2 instance you launched in *Project Task 12.3*
3. Select `Terminate (delete) instance` from the **Instance state** drop-down list
4. In the dialog box that appears, click the **Terminate (delete)** button, and your EC2 instance will be terminated
5. From the search bar at the top of the AWS Management Console webpage, search for and navigate to the EventBridge service
6. From the left-hand menu, click `Rules` in the **Buses** section
7. In the right-hand pane, select the rule you created earlier in *Project Task 12.2* and then click the **Delete** button
8. Confirm that you wish to delete the rule by typing `delete` in the text box that appears, and then click the **Delete** button
9. The rule will now be deleted
10. From the search bar at the top of the AWS Management Console webpage, search for and navigate to Amazon SNS
11. From the left-hand menu, click on **Topics**
12. In the right-hand pane, select the topic you created earlier in *Project Task 12.1*
13. Click the **Delete** button at the top of the webpage
14. In the dialog box that appears, type in `delete me` and then click the **Delete** button

You have now successfully terminated the resources you created in this project. This project task demonstrated how you can use AWS EventBridge to build event-driven workflows. This can be particularly useful as part of your overall management of resources, as in the case of this example. However, you can also use AWS EventBridge for application-level workflows.

Event-driven architectures can be particularly useful to build efficient systems and application design patterns, ensuring that resources and workloads are only triggered and consumed when a matching event occurs or at designated schedules.

Summary

AWS offers a vast array of services that you can use to design and build decoupled and distributed architectures for your applications. Depending on your business use case, moving away from a monolithic architecture to a microservices-based, event-driven design provides several benefits, including reduced single points of failure, independent component scalability, and improved availability.

To design decoupled architectures, you need a way to separate your application components, such as frontend and backend services. This is only possible if those components can communicate in a manner that facilitates independent operation and scalability. The use of message queuing systems like Amazon SQS plays a critical role in bringing this type of architecture to life.

Furthermore, designing your application stack so that each component communicates asynchronously and responds to events as they occur ensures that resources are only consumed when required. Amazon EventBridge enables you to build such event-driven applications, helping you avoid idle resources and unnecessary costs.

Finally, when designing complex, distributed, and decoupled architectures, the use of orchestration services such as Amazon Step Functions gives you the ability to design application workflows quickly and efficiently.

In the next chapter, you will learn how you can use AWS to analyze the vast array of data your business collects and stores, both for auditing purposes as well as for specific application requirements. AWS offers a number of different analytical tools enabling you to perform real-time data ingestions, perform ad-hoc queries, and even Big Data analytics.

Exam Readiness Drill – Chapter Review Questions

Apart from mastering key concepts, strong test-taking skills under time pressure are essential for acing your certification exam. That's why developing these abilities early in your learning journey is critical.

Exam readiness drills, using the free online practice resources provided with this book, help you progressively improve your time management and test-taking skills while reinforcing the key concepts you've learned.

HOW TO GET STARTED

- Open the link or scan the QR code at the bottom of this page
- If you have unlocked the practice resources already, log in to your registered account. If you haven't, follow the instructions in *Free Benefits with Your Book* section in this book's *Preface* and come back to this page.
- Once you log in, click the START button to start this chapter's quiz
- We recommend attempting a quiz multiple times till you're able to answer most of the questions correctly and well within the time limit.
- You can use the following practice template to help you plan your attempts:

Working On Accuracy		
Attempt	**Target**	**Time Limit**
Attempt 1	40% or more	Till the timer runs out
Attempt 2	60% or more	Till the timer runs out
Attempt 3	75% or more	Till the timer runs out
Working On Timing		
Attempt 4	75% or more	1 minute before time limit
Attempt 5	75% or more	2 minutes before time limit
Attempt 6	75% or more	3 minutes before time limit

The above drill is just an example. Design your drills based on your own goals and make the most out of the online quizzes accompanying this book.

Link to this Chapter's Quiz

You need to unlock the online practice resources to access the link below. Check the *Free Benefits with Your Book* section in the *Preface* for detailed instructions on how to do this. You only need to unlock the resources once.

Open Quiz `https://packt.link/clf_c02_ch12`or scan the QR code

13

Analytics on AWS

Data is the ultimate currency of the 21st century. Businesses today can either gain a massive competitive advantage through how they analyze and consume data—or, at worst, go completely out of business due to data leaks and mismanagement. Companies use data to understand their markets, identify trends, predict sales, and ultimately gain a competitive edge.

Furthermore, in this era of **machine learning** (**ML**) and **artificial intelligence** (**AI**), understanding vast amounts of data has become easier. Organizations can now query their data, identify complex patterns, and discover outliers much faster. Today's analytical tools, powered by AI and ML, enable businesses to build solutions that deliver better customer service, prevent fraud, identify and even predict technical issues or bugs in application code—and much more.

AWS offers a vast array of analytical services, each designed for different use cases. Whether you need to process streaming data in real time, run ad-hoc queries, or host an entire data warehousing solution for your global enterprise, AWS has a service for it.

In this chapter, you will learn about these services, their use cases, and best practices for configuring them for your specific needs—enabling you to ingest, store, and analyze your data efficiently.

The following topics are discussed in this chapter:

- Streaming data with Amazon Kinesis
- Understanding your data structure with AWS Glue
- Performing ad hoc analytics with Amazon Athena

- Searching and processing large-scale data with Amazon OpenSearch Service and Amazon EMR
- Learning about business intelligence with Amazon Quick Suite

Streaming data with Amazon Kinesis

A wide range of applications today generate streaming data that must be captured, ingested, processed, and analyzed in real time. Examples include **logs** generated by applications (used to identify access patterns or errors), **clickstream data** from websites (to uncover trends and customer behaviors), and **Internet of Things** (**IoT**) **data** (used to monitor sensors, images, videos, and other connected devices).

Organizations need a reliable mechanism to capture massive volumes of streaming data and ingest it in real time. This data then needs to be processed and consumed by business intelligence applications to provide reporting, analytics, and visualizations that support critical decision-making.

AWS offers **Amazon Kinesis**, a suite of fully managed, serverless services that lets you process streaming data as it arrives. It enables real-time and near-real-time analytics in a cost-effective manner—without the need to provision or manage any underlying infrastructure.

The Amazon Kinesis product suite comprises four key services:

- Amazon Kinesis Data Streams
- Amazon Kinesis Video Streams
- Amazon Data Firehose
- Amazon Managed Service for Apache Flink

In the coming sections, you will examine each of these services, starting with Amazon Kinesis Data Streams and its core capabilities.

Amazon Kinesis Data Streams

You can use **Amazon Kinesis Data Streams** to ingest and process continuous streams of data in real time. Data is ingested into the stream from producers that capture information from a wide range of sources, as shown in *Figure 13.1*:

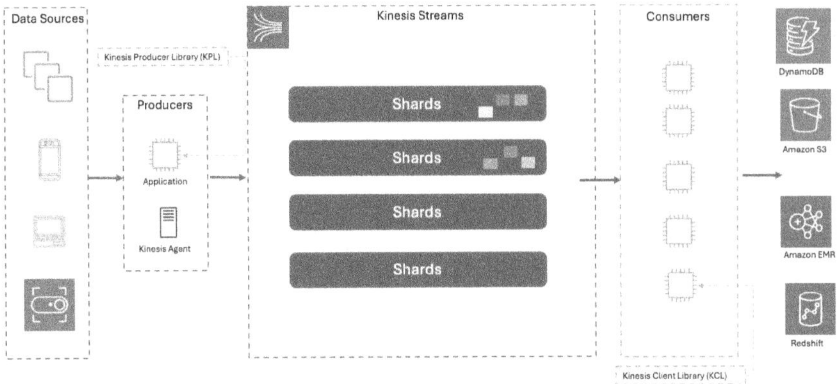

Figure 13.1: Amazon Kinesis Data Streams

You can create Kinesis data stream applications using the **Kinesis Client Library** (**KCL**) and Amazon EC2 instances to read data from the streams (known as **consumers**) and process it according to your specific business use case. For example, you can use streaming data to build real-time dashboards, perform anomaly detection to identify fraudulent activities, dynamically adjust pricing, modify advertising strategies, and much more.

As illustrated in *Figure 13.1*, Kinesis Data Streams uses the concept of **shards**, which represent units of capacity and contain data records within a stream. A stream can consist of multiple shards, and the total capacity of the stream is the sum of all shard capacities. The overall cost is determined by the number of shards provisioned, as you are charged per shard per hour.

An important feature of Amazon Kinesis is that data remains in the stream and is accessible for up to **24 hours by default**. This soft limit can be extended to **7 days** using the *extended data retention* feature. You can also enable *long-term data retention*, which allows data to be stored for up to **365 days**. This ensures that consuming applications have sufficient time to process all incoming data streams.

While Amazon Kinesis Data Streams allows you to capture and process streaming data in real time, it requires you to build and manage the consumer applications that process and store that data. However, sometimes all you need is a reliable way to deliver large volumes of streaming data directly into storage or analytics services without managing the underlying infrastructure.

This is where Amazon Data Firehose becomes useful. Amazon Data Firehose automatically delivers streaming data to a wide range of AWS services and external storage endpoints, making it easier to load large amounts of data into storage services for later analysis.

Amazon Data Firehose

Businesses need to ingest and load raw data into a wide range of technology services to perform analytics, store historical data for compliance and regulatory requirements, and feed data into tools like Amazon OpenSearch Service for near real-time analytics using a variety of business intelligence platforms.

Amazon Kinesis Data Firehose can also deliver data to external third-party services such as Datadog, New Relic, and Splunk, among others, enabling you to continue using the tools your organization is already familiar with. The service can batch, process, compress, and transform data before loading it into these third-party targets. You can also encrypt this data to strengthen your overall security posture.

Kinesis Data Firehose buffers incoming data before delivering it to destinations such as Amazon S3, Amazon Redshift, or Amazon OpenSearch Service. This buffering introduces a small delay (typically around 30 to 60 seconds), depending on the buffer size and interval settings. This is why Amazon Kinesis Data Firehose is considered a *near* real-time data loading service.

You can think of Amazon Kinesis Data Streams as a live news broadcast service. You process data as soon as it's ingested. In contrast, Amazon Kinesis Data Firehose is more like a news highlights feed; you receive updates every minute, bundled and ready for easy consumption.

Amazon Kinesis Data Streams and Amazon Data Firehose are commonly used to process streaming data such as application logs, clickstream data, and telemetry information. However, these services are not designed for continuously streaming video feeds. For video streaming workloads, AWS provides Amazon Kinesis Video Streams, which you will explore in the next section.

Amazon Kinesis Video Streams

Businesses today stream a vast array of different content types, and this includes video footage that needs to be analyzed, documented, processed, and used for live or on-demand viewing. **Amazon Kinesis Video Streams** enables you to capture live video data from a wide range of sources, including CCTV cameras, webcams, drones, and other sources.

Amazon Kinesis Video Streams can also be used to send non-video time-serialized data, such as audio, radar, thermal imaging, and much more. Amazon Kinesis Video Streams will store your raw footage in Amazon S3, ensuring high levels of durability for your data. You can then search for and retrieve those footages based on devices and timestamps.

A key use case for Amazon Kinesis Video Streams is that you can use downstream services on AWS to then analyze those footages and apply the data to real-world solutions. For example, you can integrate your application architecture to have **Amazon Rekognition**, a computer vision machine learning service on AWS, identify objects, people, text, scenes, and activities in the images and videos.

Figure 13.2 illustrates a use case for Amazon Kinesis Video Streams services:

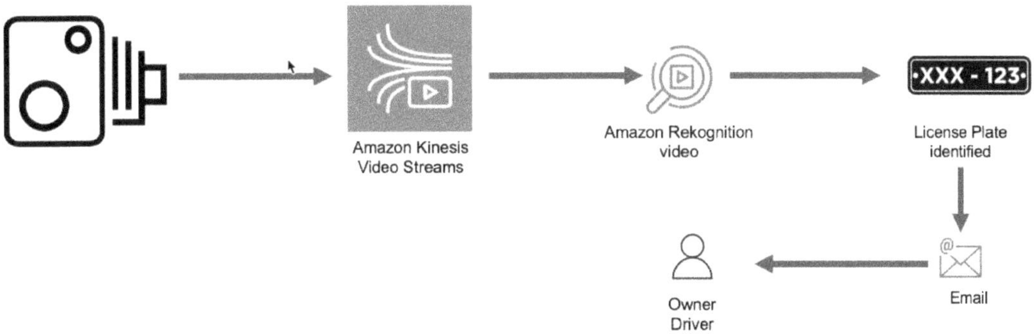

Figure 13.2: Amazon Kinesis Video Streams

In this scenario, Amazon Rekognition is used to identify the license plate of any vehicle that crosses the speed limit and interfaces with a backend database to send an email to the owner/driver of a fine that needs to be paid for the violation.

Another example of using Amazon Kinesis Video Streams is for smart home devices such as doorbells. Amazon Kinesis Video Streams can ingest, index, and live-play those streams to your smartphone app, allowing you to monitor and communicate with the person knocking on the door.

Some businesses may already use streaming frameworks in their on-premises environments and want to migrate these workloads to AWS. To support open-source stream processing tools such as Apache Flink, AWS provides Amazon Managed Service for Apache Flink. This is a fully managed service that allows you to run Flink applications without managing infrastructure and is covered in the next section.

Amazon managed service for Apache Flink

Many businesses today use an open-source, real-time stream processing engine called **Apache Flink** to ingest and process large volumes of data, either in real time or in batches. The service provides powerful capabilities for running complex computations on streaming data, such as filtering, aggregating, and joining data streams with very low latency.

Rather than designing, building, and managing your own expensive infrastructure to run this streaming service, Amazon Managed Service for Apache Flink offers a pay-as-you-go model where AWS handles all infrastructure management, scaling, and fault tolerance. You simply write your Flink application code using SQL, Java, or Python to analyze data coming from Kinesis Data Streams or Kinesis Data Firehose, without the need to manage servers or clusters.

Businesses store vast amounts of data in a variety of formats and locations, including databases and spreadsheets. Often, this data needs to be extracted, transformed into a format suitable for analysis, and then loaded into services that can perform analytics and support the creation of business intelligence solutions. The next section introduces you to **AWS Glue**, a service designed specifically for this purpose.

Understanding your data structure with AWS Glue

AWS Glue is a serverless **Extract, Transform, and Load** (**ETL**) service. Businesses can use AWS Glue to discover, prepare, enrich, clean, and transform data so that downstream services can easily consume it.

The service offers the ability to crawl your raw datasets and discover their structure, also known as a **schema**. For example, AWS Glue can analyze CSV files to identify column names and their data types (such as string, number, or Boolean). This makes it easier to ingest the data into analytics and **business intelligence** (**BI**) tools for further analysis and visualization.

You can use the crawler to scan various data repositories, classify datasets, and infer their schemas. The resulting metadata is then stored in the AWS Glue Data Catalog, which can be used to automatically generate ETL scripts that transform, flatten, or enrich your datasets. You can also define events or schedules to run crawlers regularly against your ingested datasets as batch jobs, ensuring your data remains continuously prepared for analysis by downstream services such as Amazon QuickSight and Amazon Athena.

While some customers continuously stream, process, and analyze data in real time, others may only need a cost-effective approach to run ad-hoc queries against data that has been captured over time. In such cases, hosting a fully-fledged database or data warehouse solution like Amazon Redshift can be excessive. The next section introduces you to Amazon Athena, a service designed to run ad-hoc queries directly against data stored in Amazon S3, without the need to provision or manage traditional database infrastructure.

Performing ad hoc analytics with Amazon Athena

Many companies store data as files in object storage services such as **Amazon S3**. Much of this data is only occasionally accessed for point-in-time analysis and then stored for historical reference. In other words, these datasets do not need to be stored in active databases such as Amazon RDS or NoSQL databases like Amazon DynamoDB, since the data is not regularly queried.

Nevertheless, ad-hoc analysis of such data, for example, running daily batch jobs or performing historical analysis, may still be required. In such cases, provisioning entire databases and ingesting large datasets for a one-time or infrequent analysis can be unnecessary and costly.

AWS offers **Amazon Athena**, a fully managed, serverless query service that allows you to interactively analyze raw data directly in Amazon S3 using standard **SQL** (**Structured Query Language**). You don't need to provision or manage any infrastructure, nor do you need to spin up expensive database instances to perform ad-hoc queries.

Amazon Athena uses **Presto**, an open-source SQL query engine designed for running fast, interactive queries. It supports ANSI SQL, enabling you to work with features like large joins, window functions, and arrays.

With Amazon Athena, you can run queries against structured and semi-structured datasets. To perform your queries, you must create a database table within Athena that defines the schema of your raw data stored in Amazon S3. This means Athena only needs to understand the data structure; the data itself remains in S3. Athena simply uses the table definition to query the underlying raw data, without needing to move or ingest it.

You can also use AWS Glue, which you learned about in the previous section, to crawl your raw data in Amazon S3 and automatically generate the required schema for your Athena tables.

Once your tables are registered, you can run `SQL SELECT` statements to query them, and you can even store query results in Amazon S3 in a location of your choice. A typical use case where Belly Brew Co. Limited might use Amazon Athena is if it needs to run a query like "What were our top 10 Kombucha flavors last month?"

In the next section, you will learn about **Amazon OpenSearch Service** and **Amazon EMR**, which offer additional capabilities for large-scale search and big data analytics.

Searching and processing large-scale data with Amazon OpenSearch Service and Amazon EMR

While Amazon Athena is designed to analyze static and historical data directly from Amazon S3, there are times when you need a robust, ultra-fast search solution capable of delivering results within milliseconds. That's where Amazon OpenSearch Service comes in.

For example, you might use Athena to run a query like, "What were our top 10 Kombucha flavors last month?" Whereas with OpenSearch, you could perform a search like "Show me all error logs containing the word 'timeout' from the last hour."

Amazon OpenSearch Service is designed for searching, filtering, and visualizing log or text data in real time. It scales seamlessly, supporting up to 25 petabytes of attached storage and up to 1002 data nodes running on Amazon EC2 instances.

OpenSearch enables you to perform full-text search, log analytics, and clickstream analytics. The traditional deployment model requires provisioning the necessary EC2 instances within an OpenSearch cluster. However, AWS also offers a **serverless** edition, allowing you to run petabyte-scale workloads without configuring, managing, or scaling any infrastructure.

Additionally, Amazon OpenSearch Service includes a **vector engine** that provides vector storage and search capabilities for ML-augmented applications and generative AI solutions—without the need to host and manage your own vector database.

Another service offered by AWS is **Amazon EMR** (**Elastic MapReduce**). This service enables you to process **big data analytics** using industry-recognized open-source frameworks, such as Apache Spark, Apache Hive, Apache HBase, and Presto.

Amazon EMR automatically provisions and scales the required infrastructure to run petabyte-scale analytics workloads efficiently. The service supports running workloads on Amazon EC2 instances, Amazon EKS clusters, and even on on-premises environments through **Amazon EMR on AWS Outposts**.

While streaming, loading, analyzing, and searching data form a substantial part of a business's data analytics functions, the ability to visualize that data, enabling decision-makers to take real action, is equally critical. The next section introduces you to Amazon QuickSight, AWS's BI solution.

Learning about business intelligence with Amazon Quick

Amazon Quick is a collection of tools and capabilities that provides traditional business intelligence services enhanced with modern AI assistance. It enables you to connect to a wide range of data sources, whether on-premises data stores, AWS databases, cloud storage services such as **Amazon RDS** and **Amazon S3**, or external SaaS and B2B applications.

You can use Amazon Quick to process and transform raw data, create rich visualization dashboards, and generate insightful reports. These insights help you better understand your organization's operations, sales performance, profitability, customer acquisition trends, and much more.

Amazon Quick includes five core services that work seamlessly together:

- **Amazon QuickSight** – for data visualization and interactive dashboards
- **Amazon QuickFlows** – for workflow automation
- **Amazon QuickAutomate** – for process optimization

- **Amazon Quick Index** – for data discovery
- **Amazon QuickResearch** – for comprehensive analysis

In addition to its AI integration, you can deploy extensions for familiar tools such as web browsers, Slack, and Microsoft Office applications.

Now that you know about the core analytical services offered by AWS, it's time to put your learning into practice. In the next section, you will complete a series of exercises to gain hands-on experience with some of AWS's analytical tools.

Project task 13 – Analyzing Belly Brew Co. Limited's kombucha casks for pH balance

In *Chapter 1*, you were introduced to a fictitious company called Belly Brew Co. Limited, which is a manufacturer and supplier of gut-friendly beverages across the UK. The company supplies a large range of these beverages to supermarkets, grocery stores, restaurants, cafes, and hotels.

One business requirement mentioned was the issue of assuring the health and safety of the kombucha casks that are fermenting for several days before being bottled and shipped. Specifically, the pH level of the beverage must adhere to a specific range of 2.5 to 3.5.

Currently, the manufacturing plants use outdated pH analyzer equipment that records the pH level of each cask at regular intervals and produces a report in CSV format. This report must be printed out and manually reviewed to identify any casks that need to be removed from distribution whose PH levels are outside of the acceptable range. The reports must be reviewed daily, and the results of the analysis must be completed by 5 PM daily.

You have been tasked with designing a solution that will automatically analyze the data and produce a report of all casks that must be removed from the batch each day.

This project task will introduce you to the architectural concepts and then provide step-by-step instructions to build a solution in your AWS account that the company can use. This will only be a partial solution, as the supplier of the pH meters will need to update their software to deliver the CSV reports directly to your application stack. As such, you will also appreciate that solutioning may involve working with third parties too.

The proposed architecture

The project briefing provided earlier and in *Chapter 1* explained that the PH analyzer tool can produce CSV files with reports of the PH levels of all casks being monitored.

Given that the CSV files can be hosted on a file share, you can redirect the repository to an Amazon S3 bucket, which could be used to host the files for analysis. You have also been informed that the analysis needs to be carried out every day and the results available at 5 PM daily.

In previous chapters, you have learned about various AWS services that can be used to help you automate this requirement and perform the analysis. For example:

- **Amazon S3** to host the CSV files. You can also use the same bucket to host the results in a separate folder.
- **Amazon Athena** can be used to run queries against the raw data and identify the casks that need to be removed. Given that the analysis task needs to be performed only once a day, there is no requirement to store the data in a database like Amazon RDS. Database solutions like Amazon RDS would add complexity and incur unnecessary costs because you pay for every second that the database instance is in a running state. This is unlike Amazon Athena, where you only pay for the cost of performing the queries.
- **AWS Lambda** to perform the actual analysis by identifying the raw data and invoking the query in Amazon Athena. You are using Lambda because it can be used to run the query in Amazon Athena automatically if triggered by another service, such as Amazon EventBridge. The Lambda service is also designed to ensure that the analysis is stored in date order to ensure that future audits would be easy to perform if required, thereby maintaining a date-ordered trail.
- **Amazon EventBridge** configured with a scheduled rule to trigger the Lambda function at 5 PM

The high-level architecture of your build is depicted in the following diagram in *Figure 13.3*:

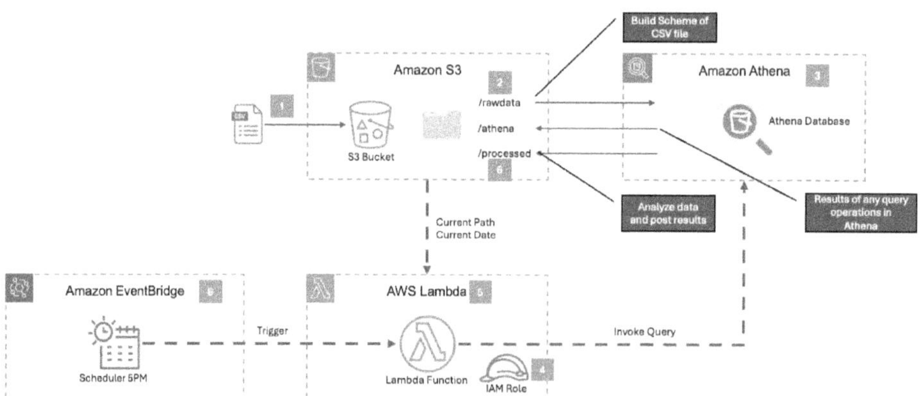

Figure 13.3: Architecture of the solution to analyze the cask PH levels data

The following outlines the key architectural design pattern for this solution, as shown by the numbering in the diagram:

1. The CSV data is uploaded to an Amazon S3 bucket that you will create for this project
2. The CSV file will be stored in a folder called `rawdata`. In a real-world scenario, you would work with the vendor of the pH analysis tool to ensure that the CSV files are delivered directly to the S3 bucket you have created. Additional folders would also be required. These include the `athena` folder, which allows Amazon Athena to store query results and temporary files, and the `processed` folder, which will store the results of the query analysis.
3. You will configure Amazon Athena to point to the S3 bucket that contains this raw data. As part of the configuration, you will specify the `athena` folder you created in *Step 2* as the location for query results. In addition, you will create a database. This database is used to store the table definition so that Amazon Athena understands the structure of the raw data stored in the CSV file. Remember that you do not import the data into Amazon Athena. Instead, Athena uses the schema definition and queries the raw data directly from Amazon S3.
4. You will configure an IAM role to ensure that the Lambda function has the required permissions to access both the Amazon S3 bucket and Amazon Athena
5. When triggered, the Lambda function will capture the current date and determine the path of the raw data. This ensures that the analysis is performed on the current day's CSV file. The Lambda function will then invoke a query in Amazon Athena to analyze this raw data. Query results are stored in the `athena` folder in the Amazon S3 bucket. Once the analysis is complete, the resulting dataset highlighting all casks that fall outside the pH range is written to the `processed` folder in the same S3 bucket.
6. To trigger the Lambda function at 5 PM each day, you will configure Amazon EventBridge with a scheduled event rule. At 5 PM, this rule will automatically invoke the Lambda function.

Now that you have reviewed the core architectural design pattern, it's time to build out the solution. The next section provides details on where you can access the Python code for this task.

Technical requirements

To complete the exercises in this project task, you must log in to your AWS Development account as the IAM user, Alice. Ensure you are in the London region. You must also download the following two files from the GitHub repository (`https://github.com/PacktPublishing/AWS-Certified-Cloud-Practitioner-CLF-C02-Exam-Guide`) in the *Chapter 13* folder and store them on your desktop for easy access:

- `kombucha_casks.csv`: the sample raw data of casks being tested
- `lambdafunction.py`: the Lambda function written in Python

Next, you will proceed to the first task, which is to create the Amazon S3 bucket to store your raw data.

Project task 13.1 – Creating an Amazon S3 bucket

In this project task, you will create the Amazon S3 bucket to which you will upload your sample CSV file. You will need to create three folders – rawdata, athena, and processed.

The following are the steps required to complete this task:

1. Ensure you are logged into your AWS account and in the London region
2. From the search box at the top of the web console, search for and navigate to the Amazon S3 web console
3. From the left-hand menu, click **General purpose buckets**
4. In the right-hand pane, click the **Create bucket** button
5. In the Create bucket webpage that appears, provide a name for your bucket, such as "`bellybrewcaskdata`" – Remember when using the **Global namespace** option, bucket names are unique globally, and so you will need to choose a unique name for your bucket
6. Scroll to the bottom of the webpage and click the **Create bucket** button again
7. You will see a notification confirming that the bucket has been successfully created. In the **Objects** tab, click the **Create folder** button as depicted in the screenshot in *Figure 13.4*:

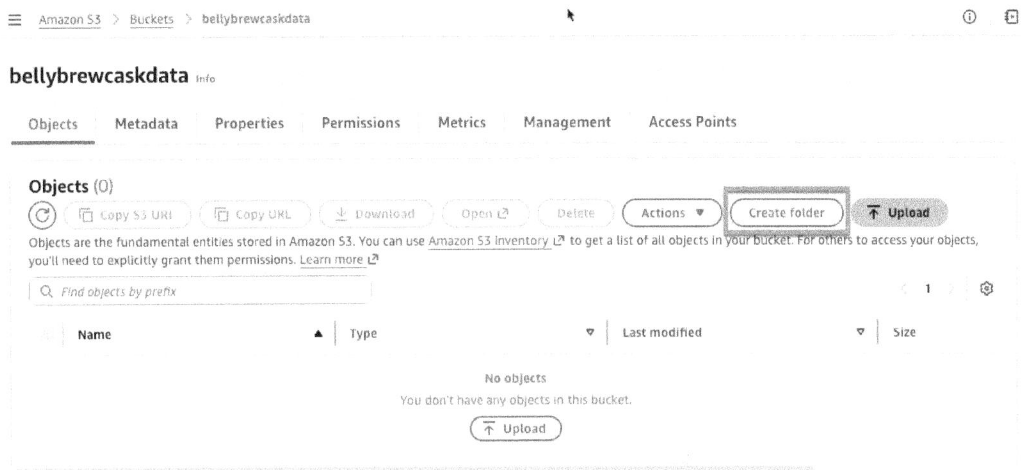

Figure 13.4: Creating folders in your bucket

8. In the webpage that appears, provide a name for your first folder, which will be used to store the raw data, such as 'rawdata'. Scroll to the bottom of the webpage and click **Create folder**
9. Next, repeat the process to create two additional folders, one called `athena` and the other called `processed`. Your final structure should look like the screenshot depicted in *Figure 13.5*:

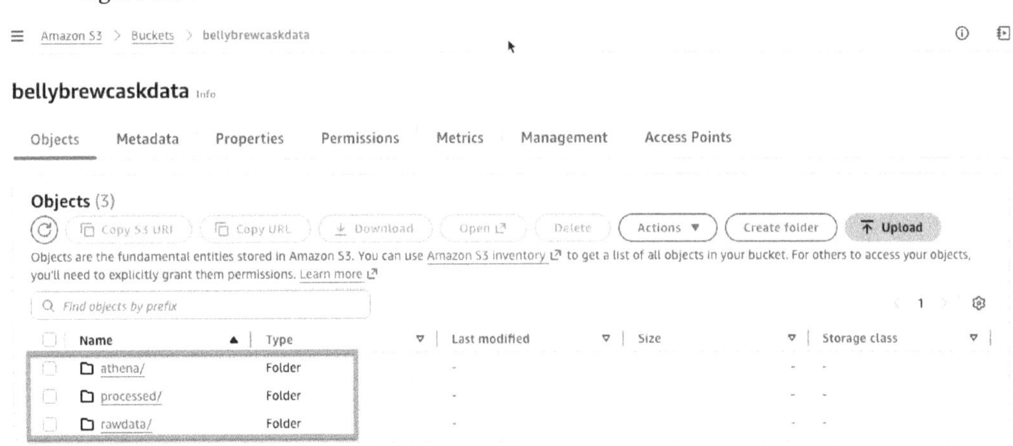

Figure 13.5: Creation of subfolders for raw data analysis

Once you have the three folders created, you can proceed to the next project task, where you will configure Amazon Athena to use this bucket for processing the raw data files.

Project task 13.2 – Configuring Amazon Athena

In this project task, you will configure Amazon Athena to point to the Amazon S3 bucket you created in *Project Task 13.1*. In addition, you will create a database that will be used to host the data structure so that Athena can query the file in Amazon S3.

The following are the steps required to complete this task:

1. From the search bar at the top of the AWS Management console, search for and navigate to the Athena console. Ensure you are in the London region.
2. From the left-hand menu, click on the hamburger icon and then click **Query editor tabs**
3. Before you can run any queries, you need to set up the query results location in Amazon S3. Click the **Edit settings** button.
   If you don't see the text box with the **Edit settings** button, you can click on **Query settings** instead to configure the query location, as depicted in the following screenshot in *Figure 13.6*.

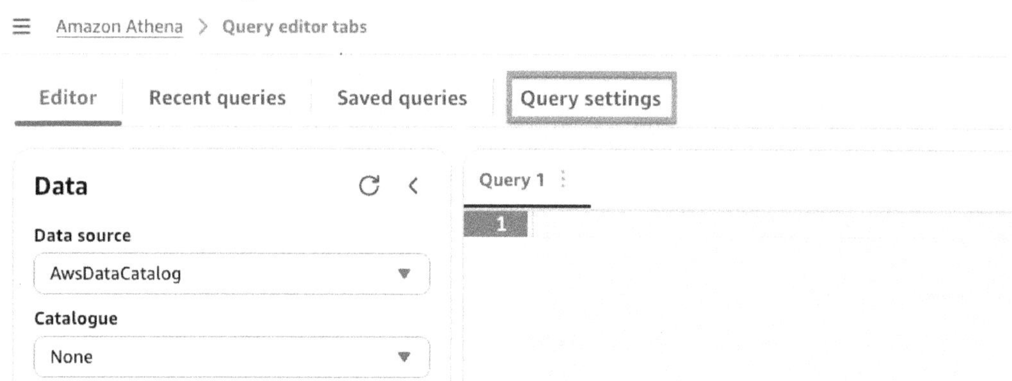

Figure 13.6: Configure the query locations setting for Amazon Athena

4. Click the **Manage** button in the **Query results encryption** section of the **Query settings** page
5. In the dialog box that appears, click the **Browse S3** button. Click the Amazon S3 bucket you created in *Project Task 13.1* and then select the **athena** folder as per the following screenshot in *Figure 13.7*.

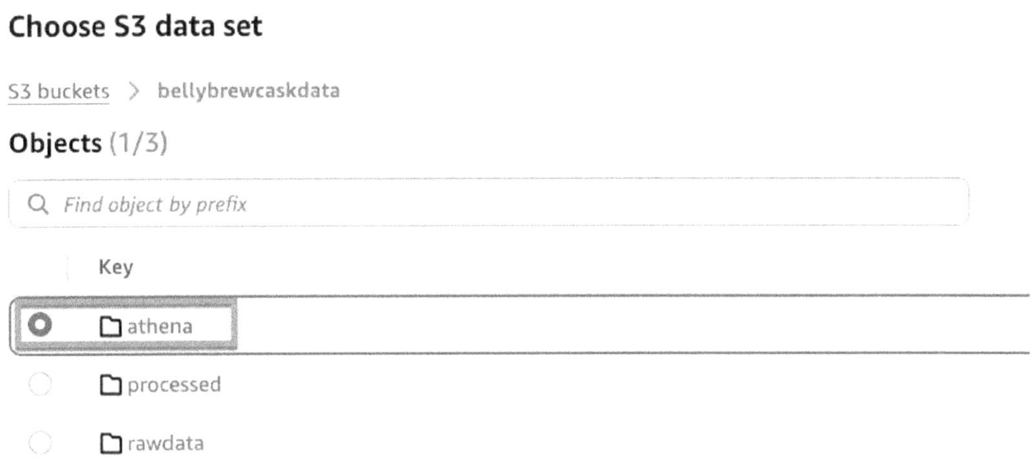

Figure 13.7: Selecting the S3 bucket and folder for query results

6. Then click the **Choose** button
7. Then click **Save**
8. You will be notified that the settings have been updated. Click the **Editor** tab.
9. Next, you must run a command to create a database. Remember, the database is just created to store the CSV file structure, not the actual data. In the **Query 1** dialog box, type in the following command: `CREATE DATABASE bellybrewanalysis_db`
10. Next, click the **Run** button as per the following screenshot in *Figure 13.8*

Figure 13.8: Create a database to store CSV structure

11. You will receive a confirmation that the command **Completed**
12. In the left-hand menu, you will also note that the Database drop-down list is now populated with the one you just created. If not, click the drop-down arrow and select the `bellybrewanalysis_db` database from the list as per the screenshot in *Figure 13.9:*

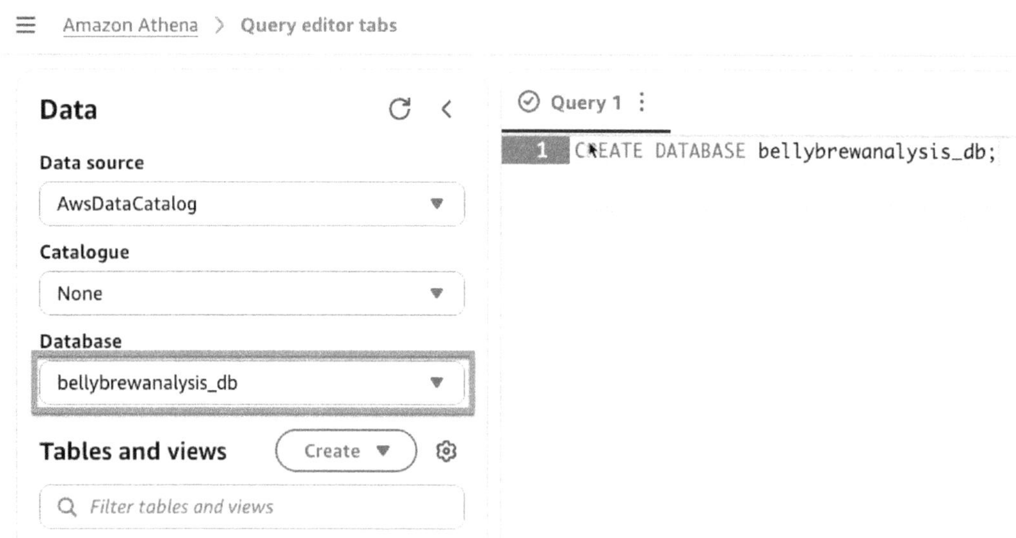

Figure 13.9: bellybrewanalysis_db database must be selected

Now that you have configured Amazon Athena correctly, you must create the IAM role with the necessary permissions for your Lambda functions to access both Athena and Amazon S3. The next project task provides the required step-by-step guide.

Project task 13.3 – Creating an IAM role

In this project task, you will create an IAM role with permissions to enable your Lambda function to access the Amazon S3 bucket and invoke queries in Amazon Athena.

The following are the steps required to complete this task:

1. From the search bar at the top of the web management console, search for and navigate to the IAM (preferably in another browser tab)
2. From the left-hand menu, click **Roles**
3. In the right-hand pane, click **Create role**
4. For the **Trusted entity type**, ensure that **AWS service** is selected
5. Next, select **Lambda** from the **Service or use case** drop-down list
6. Click **Next**
7. In the **Add permissions** webpage that appears, search for and select the following managed policies. You will need to search for each policy one at a time and click the checkbox next to it to have it selected.
    a. `AmazonS3FullAccess`
    b. `AmazonAthenaFulAccess`
    c. `AmazonAPIGatewayPushToCloudWatchLogs`

    > **Note**
    >
    > The `AmazonAPIGatewayPushToCloudWatchLogs` is simply to ensure that the results of the query will be stored in CloudWatch Logs.

8. Click **Next**

9. Provide a name for your IAM role, such as `belly-brew-iam-role`
10. Scroll down and click `Create role`

Your IAM role has now been created. In the next project task, you will create the Lambda function.

Project task 13.4 – Creating a Lambda function

To complete this project task, you must download the Python file: `lambdafunction.py` to your desktop as explained in the *Technical requirements* section earlier.

The following are the steps required to complete this task:

1. From the search bar at the top of the AWS management console, search for and navigate to the Lambda console
2. In the splash screen that appears, click **Create a function**. Alternatively, from the left-hand menu (click the hamburger icon), click **Functions** and then in the right-hand pane, click **Create function**
3. In the **Create function** webpage that appears, ensure that **Author from scratch** is selected
4. Provide a name for your function such as `belly-brew-athena-function`
5. Next, select **Python 3.14** from the **Runtime** drop-down list
6. Next, scroll further down and enable the toggle switch for **Custom execution role**
7. In the sidebar that opens from the right-hand pane, select the IAM role you created in *Project Task 13.3* from the **Choose an existing role** drop-down list
8. Click the **Save** button
9. Scroll further down and click **Create function**
10. You will receive a notification confirming that your function has been created. Close the **Getting started** pop-up window if it appears
11. In the main Lambda function webpage, click on the **Configuration** tab as depicted in the following screenshot in *Figure 13.10*:

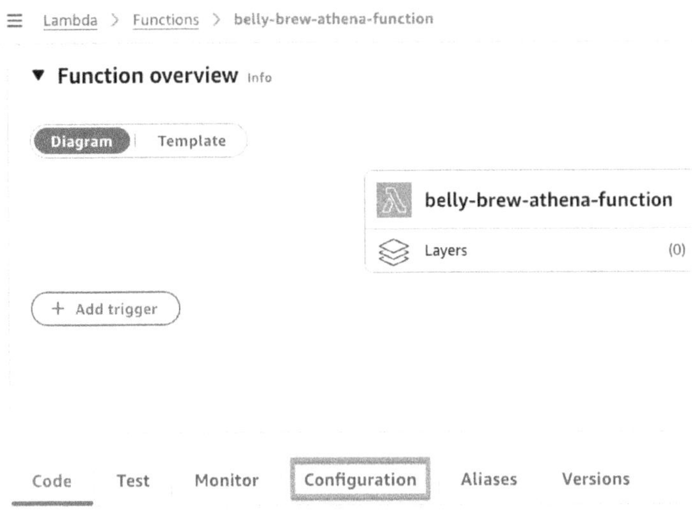

Figure 13.10: Lambda function configuration

12. From the left-hand menu, click **General configuration**. In the right-hand pane, click the **Edit** button
13. Set the default **Timeout** period from `3 sec` to `1 min`. This will ensure the function has sufficient time to complete the query.
14. Click **Save** at the bottom of the webpage
15. Next, you must paste the Lambda code into the code section of the function. Before doing so, you must edit the code.
    a. Open the `lambdafunction.py` file using Notepad or an IDE such as Visual Studio Code
    b. Update lines 10 and 11 with your Amazon S3 bucket name and your Amazon Athena database name that you defined earlier in *Project Tasks 13.1* and *13.2*, respectively. Note the placeholders in the screenshot in *Figure 13.11*. Ensure you replace these with your actual names, making sure to also remove the square brackets.

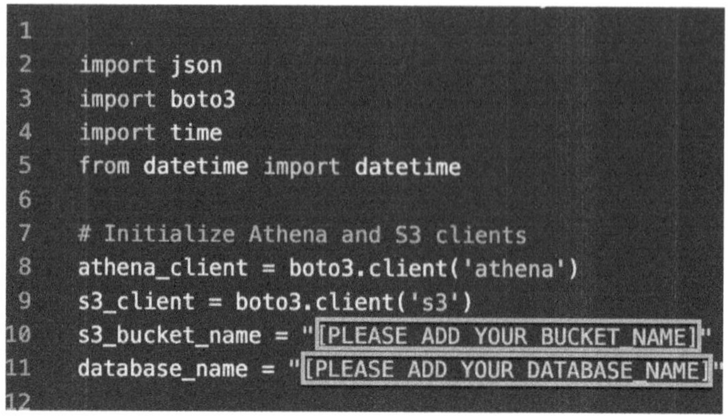

Figure 13.11: Lambda function code

   c. Save the file
   d. Copy the entire contents of the file to your clipboard

16. In the Lambda console, click on the **Code** tab
17. You will see an existing Lambda function template. Highlight the entire code template and delete it.
18. Next, paste your Lambda function code, which you edited earlier in *Step 15.b*. Ensure the entire code has been copied across as per the following screenshot in *Figure 13.12*:

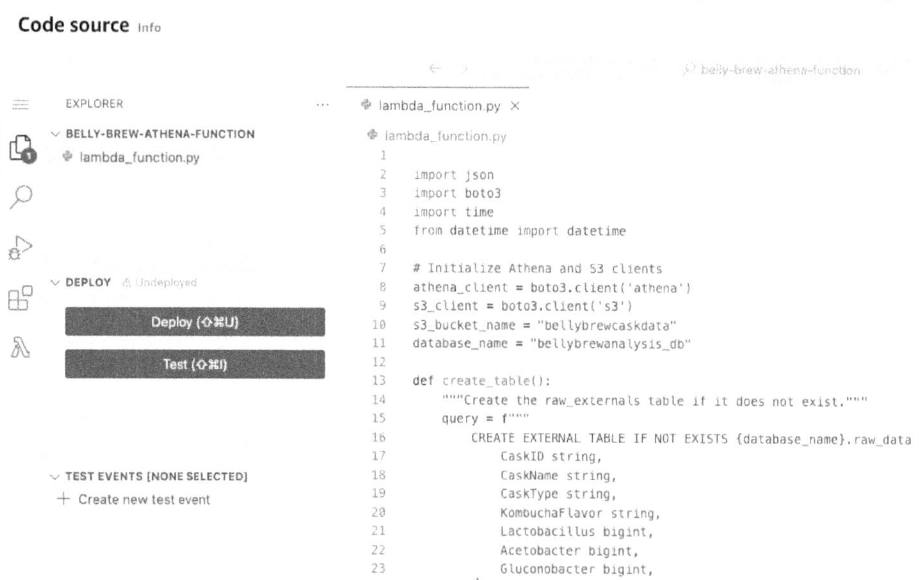

Figure 13.12: Updated Lambda Function Code

19. Next, click **Deploy**
20. Your Lambda code will now be deployed, and you should see a notification informing you that the function was successfully updated

In the next project task, you will proceed to create an EventBridge Scheduled Rule. This is because you want the Lambda function to be triggered at 5 pm as per the requirements of this project.

Project task 13.5 – Creating an EventBridge schedule rule

As per the requirements stated earlier, the analysis of the CSV file must be done at 5 pm to identify which Kombucha casks, if any, do not meet the pH balance requirements for bottling and distribution. Any casks that fall outside of the specified range are to be removed from the production line.

The following are the steps required to complete this task:

1. From the search bar at the top of the AWS management console, search for and navigate to the EventBridge web console
2. From the left-hand menu, click **Schedules** under **Scheduler**
3. In the right-hand pane, click **Create schedule**
4. Provide a name for your schedule rule such as `belly-brew-cask-analysis-scheduler`
5. Scroll further down and select the **Recurring schedule** option
6. Ensure you set the time zone to your time zone. For example, if you are in Sydney, Australia, you would set it to `UTC+11:00` –; your time zone may also vary based on whether you operate daylight savings.
7. Next, select the option for **Cron-based schedule**
8. Next, you will need to provide a Cron expression that represents 5 pm, Monday to Friday, every weekday of the month, every month, and every year. A cron expression is a time-based schedule written in a specific format that tells a system when to automatically run a task or job. You can use the following expression: `0 17 ? * MON-FRI *`.
9. Add these values in the appropriate boxes as shown in the screenshot in *Figure 13.13*. Note the resulting schedule highlighted below.

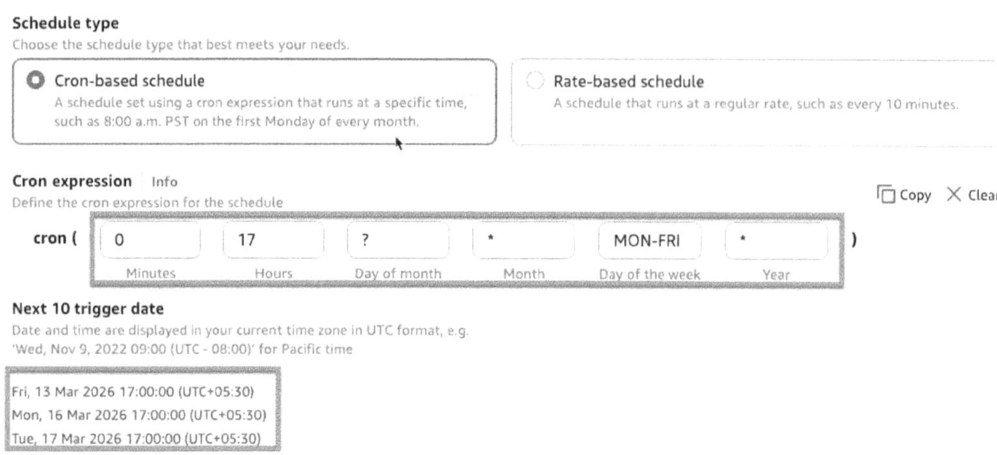

Figure 13.13: Cron expression for schedule

> **Tip**
>
> You can learn more about cron expressions and how to define them at `https://docs.aws.amazon.com/scheduler/latest/UserGuide/schedule-types.html?icmpid=docs_console_unmapped#cron-based`

10. Scroll a bit further down and select **OFF** from the **Flexible time window** drop-down list
11. Click **Next**
12. In the **Target detail** webpage, select `AWS Lambda`
13. Scroll a bit further down and select the Lambda function you created from the drop-down list in the **Invoke** section of the webpage
14. Scroll to the bottom of the webpage and click **Next**
15. In the **Settings – optional** webpage, select **None** from the **Action after schedule completion** drop-down list. This is because you want the Lambda function to be invoked daily, as would be the case for the real-world scenario.
16. Scroll to the bottom of the webpage and ensure that the option **Create new role this schedule** for the **Execution role** is selected. This role is used by EventBridge to invoke the Lambda function

17. Click **Next**
18. You will now be on the **Review and create schedule** webpage. Scroll to the bottom of the webpage and click **Create schedule**

Your EventBridge schedule rule will be created, and you should see that **Status** is set to **Enabled** as per the following screenshot in *Figure 13.14*:

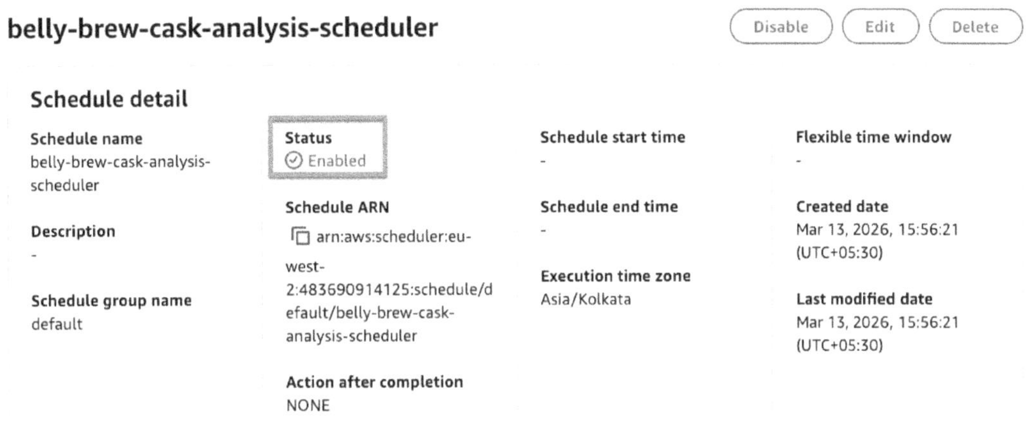

Figure 13.14: EventBridge Scheduler Status: Enabled

In the next project task, you will upload a sample CSV file to the rawdata folder in your S3 bucket to run a test.

Project task 13.6 – Uploading sample CSV to S3

In this project task, you will upload the sample CSV file you downloaded from the GitHub repository to your Amazon S3 bucket. If you look at the file by opening it in Excel or another suitable application, you will note that there are more than 500 entries of casks that need to be analyzed. You will also note that some casks are not suitable as their pH levels are outside of the range of 2.5 to 3.5, as depicted in the screenshot in *Figure 13.15*:

	A	B	C	D	E	F	G	H	I	J	K
1	CaskID	CaskName	CaskType	KombuchaFl	Lactobacillus	Acetobacter	Gluconobact	PH Level	LS-Code	Weight	Temperature
2	1	Derek	Port casks	Raspberry	458	330	33	3.37	5349684-C	72.8	77
3	2	Alice	Port casks	Raspberry	460	333	34	2.52	1388758-B	72.88	80.6
4	3	Oscar	Port casks	Blackcurrant	458	332	34	2.8	5210678-A	72.84	77.2
5	4	Alice	Port casks	Mojito	460	333	36	2.91	6793789-B	72.8	81.6
6	5	Emily	Port casks	Blackcurrant	454	332	35	2.89	1024747-B	72.89	75.3
7	6	Vince	Port casks	Ginger & Lem	460	337	37	2.55	0230733-A	72.85	81.6
8	7	Lydia	Port casks	Blackcurrant	457	334	36	3.4	7731297-C	72.86	80.5
9	8	Alice	Port casks	Ginger & Lem	452	333	37	2.88	0195438-C	72.81	80.5
10	9	Alice	Port casks	Raspberry	454	333	33	3.26	5268786-C	72.81	79.1
11	10	Olive	Port casks	Raspberry	455	336	33	3.46	6954610-C	72.8	78.4
12	11	Jonah	Port casks	Peach	459	335	37	2.89	4959300-A	72.82	79.3
13	12	Miles	Port casks	Ginger & Lem	458	333	37	2.75	5303026-C	72.84	77.5
14	13	Zara	Port casks	Blueberry	459	338	36	2.96	6657967-E	72.82	81.9
15	14	Emily	Port casks	Blackcurrant	457	332	36	2.73	1763673-A	72.81	81.9
16	15	Alice	Port casks	Raspberry	457	340	35	2.57	8570180-E	72.89	83.2
17	16	Alice	Port casks	Peach	456	340	36	4.72	1646768-D	72.9	80
18	17	Simon	Port casks	Blueberry	454	333	37	3.46	1661254-B	72.86	78.7
19	18	Derek	Port casks	Peach	455	330	35	4.59	3461315-E	72.84	82.5
20	19	Miles	Port casks	Blackcurrant	459	332	37	2.7	4497510-B	72.9	80.5
21	20	Lydia	Port casks	Peach	459	334	34	3.2	9186649-C	72.86	76.5
22	21	Oscar	Port casks	Peach	453	334	37	2.64	9695341-A	72.83	79.7

Figure 13.15: Sample CSV file

The Lambda function will trigger a query in Amazon Athena to identify these casks that are out of range and create a separate report for you, placing them in the `processed` folder of your S3 bucket.

The following are the steps required to complete this task:

1. From the search bar at the top of the AWS management console, search for and navigate to Amazon S3
2. From the left-hand menu, click **General purpose buckets**
3. In the right-hand pane, click the bucket you created in *Project Task 13.1*
4. Click the `rawdata` folder to access it, as per the following screenshot in *Figure 13.16*:

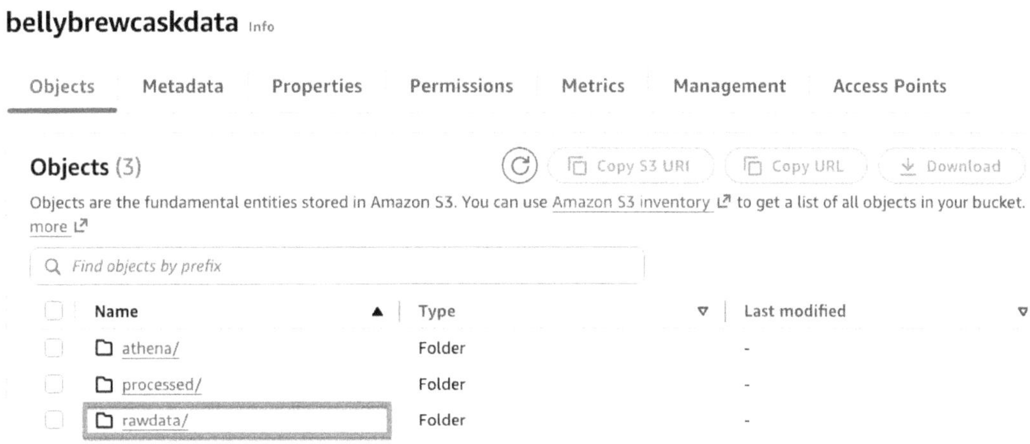

Figure 13.16: Amazon S3 Bucket – Upload CSV file to rawdata

5. Because this task is being performed daily and your CSV file is generated once a day by the third-party pH analyzer equipment, you want to ensure that you only analyze the current day's data. For that reason, create a subfolder and name the folder with today's date in the format `yyyy-mm-dd`. For example, if today is 13 March 2026, create a folder like `2026-03-13`
6. Next, click this subfolder to navigate into it as per the following screenshot in *Figure 13.17*:

Figure 13.17: Create a subfolder with today's date

7. Click the **Upload** button
8. Click **Add files**
9. In the File Explorer or Finder window that appears, navigate to your Desktop where you saved the sample CSV file and double-click on it
10. Your file is now selected. Scroll to the bottom of the webpage and click **Upload**

Your file should now be in the rawdata folder of the Amazon S3 bucket you created for this project. At 5 pm in your designated time zone, the EventBridge schedule should trigger the Lambda function to run the query in Amazon Athena. The query is designed to identify all Kombucha casks that have reported a pH level outside the range of 2.5 to 3.5.

In the next project task, you will review the results of the analysis and clean up the resources to avoid unnecessary usage of credits.

Project task 13.7 – Testing the application

This part of the project can only be completed after 5 pm on the day your Lambda function is invoked. If you managed to complete all the project tasks before 5 pm, then you will just have to wait till after 5 pm to check the results. You can run the test against your Lambda function directly, bypassing the EventBridge scheduler, but it's well worth the wait to see how this all works automatically.

The following are the steps required to complete this task:

1. From the search bar at the top of the AWS Management Console, search for and navigate to Amazon S3
2. From the left-hand menu, click **General purpose buckets**
3. In the right-hand pane, click the bucket you created in *Project Task 13.1* to access it as per the following screenshot in *Figure 13.18*:

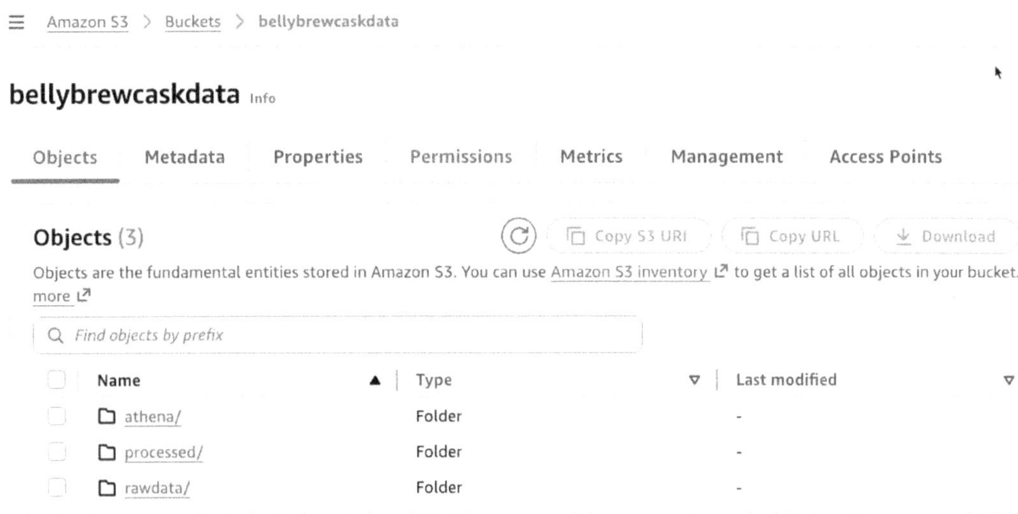

Figure 13.18: Amazon S3 Bucket with rawdata

4. Next, click the **processed** folder to open it
5. You will note that there is a folder created with the current date. Navigate into that folder
6. You should find two files in that folder – one file will have a .csv extension
7. Select the file by clicking on the check box next to it, and click the **Download** button. This will download the file to your local Downloads folder.
8. Navigate to your Downloads folder using File Explorer/Finder and then open it in Excel or another suitable application
9. If the Lambda function successfully calls Amazon Athena to run the required query, the CSV file will contain a list of casks that have reported pH levels outside of the acceptable values, as depicted in the following screenshot in *Figure 13.19*:

	caskid	caskname	casktype	kombuchaflavor	lactobacillus	acetobacter	gluconobacter	ph level	s-code	weight	temperature
2	16	Alice	Port casks	Peach	456	340	36	4.72	646768-D	72.9	80
3	18	Derek	Port casks	Peach	455	330	35	4.59	461315-E	72.84	82.5
4	25	Alice	Port casks	Blackcurrant	457	336	33	5.04	110261-B	72.85	80.6
5	58	Derek	Port casks	Strawberry	457	339	34	4.51	668396-C	72.87	75.1
6	143	Olive	Port casks	Ginger & Lemon	457	334	36	4.58	729676-D	72.87	84.7
7	179	Alice	Port casks	Strawberry	459	336	36	5.36	441975-B	72.82	80.1
8	204	Zara	Port casks	Peach	452	337	37	4.67	514967-D	72.89	80.2
9	252	Emily	Port casks	Ginger & Lemon	451	340	36	4.62	947475-E	72.84	82.7
10	272	Helen	Port casks	Blackcurrant	452	334	34	4.54	858846-C	72.8	81.4
11	341	Mason	Port casks	Mojito	459	331	37	5.19	909784-E	72.86	84.2
12	346	Vince	Port casks	Peach	460	336	36	4.78	046671-D	72.87	76.3
13	364	Simon	Port casks	Blackcurrant	457	337	37	5.1	131722-D	72.89	83.6
14	377	Miles	Port casks	Peach	460	333	33	4.52	707338-B	72.86	78
15	408	Olive	Port casks	Strawberry	460	340	37	5	332381-E	72.87	79.4
16	422	Zara	Port casks	Strawberry	454	337	35	4.97	447158-B	72.81	79.5
17	429	Simon	Port casks	Ginger & Lemon	454	332	37	5.63	890267-A	72.89	78.3

Figure 13.19: Resultant CSV file reporting list of casks outside the acceptable pH values

Congratulations, you have now successfully completed this project task and fulfilled the second requirement of Belly Brew Co. Limited. Assuming that there are no additional changes or modifications required to the solution, you would work with the third-party supplier of the pH analyzer equipment to integrate their system with your application. Specifically, you must ensure the pH analyzer tool uploads the recorded data in CSV format to the Amazon S3 bucket.

The overall design would need to consist of the necessary business logic to ensure that the uploads of the raw data are placed in sub-folders within the `rawdata` folder that are labeled in the date format of the day of the upload.

In the next project task, you will perform a cleanup exercise to terminate the resources you have created to avoid unnecessary consumption of your AWS credits and/or charges.

Project task 13.8 – Cleaning up

In this project task, you will terminate the resources you created.

The following are the steps required to complete this task:

1. Terminate the EventBridge Schedule:
    a. Using the search bar at the top of the AWS Management console webpage, search for and navigate to EventBridge
    b. From the left-hand menu, click **Schedules**
    c. In the right-hand pane, select the schedule you created in *Project Task 13.5*
    d. Click the **Delete** button
    e. Click the **Delete** button again in the popup window that appears

2. Delete the Lambda Function:
    a. Using the search bar at the top of the AWS Management Console, search for and navigate to Lambda
    b. From the left-hand menu, click **Functions**
    c. In the right-hand pane, select the function you created in *Project Task 13.4*
    d. From the **Actions** drop-down list, select **Delete**
    e. In the dialog box that appears, type in `confirm` and then click **Delete**. This will remove the function
3. Delete the Amazon Athena Database
    a. Using the search bar at the top of the AWS Management Console, search for and navigate to Athena
    b. From the left-hand menu, click **Query editor tabs**. As depicted in the screenshot in *Figure 13.20*, you will note that the database and table were created by the Lambda function

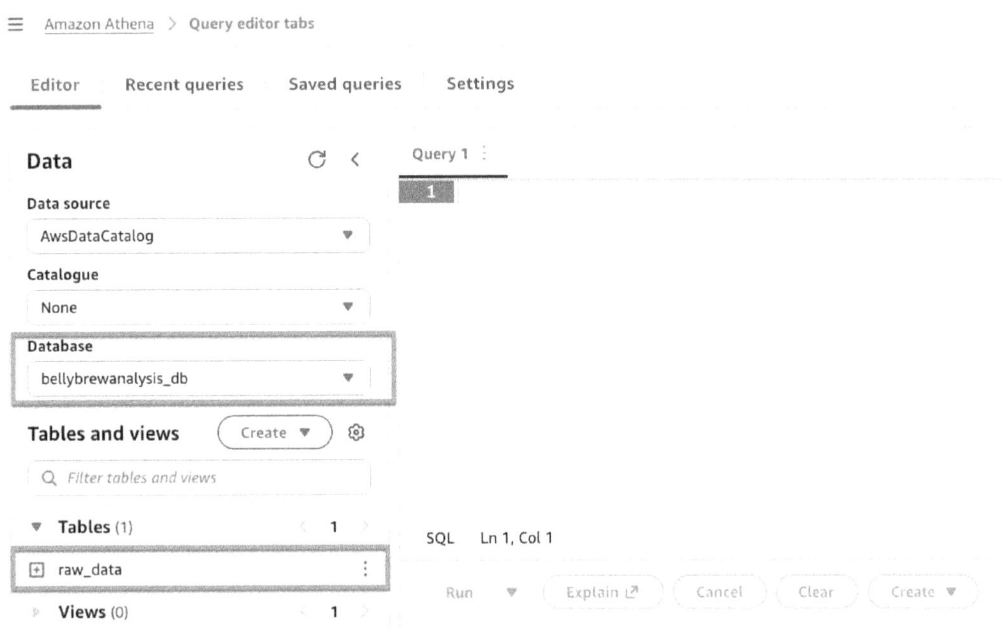

Figure 13.20: Athena database and table for Belly Brew Co. Limited

   c. To remove the table type the SQL query `DROP TABLE bellybrewanalysis_db.raw_data;` in the Query1 text area and click the **Run** button. This will delete the table
   d. To remove the database, type the SQL query `DROP DATABASE bellybrewanalysis_db;` in the Query1 text area, replacing the previous query, and click the **Run** button. This will delete the Database
4. Delete the S3 bucket
   a. Using the search bar at the top of the AWS Management Console, search for and navigate to Amazon S3
   b. From the left-hand menu, click **General purpose buckets**
   c. In the right-hand pane, select the bucket you created in *Project Task 13.1*
   d. Click the **Empty** button – this is necessary because you cannot delete a bucket that has objects in it
   e. In the **Empty bucket** webpage that appears, type in `permanently delete` in the text box under **Permanently delete all objects in bucket "name of your bucket"**
   f. Click the **Empty** button
   g. Click **Exit**
   h. Select the bucket again from the list of buckets
   i. Next, click the **Delete** button
   j. Type in the name of the bucket in the text box under **Delete bucket "your bucket name"?**
   k. Click **Delete bucket**
5. Delete the CloudWatch Logs Group. When you create a Lambda function, it creates a log group in CloudWatch. You will learn more about CloudWatch in *Chapter 16*. For now, you simply want to delete this log group to keep things tidy.
   a. Using the search bar at the top of the AWS Management Console, search for and navigate to CloudWatch
   b. In the left-hand menu, click **Log Management** under the **Logs** section
   c. In the right-hand pane, select the log group related to your Lambda function, as depicted in the screenshot in *Figure 13.21*:

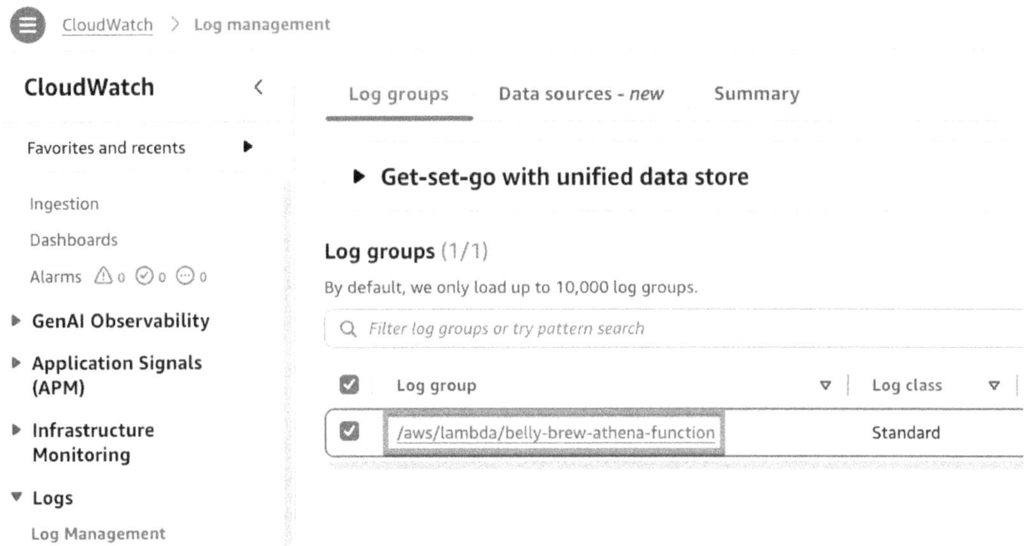

Figure 13.21: AWS CloudWatch Logs Group

d. Click **Delete log group(s)** from the **Action** drop-down list

e. Click the **Delete** button in the pop-up window that appears

You have successfully terminated all resources related to this project. This project showcased how you would use a wide range of serverless technologies to help you build end-to-end architectures and solutions for real-world use cases such as that of Belly Brew Co. Limited.

Summary

Data is the new currency for businesses, and the ability to analyze large volumes of data in the shortest possible time is critical for any company. AWS offers a wide range of analytical tools designed to help you stream, ingest, process, transform, and analyze your datasets. You have a wide range of tools available at your disposal, many of which are fully managed, requiring no infrastructure services to be managed by the customer.

You can use streaming tools like Amazon Kinesis that allow you to process and analyze data in real-time. Services like Amazon Data Firehose can be used to load data onto a wide range of AWS and third-party services, including Amazon S3, Redshift, Splunk, and much more.

If you need to perform ad-hoc queries against your data in Amazon S3, you have access to Amazon Athena – a service you can use to perform ad-hoc analysis of your data. You can use Amazon Glue to perform ETL jobs and discover the structure of the schema of your data.

Finally, you can use Amazon Quick to perform business intelligence analysis and build a visualization dashboard and reporting for your organization.

The ability to understand data is critical for any business. However, in addition to that, the ability to query data in a manner that is more human and easily digestible is just as important. In addition, using past historical data to predict trends and make recommendations is a powerful tool for any organization competing in today's global marketplace. AWS offers a wide range of machine learning and artificial intelligence services that can help you perform trend analysis, predict consumer behavior, and access information hidden in big data sets in a matter of minutes. These topics are discussed in the next chapter.

In this chapter, we explored how AWS analytics services help businesses stream, prepare, query, search, process, and visualize data using services such as Amazon Kinesis, AWS Glue, Amazon Athena, Amazon OpenSearch Service, Amazon EMR, and Amazon QuickSight. In the next chapter, you will build on that data foundation by looking at AWS machine learning and artificial intelligence services that can recognize images, convert text to speech, transcribe audio, translate text, extract information from documents, analyze sentiment, and support custom model development.

Exam Readiness Drill – Chapter Review Questions

Apart from mastering key concepts, strong test-taking skills under time pressure are essential for acing your certification exam. That's why developing these abilities early in your learning journey is critical.

Exam readiness drills, using the free online practice resources provided with this book, help you progressively improve your time management and test-taking skills while reinforcing the key concepts you've learned.

HOW TO GET STARTED

- Open the link or scan the QR code at the bottom of this page
- If you have unlocked the practice resources already, log in to your registered account. If you haven't, follow the instructions in *Free Benefits with Your Book* section in this book's *Preface* and come back to this page.
- Once you log in, click the START button to start this chapter's quiz
- We recommend attempting a quiz multiple times till you're able to answer most of the questions correctly and well within the time limit.
- You can use the following practice template to help you plan your attempts:

Working On Accuracy		
Attempt	**Target**	**Time Limit**
Attempt 1	40% or more	Till the timer runs out
Attempt 2	60% or more	Till the timer runs out
Attempt 3	75% or more	Till the timer runs out
Working On Timing		
Attempt 4	75% or more	1 minute before time limit
Attempt 5	75% or more	2 minutes before time limit
Attempt 6	75% or more	3 minutes before time limit

The above drill is just an example. Design your drills based on your own goals and make the most out of the online quizzes accompanying this book.

Link to this Chapter's Quiz

You need to unlock the online practice resources to access the link below. Check the *Free Benefits with Your Book* section in the *Preface* for detailed instructions on how to do this. You only need to unlock the resources once.

Open Quiz `https://packt.link/clf_c02_ch13`or scan the QR code

14

Machine Learning and Artificial Intelligence

Machine learning (**ML**) and **artificial intelligence** (**AI**) have taken the world by storm. Now considered cutting-edge and among the most impactful technologies of our time, it has become almost imperative for anyone pursuing a career in cloud computing to be familiar with the wide range of AI and ML services available on modern cloud platforms—and to understand how to use and support many of their managed AI/ML offerings.

Furthermore, with Generative AI rapidly transforming businesses and driving major gains in efficiency and productivity, now is the ideal time to learn how these tools work and how to build solutions around them. Companies are actively seeking expertise in GenAI services: understanding customer interactions and sentiment, building chatbots that deliver human-like conversations, and performing ultra-fast translations, transcriptions, and summarizations.

In this chapter, you will be introduced to a wide range of AI/ML services. For the AWS Certified Cloud Practitioner exam, it is imperative that you understand these technologies at a high level and are familiar with their primary use cases.

The topics covered in this chapter include:

- Recognizing images, videos, and text with Amazon Rekognition
- Converting text to speech with Amazon Polly
- Using AWS services for transcription, translation, and text extraction
- Understanding sentiment with Amazon Comprehend
- Building your own models with Amazon SageMaker

Recognizing images, videos, and text with Amazon Rekognition

Amazon Rekognition is a fully managed service that enables you to add computer vision capabilities to your applications. You can use Amazon Rekognition to analyze images and video files stored in Amazon S3 buckets.

Amazon Rekognition can detect objects and text in images and video, as well as compare faces, perform facial analysis, and identify attributes, such as age, gender, and emotions.

Several use cases include:

- Searchable and labeled media libraries
- Face-based identity verification systems
- Detection of **personal protective equipment** (**PPE**)
- Celebrity recognition
- Identification of unsafe content
- Text detection, and much more

Another capability of Amazon Rekognition is **Face Liveness**. Many applications require live verification using your mobile phone. For example, applying for a new passport or completing **KYC** (**Know Your Customer**) verification. In addition to uploading identity documents, you are often required to log in to a web app using your mobile device and camera, where the app scans your face as part of the live verification process.

Amazon Rekognition can detect whether the verification is being performed by a live person or if a bad actor is attempting to spoof the system using digital photos, digital videos, or 3D masks. These features make Amazon Rekognition the go-to service for image and video recognition and analysis.

While Amazon Rekognition can detect text embedded in images, it is not designed to offer a complete text extraction and analysis service. AWS offers a wide range of other services such as being able to extract text from pages of handwritten notes. Also, you may have text-based documents that need to be converted to speech for audio books or for converting voice narrations to text using a transcription service. In the next section, you will learn about another service that enables you to build text-to-speech applications.

Converting text to speech with Amazon Polly

Amazon Polly is an artificial intelligence service that uses deep learning to synthesize speech into a human-like voice with just text inputs. You can select from a wide range of voices across different accents and languages for both genders.

You can send your text data to Amazon Polly via API calls and have it immediately converted to an audio stream, which you can play back as part of your application. Amazon Polly supports standard audio formats like MP3.

Amazon Polly also offers **Neural Text-to-Speech** (**NTTS**) voices that support features like Newscaster speaking styles, enabling the delivery of flash news updates by TV and radio newscaster organizations.

With Amazon Polly, you can also use custom lexicons to modify pronunciation for particular words, use acronyms, and neologisms. To customize pronunciations, you can upload an XML file with lexical entries. For example, some TTS systems pronounce the common English word "often" incorrectly as "off-ten." Any time Polly encounters that word in your speech output, it will use your custom pronunciation.

An example lexicon XML file is provided as follows:

```
<lexicon version="1.0"
         xmlns="http://www.w3.org/2005/01/pronunciation-lexicon"
         alphabet="ipa"
         xml:lang="en-US">

  <lexeme>
    <grapheme>often</grapheme>
    <!-- Correct pronunciation: "aw-fn" -->
    <phoneme>ˈɔːfən</phoneme>
  </lexeme>

</lexicon>
```

Notice how you can use the `<phoneme>` element to explicitly define the correct pronunciation. This allows Amazon Polly to speak words exactly the way you intend, ensuring natural-sounding and accurate text-to-speech output—even for words that are commonly mispronounced.

You can use Amazon Polly for a wide range of voice applications, such as **interactive voice response** (**IVR**) systems, educational content narration, accessibility tools, real-time announcements, audiobook generation, and creating natural-sounding voices for websites and mobile apps.

After looking at how Amazon Polly turns text into speech, it is useful to look at services that work in the other direction or with related language-processing tasks, such as converting speech to text, translating content, and extracting text from documents.

Using AWS services for transcription, translation, and text extraction

AWS provides several AI services that help you process spoken, written, and document-based content. Amazon Transcribe converts speech into text, Amazon Translate converts text between languages, and Amazon Textract extracts text and structured data from documents and images.

Amazon Transcribe

Amazon Transcribe is a fully managed automatic speech-to-text transcription service. You can use Amazon Transcribe either as a standalone service—by pointing it to your audio files stored in Amazon S3—or integrate it directly into your own transcription applications. This is particularly useful when you need on-demand transcription of streaming audio, such as for closed captioning, thanks to its deep learning technology.

Amazon Transcribe can help you extract business insights from meetings, customer calls, and video files. You can also use it to automatically transcribe clinical conversations, and the service is **fully HIPAA compliant**. For added privacy, you can have sensitive and **personally identifiable information** (**PII**) automatically redacted from your transcripts, ensuring compliance with regulatory requirements.

There are no upfront costs or infrastructure charges. You can access the service on demand, and you only pay for the seconds of audio transcribed, billed monthly.

Next, you will learn about Amazon Translate.

Amazon Translate

Amazon Translate is a text translation service that enables you to perform high-quality translations. The service uses advanced machine learning technologies to enable you to translate unstructured text and documents across multiple languages. You can build applications and solutions that leverage Amazon Translate to automatically translate web pages, meeting minutes, technical reports, knowledge bases, posts, and more.

The service can be used to support interpersonal communications such as email, within gaming applications, and customer service chat, enabling your employees to connect in their preferred languages.

Amazon Translate supports multiple languages and can auto-detect the source language. *Figure 14.1* depicts the translation of text between English and French.

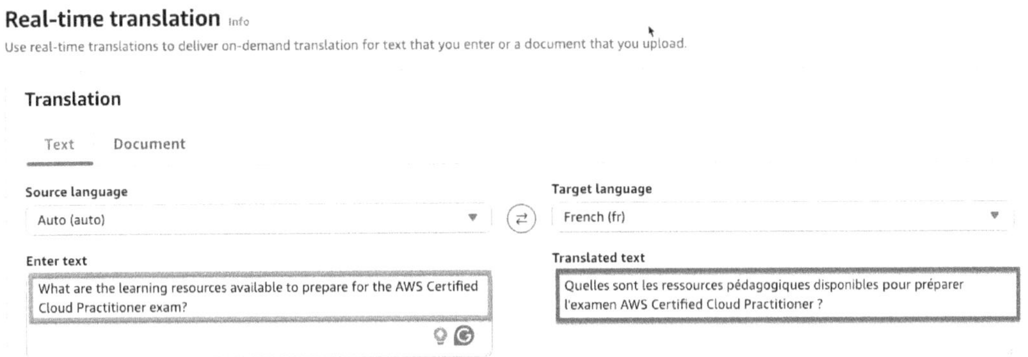

Figure 14.1: Amazon Translate example

You can use Amazon Translate to perform real-time translations or perform batch translation jobs for a large collection of documents up to 5 GB in size. Batch processing is ideal for short documents, social media postings, user reviews, and any other tasks not requiring real-time translations.

Next, you will learn about another service that allows you to capture text data from a wide range of document formats, including printed text, handwriting, and layout elements.

Amazon Textract

Many companies manually extract data from scanned documents, images, PDFs, tables, and forms using a wide range of tools and **optical character recognition** (**OCR**) software. However, often these software solutions are not adequate for every use case and require manual configurations whenever the source is changed, such as changes in the form layout of a PDF document.

Amazon Textract uses machine learning to read and process any type of document or image and can extract text data accurately from a wide range of sources, including tables and handwritten documents.

Figure 14.2 showcases how the content of a payslip form is extracted:

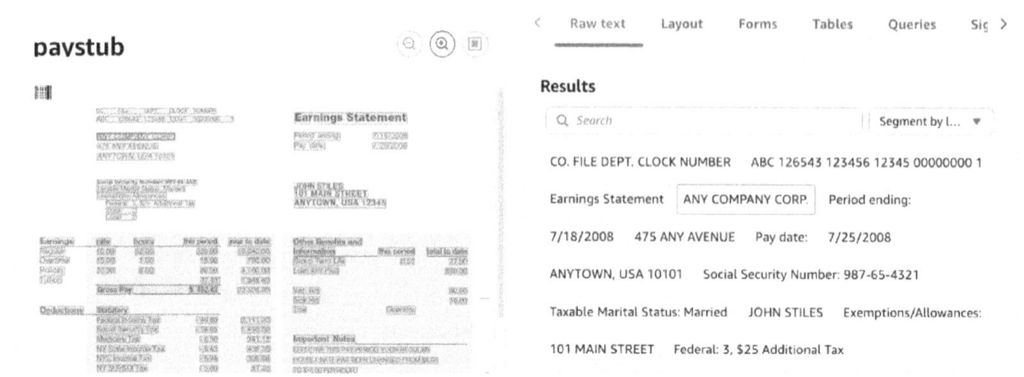

Figure 14.2: Amazon Textract example

The extracted data can then be used to update backend databases. For example, the extracted payslip data in *Figure 14.2* can be ingested into an accounting application to complete the annual tax return calculations.

Amazon Textract can also preserve the data structure stored in tabular formats during extraction, ensuring that context remains intact and making it ideal for extracting information from financial records, medical records, and any data in a column-row format.

Amazon Textract can also detect text in handwritten documents and notes. It can detect signatures on any document or image, enabling you to leverage the service for processing loan application forms, claim forms, and much more.

In the next section, you will learn about an Amazon AI service that enables you to understand the context and meaning of your textual data. This is particularly useful when you need to perform sentiment analysis, for example, how customers feel about the customer service they receive from your helpdesk team.

Understanding sentiment with Amazon Comprehend

Amazon Comprehend is an AI service that uses deep learning technology to accurately analyze text and is designed to understand its context and meaning. You can use Amazon Comprehend to analyze millions of documents and gather insights. The service uses **Natural Language Processing** (**NLP**) to automatically detect the following in textual documentation:

- **Entities**: Names of people, places, companies
- **Key phrases**: The main ideas in the text
- **Sentiment**: Whether the text is positive, negative, neutral, or mixed
- **Language**: Which language is the text written in

You can use Amazon Comprehend to build smart applications, such as an application that identifies and prioritizes customer reviews that have a negative connotation, so that you can handle those customers' issues promptly.

Amazon Comprehend uses pre-trained models to analyze documents and gather insights – the model is continuously trained on a large body of text. In addition, you can customize the service to your specific requirements by building custom NLP models using your proprietary data. Here, you can define custom classification and custom entity recognition.

Although AWS offers a wide range of AI and ML tools pretrained with massive datasets, sometimes you need to build custom models with your training data. Amazon SageMaker AI enables you to design and build your own models and is discussed next.

Building your own models with Amazon SageMaker AI

Businesses may often need to build their own machine learning models based on their industry and specific requirements. To that end, Amazon offers its machine learning solution called **Amazon SageMaker AI**. Previously known as just Amazon SageMaker, this service enables your data scientists and developers to quickly build, train, and deploy ML models into a production-ready hosted environment. You do not need to procure and manage expensive hardware, allowing you to focus on building and developing your ML workflows.

You build your machine learning models to generate predictions or insights by training them with an algorithm and sample data. Once the model has been trained, you embed it into your application so it can produce real-time, scalable inferences. The workflow is depicted in *Figure 14.3*:

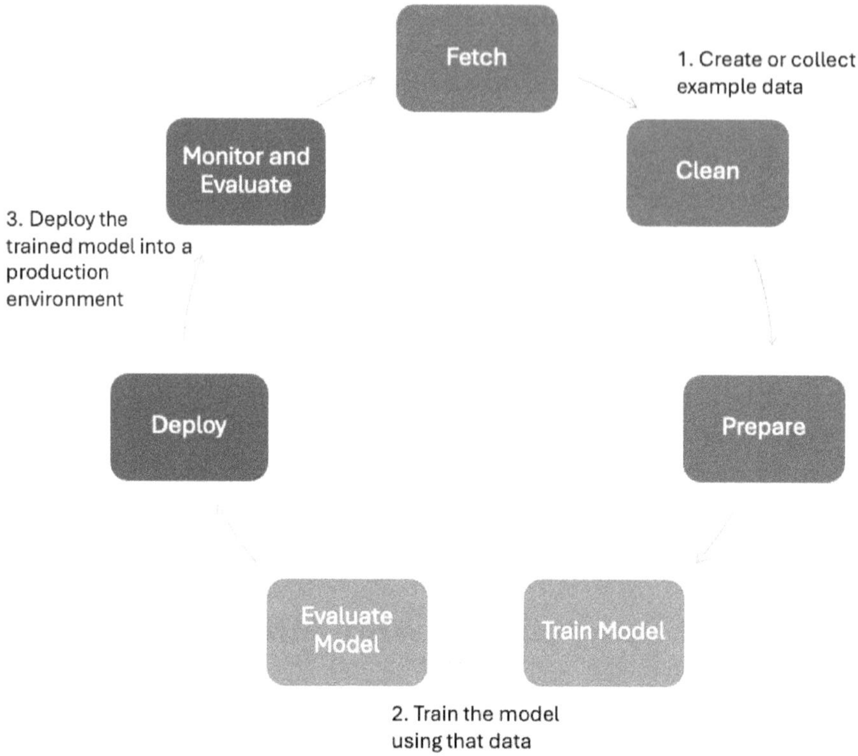

Figure 14.3: Training a model

A typical machine learning workflow follows a three-step, iterative cycle:

1. Create or collect example data
2. Train the model using that data
3. Deploy the trained model into a production environment

If necessary, you may need to continue training and fine-tuning your model before reaching the third stage of deployment.

In the next section, you will implement a project for Belly Brew Co. Limited that uses the AWS Transcribe service to automatically convert incoming customer calls to text, which can be stored for later retrieval or used to automate additional workflows like placing an order or making a complaint.

Project task 14 – Building a customer call transcription service for Belly Brew Co. Limited

In this project task, you will build out a portion of the overall architecture required by Belly Brew Co. Limited. The company receives lots of calls from both existing and potential customers. Some of those calls end up as voicemails and need to be transcribed so that they can be used by other applications, such as order placement or customer support.

In this project task, you will build a simple sub-section of the application that reads audio recordings from an Amazon S3 bucket and transcribes those audio files into text. In a larger end-to-end architecture, these text files would be consumed by applications like order processing.

The architecture is depicted in *Figure 14.4*:

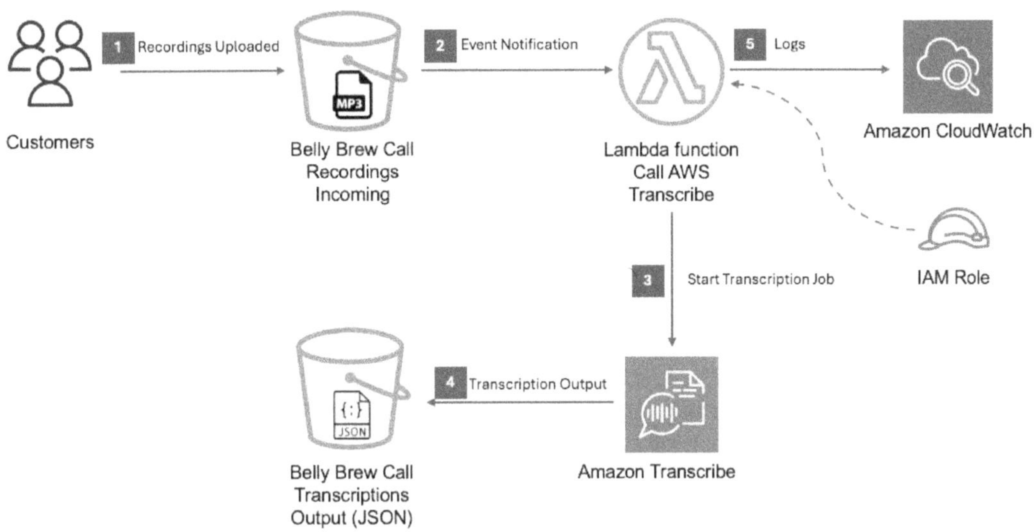

Figure 14.4: Belly Brew Co. Limited transcription project

Key steps of the application workflow are:

1. Customers' recordings are uploaded to an Amazon S3 bucket. Normally, an application, such as the voice system application, will perform this upload.
2. An Event Notification is configured on the Recordings bucket to send a notification to a Lambda function that will start the transcription service
3. The Lambda function will provide the audio file to AWS Transcribe to carry out the transcription and provide a simple JSON transcript file of the audio

4. AWS Transcribe will complete the transcription process, and the same Lambda function then instructs AWS Transcribe to upload the file to the Transcripts bucket in the output folder
5. Finally, Lambda automatically captures critical events and details of the execution and pushes those logs to CloudWatch logs

> Note
>
> To ensure appropriate authorization, you must also create an IAM role with the necessary permissions.

Technical requirements

To complete the project exercises in this chapter, ensure you are logged in to your AWS Development account as the IAM user Alice and are in the London region to complete the project tasks. Also, ensure that you download the mp3 audio file from the Packt GitHub repo at: `https://github.com/PacktPublishing/AWS-Certified-Cloud-Practitioner-CLF-C02-Exam-Guide`. Store the mp3 file on your desktop for easy access, as you will need to upload this to an S3 bucket in your AWS account. Two additional files in the repo will also be required—the lambda function written in Python and an IAM policy for an IAM role you will need to create to grant the necessary permissions. Download both files and store them on your desktop for easy access.

Project task 14.1 – Setting up Amazon S3 buckets

In this project task, you will create two Amazon S3 buckets; the first one will be used to host the incoming audio files. A sample call recording is available in the GitHub repo. The second bucket will be used to host the transcriptions.

The following are the step-by-step instructions to create both Amazon S3 buckets:

1. Ensure that you are logged into the AWS Development account as the IAM user Alice and navigate to the Amazon S3 web management console
2. Ensure that you are in the London region by selecting it from the drop-down menu in the top right-hand corner of the management console page
3. From the left-hand menu in the Amazon S3 management console, click on **General purpose buckets**
4. In the right-hand pane, click the **Create bucket** button
5. Ensure that **Global namespace** is selected under **Bucket namespace**. Provide a name for your bucket, such as `bellybrew-call-recordings` (remember that bucket names

must be unique, so you will need to choose a name of your choice that hasn't already been used)

6. Scroll to the bottom of the web page and click the **Create bucket** button. You will then be redirected to the bucket and be able to see its details page as per the screenshot in *Figure 14.5*.

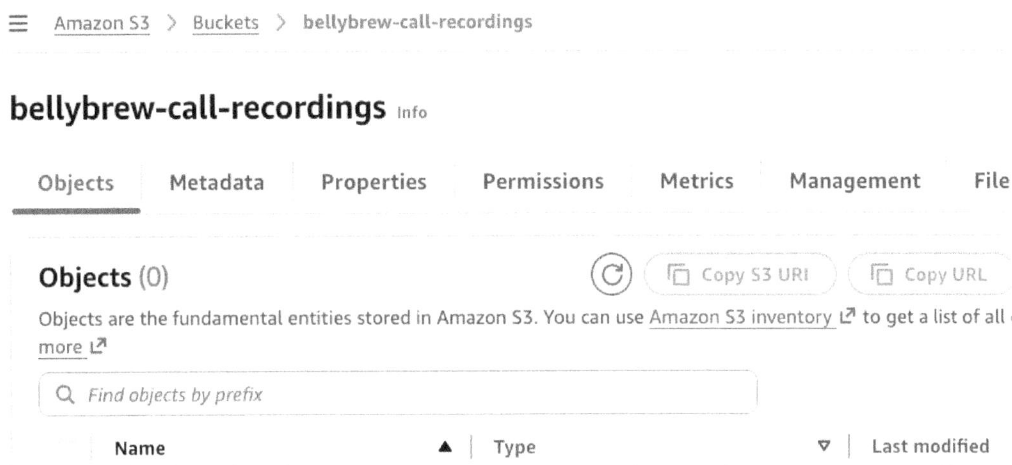

Figure 14.5: Bellybrew-call-recordings bucket

7. In the **Objects** tab of the bucket, click the **Create folder** button. This folder will be used to store the mp3 audio files.
8. Name the folder as `incoming`
9. Scroll to the bottom of the webpage and click the **Create folder** button
10. Next, you must create another **General purpose bucket** that will be used to store all the transcriptions by following *steps 3 to 6* again. Create this second bucket with a name like `bellybrew-transcripts`. Remember your bucket name will need to be different from the one shown in this book as they need to be unique. Within this bucket, create a folder for storing the transcripts outputs and name the folder `output` by following *steps 7 and 8* again.

Next, you will need to create an IAM role for AWS Lambda, which will grant your function the permissions to read and write to the Amazon S3 buckets and start the transcription jobs.

Project task 14.2 – Creating an IAM role

In this project task, you will create an IAM role to ensure that your Lambda function has the right permissions to access and process the incoming recordings and use AWS Transcribe to complete the transcription tasks.

To complete this project, ensure that you have downloaded the sample `iamrole.json` file from our GitHub repo and open it up in Notepad or your favorite IDE, such as Visual Studio Code.

You will need to update the policy, replacing the placeholder values shown in the screenshot in *Figure 14.6* with your bucket names of the buckets you created in *Project Task 14*, which will be used to store the audio files and the transcripts. Once you update the policy, save the file.

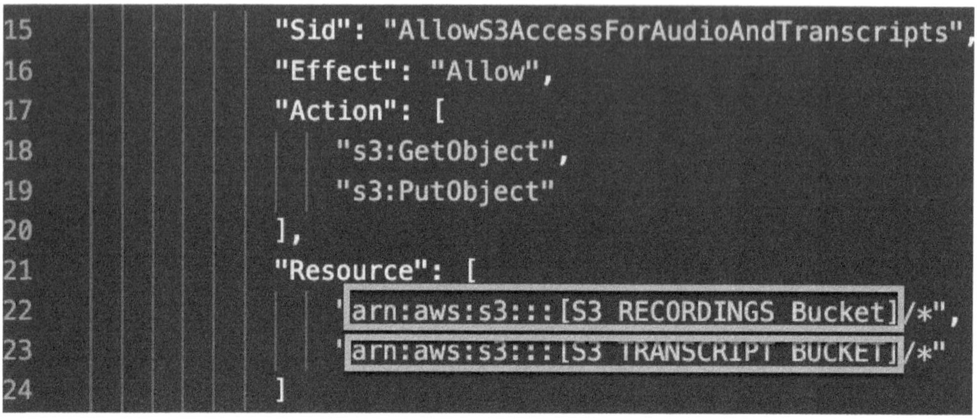

Figure 14.6: IAM role policy with placeholders to update bucket names

The following steps will guide you through the process of creating the IAM role with the necessary permissions for your Lambda function:

1. Ensure that you are still logged into the AWS Development account
2. From the search bar at the top of the webpage, search for and navigate to the IAM dashboard
3. From the left-hand menu, click **Policies**
4. In the right-hand pane, click the **Create policy** button
5. For the **Policy editor**, click the **JSON** option
6. Delete the existing sample policy in the **Policy editor** window and copy and paste the policy you downloaded earlier with the updated bucket names into this window
7. Scroll to the bottom of the webpage and click the **Next** button
8. Provide a name for the policy, such as `BellyBrewTranscriptionPolicy`
9. Click the **Create policy** button at the bottom of the webpage
10. Next, from the left-hand menu, click **Roles**
11. In the right-hand pane, click the **Create role** button
12. Next, select **AWS service** as the **Trusted entity type**

13. For the **Use case**, select **Lambda** from the **Service or use case** drop-down list
14. Click **Next**
15. In the search under **Add permissions**, search for the policy you created earlier and select it by clicking the checkbox next to the policy name
16. Click **Next**
17. Provide a name for your role, such as `BellyBrewTranscriptionRole`
18. Click the **Create role** button at the bottom of the webpage

In the next project task, you will create the Lambda function, which will be used to respond to an S3 event when an audio file is uploaded to the call recordings bucket and trigger AWS Transcribe to perform the transcription task.

Project task 14.3 – Creating Lambda function

In this project task, you must create the Lambda function. The function will be triggered by Amazon S3 Event Notifications when you upload an audio file to the incoming folder of the recordings bucket, and then it will trigger the transcription task by calling the AWS Transcribe service.

Ensure you have downloaded the Lambda functions source code from the GitHub repo and have it accessible from your desktop.

The following are the steps to follow to create, edit the code and deploy the Lambda function:

1. Open the Lambda function source code you downloaded in Notepad or your favorite IDE and update line number 22 with the bucket name of your transcription bucket you created in *Project Task 14.1* as shown in *Figure 14.7*:

```
20                'MediaFileUri': media_uri
21            },
22            OutputBucketName="[Belly Brew Output Bucket]",
23            OutputKey=f"output/{job_name}.json"
24        )
```

Figure 14.7: Update the Lambda function code with the name of your transcription bucket

2. Ensure you are still logged into the AWS Development account and in the London region
3. From the search bar at the top of the web management console, search for and navigate to the **AWS Lambda service**
4. Access the left-hand menu by clicking on the hamburger icon and select **Functions**

5. In the right-hand pane, click the **Create function** button. You will be presented with the **Create function** configuration page.
6. Ensure that **Author from scratch** is selected
7. Provide a name for your function, such as `bellybrewtranscribefunction`
8. Select **Python 3.14** as the **Runtime**
9. Ensure that **x86_64** is selected as the **Architecture**, as shown in *Figure 14.8*:

Figure 14.8: Create function configuration page

10. Expand the **Additional settings** section
11. Enable the **Custom execution role** toggle switch. This will open a side window on the far right of the webpage titled **Configure custom execution role**
12. Select the IAM role you created in *Project Task 14.2* earlier from the **Execution role** drop-down list and click **Save**
13. Click the **Create function** button at the bottom of the webpage
14. If you get a **Getting started** pop-up window, click **Dismiss**
15. You will be presented with the **Function overview** page. Scroll a bit further down and select the **Code** tab (if it is not already selected)
16. A sample code will be provided in the `lambda_function.py` code window of the **Code source** section
17. Copy and paste the Python code you downloaded earlier from the GitHub repository into the code window, replacing the sample code as depicted in *Figure 14.9*:

Figure 14.9: Copy and paste the Lamba function into Code source section

18. From the left-hand pane, click the blue **Deploy** button. This will deploy your Lambda function
19. Next, you must update the timeout configuration. Click the **Configuration** tab
20. Click **General configuration** from the left-hand menu and then click the **Edit** button in the right-hand pane
21. The Timeout period is by default set to 3 seconds. Change this to `10 seconds`.
22. Click the **Save** button. Your function will now be updated.

In the next section, you will configure an Amazon S3 Event Notification on the recordings bucket you created in *Project Task 14.1*.

Project task 14.4 – Configuring Amazon S3 event notifications

In this project task, you will configure the recordings S3 bucket, which will be used to upload the audio files to, with an Event Notification such that whenever an mp3 file is uploaded to it, the Lambda function you created in *Project 14.3* will be invoked and the transcription of the audio will be completed. The output of which will be uploaded to the transcription bucket.

1. Ensure you are still logged into the AWS Development account and navigate to the Amazon S3 management console
2. From the left-hand menu, click on **General purpose buckets**
3. In the right-hand pane, click the recordings bucket, e.g., `bellybrew-call-recordings`
4. Click the **Properties** tab

5. Scroll down to the **Event notification** section of the page and click the **Create event notification** button
6. In the **Create event notification** webpage, provide a name for your event, such as `bbrecordings`
7. In the **Prefix – optional** text box, add the prefix `incoming/` (with the slash at the end)
8. For the suffix, add `.mp3` – this will ensure that only mp3 audio files will invoke the Lambda function as shown in *Figure 14.10*:

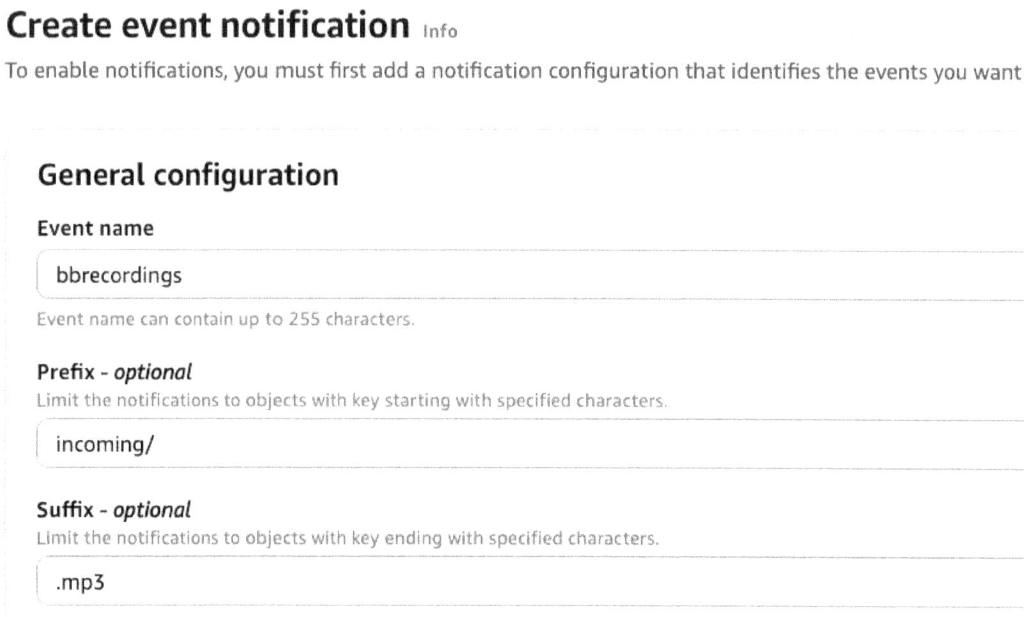

Figure 14.10: Create event notifications settings

9. Next, in the **Event types** section, select the **Put** object creation event. This event type is generated when you upload objects to the bucket.
10. Scroll further to the bottom and in the **Destination** section, ensure that **Lambda function** is selected
11. Select the Lambda function you created in *Project Task 14.3* from the **Lambda function** drop-down list
12. Click **Save changes**

In the next section, you will test out the application workflow. You will upload a sample audio file (available in the same GitHub repo) to the recordings S3 bucket in the `incoming` folder. This will trigger the event notification to invoke the Lambda function, which in turn will trigger

AWS Transcribe to perform a transcription on the audio file and post the transcription to the second bucket.

Project task 14.5 – Testing the application

In this project task, you will test out the application with the sample audio provided.

The following steps will guide you through the process of testing out the application. You will upload an mp3 file to the recordings bucket, which should trigger the Lambda function to use AWS Transcribe to transcribe the audio to text. The resultant transcription will be saved to your transcription bucket:

1. Ensure you are logged into the AWS management console in the London region and navigate to the Amazon S3 management console
2. Click on the recordings bucket to open it in the browser window
3. Next, ensure you are in the **Object** tab, where you can upload the sample audio
4. Click the `incoming` folder
5. Click the **Upload** button, and this will take you to the **Upload** webpage
6. From your desktop, drag and drop the audio file you downloaded from your desktop repository as depicted in *Figure 14.11*:

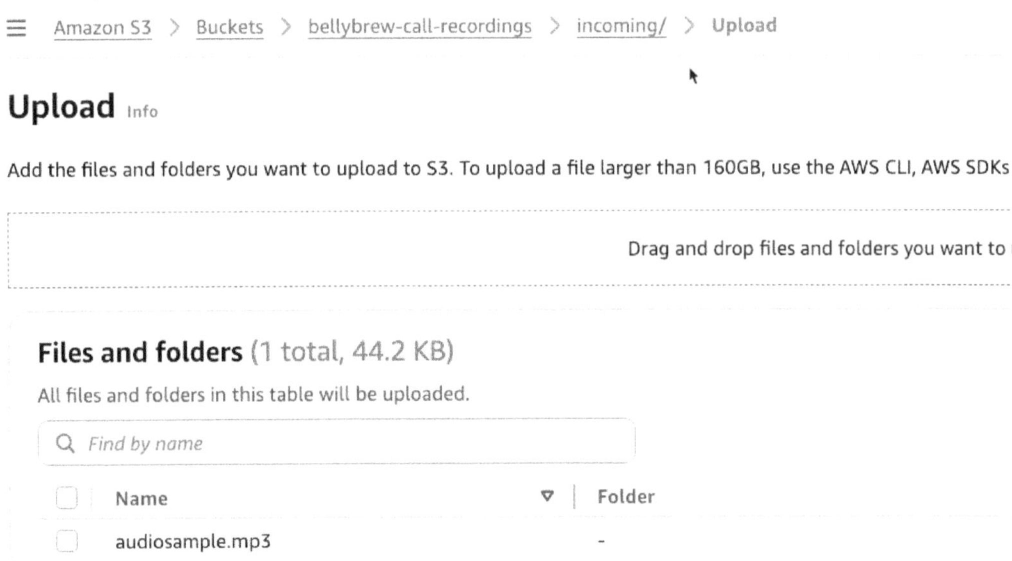

Figure 14.11: Upload the sample audio to the Recordings S3 bucket

7. Click the **Upload** button
8. Wait for a few seconds and navigate to the `Output` folder of the transcription S3 bucket

9. You should then find two files created as shown in *Figure 14.12*:

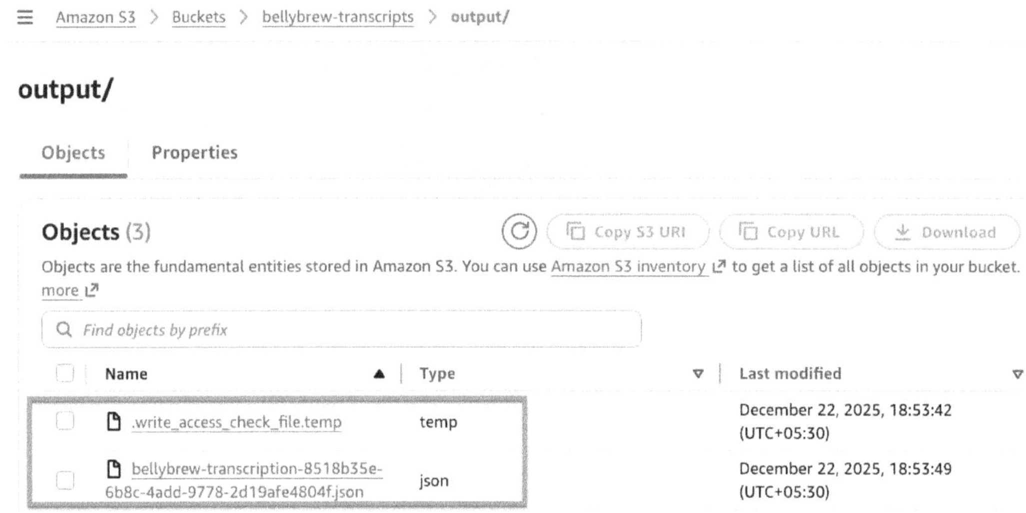

Figure 14.12: Transcripts output files

10. Click to select the JSON file and then click the **Download** button
11. You will now find the JSON transcript file in your downloads folder and you can open it in Notepad or your favorite IDE, such as VS Code. A screenshot of the JSON file is shown in *Figure 14.13*:

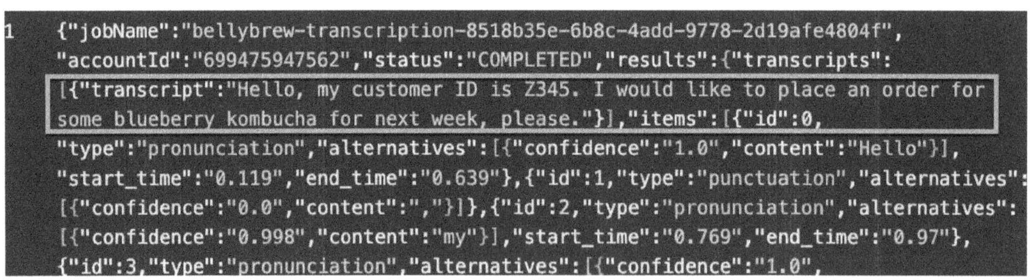

Figure 14.13: Transcript file

12. Notice the highlighted text is the actual transcript of the sample audio

This project task demonstrates how you would use a service like AWS Transcribe as part of an overall architectural design for an application.

Summary

In this chapter, you learned about several Machine Learning tools and AI services. AWS offers a vast array of fully managed machine learning tools that you can use to build complex AI- and ML-driven applications for your business requirements.

As part of your exam preparation, ensure that you are fully aware of core machine learning tools such as the ones discussed in this chapter. Each machine learning service is designed to offer specific functions, such as Amazon Polly, which converts text to speech, and Amazon Transcribe, which can transcribe audio files into text.

Amazon ML tools such as Amazon Rekognition, Polly and others are fully managed, so you do not need to procure or manage your own infrastructure. Even if you need to build your own training models for custom use cases, AWS offers the SageMaker suite of tools and services enabling you to focus on your business goals and objectives.

So far you have manually designed and deployed various infrastructure services such as S3 buckets, EC2 instances, and RDS databases using the AWS management console. However, businesses do not want to spend time building, configuring, and managing underlying infrastructure. Furthermore, using the AWS management console to manually create resources using mouse clicks and keyboard entries often leads to inconsistencies in how components are configured.

The next chapter introduces you to tools to automate the design, build, and deployment of infrastructure using PaaS tools and **Infrastructure as Code** (**IaC**). These services enable you to build infrastructure resources in a manner that is consistent, repeatable, and predictable.

Exam Readiness Drill – Chapter Review Questions

Apart from mastering key concepts, strong test-taking skills under time pressure are essential for acing your certification exam. That's why developing these abilities early in your learning journey is critical.

Exam readiness drills, using the free online practice resources provided with this book, help you progressively improve your time management and test-taking skills while reinforcing the key concepts you've learned.

HOW TO GET STARTED

- Open the link or scan the QR code at the bottom of this page
- If you have unlocked the practice resources already, log in to your registered account. If you haven't, follow the instructions in *Free Benefits with Your Book* section in this book's *Preface* and come back to this page.
- Once you log in, click the START button to start this chapter's quiz
- We recommend attempting a quiz multiple times till you're able to answer most of the questions correctly and well within the time limit.
- You can use the following practice template to help you plan your attempts:

Working On Accuracy		
Attempt	Target	Time Limit
Attempt 1	40% or more	Till the timer runs out
Attempt 2	60% or more	Till the timer runs out
Attempt 3	75% or more	Till the timer runs out
Working On Timing		
Attempt 4	75% or more	1 minute before time limit
Attempt 5	75% or more	2 minutes before time limit
Attempt 6	75% or more	3 minutes before time limit

The above drill is just an example. Design your drills based on your own goals and make the most out of the online quizzes accompanying this book.

Link to this Chapter's Quiz

You need to unlock the online practice resources to access the link below. Check the *Free Benefits with Your Book* section in the *Preface* for detailed instructions on how to do this. You only need to unlock the resources once.

Open Quiz `https://packt.link/clf_c02_ch14` or scan the QR code

Part 4

Automation, Management and Governance, and Security on AWS

Building applications and provisioning infrastructure using **Infrastructure as Code** (**IaC**) and **Platform as a Service** (**PaaS**) solutions helps ensure architectures and resources are deployed in a repeatable and consistent manner. Whether you deploy a set of resources once or multiple times, you can be confident that the architecture is provisioned with the correct configuration and follows the intended design every time. Services such as CloudFormation and Elastic Beanstalk are designed specifically for this purpose. In addition, following DevOps practices and implementing a **Continuous Integration/Continuous Deployment** (**CI/CD**) pipeline enables you to deliver application updates and enhancements more efficiently and reliably.

This part also covers the core management and governance services required to manage, monitor, and support workloads, applications, and infrastructure resources deployed on AWS. Finally, security must be considered from the outset of any cloud solution. You will learn about key security best practices, including encryption and network auditing, and explore a range of tools and services available to help protect your applications and infrastructure from malicious attacks.

This part of the book includes the following chapters:

- *Chapter 15, Automation, Deployment, and Additional AWS Services*
- *Chapter 16, Management and Governance on AWS*
- *Chapter 17, Security Fundamentals and Tools on AWS*

15

Automation, Deployment, and Additional AWS Services

Businesses use cloud services to either offload their on-premises workloads, build hybrid cloud solutions, or develop cloud-native applications. Companies do not want to really concern themselves with provisioning and managing core underlying infrastructure if possible – their primary concern is the ability to host scalable, highly available, secure, and cost-effective applications for their internal business needs or customer-facing requirements.

To that end, businesses want to be able to deploy their applications that consume less administrative burden and ensure smooth ongoing releases and updates. Businesses must focus on what matters most to them – not the underlying heavy lifting of infrastructure services and resources.

In *Chapter 10*, you deployed a complete marketing campaign website for Belly Brew Co. Limited. However, you had to manually provision all the underlying infrastructure resources such as VPCs, EC2 instances, load balancers, auto scaling groups, and databases. What if you could automate the deployment of these resources using a **Platform as a Service** (**PaaS**) tool? Services like **Amazon Elastic Beanstalk** allow you to upload your application code, select the appropriate language and framework, and provision all the necessary resources for you, rather than you having to manually use the console to deploy the required resources.

Another approach is to provision your resources using code – specifically, **Infrastructure as Code** (**IaC**) solutions that require you to use a declarative language script to build out the configurations of your resources. AWS provisions these resources exactly as you define them in your code. This approach ensures repeatable deployments, making it easier to deploy the architecture across multiple accounts and environments with a single click. You get consistency in your deployment configurations, the ability to version your build solutions, and faster provisioning.

In this chapter, you will learn about these automation provisioning tools and the PaaS solution. You will also be introduced to the basic concepts of DevOps and how organizations manage their application releases and updates using **Continuous Integration and Continuous Deployment** (**CI/CD**) tools.

The following topics are covered in this chapter:

- Deploying applications using AWS Elastic Beanstalk
- Architecting and deploying infrastructure using AWS CloudFormation
- Introducing CI/CD with AWS Developer tools
- Introducing Amazon Q

Deploying applications using AWS Elastic Beanstalk

AWS Elastic Beanstalk is a PaaS offering that enables you to upload and deploy your application without having to manually configure any underlying resources. AWS provisions all necessary infrastructure, such as EC2 instances, load balancers, auto scaling groups, and even databases, based on your specified requirements for the application stack. This means you do not need to spend hours managing infrastructure resources, and your developers get to focus on the application layer rather than the minute infrastructure configuration.

The service also offers management and logging capabilities, includes capacity provisioning and health monitoring, and ensures high availability and scalability. You simply upload your code in a supported language and framework, and AWS provisions the necessary resources and deploys your application.

Some of the more popular languages supported include:

- Go
- Java
- Dot Net
- Node.js
- PHP
- Python

In addition to standard applications built using any supported language, Elastic Beanstalk also supports Docker containers. This means you have additional flexibility because you can configure your runtime environments for other languages and platforms that are packaged as containers.

With AWS Elastic Beanstalk, you have the same range of flexibility in how you configure and deploy your resources as any manual deployment—you can choose your EC2 instance type, decide on auto scaling policies, and define how your load balancers should be configured. These features allow you to retain control but without the complexity of manual configurations.

Next, you will learn more about some of the core components of AWS Elastic Beanstalk.

Core components of AWS Elastic Beanstalk

When working with AWS Elastic Beanstalk, you create an **application**. Think of this as a folder in Elastic Beanstalk that groups related environments and versions of the same app. It is within the application container that you manage all the Elastic Beanstalk objects related to your application.

An application can have multiple versions, enabling you to test the differences between them. It is a pointer to a ZIP/WAR file in an Amazon S3 bucket that contains the application code.

Before you deploy your application, you must create an **environment**, which is a collection of AWS resources that will run the application, such as EC2 instances, load balancers, runtimes, and language frameworks. Each environment can only run one application version at a time; however, you can run multiple environments simultaneously. This is how you can host different stages of your application, such as:

- **Development**: used by developers to build new features or fix bugs
- **Testing**: used for alpha and beta testing
- **Production**: the live environment accessed by end users

When you create an environment, you must define the **environment tier**. The environment tier describes how traffic reaches your application and tells AWS what resources to provision. There are two tiers:

- **Web Server environment**: used for applications' HTTP and HTTPS requests (for example, websites and API calls)
- **Worker environment**: used for background processing applications that receive jobs from a queue

Figure 15.1 depicts the two Elastic Beanstalk environment tiers for a typical application that comprises a frontend and backend workload.

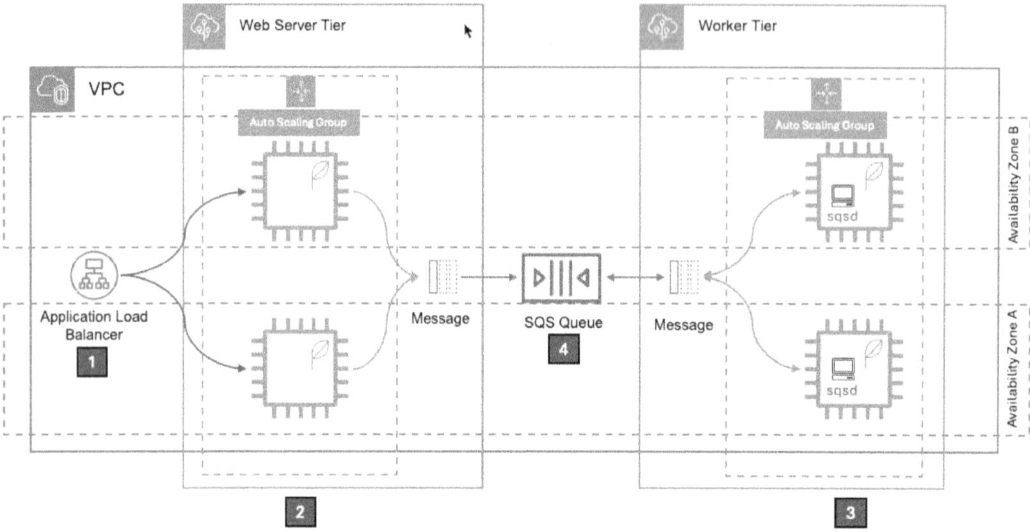

Figure 15.1: AWS Elastic Beanstalk environments

The following are the key components of the architecture as depicted in *Figure 15.1*:

1. The application is served by an Application Load Balancer that accepts requests using standard HTTP and HTTPS protocols. This is typical of a website or web application delivery.
2. The Web Server Tier comprises the EC2 instances, which host the frontend user interface (UI) of the application and may be supported by an auto-scaling group that is managed by the Elastic Beanstalk service. Incoming requests to the Application Load Balancer are evenly distributed to the available EC2 instances across the availability zones.
3. The Worker Tier is designed to process background application logic. It is supported by an auto-scaling group to scale as required based on the number of requests held in the SQS queue, which is designed to decouple the application stack. The Elastic Beanstalk service will install a daemon on each EC2 instance in the fleet. The daemon is used to read messages from the SQS queue and send this data to the application servers running in the worker environment for processing.
4. The Amazon SQS queue is used to store messages as requests from the front-end web server tier, which the resources in the worker tier will pull based on capacity and availability. This ensures a decoupled architecture and reduces overburdening the backend application services.

In this section, you learned about the AWS Elastic Beanstalk service, which is a PaaS solution. The service is designed to handle the infrastructure heavy lifting, provisioning, managing, and maintaining all the required underlying resources so that developers can focus on their application code and business logic.

In the next section, you will learn about another automation tool designed to help you architect and deploy infrastructure resources using **Infrastructure as Code** (**IaC**) – specifically, AWS CloudFormation.

Architecting and deploying infrastructure using AWS CloudFormation

Infrastructure as Code (**IaC**) is a process by which you define and describe your infrastructure resources and their configurations in a scripted template written using a data serialization language such as YAML or JSON.

Data-serialization languages are used to convert structured data into a format that can be stored, transmitted, and read by another system, without losing its meaning.

AWS CloudFormation uses data-serialization languages like YAML and JSON to read the structured description of your AWS resources, build a dependency graph, and then provision the infrastructure automatically. This is also known as declarative scripting.

This is different from imperative scripting using languages like Python or Java, which require you to explicitly describe the step-by-step instructions on how to carry out those configurations.

The following table compares the two styles of scripting:

Feature	**Declarative IaC**	**Imperative Scripting**
Focus	Defines the desired end state of infrastructure	Defines the step-by-step actions to be performed
How It Works	The tool determines how to achieve the target state	The script explicitly controls every action
Idempotency	Typically idempotent and repeatable	May produce different results if run multiple times
Examples	AWS CloudFormation, Terraform	Bash, PowerShell, Python scripts

Table 15.1: Declarative Infrastructure as Code (IaC) vs. Imperative Scripting

The next section provides further details on how these templates are defined.

CloudFormation templates

AWS CloudFormation uses templates, which are text files written in JSON or YAML. The script describes the resources to provision, along with mandatory and optional configuration options required to provision the resources.

For example, if you need to deploy an EC2 instance in the default VPC, in a default subnet, and attach it to the default security group, you can provide a CloudFormation template such as the YAML code below:

```
AWSTemplateFormatVersion: "2010-09-09"
Description: >
  Basic CloudFormation template to launch a single EC2 instance in the default
VPC and default subnet.
Resources:
  MyEC2Instance:
    Type: AWS::EC2::Instance
    Properties:
      # Use an Amazon Linux 2023 AMI us-east-1 Region (update AMI ID per region!)
      ImageId: ami-07ff62358b87c7116
      InstanceType: t2.micro   # Define Instance Type
      # By not specifying a SubnetId, EC2 will launch in the default subnet
      # By not specifying the Security Group, EC2 will launch with the default
Security Group
      Tags:
        - Key: Name
          Value: MyFirstCFNInstance
```

Some key points to note in the code:

- The AWS template format version is set to `"2010-09-09"` and is the current and only supported version.
- A `Description` field is used to explain the purpose of the template.
- There are various sections of the templates, such as `Parameters`, `Mappings`, `Resources`, `Outputs`, and others.
- The `Resources` section is the only mandatory section. This section is used to describe what AWS resources will be created. In this case, it's the `AWS::EC2::Instance` resource.

- An `AMI ID` must be specified when launching an EC2 instance. AMIs are region-specific, so you must provide an AMI ID that exists in the region where the resources are being provisioned. You can use the `Mappings` section to define AMIs based on the region the template is being deployed in, making the template more dynamic.
- Some properties such as `InstanceType`, `SubnetId`, and `SecurityGroupIds` may need to be defined depending on your requirements. If `SubnetId` and `SecurityGroupIds` are not specified, AWS automatically uses the `default subnet and default security group` of the default VPC.

Once the template is defined, it is uploaded to AWS CloudFormation to create a **stack**, which provisions the actual AWS resources. CloudFormation passes the properties to the EC2 service. When `SubnetId` or `SecurityGroupIds` is missing, EC2 automatically applies the default VPC, default subnet, and default security group.

In the next section, you will learn more about CloudFormation stacks.

CloudFormation stacks

When you create and upload a CloudFormation template, you deploy what is known as a **Stack**. A stack is a collection of one or more AWS resources that are deployed and managed as a single unit using CloudFormation. For example, using a single template, you can provision a VPC, load balancers, auto-scaling groups to provision EC2 instances, and even a backend Amazon RDS database, all part of that single stack.

How you build out your stack deployment is also critical. For example, you can use more advanced techniques to modularize the various infrastructure elements of your environment as separate templates. You can then use either:

- **Cross-Stack References**: Where you build a base stack, such as a VPC, and allow other stacks to reference values from it (for example, Subnet IDs or Security Groups) so that compute or database resources can be deployed into the same underlying environment without being part of the same stack.
- **Nested Stacks**: Where you modularize each infrastructure element, such as VPCs, EC2 instances, and RDS instances, as separate templates and invoke them from a main parent template to build a complete end-to-end infrastructure for an application. This allows you to organize infrastructure into logical components while still managing everything through a single parent stack, making updates and ongoing management easier

When you need to delete the resources deployed by CloudFormation, you simply delete the stack. AWS will then terminate all the resources it created following your template. This ensures orphan resources are not left lingering, which often happens when you manually delete several infrastructure resources.

Sometimes you may need to update or modify a stack. For example, when you need to upgrade an EC2 instance type from a t3.micro to a t3.large. In the next section, you will learn more about how you can achieve this using **AWS CloudFormation Change Sets**.

AWS CloudFormation change sets

If you need to change the configuration of your cloud resources to cope with changing requirements or demand, you need a way to upgrade or modify existing resources without having to rebuild the entire stack. This is particularly true if the change you need to make should not affect the application.

AWS CloudFormation offers a feature known as **Change Sets**, which is where you upload a modified version of your template or even supply a new template as a *change* to the existing stack configuration. AWS CloudFormation will then provide a visual representation of your proposed changes and notify you if the change will require resource replacements.

In *Figure 15.2*, you will note that a change set has been requested to upgrade the EC2 instance type from a `t3.micro` to a `t3.small`.

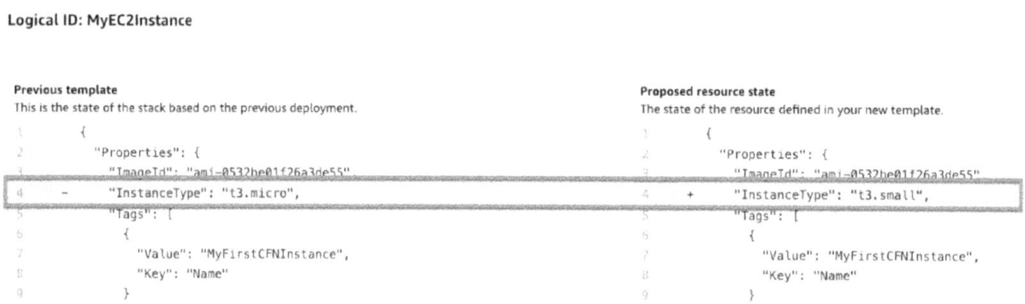

Figure 15.2: Change Set request to upgrade the EC2 instance type from t3.micro to t3.small

Once you have reviewed the proposed change, you can then execute the change set, and AWS will perform the modifications as required.

Change sets are particularly useful in highlighting how the change proposed will impact the existing architecture and if any resources will be affected. You can then take any necessary precautions, such as performing backups and taking manual snapshots before executing the change.

AWS CloudFormation makes it easy to build infrastructure solutions in a consistent, repeatable manner with predictable outcomes. You can build a wide range of templates to quickly deploy your resources using CloudFormation rather than manually configuring each resource using the web console, which often leads to inconsistencies and errors.

In addition to automating your infrastructure provisioning and deployment using tools like Elastic Beanstalk and CloudFormation, you must also consider your application lifecycle that runs on the provisioned infrastructure. Modern architectures recommend applying **DevOps** principles and best practices when designing how your applications are deployed, updated, and released into production environments. The next section introduces you to this concept and the tools offered by AWS to build an effective DevOps pipeline.

Introducing CI/CD with AWS developer tools

Managing the application lifecycle is crucial to ensure that users always have access to the latest and most reliable version of an application, without bugs or performance issues. This means development teams must continuously enhance the application, introduce new features based on customer feedback, and resolve issues in a timely manner. In addition, releasing the application into production must follow a carefully planned strategy, ensuring that new features and bug fixes are deployed with minimal disruption and that rollbacks are simple if something goes wrong.

DevOps is a set of practices that brings development (Dev) and operations (Ops) teams together to collaborate across the entire application lifecycle. Rather than delivering large releases every few months or once a year, DevOps promotes small, frequent, and incremental releases aligned with the principles of CI/CD (Continuous Integration and Continuous Delivery/Deployment). Instead of working in silos, DevOps encourages automation and continuous feedback, allowing applications to be released faster, more reliably, and with fewer errors.

AWS provides a wide range of tools and services to build, test, deploy, and operate applications, while improving quality, stability, and customer satisfaction.

In the following subsections, we will look at a high-level overview of some of these tools.

AWS CodeCommit

Developers write and maintain code for their applications, which must be continuously updated, revised, and versioned as new features are added and bugs are fixed. **AWS CodeCommit** is a fully managed, secure source control service that hosts Git-based repositories, enabling teams to manage source code versions and track changes efficiently.

CodeCommit can be used to store application source code, configuration files, scripts, and documentation. It works with standard Git tools and commands, making it easy for developers who already use Git on other platforms to adopt CodeCommit without changing their existing workflows.

AWS CodeBuild

AWS CodeBuild is a fully managed build service. Developers use CodeBuild to compile source code, run unit tests, and build artifacts that can then be deployed on AWS. There is no need to provision your own build servers, and the service offers prepackaged build environments for popular languages and build tools. All you need to do is provide a buildspec file, which is a collection of build commands and related settings, in YAML format. AWS CodeBuild uses this file to run a build.

Finally, you are charged on a pay-as-you-go model, making the offering very cost-effective rather than hosting your own build servers.

AWS CodeDeploy

Once an application has been built and compiled, **AWS CodeDeploy** can be used to automate the deployment of the application to Amazon EC2 instances, **Amazon Elastic Container Service** (**ECS**), AWS Lambda functions, and on-premises servers. CodeDeploy helps ensure that application updates are delivered in a consistent and repeatable way.

CodeDeploy deploys application revisions and supporting artifacts that are typically stored in services such as Amazon S3 or external repositories like GitHub and BitBucket. The service enables rapid and reliable application releases, including updating Lambda function versions, while helping to avoid application downtime during deployments. This is achieved using different deployment strategies, such as in-place deployments, where instances are updated gradually (for example, by taking a defined number of instances offline at a time), and **blue/green deployments**, where the existing application version (blue environment) continues to run while a new version is deployed to a separate environment (green environment). Once testing and approvals are complete, traffic can be shifted to the new version.

One of the key benefits of AWS CodeDeploy is its **centralized control** over application deployments, including the ability to monitor deployment status, stop deployments, and roll back automatically if errors occur.

AWS CodePipeline

AWS CodePipeline is a fully managed continuous delivery solution you can use to automate your application releases and updates. CodePipeline integrates with the previously mentioned tools (CodeCommit, CodeBuild, and CodeDeploy) to automate the build, test, and deployment of your application releases every time your code changes, as depicted in the following workflow in *Figure 15.3*:

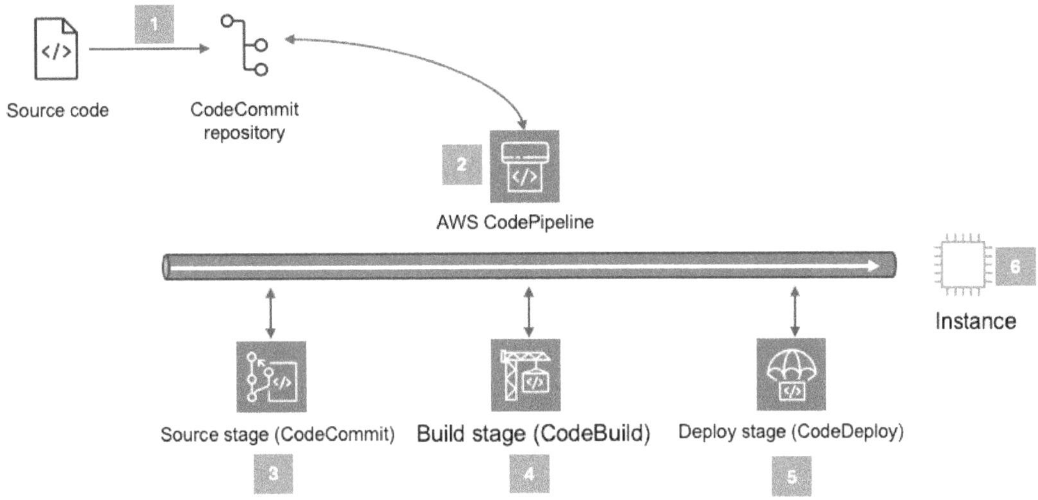

Figure 15.3: AWS CodePipeline orchestration

The following steps explain the workflow of the AWS CodePipeline service:

1. The developer pushes the source code to the AWS CodeCommit repository
2. A commit to CodeCommit triggers an AWS CodePipeline workflow
3. The Source stage of CodePipeline pulls the latest code from the CodeCommit repository
4. The Build stage uses AWS CodeBuild to compile, test, and package the application
5. The Deploy stage uses AWS CodeDeploy to deploy the application
6. AWS CodeDeploy then deploys the application to the target EC2 instance

CodePipeline doesn't store code, build applications, or deploy workloads; it simply orchestrates the entire CI/CD workflow.

In the next section, you will learn how developers can use AI tools on AWS to help them write code and design application workflows using a product called **Amazon Q**.

Introducing Amazon Q

Amazon Q is a fully managed generative AI service that acts as an intelligent assistant for working with AWS. Using **natural language processing** (**NLP**), you can ask questions about AWS architectures, best practices, troubleshooting, cost, and the state of your own resources — all in plain English.

Amazon Q is powered by Amazon Bedrock, a fully managed service that provides access to a wide range of **foundation models** (**FMs**) through standard API calls. This is what allows

Amazon Q to understand your questions and respond with context-aware, AWS-specific guidance.

In practical terms, Amazon Q supports you throughout the application lifecycle. For example, you can describe a requirement — such as building a secure web application or creating an Amazon ECS Fargate environment — and Amazon Q can suggest suitable AWS services aligned with best practices, recommend architectural patterns, and explain unfamiliar configurations. Directly inside the AWS Management Console, you can also ask Amazon Q about your existing resources and costs and have it return the answers as tables and charts. This enables even non-developers to move from idea to working solution faster while staying aligned with AWS Well-Architected design principles.

In the next section, you will learn how to deploy an Amazon EC2 instance using the AWS CloudFormation service. Understanding the fundamentals of IaC is critical for anyone seeking a solid career in cloud computing across a wide range of roles. By using IaC, you can ensure that your solutions are provisioned in a consistent, repeatable, and reliable manner.

Project task 15 – Deploying an EC2 instance using AWS CloudFormation

In this project task, you will deploy a simple YAML template using AWS CloudFormation to provision an EC2 instance in the us-east-1 (North Virginia) region. This will give you hands-on experience in how CloudFormation templates work and how you can provision consistent and repeatable workloads using templates.

Technical requirements

To complete the project exercises in this chapter, ensure you are logged in to your AWS Development account as the IAM user Alice to complete the project tasks. Also, ensure that you download the YAML template from the Packt GitHub repo at `https://github.com/PacktPublishing/AWS-Certified-Cloud-Practitioner-CLF-C02-Exam-Guide`. Store the template on your desktop for easy access, as you will need to update it with the correct EC2 AMI ID before uploading it to AWS CloudFormation.

Project task 15.1 – Modifying the YAML template

In this project task, you will update the YAML template that you downloaded from the GitHub repository. Specifically, you will be deploying the EC2 instance in the `us-east-1` (North Virginia) region, and you must ensure the AMI you use for the EC2 instance is available in this region.

1. Log in to the AWS Management console as Alice. Use the search bar at the top of the console to search for and navigate to the EC2 service

2. Ensure that you are in the `us-east-1` region by selecting it from the drop-down list in the top left-hand corner of the webpage
3. From the left-hand menu, click on **Instances**
4. In the right-hand pane, click **Launch instance**. Note that you will not actually launch an instance; this procedure is just so you can obtain the latest AMI ID from the console screen
5. In the **Launch an instance** webpage that appears, select `Amazon Linux AMI` from the **Quick Start** tab in the **Application and OS Images (Amazon Machine Image)** section
6. From the **Amazon Machine Image (AMI)** drop-down list, ensure that the **Amazon Linux 2023 kernel-6-1 AMI** is selected
7. Next, make a note of the `AMI ID` for this operating system as per the following screenshot in *Figure 15.4*. You will update the template you downloaded from our GitHub repository with this AMI ID.

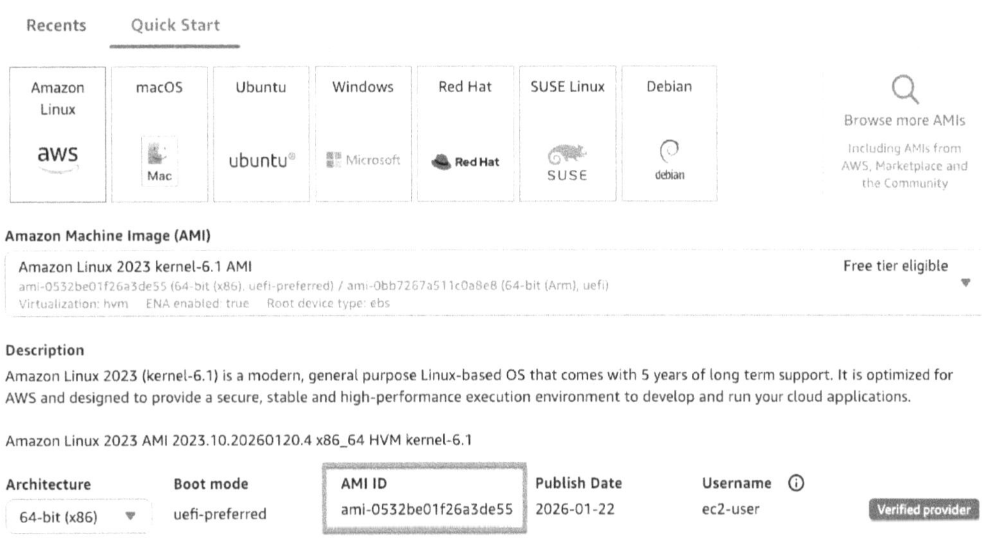

Figure 15.4: Amazon Linux AMI ID

8. Scroll to the bottom of the webpage and click the **Cancel** link to cancel the instance launch
9. Next, open the YAML template you downloaded from the GitHub repository using Notepad or your favorite IDE, such as Visual Studio Code

10. Replace the AMI ID Placeholder with the actual ID you noted earlier in *Step 8*. See the screenshot in *Figure 15.5* – ensure that you remove the square brackets '[ ]' too.

```
AWSTemplateFormatVersion: "2010-09-09"
Description: >
  Basic CloudFormation template to launch a single EC2 instance in the default VPC and de
Resources:
  MyEC2Instance:
    Type: AWS::EC2::Instance
    Properties:
      # Use an Amazon Linux 2023 AMI us-east-1 Region (update AMI ID per region!)
      ImageId: [Provide AMI ID]
      InstanceType: t2.micro   # Define Instance Type
      # By not specifying a SubnetId, EC2 will launch in the default subnet
      # By not specifying the Security Group, EC2 will launch with the default Security G
      Tags:
        - Key: Name
          Value: MyFirstCFNInstance
```

Figure 15.5: CloudFormation YAML template – Replace the placeholder with AMI ID

11. Save the file

In the next project task, you will use this template to create a CloudFormation stack and deploy an EC2 instance.

Project task 15.2 – Creating a CloudFormation stack

In this project task, you will upload the amended YAML template and create a CloudFormation stack to deploy an EC2 instance in a default VPC in the `us-east-1` region. The EC2 instance will be deployed in a default subnet and associated with the default security group.

1. From the AWS management console, search for and navigate to the CloudFormation service
2. Click the Hamburger icon in the far left of the webpage to expand the CloudFormation menu, as shown in *Figure 15.6*:

Figure 15.6: Expand the CloudFormation menu

3. In the right-hand pane, click the **Create stack** button
4. Ensure that **Choose an existing template** is selected in the **Prepare template** section
5. Click the **Upload a template file** option in the **Specify template** section of the webpage
6. Click the **Choose file** button that appears and then navigate to the location of your template file, which you updated earlier, and select the file. The file name will appear in the text box below the **Choose file** button as shown in *Figure 15.7*:

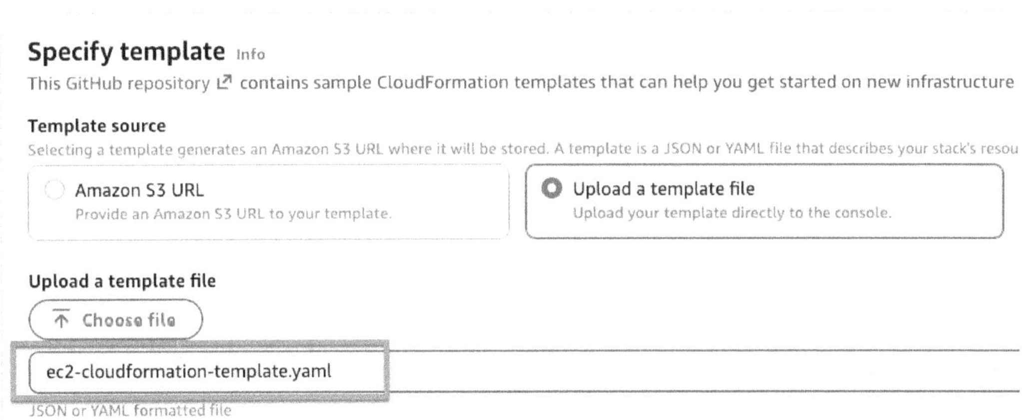

Figure 15.7: Specify YAML template to build stack

7. Click **Next**
8. Provide a name for your stack, such as `MyFirstStack`
9. Click **Next**

10. The **Configure stack options** webpage that appears enables you to define additional options such as tags and permissions. For now, simply scroll to the bottom of the webpage and click **Next**.
11. Review your configuration in the **Review and create webpage**, scroll to the bottom of the page, and click **Submit**
12. AWS CloudFormation will now use the template to deploy your EC2 instance. You will be redirected to the **Events** tab of the stack, as shown in *Figure 15.8*, where you can monitor the events of the deployment.

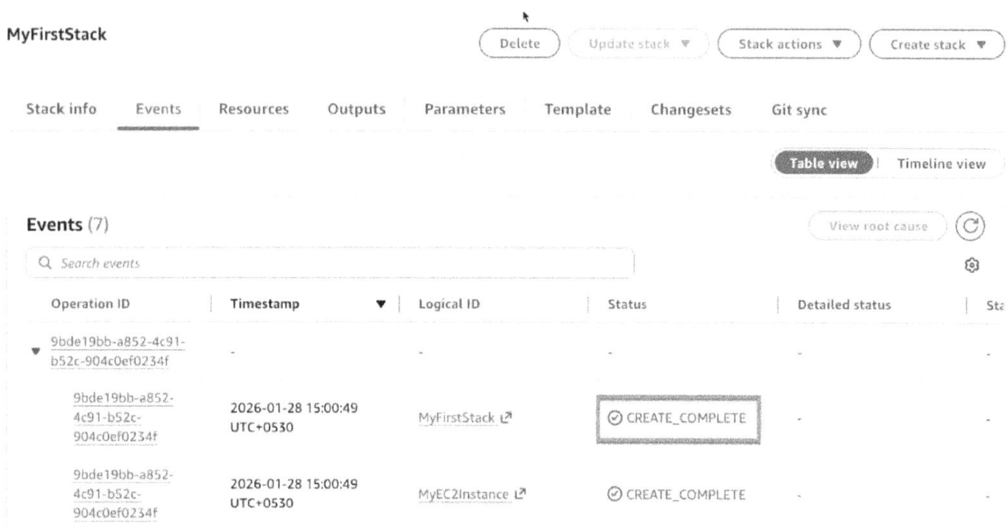

Figure 15.8: Events tab of the stack

13. With the stack now fully deployed and the status defined as `CREATE_COMPLETE`, you have now successfully deployed your stack
14. From the search bar at the top of the AWS management console, search for and navigate to the EC2 web console
15. Click **Instances** from the left-hand menu
16. In the right-hand pane, you should see your EC2 instance, which was deployed using CloudFormation as shown in *Figure 15.9*:

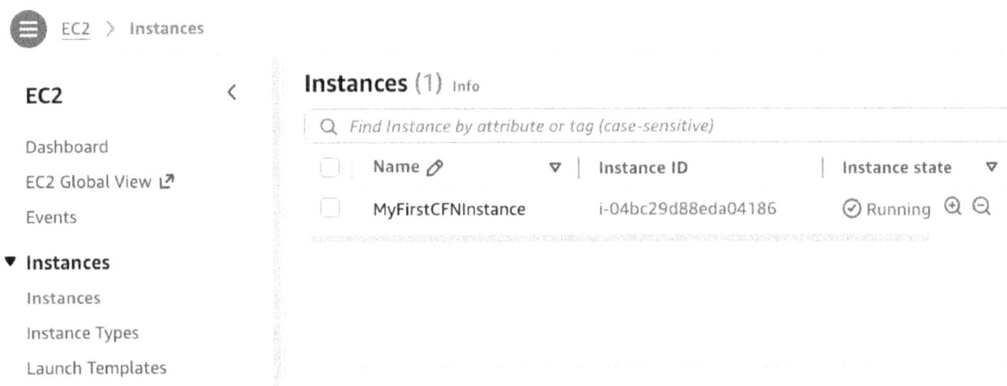

Figure 15.9: Confirmation of EC2 deployment using CloudFormation

Your instance is now fully deployed and in the running state. In the next section, you will terminate this instance by deleting the CloudFormation template.

Project task 15.3 – Cleaning up

In this project task, you will terminate the EC2 instance by deleting the CloudFormation stack. You should not manually terminate resources deployed by CloudFormation as this causes a configuration drift with the stack. Always delete the stack in CloudFormation, and the service will delete any resources that belong to the stack. You can also define deletion policies to retain any resources you might need after stack deletions, such as a backup of a database.

1. Navigate back to the AWS CloudFormation console
2. From the left-hand menu, click on **Stacks**
3. In the right-hand pane, select your stack
4. Click the **Delete stack** button
5. In the pop-up window that appears, type in the name of your stack in the text box and click the **Delete stack** button

Your stack will now be deleted, and any resources created, such as the EC2 instance, will be terminated.

Summary

In this chapter, you discovered how businesses want to be able to focus on their application design and development rather than the underlying heavy lifting associated with infrastructure provisioning, deployment, and management. Companies do not want to spend hours maintaining and managing their infrastructure and instead need to focus on building new features and resolving bugs within their applications.

Furthermore, the ability to automate infrastructure provisioning and management in a repeatable and consistent manner is critical to avoid potential discrepancies in minute configuration items of those resources, which often lead to confusion and delayed troubleshooting exercises.

To help customers automate and manage their infrastructure resources efficiently, AWS offers PaaS tools such as Elastic Beanstalk and IaC solutions such as CloudFormation.

AWS Elastic Beanstalk is designed to help developers focus on their code. Developers can upload their code in a supported language and framework and have Elastic Beanstalk provision all the necessary infrastructure resources to host the application.

AWS CloudFormation is an IaC platform, enabling you to define your infrastructure resources using YAML or JSON templates. You can create templates that define complete end-to-end architecture patterns and deploy the required resources as stacks fully managed by the CloudFormation service.

Finally, you learned about various developer tools that support your application and **software development lifecycle** (**SDLC**) process using CI/CD services such as AWS CodeCommit, CodeBuild, CodeDeploy, and CodePipeline.

In the next chapter, you will learn about monitoring and managing your resources on AWS. While architecting, building, and deploying solutions play an important role as a Cloud Practitioner, supporting existing environments, managing, and maintaining workloads so that they operate at optimal levels is just as critical. The chapter introduces you to tools that help you analyze the health and performance of your resources and take appropriate actions to ensure reliability and stability. You will also learn how to audit access and enforce governance while also understanding concepts related to change management. In addition, you will learn about various tools to help you efficiently manage fleets of resources.

Exam Readiness Drill – Chapter Review Questions

Apart from mastering key concepts, strong test-taking skills under time pressure are essential for acing your certification exam. That's why developing these abilities early in your learning journey is critical.

Exam readiness drills, using the free online practice resources provided with this book, help you progressively improve your time management and test-taking skills while reinforcing the key concepts you've learned.

HOW TO GET STARTED

- Open the link or scan the QR code at the bottom of this page
- If you have unlocked the practice resources already, log in to your registered account. If you haven't, follow the instructions in *Free Benefits with Your Book* section in this book's *Preface* and come back to this page.
- Once you log in, click the START button to start this chapter's quiz
- We recommend attempting a quiz multiple times till you're able to answer most of the questions correctly and well within the time limit.
- You can use the following practice template to help you plan your attempts:

Working On Accuracy		
Attempt	**Target**	**Time Limit**
Attempt 1	40% or more	Till the timer runs out
Attempt 2	60% or more	Till the timer runs out
Attempt 3	75% or more	Till the timer runs out
Working On Timing		
Attempt 4	75% or more	1 minute before time limit
Attempt 5	75% or more	2 minutes before time limit
Attempt 6	75% or more	3 minutes before time limit

The above drill is just an example. Design your drills based on your own goals and make the most out of the online quizzes accompanying this book.

Link to this Chapter's Quiz

You need to unlock the online practice resources to access the link below. Check the *Free Benefits with Your Book* section in the *Preface* for detailed instructions on how to do this. You only need to unlock the resources once.

Open Quiz `https://packt.link/clf_c02_ch15`or scan the QR code

16

Management and Governance on AWS

As a cloud practitioner, you must ensure that the wide range of resources you provision to host your application are highly available, secure, and perform as expected. You must continuously monitor your underlying resources and identify any potential performance issues that could cause bottlenecks. These issues should be addressed at the earliest and, with the help of monitoring and logging solutions available on AWS, even prevented.

You must also be able to audit your environment to ensure that you prevent any unauthorized access or deployments and detect anomalies that may indicate performance or security issues. Furthermore, you must enforce proper change management processes to ensure that all changes made to resources are compliant with organizational requirements and to prevent unauthorized changes.

Finally, as part of your day-to-day management, you must also be able to effectively manage your resources—such as patching, performing updates, and automating maintenance tasks.

In this chapter, you will look at a series of AWS services that enable you to effectively monitor and manage your AWS resources. You can use these services to ensure your resources operate efficiently and within acceptable performance standards. You can also audit and log all requests made in your AWS account to ensure you have a trail of all activities, enabling you to stay compliant. Finally, you can enforce rules to ensure resources provisioned, or changes made to existing ones, are in accordance with business goals and objectives.

The following topics are covered in this chapter:

- Observing workloads with Amazon CloudWatch
- Meeting compliance requirements with AWS CloudTrail
- Managing change control with AWS Config
- Automating resource administration with AWS Systems Manager
- Improving workloads with AWS Trusted Advisor

Observing workloads with Amazon CloudWatch

Amazon CloudWatch is a fully managed monitoring and logging service designed to help you monitor and analyze the health of your AWS resources and applications. With Amazon CloudWatch, you can see how your resources are performing in real time. You can collect measurements (called **metrics**) from your resources hosted on AWS as well as from on-premises locations.

A metric represents a time-ordered set of data points that are published to CloudWatch. An example of a metric is CPU Utilization for an EC2 instance, expressed as a percentage over time. If a particular instance is consuming more than 95% CPU utilization for an extended period, you may wish to investigate it, as this could affect performance for your end users.

You can also use Amazon CloudWatch to collect application log data as key-value pairs, which can be used to identify issues with applications such as errors, timeouts, and more. Thus, in addition to capturing metric data from resources such as EC2 instances, RDS databases, and DynamoDB tables, you can also obtain logging information for applications, such as Apache web servers, Nginx, WordPress, and more.

Some typical use cases for Amazon CloudWatch include the following:

- **Infrastructure monitoring and troubleshooting:** Monitor resource metrics and logs and visualize trends over time to identify potential bottlenecks. This can be used to conduct root cause analysis to resolve incidents and problems.
- **Proactive resource optimization:** Configure alarms that monitor metric values and are triggered when defined thresholds are crossed for a specified period. You can also define automated remediation actions, such as configuring Auto Scaling to launch additional resources to distribute load or restarting or terminating instances.

- **Log analytics:** Analyze log files from a wide range of application sources to identify operational issues, bugs, and potential security exploits, as well as to determine application performance and health.

In the next section, you will learn more about how Amazon CloudWatch organizes and categorizes metrics data so that it is easy to consume and analyze.

CloudWatch namespaces, dimensions, and metrics

Before using Amazon CloudWatch, it is important to understand how the service captures metric and log data and how it categorizes this data. Amazon CloudWatch uses the concepts of **namespaces**, **dimensions**, and **metrics**. Let's look at them in a bit more detail:

- **CloudWatch namespaces:** A **namespace** is a logical container used to group metric data that belongs to a specific AWS service. The screenshot depicted in *Figure 16.1* showcases a few common namespaces. So, for example, you have a namespace called **AWS/EC2** to capture all metrics related to your EC2 instances.

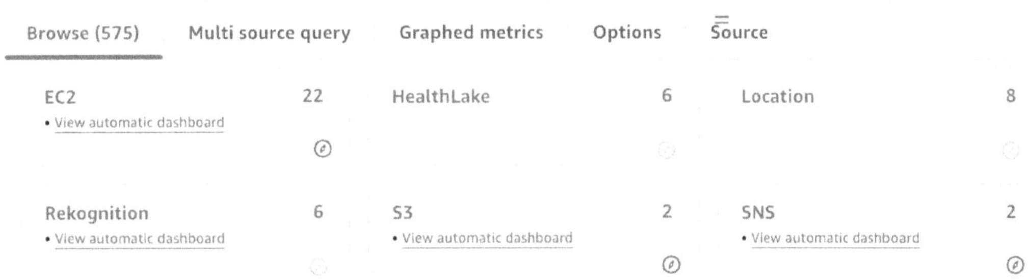

Figure 16.1: CloudWatch metrics namespaces

  In addition to the standard namespaces defined by AWS, you can create custom namespaces to capture custom metrics, such as those related to third-party applications running on your EC2 instances.

- **CloudWatch dimensions:** Dimensions represent the individual resource that you are monitoring. For example, dimensions related to your EC2 instances include the individual instance ID whose metrics you are monitoring, as depicted in *Figure 16.2*:

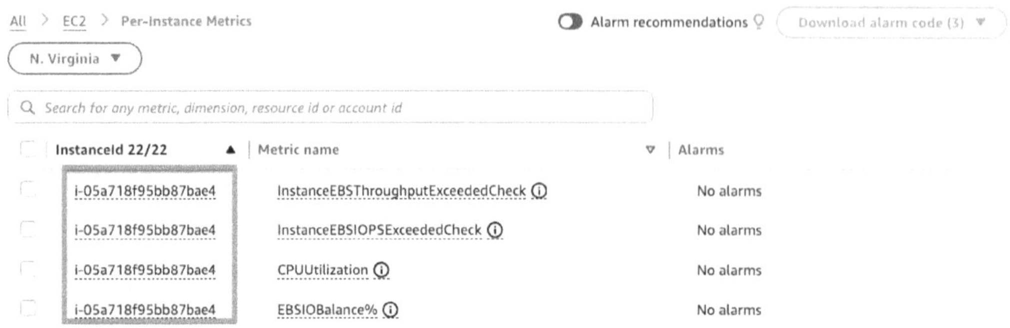

Figure 16.2: Individual instances represent the dimensions of the EC2 namespace

- **CloudWatch metrics:** These are the individual measurements for the resource you are monitoring, such as CPU Utilization, Network Bytes In/Out, Disk Read/Write, and more.

In the next section, you will explore CloudWatch metrics in greater depth.

More on CloudWatch metrics

Amazon CloudWatch metrics are time-ordered sets of data points. Resources that you provision on AWS will report a wide range of standard metrics to CloudWatch by default. For example, you could monitor the CPU Utilization metric consumed by a specific EC2 instance as a percentage over a period. This can help you track performance trends, identify spikes, and determine if the resource is being overutilized.

Figure 16.3 depicts the CPU Utilization of an EC2 instance running in the us-east-1 region. This instance is a t3.micro instance (it has 1 vCPU and 1 GB RAM).

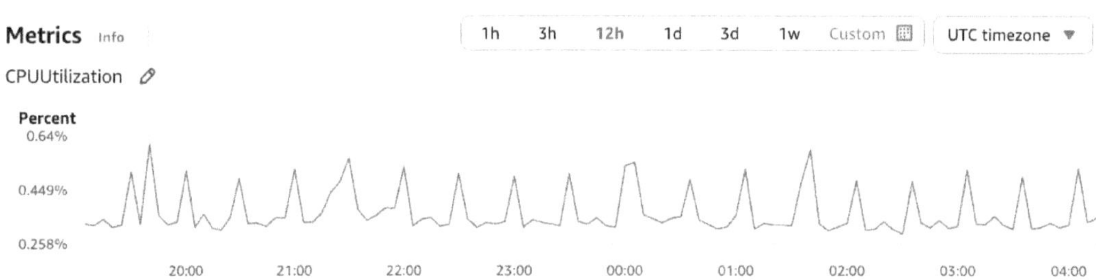

Figure 16.3: CPU utilization for a t3.micro instance over a 12-hour period

Using the data points captured, you can identify any bottlenecks or potential issues over time.

Amazon CloudWatch offers a wide range of built-in metrics across its vast array of services and resources. However, you may also need to collect custom metrics, as discussed next:

- **Built-in metrics:** Amazon CloudWatch allows you to collect a wide range of default metrics. These metrics are captured from the underlying infrastructure, such as the host machines and the hypervisor layer. An example of this is CPU utilization, which captures how much CPU is being consumed from the allocated capacity at the hypervisor level. Other examples include disk read/write and data transfer metrics.
- **Custom metrics:** If you need to capture operating system-level or application-level metrics, you must install a CloudWatch agent on the resource, such as an EC2 instance. Examples include web application load times, request error rates, and more. Another example of a custom metric is operating system memory consumption. This is because, unlike CPU utilization, which monitors underlying hardware CPU usage patterns, memory metrics operate at the OS level and are not monitored by default.

While capturing all these different metrics over a period is useful, the ability to present the data in an *easily digestible* form is crucial for quickly identifying trends and issues. Amazon CloudWatch offers the ability to create custom dashboards, which are discussed next.

CloudWatch dashboards

Amazon CloudWatch offers a dashboard feature enabling you to present captured metrics and logging data that offer visualization capabilities through charts and graphs.

You can use CloudWatch dashboards to provide insights into your resources' health across AWS accounts and regions using the cross-account functionality and integrate this with AWS organizations. This enables you to create cross-account dashboards.

An example of how you can represent your captured metrics data using dashboards is depicted in *Figure 16.4*:

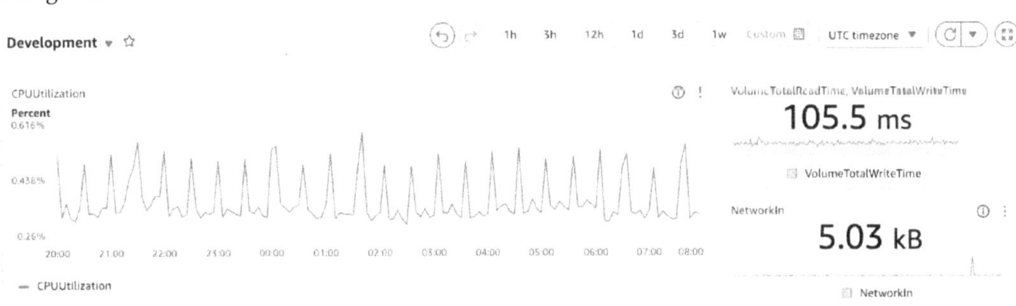

Figure 16.4: Amazon CloudWatch dashboards

In addition to monitoring your resources using CloudWatch dashboards, you can also create alarms that trigger when specified threshold values are breached. This is discussed in the next section.

CloudWatch alarms

You can configure **CloudWatch alarms** to monitor a given resource's metrics, for example, the average CPU utilization of an EC2 instance. If the metric crosses a specific threshold value that you define, it can trigger an alarm. Note that the alarm will only trigger once the threshold value is breached for more than a defined period. This helps prevent false positives caused by momentary spikes.

For example, you may wish to trigger an alarm if the CPU utilization on an EC2 instance is over 90% for more than 15 minutes.

CloudWatch alarms can be in any one of three states:

- **OK:** Occurs when the metric is within the range defined as acceptable
- **Alarm:** Occurs when the metric is outside the specified range. This can be either above or below the defined threshold
- **Insufficient data:** Occurs when the data needed to determine the alarm state is missing or incomplete. Typically, an alarm is in this state when it is first created, while it begins collecting metric data

Once an alarm has been triggered, you can automate certain actions to be taken in response. These include:

- **Simple Notification Service (SNS) notification:** You can send an automatic notification to an administrator or push the notification to an application or a Lambda function to perform an automated remediation task
- **Auto Scaling action:** For EC2 instances, you can trigger an Auto Scaling action when the alarm is triggered to launch or terminate instances as required, ensuring that the metric falls back within acceptable ranges
- **EC2 action:** You can configure an alarm to trigger an EC2 instance action, such as stopping or restarting the instance. For certain instance types, you can also perform an instance recovery, which means the instance is relaunched on different host hardware. This is particularly useful if the underlying hardware on which the EC2 instance was originally running is experiencing an issue

You can also publish your alarms to CloudWatch dashboards, giving you instant visibility when alarms are triggered.

In addition to metrics, CloudWatch allows you to ingest logging data across both AWS services and third-party applications. **CloudWatch Logs** is discussed in the next section.

CloudWatch logs

Amazon CloudWatch also offers the ability to capture logging data across a wide range of AWS services, as well as third-party applications that you host on Amazon EC2 instances, Amazon ECS clusters, and AWS Lambda functions. For example, you can ingest VPC Flow Logs into CloudWatch Logs, which allows you to analyze network traffic flowing into and out of your VPCs. You can also capture logs from services such as AWS CloudTrail, Amazon Route 53, and many more. Examples of third-party application logs that you can capture include web server access logs, error logs, and operating system event logs.

You can ingest logs regardless of their source, and they are stored as a series of time-ordered events that you can query, analyze, search, and filter for specific patterns or error codes. You can also visually analyze your logging data using CloudWatch dashboards.

Logging data can be retained indefinitely for historical analysis, although many organizations configure retention periods ranging from 1 day to 10 years to meet compliance requirements. You can also archive your logging data to Amazon S3 buckets and use one of the Amazon S3 Glacier storage classes to keep costs to a minimum.

In the next section, you will learn about another management and governance service known as **AWS CloudTrail**. This service is designed to help you audit access patterns and enforce governance and compliance.

Meeting compliance requirements with AWS CloudTrail

As part of your overall management, governance, and security toolkit, you must monitor access patterns and track all actions that take place in your AWS account – be they provisioning or terminating resources, or even as simple as an IAM user logging into your AWS account, having read access to those resources and applications. Amazon CloudTrail is an auditing service that records every single API call made to your AWS account and the resources contained within.

Amazon CloudTrail is enabled by default and records all activities you perform in your AWS account. For example, if a user Alice logs in to the account and launches an EC2 instance, and then later terminates it, all these individual actions are recorded as depicted in the following screenshot in *Figure 16.5*.

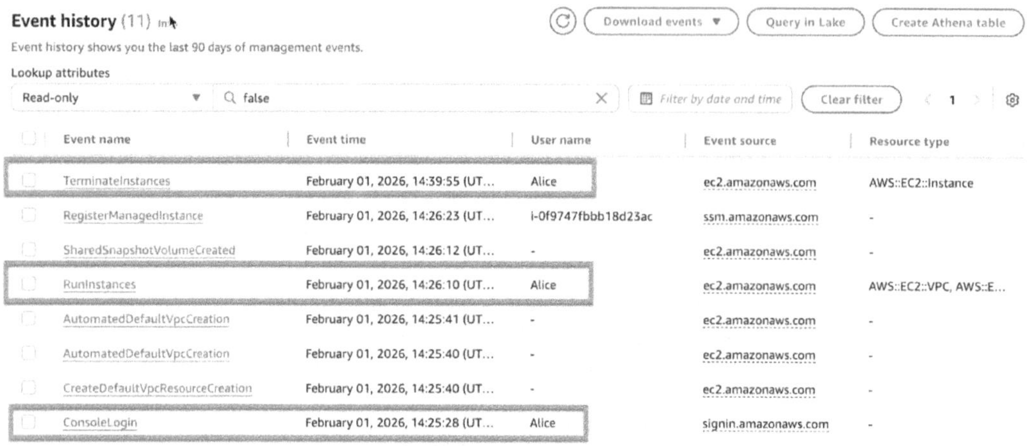

Figure 16.5: Amazon CloudTrail event history

With Amazon CloudTrail, you can monitor and enforce compliance and governance by responding to the recorded **time-ordered series of events** that take place in your AWS account. You can ingest these events into Amazon CloudWatch and Amazon EventBridge to trigger automated remediation actions, such as invoking AWS Lambda functions or sending alert notifications using Amazon SNS.

Amazon CloudTrail provides a history of both **API and non-API activities**. API activities include actions such as launching an EC2 instance or deleting an Amazon S3 bucket. Non-API activities include actions such as logging in to the AWS Management Console.

Amazon CloudTrail allows you to record the following types of events:

- **Management events:** These provide information about management operations that you perform in your AWS account. Also known as *control plane operations*, examples include API calls such as the `RunInstances` operation when you launch a new EC2 instance. Management events include both **write-only** and **read-only** events. For example, when Alice launches an EC2 instance (as shown in *Figure 16.5*), she performs a write-only event. A read-only event would include an API operation such as `DescribeInstances`, which returns a list of EC2 instances without making any changes. Management events can also include non-API activities, such as when a user logs in to the AWS Management Console.
- **Data events:** These provide information about operations performed **on or within a resource** in your AWS account. For example, when you upload an object to an Amazon S3 bucket, you perform the `PutObject` API operation. Another example of a data event is adding items to a DynamoDB table, which results in a `PutItem` API operation.

Data events are known as **data plane operations** and are generally high volume. Data events are not logged by default, and you must explicitly configure a trail and specify the supported resources or resource types for which you want to collect these events.

- **Insight events:** These provide details about **unusual activities** in your AWS account. You must enable Insight events to allow CloudTrail to detect such behavior. For example, if your account normally logs one or two Amazon S3 `DeleteBucket` API calls per minute, but suddenly starts logging 200 `DeleteBucket` calls per minute, this may be recorded as unusual activity.

Amazon CloudTrail Events stores all management events for up to 90 days, which you can view in the console or download. Furthermore, the event history will not provide any information on data events—for these, you must create a trail, which is discussed in the next section.

Regional and global trails

If you need to store data events or management events beyond the default 90-day retention period, you must create a specific Amazon CloudTrail **trail**. A trail is a configuration that enables CloudTrail to record specific types of events and store them in Amazon S3 and optionally in AWS CloudWatch Logs.

Trails can be configured to record events from a single region or across all regions:

- **All-Regions trail:** CloudTrail records events in each AWS region and delivers them as log files to the Amazon S3 bucket that you specify. When you configure CloudTrail to record events from all regions, any new regions launched by AWS are automatically included. The All-Regions trail is also the default option when you create a trail using the CloudTrail console.
- **Single-Region trail:** In some cases, you may only require trail data from a specific region. You can configure a trail to record log files and event data from a single region and have them delivered to an Amazon S3 bucket of your choice.

You can also create an **AWS Organization trail**, which records events from the management account as well as all member accounts in the AWS Organizations environment. This approach ensures that you record important management events across all member accounts, supporting centralized auditing, and compliance requirements.

In the next section, you will learn about another service that allows you to analyze and evaluate changes to your resources over a period. This is particularly useful when you want to enforce change management processes and ensure that any configuration you implement is in alignment with corporate governance and rules.

Managing change control with AWS Config

AWS Config is a service that enables you to monitor how your resources are configured and track changes to those configurations over time. You can also gain insights into how those resources were configured in the past, including resources that have since been deleted.

In addition, you can define rules to ensure that any resources created are compliant with predefined configurations. For example, you may wish to enforce a rule that all Amazon S3 buckets have versioning enabled. If versioning has not been set, AWS Config will flag the bucket as non-compliant.

With AWS Config, you can monitor changes to **individual configuration items** of your resources. A configuration item is a point-in-time snapshot of the attributes for a given resource in your AWS account. A configuration item includes information such as metadata, attributes, relationships with other resources, and the resource's current configuration.

For example, when you deploy an EC2 instance, one configuration item is the instance type. If you select the `t3.micro` instance type, that value represents a configuration item for the EC2 instance being deployed.

When you make changes to a resource, you modify its configuration items—for example, when you upgrade an instance type from `t3.micro` to `t3.small`. This change is recorded in a JSON **diff file**, highlighting the fields that have changed, as shown in *Figure 16.6*:

Figure 16.6: AWS Config monitoring changes to resource config

AWS Config can also help businesses manage their change management workflows by providing evidence of configuration changes, which can be used for troubleshooting purposes.

So far, you have learned about various tools that help you monitor resources, capture metrics and logging data, audit activity, and document resource changes, as well as enforce resource configurations using rules. As part of the management and governance toolkit, you also need mechanisms to automate management tasks across your resources, such as patching EC2 instances, implementing automation workflows, and administering your environments. In the next section, you will learn about AWS Systems Manager, which offers a wide range of tools to help you efficiently manage and administer your AWS resources.

Automating resource administration with AWS Systems Manager

AWS Systems Manager is a suite of services that enables you to centrally manage and administer your AWS resources. With AWS Systems Manager, you gain visibility into the resources provisioned in your AWS account, as well as the ability to automate and perform day-to-day operational tasks.

AWS Systems Manager uses the concept of **documents**, which are written in JSON or YAML format and define the actions to be taken against those resources. AWS offers a wide range of predefined documents, or you can create your own. For example, the **AWS-ArchiveEBSVolumeSnapshots** document can be used to identify EBS snapshots that match a specific tag key and value, evaluate them against a defined retention policy, and then archive them to reduce storage costs. A screenshot is presented in *Figure 16.7*:

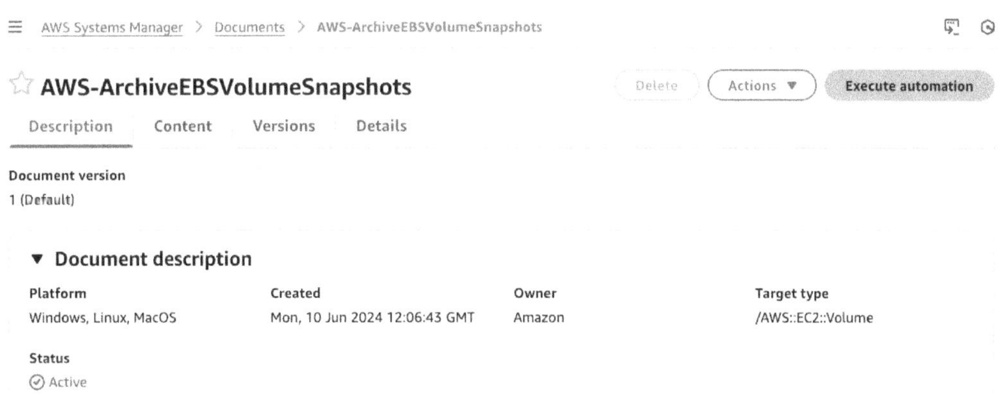

Figure 16.7: AWS Systems Manager documents

AWS Systems Manager offers a wide range of tools and services to enable your operations team to centrally and efficiently manage all resources deployed in your AWS account. These include:

- **Run Command**: The Run Command is a feature that enables you to remotely run Linux shell scripts and Windows PowerShell commands across your fleet of EC2 instances. This allows you to deploy configuration changes or install and update applications across multiple instances in one shot, without individually connecting to each instance.
- **State Manager**: This offers the ability to design and maintain consistent configurations across your EC2 instances, such as firewall settings, antivirus configurations, and more.
- **Inventory**: This service enables you to capture software configuration information about your EC2 instances. These include details about how the operating system configuration, including DHCP settings, agent details, and any custom items. You can run queries to track and audit your systems.
- **Maintenance Window:** Part of the change management capability, the Maintenance Window service enables you to schedule times when administrative tasks, such as installing patches, can be performed.
- **Patch Manager:** This service enables you to automate patch deployments to your EC2 instances. You can obtain information on which patches have been deployed and which patches are pending across both operating systems and application patches.
- **Parameter Store:** This service enables you to store sensitive information such as database endpoints, usernames and passwords, API keys, and other configuration details in an encrypted store. Application running on your instances can reference these configuration details by making API calls to Parameter Store when required. This ensures that you do not need to hardcode sensitive data in application code or store it on instances in plain text.
- **Session Manager:** This service enables you to remotely access your Linux and Windows-based instances using a browser-based interactive shell and CLI. The service uses standard HTTPS (`port 443`) to connect you to the shell interface of your instance, meaning that you do not need to open unnecessary ports for remote administration. This also means you do not need to provision Bastion Hosts in public subnets, which can increase security risks.

AWS Systems Manager has several additional tools to help you efficiently manage your resources, such as your EC2 instances in your AWS account. In the next section, you will learn about the AWS Trusted Advisor service, which enables you to inspect your AWS environment and identify whether your resources have been configured in accordance with best practices.

Improving workloads with AWS Trusted Advisor

AWS Trusted Advisor is a service that enables you to analyze your workloads and how they are configured against AWS-recommended best practices across five different categories.

These best practices help you identify opportunities to improve resource performance, reliability, security, and cost-effectiveness. AWS Trusted Advisor uses a **color-coded system** to highlight key configuration findings, as follows:

- **Green:** Trusted Advisor has not identified any issues, and your resources comply with best practices
- **Yellow**: Trusted Advisor detects a potential issue and recommends reviewing your configuration. For example, if you are consuming more than 80% of a particular service limit, this will be highlighted
- **Red**: Trusted Advisor recommends that you take immediate action to resolve critical issues. For example, if you have opened `port 3389 (RDP)` to allow access to a Windows EC2 instance from the entire internet (`0.0.0.0/0`), this is considered a security risk

The five categories used to guide how your resources should be configured are:

- **Performance:** Provides recommendations on how you can modify your existing infrastructure architecture and configurations to improve performance. This category helps identify over-utilized resources and recommends upgrades where appropriate
- **Security:** Reports on resources that are not configured in accordance with security best practices. For example, if **multi-factor authentication** (**MFA**) is not enabled on the root user account, AWS highlights this as a critical security risk.
- **Fault tolerance:** Identifies resources that should be reconfigured to improve resilience and reduce single points of failure
- **Cost optimization:** Performs checks to identify opportunities to reduce costs and avoid waste. This may include recommendations such as moving from On-Demand pricing to Reserved Instances or using appropriate Savings Plans
- **Service limits:** Checks whether your AWS resources are approaching service limits or quotas and alerts you accordingly

AWS Trusted Advisor is a go-to tool for obtaining a detailed breakdown of how your AWS resources are configured and for analyzing recommendations to align them with industry best practices and AWS guidance.

It is important to note that AWS Trusted Advisor is not entirely free. The available checks and reporting features depend on the AWS Support plan you have subscribed to. With the **Basic**

Support plan, you only have access to a limited set of core checks. To gain access to the full range of recommendations across all five categories, you must subscribe to at least the **Business Support** plan.

In the next section, you will carry out a project task to monitor a resource using Amazon CloudWatch and configure alarms.

Project task 16 – Configuring CloudWatch alarms for EC2 monitoring

In this project task, you will deploy an EC2 instance and configure it with a tool that will allow you to overload the CPU. You can also create an AWS CloudWatch Alarm to monitor the CPUUtilization metric from the instance and configure an alarm so that when the CPUUtilization is equal to or greater than 70% for more than 5 minutes, it will trigger an alarm. The workflow is depicted in the diagram in *Figure 16.8*.

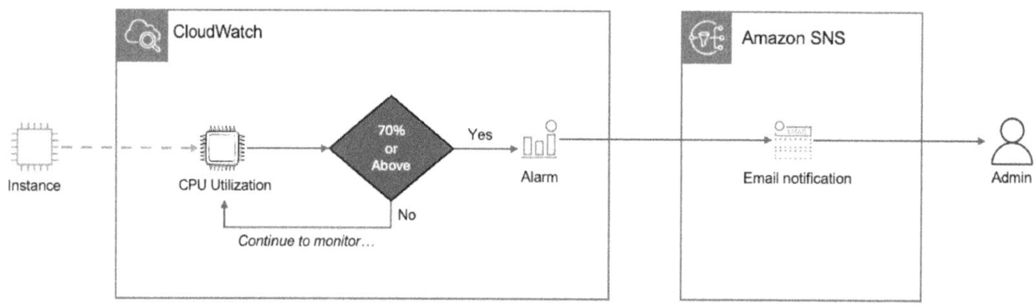

Figure 16.8: Amazon CloudWatch configuration

You will also configure the CloudWatch alarm to send an Amazon SNS email notification to an email address of your choice. This will illustrate how you could send alerts to administrators in your organization.

Technical requirements

To complete the project exercises in this chapter, ensure you are logged in to your AWS Development account as the IAM user Alice to complete the project tasks.

Project task 16.1 – Deploying an EC2 instance

In this project task, you will deploy an EC2 instance in the default VPC in the us-east-1 (North Virginia) region.

1. Log in to the Belly Brew Co. Limited AWS Development account
2. From the main search bar at the top of the AWS Management Console, search for and navigate to the **EC2 dashboard**

3. Ensure that you are in the `us-east-1 region (N.Virginia)` by selecting it, if necessary, from the region drop-down menu at the top right-hand corner of the webpage
4. From the left-hand menu, select **Instances**
5. In the right-hand pane, click the **Launch instances** button
6. Provide a name for your instance, such as `bb-stress-server`
7. Ensure that you select the Amazon Linux 2023 kernel-6.1 AMI from the **Amazon Machine Image (AMI)** drop-down menu
8. Scroll down and for the **Instance type** ensure you have selected the `t3.micro` instance
9. Next, select **Proceed without a key pair (Not recommended)** from the **Key pair (login)** drop-down. Instead of key pairs, you will be using the EC2 Connect Instance feature to connect to the instance
10. Ensure that the **Default VPC** is selected in the **Network settings** section
11. Next, ensure that the **Create security group** option is selected under **Firewall (security groups)** and the **Allow SSH traffic from** is set to **Anywhere (0.0.0.0/0)** as per the screenshot shown in *Figure 16.9*:

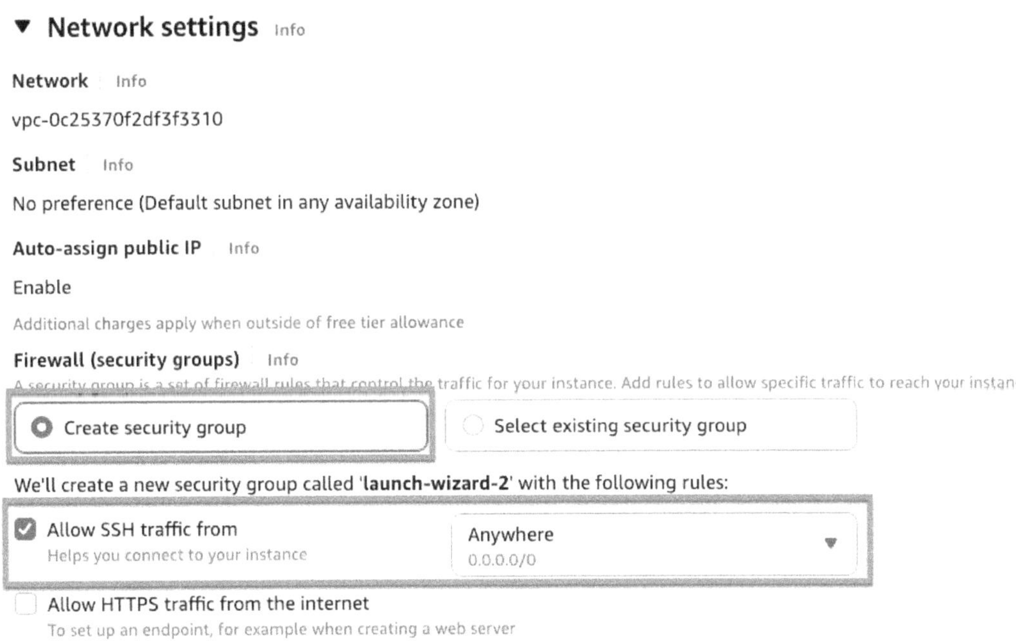

Figure 16.9: Network and security group settings

12. Scroll to the bottom of the web page and click the **Launch instance** button

13. Your instance will now launch, and you can navigate to the list of instances by clicking the **Instances** link from the breadcrumb at the top of the webpage or the left-hand menu
14. Allow your instance to undergo the **Status check** as per the following screenshot in *Figure 16.10*:

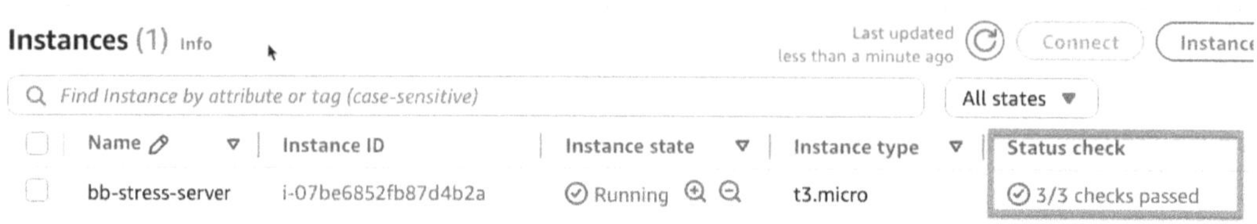

Figure 16.10: EC2 instance status check

Allow the instance to run for at least 15 minutes before performing the next project task so that it is visible in CloudWatch.

Project task 16.2 – Configuring CloudWatch alarm

In this project task, you will create a simple alarm to monitor if the EC2 instance has a high CPU load of over 70% for more than 5 minutes. If it crosses this threshold value, you will receive an email alert using Amazon SNS, and the alarm will be triggered.

1. Ensure that you are still logged into the AWS Development account and in the `us-east-1` region
2. From the search bar at the top of the AWS management console. Search for and navigate to **CloudWatch**
3. From the left-hand menu, click **Alarms**
4. In the right-hand pane, click the **Create alarm** button
5. You will be presented with a step-by-step wizard to create the alarm. Select the **Select metric** button in the **Specify metric and conditions** webpage
6. In the dialog box that appears, ensure the **Browse** tab is selected
7. Click the **EC2** link
8. Next, click **Per-Instance Metrics**
9. From the list that appears, scroll to find the metrics related to **bb-stress-server**. Select the check box next to the **bb-stress-server** that corresponds with the `CPUUtilization` metric as per the screenshot shown in *Figure 16.11*:

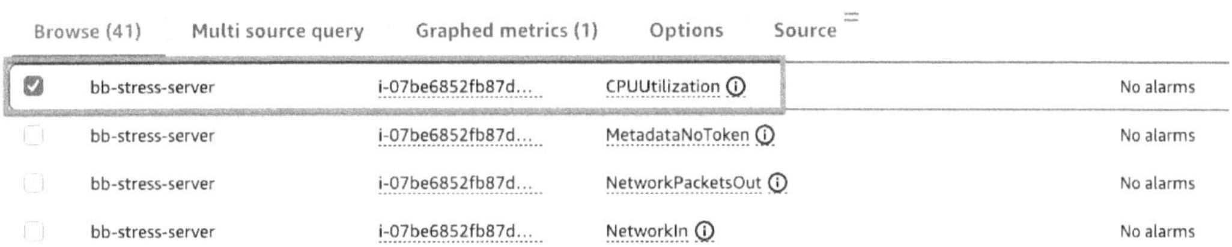

Figure 16.11: Bb-stress-server CPUUtilization metric

10. Click the **Select metric** button at the bottom of the webpage. You will be presented with the **Metric** graph and the details page
11. Scroll down to the **Conditions** section and select the option **Greater/Equal >= threshold**
12. In the text box under **than...** type in the value `70`. This is the percentage value that you define as a threshold. So if the CPU Utilization is equal to or greater than 70%, you want the alarm to be triggered
13. Leave the default values in the **Additional configuration** section and click **Next**
14. In the **Configure actions** section, ensure that **In alarm** is selected
15. Click the **Create new topic** option under **Send a notification to the following SNS topic**
16. Provide a topic name such as `bb-stress-server-alarm` in the **Create a new topic...** text box
17. Next, provide your email address in the text box under **Email endpoints that will receive the notification...**
18. Click the **Create topic** button
19. Scroll down to the bottom of the webpage and click **Next**
20. Provide a name for your alarm, such as `bb-stress-server-alarm`
21. Click **Next**
22. Click the **Create alarm** button. Your alarm will now be created. You will also see a notification informing you that your email subscription for the notification is pending confirmation. You must log in to your email account and click on the confirmation link that AWS sends you to confirm the alert subscription.

Tip

Note that sometimes the confirmation request can end up in your Spam folder, so make sure to check that out if you don't see the email in your inbox.

23. Once you have confirmed your subscription, you can go back to the CloudWatch Alarms console and refresh the webpage. You should see that the Alarm is defined and the **current state** is set to **OK** as per the following screenshot in *Figure 16.12*. This is because the alarm has not been breached yet, as the instance is not being overloaded.

    Note

    The **State** may show up as `Insufficient Data` for a short while before it changes to the `OK` state. This is because it takes a short while to capture the metrics data.

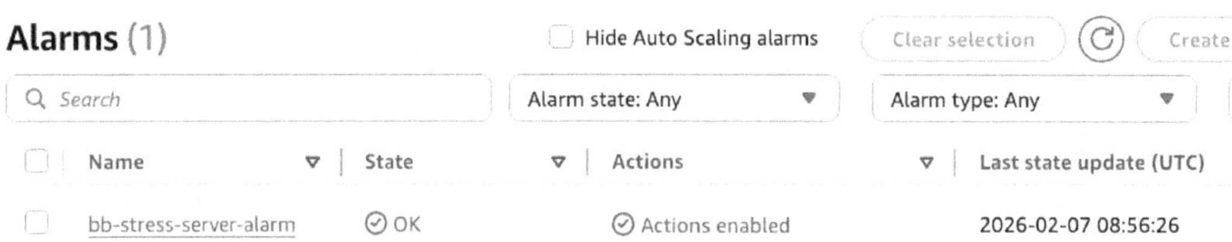

Figure 16.12: CloudWatch alarm status

As the alarm has now been configured, in the next project task, you will run a stress tool on the server to trigger the alarm.

Project task 16.3 – Installing and running stress tool on EC2 instance

In this project task, you will remotely connect to the EC2 instance, install a stress tool, and run it to trigger an alarm.

1. Ensure that you are still logged into your AWS Development account
2. Navigate to the **EC2** dashboard as you did earlier
3. From the left-hand menu, click **Instances**
4. In the right-hand pane, select the instance **bb-stress-server**
5. Click the **Connect** button. You will be redirected to the **Connect to instance** webpage
6. Ensure that the **EC2 Instance Connect** tab is selected

7. Click the **Connect** button
8. Another webpage will be launched in another tab window, which will connect you to your EC2 instance
9. Elevate your privileges to root by typing in the command `sudo su` and then pressing *Enter*
10. Update the operating system by typing in the command `dnf update -y` and pressing *Enter*. If there are any updates, these will now be installed.
11. Once completed, install the stress tool by typing in the command `dnf install -y stress` and then pressing *Enter*. Wait for the installation to complete.
12. Next, you will run the stress test. While still in the EC2 instance connect session, type in the command `stress -c 2 -t 600` and press *Enter*. The stress tool will now run, and this will add load to the CPU:
    - The `-c` switch defines the number of vCPUs. Since you are running a `t3.micro`, this only has 2 `vCPUs`
    - The `-t` defines the timeout period. `600` represents 10 minutes
13. Wait for about five minutes and then navigate to the AWS CloudWatch dashboard using the previous EC2 dashboard browser window
14. From the left-hand menu, click **All alarms**
15. In the right-hand pane, click the **alarm** you created in *Project Task 16.2*. You will notice the **CPUUtilization** graph, as shown in the following screenshot in *Figure 16.13*:

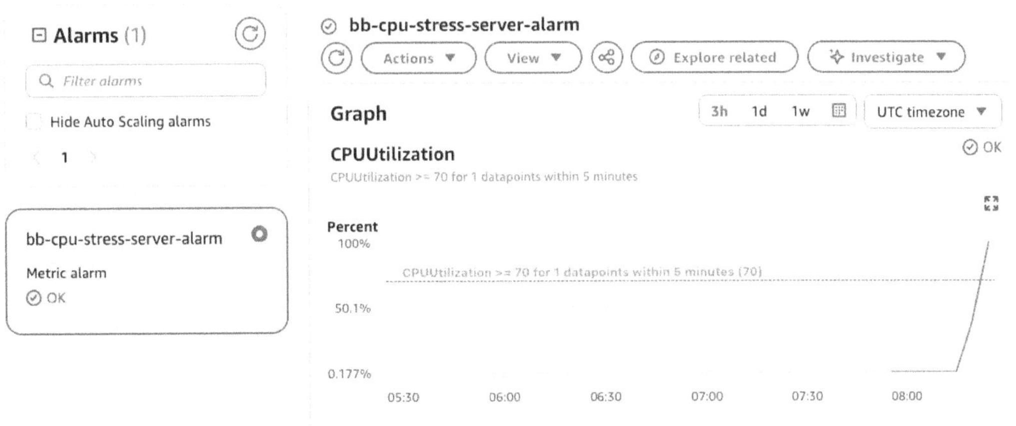

Figure 16.13: CPUUtilization graph

16. As you can see, the CPU is overloaded on the server and crosses the 70% threshold. Once this stays above 70% for more than five minutes, it will trigger an alarm, and you will see the state as per the following screenshot in *Figure 16.14*:

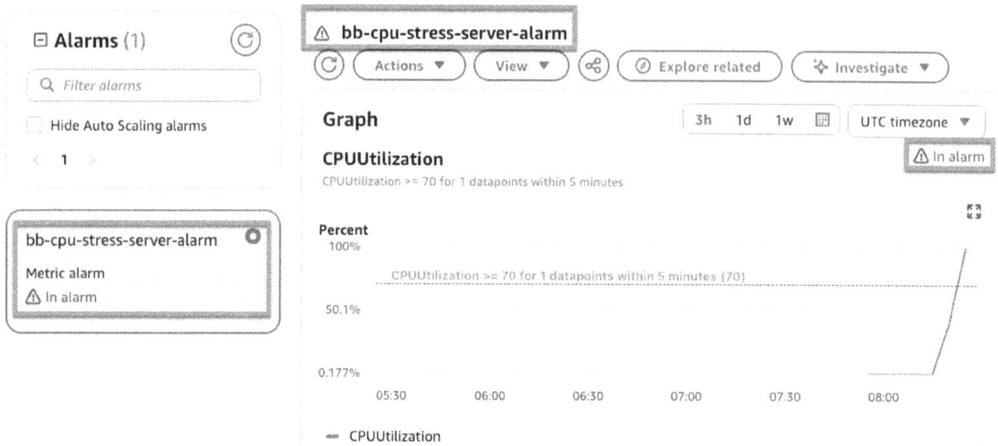

Figure 16.14: CloudWatch alarm

17. Next, log in to your email account, and you should find an email from AWS about the alarm

In this project task, you simulated an alarm state by running a stress test tool on your EC2 instance. In the next project task, you will perform a clean-up exercise to remove the resources you have created.

Project task 16.4 – Cleaning up

In this project task, you will delete the alarm and terminate the EC2 instance.

1. While still in the AWS CloudWatch dashboard, click on **Alarms** from the left-hand menu
2. In the right-hand pane, select your alarm and select **Delete** from the **Actions** drop-down list
3. In the pop-up window that appears, click the **Delete** button
4. Navigate back to the EC2 dashboard
5. From the left-hand menu, click **Instances**
6. In the right-hand pane, select the **bb-stress-server** instance
7. Select **Terminate (delete) instance** from the **Instance state** drop-down list
8. Click the **Terminate (delete)** button

Your instance will now be terminated. As you can see, you can create alarms to monitor a wide range of metrics and have alerts sent to you if any of the resources enter an alarm state. You can also automate remediation actions and invoke Lambda functions to address any alarms.

Summary

This chapter focuses on how you can monitor, manage, and administer your workloads in an efficient and proactive manner. To host your applications in the cloud, you need to design end-to-end infrastructure resources that fulfill the core requirements of compute, networking, storage, and database services, while also incorporating security best practices and cost optimization.

To manage your workloads effectively, you must monitor and observe the health of your resources, ensuring high performance and reliability while mitigating potential bottlenecks. Here, **Amazon CloudWatch** offers a suite of features to help you monitor your workloads, identify resource utilization, and perform extensive observability tasks required to ensure you consistently deliver optimal performance.

Security, along with the ability to audit access, is critically important to prevent unauthorized access and minimize attack surfaces. Using **AWS CloudTrail**, you can audit management and data access patterns, providing visibility into potential malicious activities within your AWS accounts.

In addition, tracking changes to resource configurations plays a vital role in cloud operations. You want to avoid misaligned configuration changes and ensure that all changes and resource configurations remain compliant with industry-standard best practices and corporate governance requirements. **AWS Config** helps you manage change control across your cloud workloads

This chapter also introduced **AWS Systems Manager**, a suite of tools designed to help you efficiently administer your resources in a secure and automated manner.

Together, these tools and services play a critical role in ensuring the smooth operation of the underlying infrastructure that supports your application requirements and overall customer experience.

In this chapter, you learned how to monitor, audit, manage, and govern AWS resources using services such as Amazon CloudWatch, AWS CloudTrail, AWS Config, AWS Systems Manager, and AWS Trusted Advisor. In the next chapter, you will build on that operational foundation by focusing on security: understanding the Shared Responsibility Model, meeting compliance requirements, securing data and applications, and using AWS tools such as WAF, Shield, Inspector, Macie, GuardDuty, and Detective to protect cloud workloads.

Exam Readiness Drill – Chapter Review Questions

Apart from mastering key concepts, strong test-taking skills under time pressure are essential for acing your certification exam. That's why developing these abilities early in your learning journey is critical.

Exam readiness drills, using the free online practice resources provided with this book, help you progressively improve your time management and test-taking skills while reinforcing the key concepts you've learned.

HOW TO GET STARTED

- Open the link or scan the QR code at the bottom of this page
- If you have unlocked the practice resources already, log in to your registered account. If you haven't, follow the instructions in *Free Benefits with Your Book* section in this book's *Preface* and come back to this page.
- Once you log in, click the START button to start this chapter's quiz
- We recommend attempting a quiz multiple times till you're able to answer most of the questions correctly and well within the time limit.
- You can use the following practice template to help you plan your attempts:

Working On Accuracy		
Attempt	**Target**	**Time Limit**
Attempt 1	40% or more	Till the timer runs out
Attempt 2	60% or more	Till the timer runs out
Attempt 3	75% or more	Till the timer runs out
Working On Timing		
Attempt 4	75% or more	1 minute before time limit
Attempt 5	75% or more	2 minutes before time limit
Attempt 6	75% or more	3 minutes before time limit

The above drill is just an example. Design your drills based on your own goals and make the most out of the online quizzes accompanying this book.

Link to this Chapter's Quiz

You need to unlock the online practice resources to access the link below. Check the *Free Benefits with Your Book* section in the *Preface* for detailed instructions on how to do this. You only need to unlock the resources once.

Open Quiz `https://packt.link/clf_c02_ch16` or scan the QR code

17

Security Fundamentals and Tools on AWS

Over the last few years, you may have heard about several high-profile security breaches and data leaks involving household brand names in the news. Cyber-attacks of all kinds have been on the rise, and given the advancement in technology, you would be forgiven for thinking that such security issues would decrease.

On the contrary, popular online applications offering email services, trading platforms, and storage services have had to enforce stricter security protocols to protect user accounts. These include mandatory **multi-factor authentication** (**MFA**) and stricter **Know Your Customer** (**KYC**) documentation requirements. These measures have become necessary in recent years.

In this chapter, you will learn about the importance of designing, deploying, and managing your applications and resources using a **zero-trust approach**. You will explore the fundamentals of the **Shared Responsibility Model** between the cloud provider and the customer, understand the need for regulatory compliance, and discover the various AWS tools and services that can help you efficiently secure your workloads.

As you architect and build solutions, you must integrate security measures and protocols in accordance with best practices at every layer — from the physical infrastructure where resources reside, such as cloud provider data centers, through the network and transport layers, all the way up to the application layer. Each layer must be protected.

The following topics are covered in this chapter:

- Applying the Shared Responsibility Model
- Meeting compliance requirements with AWS programs
- Testing workload security with AWS vulnerability scanning
- Securing data with AWS encryption services
- Protecting web applications with AWS WAF
- Mitigating DDoS attacks with AWS Shield
- Identifying vulnerabilities with Amazon Inspector
- Discovering, detecting, and investigating threats with Amazon Macie, GuardDuty, and Detective

Applying the Shared Responsibility Model

With on-premises networks and data centers, you are solely responsible for the security you architect and implement for your applications — from the physical security that determines who can enter data center facilities and server rooms, through to how the application is made accessible over the Internet and other external networks.

With cloud providers, however, the responsibility for designing and implementing the same high level of security best practices does not fall on the provider alone. Instead, it is shared between the customer and the cloud service provider.

You can rest assured that AWS designs and enforces physical security measures to ensure that only authorized personnel are granted access to the underlying infrastructure hosting your cloud resources and applications. AWS implements security controls to protect the physical network, underlying firewall services, and all security layers up to the hypervisor that runs your compute resources.

With managed services such as Amazon RDS and DynamoDB, additional security protocols are followed — for example, ensuring that the infrastructure supporting these services is regularly patched with critical security updates.

However, as a customer, you are responsible for securing how you build and deploy your applications in the cloud. You must ensure that your data is encrypted using the security tools provided by AWS. This is where the concept of the Shared Responsibility Model comes in. The diagram in *Figure 17.1* illustrates how the Shared Responsibility Model is structured:

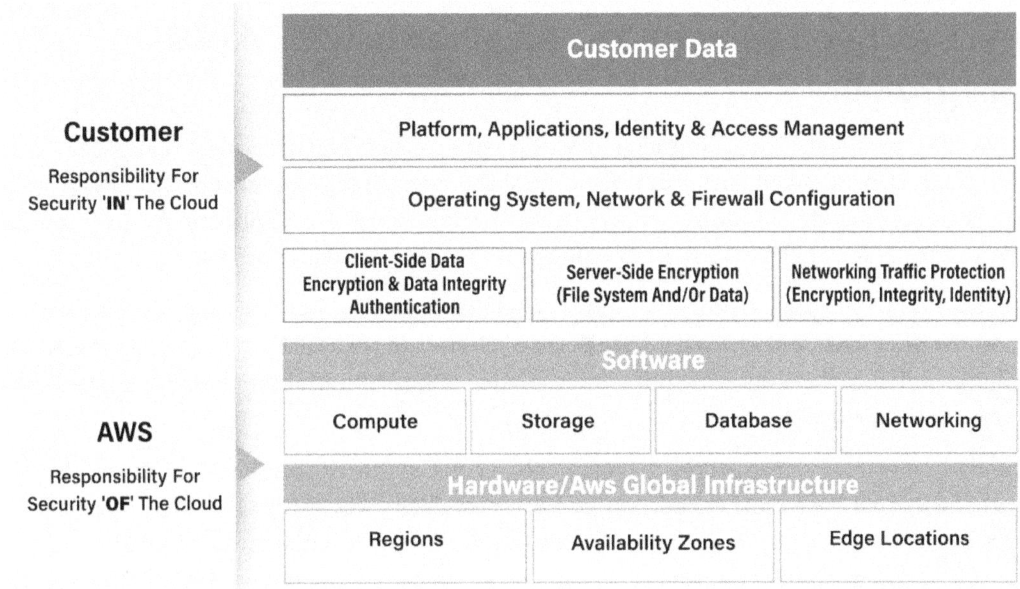

Figure 17.1: AWS Shared Responsibility Model

AWS is responsible for the security *of* the cloud. This includes enforcing strict security protocols across the global infrastructure — its data centers (located across Regions and Availability Zones), edge locations, content delivery infrastructure, storage systems, networking components, and the hypervisors that support compute services.

As a customer, you are responsible for security *in* the cloud. This includes:

- Implementing strong IAM policies
- Enforcing MFA
- Securing applications with authentication and authorization controls
- Encrypting data
- Patching EC2 instances to address vulnerabilities
- Protecting data stored in services such as Amazon S3

Ultimately, if you can configure a resource, for example, an Amazon S3 bucket used to host your data, then how that resource is configured is your responsibility.

In the next section, you will learn about how AWS ensures compliance with regulatory requirements.

Meeting compliance requirements with AWS programs

AWS offers compliance programs aligned with a wide range of global regulatory and legal standards. Depending on the nature of your business, you may need to ensure that any applications or workloads hosted on AWS meet specific compliance requirements. To that end, you can verify whether AWS participates in the necessary compliance programs.

For example, if you plan to process and store credit card information, your application must meet the **Payment Card Industry Data Security Standard** (**PCI DSS**). At the same time, AWS must ensure that the underlying infrastructure used to host the application is also aligned with these requirements.

Similarly, if you are a healthcare organization based in the United States, you must comply with the **Health Insurance Portability and Accountability Act** (**HIPAA**) of 1996. This means your application must be designed to be HIPAA-compliant. Any patient information stored must be secured, confidential, and encrypted. Access to patient **Protected Health Information** (**PHI**) must be granted only to authorized personnel.

While there is no formal HIPAA certification for a **cloud service provider** (**CSP**) such as AWS, AWS aligns with HIPAA's risk management expectations through frameworks such as FedRAMP and NIST 800-53. These are higher security standards that map to the HIPAA Security Rule and support compliance.

In addition to its wide range of compliance programs, AWS also offers **AWS Artifact** — a self-service portal that provides on-demand access to security and compliance reports (such as ISO, SOC, and PCI) as well as agreements like the **Business Associate Addendum** (**BAA**) and **Non-Disclosure Agreements** (**NDAs**).

When it comes to security, prevention is always better than a cure. As a business, you must be able to demonstrate that your resources and application workloads are well secured and resilient against potential threats. One way to assess your security posture is to run simulated tests to evaluate how penetrable your environment may be.

In the next section, you will learn more about AWS Vulnerability Scanning options.

Securing data with AWS encryption services

As an AWS customer, you must ensure that the workloads and applications you deploy are highly secure and accessible only to authorized entities. However, unless you actively test your security posture, you cannot be certain that your configurations and architecture align with your security requirements.

AWS allows you to run specific types of scans against your own cloud workloads to identify potential vulnerabilities. Also known as **penetration testing**, this involves simulating cyber-attacks against your computing resources to uncover weaknesses. These activities should be carried out by internal or authorized security teams.

That said, not all types of scans and simulated attacks are permitted. For instance, you are prohibited from using tools to perform **Denial of Service** (**DoS**) testing. Simulated **Distributed Denial of Service** (**DDoS**) attacks may only be conducted by an **AWS Partner Network** (**APN**) partner that has been pre-approved by AWS to perform such testing.

The following table provides a quick overview of some of the permitted services you can run scans against, as well as certain types of simulations that are prohibited.

Permitted Service	**Prohibited Activities**
Amazon EC2 instances, WAF, NAT Gateways, and Elastic Load Balancers	DS zone walking via Amazon Route53 hosted zones
Amazon RDS	DoS, DDoS, simulated DoS
Amazon CloudFront	Port flooding
Amazon Aurora	Protocol flooding
Amazon LightSail resources	Request flooding
Amazon API Gateway	Outbound penetration testing from API Gateway; request flooding, including API request flooding; DoS/DDoS or simulated DoS/DDoS |

Table 17.1: AWS permitted services and prohibited activities for penetration testing

> **Tip**
>
> These prohibited activities apply across AWS security assessments and are not always specific to a single service. Always review the latest AWS Customer Support Policy for Penetration Testing before conducting any assessment.

Ensure that the tests you run are against your own workloads. As a customer, you are not permitted to conduct any security assessments of AWS infrastructure or the AWS services themselves.

In *Chapter 6*, you were introduced to Amazon S3 encryption, which focused on how you can encrypt the data you store in your Amazon S3 buckets. However, encryption options can also be applied to other resource types, such as encrypting your EBS volumes or RDS Databases. In the next section, you will learn more about encryption options on AWS.

Securing data with AWS encryption services

Encryption is the process of making data unreadable to unauthorized users and applications. Plain text data is scrambled using an encryption key and an algorithm. The only way to get back the plain text is to have the appropriate decryption key.

There are two types of encryption:

- **Encryption in transit**: This is when data is being transmitted across networks, such as when you access a website using a browser
- **Encryption at rest**: This is when data is being stored on a storage medium, such as a hard drive

AWS offers services to help you design and implement encryption for data both in transit and at rest.

For data in transit, you must transmit the data using **Secure Sockets Layer/Transport Layer Security** (**SSL/TLS**). This requires the sending and receiving nodes to establish a secure connection, such as the HTTPS protocol. To establish the encrypted connection, you must use X.509 certificates that you can either purchase from a third-party certificate authority or create using the **AWS Certificate Manager** (**ACM**) service.

To protect data at rest, you must create an encryption key to encrypt and decrypt data as it is stored and retrieved from a given storage medium, such as an Amazon EBS volume or an EFS file store. Encryption and decryption keys are data files containing a long series of numbers and/or letters that are used by a cryptographic algorithm to encode and decode data. Examples of algorithms you may have heard of include Triple DES or **Advanced Encryption Standard** (**AES-256**) encryption.

An encryption key can be either **symmetric** or **asymmetric**:

- **Symmetric keys use** the same key for both encrypting and decrypting the data.
- **Asymmetric keys are** a combination of a public/private key pair. You use the public key to encrypt the data, and only someone who has access to the private key of that pair can decrypt it.

In an on-premises environment, you may need to procure the necessary infrastructure to create and manage encryption and decryption keys, as well as perform the actual task of encrypting and decrypting data yourself. However, AWS offers its **Key Management Service** (**KMS**), which takes away much of the underlying heavy lifting from you.

With KMS, you can create and manage **customer-managed keys** (**CMKs**), which are used in conjunction with AWS services that integrate with KMS to encrypt the data those services store on your behalf. Using customer-managed keys gives you a higher level of control over the lifecycle and usage of your keys.

AWS also provides **AWS-managed keys**, which are created and managed automatically by AWS on behalf of a service (for example, `aws/ebs` or `aws/rds`). These keys are free to use but offer limited control compared to customer-managed keys and are commonly used as the default encryption option for many AWS services.

You can also use **AWS-owned keys** if you do not want the overhead of managing keys or paying for customer-managed keys. AWS-owned keys are fully managed by AWS and are used automatically by some services behind the scenes. You can use these keys to encrypt and decrypt your data, but you do not have control over the lifecycle of the key, and you do not see them in your account. You are also not charged for using these keys.

The AWS **Key Management Service** (**KMS**) uses shared hardware security modules to generate the necessary key material that is then used to create your encryption keys. Although this is highly secure and uses **Federal Information Processing Standards** (**FIPS 140-2**) validated hardware, it is nevertheless shared with other customers, which means you do not have complete control over the hardware security modules. In some cases, this might be unacceptable depending on the industry your business operates in.

In the next section, you will learn more about how you can use your own hardware security modules in the cloud to create and manage your keys.

AWS CloudHSM

AWS CloudHSM is a dedicated hardware security module (HSM) that allows you to generate and manage your encryption keys for use with AWS services to encrypt and decrypt your data. These hardware modules are placed in your VPC and managed by AWS. While AWS takes care of provisioning these hardware modules, you are fully responsible for generating, storing, importing, and exporting your cryptographic keys. AWS does not have access to your keys and cannot recover them if you lose those keys. It is recommended that you have at least a minimum of two CloudHSM devices for failover and to avoid a single point of failure. This obviously increases the cost, but it is highly advised.

AWS CloudHSM complies with FIPS 140-3 (Level 3) and is ideal when AWS KMS is not enough from a control, compliance, and trust perspective. For example, a government organization may prefer to have its own CloudHSM devices rather than use KMS.

Protecting your data using encryption technologies is fundamental to enforcing your security posture. However, you must also ensure that your applications are secured and protected from malicious attacks. In the next section, you will learn about an AWS service designed to protect your application from common web exploits and attacks.

Protecting web applications with AWS WAF

AWS **Web Application Firewall** (**WAF**) is designed to offer firewall protection at the application layer, protecting your workloads over standard HTTP and HTTPS protocols. The service integrates with various application layer entry points published through Amazon CloudFront, Amazon API Gateway REST APIs, and Application Load Balancers.

This allows you to protect your applications against common web exploits such as cross-site scripting and SQL injection attacks. With AWS WAF, you create web access control lists (web ACLs), define rules that fall within specific criteria, and specify the actions to take if any web request matches that criterion, such as dropping requests suspected to be malicious.

Next, you will learn about another security tool that helps prevent network attacks.

Mitigating DDoS attacks with AWS Shield

AWS Shield offers protection against **Distributed denial of service** (**DDoS**) attacks. This is an attack type where bad actors attempt to overwhelm your applications, networks, and resources by sending a flood of internet traffic. Your resources cannot cope with the load and end up denying access to authorized users, resulting in customer dissatisfaction, reputational damage, and ultimately financial loss.

AWS offers two tiers for the AWS Shield service. These are:

- **AWS Shield Standard**: This is offered free of cost for AWS customers and protects against common network and transport layer DDoS attacks on your websites and applications. AWS Shield Standard can be used with Amazon CloudFront and Route 53 to provide layered protection against known infrastructure attacks. This means that to benefit from the standard offering, your architecture must make use of these services.
- **AWS Shield Advanced**: This tier offers additional protection against attacks on your EC2 instances, load balancers, CloudFront distributions, Global Accelerator, and more. The service offers real-time detection, proactive monitoring, and automatic mitigation of application layer (Layer 7) attacks. In addition, when you subscribe to the advanced version, you get access to the AWS **Shield Response Team** (**SRT**), an expert team available 24/7 for manual intervention and support. AWS also reimburses costs for scaling resources, such as auto-scaling your EC2 instances due to DDoS attacks.

Note that when you subscribe to AWS Shield Advanced, you get access to AWS WAF with up to 50 billion requests per month included in the cost. The Shield Advanced service is available at a cost of $3,000 per month.

In the next section, you will learn how to protect your EC2 instances from unintended network access and manage operating system vulnerabilities through effective patch and update monitoring.

Identifying vulnerabilities with Amazon Inspector

AWS offers a wide range of tools to protect your network, infrastructure resources as well as your applications from malicious attacks. However, prevention is always better than cure, and one such service that you must add to your toolkit is **AWS Inspector**. This service continuously assesses the network exposure and software vulnerabilities of your EC2, Lambda functions, and code scans, as well as container workloads.

With AWS Inspector, you can detect open ports and identify whether the operating system or applications running on your instances are known to have vulnerabilities that need to be patched.

AWS Inspector integrates with AWS Systems Manager to collect telemetry data from your instances. The service automatically scans your workloads and compares findings against security intelligence sources such as the **Common Vulnerabilities and Exposures** (**CVE**) database.

AWS Inspector evaluates:

- **Network exposure**: Identifying instances that may be reachable from the internet
- **Software vulnerabilities**: Detecting known vulnerabilities in operating systems and installed applications

The findings are presented in the AWS Inspector dashboard with granular data to help you identify potential vulnerabilities. You can then take necessary action to resolve these.

While analyzing your EC2 instances, Lambda code, and containers to detect vulnerabilities is crucial, you must also ensure that your data is protected from unauthorized access. Specifically, you must ensure that you protect **personally identifiable information** (**PII**) and track how it is being used, enforcing guardrails to prevent unauthorized access.

This is where services such as Amazon Macie, GuardDuty, and Detective become useful, as they help you identify sensitive data, detect suspicious activity, and investigate potential security issues across your AWS environment.

Discovering, detecting, and investigating threats with Amazon Macie, GuardDuty, and Detective

The following services approach security from different but complementary angles. Amazon Macie focuses on discovering and protecting sensitive data, GuardDuty helps detect potential threats and malicious activity, and Detective supports deeper investigation when you need to understand the root cause of a security finding.

Amazon Macie

Amazon Macie is a fully managed data security and privacy service designed to help protect **Personally Identifiable Information** (**PII**) and **Protected Health Information** (**PHI**) stored in your Amazon S3 buckets.

Amazon Macie uses machine learning and pattern-matching capabilities to discover sensitive data and track changes to your buckets by identifying new or modified objects over time. The service can be used to perform on-demand analysis or run automated data discovery jobs, reporting its findings through dashboards and alerts.

Amazon Macie can also be used in a multi-account architecture by monitoring your buckets across multiple accounts within an AWS Organizations configuration. This means you can designate a single Macie administrator account to centrally manage and help prevent data leaks across all member accounts.

In the next section, you will learn about another service designed to detect malicious activity against your AWS account.

AWS GuardDuty

AWS GuardDuty is a threat detection service designed to help you identify potential malicious activity against your AWS accounts and applications.

The service uses various threat intelligence feeds, such as known malicious IP addresses and domains, and applies machine learning to analyze data from Amazon CloudTrail event logs, VPC Flow Logs, and Route 53 DNS logs.

AWS GuardDuty can detect the use of compromised credentials, communication with malicious IP addresses, as well as unusual activity carried out in your AWS account based on past behavior — for example, if a fleet of EC2 instances is launched in a region you do not normally operate in, or if Amazon S3 API calls originate from an unexpected remote host, or if unauthorized access attempts are made from known malicious IP addresses.

AWS GuardDuty provides detailed findings in the GuardDuty console, integrates with Amazon EventBridge and AWS Security Hub, and makes it easier to identify potential malicious activity that you can act on to better protect your environment.

Next, you will learn about another AWS service designed to help identify the root cause of potential security issues.

Amazon Detective

So far, you have learned about various security tools that can help you detect data leaks, potential malicious activity, and even protect against DDoS attacks. In addition, you have access to logging and monitoring data from tools such as Amazon CloudWatch and AWS CloudTrail. If you need to analyze all this data and identify the root cause of security issues, you will traditionally have to extract these individual data sources and build an **Extract, Transform, and Load** (**ETL**) solution to perform a deep-dive analysis.

AWS offers **Amazon Detective**, designed to help you perform root cause analysis of your security issues without the need to build complex ETL processes. The service automatically collects and analyzes time-based events such as login activity and network traffic from AWS CloudTrail and VPC Flow Logs, and ingests findings from AWS GuardDuty to build visualizations and identify behaviors over time.

Ultimately, Amazon Detective helps you perform a deeper analysis of your security data and identify the root cause of security breaches and malicious activity.

In the next section, you will have the opportunity to configure Amazon Macie to analyze raw data held in an Amazon S3 bucket and identify potential PII that must be protected.

Project task 17 – Preventing employee data leaks at Belly Brew Co. Limited

The HR team at Belly Brew Co. Limited has been extremely busy over the past week preparing for a new Point of Sales training program across various cafes in the UK. They recently uploaded employee records documents to a folder in Amazon S3 to support internal workforce analysis. However, the data was mistakenly uploaded to the wrong S3 bucket.

Although the bucket belonged to HR, it was intended for storing only training materials — not employee personal records. As a result, sensitive information such as employee contract details, dates of birth, and National Insurance numbers was stored in an inappropriate location.

Amazon Macie can be configured to analyze the contents of these buckets and identify the presence of any **Personally Identifiable Information** (**PII**).

Organizations can quickly detect such issues and take appropriate action. In this case, the issue was not permissions-driven because HR had access to multiple buckets and happened to upload the data to the wrong one.

In this project task, you will use Amazon Macie to detect PII data and identify a potential data leak issue.

Technical requirements

To complete the tasks in this project exercise, you must be logged into the AWS Development Account as the IAM user Alice. All tasks will be performed in the `us-east-1` region. Ensure you download the CSV file from the GitHub (`https://github.com/PacktPublishing/AWS-Certified-Cloud-Practitioner-CLF-C02-Exam-Guide`) repository and save it to your desktop for easy access.

Project task 17.1 – Creating an Amazon S3 bucket

In this project task, you will create an Amazon S3 bucket and upload the CSV file you downloaded from the GitHub repo.

1. Ensure you are logged into the AWS Development account and that you are in the **us-east-1 (North Virginia)** region
2. From the search bar at the top of the management console, search for and navigate to the **Amazon S3 service**
3. From the left-hand menu, click the **general purpose buckets** link
4. In the right-hand pane, click the **Create bucket** button
5. Provide a name for your bucket, such as `bellybrew-hr-training`
6. Scroll to the bottom of the webpage and click the **Create bucket** bucket
   Your bucket has now been created as shown in the screenshot provided in *Figure 17.2*:

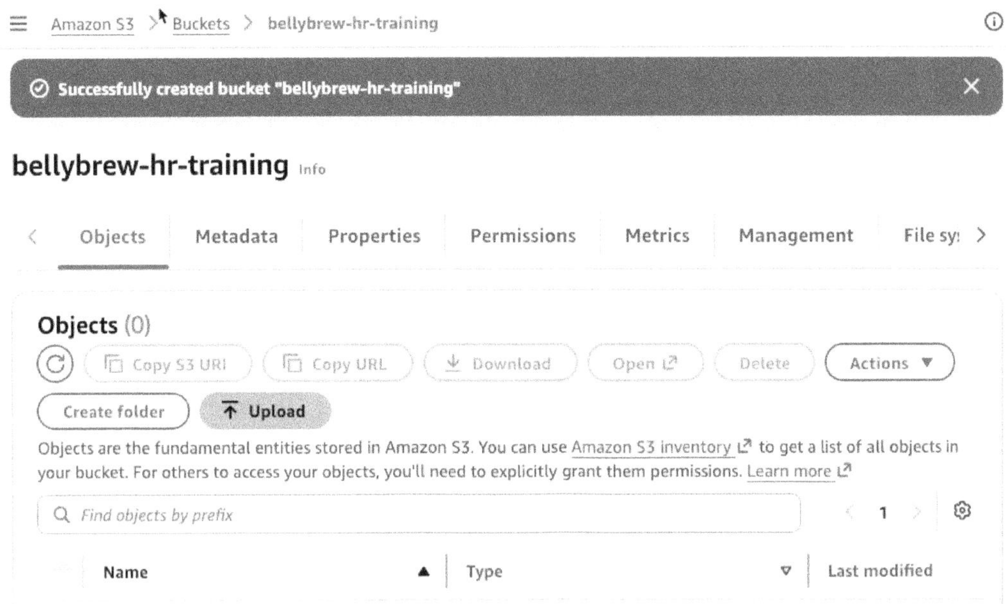

Figure 17.2: Amazon S3 buckets

7. Ensure the **Objects** tab is selected, and click the **Upload** button
8. Next, in the **Upload** webpage that opens, drag and drop your CSV file from the desktop. Alternatively, click the **Add files** button, navigate to the desktop location, and select the CSV file.
9. Scroll to the bottom of the webpage and click the **Upload** button
10. You will get a confirmation stating that the upload succeeded. Click the **Close** button at the top right-hand of the webpage.

Now that the CSV file has been uploaded, you can proceed to configure Amazon Macie in the next project task.

Project task 17.2 – Configuring Amazon Macie

In this project task, you will configure Amazon Macie to analyze the data in this S3 bucket.

1. From the search bar at the top of the management console, search and navigate to **Amazon Macie**
2. If this is the first time you have accessed Amazon Macie, you will see a splash screen as depicted in *Figure 17.3*:

Figure 17.3: Configuring Amazon Macie

3. Click the **Get started** button
4. Next, click the **Enable Macie** button
   Amazon Macie will run an initial scan. Wait for it to complete and for the summary to be displayed as shown in the following screenshot in *Figure 17.4*:

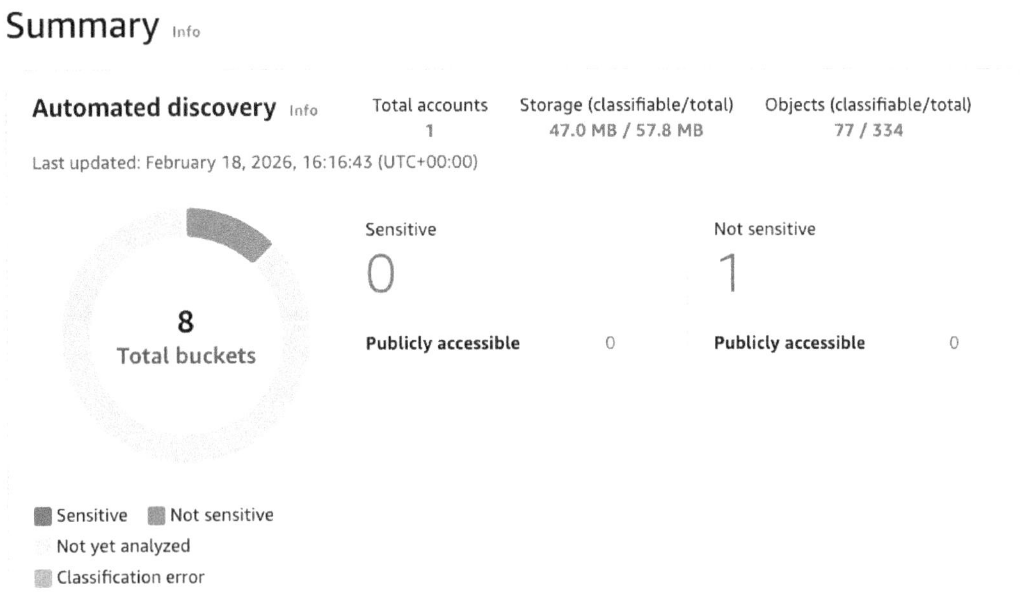

Figure 17.4: Amazon Macie summary

5. From the left-hand menu, click **Jobs**
6. From the right-hand pane, click the **Create job** button
7. You may see a dialog box informing you that the **Create job** action is not part of the 30-day free trial. Go ahead and click **Yes**, as you will delete this job after the task.
8. In the right-hand pane, for **Step 1**, go ahead and select the bucket you created in *Project Task 17.1* and click **Next**
9. In **Step 2**, go ahead and click **Next**
10. In **Step 3**, select the **One-time job** option and then click **Next**
11. In **Step 4**, leave the **Recommended** option selected and click **Next**
12. In **Step 5**, click **Next**
13. In **Step 6**, click **Next**
14. In **Step 7**, provide a name for the job, such as `bellybrew-hr-analysis`, and click **Next**
15. In **Step 8**, review your configuration, scroll to the bottom of the webpage, and click **Submit**
16. You will be redirected to the **Jobs** webpage and will note the job currently in the **Active (Running)** state

17. Wait for about five minutes and then click the job name. A sidebar will open as shown in the screenshot in *Figure 17.5*:

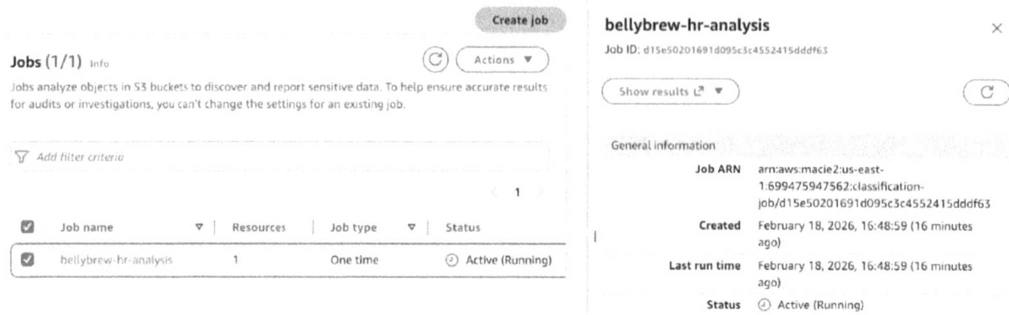

Figure 17.5: Active Macie Job

18. From the **Show results** drop-down menu, click **Show findings**. A new webpage will open in another tab, and you will note the detailed findings of the objects in this bucket.
19. Note the **Severity** of the objects in the bucket is defined as **High**, and the resource identified as the **bellybrew-employees.csv** file, as shown in the following screenshot in *Figure 17.6*:

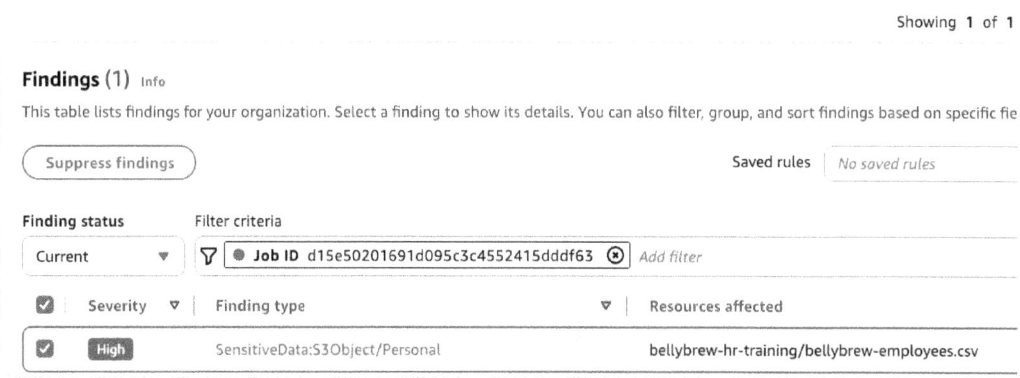

Figure 17.6: Findings of sensitive data in the CSV file

Amazon Macie also generates a JSON file that contains details of the actual PII data captured.

In the next project task, you will proceed to disable Amazon Macie to ensure you do not incur any costs after the 30-day trial.

Project task 17.3 – Disabling Amazon Macie

In this project task, you will disable Amazon Macie to ensure you do not incur any unnecessary costs:

1. Ensure you are still logged into your AWS account, and, if necessary, navigate back to the Amazon Macie console
2. From the left-hand menu, click **Settings**
3. In the right-hand pane, scroll to the bottom of the webpage and click the **Disable Macie** button
4. Type in `Disable` in the text box provided and then click the **Disable** button

You have now successfully disabled the Macie Service.

Summary

Security is a shared responsibility when you host your applications and workloads with a cloud provider. AWS offers high security standards across all layers, but is only responsible for the infrastructure and managed services it provides. This is known as **Security of the Cloud**.

It remains the customer's responsibility to ensure that their applications are built with security in mind and that appropriate authentication and authorization mechanisms are configured to ensure access follows the principle of least privilege. The customer is responsible for **Security in the Cloud**, meaning they must ensure that the data they store is protected, encrypted, and accessible only to authorized entities.

AWS aligns with industry best practices, compliance programs, and regulatory requirements, ensuring that you can trust the services to meet necessary legal and governance standards. Nevertheless, how you design your application is just as important in ensuring that your solutions are secure.

This chapter also provided a high-level overview of the various encryption approaches available, including encryption in transit and at rest, as well as use cases where you may wish to host your own hardware security modules for encryption key isolation.

You also learned about a wide range of security tools, such as:

- AWS WAF to protect your web applications from common exploits
- AWS Shield to protect against DDoS attacks, with the advanced version providing access to the SRT team for support during attacks
- Amazon Inspector to identify vulnerabilities in your EC2 instances and workloads
- Amazon Macie to detect and help protect sensitive data such as PII and PHI
- AWS GuardDuty to identify potential malicious activity and threats
- Amazon Detective to help identify the root cause of security incidents and breaches

It is critical that you design and build your solutions with security applied at all levels. Security should never be an afterthought.

In the next chapter, we will turn to cloud economics, learning how AWS pricing works, how to estimate costs before deployment, and how to monitor, forecast, and control spend using tools such as the AWS Pricing Calculator, Migration Evaluator, Cost Explorer, and AWS Budgets.

Exam Readiness Drill – Chapter Review Questions

Apart from mastering key concepts, strong test-taking skills under time pressure are essential for acing your certification exam. That's why developing these abilities early in your learning journey is critical.

Exam readiness drills, using the free online practice resources provided with this book, help you progressively improve your time management and test-taking skills while reinforcing the key concepts you've learned.

HOW TO GET STARTED

- Open the link or scan the QR code at the bottom of this page
- If you have unlocked the practice resources already, log in to your registered account. If you haven't, follow the instructions in *Free Benefits with Your Book* section in this book's *Preface* and come back to this page.
- Once you log in, click the START button to start this chapter's quiz
- We recommend attempting a quiz multiple times till you're able to answer most of the questions correctly and well within the time limit.
- You can use the following practice template to help you plan your attempts:

Working On Accuracy		
Attempt	**Target**	**Time Limit**
Attempt 1	40% or more	Till the timer runs out
Attempt 2	60% or more	Till the timer runs out
Attempt 3	75% or more	Till the timer runs out
Working On Timing		
Attempt 4	75% or more	1 minute before time limit
Attempt 5	75% or more	2 minutes before time limit
Attempt 6	75% or more	3 minutes before time limit

The above drill is just an example. Design your drills based on your own goals and make the most out of the online quizzes accompanying this book.

Link to this Chapter's Quiz

You need to unlock the online practice resources to access the link below. Check the *Free Benefits with Your Book* section in the *Preface* for detailed instructions on how to do this. You only need to unlock the resources once.

Open Quiz `https://packt.link/clf_c02_ch17`or scan the QR code

Part 5

Cloud Economics and AWS Pricing

One major reason for moving to the cloud is the promise of moving from a CapEx mode of investment in IT to an OpEx mode – meaning that as an organization, you are charged for your IT services on a pay-as-you-go model or, more importantly, on a *pay-as-you-consume* model. This is analogous to how you pay for electricity, gas, or water supply. Ultimately, this means that you do not have to tie up vast amounts of capital in hardware infrastructure that you must procure if you were self-hosting resources to host your applications. However, cloud can become very expensive really quickly if you do not plan your solutions well, if you leave unused resources running, and if you are not diligent to avoid waste.

This penultimate part focuses on cloud economics and the AWS billing and pricing models, enabling you to design your solutions in the most cost-effective manner. You must learn the fundamentals of how AWS charges for its services, where you can save on costs through volume pricing or reserving capacity, and how to calculate your estimated monthly costs using the tools provided. FinOps is a huge career pathway you can consider, and this part of the AWS Certified Cloud Practitioner study guide introduces the core concepts of cost optimization in the cloud.

This part of the book includes only the following chapter:

- *Chapter 18, Cloud Economics and Pricing Strategies on AWS*

18

Cloud Economics and Pricing Strategies on AWS

Companies often consider moving to the cloud because they have heard about the cost benefits associated with shifting from a **CAPEX** model of IT investment to an **OPEX** model. CAPEX refers to capital expenditure associated with procuring hardware such as servers, storage, and networking equipment. Although these can be considered assets for the business, it is worth bearing in mind that such assets often depreciate very quickly and inevitably need to be replaced. Computing hardware typically has a lifecycle of around **three to five years**, and that does not even consider the replacement of failed hardware components during that time.

OPEX, on the other hand, refers to operational expenses, which can vary depending on usage and consumption. Unlike CAPEX, where once you purchase hardware, the cost remains the same regardless of whether you fully utilize it or not, OPEX allows you to benefit from a **pay-as-you-consume model**. This helps organizations operate more cost-efficiently because they only pay for the resources they use. Depending on how you design and build your solutions and architectures, the overall IT spend can be significantly lower compared to following a traditional CAPEX model.

Cloud providers invest massive amounts of capital into computing infrastructure and make those resources available to customers through this **pay-as-you-go consumption model**. This ultimately gives organizations the opportunity to reduce their overall IT expenses while maintaining flexibility and scalability.

In this chapter, you will learn about some basic cost optimization principles, followed by a review of some specific tools and services to help you manage your costs more effectively.

The following are the main topics covered in this chapter:

- Learning the fundamentals of AWS billing and pricing strategies

- Introducing AWS cost calculators (Pricing Calculator)
- Estimating migration costs with Migration Evaluator
- Understanding the basics of AWS Cost Explorer
- Configuring AWS Budgets

Learning the fundamentals of AWS billing and pricing strategies

As a minimum, AWS charges you for the resources you consume based on three primary core elements:

- **Amount of computing capacity**: For instance, the EC2 or RDS instance type you use for a given number of seconds
- **Storage**: The total storage consumed; for example, 100 GB of EBS GP3 Volume
- **Outbound data transfer**: The total data transferred out of a region, for example, 1 TB of data transfer from eu-west-2 (London region) to your local data center

The following subsections provide a broad overview of how you might strategically choose the resource types you use to optimize costs.

Compute services

How you are charged for your compute resources depends very much on the pricing model you choose. For example, if you deploy an EC2 instance using the **On-Demand pricing model**, you pay a fixed rate per second (with a 60-second minimum) depending on the instance type that defines the CPU, memory, storage, and network capabilities.

You could also purchase a **Reserved Instance** for the same instance and benefit from a discounted hourly rate. The level of discount varies depending on the length of the reservation, such as a 1-year or 3-year term, and whether you choose to pay for the reservation all upfront, partially upfront, or with a no-upfront payment option.

The decision to choose between On-Demand and Reserved Instances depends on your use case. If you plan to have your instances running 24/7 throughout the year, then you will benefit from purchasing those instances using the Reserved Instance pricing model. Bear in mind that regardless of your consumption patterns, once you purchase a Reserved Instance, you are committed to the discounted hourly charge for the duration of the contract.

Therefore, if you plan to use the compute resources for only a short period, such as a few weeks or months, it might work out more cost-effectively to opt for the On-Demand pricing model.

Spot Instances are another option for applications that can tolerate interruptions and do not require stateful environments. These could be ideal for short batch jobs, for example, where you could provision a fleet of Spot Instances with up to a 90% discount off the On-Demand price for the same instance type.

Another option to reduce costs is to consider using **Savings Plans**. With Savings Plans, you commit to a minimum hourly dollar spend and can provision resources at a discounted rate.

Savings Plans for compute resources are available in two options:

- **Compute Savings Plans**: Designed to provide flexibility to help you reduce your costs across compute resources such as EC2 instances, ECS Fargate, and even Lambda usage. With Compute Savings Plans, you can reduce your costs by up to **66%**. It provides flexibility to move workloads from EC2 to Fargate or Lambda at any time and continue to benefit from the discounted rate.
- **EC2 Instance Savings Plans**: Designed to offer a discount of up to **72%**, but limited to EC2 instances only. You can also move between instance families, operating systems such as Windows to Linux, and across regions such as N. Virginia to London, and continue to benefit from the discounted rate.

The next section provides a high-level overview of how storage is charged.

Storage services

Depending on the type of storage you consume, you are charged based on the total storage allocated or consumed, plus additional parameters, such as the number of requests made to your storage service. Pricing will also vary depending on the region your storage resource is created in. The following provides a broad-level overview of this:

- **Amazon S3**: You are charged for the total storage costs of your object's size and how long you store the objects for each month. The cost also depends on the storage class you place your objects in. Additional features such as monitoring and automated transitions between classes are also applicable for S3 Intelligent-Tiering, as are per-request ingest charges when using `PUT`, `COPY`, or lifecycle rules to move data between storage classes.
- **Amazon EBS Volumes**: You are charged for the total volume you provision, regardless of whether you consume that storage or not. Additional charges may be incurred depending on the volume type and the number of provisioned IOPS (Input/Output Operations Per Second). You are also charged for snapshots you create, store, and copy across regions. You will find more details at `https://aws.amazon.com/ebs/pricing/`.
- **EFS File Systems**: With EFS file systems, you pay for the storage you consume. However, there are also charges based on the type of storage, such as **Standard**, **Infrequent Access**, or **Archive**, as well as the throughput configuration.

Other services are charged based on the number of requests you make. For example, the total number of reads and writes to a DynamoDB table, meaning that you are charged based on reading, writing, and storing data in your DynamoDB tables. Pricing will also vary depending on whether you opt for on-demand or provisioned throughput.

Overall, it's important to understand the specific use case that you are provisioning your resources for and choose the most appropriate pricing option.

In the next section, you will learn about a tool you can use to estimate your monthly costs on AWS.

Introducing AWS cost calculators (Pricing Calculator)

The AWS Pricing Calculator available at `https://calculator.aws/` is a tool you can use to estimate your monthly costs for a given workload. You can select and document a vast array of services you plan to use and the resources you provision, and the pricing calculator will provide a monthly estimate of your total cost.

You can view the prices per service or per group of services to analyze your proposed architecture costs for potential projects. To illustrate how the pricing calculator works, refer to the following architectural diagram for a proposed design as depicted in *Figure 18.1*:

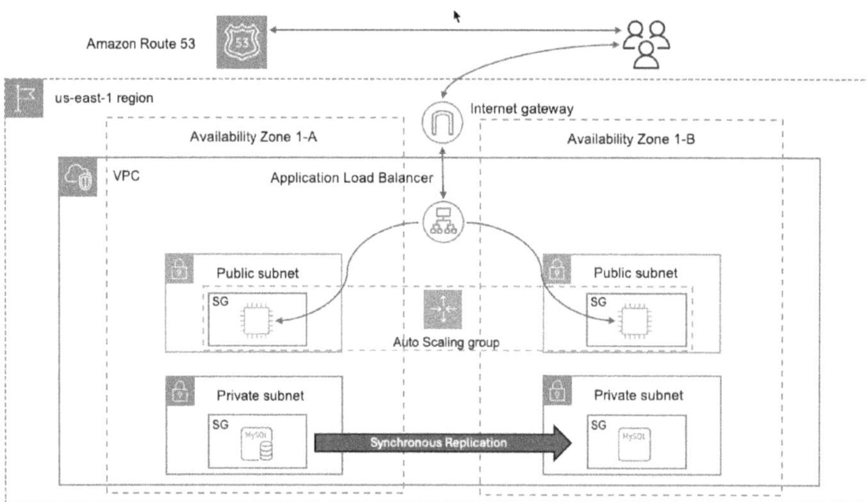

Figure 18.1: AWS architecture example

In the architecture defined in *Figure 18.1*, you will note that several different resources have been provisioned across compute, network, and database services. The core resources provisioned include:

- A **VPC** in the **us-east-1 region**, with four subnets, spread across two availability zones. The VPC hosts an Internet Gateway, giving the resources in the public subnet access to the Internet.
- An **Application Load Balancer** (**ALB**) to allow inbound traffic to be evenly distributed across the web servers (EC2 Instances), which host the Belly Brew Co. Limited web application.
- Two **EC2 Instances**, one in each availability zone, to offer high availability in case of a single AZ outage. The instances are managed by an Auto-Scaling Group, which, for simplicity, is configured to always ensure there are two instances always running with no additional scaling. In real-world use cases, you probably define a scaling policy to handle different loads.
- An Amazon RDS database running the MySQL engine, configured in standard multi-AZ configuration to offer high availability and failover capabilities in case the primary instance has an outage or during maintenance periods.

To determine the costs of these resources, you need to obtain additional pieces of information, such as EC2 instance size for your web servers, the size and type of EBS volumes attached to the instance, the amount of traffic in and out of the VPC, and the database instance type. Additional details like whether you require a multi-AZ configuration for your database, the storage consumed, and the number of requests will also affect the estimated cost.

Using the AWS Pricing Calculator, you would need to provide these details to work out an estimate of the cost of those resources. The screenshot in *Figure 18.2* depicts the calculator where you would select services, resource types, and configurations to enable the calculator to estimate your costs.

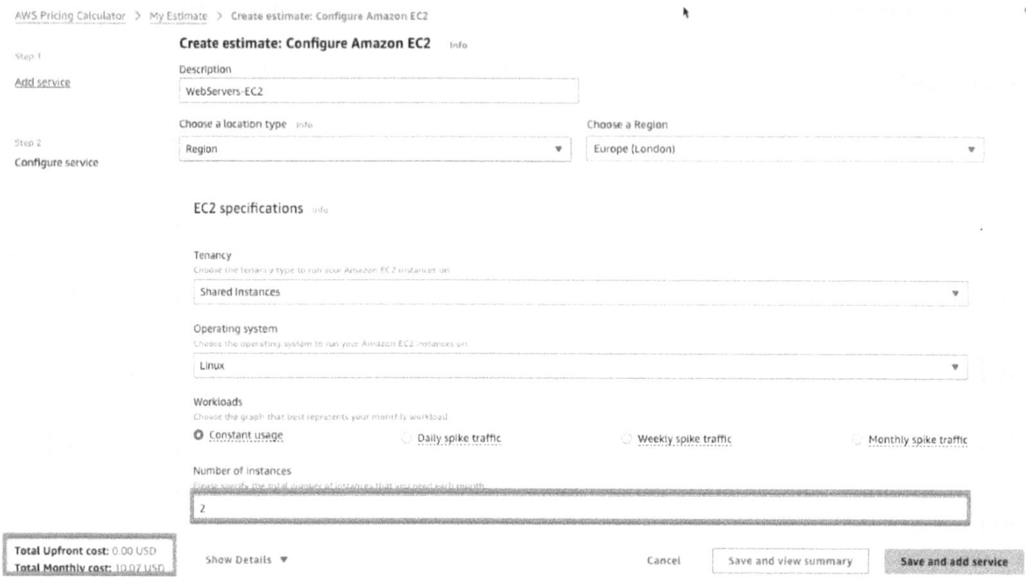

Figure 18.2: Pricing calculator estimate – Monthly costs

The screenshot in *Figure 18.2* only shows a portion of the configuration webpage to calculate the cost of the EC2 instances that will be deployed for the Belly Brew Co. Limited web application, as discussed earlier.

Once you have provided the details of your configuration, you can produce an estimate like the one shown in the screenshot in *Figure 18.3*:

Service	Configuration Summary	Monthly Cost USD ($)
Amazon Virtual Private Cloud (VPC)	DT Inbound: All other regions (0 TB per month), DT Outbound: Europe (British Telecom) - Manchester (25 GB per month), DT Intra-Region: (25 GB per month), Data transfer cost (0.5)	0.50
Application Load Balancer	Number of Application Load Balancers (1)	25.45
Amazon EC2	Tenancy (Shared Instances), Operating system (Linux), Workload (Consistent, Number of instances: 2), Advance EC2 instance (**t3.small**), Pricing strategy (Compute Savings Plans 3yr No Upfront), Enable monitoring (disabled), DT Inbound: Not selected (0 TB per month), DT Outbound: Not selected (0 TB per month), DT Intra-Region: (0 TB per month)	20.15
Amazon Elastic Block Store (EBS)	Number of volumes (2), Average duration of volume (730 hours per month), Storage amount per volume (60 GB), Snapshot Frequency (Daily), Amount changed per snapshot (500 MB), Provisioning IOPS per volume (gp3) (3000), General Purpose SSD (gp3) - Throughput (125 MBps)	18.28
Amazon RDS for MySQL	Storage amount (100 GB), Storage for each RDS instance (General Purpose SSD (gp2)), Nodes (2), Instance type (db.t4g.micro), Utilization (On-Demand only) (100 %Utilized/Month), Deployment option (Multi-AZ), Pricing strategy (OnDemand), Additional backup storage (250 GB)	167.26
Amazon Route 53	Hosted Zones (1)	1.50
Total Monthly Cost		**233.14**

Figure 18.3: Table showing monthly estimated costs

You will also note that the configuration summary provides details of how the resources are defined. For example, the Amazon RDS database has been configured with the multi-AZ settings, which have an impact on the price.

The **Pricing Calculator** is an excellent tool you can use to build cost estimates for your clients when proposing your solutions.

The next section provides a high-level overview of another tool known as the Migration Evaluator.

Estimating migration costs with Migration Evaluator

Many companies looking to move their on-premises workloads to AWS will ask the ultimate question – how much is this going to cost? As a Cloud Practitioner, you must not only be able to design technical solutions for the workloads you plan to host on AWS but also be able to guide the customer on the potential costs involved. Many companies have heard that moving to the cloud could reduce their total expenditure, and often, you need to demonstrate that as part of your client engagement process.

The AWS Migration Evaluator has been designed to help you assist customers in understanding their current on-premises cost structures by modeling their compute, storage, and network patterns, and showing the projected costs of rehosting those workloads in the cloud.

The following are key features of the Migration Evaluator:

- **Inventory Collection**: To collect inventory data from your on-premises resources, you must install an agentless collector on your on-premises servers that will have read-only access to your VMware and Hyper-V environments, hosting servers running Linux, Windows, Active Directory, Exchange, SQL Server, and more.
- **Migration Evaluator Quick Insights**: This feature provides visibility into the projected costs of running your on-premises application in the cloud. It comes with a summary page highlighting the potential savings of moving your workloads to the cloud. It also offers detailed per-server configuration details that your technical team will find useful.
- **Server Dependency Mapping**: This feature offers technical details of your server architecture as well as network connectivity configuration to provide a visual representation of your server-to-server dependencies, ensuring that you know the best order to follow to complete the migration.
- **AWS Migration Expertise**: AWS offers a team of solutions architects to understand your migration goals, such as consolidating licensing, migration of data and shifting from CAPEX to OPEX. These subject matter experts can provide expert guidance and help strategize your migration plans.

AWS Migration Evaluator can help you define and create necessary business case reports to illustrate the cost benefits of moving your workloads to the AWS cloud.

In the next section, you will learn about a service that can be used to visualize your monthly historical costs as well as forecast future costs based on current and past usage patterns.

Understanding the basics of AWS Cost Explorer

AWS Cost Explorer is a visualization tool designed to help you view your monthly costs over a period. You can use the services to look at historical costs and understand what your average monthly spend is for a given AWS account. *Figure 18.4* depicts a snapshot of the total cost and average monthly costs:

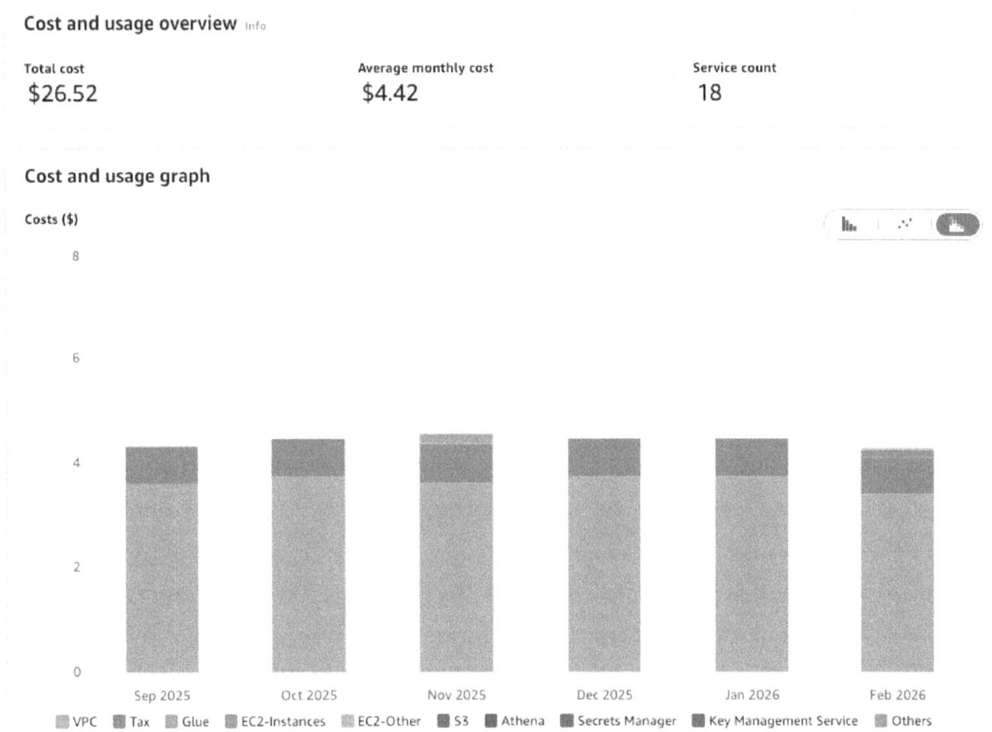

Figure 18.4: AWS Cost Explorer

You can generate reports and graphs to provide a visual representation of how your total spend is allocated across services consumed in your account. You can also forecast up to 18 months ahead and understand how predictions are calculated with AI-powered explanations.

The following screenshot in *Figure 18.5* depicts the forecasted costs for March, April, and May 2026:

Figure 18.5: AWS Cost Explorer with costs forecasts

In addition to visualizing your current and historic spend, as well as forecasting future monthly costs, there are several reports you can generate with the AWS Cost Explorer services. These include:

- **Reserved Instance (RI) Utilization**: This report enables you to identify the savings made from using reserved instances over on-demand options for Amazon EC2, Amazon RDS, and others. It also suggests any recommendations for future purchases.
- **Reserved Instance (RI) Coverage**: This report details what percentage of your compute consumption has been covered by RI instances you have purchased in your account.
- **Cost Anomaly Detection**: Another feature is the ability to detect anomalies in your normal spending patterns. In most cases, these might be approved changes you made in your account, such as launching additional resources for a new project. However, the root case feature helps pinpoint the additional spend, which you can then investigate further.

In the next section, you will learn how you can use cost allocation tags to help you identify which services and resources you are consuming and spending on.

Cost allocation tags

You can tag most resources you create in AWS to help you identify that resource and what purpose that resource serves. Tags consist of a key and a value pair, and you can attach up to 50 such key-value pair tags for every single resource you create in AWS (this can vary slightly by service). For example, in addition to using a tag to name your resource, you can also tag it as being part of a given project, for a specific department, and other similar categories.

You can also use cost-allocation tags to help you identify your spending patterns against your resources. Here, AWS offers two types of cost-allocation tagging options:

- **AWS-generated tags**: These are created and managed by AWS services
- **User-defined tags**: These are created and managed by you using your preferred corporate naming conventions. These tags help you track usage and cost across your AWS resources

You must activate cost-allocation tags to be able to produce reports with those tags and understand your usage and consumption patterns.

Another service you can use to help you create chargeback capabilities with your customers is called the AWS Billing Conductor, and this is discussed in the next section.

AWS Billing Conductor

The **AWS Billing Conductor** enables you to customize your monthly billing data so that you can visualize the billing relationship between you and your customers or internal business units with which you have a chargeback relationship. This is also useful if you charge external customers for your services as an AWS Partner. The service also allows you to distribute credits, fees, and shared overhead costs, which is particularly useful to attribute costs to the correct internal teams and business units.

The service allows you to generate and display rates to customers over a billing period, and you can use it to generate and display custom rates you charge to your customers for a given billing cycle.

In the next section, you will learn how you can create and manage budgets on AWS.

Configuring AWS Budgets

In *Chapter 4*, you were introduced to AWS Budgets as part of *Project Task 4.3*. This service is designed to help you define budgets that you can use to track costs and usage across different types of projects, business units, and departments.

Different departments and business units may have different application workloads that need to run in your AWS account. You can configure budgets to keep track of the costs incurred by those workloads and apply guardrails to avoid overspending.

You can define threshold values for both actual and forecasted budgets and configure specific actions to take if the budget threshold value is crossed. For example, you can specify an IAM policy that denies the ability for a user or group to launch new EC2 instances if the monthly budget for EC2 has been exceeded.

With **AWS Budgets**, you can also configure alerts using Amazon SNS so that specific individuals or groups can be notified when the actual spend has crossed specific threshold values of the budget, such as at 75% or 90%, and so on.

There are several types of budgets you can create, including:

- **Cost budgets**: Define a specific amount you are willing to spend over a period, such as monthly
- **Usage budgets**: Define how much of a specific service you wish to consume
- **RI utilization budgets**: Specify a utilization threshold amount and configure alerts to send you a notification if you use less than the threshold value. This is particularly useful when you want to identify if your RI resources are being underutilized
- **RI coverage budgets**: Identify how much of your instance usage is covered by the reservation
- **Savings Plans utilization budgets**: Identify when your Savings Plans utilization falls below a specific threshold value, which can be used to identify if any Savings Plans are underutilized
- **Savings Plans coverage budgets**: Identify how much of your instance usage is covered by the Savings Plans

AWS Budgets are designed to help you ensure your company does not overspend and to keep track of all projects and workloads you run in your AWS account. Additionally, you can identify opportunities, such as procuring additional Reserved Instances or using Savings Plans, that might help you be more cost-effective.

The next section gives you an opportunity to get some hands-on practice with AWS Cost Explorer.

Project task 18 – Forecasting spending with AWS Cost Explorer

In this project task, you will configure the AWS Cost Explorer to report on forecasted costs for the upcoming months in your AWS Development account. You have already deployed various resources while completing previous project tasks, so this is an opportunity to see what your costs might look like in the future. Note that if you have set up a free plan account, you should not be incurring an actual bill just yet because the project tasks you deployed would have consumed some of the credits AWS provided when you set up the account.

Technical requirements

To complete the tasks in this project exercise, you must be logged into the AWS Development Account as the IAM user Alice.

Project task 18.1 – Forecasting monthly costs using Cost Explorer

In this project task, you will forecast the costs likely to occur in the upcoming months.

The following steps will guide you through the process:

1. Ensure you are logged into the AWS Development account, this time as the root user (Not Alice)
2. In the AWS Management Console, click on your **Account Name** (e.g., Development) in the top right-hand corner of the webpage
3. From the list that appears, click **Billing and Cost Management**
4. In the webpage that appears, click **Cost Explorer** under **Cost and Usage Analysis** from the left-hand menu
5. In the right-hand pane, you will have the option to create a **New cost and usage report**. In the far-right pane, under **Report parameters**, do the following:
    1. Click the **Date Range** textbox and set the range from the current month to three months ahead in the future. For example, if the current month is February and the year is 2026, set the range as `2026-02-01 - 2026-05-31`
    2. Click the **Apply** button
6. The middle pane should now be updated with a graph and a table showing the current month's spending and the three upcoming months, as shown in the following screenshot in *Figure 18.6*:

Figure 18.6: Cost Explorer forecasts

Note the current month's cost and the upcoming forecasted costs for your workloads. In the example shown in *Figure 18.6*, you will note that there were no costs incurred in February. This is because the AWS credits are still available in this account and are being consumed for any workloads deployed. However, this account has been used for running projects too, and so you will note that in March, the forecasted cost is going to be around $30. Hopefully, your cost explorer window shows no forecasted charges (because you were careful to terminate all unwanted resources).

Summary

Businesses across the globe are keen to reduce their overall costs and often look to move to the cloud because of the promise of significant savings, driven by greater economies of scale. Cloud providers like AWS, Azure, and Google Cloud compete not only on delivering advanced technologies but also on price, making it an ideal opportunity to consider cloud hosting rather than an on-premises approach to building IT infrastructure.

However, simply rehosting your workloads in the cloud is not going to save you money if your architectural design strategy is not cost-optimized. Providers like AWS charge you by the second for many of their services, and unless you closely monitor your consumption—

ensuring you reduce wastage by not running idle resources in the middle of the night when no one is accessing your application, costs can quickly add up. It is even possible to spend vast amounts on cloud resources, making on-premises infrastructure seem more cost-effective. The reality, however, is that cloud services can be highly cost-efficient so long as you ensure your design patterns are aligned with your cost optimization goals.

With AWS, you also benefit from a range of free tier options. For example, you get 1 million free invocations of Lambda functions before incurring any costs. While these features help reduce overall spend, it's important to note that runaway applications, bugs, or malicious code can quickly consume these free-tier allowances. In addition, there are several ways to reduce costs further, such as using Reserved Instances or Savings Plans.

Beyond design considerations, you have access to a variety of tools and services to help you gain visibility into your costs, define budgets, enforce rules when thresholds are exceeded, and access detailed reports to maximize utilization and achieve better value for money.

Finally, tools like the AWS Pricing Calculator and Migration Evaluator help you estimate the costs of workloads you plan to move to the cloud.

In the final chapter, you will take a deep dive into the core architectural best practices for building solutions in the cloud using the AWS Well-Architected Framework. This framework is built around six key principles, or pillars, that form the foundation of any cloud solution you choose to develop. It provides best-practice guidance and recommendations covering reliability, performance, security, cost optimization, operational excellence, and sustainability—concepts that are critical in today's cloud-driven world. You will also learn about the AWS **Cloud Adoption Framework** (**CAF**), a business-focused collection of best practices and methodologies designed to help organizations transform from traditional IT environments and legacy systems to modern architectures and cloud-hosted applications.

Exam Readiness Drill – Chapter Review Questions

Apart from mastering key concepts, strong test-taking skills under time pressure are essential for acing your certification exam. That's why developing these abilities early in your learning journey is critical.

Exam readiness drills, using the free online practice resources provided with this book, help you progressively improve your time management and test-taking skills while reinforcing the key concepts you've learned.

HOW TO GET STARTED

- Open the link or scan the QR code at the bottom of this page
- If you have unlocked the practice resources already, log in to your registered account. If you haven't, follow the instructions in *Free Benefits with Your Book* section in this book's *Preface* and come back to this page.
- Once you log in, click the START button to start this chapter's quiz
- We recommend attempting a quiz multiple times till you're able to answer most of the questions correctly and well within the time limit.
- You can use the following practice template to help you plan your attempts:

Working On Accuracy		
Attempt	**Target**	**Time Limit**
Attempt 1	40% or more	Till the timer runs out
Attempt 2	60% or more	Till the timer runs out
Attempt 3	75% or more	Till the timer runs out
Working On Timing		
Attempt 4	75% or more	1 minute before time limit
Attempt 5	75% or more	2 minutes before time limit
Attempt 6	75% or more	3 minutes before time limit

The above drill is just an example. Design your drills based on your own goals and make the most out of the online quizzes accompanying this book.

Link to this Chapter's Quiz

You need to unlock the online practice resources to access the link below. Check the *Free Benefits with Your Book* section in the *Preface* for detailed instructions on how to do this. You only need to unlock the resources once.

Open Quiz `https://packt.link/clf_c02_ch18` or scan the QR code

Part 6

Architectural Best Practices and Digital Transformation

The final part of this book focuses on core architectural best practices and how to build cloud solutions by following the principles of the AWS Well-Architected Framework. Doing so helps ensure that your applications and workloads are designed with security in mind, are scalable and resilient, and can adapt to changing levels of demand. The six pillars also provide best-practice guidance to help optimize costs and ensure the architectures you build are environmentally sustainable.

In addition, you will learn about the AWS Cloud Adoption Framework—a set of guidelines designed to help organizations adopt cloud technologies and digitally transform their businesses. The framework provides a structured approach to business transformation, enabling organizations to modernize their operations and compete more effectively in today's digital economy.

This final part of the book includes only the following chapter:

- *Chapter 19, AWS Cloud Adoption Framework (CAF) and Well-Architected Framework*

19

AWS Cloud Adoption Framework (CAF) and Well-Architected Framework

Businesses move to the cloud to become more agile, access cutting-edge technologies to gain a competitive advantage, enforce high levels of security, and ultimately reduce costs while avoiding the **capital expenditure** (**CAPEX**) typically associated with on-premises infrastructure.

However, without the right guidance and adherence to industry best practices, cloud adoption can become inefficient, leading to poor architectural choices, security risks, and uncontrolled spending.

AWS provides two key frameworks designed to help organizations successfully navigate their cloud transformation journey:

- **The AWS Cloud Adoption Framework** (**CAF**) – which outlines how organizations plan and manage their cloud transformation initiatives
- The AWS Well-Architected Framework (**WAF**) – which provides best practices for designing and operating workloads that are secure, reliable, performant, cost-effective, and sustainable

Together, these frameworks provide a structured approach to both the business and technical aspects of cloud adoption.

In this chapter, you will cover the following main topics:

- Understanding the AWS Cloud Adoption Framework
- Applying the six pillars of the AWS Well-Architected Framework
- Assessing workloads with the AWS Well-Architected Tool

Understanding the AWS Cloud Adoption Framework

The AWS **Cloud Adoption Framework** (**CAF**) provides a structured approach to help organizations plan and execute their cloud transformation through four key transformation domains—Technology, Process, Organization, and Product. The following is a high-level overview of these domains:

- **Technology**: Focuses on cloud services to help migrate and modernize legacy systems, ultimately reducing costs, improving security posture, and decreasing downtime
- **Process**: Focuses on digitizing, automating, and optimizing business operations. This may involve using cutting-edge technologies like machine learning and artificial intelligence to improve customer experience, enhance employee productivity, conduct fraud detection, and accurately forecast business performance
- **Organization**: Focuses on enhancing teams and departments to better collaborate and work efficiently together, enabling rapid iterative improvements to products and services while gaining a competitive advantage
- **Product**: Focuses on creating value propositions and new revenue streams, enabling organizations to reach more customers and increase market share

These domains represent the primary areas of change required to enable successful cloud adoption.

Underpinning these domains are six perspectives—Business, People, Governance, Platform, Security, and Operations—which together enable organizations to achieve key business outcomes such as reduced risk, improved operational efficiency, and increased business value, as illustrated in the cloud transformation value chain shown in *Figure 19.1*.

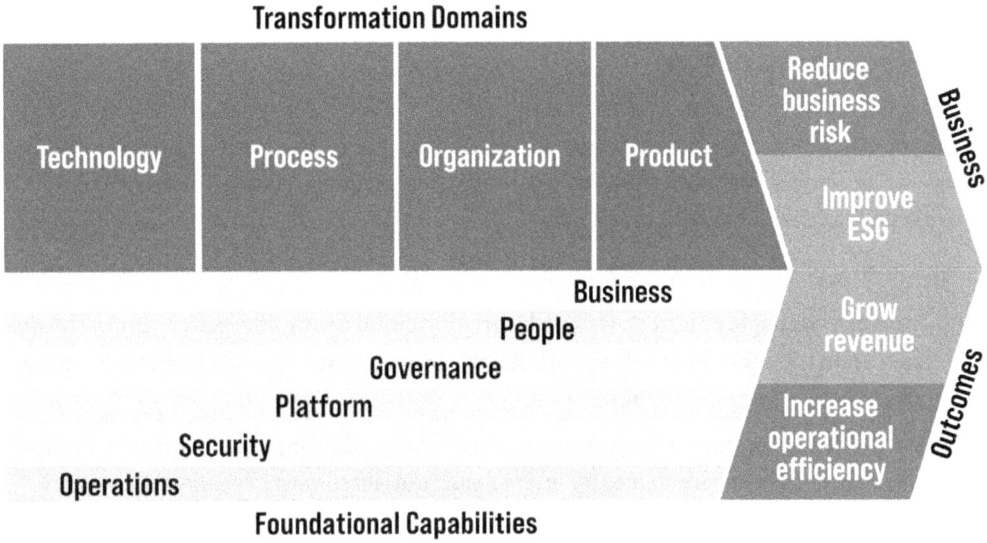

Figure 19.1: AWS CAF workflow

Each perspective comprises a set of capabilities that enable you to leverage processes and best practice guidance, helping you improve your cloud readiness and deliver a successful cloud adoption and transformation. These perspectives and their associated capabilities are depicted in *Figure 19.2*.

Business	People	Governance	Platform	Security	Operations
Strategy Management	Culture Evolution	Program & Project Management	Platform Architecture	Security Governance	Observability
Portfolio Management	Transformational Leadership	Benefits Management	Data Architecture	Security Assurance	Event Mgmt (AIOps)
Innovation Management	Cloud Fluency	Risk Management	Platform Engineering	Identity & Access Management	Incident and Problem Mgmt
Product Management	Workforce Transformation	Cloud Financial Management	Data Engineering	Threat Detection	Change & Release Management
Strategic Partnership	Change Acceleration	Application Portfolio Mgmt	Provisioning and Orchestration	Vulnerability Management	Performance and Capacity Mgmt
Data Monetization	Organization Design	Data Governance	Modern App. Development	Infrastructure Protection	Configuration Management
Business Insights	Organizational Alignment	Data Curation	CI/CD	Data Protection	Patch Management
Data Science				Application Security	Availability and Continuity Mgmt
				Incident Response	Application Management

Figure 19.2: AWS CAF perspectives and their capabilities

The following is a breakdown of the individual perspectives and their capabilities:

Business perspective

The Business perspective focuses on ensuring that your investments are used effectively to achieve your digital transformation goals and objectives, delivering positive business outcomes. Common stakeholders typically include senior leadership and the board of directors, such as the CEO and CTO.

Key capabilities for this perspective are:

- **Strategy management**: Focuses on leveraging cloud technologies to optimize business operations, identify new value propositions and revenue models, capture new markets, and expand the customer base.
- **Portfolio management**: Examines current product offerings and prioritizes cloud-native initiatives to accelerate business goals and outcomes. Leverages the seven migration strategies (known as the **7 Rs of migration**) to rationalize the product portfolio, identify short- and long-term opportunities, and determine where the business can benefit from innovation and financial gains.
- **Innovation management**: Focuses on developing new and improving existing processes and products. Leverages the cloud to provision and decommission resources on demand using a consumption-based model. Encourages incremental improvements while supporting new business ideas and models.
- **Product management**: Focuses on managing cloud-enabled products that deliver continuous value to customers throughout their lifecycle. This involves building a balanced product portfolio, organizing small cross-functional teams, defining product ownership and roadmaps, and using agile methods to iterate rapidly.
- **Strategic partnerships**: Focuses on developing strategic partnerships with cloud providers, particularly when building cloud-hosted solutions, integration products, and services. Enables organizations to benefit from partner programs, promotional offerings, and funding opportunities.
- **Data monetization**: Focuses on leveraging data to develop long-term monetization strategies by identifying opportunities to improve operations, customer and employee experience, and decision-making, while enabling new business models. Examples include personalization, localization, segmentation, and customer loyalty programs.
- **Business insights**: Focuses on gaining real-time and near real-time insights into business performance to improve decision-making and optimize operations. Leverages

data catalogs to locate relevant data and uses dashboards to identify trends, patterns, and relationships.

- **Data science**: Focuses on advanced analytics and machine learning to identify data monetization opportunities. Ensures data is appropriate for building, training, and testing models, and includes human-in-the-loop validation where needed for low-confidence predictions.

Belly Brew Co. Limited uses cloud technologies to support its growth strategy by expanding online sales channels, improving customer engagement, and gaining real-time insights into product demand across its retail network. By leveraging data analytics and cloud-based services, the company can identify new market opportunities, optimize operations, and develop innovative products that deliver greater value to customers.

The next section covers the People perspective and its related capabilities.

People perspective

The people perspective focuses on encouraging constant change as a cultural norm, ensuring continuous growth, learning, and agility. By evangelizing change as progress and growth, businesses can adapt to market dynamics more quickly, operate more efficiently, and build stronger leadership and workforce capabilities. Common stakeholders typically include the CIO (Chief Information Officer), COO (Chief Operating Officer), CTO (Chief Technology Officer), and enterprise leaders.

Key capabilities for this perspective are:

- **Cultural evolution**: Focuses on leveraging your heritage and values while incorporating new behaviors and mindsets to build a workforce that is adaptable and thrives on continuous improvement and innovation. Develop a customer-obsessed approach across all aspects of your business, encouraging iterative improvements and building a culture of cross-functional teams to drive ownership and autonomy.
- **Transformational leadership**: Focuses on strengthening leadership capabilities by aligning technical and business leaders to ensure transformation progress against common goals and objectives. Develop a **Cloud Center of Excellence** (**CCoE**) to evangelize and drive transformation efforts, codifying patterns for consistency and scalability.
- **Cloud fluency**: Focuses on targeted training strategies to encourage rapid, practical, and project-focused skill development. Promote data literacy and develop advanced analytics skill sets. Combine virtual, classroom, and just-in-time training with hackathons and formal certification-based validation. Encourage and reward knowledge sharing through formal processes, peer reviews, and ongoing curation.

- **Workforce transformation**: Focuses on building a diverse and inclusive workforce with an appropriate mix of technical and non-technical skill sets. Identify gaps in roles and address them through structured hiring and training programs to improve your organization's cloud capability. Attract new talent by building a strong employer brand and promoting a clear digital vision and future-focused culture.
- Change acceleration: Focuses on driving adoption of new ways of working using structured, end-to-end frameworks designed to minimize disruption across people, culture, and roles. Align leadership around success factors, reduce potential barriers and dependencies, and enable people across the organization to adapt effectively to change.
- **Organization design**: Design your organization to align with cloud-native operating models, enabling progress throughout your transformation journey. This includes how teams are structured, enabling cross-functional collaboration, defining decision-making processes, and maintaining open communication channels. Use managed service providers to offload non-core tasks and build strong partner relationships.
- **Organizational alignment**: Ensure strong alignment across organizational structures, operations, and processes. Prioritize business outcomes such as operational resilience, agility, and product/service innovation. Build autonomous systems that focus on better decision-making and improved productivity.

Belly Brew Co. Limited invests in developing cloud and data skills across its workforce, enabling employees to adopt new technologies that improve collaboration, productivity, and innovation. By fostering a culture of continuous learning and cross-functional teamwork, the company can adapt more quickly to changing customer demands while supporting its long-term digital transformation goals.

The next section covers the Governance perspective and its related capabilities.

Governance perspective

The Governance perspective is designed to help you orchestrate your cloud initiatives in a way that reduces risk to business operations while ensuring alignment with future goals and objectives. Key stakeholders typically include members of the board of directors, such as the CIO and COO.

Key capabilities for this perspective are:

- **Program and Project Management**: Focuses on delivering carefully coordinated, cross-functional cloud transformation initiatives. The emphasis is on strong program management to oversee critical interdependencies and manage costs, schedules, and effort effectively. This capability also ensures that you continuously monitor progress, validate roadmaps with business sponsors, and escalate issues to senior leadership in a timely manner.

- **Benefits management**: Focuses on clearly identifying the business benefits of cloud initiatives upfront and tracking transformation progress over time. This includes defining metrics to measure and demonstrate desired outcomes and communicating these results to stakeholders. Regularly measuring benefits against proposed roadmaps is fundamental to this capability.
- **Risk management**: Focuses on how cloud services can be used to reduce business risk. This includes identifying and quantifying risks related to availability, security, performance, and business reputation, and defining how cloud adoption can mitigate those risks. It also highlights reducing large upfront infrastructure investments by leveraging on-demand, scalable, and reliable cloud resources.
- **Cloud financial management**: Focuses on planning, measuring, and optimizing cloud spend by aligning services and resources with the most appropriate pricing models for each use case. This includes budgeting, dynamic forecasting, and identifying cost anomalies early. It emphasizes the use of tagging strategies, such as cost allocation tags, to understand which projects, business units, and departments are incurring costs. It also includes strategies to benefit from volume discounts through consolidated billing, enforcing guardrails where necessary, and avoiding technical debt.
- **Application portfolio management**: Focuses on managing and optimizing your application portfolio to support business strategy. This involves creating an accurate inventory of applications, identifying opportunities for consolidation, migration, and modernization, and prioritizing critical applications based on business impact. It also includes mapping applications to the underlying infrastructure and ensuring scalability, high availability, and security.
- **Data governance**: Focuses on managing and controlling data to ensure it is accurate, consistent, secure, and fit for business use. This involves defining standards and policies, along with continuously monitoring and improving data quality throughout its lifecycle.
- **Data curation**: Focuses on organizing data so it can be easily found, understood, and used. This includes creating and maintaining a data catalog that acts as a searchable index, enabling self-service access for analysts and stakeholders. It also involves enriching data with metadata to improve discoverability and usability.

Belly Brew Co. Limited uses governance processes to ensure its cloud investments deliver measurable business value while maintaining control over costs, security, and operational risks. By implementing financial monitoring, data governance policies, and structured project oversight, the company can support sustainable growth while ensuring cloud initiatives remain aligned with strategic business objectives.

The next section covers Platform perspective and its related capabilities.

Platform perspective

The Platform perspective focuses on enabling and accelerating the delivery of cloud workloads using enterprise solutions that are scalable, resilient, and secure. It also considers hybrid design models, particularly when connecting on-premises workloads with cloud resources.

Key capabilities for this perspective are:

- **Platform architecture**: Focuses on enabling you to create and maintain guidelines, principles, and patterns to accelerate cloud adoption while reducing risk. It involves creating blueprints and guardrails to support authentication, security, logging, and auditing. You may also need to consider workloads that must remain on premises due to latency or data residency requirements, where hybrid models are appropriate.
- **Data architecture**: Focuses on building well-designed data and analytics architectures that are fit for purpose while reducing complexity, cost, and technical debt. Consider a layered approach where the right tools are used for the right use cases, and improvements are made incrementally. Leverage serverless technologies and managed services to simplify the management of underlying resources.
- **Platform engineering**: Focuses on building multi-account environments to separate workload stages such as development, testing, and production. Enforce preventative and detective guardrails to ensure only approved services and resources are used. Consider identity federation to simplify authentication using existing credentials. Use **Infrastructure as Code** (**IaC**) to create consistent and repeatable configurations.
- **Data engineering**: Focuses on automating data and analytics platforms to improve productivity and time to market. Use metadata to automate data pipelines that ingest raw data and produce optimized datasets. Establish cross-functional teams that bring together expertise from infrastructure, software engineering, and data management.
- **Provisioning and orchestration**: Focus on defining approved cloud products using service catalogs. Maintain consistent infrastructure provisioning through IaC and design self-service portals to enable teams to access and consume approved resources.
- **Modern application development**: Focuses on adopting well-architected, cloud-native design patterns. Use containers and serverless architectures to optimize resource

utilization and decouple applications into independent microservices and event-driven components. Ensure security is implemented throughout the application lifecycle.

- **Continuous integration and continuous delivery (CI/CD)**: Focuses on adopting DevOps practices to build agile and iterative application delivery processes. Implement CI/CD pipelines to accelerate innovation, encourage early testing such as unit tests, and use deployment strategies such as in-place, rolling, immutable, and blue/green deployments.

Belly Brew Co. Limited uses cloud platforms to build scalable, secure, and resilient systems that support online ordering, inventory management, production planning, and business analytics. By adopting cloud-native services, automation, and **Infrastructure as Code** (**IaC**), the company can deploy new solutions faster, improve operational efficiency, and support future business growth.

The next section covers the Security perspective and its related capabilities.

Security perspective

The Security perspective focuses on achieving confidentiality, integrity, and availability of your data. It emphasizes applying security best practices across all layers of the application stack, from the underlying physical resources through to the application itself. Key stakeholders include the CISO, CCS, internal auditors, and security engineers.

Key capabilities for this perspective are:

- **Security governance**: Focuses on establishing effective security roles, responsibilities, policies, and procedures with clear lines of accountability. It examines compliance requirements and ensures adherence to regulatory and legal obligations. It also emphasizes your responsibility for security in the cloud—how you configure and manage workloads and applications, and how you secure your data. Regular risk assessments are encouraged to identify vulnerabilities and define mitigation strategies.
- **Security assurance**: Focuses on continuously monitoring and improving security and privacy programs. It emphasizes the importance of documented controls, regular review of audit reports, and alignment with compliance programs. It also ensures the operational effectiveness of controls and ongoing review of security policies, processes, and procedures.
- **Identity and access management**: Focuses on managing identities and granting permissions based on the principle of least privilege. It encourages the use of centralized IAM solutions or federation with existing **identity providers** (**IdPs**), along with **multi-factor authentication** (**MFA**). It also promotes the use of **attribute-based access control** (**ABAC**) to enable scalable and dynamic policy enforcement.

- **Threat detection**: Focuses on identifying potential security misconfigurations, anomalies, and suspicious behaviors that could lead to breaches. It involves using monitoring tools and services to collect and analyze data from multiple sources, including network traffic, operating systems, applications, databases, and endpoints, to improve visibility and response times.
- **Vulnerability management**: Focuses on regularly scanning for vulnerabilities and prioritizing remediation based on risk. It also recommends practices such as penetration testing and red teaming to identify weaknesses across the application stack and infrastructure configurations, ensuring appropriate authorization is obtained beforehand.
- **Infrastructure protection**: Focuses on protecting infrastructure from unintended and unauthorized access. It applies a defense-in-depth approach, including network security controls such as network access control lists and security groups, endpoint protection for services like EC2 and operating systems, and application-layer protections such as web application firewalls and authentication mechanisms.
- **Data protection**: Focuses on ensuring data is protected from unauthorized access. It recommends classifying data based on sensitivity and criticality (e.g., PII and PHI), defining data lifecycle policies, and enforcing encryption both at rest and in transit.
- **Application security**: Focuses on identifying and addressing vulnerabilities within applications. It promotes best practices such as avoiding hardcoding sensitive data or credentials, performing regular code scans, and applying timely patching at the software layer.
- **Incident response**: Focuses on ensuring a rapid and effective response to security incidents. It includes educating staff on security operations, developing runbooks and incident response procedures, and conducting simulated incidents to identify gaps. Lessons learned should be used to continuously improve response processes.

Belly Brew Co. Limited implements security controls to protect sensitive customer, employee, and business data while ensuring its cloud-based systems remain available and resilient. By applying security best practices such as identity and access management, encryption, continuous monitoring, and incident response planning, the company can reduce risk, maintain customer trust, and support regulatory compliance.

The next section covers the Operations perspective and its related capabilities.

Operations perspective

The Operations perspective focuses on automating and optimizing operations to ensure your workloads are scalable, reliable, and managed in accordance with best practices. Key stakeholders include infrastructure and operations leaders, site reliability engineers, and service managers.

Key capabilities for this perspective are:

- **Observability**: Focuses on using tools to capture telemetry data, including logs, metrics, and traces, to understand the internal workflows of your application stack. Traces help track requests as they move through application components and can be used to identify bottlenecks. You can also use synthetic monitoring to create canaries—configurable scripts that run on a schedule to capture detailed information about your endpoints and APIs. Consider using Business Intelligence (BI) tools to visualize findings and turn raw data into actionable insights.
- **Event management (AIOps)**: Focuses on monitoring events in your cloud environments to understand their impact on workloads. It helps filter out noise and focus on what matters. Machine learning can be used to detect unusual behavior, predict potential issues, and automate alert generation.
- **Incident and problem management**: Focuses on restoring operations quickly and minimizing business impact. Automating responses can accelerate resolution and improve uptime. As cloud systems are often distributed, ensure teams are aligned and tools are integrated to resolve issues efficiently. This includes defining clear escalation paths and using runbooks to guide response actions.
- **Change and release management**: Focuses on making change and release processes more iterative and reliable, with rollback capabilities to reduce the risk of outages. Implement automated approval workflows where possible and enable automated rollback to a known good state when issues occur.
- **Performance and capacity management**: Focuses on monitoring workload performance and ensuring capacity meets both current and future demands. Incorporate Auto Scaling while adhering to service quotas and use capacity reservations where necessary. Continuously monitor utilization and analyze trends to align capacity with demand patterns.

- **Configuration management**: Focuses on maintaining an accurate and complete record of your cloud resources and their relationships as they change over time. Use **Infrastructure as Code** (**IaC**) to ensure consistent and repeatable configurations, avoid configuration drift, and integrate version control systems.
- **Availability and continuity management**: Focuses on ensuring the availability of business-critical applications. Design for disaster recovery by understanding business **RTO** (**Recovery Time Objective**) and **RPO** (**Recovery Point Objective**) requirements and selecting appropriate backup and recovery strategies. Consider leveraging chaos engineering to improve resilience in controlled environments.
- **Application management**: Focuses on monitoring, managing, and resolving issues within the application stack. It involves aggregating application data into a single management interface to provide end-to-end visibility and control.

Belly Brew Co. Limited uses cloud operations and automation to monitor production, sales, and business applications, ensuring systems remain reliable, scalable, and available as the business grows. By implementing monitoring, automated scaling, backup and recovery processes, and IaC, the company can improve operational efficiency, reduce downtime, and maintain business continuity.

As a set, these six perspectives provide a roadmap to enable Belly Brew Co. Limited to embark on its digital cloud transformation journey:

- Business: Why Belly Brew Co. Limited is adopting the cloud
- People: How employees and leaders support the transformation
- Governance: How cloud adoption is controlled and measured
- Platform: The technical foundation enabling cloud workloads
- Security: How data and systems are protected
- Operations: How workloads are monitored, maintained, and optimized

Using the AWS Cloud Adoption Framework and understanding the underlying perspectives and their capabilities can help organizations accelerate their cloud digital transformation journeys. By incorporating these capabilities into your transformation strategy, you can build end-to-end cloud solutions that align with your business goals and objectives.

Critical to this is the transformation journey itself, which should be incremental and demonstrate value-added improvements quickly. In addition, taking an iterative approach helps maintain momentum and allows you to continuously evolve your roadmap as you progress.

The AWS CAF recommends four iterative and incremental cloud transformation phases. These are depicted in the following diagram in *Figure 19.3*:

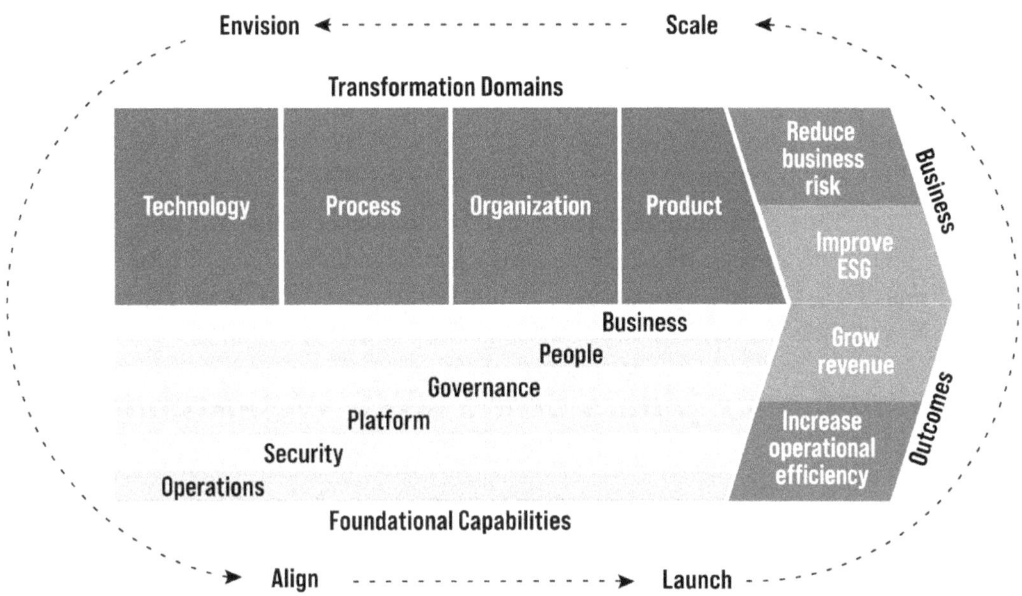

Figure 19.3: The four phases of transformation

The four phases are:

- **Envision phase**: Focuses on identifying and prioritizing opportunities across the four transformation domains and defining a target state that aligns with business goals and objectives. This includes creating business cases, identifying key opportunities, and building a cloud adoption roadmap.
- Align phase: Focuses on understanding your current environment and identifying gaps across the six AWS CAF perspectives that must be addressed for successful cloud adoption. This phase involves identifying key stakeholders, assessing existing capabilities, and building awareness of how the cloud can deliver business value.

- Launch phase: Focuses on building and deploying the initial cloud environment and pilot initiatives. It is important to establish foundational capabilities, such as governance, security, and platform architecture to demonstrate value and validate the approach.
- Scale phase: Focuses on expanding pilot initiatives into full production workloads with scalable capabilities. This involves optimizing operations, improving processes, and accelerating migration efforts to realize business value.

The six perspectives of the AWS Cloud Adoption Framework enable businesses to embark on their cloud adoption journey in a controlled and systematic manner—aligning the whole organization to a common goal, reducing risk, improving operational efficiency, increasing business value, and ultimately staying competitive in the market.

While the AWS **Cloud Adoption Framework** (**CAF**) focuses on broader business transformation goals and objectives, the Well-Architected Framework focuses on the architectural design patterns of your workloads and applications in the cloud. The next section introduces you to this framework and its six pillars of success.

Applying the six pillars of the AWS Well-Architected Framework

The AWS Well-Architected Framework provides a set of best practice guidelines that help you design, build, and operate your applications and workloads in a secure, reliable, high-performing, cost-effective, and sustainable manner.

It is built around six key pillars as depicted in the diagram in *Figure 19.4*, with each pillar focusing on a specific area of cloud architecture:

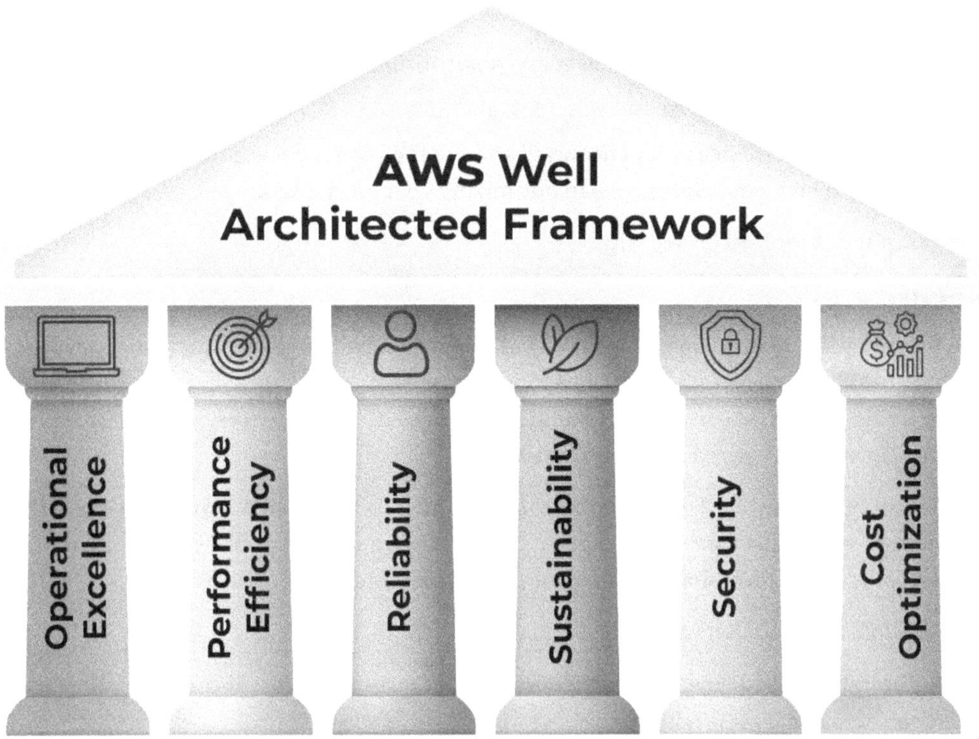

Figure 19.4: AWS Well Architected Framework

By understanding these pillars, you can make informed design decisions and ensure your solutions align with AWS's recommended best practices.

Operational Excellence pillar

The Operational Excellence pillar focuses on how well you manage and run your workloads, ensuring continuous improvements, and analyzing data for further optimization over time. You want to ensure that your workloads incur minimum administrative overhead, and often this requires incorporating DevOps practices and Site Reliability Engineering principles.

Key principles of this pillar include:

- Consider automating procedures and configurations using IaC
- Making small, frequent, and reversible changes that are easier to roll back and reduce risk
- Continuously review and improve operational processes

- Design for failure (so nothing fails) and perform rigorous testing and simulations, such as hackathons and game days
- Conduct *lessons* learned exercises and share insights with key stakeholders
- Implement and analyze metrics, logs, and KPIs

The Operational Excellence pillar encourages you to focus on reducing the time spent firefighting and being more proactive in optimizing your workloads.

The next pillar is focused on security.

Security pillar

The Security pillar focuses on ensuring your data is protected while in transit and at rest. It provides best practice recommendations for designing solutions that meet the principle of least privilege access, ensuring that your applications, access to services, and resources are accessed only by authorized users and systems.

The Security Pillar emphasizes the importance of understanding the **Shared Responsibility Model** from an architectural design approach and how you must control specific areas of the cloud resources you provision in accordance with recommended practices.

Key principles of this pillar include:

- Design and implement strong identity and access management controls following the principle of least privilege
- Apply security at all layers (network, application, and data)
- Enable traceability using logging, monitoring, and auditing tools and services
- Encrypt data in transit and at rest
- Automate security controls that scale
- Test your security posture through game days and conduct lessons learned exercises

The Security Pillar focuses on designing your solution with security in mind, deciding what controls to put in place, how to handle security incidents, and how to protect your systems and data.

The next pillar is focused on Reliability.

Reliability pillar

The Reliability Pillar provides best practice guidelines to help you design your application and workloads as they are intended to function and quickly recover from any failures.

Cloud environments and the services offered can be used to build robust and resilient systems that are highly available, scalable, and able to offer fault tolerance, provided your architecture is designed in accordance with recommended best practices. Attempting to build a similar architecture for on-premises infrastructure is usually not possible due to limitations of resources and capital costs associated with such architectures.

Key principles of this pillar include:

- Designing infrastructure services to automatically recover from failures using monitoring and automation tooling
- Testing recovery procedures to ensure entire systems can be restored quickly
- Scaling horizontally to avoid single points of failure
- Using Auto Scaling services to avoid capacity guessing and peak load provisioning
- Manage changes through automation

The Reliability Pillar emphasizes the importance of designing for failure and recovery. If your architecture is built to handle failure, you will be able to ensure high availability and a consistent user experience.

The next pillar is focused on Performance Efficiency.

Performance Efficiency pillar

The Performance Efficiency pillar focuses on using your cloud services efficiently while maintaining performance levels even as demand changes. AWS offers several tools and best practice recommendations to help you efficiently spin up and manage underlying infrastructure resources.

Key principles of this pillar include:

- AWS recommends using managed services to avoid operational complexity. For example, use Amazon RDS databases instead of installing your database engines on EC2 instances.
- Deploy workloads globally to reduce latency issues for users – consider utilizing global services like Amazon CloudFront and Amazon Route 53 for this purpose
- Consider building serverless architectures to eliminate infrastructure management
- Experiment with different configurations and test different resource types (for example, EC2 instance types or EBS volume types) to optimize performance
- Select the right technologies for your workload's environments

The Performance Efficiency pillar focuses on being adaptable and ensuring your resources offer the best performance for the required use case while still being utilized efficiently.

The next pillar is focused on Cost Optimization.

Cost Optimization pillar

The Cost Optimization pillar focuses on ensuring you deliver maximum business value at the lowest possible costs. Cost management in the cloud is a critical component if businesses are to benefit from moving their on-premises workloads to cloud-hosted services.

Key principles of this pillar include:

- Implement cloud financial management (FinOps) best practices
- Adopt a consumption model, meaning that you should only pay for what you use. For example, if you are running an EC2 instance that is only being used during business hours using the On-Demand pricing model, consider turning the instance off during non-business hours.
- Measure costs against business output to determine efficiency
- Use managed services instead of unnecessary infrastructure provisioning and management
- Analyzing and attributing costs to individual workloads or teams and using cost allocation tags correctly
- Consider consolidated billing options, reserved instance pricing options, volume discounts, and savings plans to benefit from lower costs where necessary

The Cost Optimization Pillar requires consistent monitoring and alerting processes to ensure you maximize your return on investment.

The next pillar is focused on Sustainability.

Sustainability pillar

The Sustainability pillar focuses on reducing environmental impact, such as the carbon footprint of running cloud infrastructure and workloads. AWS offers a wide range of tools to help you build more energy-efficient architectures when compared to on-premises data centers.

Key principles of this pillar include:

- Measuring and understanding the environmental impact of your workloads – consider consolidating your instances, opting for containerized solutions, or serverless architectures
- Setting sustainability goals and aligning your architecture design patterns accordingly
- Maximize utilization through right-sizing and efficient design
- Use managed services to reduce overall resource consumption

- Adopt new, more energy-efficient technologies
- Minimize downstream impact for your users

The Sustainability pillar helps businesses become more environmentally responsible and, in many cases, also fulfill regulatory requirements for environment-related policies.

The six pillars of the AWS Well Architected Framework examine how you can technically architect your cloud solutions to ensure you offer applications that are secure, reliable, high-performing, cost-efficient, operationally effective, and environmentally sustainable.

In the next section, you will learn about the Well Architected Tool—a free service designed to help you evaluate and analyze your cloud solutions to ensure alignment with the AWS Well Architected Framework.

Assessing workloads with the AWS Well-Architected Tool

The **AWS Well-Architected Tool** is a free AWS service designed to help you review your cloud applications and workloads to ensure that they are designed in accordance with AWS best practices. The Well-Architected Tool also enables you to identify gaps and opportunities for improvement.

You use the tool to answer a series of questions about your application architecture against the six pillars of the Well-Architected Framework and identify how your workloads have been built in alignment with those best practices. AWS generates a report identifying risks, recommendations, and options for optimization based on those six pillars as guidelines to follow when building cloud solutions.

Table 19.1 provides a breakdown of the core benefits of the AWS Well-Architected Tool:

Feature	Description
Workload Reviews	Assess applications and infrastructure against AWS best practices
Risk Identification	Highlights **High Risk Issues** (**HRIs**) that could affect reliability, security, performance, or cost
Improvement Plans	Provides recommendations and remediation guidance

Feature	Description
Continuous Assessment	Track architectural improvements over time
Lens Support	Apply specialized guidance for specific workloads such as serverless, SaaS, machine learning, and financial services

Table 19.1: AWS Well-Architected Tool

Belly Brew Co. Limiteduses the AWS Well-Architected Tool to assess its email capture website and internal manufacturing applications against the six pillars of the AWS Well-Architected Framework. The review helps the company identify potential risks, improve operational resilience, strengthen security controls, and optimize cloud costs.

The AWS Well-Architected Tool is offered free of cost, built directly into AWS, and provides actionable recommendations. Organizations can also use the tool to prepare for audits and reviews, and it encourages continuous architectural improvements.

Summary

As a business, you must ensure that your IT workloads and applications are designed to be reliable, scalable, highly available, secure, and cost-effective.

To successfully adopt cloud and drive real transformation for your business, there are two key areas where you must focus and build momentum:

- **Business goals and transformation (The "why" and "who")**: Focusing on this area involves:
    - Aligning business goals with digital transformation initiatives
    - Building a cloud-first culture with a willingness to adapt and evolve
    - Ensuring all solutions meet legal, compliance, and governance requirements
    - Maintaining a strong security posture across the organization
    - Driving productivity and operational efficiency

The **AWS Cloud Adoption Framework** (**CAF**) provides a structured approach through six perspectives, helping organizations align people, process, and technology to accelerate their cloud journey.

- **Technical design and best practices (The "how")**: Focusing on this area involves:
  - Designing solutions that reduce operational overhead through automation and resilient architectures
  - Implementing security at every layer, following least privilege and the shared responsibility model
  - Designing for failure so that issues in one component do not impact the entire system
  - Building highly performant and scalable systems that can adapt to changing demand
  - Continuously optimizing for cost
  - Designing with sustainability in mind, reducing environmental impact

The **AWS Well-Architected Framework** provides six pillars that guide you in building secure, reliable, high-performing, cost-optimized, and sustainable solutions. The AWS CAF helps you transform the business, while the AWS Well-Architected Framework helps you build the right solutions.

Together, they ensure you can move to the cloud quickly, safely, and efficiently—without compromising security, stability, or cost.

Designing, building, and deploying cloud solutions that are highly reliable, available, scalable, secure, and cost-effective is a critical skill that organizations around the world demand. Understanding core cloud fundamentals and architectural best practices before implementing any solution is essential, as is the ability to rapidly iterate, enhance, and improve applications to remain competitive in today's market.

AWS offers a wide range of services, tools, best-practice guidance, and support to help organizations gain a competitive advantage. Unlike traditional IT environments that often require significant upfront capital investment, AWS enables businesses to access scalable resources on demand and reach customers across a global market.

This brings us to the end of the book. As you close this study guide, remember that the *AWS Certified Cloud Practitioner* exam is not just a test of service names. It is a test of how well you understand cloud value, shared responsibility, security, cost, reliability, and the choices that shape real cloud solutions. Keep revisiting the hands-on projects, use the chapter quizzes to strengthen weak areas, and treat this foundation as the first step toward deeper AWS learning and practical cloud architecture.

Exam Readiness Drill – Chapter Review Questions

Apart from mastering key concepts, strong test-taking skills under time pressure are essential for acing your certification exam. That's why developing these abilities early in your learning journey is critical.

Exam readiness drills, using the free online practice resources provided with this book, help you progressively improve your time management and test-taking skills while reinforcing the key concepts you've learned.

HOW TO GET STARTED

- Open the link or scan the QR code at the bottom of this page
- If you have unlocked the practice resources already, log in to your registered account. If you haven't, follow the instructions in *Free Benefits with Your Book* section in this book's *Preface* and come back to this page.
- Once you log in, click the START button to start this chapter's quiz
- We recommend attempting a quiz multiple times till you're able to answer most of the questions correctly and well within the time limit.
- You can use the following practice template to help you plan your attempts:

Working On Accuracy		
Attempt	**Target**	**Time Limit**
Attempt 1	40% or more	Till the timer runs out
Attempt 2	60% or more	Till the timer runs out
Attempt 3	75% or more	Till the timer runs out
Working On Timing		
Attempt 4	75% or more	1 minute before time limit
Attempt 5	75% or more	2 minutes before time limit
Attempt 6	75% or more	3 minutes before time limit

The above drill is just an example. Design your drills based on your own goals and make the most out of the online quizzes accompanying this book.

Link to this Chapter's Quiz

You need to unlock the online practice resources to access the link below. Check the *Free Benefits with Your Book* section in the *Preface* for detailed instructions on how to do this. You only need to unlock the resources once.

Open Quiz `https://packt.link/clf_c02_ch19` or scan the QR code

20

Unlock the Code Bundle and the PDF Version

Your copy of this book includes the following exclusive benefits:

Complete Code Bundle

Download the full source code for this book's examples and projects.

DRM-Free PDF Version

Download DRM-free PDF and ePub copies of this book.

7-Day Packt Library Access

Get 7-day unlimited access to 8,000+ books and videos. No credit card required.

Available for first-time Packt+ trial users only.

Next-Gen Reader Access

Read this book on Packt Reader with progress sync, dark mode and note-taking.

Follow this guide to unlock them. The process takes only a few minutes and only needs to be completed once.

Unlock this book's free benefits in three easy steps

Step 1

Have your purchase invoice ready for *step 3*. If you have a physical copy, scan it using your phone and save it as a PDF, JPG, or PNG.

For more help on finding your invoice, visit `https://www.packtpub.com/unlock-benefits/help`.

> Note
>
> **Note**: If you bought this book directly from the Packt website, no invoice is required. After *step 2*, you can access your exclusive content right away.

Step 2

Scan the QR code or go to `packtpub.com/unlock`.

On the page that opens (similar to *Figure 20.1* on desktop), search for this book by name and select the correct edition.

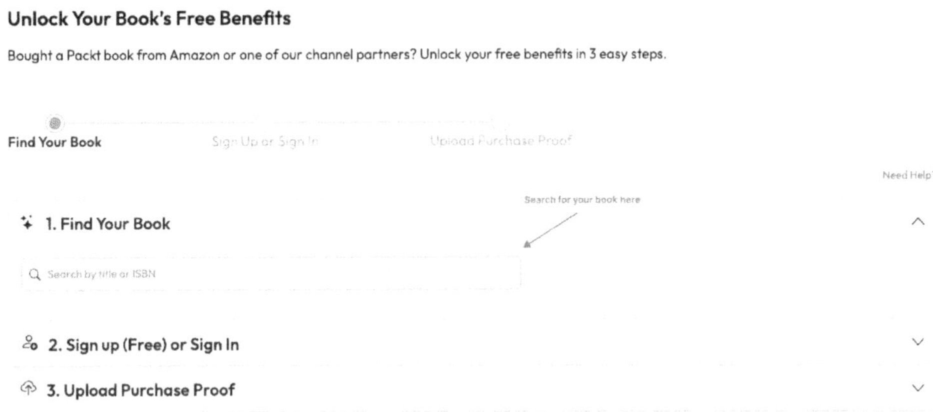

Figure 20.1: Packt unlock landing page on desktop

Step 3

After selecting the book, sign in to your Packt account or create one for free. Then, upload your invoice (PDF, PNG, or JPG, up to 10 MB). Follow the on-screen instructions to finish the process.

Need help?

If you get stuck and need help, visit `https://www.packtpub.com/unlock-benefits/help` for a detailed FAQ on how to find your invoice and more. This QR code will take you to the help page.

Note

Note: If you are still facing issues, reach out to `customercare@packt.com`.

Other Books You May Enjoy

The Self-Taught Cloud Computing Engineer

Dr. Logan Song

ISBN: 978-1-80512-370-5

- Develop core skills needed to work with AWS, Azure, and GCP
- Gain proficiency in compute, storage, and networking services across multi-cloud and hybrid-cloud environments
- Integrate cloud databases, big data, and machine learning services in multi-cloud environments
- Design and develop data pipelines, encompassing data ingestion, storage, processing, and visualization in the clouds
- Implement machine learning pipelines in multi-cloud environment
- Secure cloud infrastructure ecosystems with advanced cloud security services

AWS for Solutions Architects

Saurabh Shrivastava, Neelanjali Srivastav, Dhiraj Thakur

ISBN: 978-1-83664-193-3

- Gain expertise in GenAI, MLOps, AIOps, and mobile edge computing
- Optimize performance and handle errors in cloud-native applications
- Prepare for new AWS certifications, including those focused on AI and data engineering
- Apply best practices for security, compliance, and AWS Learning Badges
- Explore the updated Well-Architected Framework with six pillars
- Get in-depth knowledge of new storage options and security group configurations

Packt is searching for authors like you

If you're interested in becoming an author for Packt, please visit `authors.packt.com` and apply today. We have worked with thousands of developers and tech professionals, just like you, to help them share their insight with the global tech community. You can make a general application, apply for a specific hot topic that we are recruiting an author for, or submit your own idea.

Share your thoughts

Now you've finished *AWS Certified Cloud Practitioner (CLF-C02) Certification Guide; Second Edition* we'd love to hear your thoughts! Scan the QR code below to go straight to the Amazon review page for this book and share your feedback or leave a review on the site that you purchased it from.

https://packt.link/r/1835464297

Your review is important to us and the tech community and will help us make sure we're delivering excellent quality content.

Index

Symbols

A

B

D

E

F

G

K

L

M

N

O

P

R

www.ingramcontent.com/pod-product-compliance
Lightning Source LLC
LaVergne TN
LVHW080801011026
849160LV00015B/1496
* 9 7 8 1 8 3 5 4 6 4 2 9 8 *